LONGMAN

Advanced Learners' Grammar

A self-study reference & practice book with answers

Mark Foley & Diane Hall

Pearson Education Limited
Edinburgh Gate
Harlow
Essex
CM20 2JE
England
and Associated Companies throughout the world.

www.Longman.com

Printed in China GCC/01

Development editor: David Lott. Produced for the publishers by Bluestone Press, Charlbury, Oxfordshire, UK. Design by Keith Rigley. Copy-edited by Sue Harmes. Illustrations by Anthony Seldon (pages 55, 72, 74, 109, 111, 125, 137, 161, 188, 195, 203, 208, 213, 215, 232, 278, 298, 303, 324, 327), Anthony Maher (pages 59, 64, 65, 80, 98, 124, 133, 191, 206, 290, 294, 297, 314, 322) and Jean de Lemos (pages 76, 91, 116, 166), all of Graham-Cameron Illustration.

Set in ITC Symbol Medium

ISBN 0582 403839

ACKNOWLEDGEMENTS

We are grateful to the following for permission to reproduce copyright material:

Atlantic Syndication Partners for an extract adapted from "How over-protective parents may harm their children's health" by Beezy Marsh published in *The Daily Mail* 24th June 1999; Guardian Newspapers Limited for headlines "Police chief admits China visit errors" by Paul Baldwin, "Radio 1 outshines commercial rivals" by Janine Gibson, "Prisons chief urges release of Bulger killers" by Alan Travis, "DiCaprio film-makers face storm over paradise lost" by John Vidal published in *The Guardian* 29th October 1999 © The Guardian 1999 and "Judge blocks ban on tobacco adverts" by Sarah Boseley, "India snubs Pope on eve of visit" by Suzanne Goldenberg published in *The Guardian* 30th October 1999 © The Guardian 1999, and extracts adapted from "Lobster's whiter shade of pale puts fishmonger £20,000 in red" by Luke Harding published in *The Guardian* 9th December 1997 © The Guardian 1997, "Stephen King's latest thriller – will the minivan get it?" by Julian Borger published in *The Guardian* 30th October 1999 © The Guardian 1999, "A word in your year, from 1900 to now" by John Ezard published *in The Guardian* 30th October 1999 © The Guardian 1999 and "Why that joke email could get you the sack" by Philip Inman and Jamie Wilson published in *The Guardian* 2nd December 2000 © The Guardian 2000; the author's agent for an extract adapted from "Dramatic tension" by Mark Lawson published in *The Guardian* 2nd August 1999; and Michael O'Mara Books Limited for extracts adapted from *The One Hundred Stupidest Things Ever Done* by Ross and Kathryn Petras.

In some instances we have been unable to trace the owners of copyright material and we would appreciate any information that would enable us to do so.

We are grateful to the following for permission to reproduce copyright photographs:

Aviation Images for page 221; Bloomsbury for page 254; Corbis Images for page 343; DK Picture Library for page 79; Image Bank for page 231; The Kobal Collection for pages 69, 94 & 154; Penguin Readers for page 61; Rex Features for pages 288 & 311; Ronald Grant for page 317.

The authors would like to thank David Lott, Kenna Bourke and Christina Ruse for their editorial input into this book. They would like to acknowledge the assistance of staff and students at the following institutions for piloting the materials: Wimbledon School of English, Westminster Kingsway College, and the College of North West London.

They would also like to thank the following for reporting on the manuscript: Valeria Arva, Centre for English Training, ELTE University, Budapest, Hungary; Rolf Donald, Eastbourne School of English, UK; Özden Ergül, TC Maltepe Üniversitesi, Istanbul, Turkey. Tatyana Goucher, Diplomatic Academy, Moscow, Russia; Bernie Hayden, UK; Olha Madylus, British Council, Thessaloniki, Greece; Michael Nutt, UK; Ludmilla Pastushenko, National Taras Shevchenko University of Kyiv, Ukraine; Jelena Timotijevic, University of Brighton, UK; Dorina Vant, Liceul de Informatica Brasov, Brasov, Romania; Berrin Yildiz, Doğuş Üniversitesi, Istanbul, Turkey.

Contents

Introduction

The *Advanced Learners' Grammar* is a comprehensive advanced level grammar of the English language with cross-referenced practice exercises and a full set of diagnostic tests.

What's in this book? The *Advanced Learners' Grammar* consists of:

- 36 diagnostic tests and a test key
- 36 units of grammar explanation with practice exercises
- double-page Round ups of key areas of grammar
- an answer key for practice exercises

Who is it for? The *Advanced Learners' Grammar* is for students who are at or above the level of the Cambridge First Certificate Examination (or equivalent). It can be used by students preparing for the Cambridge Advanced or Proficiency or other similar examinations, or by advanced students who are not preparing for examinations at all.

What kind of grammar? In addition to describing traditional grammar 'rules', the *Advanced Learners' Grammar* examines the close relationship between grammar and vocabulary in English. The grammar explanations cover areas such as multi-word verbs, prepositions and reporting verbs and many where grammar and vocabulary are closely linked; useful word lists, charts and Round ups are also included. The explanations highlight common errors and areas of potential confusion and explain the differences between British and American usage. The importance of context and levels of formality are fully described, and examples are given which reflect up-to-date, idiomatic speech and writing. Many of the examples have been taken from the BNC/Longman corpus. The *Advanced Learners' Grammar* also contains units on text structure and discourse, as these areas are essential for the advanced student to develop beyond the confines of simple grammar and sentence structure.

What kind of practice? The *Advanced Learners' Grammar* generally contains four pages of practice exercises for every four pages of grammar explanation. There is a variety of types of exercises, ranging from simple gap-filling, matching and transformation tasks to complex manipulation of text. Each unit contains at least one exercise that is typical of the tasks found in advanced level examinations such as the Cambridge Advanced and Proficiency.

How do I use it? You can use the *Advanced Learners' Grammar* in a number of different ways.

Either:

- Use the Contents (pages 3–7) to find a unit which interests you.

Read through the explanation sections and do the practice exercises which follow. You can check your answers to the exercises in the key.

Or:

- Use the index (pages 374–384) to find a particular area in which you need practice.

> **predictions**
> about the future 4.1A, 4.1C–D, 4.4C, 18.1A
> *be going to* + infinitive 4.1B

- The explanations are composed of sections which are divided into sub-sections.

> **4.1 PREDICTION**
>
> 4.1A *will/won't* + infinitive — We use *will/won't* (the future simple) to talk about predictions which are based on guesswork, analysis or judgement. We use *will/won't* with all persons and with personal and impersonal subjects:

- Read the sections or sub-sections that are listed in the index and then do the related practice exercises. There is a reference above each exercise which shows which section or sections it is practising.

> **1** **4.1, 4.2**
>
> **Complete the dialogues according to the cartoons and using the verbs in brackets. Use *will/won't*, *will/won't be* + verb *-ing*, *will/won't have* + past participle or *be going to*.**

Or:

- Use the diagnostic tests (pages 10–45) to identify your areas of weakness. Do the test for a particular area of grammar, for example, the future.

> Diagnostic test 4
>
> **The future (1)**
>
> **Write the correct form of the verb in brackets to complete these sentences. Use one of these structures: will/won't, shall, be going to, *will/won't be* + *-ing*, *will/won't have* + past participle, *will/won't have* + *been* + *-ing*, present continuous or present simple.**

- Then check your answers in the key to the diagnostic tests (pages 344–353). Each answer contains one or more reference numbers. Circle the reference numbers for the items you answered incorrectly, read those sub-sections in the explanation section and then do the related practice exercises.

> **TEST 4**
> 1 will find ▶ **4.1A**
> 2 'll probably sell ▶ **4.1A, 4.4C**
> 3 are going to win ▶ **4.1B**

Tip: when doing the diagnostic tests, it may be better to write your answers on a separate sheet of paper, so that you can refer to it easily when you check the key.

Symbols The following symbols are used in the grammar explanations:

❗ = particular problem or exception; take note
▶ = refer to this particular section in another unit
✔ *example* = grammatically correct
✘ ~~*example*~~ = grammatically incorrect
[*example*] = non-standard usage

Diagnostic test 1

Present tenses

Write the correct form of the words in brackets to complete the sentences. Use only the present simple (e.g. *arrives/doesn't arrive*) or the present continuous (e.g. *is/are arriving*).

Example
It's nearly half past ten. ...*Do they always eat*... (they/always/eat) this late in Spain?

1 Carina .... (enjoy) hospital dramas so she .... (watch) *ER* every week.

2 Japanese cooking .... (not use) a lot of dairy food.

3 .... the interest rate .... (usually/change) because of inflation?

4 Graham won't give up cigarettes. He .... (smoke) about fifty a day.

5 Britney Spears .... (stay) in the Waldorf Astoria on this visit to New York.

6 We .... (take) a two-week winter holiday in Gstaad every year.

7 I .... (feed) the neighbour's cat this week while she's in hospital.

8 The court .... (not/usually/send) first-time offenders to prison, but it is possible in exceptional circumstances.

9 Then you .... (mix) all the ingredients together quickly and .... (put) the mixture in a hot oven for twenty minutes.

10 I can see the leaders. The three front runners .... (turn) the corner into the stadium complex now.

11 Julie, listen to this. It's Thursday evening and I .... (get) home really late from the club, and she .... (say) to me ...

12 Hewitt certainly .... (not/play) his best tennis at the moment.

13 Hurry up and buy your sandwich! Here .... (come) the bus!

14 'Sorry I haven't phoned. I lost my address book.' 'Oh, you .... (always/lose) your address book! Why don't you keep everything on the computer?'

15 The part-time philosophy course .... (consist of) twenty evening lectures and five full-day seminars.

16 .... (you/think) we should allow more than an hour to get to the station?

17 We can't leave a ten-year-old child on her own. What on earth .... (you/think) of?

18 Don't ask him! He .... (be) really difficult at the moment.

19 Would you like to try these champagnes? We .... (taste) them to write a review for the wine club newsletter.

20 We .... (guarantee) that you won't be disappointed with the performance of our new washing machine.

Diagnostic test 1 key ▶ **page 344**

Diagnostic test 2

Past tenses

Underline the correct verb form in *italics*.

Example
The Incas *didn't have/weren't having* a written script.

1 The pool in the hotel was absolutely filthy so we didn't *swam/swim* in it.

2 We *stoped/stopped* at the first service station we came across.

3 The thieves ran out of the bank, *jumped/were jumping* into their car and sped away up the high street.

4 Rameses II *was ruling/ruled* over ancient Egypt for more than fifty years.

5 Intervention was urgently required – the starving children *grew/were growing* weaker by the day and there *was/was being* little sign of an end to the drought.

6 By the middle of the nineteen sixties many parts of Europe *experienced/were experiencing* a tremendous economic boom.

7 Jim *left/was leaving* on the early flight the next morning so he made his excuses and left the party before midnight.

8 Many of the survivors *worked/were working* in the fields when the earthquake struck.

9 Phil stood at the door soaked from head to toe; he *had been running/was running* in the rain.

10 Denise had to leave school early on Wednesday because she *took/was taking* her driving test.

11 By the third month of the war rebel forces *took/had taken* most of the province.

12 At the time of the trial last summer Hinkley *had been/was* in prison for eight months.

13 We missed the first act of the play because when we arrived at the theatre the performance *already started/had already started*.

14 At midnight Mr Rochester *had climbed/climbed* the stairs and went into his bedchamber.

15 The early rains were a disappointment as we *expected/had expected* to reach the coast before the monsoon set in.

16 At the time of the take-over the company's shares *had declined/had been declining* in value for several months.

17 Brendan was surprised to find the gas tank empty as he *had only been using/had only used* the truck twice that week.

18 Before the advent of satellite television viewers didn't *used to have/use to have* a very wide selection of channels.

19 The staff *were used/used* to be paid weekly but now they receive a monthly salary.

20 Things have certainly changed – there *would be/used to be* loads of small shops around here when I was young.

Diagnostic test 2 key ▶ **page 344**

Diagnostic test 3

Past to present tenses

Underline the best choice of words in *italics*.

Example
Has the package arrived/Did the package arrive safely yesterday?

1 We still hold meetings in the old manor house, which *stood/has stood* on the same spot for over two hundred years.

2 Beethoven *has written/wrote* some of the most accomplished symphonies you will ever listen to.

3 I *didn't see/haven't seen* Keith at all yesterday morning.

4 The nurses' strike *increased/has increased* the current waiting time for minor surgery by two to three weeks.

5 Only one British female astronaut *spent/has spent* time on a space station.

6 News is coming in of an incident in Parliament. A group of armed men *surrounded/has surrounded* the building and is holding hostages.

7 He's really much more handsome in the flesh than I *thought/have thought*.

8 We *eat/have been eating* much less beef recently because of the crisis, but we think it's safe to start again now.

9 This country *has been welcoming/has welcomed* the latest influx of political refugees from the Balkans.

10 The incidence of street crime *has risen/has been rising* by five per cent in the last two months.

All of the sentences below contain a grammatical mistake. Find and correct the mistakes.

Example
My family ~~is living~~ in this country for over twenty years. .....*has been living/has lived*.....

11 Hurry up! We have been waited for you for twenty minutes! ....

12 We have been using this supplier since two years and we've never had problems before. ....

13 There were seven police dramas on TV so far this week – and it's only Thursday! ....

14 Only halfway through the financial year and British Aerospace already announced that its pre-tax profits will be down by seventy per cent. ....

15 The Indian Government has imposed a ban on tiger hunting five years ago. ....

16 Several drivers have been badly injured during the 1999 racing season. ....

17 This farm is growing organic vegetables for more than ten years now. ....

18 She has been playing with the symphony orchestra three times this season. ....

19 'I haven't seen you for ages.' 'No, I've travelled in South-East Asia.' ....

20 Oasis has been recording a new album. It was a great success on its release last week. ....

Diagnostic test 3 key ▶ **page 344**

Diagnostic test 4

The future (1)

Write the correct form of the verb in brackets to complete the sentences. Use one of these structures: *will*, *shall*, *be going to*, *will be* + *-ing*, *will have* + past participle, *will have* + *been* + *-ing*, present continuous or present simple.

Example
'Have you booked a holiday yet for this year?' 'Yes, we ....*are taking*......... (take) a cruise around the Caribbean in November.'

1 I've taken the 10.40 to Bristol every Friday for three years and it's always half empty. Believe me, you .... (find) a seat.

2 My father's approaching retirement age, so he .... (probably/sell) the business next year.

3 Going by all of the recent polls, the social democrats .... (win) next week's election by a huge majority.

4 Look at those black clouds. It .... (rain) this afternoon.

5 I'm going on holiday tomorrow. This time next Tuesday afternoon I .... (ski) down a mountain!

6 At our next wedding anniversary we .... (be/married) for twenty-five years.

7 'You speak very good Chinese.' 'Thank you. It's not surprising; I .... (live) in Beijing for eight years next month.'

8 Sit down and watch the TV; I .... (just/finish) this letter quickly before I join you.

9 Your driving test is next Tuesday, so .... (we/have) a two hour session on Monday?

10 'Have your parents decided whether you can come to the festival next weekend?' 'Not yet, but they can't stop me. I .... (come) with you.'

11 I've won the jackpot on the lottery and I .... (spend) it all straight away!

12 I've just been to the council meeting. It looks like they .... (build) a new shopping centre in town.

13 I've just heard a rumour that your favourite jazz singer .... (come) to give a concert in our village!

14 'Have you looked at the new financial report yet?' 'No, but I .... (stay) at home this evening so I can study it then.'

15 The takeover is going ahead, I'm afraid, so we .... (make) some redundancies in the New Year.

16 Erm, I don't want to be rude, but .... (you/stay) with us for long when you come over to Britain?

17 The plane .... (take off) at 10.45, so we had better check in by 8.45.

18 Sunrise .... (be) at 6.40 a.m. tomorrow.

19 Mr Fellows .... (play) golf tomorrow afternoon, as usual, so you can catch him on the golf course.

20 The decorator won't finish the work until you .... (pay) him what you owe.

Diagnostic test 4 key ▶ **page 344**

Diagnostic test 5

The future (2)

Choose the correct word or phrase (a–c) to complete the sentences.

Example
Shh! You ...*b*... disturb your mother.
a are due to b are not to c are to

1 The Mayor of Paris .... attend the service tomorrow before leaving the city.
a is about to b is to
c is on the point of

2 These pills are .... with any other medicine.
a not to be taken b not take
c due to be taken

3 The timetable .... be published on 1st May.
a is due to b is about to
c is on the point of

4 Hurry! Run! The train's just .... leave without us!
a to b due to c about to

5 Because of the erosion of their habitats, some species are .... extinction.
a about to b on the verge of
c likely to

6 He's very .... to accept the position as we can't match his current salary.
a unlikely b likely c sure

7 We .... promote trainees within two to three years of qualifying.
a are about to b expect to
c anticipate to

8 'I'm sorry about spilling wine on your dress last week.' 'Don't worry. I .... take it to the cleaner's anyway.'
a was going to b would c was to

9 As he raised his arm she realised that he .... strike her again.
a was due to b was to
c was about to

10 I'm really sorry. We .... to stop at a service station and phone you, but we didn't want to waste any more time.
a were due to b were going to
c were to

Now choose two correct answers (a–c) to complete the sentences.

Example
Everyone was getting impatient. The trial of the century ....*b, c*........ start in two minutes.
a would to b was to c was due to

11 Crash investigators .... release their findings to the press later today.
a are about to b are due to c are to

12 The exam starts at three. .... arrive at the hall at least five minutes before the start.
a Be sure to b You are to
c Be bound to

13 Hurry up. The tour group is .... If you don't come now, they'll go without us!
a to leave b about to leave
c on the point of leaving

14 Do you believe we are .... a really exciting breakthrough here?
a on the point of b forthcoming
c on the verge of

15 Standing underneath the stricken building, no one seemed aware of the .... danger.
a impending b imminent c bound

16 'Do you think the judges will like my entry?' 'Of course. They're .... to like it!
a sure b bound c unlikely

17 We .... one hundred per cent customer satisfaction with this new vacuum cleaner!
a hope b guarantee c anticipate

18 The society .... expand its membership by twenty per cent in the next year.
a hopes to b may c envisages

19 Look, I didn't put the rubbish out this morning because I thought you .... do it!
a were going to b would c were to

20 The new department store .... on 2nd January, but the explosion prevented this.
a was to open b would open
c was to have opened

Diagnostic test 5 key ▶ **page 345**

Diagnostic test 6

Negation

In each group of sentences below (a–c), two are grammatically correct. Tick (✔) the correct sentences.

Example
a He's no actor! ✔   b He's not an actor! ✔
c He's any actor!

1 'Where's Suzy?'
a 'She isn't at home.'
b 'She's not at home.'
c 'She's no at home.'

2 Hannah .... tell the rest of the family.
a begged her sister don't
b begged her sister not to
c didn't beg her sister to

3 He found her ....
a not attractive, but strangely appealing.
b inattractive, but strangely appealing.
c unattractive, but strangely appealing

4 a They'll get no help from Janice.
b They'll get none help from Janice.
c They won't get any help from Janice.

5 There were .... bookings for the restaurant on its opening night.
a any
b few
c no

6 He says he .... about the robbery.
a knows nothing
b doesn't know anything
c doesn't know nothing

7 a We think that the conference won't be a failure.
b We don't think the conference to be a failure.
c We don't think that the conference will be a failure.

8 The woman in the photo .... to be happy.
a seems not
b doesn't seem
c isn't seem

9 Hasn't Stella contacted her solicitor yet?
a Yes, she has.   b Yes, she hasn't.
c No, she hasn't.

10 .... come with us to the beach tomorrow?
a Don't you
b Will you
c Won't you

11 Many managers .... prepare for meetings.
a don't hardly
b hardly ever
c hardly

12 That kind of crime .... these days, does it?
a rarely happens
b doesn't rarely happen
c seldom happens

Rewrite the underlined part of each sentence to make it negative. Use *not*, *n't*, *neither* ... *nor* or a negative prefix.

Example
<u>I expect there'll be</u> a movie on the flight.
I don't expect there'll be a movie on the flight.

13 The professor ordered him <u>to leave</u> the room.
....

14 <u>Having seen</u> the film, I don't understand the hype.
....

15 <u>Many</u> antique watches of this type are available these days.
....

16 They've booked <u>either to go on a cruise or to visit the Pyramids</u>.
....

17 The followers of this sect <u>believe that</u> there <u>is</u> life after death.
....

18 <u>Have you seen</u> Harrison Ford's new film yet?
....

19 The suspects <u>denied</u> all of the allegations against them.
....

20 The new Financial Director was generally thought to be <u>honest</u>.
....

Diagnostic test 6 key ▶ **page 345**

Diagnostic test 7

Questions

Nine of these questions contain mistakes of grammar or formality. Tick [✔] the correct questions, then find and correct the mistakes.

Example
What did you buy else at the shops?
What else did you buy at the shops?

1 What means 'heliotrope'? I can't find it in the dictionary.
....

2 How long you had been living there before the war broke out?
....

3 According to the recipe, what time should I turn the oven off?
....

4 'There was an awful explosion in town yesterday.' 'Really? What did happen?'
....

5 Who exactly presents the certificates at the graduation ceremony?
....

6 How on earth will you get there? The buses have all been on strike for a week.
....

7 'I didn't think much of that film, did you?' 'Yes, I thought it was terrible.'
....

8 Let's give the evening class a miss tonight and stay in, don't we?
....

9 'I'm going to have to cancel this evening. I'm still at work.' 'Oh, things are still really hectic, are they?'
....

10 Can you let me know what time does the train from Croydon arrive?
....

11 Could you possibly let us know if or not the tree roots will affect the foundations?
....

12 Do you know if the victim had been staying in this hostel immediately prior to the attack?
....

13 Honestly, I can't trust you to do anything right. You can't have lost your passport. Could you tell me where you put it after the holiday?
....

14 'They didn't give the concert after all last night.' 'Did they? Why not?'
....

15 'I love seeing Robbie Williams live. He's such a good dancer.' 'Yes, isn't he?'
....

Write an appropriate question tag (e.g. *isn't it?*) to complete each question.

Example
You don't really believe in ghosts, ...*do you*...?

16 Surely your parents will help you to get the food ready, ...?

17 Look at the time. We ought to go now to get the last bus, ...?

18 She needn't pay for the whole course in advance, ...?

19 'Have you seen my new puppy? He's worth £250.' 'He's lovely. He's a pedigree, then, ...?'

20 Don't forget to bring me some of your fantastic carrot cake, ...?

Diagnostic test 7 key ▶ **page 345**

Diagnostic test 8

Passives, causatives and *get*

Rewrite these sentences beginning with the word(s) in bold. You will need to use passive or causative forms.

Example
My parents let me stay up late yesterday.
I ...*was allowed to stay up late yesterday*.........

1 The management have offered the workers a pay rise.
A pay rise ....

2 The mechanics are overhauling the entire fleet.
The entire fleet ....

3 They made the contestants dress in ridiculous outfits.
The contestants ....

4 The organisers should have warned us in advance.
We ....

5 Having taken advice, the committee decided not to proceed.
Advice ....

6 It was my father's final wish that they would bury him at sea.
To ....

7 We regret the fact that the landlord didn't inform us of his decision.
We regret not ....

8 The garage services my car every six months.
I ....

9 The carriers will receive instructions to return the goods to your clients by Friday.
We will have ....

10 They are going to repair Susy's car free of charge!
Susy's getting ....

11 I want you to repair that computer as soon as you possibly can.
Get ....

12 I can see that nobody's cleaned the bathroom for weeks!
The bathroom ....

Choose the correct or best sentence (a or b) in each pair.

13 a Twenty per cent of the world's oil is owned by Saudi Arabia.
b Twenty per cent of the world's oil gets owned by Saudi Arabia.

14 a Some people think *The Tempest* is Shakespeare's final play.
b *The Tempest* is thought to be Shakespeare's final play.

15 a A famous actress is resembled by my sister.
b My sister resembles a famous actress.

16 a That political party wants to increase its membership.
b Membership wants to be increased by that political party.

17 a The Golden Gate Bridge is a marvel of American technology. It was designed by Joseph B Strauss in the 1930s.
b The Golden Gate Bridge is a marvel of American technology. In the 1930s Joseph B Strauss designed it.

18 a The interviewers will interview the candidates in alphabetical order.
b The candidates will be interviewed in alphabetical order.

19 a The post has arrived at last.
b The post has been arrived at last.

20 a This programme was recorded in front of a live audience.
b We recorded this programme in front of a live audience.

Diagnostic test 8 key ▶ **page 345**

Diagnostic test 9

Reported speech

Ten of these sentences contain mistakes. Tick (✓) the two correct sentences, then find and correct the mistakes.

Example
I've already ~~said~~ you a hundred times that you're too late! ....*told* **(or:** *said to***)**........

1 The surgeon reassured Mr Ellis. 'The operation has been a resounding success,' said she. ....

2 He told that his mobile phone had been out of action all day. ....

3 Mary was fed up about her inability to complete the course. She told the lecturer I felt I couldn't complete it. ....

4 The manager told us last Friday evening that he wanted us in on time tomorrow morning to start the Saturday sale. ....

5 Susie phoned her husband and told him that she would be gone when he got home. ....

6 Janice hates the idea of growing old. She said yesterday that she wished she had still been young. ....

7 The negotiator said he's working on the details of a tentative settlement. ....

8 Laura said if anybody had reported a missing person to the police yet. ....

9 The nurse asked when exactly had started the pain. ....

10 We asked the travel agent if or not there was a swimming pool at the villa. ....

11 Several members of the Royal Family urged Edward VIII don't abdicate. ....

12 Even under great pressure O'Brien denied to have taken part in the attack. ....

Rewrite each quote in indirect speech.

Example
I've lost a contact lens so I can't see a thing!
Gary explained that ....*he had lost a contact lens so he couldn't see a thing.*..................

13 'I will remember 1st March 2000 as a great day for the nation!'
The President announced ....

14 'Publication may be delayed by one week.'
The editor told us ....

15 'You must lose at least 20 kilos.'
The doctor told me ....

16 'Intelligent life does not exist in our universe.'
Many astronomers believe ....

17 'The Ming Dynasty lasted for almost 300 years.'
The historian explained ....

18 'When do you want the sofa to be delivered?'
The shopkeeper asked my wife ....

19 'Isn't that stupid behaviour for a cyclist?'
The pedestrian complained ....

20 'You really must do at least four hours' training a day.'
The trainer urged his team ....

Diagnostic test 9 key ▶ **page 346**

Diagnostic test 10

Conditionals

Twelve of these conditional sentences contain a mistake, or may be considered incorrect by most English speakers. Tick (✓) the correct sentences, then find and correct the mistakes. (Be careful! Incorrect punctuation counts as a mistake.)

Example
I would have called you if I ~~knew~~ you were at home.
had known

1 It may be possible, if both parties desire it, to reduce the time scale.

2 If the bill is passed by both parliamentary houses then it becomes law.

3 Shall we start the decorating at the weekend if we had no other plans?

4 If you spill even something as innocuous as water on this fabric, it stains.

5 When you press the 'record' button, the green light comes on.

6 If the museum will charge for entry, a lot of people won't be able to use it.

7 Are you unhappy with any of our operatives, we will replace them immediately.

8 If you're taking some flowers to Julie, I'll take some fruit.

9 If the form has been correctly completed, the transfer will take only two days.

10 The organisers would respond positively to proposals if they are submitted by 10th June.

11 If you were to listen more carefully, you might understand a little more.

12 If I was you, I should try to see a consultant as soon as possible.

13 If he would have waited a bit longer, we would have given him the result.

14 The King of Belgium didn't attend the royal wedding. If he hadn't been there, he would have witnessed a marvellous spectacle.

15 If the company didn't want to continue sponsoring us in the future, they wouldn't renew our contract last week, would they?

16 If the authority had built new homes as planned, we would have fewer homeless people on our streets today.

17 Shh! I'd be grateful unless you made comments during the concert.

18 Always take a basic medicine kit on holiday in case you fall ill.

19 Even they go down with flu after they've had the vaccination, it's likely to be less serious.

20 Those concerned by the long-term effects of global warming believe that the damage has been done, whether we take remedial steps now.

Diagnostic test 10 key ▶ page 346

Diagnostic test 11

The subjunctive and 'unreal' uses of past forms

Five of these sentences contain grammatical mistakes. Tick (✔) the correct sentences, then find and correct the mistakes.

Example
If only we ~~can~~ see the situation through his eyes. ......*could*......

1 It is high time the country were told of the Prime Minister's intentions. ....

2 I wish I would have green eyes like Elizabeth Taylor. ....

3 The regulations require that each defendant in turn submit a sworn statement to the court. ....

4 If you only paid more attention! ....

5 It's high time we didn't act so impulsively. ....

6 If only the car would have been going more slowly! ....

7 Long lives the President! ....

8 If only that I had known. ....

Circle the best explanation (a or b).

Example
I'd sooner you paid me cash.
a I expect you to pay me soon.
(b) I prefer to be paid in cash.

9 If only I was as tall as my brother.
a I used to be as tall as my brother.
b I am shorter than my brother.

10 Get a move on! It's high time we left for the airport.
a We are late.
b We have just left.

11 Suppose we win the competition.
a I think we have a chance of winning.
b Winning is extremely unlikely.

12 He bosses everyone around as if he owned the place.
a He owns the place.
b He doesn't own the place.

13 She wishes she had a home of her own.
a She likes living in her own place.
b She would like to live in her own place.

14 If only I could wear such bright clothes.
a Bright clothes don't suit me.
b I'm the only one who can wear bright clothes.

Complete each sentence so that it means the same as the preceding sentence(s).

Example
I regret leaving the children with her.
I wish ...*I hadn't left the children with her.*...

15 You ought to start doing your homework.
It's high time you ....

16 Would you have gone if you had been invited?
Supposing you ....

17 I don't want you to bring that smelly dog into this house.
I'd rather you ....

18 I prefer wearing natural fabrics.
I'd sooner ....

19 He sounds quite convincing. Perhaps he knows what he is talking about.
He sounds as though ....

20 You are always talking with your mouth full. I want you to stop doing it.
I wish you ....

Diagnostic test 11 key ▶ **page 346**

Diagnostic test 12

-ing forms and infinitives

Write suitable forms of the word(s) in brackets, putting verbs into an *-ing* form (e.g. *returning*) or infinitive form (e.g. *to return*). You may need to change or add words.

Example
I'm looking forward to ...*her returning*... with good news. (she/return)

1 I'm afraid you'll have to move your car, sir. There is .... here. (not/park)

2 For evil .... it is only necessary that the good do nothing. (succeed)

3 Sylvia rang her doctor .... an appointment. (make)

4 The thing I most enjoy about my job is .... people with problems. (help)

5 Pressure from the board led to .... the company. (he/leave)

6 The colonel ordered a day's leave in order .... the morale of the troops. (boost)

7 We got there only .... that the concert had been cancelled. (find)

8 You're welcome .... yourself to anything from the fridge. (help)

9 It's strange that she didn't mention .... him at the party. (meet)

10 I really can't risk .... these awful programmes. (the children/see)

11 Don't disturb me, I've got a report .... by lunchtime. (write)

12 I can't stand .... animals in pain. (see)

13 I must remember .... my alarm clock tonight. (set)

14 Dean's so sorry; he really didn't mean .... you. (hurt)

15 You won't find any spare parts; they stopped .... them ages ago. (make)

16 We went on .... even after the music had stopped. (dance)

17 We regret .... the cancellation of today's service due to ill health. (announce)

18 As the plane flew over we saw the workers .... the new opera house. (build)

Five of these sentences contain mistakes. Tick (✓) the correct sentences, then find and correct the mistakes.

Example
We agreed ~~meeting~~ outside the cinema at nine.
.....*to meet*..

19 The dispensing medical aid is the main activity of the Red Cross
....

20 Everyone in the office was fed up with Brian's moaning.
....

21 The new manager is sure to looking into ways to cut costs.
....

22 He got caught when the boss found making personal phone calls.
....

23 The airline allowed us taking the wheelchair on board.
....

24 We were furious when the judge ordered to pay compensation.
....

25 Despite budget constraints the BBC continues to make innovative programmes.
....

Diagnostic test 12 key ▶ **page 346**

Diagnostic test 13

Participle and infinitive phrases

Underline the correct alternative in *italics*.

Example
Not to have/Not having an invitation, I couldn't get into the party.

1 *He didn't own/Not owning* a watch, Peter was often late.

2 Writing in the 'Evening Standard', an *article/author* complained about the lack of disabled facilities on the underground.

3 Objects *bought/buying* in junk shops can often turn out to be quite valuable.

4 Neil Armstrong was the first man *walking/to walk* on the moon.

5 'It's only me!' she said, *opening/she opened* the door.

6 Their long-term plan was *the company/for the company* to expand into Asia.

7 Hilary got to the station only *finding/to find* that the train had already left.

8 Generally *to speak/speaking*, our best business comes via our website.

Complete each sentence using the number of words indicated in brackets, so that the sentence means the same as the one(s) before it.

Examples
Sally's only regret was that she hadn't had any children.
Not having had any children was Sally's only regret. (3 words)
Brian moved to Manchester so that he could be closer to his ailing parents.
Brian moved to Manchester *to be* closer to his ailing parents. (2 words)

9 They couldn't buy the house owing to the fact that the bank had refused their loan application.
Their loan application ...., they weren't able to buy the house. (3 words)

10 He is not rich so he won't be able to afford it.
.... rich, he won't be able to afford it. (2 words)

11 If you service it regularly, the engine should last for 200,000 kilometres.
.... regularly, the engine should last for 200,000 kilometres. (1 word)

12 Hilary left the team when she had completed her project.
Her project .... Hilary left the team. (1 word)

13 My proudest possession is this watch. My grandfather left it to me.
The watch .... to me by my grandfather is my proudest possession. (1 word)

14 John felt too ashamed to carry on because he hadn't kept his word.
.... his word, John felt too ashamed to carry on. (3 words)

15 The children always had plenty to do because they lived near the sports centre.
.... near the sports centre, the children always had plenty to do. (1 word)

16 As he had already passed his medical, Dean was able to start immediately.
.... his medical, Dean was able to start immediately. (2 words)

17 Their worst mistake was that they did not apply sooner.
Their worst mistake was .... sooner. (4 words)

18 We often find that the larger sizes are the first ones which we sell.
We often find the larger sizes are the first .... (2 words)

19 David bought a laptop so that he could access his e-mails when he was travelling.
David bought a laptop .... his e-mails when he was travelling. (2 words)

20 My honest opinion is that I really didn't enjoy it.
I really didn't enjoy it, ... honest. (2 words)

Diagnostic test 13 key ▶ page 347

Diagnostic test 14

Multi-word verbs

Rewrite these sentences replacing the underlined words with the words in brackets. Make any necessary changes to word order.

Example
She repaid the debt punctually. (on time/paid/back/it)
She paid it back on time. ....

1 The whole story was invented by Suzy's brother. (by/him/made/was/up)
....

2 Maintain the good work. (up/it/keep)
....

3 Make sure you carefully follow the guidelines. (strictly/to/stick)
....

4 This tie doesn't match that shirt.....(it/with/go)
....

5 We met my wife's cousin by chance at the museum. (into/him/ran)
....

6 These are the beliefs our movement upholds. (stands/which/for/our movement)
....

7 The company won't tolerate this kind of behaviour. (with/it/put/up)
....

8 I revealed the secret to Elizabeth. (it/her/in/let/on)
....

Eight of the following sentences contain grammatical mistakes or an inappropriate verb or multi-word verb. Tick (✓) the correct sentences and correct the others.

Examples
They're a company with which we've been dealing for many years. .....✓..........................
Her Majesty ~~turned up~~ at the ceremony in the dazzling Imperial State Coach.
.........*arrived*.............

9 That division was taken by head office over.
....

10 The very first breakout of the disease was reported in Namibia. ....

11 Steve was left by his ex-girlfriend out from her wedding invitation list.
....

12 It is a condition of receiving this Internet account that you do not give away your confidential PIN number to any third party.
....

13 Could you activate the kettle, darling? I'm dying for a cup of tea.
....

14 He fell down the floor and hurt himself.
....

15 Come on! We're going to be late!
....

16 The plane took off the ground at incredible speed. ....

17 The government brought recently in some legislation to deal with the problem.
....

18 There are few people for whom he cares so deeply. ....

19 They took Clive up on his invitation.
....

20 We look forward eagerly to your wedding.
....

Diagnostic test 14 key ▶ **page 347**

Diagnostic test 15

Dependent prepositions

Thirteen of these sentences contain mistakes. Tick (✔) the correct sentences, then find and correct the mistakes.

Example
The primary purpose of the police is to protect people ~~of~~ criminals. ......*from*............

1 The supervisor said I shouldn't have shouted at the client so I had to apologise to. ....

2 I never really know whether I should insist on sit at the top table or not. ....

3 The waiter was quite amazed at our eating everything so quickly. ....

4 All my friends agree to the government's new policy on third world debt. ....

5 Sylvia was astonished at that her boyfriend had behaved so atrociously. ....

6 You know I'm really not that interested in if he's coming with us or not. ....

7 David's quarrelled his wife over selling the house. ....

8 Please make an effort. The children are really depending on you their party costumes. ....

9 Can you tell us if the minister has stopped the by-pass from going ahead? ....

10 I blame my parents for my bad habits. ....

11 The old persons' home will provide Sam for a room. ....

12 Don't worry, the guide's going to fully explain me all the details. ....

13 He succeeded in winning the first round but I'm afraid he didn't have any success in beating his second opponent. ....

14 The auditors initially issued a demand for full repayment but then changed their minds and simply demanded for a token contribution. ....

15 Lack of nutrients caused serious damage to growing. ....

16 Wendy's sarcastic comments made me curious about her motives. ....

17 We were absolutely furious by their outrageous prices. ....

18 I don't mind driving but I'm really scared by flying. ....

19 I'd prefer somewhere else; I'm not too keen on Thai food. ....

20 Apparently Donna's angry with her boss; he's given her the late shift yet again. ....

Diagnostic test 15 key ▶ **page 347**

Diagnostic test 16

Modal verbs (1): *can*, *could*, *may*, *might*, *be able to*

Fifteen of the sentences below contain mistakes with modal verbs. Tick (✓) the correct sentences, then find and correct the mistakes.

Examples

We took an exam yesterday and I couldn't answer any of the questions.
...........✓...........

I ~~could be~~ promoted last year but I preferred to stay on the shop floor. ...*could have been*....

1 When I finish the course next year I can speak perfect French. ....

2 You'll have to call a cab. I can't have been able to drive since I broke my arm last June. ....

3 This computer is so simple that it is able to be operated by anyone. ....

4 The job interview was a disaster; I could only answer half the questions! ....

5 When she was riding in the woods last week, Helen fell off her horse but luckily she could get back on and ride home. ....

6 It's really annoying. Surely you knew they didn't accept traveller's cheques at that hotel. You could warn me before I left! ....

7 These days she is rather slow but as a child she could run like the wind. ....

8 What an excellent choice of restaurant. I can't have chosen better if I'd made the reservation myself! ....

9 There can be life on Saturn. ....

10 My father could be a star in the 1980s, it's a pity that he never really tried. ....

11 Watching TV soaps can become very addictive. ....

12 Jane's late. She can be stuck in a traffic jam. ....

13 A new car! What can she be thinking of! ....

14 I heard your sales results were excellent. May you get a bonus this year? ....

15 Don't get too anxious; there may well be a simple explanation for it. ....

16 Don't bother replying as I may have changed address by the time you read this. ....

17 Steve couldn't steal it. I'm sure he was at home all week. ....

18 Elizabeth can get better results if she paid more attention to her homework. ....

19 I'll be able to meet you after the lesson. ....

20 I'm not sure about tomorrow night. I may be on call. ....

21 Excuse me. Am I able to use your phone? ....

22 Well, don't worry. You could always try again tomorrow. ....

23 I could leave work early yesterday – my boss gave me permission. ....

24 You might get me some bin liners if it's not too much trouble. ....

25 People might not smoke on British Airways flights; it's forbidden. ....

Diagnostic test 16 key ▶ **page 348**

Diagnostic test 17

Modal verbs (2): *must*, *should*, *ought to*, *have to*, *need to*

Underline the best choice of word(s) in *italics* in each of these sentences.

Example
As they get older, teenagers <u>*should*</u>/*had better* be treated more like adults.

1 *To must*/*Having to* listen to hip-hop music all evening is my idea of torture!

2 The landlord *ought to*/*ought* have taken his responsibilities more seriously.

3 This company is awful to work for. We *must*/*have to* account for every minute of the day.

4 Do you know if we *must*/*have to* have visas for the Caribbean?

5 The newspaper *shouldn't have*/*mustn't have* printed the rumour without concrete evidence.

6 What a state my shoes are in! They *need*/*must* repairing.

7 We *have to*/*are supposed to* put our bags in the lockers, but most people take them into the gym.

8 We *couldn't go*/*mustn't have gone* into the disco because we were too young.

9 Polite notice: children *do not have to*/*are not allowed to* play on the grass.

10 This offer is not open to current employees. Participants *must not have*/*need not have* been employed by the company in the last four years.

11 We *needn't*/*needn't to* have booked the tickets in advance; there were plenty left.

12 With our new range of hair products, you *mustn't*/*don't have to* spend hours caring for your hair.

13 There wasn't anyone on the nightclub door so we *didn't need to show*/*needn't have shown* proof of our age.

14 As we're getting a lodger, we'd *better*/*better to* have some more keys cut.

15 Our advice is that even people as young as twenty-five *should*/*must* consider a personal pension.

16 You *won't have to*/*had better not* tell Shirley what you saw – it will only upset her and she'll blame you.

17 The ground's soaking outside – it must *raining*/*be raining* quite heavily.

18 If you bring your receipt, there *shouldn't*/*mustn't* be any difficulty with a refund.

19 Lewis *must have*/*should have* been training very hard to develop muscles like that!

20 I walked into the showroom and saw the car, and I knew I *had to have*/*must have had* it.

Diagnostic test 17 key ▶ **page 348**

Diagnostic test 18

Modal verbs (3): *will, would, shall*

Complete the sentences with *will*, *'ll*, *won't*, *would*, *wouldn't* or *shall* and the correct form of the words in brackets.

Example
The new play on Broadway is really good, but I don't like Sean Penn in it. Kevin Bacon ....*would be*.......... (be) much better.

1 We had to hurry to get him to the hospital. We knew it .... (be) too late otherwise.

2 'I wonder where Dad is.' 'He .... (drive) to the airport, I should think.'

3 'Oh dear. The lecture starts at nine o'clock. I'm late!' 'Don't worry. This lecturer's always late. He .... (not/start) yet.'

4 At this point in the season, the parents .... (eat) their young rather than allow a predator to attack them.

5 The doctor .... (act) as a witness to your signature. She doesn't mind doing that sort of thing.

6 The PA .... (not/book) my flights. She says it isn't in her job description.

7 Dad .... (always/help) us out financially when we were at university, however difficult it was for him.

8 The police interrogated the terrorist for more than four hours, but she .... (not/reveal) the names of her co-conspirators.

9 You look tired. .... (I/make) supper this evening?

10 What .... (we/do) with Tom if he doesn't get into university?

11 .... (you/be) so kind as to help me across the road, young man?

12 We .... (like) everyone in this room to feel comfortable with the proposal.

Circle the correct meaning or interpretation (a or b) for each sentence.

Example
It would be so nice to live by the sea.
a The speaker lives by the sea.
(b) The speaker doesn't live by the sea.

13 If anyone rings in the next few minutes, I'll be in the storeroom.
a I'm in the storeroom now.
b I'm going to the storeroom.

14 Ralph isn't here right now, I'm afraid. He'll be at the office.
a He is at the office now.
b He's on his way to the office.

15 I've tried it again and again but the computer just won't accept my disc. I don't understand it.
a I'm annoyed with the computer.
b I am not concerned about the computer.

16 It's a relief that Annie's changed class. She would argue with everything I said.
a I didn't mind the arguments.
b The arguments annoyed me.

17 The secretary shall minute the proceedings of each meeting.
a The secretary is offering to do it.
b The secretary is instructed to do it.

18 'It looks as though the fuel crisis is over.' 'I wouldn't be too sure.'
a The second speaker agrees.
b The second speaker doesn't agree.

19 It would be so nice to have a little cottage in the country.
a The speaker doesn't have a cottage.
b The speaker has a cottage.

20 I would have liked to meet the professor while he was here.
a The speaker met the professor.
b The speaker didn't meet the professor.

Diagnostic test 18 key ▶ page 348

Diagnostic test 19

Auxiliaries, *have (got)*, *do*

Ten of these sentences contain mistakes or errors of style. Tick (✔) the correct sentences, then find and correct the mistakes. Note that some sentences may be correct in spoken English, not in written English.

Example
~~We'ven't~~ been able to access the website since yesterday evening. ....*We haven't*....

1 The builders were certainly working hard; they were plastering the kitchen, were painting the staircase and were tiling the bathroom. ....

2 Kevin's exhausted; its been a hectic day. ....

3 'The battery's flat. You didn't turn the lights off, did you?' 'Yes, I did turn them off, I remember it distinctly.' ....

4 'Miranda's over the moon. She's always wanted to have got a sports car.' ....

5 They won't have anyone smoking in their house. ....

6 He's watching television when she arrived at the flat. ....

7 'Why didn't you ask Graham about the reorganisation plan?' 'What was the point? He wouldn't've known anything about it.' ....

8 Will you have got a good weekly income from your pension when you retire? ....

9 She's such a naughty child; she could really do some strict discipline! ....

10 Do help yourself to a drink. ....

11 A shower was had by John before he came to work. ....

12 'Excuse me. Is there a post office near here?' 'Sorry, I haven't a clue. I'm a stranger here myself.' ....

13 Members can have got two cards each. ....

14 I see the Red Sox have gotten themselves a new striker this season. ....

15 We used to have got a house in the country before Jack lost his job. ....

Diagnostic test 19 key ▶ **page 348**

Diagnostic test 20

Confusing verbs

Replace the expressions in *italics* in these sentences using a suitable form of *make* or *do*.

Example
I like listening to the radio while *washing* the dishes. ......doing..................

1 Sammy *earns* a lot more than I did at his age. ....

2 That old curtain fabric *has become* a marvellous ball gown. ....

3 You can go out after you *have completed* your homework. ....

4 What an awful outfit; you'd think she *had sewn* it herself! ....

5 We *carry out* the staff appraisals once every six months. ....

6 She is *undertaking* research into brand name recognition ....

7 Make sure you *brush* your teeth before you go to bed. ....

8 Stop dithering. You must *come up with* a decision now. ....

Underline the best form in *italics* in each of these sentences.

Example
Would you mind if I *did*/<u>*made*</u> a suggestion about this?

9 Sue's *had/taken* a real dislike to her new supervisor.

10 It's high time the committee *had/took* action over this flagrant abuse.

11 Grace has *gone/been* on holiday in Jamaica and she's come back with a lovely tan.

12 I'm a little faint. Could I *lie/lay* down on the sofa for a minute?

13 The men have just *lain/laid* a brand new carpet in the bedroom.

14 I was so tired yesterday that I *lay/lied* in bed for most of the day.

15 Anatoly *speaks/talks* English with a strong accent.

16 The Prime Minister *spoke/talked* at the international conference in Geneva.

17 She's such a chatterbox, we were up half the night *speaking/talking*!

18 What do you think of that plan to *rise/raise* the 'Titanic' from the seabed?

19 I'm afraid a rather serious problem has *raised/arisen*.

20 Tax rates always seem to be *rising/raising* these days.

21 They *robbed/stole* my purse in broad daylight!

22 I regret to inform you that the bank will be unable to *lend/borrow* the sum you have requested.

23 Graham and Lucy are coming here for the weekend and I think they are *bringing/taking* the children with them.

24 Sorry I'm home so late, I *took/brought* the car to work today and I got stuck in a traffic jam.

25 Would you mind *bringing/fetching* the children from school next Tuesday?

Diagnostic test 20 key ▶ **page 348**

Diagnostic test 21

Adjectives

Fifteen of these sentences have mistakes. These may be an incorrect word, a spelling mistake or an error in word order. Tick (✔) the five correct sentences, then underline the mistakes in the others and write the corrections.

Examples

I'm afraid the only seat available is on the early morning flight.

.......................✔.......................

Our ~~squad national~~ is one of the best this country has ever produced.

....*national squad*....................................

1 London features numerous historics sites such as Westminster Abbey.

....

2 I'm writing a report on the political attitudes of the young's.

....

3 The health care needs of the old are a major problem for many western countries.

....

4 We've won first prize? What amazing!

....

5 A plant being built outside the town is chemical.

....

6 Try not to disturb the asleep children.

....

7 They are doing experiments on alive animals.

....

8 Please don't tell me negative anything.

....

9 I'm afraid that's the only answer possible.

....

10 Our latest release is a film suitable for all ages.

....

11 The involved people will be caught and severely punished.

....

12 We will be supplying an antidote to all those infected by the virus.

....

13 To avoid theft please make use of the provided security boxes.

....

14 The report into the rail crash was rather worried.

....

15 I always seem to play for the lost team!

....

16 Interest in Latino music is no longer confined to speaking Spanish audiences.

....

17 We've inherited a dining mahogany table from my great aunt.

....

18 They're selling that Victorian wonderful house on the corner.

....

19 The players will be wearing blue and red striped shirts for today's match.

....

20 The interview panel felt the applicant was well-informed and honest, capable.

....

Diagnostic test 21 key ▶ **page 349**

Diagnostic test 22

Comparison

Nine of these sentences contain mistakes. Tick (✓) the correct sentences, then find and correct the mistakes.

Example
Which of these three houses is the ~~expensivest~~?
......*most expensive*......

1 Come on, you've got to admit she's much slimer than you! ....

2 She's always saying she's better looking than I. ....

3 Our cat Whiskers has been much more lively since we added vitamin supplements to her diet. ....

4 We felt the male character was realer than the female, who seemed very artificial. ....

5 'Which do you prefer, darling, the brown or the green?'
'Oh, the green is definitely the best.' ....

6 I'm most proudest of this one. I won it against really stiff competition. ....

7 The divorce has made him the most unhappy man in the street, don't you think? ....

8 That special diet has worked miracles. He's much less fat than he used to be. ....

9 The eldest piece in the museum is this Egyptian amulet from the Third Dynasty. ....

10 Hasn't their eldest son just landed some sort of job in Seattle? ....

11 Our new social security scheme is lots more generous than the previous Government's. ....

12 Windsor Castle is the largest occupied castle of Britain. ....

13 Things are about as worse as they can get. ....

14 Children these days seem to get ruder and ruder and ruder. ....

15 I'm angrier than upset. ....

Complete each sentence so that it means exactly the same as the preceding one. You must include the word(s) in brackets.

Example
I predicted the weather would be very hot and I was right. (just as)
The weather ...*was just as hot as I predicted.*...

16 The *Hyperlink* modem is much faster than all the others in our catalogue. (by far)
Of all the modems ....

17 Jan and Lucy are equally good at tennis. (no).
Jan is .... Lucy at tennis

18 Getting a made-to-measure suit was much cheaper than I expected. (not nearly)
Getting a made-to-measure suit ....
....

19 I couldn't open the lock because it was very cold. (that)
It .... open the lock.

20 He gets increasingly angry as he becomes more frustrated. (angrier)
The more .... he gets.

Diagnostic test 22 key ▶ **page 349**

Diagnostic test 23

Gradable and ungradable adjectives

Five of these sentences contain mistakes with the adverbs and adjectives. Tick (✔) the correct sentences and underline the mistakes.

Examples
Some of these new laptops are hideously expensive. ✔
As usual he bought me something absolutely cheap.

1 Iceland is colder than Sweden.

2 Casualties during the Crimean War were very enormous.

3 Steve's new girlfriend is very attractive.

4 Clients are advised that Miami tends to be more boiling than Los Angeles during the winter months.

5 Milan cathedral is slightly huge.

6 Thank you. That really was a most delicious meal!

7 In many areas of Europe the wolf is virtually extinct.

8 My friend told me the film was dead exciting.

9 Last night's episode was really gripping.

10 I can't stand that actor; he's absolutely ugly.

11 The club's very empty for a Saturday night.

12 It's slightly free to get in; less than one Euro, in fact.

Choose the most appropriate adverb a, b or c, to fill each gap.

13 Jim hates speaking in public; he's .... shy.
a absolutely b completely c painfully

14 The Wimbledon final was .... exciting.
a absolutely b utterly c terribly

15 Your new bracelet's beautiful. It looks .... expensive.
a very b completely c absolutely

16 I think I'd better lie down; I feel .... sick.
a practically b a little bit c virtually

17 Yes, sir. You're .... correct. I'll give you a refund.
a quite b very c rather

18 Since the accident Clive has been .... paralysed.
a totally b absolutely c very

19 After a month with no rain the grass is .... dead.
a slightly b almost c somewhat

20 I wasn't expecting much but, surprisingly, the play was .... good.
a nearly b absolutely c quite

Diagnostic test 23 key ▶ **page 349**

Diagnostic test 24

Adverbs

Underline the correct form or phrase in *italics*.

Example
I haven't seen that much of them *late*/*lately*.

1 You're bound to be promoted; the boss thinks very *high*/*highly* of you.

2 The elephant trek took us *deep*/*deeply* into the rainforest.

3 In our school *fifty roughly*/*roughly fifty* students have mobile phones.

4 As we descended the hill the car began to go *more fast*/*faster*.

5 I've had a lot of insomnia recently. *I only slept yesterday*/*Yesterday I only slept* four hours.

6 *Weekly I get paid*/*I get paid weekly*, so I can pay the rent on Saturday.

7 *Here lies the tomb*/*The tomb here lies* of Sir Jasper Willoughby.

8 The train strike won't affect her, she *arrives usually*/*usually arrives* by taxi.

9 Liz isn't our most punctual member of staff, she *is often*/*often is* late for work.

10 I'm afraid that we *still don't*/*don't still* know his name.

11 You'll never get your money back because the company isn't *trading any longer*/*any longer trading*.

12 My parents aren't very sociable, in fact they *go out hardly ever*/*hardly ever go out*.

13 I'm sorry that the kids *badly behaved*/*behaved badly* while you were babysitting.

Rewrite these sentences, putting the adverb in brackets in the correct position.

Example
She has got a place in the shortlist. (definitely)
She has definitely got a place in the shortlist.

14 I thought his performance was good. (pretty)

....

15 The patient's body is now entirely free of symptoms. (almost)

....

16 These days I take my health much more seriously. (probably)

....

17 She's my worst enemy and I don't like her. (really)

....

18 Rejected, Harriet turned to food for comfort. (emotionally)

....

19 I bumped into your brother at the supermarket. (incidentally)

....

20 I understood everything because the teacher answered the question. (clearly)

....

Diagnostic test 24 key ▶ page 349

Diagnostic test 25

Nouns and noun phrases

In each sentence, either one or both of the forms in *italics* is correct. Tick (✓) the sentences where both forms are correct. Underline the correct form in the others.

Example
Mumps *is/are* not too problematic if contracted in childhood, but can be dangerous in later life.

1 The *chair/chairwoman* has just phoned to say she's been delayed in traffic.

2 For really good electric *pianos/pianoes*, have a look in Marston's.

3 Corn circles are one of the strangest *phenomenons/phenomena* of recent times.

4 Parliament consists of 653 *MP's/MPs*, about two-thirds of whom belong to the Government.

5 For this dish, you need to weigh the ingredients carefully on the *kitchen scale/kitchen scales*.

6 The Asthma Helpline will be able to give you *advice/an advice*.

7 This checkout is for customers with *fewer/less* than five items only.

8 He was hit on the head by *stone/a stone* and had to go to hospital.

9 The supermarket is doing a lot of different *fruit/fruits* from the Far East at the moment.

10 The most exciting event for most British viewers in the Sydney Olympics *was/were* the rowing finals.

11 The Society's President, against the wishes of the other founder members, *has/have* agreed to the sale.

12 Bread and butter *is/are* eaten with meals by most people in the North of England.

13 'The Three Kings' *was/were* a great success for George Clooney.

14 Have you thought about doing gymnastics? I think *it's/they're* very good for you.

15 Recent events prove the saying that twenty-four hours *is/are* a long time in politics.

16 The Council's team of social workers *is/are* to be commended for their actions.

17 The United Nations *is/are* sending a special envoy to the conflict zone.

18 I'll take you to the station if you give me *shout/a shout* when you're ready.

19 *The attack on the Minister was/The people attacked the Minister and it was* unprovoked and extremely vicious.

20 The first *outbreak/breakout* of the epidemic was in Zaire in the 1980s.

Diagnostic test 25 key ▶ **page 350**

Diagnostic test 26

Possessives and compound nouns

Eighteen of these sentences contain mistakes. Tick (✓) the correct sentences, then find the mistakes and correct them.

Example
Have you met the new girlfriend of my stepson yet?
Have you met my stepson's new girlfriend yet?

1 Did you notice that greasy stain on a side of our sofa? ....
2 Dave's company has been awarded a contract to repair all the buses' engines. ....
3 People in this street are very proud of their's manicured front lawns. ....
4 Isn't she your secretary's brother's boss? ....
5 These gloves look familiar; I think they're Joe's. ....
6 The villa we're borrowing belongs to my sister's-in-law's parents. ....
7 I adore Lennon's and McCartney's music, especially the early stuff. ....
8 This is Mario, he's a colleague of Professor Grigson. ....
9 I might be able to get you an interview; the owner's a friend of me. ....
10 Is that the new car of Hilary? ....
11 Elizabeth's the youngest daughter of Mr Granger. ....
12 Jem saw a fantastic article in the local paper of today. ....
13 Galileo was NASA's biggest project. ....
14 It's in a great location, only five minutes' walk from the supermarket. ....
15 Could you give me a dollar's worth of those bananas, please? ....
16 How about all of us going back to the house of my brother for some coffee? ....
17 Did you manage to get an appointment at the doctor's? ....
18 Oh, for the sake of heaven, can't you get a move on? ....
19 He's doing some research for his dissertation on anthropology's history. ....
20 The celebrities acknowledged the crowd's cheers who lined the street. ....
21 Astronomers predict an eclipse of the sun on April the thirteenth's morning. ....
22 Inspector Walters achieved fame with the famous serial killer's arrest. ....
23 Commentators have been stunned by the scale of the scandal. ....
24 The processor is the computer's main component, wouldn't you agree? ....
25 This term the class will be reading the short stories' collection of Graham Greene. ....
26 Everyone's been admiring my expensive wife's car. ....
27 If there's one thing I can't stand it's fussy children's clothes. ....
28 There's a beautiful old house for sale at the local estate's agent's. ....
29 If you want a really unique wedding dress, you need to find a good maker of dresses. ....
30 Great news – the college is going to give me a one-year sabbatical. ....

Diagnostic test 26 key ▶ page 350

Diagnostic test 27

Pronouns

Ten of these sentences contain mistakes. Tick (✔) the correct sentences, then find and correct the mistakes.

Example
Someone he called in the middle of the night – I don't know who it was.
Someone called in the middle of the night

1 We always wash up the dog's dishes separately. This cloth is for our dishes and that one is for its.
....

2 It's not their deckchair. It's our! Don't you recognise it?
....

3 E-mails they have become a real nuisance. I receive about thirty a day now.
....

4 Those plastic cakes look good enough to eat them!
....

5 The ski instructor didn't actually ski any better than me.
....

6 Don't tell anyone else about the surprise party. It's between you and I!
....

7 Could all of you people move a few metres to the left, please?
....

8 If you'd like a new tennis racket, I can get you a one very cheaply.
....

9 It's been an excellent course. I've enjoyed very much.
....

10 Some elderly people have difficulty in remembering themselves what happened only a few hours before.
....

11 Myself, I'm really not keen on savoury and sweet flavours together.
....

12 After John had been in captivity for three years, he and his wife had a lot to tell themselves.
....

13 They haven't cleaned the stairwells in our flats for over a month now.
....

14 The refugees have arrived and everybody seem quite happy with the living arrangements.
....

In the following sentences, one, two or all three of the answers (a–c) may be correct. Tick (✔) all of the correct answers.

Example
Each interviewee should arrive promptly for .... interview.
a his ✔ b his/her ✔ c their ✔

15 It's .... who asked for the music to be turned down.
a them b them ones c they

16 Come on! Own up! Who's left .... muddy boots in the kitchen again!
a their b his/her c her

17 We had to take Damon to the vet yesterday. .... 's got ear mites again.
a It b He c Himself

18 I'd like to treat .... to a night at the opera.
a you b yourself c myself

19 The hostile tribes went to war with ....
a one another b each other
c themselves

20 In cases like these, ... can understand the motive behind the attack.
a one b you c we

Diagnostic test 27 key ▶ **page 350**

Diagnostic test 28

Determiners

Complete each sentence with *a/an*, *the* or – (no article).

Example
All our towels are made of ..–.. Egyptian cotton.

1 Ruthless poachers hunt .... elephant for the valuable ivory of its tusks.

2 Next week I'll be reviewing a stunning new film. .... film stars Michael Douglas and is directed by Curtis Hanson.

3 Yesterday evening's *Nature Scope* about .... sun's future worried a large number of viewers.

4 Muhammad Ali was voted .... greatest sports personality of the twentieth century.

5 It is commonly accepted today that .... brown bread is good for you.

6 Many research scientists are inspired by .... hope of curing diseases by genetic engineering.

7 Fewer people attend .... church regularly now than twenty years ago.

8 Julianne studied for seven years to become .... criminal lawyer.

9 Like many people, I learnt to play .... piano when I was a child, but gave it up in my teens.

10 We recommend that children and teenagers are inoculated against .... meningitis.

Underline the correct determiner or determiners in each sentence (– = no article). In some cases two may be correct.

Example
None/Some/Both neighbours rushed to the aid of the elderly woman.

11 It costs £10 *a/an/–* hour to hire the squash court.

12 There's *a/the/–* good wine bar in the town centre, isn't there?

13 *A/The/–* Mr Jones came to see you this afternoon.

14 My parents grew up in the 1950s. In *the/these/those* days there was far less freedom than there is now.

15 *This/That/A* woman I'd never met before came up to me in the bank and asked if she could borrow £10!

16 It's freezing! I've never known a winter *–/this/that* cold before.

17 Isn't there *any/some/the* way that you can ensure delivery tomorrow?

18 *Every/All/Each* the children in the school have to take up at least one sport.

19 We have asked our retail outlets to return *both/both of/some* the new models for further inspection.

20 *Much/A lot/A few* depends on the final outcome of the negotiations.

Diagnostic test 28 key ▶ page 351

Diagnostic test 29

Prepositions

Tick (✔) the correct answer.

Example
The animal spun round suddenly and hissed violently .... me.
a to b by c at ✔

1 We used to be able to hear the sonic boom of Concorde as it flew ..... the house.
a above b over c on top of

2 Is the rank of sergeant ..... the rank of corporal in the British army?
a underneath b behind c below

3 The Grand Bazaar ..... Istanbul is the largest covered market in the world.
a at b in c by

4 The Council is building a new office .... the car park of the Multiplex cinema.
a at b behind c after

5 The zookeeper was amazing – he calmly walked ..... the lion and took the bag out of its mouth.
a near b up to c towards

6 Your appointment with the consultant is at 6.30 ..... the evening of the 11th.
a in b at c on

7 The new soap opera on BBC2 is starting ..... tomorrow.
a at b – c on

8 The walking tour will be leaving promptly ..... time in order to cover the itinerary.
a on b in c at

9 Louis was unable to name one person ..... all his acquaintances that he could truly call a friend.
a between b under c among

10 The hotel's bedding is made only ..... the finest cottons and linens.
a of b in c with

11 Well, ... my opinion, our neighbours could be a lot noisier and more disruptive than they actually are.
a from b according to c in

12 Despite ..... no rain for weeks, the garden appears to be flourishing.
a have b that we have had c having

Six of these sentences contain mistakes with prepositions in *italics*. Tick (✔) the correct sentences, then find and correct the mistakes.

Example
The house was undamaged in the floods, *except* the carpets. ......*except for*......

13 We had to put up with her moaning for the whole journey *up to* Glasgow! ....

14 Harriet advanced to her position in the company *by means* some strategic friendships. ....

15 The post office is *behind just* the petrol station. You can't miss it. ....

16 Why don't you go *towards* that police officer and ask him the way? ....

17 The divorce became much more expensive and messier *because of that solicitors became involved*. ....

18 *From what they said on the weather forecast* yesterday, we're in for a good weekend. ....

19 *Apart from to dismantle the lighting*, the band took only fifteen minutes to pack up. ....

20 I've been offered the job in Helsinki *for that I applied*. ....

Diagnostic test 29 key ▶ **page 351**

Diagnostic test 30

Word order and verb patterns

For each sentence below, you are given three possible ways of completing it. Only two are correct. Tick (✔) the correct ones.

Example
Although the girl was clearly in her teens, she appeared ...
a the child's mother.
b to be the child's mother. ✔
c fond of the child. ✔

1 During an interview the Minister told ...
a the nation that she would be resigning.
b to the nation that she would be resigning.
c the interviewer a lie about his resignation.

2 Passengers stumbled and luggage flew from the racks as the driver suddenly ...
a stopped. b stopped the train.
c stopped to the train.

3 The low turnout of townspeople at the meeting made the new councillor ...
a to get angry. b angry.
c chairman of the committee.

4 Surely you don't always want to remain ...
a a shop worker? b to be a shop worker?
c in his shadow?

5 When Jean-Paul Gaultier arrived on the scene, he appeared ...
a the natural successor to Westwood.
b to be the natural successor to Westwood.
c refreshingly new and different.

6 As part of their launch, the new travel company offered ...
a their first customer a free holiday.
b a free holiday to their first customer.
c to their first customer a free holiday.

7 The girl's passion for the man made her ...
a sign the confession.
b to sign the confession.
c blind to his faults.

8 The never-ending care and devotion of the nurses in the hospital helped ...
a to overcome cancer my father.
b my father overcome cancer.
c my father to overcome cancer.

The words in brackets are in the wrong order. Rewrite them in the correct order.

Example
When we won the lottery last year, [new/we/our/house/parents/bought/a].
........*we bought our parents a new house.*........

9 In the play, [the/Princess/Duke/really/the/loves], but unfortunately his love isn't reciprocated. ....

10 [quote/you/could/provide/a/formal]? If you put it in writing, we'll accept it. ....

11 [secret/kept/Duncan/to/her/Katharine/marriage/a] for several months before she dared to tell her parents. ....

12 [Bettina/yacht/named/John/the] after his wife, who had recently passed away.
....

13 The arrival of the Shakespearean actor [amount/company/of/the/brought/certain/class/a]. ....

14 The Millers are just leaving. [will/show/motorway/them/the/you/way/to/the]? You go past the slip road, don't you?
....

15 The children at the party were delighted when [rabbit/hat/from/a/the/magician/pulled/his]. ....

16 The warden told [that/want/see/visitors/prisoner/the/didn't/them/the/to].
....

17 [machine/me/use/show/can/you/how/to/this]? I'm useless with anything mechanical.
....

18 We have to take on the third applicant; [enough/she/well-qualified/had/experience/and/was/she]. ....

19 The new design of the magazine [brighter/is/the/one/previous/much/than].
....

20 The play was a total disaster! [left/first act/we/as soon as/over/the/was].
....

Diagnostic test 30 key ▶ page 351

Diagnostic test 31

Relative clauses

Underline the correct alternative in *italics*.

Example
Do you know anyone *which/who* can repair cigarette burns on clothes?

1 It's usually children from deprived backgrounds *that/which* cause the worst problems.

2 *Captain Corelli's Mandolin*, *that/which* topped the best-seller lists for weeks on end, was never formally publicised.

3 The Council provides bins in *that/which* waste paper can be deposited for recycling.

4 All cows over 30 months *who/which* may have been exposed to BSE will be destroyed.

5 Address the reference 'to *who/whom* it may concern', as it's very formal.

6 The town hall clock played a different tune at twelve every day, *which/what* amused the locals and attracted tourists.

7 'There's a lucky person in this hall *who/whose* lottery ticket has just won them £2,000!'

8 'Why don't you tell the police *which/what* you told me yesterday?'

9 The film is set in the period *where/when* the divide between rich and poor was much greater than it is now.

10 You can put the photo *whichever/wherever* you think it looks best.

Each sentence below contains a mistake. Find the mistakes and correct them.

Example
Orders for ~~that~~ we have received payment will be processed immediately. ......*which*..............

11 The jackets which this shop makes them are of excellent quality. ....

12 Jack has prepared his favourite dish from Delia Smith's recipe book, which he is about to eat. ....

13 Can you get me one of those chocolate bars have got toffee in the middle?
....

14 The charity event raised over £1,000 for St Andrew's Hospice which opened last year.
....

15 I'd always wanted to take Graham to the city where I grew up in. ....

16 Have you invited the residents who living here on a temporary basis to the meeting?
....

17 He presented the visiting ambassador with a genuine Ming vase, that was worth over \$10,000. ....

18 The bank robbery what I told you about is in the local newspaper. ....

19 High taxation is often the main reason which governments fall. ....

20 The new buyer identified a dozen new sources for the material, most of them proved to be reliable. ....

Diagnostic test 31 key ▶ page 351

Diagnostic test 32

Contrast

Fourteen of these sentences contain a mistake. Tick (✓) the correct sentences, then correct the mistakes. (Some of the mistakes are in word order and level of formality.)

Example
We didn't have a lot of success with the garden, despite we worked hard on it.
...*We didn't have a lot of success with the garden, although we worked hard on it.*.......

1 I'm Gemini even though my mother is Capricorn. ....

2 My partner enjoys adventure holidays, whereas I prefer to laze on a beach.
....

3 But they'd travelled round the world, they had little experience of their own country.
....

4 Although the watch looked just like a Rolex, it had cost only $50 in a market in Hong Kong. ....

5 The girl was released from prison, she had served although only a fraction of her sentence. ....

6 Even although there was a Force 9 gale, the ship remained stable.
....

7 Visitors to tropical resorts still stay out in the sun too long, even they have had plenty of warning about the dangers of the sun's rays.
....

8 These exclusive villas are only a five-minute walk from the busy centre of the resort. They are a haven of peace and tranquillity yet.
....

9 Her face, although deathly pale, was as stern as ever.
....

10 Ideal the house may appear at first sight, be sure to have a full structural survey.
....

11 In spite of he had a full course of driving lessons, he failed the test four times.
....

12 Despite she was a woman, Marie Curie made a successful career for herself in a male-dominated world.
....

13 Despite having to do it in the dark, we managed to pitch the tent without problems.
....

14 Although the fact that the machine was under guarantee, the company refused to replace it.
....

15 We had a really horrible flight back – it was terrifying. The plane was all over the place and people were throwing up everywhere and screaming. Nonetheless, we got back safely.
....

16 However a dog may be a good companion for the elderly, the need to take it for walks may be a disadvantage.
....

17 Australian wines have long impressed European wine lovers. Australian, by contrast, champagne is a relative newcomer.
....

18 Most people appreciate the damage being done to the environment by cars. They won't stop using their own vehicles, however.
....

19 The new designs are not as innovative as the competition. They will certainly be popular as they are realistically priced, still.
....

20 The plumber charged $100 for an hour's work. He did a good job, mind you.
....

Diagnostic test 32 key ▶ **page 352**

Diagnostic test 33

Introductory *there* and *it*

Complete the sentences with *it* or *there* (and a suitable form of *be* if necessary).

Examples

In the state of Texas alone ...*there are*.. thought to be more than thirty prisoners on death row.

She found .....*it*............ strange that he never talked about his childhood.

1 Once upon a time .... an old woman who lived in a shoe.

2 During tomorrow's show .... an interval of fifteen minutes.

3 Luckily, ... not any difficulty finding the shop yesterday.

4 .... a long way to the beach from here.

5 'Which street is it?' '.................... the first one on the left.'

6 .... seems to be something wrong with my modem.

7 Strange weather for June; .... freezing today!

8 .... hardly any fuel left in the car.

9 The army doesn't anticipate .... much opposition from the rebel forces.

10 .... looks as though our team's going to win, after all.

11 .... supposed to be several ticket machines outside the station.

12 Given the right monetary conditions, ... theoretically possible to achieve zero inflation.

13 From the swirling mist .... emerged a mysterious cloaked figure.

14 If the reorganisation goes ahead .... sure to be a lot of opposition from the sales force.

15 I leave .... to your conscience to decide whether to report the matter.

16 Frankly, ... not surprising that they were expelled.

17 We would appreciate .... if you wouldn't say anything about this to the children.

18 Well, Mr Green, ... nothing wrong with the heating element so perhaps we'd better look at the pump.

19 Hello, ... Azco Market Research here; I wonder if you'd have a few minutes to take part in our telephone poll?

20 The ministry didn't expect .... quite such a negative reaction from farmers.

Diagnostic test 33 key ▶ page 352

Diagnostic test 34

Emphatic structures and inversion

Make the sentences more emphatic by rewriting them, beginning with the word(s) in brackets.

Example
They are doing something quite unprecedented. **(What)**
What they are doing is quite unprecedented.

1 The shellfish made Jasmine sick. (**It was**)

2 Greg lost the office keys. (**It**)

3 He's approaching the problem from an entirely new angle. (**What**)

4 They've done something unforgivable. (**What**)

5 I came by bus because my car has broken down. (**The reason**)

6 A second chance is the only thing I want. (**All**)

7 The guy who told me about the new club was Zack. (**Zack**)

8 We have to leave our bags and coats here. (**This**)

9 They told me the same thing. (**That's**)

10 He's very unlucky in love! (**Lucky**)

11 The interactive displays were much more interesting. (**Much**)

12 The Lord Chancellor was also at the ceremony (**Also**)

13 The firefighters were unable to enter the building because the heat was so intense. (**So**)

14 A parking ticket was stuck to my windscreen. (**Stuck**)

15 Although they were defeated they managed to keep smiling. (**Defeated**)

16 A gnarled old oak tree stands beside the river bank. (**Beside**)

17 The midnight movie is after this. (**Next**)

18 The government has hardly ever suffered such an overwhelming defeat. (**Seldom**)

19 As soon as we arrived they announced that the show was cancelled. (**No sooner**)

20 Refunds cannot be given under any circumstances. (**Under**)

Diagnostic test 34 key ▶ **page 352**

Diagnostic test 35

Aspects of cohesion

Rewrite the underlined sections of these sentences to avoid repetition.

Example
The dog winced as its owner kicked the dog once again. ....*it*.......

1 The American woman stepped off the train onto the crowded platform. The American woman was so striking that a hush fell over the people waiting to greet their loved ones. ....

2 I really don't like these modern paintings. I much prefer the paintings over there. ....

3 'Would you like some of these jelly beans?' 'No, thanks. I only like the red jelly beans and there aren't any left.' ....

4 'Have you seen Billy, Martin and Greg today?' 'Yes. Billy, Martin and Greg were at the coffee bar this morning.' ....

5 I'm afraid we didn't complete the obstacle course as quickly as the other team completed it. ....

6 'This lecture is really useless. I don't want to stay any longer.' 'No, I don't want to stay any longer.' ....

7 He asked me to give up my day off to help with the stocktaking, and he said he'd pay me extra to give it up. ....

8 My boss gave me a totally unexpected pay rise. I'd better thank her for giving me the pay rise. ....

9 'Do you think that Britain will win the bid to host the next World Cup?' 'I certainly hope they don't win it! It'll be chaos!' ....

10 Ask whether your parents are doing anything this weekend, and if they aren't doing anything, invite them to our party. ....

Eight of the sentences below either contain a mistake or could be expressed more concisely. Tick (✓) the two correct sentences, then correct the mistakes.

Example
Nigel coughed nervously and Laura coughed nervously too.
...*Nigel coughed nervously and so did Laura*...

11 The best pizzas are not to be found in big, city-centre restaurants but they are to be found in small, backstreet restaurants. ....

12 The girls all wanted to watch the video of *Romeo and Juliet*. The boys weren't so keen because they didn't want to watch a romantic film. They were so enthusiastic because they knew that Romeo was Leonardo diCaprio! ....

13 'Would you like some white wine?' 'No, thanks, I prefer red one.' ....

14 The people opposite us sniffed at the acrid smell of smoke and so we did. ....

15 'You wanted me to ring you about the arrangements for the wedding.' 'So did I.' ....

16 Grabbing her bag and snatching the money from the table, Angela ran through the front door and into the waiting taxi. ....

17 Mervyn Jones failed to complete the 400 metres because tore a muscle in his leg. ....

18 'Aren't they meeting us here?' 'Well, they must, because they weren't at home when I rang a few minutes ago.' ....

19 'Go to the Tate Modern without me. I'm not that interested in it.' 'Well, you should be! It's a great gallery.' ....

20 The President was unable to put through all the reforms that he had wanted to put through. ....

Diagnostic test 35 key ▶ page 353

Diagnostic test 36

Features of discourse

Circle the better option (a or b) for each space (1–7) in the text. Both options are grammatically correct; choose the most appropriate in the context.

Jane and Tom had been looking for a new home to buy for ages and they were excited about viewing the empty house in Garfield Road. (1) .... so it was quite easy to find. Walking up to the front door they noticed that the garden was extremely unkempt and full of rubbish. (2) .... Unfortunately the inside of the house was little better. From the state of the hallway it was clear that nobody had lived there for many years. Undaunted, Jane made straight for the kitchen. (3) .... It wasn't a pleasant sight. (4) .... Jane decided to see if the reception rooms were any better and walked back into the hall. (5) .... It was empty of furniture but with growing excitement Jane noticed a large boarded-up fireplace. She shouted for Tom to come and look at it. (6) .... So few houses had big fireplaces these days, and there was nothing she loved more than a house with a blazing log fire. (7) ....

1 a They knew the old church was opposite it.
  b They knew it was opposite the old church.

2 a There was a burnt-out sofa and an old fridge which was lying on its side.
  b A burnt-out sofa and an old fridge which was lying on its side were there.

3 a In any house it was the kitchen that she always wanted to see first.
  b She always wanted to see the kitchen first in any house.

4 a Hidden under a thick layer of dust and grease were the kitchen walls and units.
  b The kitchen walls and units were hidden under a thick layer of grease and dust.

5 a She stepped into the old dining room, pushing open a creaking mahogany door.
  b Pushing open a creaking mahogany door, she stepped into the old dining room.

6 a This was exactly the kind of thing they had been hoping to find.
  b They had been hoping to find exactly this kind of thing.

7 a Ever since her childhood spent in an old farmhouse in Scotland she had loved it.
  b It was something she had loved ever since her childhood spent in an old farmhouse in Scotland.

Choose the best word or phrase (a–n) from the box below to complete each sentence. Not all the options are needed.

> **a** At first **b** Furthermore **c** Nevertheless
> **d** Due to **e** After that **f** Consequently
> **g** The Prince **h** The Prince of Wales
> **i** To know the right people.
> **j** Knowing the right people.
> **k** Cheques should be
> **l** It would be nice if your cheque was
> **m** creepy **n** unnerving

8 Proof of status must be included with each application. ...., we require a signed and dated passport-sized photograph, which is non-returnable.

9 Joseph never went to university. ...., he considered himself to be well educated.

10 The air traffic controllers have called a strike. ...., all flights are cancelled until further notice.

11 The tour of the Acropolis will take two hours. .... you will be free to go shopping.

12 The Prince of Wales announced his decision to give up playing polo today. .... has sustained a number of injuries in recent years.

13 Being in the right place at the right time. .... These are the ingredients of success in our society.

14 Invoices should be paid by cheque. .... marked 'payee only'.

15 Many critics find the scene in the attic particularly ....

Diagnostic test 36 key ▶ page 353

1 Present tenses

The present simple and the present continuous tenses are the most common ways of expressing present time in English. The present simple describes things that are generally true, while the present continuous describes things that are true at the time of speaking, but which may change. This unit looks at the present time uses of these two tenses. They can also express future time (▶ **Unit 4**) and past time (▶ **1.1E, 1.2E**).

1.1 PRESENT SIMPLE

1.1A Form

The form of the present simple verb only changes after *he*, *she* or *it*, when we add *-s* to the base form (*-es* after *o*, *s*, *sh*, *ch* and *x*; *-ies* when the base form ends in *-y*):

*I read → he read**s**; we watch → she watch**es**; they carry → it carr**ies***

✗ ~~*Carina **enjoy** hospital dramas so she **watch** 'ER' every week.*~~

✓ *Carina **enjoys** hospital dramas so she **watches** 'ER' every week.*

We form the negative and questions with the auxiliary *do* (▶ **6.1A, 7.1A**). In the negative we usually use the contracted forms *don't* and *doesn't* in speech and informal writing:

*Japanese cooking **doesn't use** a lot of dairy food.*

***Do** interest rates usually **go up** in order to reduce inflation?*

1.1B General truths and facts

We often use the present simple to state truths and to describe things which we feel are facts or permanent situations:

- Things which are generally true:
  *British people **drink** a lot of tea, while Americans **drink** more coffee.*
- Facts: *Broken bones in adults **don't heal** as fast as they **do** in children.*
- Permanent situations: *A colony of Antarctic penguins **lives** in Marwell Zoo.*

1.1C Repeated events/actions

We use the present simple to describe things that happen on a regular basis:

*As temperatures **fall** with the approach of winter, the soil **freezes** and **contracts** ...*

*The Blairs **take** their summer holiday in a quiet part of Tuscany.*

We often use the present simple with adverbs of frequency (*always*, *usually*, *often*, *sometimes*, *never*) and expressions of frequency (*every ...*, *once a ...*):

*Share prices **usually change** on a daily basis – but **often** by very little.*

*Our two chefs **provide** an excellent choice of hot meals **every day**.*

1.1D Series of events/actions

We use the present simple to describe a series of events or actions (e.g. to give directions or instructions) often with impersonal *you*:

*From here **you cross** the road, **go** through an iron gate and **follow** the path west ...*

This is similar to the imperative, but the imperative can sound more abrupt:

***Cross** the road, **go** through an iron gate and **follow** the path west ...*

We use the present simple when we want to express the immediacy of an event, e.g. in sports commentaries, particularly when the action being described is a quick one and is therefore over before the description finishes:

*France **kicks off**, Zidane **passes** to Henry, Henry **cuts** inside ...*

1.1E Other uses

If we wish to give the events of a past narrative or an anecdote more immediacy, we can use the present simple, especially in speech (compare ▶ **1.2E**):

*There's an old woman with thick glasses and a name tag. I **go** up to her and **ask** ...*

Newspaper headlines often use the present simple to express a past event, which again gives more immediacy to the event:

*Addicted Chaplin star **gets** three years for new drugs lapse.*

We use the present simple in formal speech or writing for certain actions:

*I **note** that you referred to the National Curriculum in your speech ...*

*I **look forward to** receiving a prompt reply to my enquiry.*

We can use the present simple to talk about fixed events in the future (▶ **4.4A**) or to express the future after conjunctions of time, e.g. *when*, *after*, *as soon as* (▶ **4.4D**).

1.2 PRESENT CONTINUOUS

1.2A Form

We form the present continuous with the present of the verb *be* and the present participle of the main verb:

*'What **are** the children **doing**?'*

We usually contract *is* or *are* to *'s* or *'re* in speech and informal writing:

*'Well, Alan**'s drawing** in his room and Sophie**'s watching** TV with me.'*

Note the following spelling rules for forming the present participle:

- Base form + *-ing*: *draw* → ***drawing***, *watch* → ***watching***, *speak* → ***speaking***
- Base form ending in *-e* + *-ing*: *take* → ***taking***, *receive* → ***receiving***, *create* → ***creating***
- Base form + consonant + *-ing*: *swim* → ***swimming***, *run* → ***running***

(For past, future and perfect continuous forms ▶ **2.2, 2.4, 3.3, 4.1C, 4.3B, 4.4C**.)

❶ We often omit the pronoun and auxiliary (*is* or *are*) when we repeat the present continuous in the same sentence:

*James and Sally **are spending** the evening together, **watching** a new video.*

For information on ellipsis ▶ **35.3A, B**.

1.2B Things which are true now

The present continuous describes an action in progress at the moment of speaking or around the time of speaking. The action is likely to continue after the time of speaking, but is likely to stop at some point, i.e. it is temporary:

*I'll be with you in a minute. **I'm just finishing** something in the kitchen.*

*We **are staying** with John to try and find out if his place really is haunted.*

Common adverbs with this form are *now*, *just*, *still* and *at the moment*:

*We**'re studying** the writings of Günter Grass on the German course **now**.*

We use *live*, *work*, *study* and *stay* in the continuous if the action is temporary:

✗ ~~*She **stays** in the Waldorf Astoria on this visit to New York, doesn't she?*~~

✓ *She**'s staying** in the Waldorf Astoria on this visit to New York, isn't she?*

Compare: *She always **stays** in the Waldorf Astoria on visits to New York.* (▶ **1.1C**)

❶ An exception to the use of the present continuous to describe actions in progress is *Here comes* and *There goes*, which are always in the present simple:

✗ ~~*Here **is coming** the postman. There **is going** the last bus.*~~

✓ *Here **comes** the postman. There **goes** the last bus.*

Note the inversion of the verb and subject in these phrases.

We also use the present continuous to describe things which are changing:

*British summers **are getting** hotter and winters **are getting** wetter.*

We do not use the present simple to express this:

✗ ~~*British summers **get** hotter and winters **get** wetter.*~~

The present simple describes a regular event which we see as unchanging:

*We **get** a lot of rain during the winter in this part of the world.*

1.2C Repeated events

It is possible to use the present continuous to talk about repeated events or actions, usually if they happen within a temporary period:

*I'm **feeding** the neighbour's cat this week while she's in hospital.*

Compare this with the use of the present simple for repeated actions (▶ **1.1C**):

*Graham's a confirmed smoker. He **smokes** about fifty cigarettes a day.*
(repeated action over a long period of time, possibly most of Graham's life)

*Graham's having a tough time at the office at the moment and he**'s smoking** about fifty cigarettes a day!* (repeated action in a temporary period)

We can use the present continuous with an adverb such as *always*, *forever* or *continually* to talk about repeated actions that happen very often, perhaps too often as far as the speaker is concerned:

*The baby**'s always making** cute little gurgling noises.*
*The neighbours **are forever slamming** doors and shouting during the night.*
*I**'m always forgetting** people's birthdays. It's so annoying.*

1.2D Series of events

You may hear the present continuous used in sports commentaries, when the action is in progress throughout the time of speaking:

*They**'re** now **entering** the back straight and El Garrouj **is starting** to pull away ...*
(*... and he **crosses** the line two seconds ahead of his closest rival ...* ▶ **1.1D**)

1.2E Other uses

We can use the present continuous with the present simple to give more immediacy to a past narrative. We use the continuous for actions which form a background, i.e. they started before the actions within the narrative:

*There's an old woman with thick glasses who**'s serving** the hot drinks, so I go up to her and ask ...* (She started serving before the action of the narrative.)

The present continuous can also express arrangements in the future (▶ **4.3A**).

1.3 VERBS RARELY USED IN THE CONTINUOUS

1.3A Verbs of believing, having, liking, etc.

There are a number of verbs in English which we rarely use in a continuous tense. They often describe states of being, thinking, possessing or feeling:

✗ ~~*Most people **aren't believing** in the existence of UFOs.*~~
✓ *Most people **don't believe** in the existence of UFOs.*

The most common of these verbs are:

verbs of existing or being	*be, consist of, contain, exist*
verbs of possessing	*belong to, have* (= own), *include, lack, own, possess*
verbs of feeling or wanting	*adore, desire, despise, detest, dislike, envy, hate, like, love, need, pity, prefer, trust, want, wish*
verbs of thinking or believing	*believe, doubt, expect, feel* (= think), *forget, imagine, intend, know, realise, recognise, remember, see* (= understand), *suppose, think, understand*
verbs of appearance	*appear, resemble, seem*
other verbs	*concern, depend, deserve, fit, matter, measure, mean, mind, weigh*

1.3B Using these verbs in the continuous

It is possible to use many of the verbs in 1.3A in the continuous, but the verb either has a different meaning or expresses a temporary action:

*'Is Maria ready yet?' 'No, she**'s having** a shower.'* (= is taking)
*Now that there's electricity in the village, Santos **is thinking** of getting his house connected.* (= is considering)

This table shows some of the common differences in use:

verb	use in present simple	use in present continuous
be	*Your son* ***is*** *a very obedient child, isn't he?*	*Your son* ***is being*** *very obedient at the moment.* (= is behaving obediently)
have	*They're very rich. They* ***have*** *three homes and a yacht.*	***I'm having*** *a really good time, thanks.* (= am experiencing)
think	*I* ***think*** *that the world's problems are getting worse.*	***I'm thinking*** *of contributing to Oxfam.* (= am considering)
mean	*The sign* ***means*** *'slow down'.*	*You're always* ***meaning*** *to call us, but you never do.* (= are intending)
appear	*It* ***appears*** *the police have not started the investigation.*	*The Philharmonic* ***are appearing*** *at the Palladium.* (= are performing)
weigh	*She* ***weighs*** *70 kilos.*	***I'm weighing*** *the ingredients for the cake.* (= action of weighing)

❗ Some verbs of feeling can be used in both the simple and the continuous with no change in meaning:

My wrist ***hurts/is hurting*** *again – I must go to the physiotherapist.*

I think those mussels may have been off. ***Do you feel/Are you feeling*** *OK today?*

1.3C Sense verbs

We do not usually use the continuous form with verbs which describe a sense or a form of perception, e.g. *hear, notice, see, smell, taste*:

✗ ~~*I'm noticing that your wife doesn't come to the wine tastings. Doesn't she drink?*~~

✓ *I* ***notice*** *that your wife doesn't come to the wine tastings. Doesn't she drink?*

With verbs which describe a sense, we usually use the simple form or *can/could* + the verb when we do not deliberately use the sense, i.e. the use is involuntary:

Can *you* ***smell*** *the fertiliser? We're really in the countryside now!*

With *smell* and *taste*, we can use the continuous for a deliberate action:

I ***(can) taste*** *cream in this.* (there is cream in the dish; involuntary action)

I'm tasting *the cream.* (the cream might be off; intentional action)

❗ We usually use the verbs *see* and *hear* only in the involuntary sense, unless they have a different meaning, e.g. ***I'm seeing*** *a new man at present* (= going out with). We use *look at, watch* or *listen to* for an intentional action:

✗ ~~*Can you keep the noise down? I'm hearing the afternoon play.*~~

✓ *Can you keep the noise down?* ***I'm listening to*** *the afternoon play.*

1.3D Performative verbs

We use performative verbs in the first person actually to perform an action, i.e. saying *I apologise* performs the action of apologising:

On behalf of the company, I ***apologise*** *for any inconvenience caused.*

When these verbs 'perform' the function they express, they do not usually take the continuous:

Railtrack ***apologises*** *for the disruption to services over the last three months.*

By saying this, the function of apologising is performed. However, if we use the verb to describe the action rather than to do it, we can use the continuous:

The Railtrack chief executive ***was apologising*** *profusely for the inconvenience.*

Common performative verbs are: *accept, agree, apologise, congratulate, declare, deny, disagree, forbid, forgive, guarantee, insist, invite, order, predict, promise, recommend, refuse, request, suggest, thank, warn.*

▶ **Pages 70 and 71 for Round up of present and past tenses**

Practice

The key to these exercises is on page 354.

1 1.1, 1.2

Write the correct form of the verb in brackets to complete this dialogue. Use the present simple or the present continuous.

SARAH Welcome to the programme. This afternoon I (1) .... (stand) in the middle of the northern Black Forest, Germany, with Rainer Sanger, from Friends of the Forest.

RAINER Good afternoon, Sarah.

SARAH Rainer, you're very concerned about this area of the forest, aren't you? Can you tell us why?

RAINER Yes. Much of the forest was wiped out in the hurricane last winter, as you can see. Many of the trees are dead, and more (2) .... (die) because of the irreversible damage. We at Friends of the Forest (3) .... (believe) that the authorities (4) .... (not/do) enough right now to restore this beautiful forest to its former state.

SARAH But they (5) .... (clear) the dead trees away, aren't they? I saw some men on the way here ...

RAINER Of course, but they (6) .... (do) that every year. It's the normal procedure. We need more trees now, but they (7) .... (not/plant) any new trees to replace those that died.

SARAH I see. But you have approached the authorities about this, I (8) .... (understand).

RAINER We have tried, but each time they (9) .... (say) that they haven't got enough money to restore the forest as quickly as we'd like. They (10) .... (always/use) money as the excuse. It's getting really frustrating!

SARAH But it's not just an excuse, is it? They clearly (11) .... (not/have) enough money for everything, and the hurricane was an unforeseen occurrence.

RAINER Of course, we appreciate that, and the point is that actually, we (12) .... (not/ask) for much money. We would just like their guidance – we can provide volunteers to work on the forest.

SARAH Oh, I see. Well, that's somewhat different. Now Rainer, could you tell us ...

2 1.1, 1.2

Underline the correct verb form in *italics* for each sentence.

1 The Guggenheim Museum in Bilbao *houses/is housing* Spain's largest collection of Modern Art.
2 We *try out/are trying out* a new paper supplier at the moment. The old one was too expensive.
3 The children *don't eat/aren't eating* sweets and chocolate before they go to bed at night. It's bad for their teeth.
4 These animals *display/are displaying* a great deal of aggression if disturbed.
5 We *currently show/are currently showing* the film 'Star Wars' at all Odeon cinemas in the region.
6 Quick! Get rid of all the mess! Here *come/are coming* Mum and Dad!
7 The weather forecast says there'll be wind from the north-west tonight. That always *brings/is bringing* snow with it at this time of year.
8 The rubbish collectors *come/are coming* on Fridays in this area. They *don't take/aren't taking* rubbish not left in black plastic bags.
9 You *always complain/are always complaining* and it really gets on my nerves! Why can't you just accept things and relax?
10 *Does the orchestra play/Is the orchestra playing* at the Town Hall this week? I'd really like to see their new concert.
11 Swimming *provides/is providing* exercise for more muscle groups than any other physical activity.
12 What *do you consider/are you considering* to be the lowest price they'll sell the house for?

3 1.1

Rewrite these sentences from newspaper articles as headlines to the articles. Use the underlined words and phrases to help you.

0 The chief inspector of prisons last night called for the release of the Bulger killers.

Prisons chief calls for release of Bulger killers

1 A High Court judge has blocked the proposed ban on tobacco adverts.

....

2 The chief of police admitted that errors were made during the Chinese President's visit to the UK.

....

3 Radio 1, the BBC's pop music station, has outshone all its commercial radio rivals in a recent poll.

....

4 The private member's bill on fox-hunting did not achieve the support needed last night to become law.

....

5 The government of India has snubbed the Pope on the eve of his visit to the country, as they have refused his invitation to attend a multi-faith gathering.

....

6 Makers of the latest Leonardo DiCaprio film are facing a huge protest from locals over their treatment of a beach used for filming.

....

4 1.1, 1.2

Complete this newspaper report. Write the verbs in brackets in the correct form, present simple or present continuous.

It's summer. A man is out for a quiet walk. He's walking along a country road and he (1) .... (mind) his own business when he (2) .... (be knocked down) and seriously injured by a minivan. The man, a writer of thrillers and horror fiction, (3) .... (survive) but he (4) .... (become) obsessed with the vehicle that maimed him. He doesn't bear a grudge against the driver. Instead, he (5) .... (buy) the minivan and (6) .... (hide) it.

This sounds like the plot of a Stephen King thriller, but it is in fact the latest chapter in the writer's real life. King has bought the van and he (7) .... (intend) to take a sledgehammer to it. At present King (8) .... (recover) from his injuries at home, where he (9) .... (suffer from) a broken hip, a fractured leg and a collapsed lung. The story is uncannily like the plot of his novel *Thinner* (written several years previously), in which the victim's family (10) .... (put) a curse on the driver. King, however, (11) .... (demand) only the withdrawal of the driver's licence. As for the minivan, we (12) .... (not know) if King will actually carry out his revenge or if he is simply hatching the plot for a new novel!

5 1.3

Read each pair of sentences below, A and B. The sentence which follows each pair is related to one of the sentences in the pair. (For example, it could come after the sentence or describe the sentence.) Write the letter of the correct sentence in the box.

0 A Steven's a difficult child.
B Steven's being difficult.
He isn't usually difficult. [B]

1 A This salmon weighs more than six kilos.
B We're weighing the salmon to put a price on it.
This is a characteristic of the salmon. [ ]

2 A I invite everyone present to the opening of the new superstore.
B I'm inviting everyone to the opening of the new superstore.
I'm offering this invitation to you now. [ ]

3 A The dance group appears to have arrived at the theatre.
B The dance group is appearing at the theatre.
There are performances every evening. [ ]

4 A Mmm. I taste cinnamon in this. Lovely.
B I'm tasting it to see if there's enough cinnamon in it.
I need to check the quantity of cinnamon. [ ]

5 A I think house prices will rise again next year.
B I'm thinking of selling my house next year.
This is my opinion. [ ]

6 A My sister has a baby.
B My sister's having a baby.
My sister's pregnant. [ ]

7 A I smell lavender. Is there a bush in the garden?
B I'm smelling the lavender. It's a very strong variety.
The smell has just come to my attention. [ ]

8 A He's having a shower.
B He has a fantastic power shower in the main bathroom.
Why don't you wait in the living room? [ ]

9 A We guarantee that your children will be supervised by experienced instructors.
B My husband and I are guaranteeing the loan for Mrs Knight.
The company takes full responsibility. [ ]

10 A Is this an inadequate explanation or am I being stupid?
B I'm sorry, I don't understand. Am I really so stupid?
Is this a permanent characteristic of mine? [ ]

6 ALL

In about half of the lines of the following text there is an error in the use of the present forms. For each numbered line (1–22), underline the error and write the correct form. Some lines are correct. Indicate these with a tick (✓). The exercise begins with two examples (0 and 00).

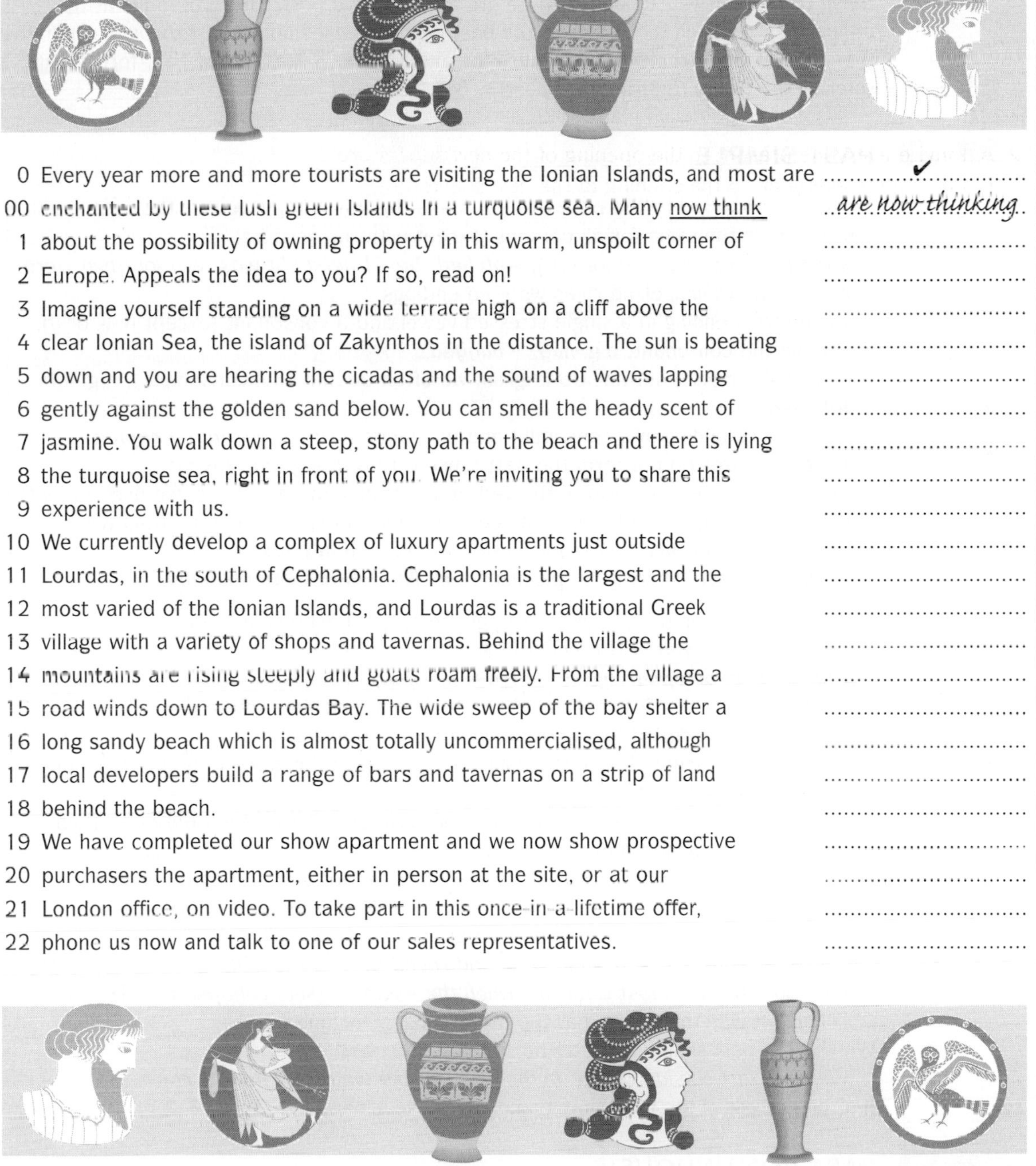

0 Every year more and more tourists are visiting the Ionian Islands, and most are ....✓............
00 enchanted by these lush green Islands In a turquoise sea. Many <u>now think</u> ..*are now thinking*..
1 about the possibility of owning property in this warm, unspoilt corner of ....
2 Europe. Appeals the idea to you? If so, read on! ....
3 Imagine yourself standing on a wide terrace high on a cliff above the ....
4 clear Ionian Sea, the island of Zakynthos in the distance. The sun is beating ....
5 down and you are hearing the cicadas and the sound of waves lapping ....
6 gently against the golden sand below. You can smell the heady scent of ....
7 jasmine. You walk down a steep, stony path to the beach and there is lying ....
8 the turquoise sea, right in front of you. We're inviting you to share this ....
9 experience with us. ....
10 We currently develop a complex of luxury apartments just outside ....
11 Lourdas, in the south of Cephalonia. Cephalonia is the largest and the ....
12 most varied of the Ionian Islands, and Lourdas is a traditional Greek ....
13 village with a variety of shops and tavernas. Behind the village the ....
14 mountains are rising steeply and goats roam freely. From the village a ....
15 road winds down to Lourdas Bay. The wide sweep of the bay shelter a ....
16 long sandy beach which is almost totally uncommercialised, although ....
17 local developers build a range of bars and tavernas on a strip of land ....
18 behind the beach. ....
19 We have completed our show apartment and we now show prospective ....
20 purchasers the apartment, either in person at the site, or at our ....
21 London office, on video. To take part in this once-in-a-lifetime offer, ...
22 phone us now and talk to one of our sales representatives. ....

2 Past tenses

We often use the past simple tense for single completed events and past states and we use the past continuous for temporary or interrupted actions. We use the past perfect tense for actions which happened before a time in the past. This unit looks at the differences between the past and the past perfect tenses and *used to/would* + infinitive. (For uses of the present perfect tense for past time ▶ **3.1**, **3.2**. For past forms which refer to the future (future in the past) ▶ **5.3**.)

2.1 PAST SIMPLE

2.1A Form

Most verbs add *-ed* to the base form to make the past simple tense. The past simple tense form is the same for all persons (except with the verb *be*):

watch – *I/he/she/it/we/you/they* ***watched***; ***be*** – *I/he/she/it* ***was***, *we/you/they* ***were***

Note the following spelling rules with *-ed* endings:

- Base forms ending in a single stressed vowel and a consonant (except *w, x* or *y*), double the consonant, e.g. *hug* → ***hugged***.
  In British English, but not US English, we often double final consonant *l*, e.g. *label* → ***labelled***.
- Base forms ending in a consonant and *y*, change *y* to *i*, e.g. *copy* → ***copied***.
- Irregular verbs do not form the past tense with *-ed*, e.g. *go* → ***went***.

We do not use the past form of the verb in questions and negatives; we use *did* (*not*) + infinitive. We usually use the contracted form *didn't* in speech and informal writing:

✗ ~~'**Did** *you* **saw** *anything suspicious?'*~~ ✗ ~~*'No, I* **didn't saw** *anything.'*~~
✓ *'**Did** you **see** anything suspicious?'* ✓ *'No, I **didn't see** anything.'*

2.1B Past actions and states

We use the past simple to describe single completed actions in the past:

*Julius Caesar **invaded** Britain in 55 BC.*
*Holland **was occupied** by the Germans in 1940.*

If the context is clear, it is not necessary to give a past time reference:

*Caesar's troops **failed** to defeat the indigenous tribes (in 55 BC).*

We use the past simple for actions which happened at the same time and also for repeated actions:

*When we got to the junction I **took** the left turn while Micky **took** the right.* (two actions at the same time)
*My brother **applied** for a visa six times before he got one.* (repeated actions)

We use the past simple for sequences of actions. Sometimes the actions follow immediately after each other, or one action causes a result:

*Silverman **ran** to the car, **jumped** in and **raced off** into the night.* (sequence of actions)
*Wall Street traders **lost** a fortune when the Asian markets **collapsed**.* (= The markets collapsed with the result that the traders lost a fortune.)

We use the past simple to describe states in the past:

*We **lived** just outside Oxford in the nineties, but we **didn't have** a car.*

(For a contrast of the past simple and the present perfect ▶ **3.1B**, **3.2**.)

2.2 PAST CONTINUOUS

2.2A Form

We form the past continuous with *was* or *were* and the present participle (▶ **1.2A**) of the main verb:

*What **were** the children **doing** while all this **was going on**?*

There are some verbs which we rarely use in the continuous tenses, including the past continuous. (For more information about this ▶ **1.3A, B, C**)

2.2B Actions in progress

The past continuous describes an action in progress at a point of time in the past, i.e. the action began before this point of time and continued after it.

*We didn't hear the intruder because we **were sleeping** on the top floor that night.*
*At the time of our arrival the city **was going through** a period of rapid expansion.*

We often use the past continuous to show that a past action was temporary, or was changing or developing:

*During my training I **was earning** a lot less than my wife.* (a temporary situation)
*His symptoms **were becoming** more pronounced each day.* (a changing situation)

We can use the past continuous to describe an ongoing action which forms the background or setting to past events. We often use the past simple for an action that happened against this background:

*Darkness **was descending** over the hushed city as James **staggered** back to college.*
(*darkness was descending* = background; *James staggered* = action)

We can use the past continuous for two actions in progress at the same time:

*We **were watching** the sky and **listening** for the first sounds of the dawn chorus.*

We usually use the past simple for repeated actions in the past (▶ **2.1B**), but we can use the past continuous if we want to emphasise that the repeated actions took place over a temporary and limited period of finished time:

*She **received** chemotherapy on a weekly basis.* (a repeated action)
*For the first three months she **was receiving** chemotherapy on a weekly basis.*
(repeated action, but only for three months)

2.2C Interrupted actions

We use the past continuous to contrast an ongoing action with a single event which interrupts it. We use the past simple for the single event:

*Elizabeth **was hunting** when messengers **arrived** with the news of Mary's plot.*
*Seventy cars **were crossing** the bridge when the pier **collapsed** into the river.*

! If the background action finishes just before the event which interrupts it, we prefer to use the past perfect continuous (▶ **2.4A, B**). Compare these examples:

Jane opened the door to let Philip in.

1 *He **was running** in the rain.*

2 *He **had been running** in the rain.*

2.2D Other uses

We can use the past continuous to describe past arrangements; the arranged event may or may not have taken place. This use is similar to the 'future in the past' (▶ **5.3**):

*Nancy **was taking** the next flight to Paris so she had to cut short the interview.*
(= Nancy had an existing arrangement to take a flight to Paris.)

We can make requests, suggestions and questions more tentative and polite by using the past continuous. We often use the verbs *think* and *wonder*:

*We **were wondering** if you would like to join us.* (= Would you like to join us ...?)
***Were** you **planning** on going somewhere else later?* (= Are you planning on ...?)

2.3 PAST PERFECT

2.3A Form

We form the past perfect with *had* and a past participle, which is the same for all persons.

By the end of the fourth day we ***had exhausted*** *most of our rations.*

I wasn't convinced that she ***had exhausted*** *all of the possibilities at that stage.*

Regular verbs have a past participle form which is the same as the past tense form (i.e. we add *-ed* to the base form ▶ **2.1A**). Irregular verbs, e.g. *see*, often have a past participle form, e.g. *seen*, which is different from the past tense form, e.g. *saw*.

We often use the contracted form of *had* (*'d*) in spoken English:

*We were exhausted; we****'d been*** *up all night with the baby.*

2.3B Actions and states before a time in the past

We use the past perfect to describe an action which is completed before a time in the past. We can include a specific time reference:

By the time the UN task force arrived, the rebel forces ***had taken*** *the province.*

We can use the past perfect for repeated actions:

The new owners found that the timbers ***had been patched up*** *several times.*

We also use the form to describe a state which existed before a past event:

At the time of her trial last year Hinkley ***had been*** *in prison for eight months.*

2.3C Sequence in the past

We can use the past perfect to make a sequence of events clear. We use the past perfect for the earlier action and the past simple for the later. Compare:

When we ***got back*** *the babysitter* ***went*** *home.*

(sequence: 1 we got back, 2 the babysitter went home)

When we ***got back*** *the babysitter* ***had gone*** *home.*

(sequence: 1 the babysitter went home, 2 we got back)

We can use *just* or *already* with the past perfect to show that the earlier action was recent or earlier than expected:

*We wanted to talk to the babysitter but she****'d just left****.*

When we got back we found that the babysitter ***had already gone*** *home.*

We can use the past perfect or the past simple with time conjunctions, e.g. *after, before, as soon as, then*:

She ushered me out of the room ***as soon as I paid/had paid*** *my subscription.*

❗ With *before* + past perfect the action in the past simple happens first:

I left university ***before I'd taken*** *the final exams.*

We can use this for a past action which prevented a later action from happening:

She ***sacked*** *him* ***before he'd had*** *a chance to explain his behaviour.*

❗ We don't usually use the past perfect if the sequence is obvious (▶ **2.1B**):

[*I* ***had opened*** *the door and let him in.*] ✔ *I* ***opened*** *the door and let him in.*

We often use the past perfect to describe the cause of a past event:

*David didn't join the band as he****'d signed up*** *with a rival label.*

2.3D Unfulfilled intentions

We use the past perfect with verbs such as *hope, expect, want, plan, think about, wish* to describe past intentions which were unfulfilled:

They ***had hoped*** *to get to the summit but Travers fell ill at base camp.*

2.4 PAST PERFECT CONTINUOUS

2.4A Form

We form the past perfect continuous tense with *had been* and the present participle:

The lake was near bursting point as it ***had been raining*** *heavily for weeks.*

The passive form of the past perfect continuous (*had been being* + past participle) is almost never used. We prefer an active form, using an 'empty' subject if necessary:

[*The unemployment figures* ***had been being underestimated*** *for decades.*]

✔ *They* ***had been underestimating*** *the unemployment figures for decades.*

There are some verbs which we rarely use in the continuous tenses, including the past perfect continuous. (For more information about this ▶ **1.3A, B, C**.)

2.4B Uses

We use the past perfect continuous to describe an ongoing situation or action which continued up to, or stopped just before, a time in the past (▶ **2.2C**):

*He **had been working** for over an hour before the auditors turned up.*

We often use this tense to explain a past result, e.g. a situation or an appearance:

*The few survivors looked painfully thin. They **had been living** on meagre rations since the accident.* (= They looked thin because they had been living on meagre rations.)

We use this tense when we want to focus on duration:

*Kubrick **had been trying** to get the film made for more than twenty years.*
*The eager fans **had been waiting** in line for over six hours.*

2.4C Contrast with other forms

We do not mention the number of times that we have done an action when we use the past perfect continuous:

✗ ~~*Jill **had** only **been watching** TV twice that week.*~~
✓ *Jill **had** only **watched** TV twice that week.* (repeated action – past perfect simple)

❗ We don't usually use the past perfect continuous for completed actions, or actions and background situations still continuing at the same time as the past simple narrative:

✗ ~~*She found her desk was empty; security **had been removing** everything.*~~
✓ *She found her desk was empty; security **had removed** everything.*
(completed action = past perfect simple)
[*We **had been living** in New York when John was made redundant.*]
✓ *We **were living** in New York when John was made redundant.*
(an ongoing situation which forms the background = past continuous)

2.5 *USED TO/WOULD*

2.5A Form and meaning

Used to is followed by an infinitive. Notice the spelling in questions and negatives:

*It **used to take** me over an hour to get to work.*
*Supermarkets **didn't use to be** open on Sundays in Britain.*
***Did** you **use to get** free milk at school?*

❗ Don't confuse *used to* + infinitive with *be/get used to* (+ verb *-ing*) which means 'be/become accustomed to':

*I **used to live** alone.* (= I lived alone at a time in the past.)
*He **wasn't used to living** on his own.* (= He wasn't accustomed to it.)
*She's **getting used to** the new technology.* (= She is becoming accustomed to it.)

2.5B Past habits

Both forms describe actions which happened regularly in the past but no longer happen (or vice versa) or now happen with more or less frequency:

*They **used to get paid** every three months.* (Now they get paid weekly.)
*We **would get up** early every Sunday to go to church.* (We don't now.)

To avoid confusion with other uses of *would*, we usually mention the past time or situation:

*He **would give** her a lift to work in the days before she passed her test.*

(For other uses of *would* ▶ **10.4, 10.5, 10.6**; ▶ **18.2B, 18.3B, 18.4, 18.5**.)

2.5C Past states

We use *used to* to describe past states which have changed:

*Lithuania **used to be** part of the Soviet Union.* (It isn't now.)
*There **didn't use to be** any crime around here in the old days.* (There is now.)

❗ We cannot use *would* for past states:

✗ ~~*France **would be** a monarchy but now it's a republic.*~~
✓ *France **used to be** a monarchy but now it's a republic.*

▶ **Pages 70 and 71 for Round up of present and past tenses**

2

Practice

The key to these exercises is on page 354.

1 2.1

Match the underlined phrases (1–10) with the explanations (A–E). Each explanation matches two phrases.

1 They ran the same test eight times before they found the bug in the software.
2 Food was in short supply throughout the war.
3 It was quite unnerving. The lights flickered while a freezing wind blew through the room.
4 Claire jumped out of her chair, ran to the balcony and grabbed the screaming child.
5 Lorenzo the Magnificent died in Florence in 1492.
6 Diplodocus dinosaurs dominated the Triassic period.
7 We had a busy morning. Steve answered the phone calls and I dealt with the e-mails.
8 The Court of Appeal rejected his case on technical grounds.
9 I'm sick of it, I can't tell you how many times we tried to contact them.
10 I threw open the doors and walked out into the bright morning sunshine.

A A single or completed action in the past.
B A sequence of actions in the past.
C Two actions which happened at the same time in the past.
D Repeated actions in the past.
E A state in the past.

2 2.1, 2.2

Complete the sentences with suitable verbs from the box. Use the past simple or past continuous.

announce blow collapse cook decide feel get up have hit leave live manage mention press run into see set off settle down soar spend stand take

1 I .... at the bus stop when I .... the speeding car slam into the lamp post.
2 The icy wind .... through the trees as we .... on our journey into the forest.
3 Brad .... exhausted so he .... onto the sofa, ... the button on the remote control and .... for an evening vegetating in front of the box.
4 The twins .... the afternoon shopping because they .... for their flatmates that evening.
5 Unfortunately for us, we .... on the wrong side of Miami when Hurricane Andrew .... the city.
6 Share prices .... when the government .... record growth figures.
7 I .... early the next morning so I .... to have an early night.
8 They say that he .... her because he found out that she .... an affair with his best friend.
9 My younger brother .... the driving test five times before he .... to pass.
10 I .... Clare at the supermarket the other day and she .... that you might be looking for work.

3 2.1, 2.2, 2.3, 2.4

Choose the best sentence (A or B) to illustrate each picture.

1 A I felt sick when I ate the pudding.
  B I felt sick when I'd eaten the pudding.

2 A When we returned to our hotel room, the maid made the bed.
  B When we returned to our hotel room, the maid had made the bed.

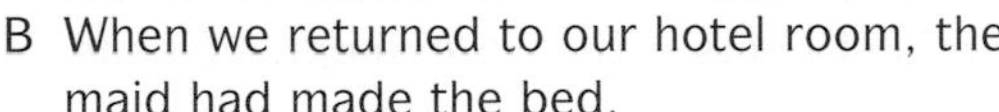

3 A I explained to my host that I'd been repairing the car.
  B I explained to my host that I was repairing the car.

4 A By the time we arrived at the zoo the elephants were having their bath.
  B By the time we arrived at the zoo the elephants had had their bath.

5 A The show started when we got there.
  B The show had started when we got there.

6 A I hoped to get a good result.
  B I had hoped to get a good result.

7 A I watched TV when Jane called round.
  B I was watching TV when Jane called round.

8 A Carrie was excited because she was travelling to Jamaica.
  B Carrie was excited because she had travelled to Jamaica.

4 2.3, 2.4

Underline the most suitable verb form in *italics*.

1 So I *turned/had turned* on my heels and walked out of the shop in disgust.
2 When we got to the station the train *had just left/just left*, so we missed our connection.
3 The mechanics *had been taking/had taken* the engine apart several times before they were able to locate the source of the mysterious rattle.
4 By 1492 the Spanish *had expelled/had been expelling* the Moors from the mainland entirely.
5 She was surprised to find the fridge empty; the children *had eaten/had been eating* everything!
6 Our lead actor turned up and he was word perfect; apparently he *was practising/had been practising* his lines all day.
7 The children wanted to go to the circus but their father *already booked/had already booked* tickets for the ice-skating spectacular.
8 Debbie couldn't understand why her computer crashed; it *had been working/was working* perfectly for as long as she could remember.
9 My niece's riding accident was rather a setback because she *hoped/had hoped* to pursue a career as a ballet dancer.
10 Mrs Lawson arrived at casualty in quite a state; she *suffered/had been suffering* from severe stomach pains for hours.

5 ALL

In about half of the lines of the following text there is a mistake in the use of past forms, *used to* or *would*. For each numbered line (1–18) underline the mistake and write the correct form. Some lines are correct. Indicate these with a tick (✔). The exercise begins with two examples (0 and 00).

Anne Frank

0 Anne Frank was a Jewish girl who was living with her family in Amsterdam ....✔..........
00 when the Germans were invading Holland in 1940. The German authorities ......invaded......
1 introduced harsh anti-Jewish laws and started to deport Jews to concentration ....
2 camps in Eastern Europe. In July 1942 Anne's father did hear a rumour that he ....
3 was going to be arrested by the police and the family resolved to find a hiding ....
4 place. They moved into an attic above Mr Frank's office and build a bookcase ....
5 to disguise the entrance to the secret apartment. Friends would bring food to the ....
6 family each morning, and they use to keep up to date with the news by listening to ....
7 the BBC on a small radio. Anne would have no friends her own age, so she ....
8 confided her feelings to a diary. In August another Jewish family joined the ....
9 Franks with their sixteen-year-old son Peter. Peter was telling Anne that the ....
10 Germans had been sending Jews to concentration camps and killing them. Anne ....
11 and Peter were becoming very fond of each other in the cramped conditions of ....
12 the secret apartment and had helped each other with their lessons. But somebody ....
13 had given away the family's secret. The German police had been watched the ....
14 hiding place for several days and on August 14th 1944 they burst in and arrested ....
15 all the occupants. The Germans were sending Anne to the Belsen concentration ....
16 camp and she was killed in February or March 1945, only a month or six weeks ....
17 before the British army arrived. Anne's father was taken to Auschwitz and ....
18 survived the war. He found Anne's diary and had published it in 1947. ....

6 ALL

Complete the text by writing the verbs in brackets in the correct tense. Read through the whole text before you begin as you may need to use passive forms and *used to/would* in your answers.

THE TRUE STORY OF TREASURE ISLAND

Treasure Island is one of the best known and most loved children's adventure stories. It (1) .... (be) first published in 1883 but remains popular to this day. People (2) .... (think) that the story was solely the work of Stevenson's imagination, but recent research has uncovered the true origin of this thrilling tale of hidden treasure and bloodthirsty pirates.

Treasure Island's author, Robert Louis Stevenson, (3) .... (be) a Scotsman born in Edinburgh in 1850. Although he (4) .... (live) abroad for many years, in 1881 he returned to the land of his birth for a holiday. With him (5) .... (be) his American wife Fanny, whom he (6) .... (meet) five years earlier in France, and his stepchildren from Fanny's first marriage. The location of their holiday was Braemar in the rugged Scottish Highlands.

The family soon settled into a relaxing routine. Each morning Stevenson (7) .... (get up) early and take them out for long walks over the hills. They (8) .... (enjoy) this for several days when the weather suddenly took a turn for the worse. Trapped indoors by the heavy rain, Robert's twelve-year-old stepson, Lloyd, (9) .... (become) increasingly bored and restless. Desperate to keep the boy amused, Robert (10) .... (get out) some drawing paper and asked the boy to do some painting.

After he (11) .... (paint) for several hours the boy (12) .... (return) to his stepfather with a beautiful coloured map of a tropical island. Robert noticed that his stepson (13) .... (draw) a large cross in the middle of the island. 'What's that?' he asked. 'That's the buried treasure,' said the boy. The thirty-one-year-old author suddenly had a flash of inspiration. He (14) .... (recently ask) to contribute stories to a children's magazine published by his friend W E Henley and he (15) .... (begin) to see the germ of an adventure story in the boy's picture. While the rain (16) .... (beat down) on the roof of his rented holiday cottage the author (17) .... (sit down) by the fire to write a story. He would make the hero a twelve-year-old boy, just like his own stepson. But who would be the villain of the piece?

For the last four years Henley (18) .... (publish) Robert's stories in his magazine, and the two had become good friends. But there was something unusual about Henley; as a young man one of his legs (19) .... (amputate) and he walked around with the aid of an artificial wooden leg. Robert (20) .... (always want) to include such a character in a story and thus Long John Silver, the pirate with a wooden leg, was born.

So, thanks to a rainy September in Scotland, a publisher with a wooden leg, and the inventiveness of a twelve-year-old American boy, we have one of the greatest adventure stories in the English language.

3 Past to present tenses

English uses the present perfect tenses (simple and continuous) to talk about actions and states which start in the past but which have a link with the present. This unit looks at the present perfect simple and continuous and compares the present perfect and the past simple. (For a detailed explanation of the past simple ▶ **2.1**.)

3.1 PRESENT PERFECT SIMPLE

3.1A Form

We form the present perfect simple with *has/have* and a past participle (▶ **2.3A**):

There ***has been*** *a serious decline in the number of people qualifying as teachers.*
Have *the printers* ***finished*** *the new brochure yet?*

We usually contract *has/have* in speech and informal writing:

*The film****'s*** *already* ***started*** *– we'd better hurry.*

In negative sentences, we usually contract *not* in speech and informal writing:

I've been to the shops today and they ***haven't started*** *the summer sales yet.*

Remember that a lot of English verbs have irregular past participles, e.g.
bring → ***brought***, *take* → ***taken***, *meet* → ***met***, *seek* → ***sought***, *swing* → ***swung***.

❗ Be careful not to drop the *have* with the present perfect:

✗ ~~*I* ***never been*** *to Madame Tussaud's.*~~
✔ *I****'ve never been*** *to Madame Tussaud's.*

3.1B Ongoing states and actions

We use the present perfect simple to talk about states that started in the past and are still continuing in the present:

The manor house ***has stood*** *on this spot for over two hundred years.* (It is still here.)

We often use the prepositions *for* (+ period of time) and *since* (+ point in time):

✗ ~~*The centre of the island* ***has not been*** *inhabited* ***since*** *fifty years.*~~
✔ *The centre of the island* ***has not been*** *inhabited* ***for*** *fifty years.*
✗ ~~*The centre of the island* ***has not been*** *inhabited* ***for*** *(the earthquake of) 1952.*~~
✔ *The centre of the island* ***has not been*** *inhabited* ***since*** *(the earthquake of) 1952.*

❗ We do not use the present simple or continuous with *for* and *since* when we refer to a state that began in the past:

✗ ~~*My family* ***lives/is living*** *in this country* ***since*** *1978.*~~
✗ ~~*My family* ***lives/is living*** *in this country* ***for*** *over twenty years.*~~
✔ *My family* ***has lived*** *in this country* ***since*** *1978/****for*** *over twenty years.*

❗ In the examples above *since* is a preposition. When we use it as a conjunction, we usually use the past simple after it:

*You****'ve been*** *really moody ever* ***since*** *that letter* ***arrived****. What's wrong?*

❗ The present continuous + *for* expresses a present situation continuing in the future:

We ***are staying*** *here* ***for*** *another three months.* (▶ **4.3A**)

We also use the present perfect to talk about actions which happened in the past but may happen again in the future. The period of time in which the action took place is unfinished, so it may be repeated. The action may have happened only once:

*I****'ve*** *only* ***been*** *to Hong Kong once, but I'd love to go again.* (My life is still continuing, so I may go to Hong Kong again.)

Or it may have happened several times (i.e. a repeated action):

NASA ***has sent*** *probes to various planets in the solar system.* (and may send more)

Sometimes we know the time is not 'finished' because of the time phrases we use:

This channel ***has shown*** *about four wildlife documentaries* ***this week****!*

Compare these two sentences:

*John Grisham **has written** some of the most successful legal thrillers.*

*Agatha Christie **wrote** a huge number of thrillers.*

In the first example the author is still alive and is able to write more successful books; in the second the author is dead and therefore can't write any more books:

✗ ~~*Agatha Christie **has written** a huge number of thrillers.*~~

We use the present perfect after superlatives, e.g. *the best/worst, the greatest*, ordinal numbers, e.g. *the first (second, third), the only*, often followed by *ever*:

*It's **the worst** sports programme I **have ever seen** and **the first** I **have ever written** to complain about!*

*Many people consider Kennedy to be **the greatest** President the USA **has had**.*

3.1C Adverbs often used with the present perfect

A number of adverbs are commonly used with the present perfect as described in 3.1B: *ever, often, seldom, never, so far, already, yet, still*:

*The Prime Minister **has seldom been put** in such a difficult position.*

*I **have never experienced** any racism in athletics.*

*We**'ve received** over 20,000 entries for the competition **so far**.*

*Only halfway through the financial year and British Aerospace **has already announced** that its pre-tax profits will be down by seventy per cent.*

*'**Have** they **announced** the date **yet**?' 'No, they **still haven't made up** their minds.'*

❶ We use *already* with the affirmative but *yet* with the negative and in questions:

✗ ~~*We've **yet** seen the film but they haven't seen it **already**.*~~

✓ *We've **already** seen the film but they haven't seen it **yet**.*

❶ It is possible in US English to use the past simple with these adverbs:

*We **already saw** the film but they **didn't see** it **yet**.*

3.1D Present relevance

We can use the present perfect simple to talk about an action completed in the past which has some relevance to the present, e.g. there is a present result of the action:

*The avalanche **has devastated** the skiing industry in the area.* (result = the skiing industry is still having big problems)

We often use this form to talk about recent actions:

*We can start the interviews now, as all the candidates **have arrived**.*

*'**Has** the government **put up** the minimum wage?' 'Yes, it's £4 per hour now.'*

Common adverbs with the present perfect in this use are *just, recently* and *lately*:

***Has** the sports centre **increased** its membership fees **lately**?*

We use *just* with very recent actions:

*I**'ve just made** a nice pot of tea. Would you like a cup?*

*The wedding of Paul McCartney and Heather Mills **has just taken place** in Ireland.*

❶ We do not use the present perfect with a definite time in the past (except with *since* or *for* ▶ **3.1B**). We usually use the past simple (▶ **2.1B**) when we give a time:

✗ ~~*Ms Brown **has arrived** half an hour ago. She's waiting in the staff room.*~~

✓ *Ms Brown **arrived** half an hour ago. She's waiting in the staff room.*

We can use the present perfect when the time is indefinite, i.e. when no time is stated, especially when the past action has some relevance to the present:

*Ms Brown **has arrived**. She's in the staff room and is ready to see you now.*

3.1E Other uses

As the present perfect simple expresses relevance to the present, news broadcasts and reports often use it to introduce a story, before moving into past tenses:

*Former Tanzanian President Julius Nyerere **has died** at the age of 77 in a London hospital. He came to London in ...*

Similarly, we often use it to introduce a new topic of conversation:

*I**'ve heard** from Maurice – he**'s been** in Australia for the last two months.*

In time clauses (e.g. *after, when*) we use the present perfect with future reference:

*We'll make a move **as soon as** the rain **has stopped**.*

3.2 PRESENT PERFECT AND PAST SIMPLE – DIFFERENCES

	present perfect	past simple
3.2A	Unfinished state/action (▶ **3.1B**) *Spain **has governed** the enclave of Ceuta since 1580.*	Finished state/action (▶ **2.1B**) *Spain **governed** the state of Western Sahara from 1958 to 1976.*
3.2B	Unfinished time (▶ **3.1B**) *I **haven't seen** Keith this morning yet.* (It's still morning.)	Finished time (▶ **2.1B**) *I **didn't see** Keith at all this morning.* (It's now afternoon/evening.)
3.2C	Present relevance (▶ **3.1D**) *The Indian Government **has imposed** a ban on tiger hunting to prevent the extinction of tigers.*	No present relevance (▶ **2.1B**) *The Indian Government **imposed** a ban on tiger hunting a few years ago.*
3.2D	Indefinite time (▶ **3.1D**) *I**'ve been** to Eurodisney twice.*	Definite time (▶ **2.1B**) *I **went** to Eurodisney in 1999 and 2000.*

3.2E Beliefs and expectations

We use the past simple, not the present perfect, to correct an incorrect belief or expectation, or to confirm a correct one:

✗ ~~*The area is far more rugged and wild than I **have expected**.*~~
✔ *The area is far more rugged and wild than I **expected**.*
✗ ~~*She is just as beautiful as I **have imagined**.*~~
✔ *She is just as beautiful as I **imagined**.*

(For a full description of uses of the past simple ▶ **2.1B**.)

3.3 PRESENT PERFECT CONTINUOUS

3.3A Form

We form the present perfect continuous with *has/have* + *been* + a present participle (*-ing* form):

*Bob Geldof **has been doing** a lot of work for charities since the mid-eighties.*
*What on earth **have** you **been doing** to that child?*

3.3B Ongoing states and actions

We use the present perfect continuous to talk about an ongoing state or action which began in the past and is still continuing or has just finished:

*Women **have been speaking out** on this issue for some time, with mixed results.*
*'Where **have** you **been**?' 'I**'ve been talking** to Jenny.'*

It is common to use *since* or *for* with this use of the present perfect continuous:

*I**'ve been looking into** the possibility of early retirement **since** the reorganisation.*

The simple form of the present perfect often focuses on the fact that an action is completed, while the continuous focuses on the fact that it is still ongoing:

- Simple: *I**'ve learnt** how to play chess.* (= I can play chess now.)
- Continuous: *I**'ve been learning** how to play chess.* (= I'm still learning.)

We use the continuous to focus on the duration of an action so we do not mention the number of times that we have done the action. With repeated actions we use the present perfect simple:

✗ ~~*I**'ve been calling** you five times this morning. Where have you been?*~~
✔ *I**'ve called** you five times this morning. Where have you been?*

The use of the present perfect continuous can suggest that the state or action may change, i.e. it is temporary. Compare this with the present simple:

*We **subscribe** to one of the satellite TV companies.* (unlikely to change)

*We**'ve been subscribing** to one of the satellite TV companies.* (not a fixed situation – we may change)

With the adverbs *lately* or *recently*, we use the present perfect continuous to talk about new developments which may be temporary:

*Helen**'s been spending** a lot of time at the club **lately**.* (= She didn't use to.)

❗ We use the present perfect continuous + *for*, not the present continuous, to specify the duration of an activity which started in the past and is still continuing:

✗ ~~*I **am learning** how to play chess for three years now.*~~

✓ *I **have been learning** how to play chess for three years now.*

❗ We do not usually use the present perfect continuous in the passive:

✗ ~~*The patient's heart rate **has been being monitored** continuously.*~~

✓ *The nurses **have been monitoring** the patient's heart rate continuously.*

3.3C Present relevance

We can use the present perfect continuous to explain a present result, e.g. a situation or an appearance. The focus is on the activity rather than the result. In this case, we don't usually use a time adverb:

*This test result is much better. It's clear you**'ve been revising**.*

*I'm sorry the hall is in such a mess. We**'ve been decorating**.*

I'm sorry the hall is in such a mess. We've been decorating.

Compare these examples of the present perfect continuous and simple:

*We **have been trialling** the new software prior to its release on the open market.*

*We **have completed** the new software trial and <u>are now ready to release it</u>.*

↑ (result)

3.4 PRESENT PERFECT SIMPLE AND CONTINUOUS – DIFFERENCES

	present perfect simple	present perfect continuous
3.4A	Completion (▶ **3.1B**) *This country **has welcomed** several hundred refugees from Kosovo in the last few weeks.*	Continuation (▶ **3.3B**) *This country **has been welcoming** political refugees for many years.*
3.4B	Repeated action (▶ **3.1B**) *She **has played** with the symphony orchestra three times this season.*	Duration of action (▶ **3.3B**) *She **has been playing** with the symphony orchestra all season.*
3.4C	Permanent situation (▶ **3.1B**) *People **have eaten** a lot less meat over the last twenty years or so.*	Temporary situation (▶ **3.3B**) *People **have been eating** less meat recently because of the crisis.*
3.4D	Focus on present result (▶ **3.1D**) ***I've done** the accounts – here they are.*	Focus on the activity (▶ **3.3C**) ***I've been doing** my accounts all afternoon.*

▶ **Pages 70 and 71 for Round up of present and past tenses**

3

Practice

The key to these exercises is on page 354.

1 3.1, 3.2

Choose the phrase or sentence (A or B), which correctly continues the text or dialogue.

0 Only halfway through the football season and Manchester United yet again leads the Premier League. The situation could easily change, however, as ...
A ... most teams played only a third of their games so far.
(B) ... most teams have played only a third of their games so far.

1 'I must remember to call my parents before I go away on Thursday. I haven't even told them about the trip yet.'
A 'Didn't you see much of them lately, then?'
B 'Haven't you seen much of them lately, then?'

2 'What do you think of our new Finance Director?'
A 'He's the most obnoxious person I ever met!'
B 'He's the most obnoxious person I have ever met!'

3 We won't be able to move back into our house for a while.
A Our tenants are living there for six months.
B Our tenants have lived there for six months.

4 Today we're previewing the new album by the top Swedish band The Cardigans, who, as I'm sure you all know, are coming to the UK on tour next month.
A The group released three albums so far.
B The group has released three albums so far.

5 Another earthquake has hit the north-west of Turkey, bringing further devastation to the area east of Istanbul, which is still suffering from the August earthquake.
A The latest tremor measured 7.2 on the Richter scale.
B The latest tremor has measured 7.2 on the Richter scale.

6 Pipeworks regrets the current inconvenience to residents of Kelvin Close.
A We have lowered the water pressure to allow essential repairs.
B We lowered the water pressure to allow essential repairs.

7 Investigators into the recent air crash have released their findings, which show a fault in the engine cooling system of the aircraft. All major airlines ...
A ... grounded aircraft of the same type for thorough checks.
B ... have grounded aircraft of the same type for thorough checks.

8 The seventeenth-century writer Cervantes is often considered the father of the modern novel. Most people only connect the name with *Don Quixote*, though Cervantes ...
A ... was a prolific writer.
B ... has been a prolific writer.

9 'With so much money being poured into medical research every year, you'd think that more breakthroughs would be made.'
'But breakthroughs are being made.
A Didn't a Colombian scientist discover a cure for malaria last year?'
B Hasn't a Colombian scientist discovered a cure for malaria last year?'

10 Most visitors to the prison are pleasantly surprised by the environment.
A It is far more open and greener than they have imagined.
B It is far more open and greener than they imagined.

2 3.1, 3.2

For each of the sentences below, write another sentence as similar as possible in meaning to the original sentence, using the word given. The word must not be altered in any way.

0 There's a cake in the oven.
baked ....*I've just baked a cake.*............

1 Most of the workers started here in 1996, when the factory opened.
since ....

2 The guest performers are all here now.
arrived ....

3 We visited the new theme park three times last summer and we intend to go this summer too.
have ....

4 Everyone in my family knows the basics of First Aid.
learnt ....

5 The latest novel by the young Indian writer Arundhati Roy is stunning. It's her best to date.
ever ....

6 There is no decision from the panel yet about the technical irregularities.
decided ....

3 3.3, 3.4

Match each sentence (A and B) in the pairs below with its meaning.

0 A I've been reading the book you lent me on genetics.
B I've read the book you lent me on genetics.
1 I've finished the book. [B]
2 I'm still reading the book. [A]

1 A The firm gives company cars to junior managers.
B The firm has been giving company cars to junior managers.
1 This is the company's usual policy. It's unlikely to change. ☐
2 This isn't the company's usual policy. It may change. ☐

2 A Something has been killing the rabbits in the woods.
B Something has killed the rabbits in the woods.
1 There are no rabbits left in the woods. ☐
2 There are some rabbits left in the woods. ☐

3 A Monsanto has placed some adverts in the national press.
B Monsanto has been placing adverts in the national press.
1 This was a one-off publicity move. ☐
2 This is a continuing publicity campaign. ☐

4 A 'Hi, Fiona. What a mess! Have you been decorating?'
B 'Hi, Fiona. This room looks great! Have you decorated it?'
1 Fiona is in the middle of decorating. ☐
2 Fiona isn't decorating any more. ☐

5 A A group of us have learnt how to play bridge.
B A group of us have been learning how to play bridge.
1 We're still learning. ☐
2 We can play it now. ☐

4 ALL

Complete the text with phrases from the box.

contained | existed | found | has allowed | have been digging | has produced | has been trying | has been | have been found | have unearthed | perished | has discovered | walked | were discovered

Palaeontologists in New Mexico (1) .... the remains of at least one dinosaur from the late Jurassic period. The palaeontologists, from Canada, (2) .... in a formerly unexplored part of the Morrison Formation – a vast fossil bed – for the last eight months. Early last week one of the group (3) .... a section of rock which (4) .... a number of bones from one, or possibly more, large herbivorous dinosaurs. Since then, the group (5) .... to release the bones from the rock and piece them together. The palaeontologists believe that the bones may form a whole dinosaur family. It is possible that the whole family (6) .... while trying to protect the young from predators.

According to Bryce Larson, the group's leader, the bones are from a large brachiosaurus. These animals (7) .... approximately 150 million years ago and are counted amongst the largest dinosaurs that ever (8) .... the Earth. Other brachiosaurus remains (9) .... in the Morrison, but these latest bones are very large and may prove to come from the largest dinosaur anyone (10) .... to date.

For a long time the Morrison Formation (11) .... one of the most productive fossil beds in the world. Since the first bones (12) .... there in 1877, it (13) .... tonnes of material. The Morrison, more than any other fossil bed, (14) .... us an insight into the late Jurassic period in North America. It seems that the latest find could reveal even more about the giants of the Jurassic.

5 ALL

Read this biography from a movie magazine. Complete the text with the verbs in brackets in the past simple or present perfect (simple or continuous).

Mel Gibson (1) .... (be) a major film star now for more than twenty years. In this time he (2) .... (become) one of the most respected Hollywood actors and he (3) .... (now start) a successful career in film directing, as well.

Gibson (4) .... (be born) in the United States in 1956 but his family (5) .... (move) to Australia in 1968. He (6) .... (complete) his school education in Sydney and (7) .... (begin) his acting career there, in the National Institute of Dramatic Art. He (8) .... (appear) in several Australian TV series, but (9) .... (get) his big break in 1979, in a film called *Mad Max*. He (10) .... (since/make) two more 'Max' films. He (11) .... (go on) to make several other successful films in Australia, for example, *Gallipoli*, before he (12) .... (move) to Hollywood.

Gibson (13) .... (make) more than thirty films, many of which (14) .... (be) great commercial successes. He (15) .... (never/be) afraid to take on challenging roles, such as *Hamlet* and *The Man without a Face*, which also (16) .... (mark) his directorial debut. He (17) .... (direct) films for the last few years. To date he (18) .... (direct) three successful films.

Unusually for the turbulent world of Hollywood romance, Gibson (19) .... (live) with the same woman for over twenty years – his wife Robyn, whom he (20) .... (marry) in 1980. Up to the present time, they have seven children.

6 ALL

You have been asked to prepare a short biography of Bruce Willis for a movie magazine. Read the notes below and write one sentence only for each numbered set of notes. Use the past simple and present perfect (simple or continuous) of the verbs in brackets, and appropriate linking words or phrases. You may add words and change the form of the words given in the notes, but do not add any extra information. The first point has been expanded for you as an example (0). (You may also wish to use the biography in Exercise 5 to help you.)

0 Bruce Willis – (be) major US film & TV star – almost 20 years

1 (become) one of most highly paid Hollywood actors, (write) filmscripts

2 born Germany 1955 – father in US army & mother German

3 family (move) back to USA (New Jersey) 1957

4 (go) Montclair State College New Jersey – (get) role in play 'Heaven and Earth'; (leave) school & (start) acting

5 1st main role = David Addison in 'Moonlighting' (hit TV show); (win) Emmys and Golden Globe awards for role

6 1st hit film = 'Die Hard', 1988; (make) two sequels since then

7 (star) mainly violent action films since 'Die Hard'; also (make) different types of film – 'Twelve Monkeys' (1995), 'The Sixth Sense' (1999)

8 (make) 40+ films, many (be) commercial success

9 (have) severe stutter ever since childhood; acting (help) him subdue it – not a problem in front of audience

10 (be) married – Demi Moore 10 years – separation 1998; (have) 3 children together

0 *Bruce Willis has been a major American film and television star for almost twenty years now.*
1 ....
2 ....
3 ....
4 ....
5 ....
6 ....
7 ....
8 ....
9 ....
10 ....

Round up: Units 1–3

Present and past tenses

form	use	example	▶
present simple	truths and facts	*British people* ***drink*** *a lot of tea.*	1.1B
	repeated events/actions	*The Blairs* ***take*** *their summer holiday in Tuscany.*	1.1C
	series of events	*You* ***cross*** *the road,* ***go*** *through a gate …*	1.1D
present continuous	actions true at time of speaking	*I'll be with you in a minute.* ***I'm just finishing*** *something in the kitchen.*	1.2B
	temporary actions	*She**'s staying** in the Waldorf Astoria this time.*	1.2B
	states in a process of change	*British summers* ***are getting*** *hotter.*	1.2B
	repeated events/actions within a temporary time	***I'm feeding*** *the neighbour's cat this week while she's in hospital.*	1.2C
	series of events in progress at time of speaking	*They**'re now entering** the back straight …*	1.2D
past simple	completed past actions	*Julius Caesar* ***invaded*** *Britain in 55* BC.	2.1B
	past states	*The Incas* ***didn't have*** *a written script.*	2.1B
past continuous	actions in progress at a time in the past	*We didn't hear him come in because we* ***were sleeping*** *on the top floor that night.*	2.2B
	past temporary/ changing situations	*His symptoms* ***were becoming*** *more pronounced as time went by.*	2.2B
	past background situations	*Night* ***was falling*** *over the beleaguered city.*	2.2B
	past interrupted actions	*They* ***were crossing*** *the bridge when the earthquake struck.*	2.2C
	past arrangements	*Nancy* ***was taking*** *the next flight.*	2.2D
past perfect simple	actions/states before a time in the past	*By the third month the rebels* ***had taken*** *most of the province.*	2.3B
	an earlier action in a past sequence	*When we got back the babysitter* ***had gone*** *home.*	2.3C
	unfulfilled intentions	*They* ***had hoped*** *to reach the summit but Travers fell ill.*	2.3D
past perfect continuous	an ongoing situation up to or just before a time in the past	*He* ***had been dreading*** *this meeting for weeks.*	2.4B
***used to* + infinitive**	past actions which no longer take place	***Did*** *you* ***use to get*** *free milk at school?*	2.5B
	past states which no longer exist	*Lithuania* ***used to be*** *part of the Soviet Union.*	2.5C

form	use	example	▶
***would* + infinitive**	past actions which no longer take place	*We **would get up** early every Saturday.*	2.5B
present perfect simple	ongoing states and actions	*The manor house **has stood** on this spot for over two hundred years.*	3.1B
	ongoing times, or actions which may be repeated in the future	*This channel **has shown** four wildlife documentaries so far this week.* *Grisham **has written** some of the most successful legal thrillers.*	3.1B
	with superlatives	*It's **the worst** sports programme I **have ever seen**.*	3.1B
	with adverbs	*I **have seldom experienced** racism in athletics.*	3.1C
	past action with present relevance (e.g. result)	*The power surge **has broken** my computer.*	3.1D
	recent actions	*I've **just made** a cup of tea.*	3.1D
	with time clauses	*We'll make a move **as soon as** the rain **has stopped**.*	3.1E
present perfect continuous	ongoing states and actions	*Women **have been speaking out** on this issue for some time.*	3.3B
	ongoing actions/states which are temporary or may change	*She**'s been drinking** a lot less recently.*	3.3B
	focus on the duration of a continuing action	*I've **been learning** to play chess for three years now.*	3.3B
	recent actions	*I've **been talking** to Jenny.*	3.3C
	explaining a present result (focus on the activity)	*I'm sorry the hall is in such a mess. We**'ve been decorating**.*	3.3C

4 The future (1)

English does not have a 'future tense', but uses a variety of forms to talk about the future. The choice of form often depends on whether we are making a prediction, expressing an intention or talking about an arrangement. This unit looks at the use of *will*, *be going to* and present tenses to talk about the future. (For other ways of talking about the future ▶ **Unit 5**.)

4.1 PREDICTION

4.1A *will/won't* + infinitive

We use *will/won't* (the future simple) to talk about predictions which are based on guesswork, analysis or judgement. We use *will/won't* with all persons and with personal and impersonal subjects:

- Personal: *We'**ll** still **be** here in twenty years.*
- Impersonal: ***Will** interest rates **rise** in the next few weeks?*

We often use *will* to predict an event which we think will happen because similar events have happened in the past:

*He'**ll be** in prison for a long time.* (Similar crimes have attracted long sentences.)
*The laptop battery **will give** you about two hours' continuous use.* (This is what previous batteries have done.)

We can use *shall/shan't* with *I* and *we*, although this is becoming dated now:

*I **shall** never **get** the hang of these new WAP phones.*

❗ We do not use *shall/shan't* with *he*, *she*, *it*, *you*, *they* for predictions:

✗ ~~*He **shall like** the idea, I'm sure.*~~
✔ *He **will like** the idea, I'm sure.*

4.1B *be going to* + infinitive

We also use *be going to* + infinitive to make a prediction, especially if there is evidence in the present to justify the prediction:

*The Roses are already a popular band and they **are going to be** massive!*
✗ ~~*Look at those black clouds. It **will rain**.*~~
✔ *Look at those black clouds. It'**s going to rain**.*

Look at those black clouds. It's going to rain.

❗ It is possible to use *will* with present evidence, but we usually use an adverb:

*Look at the sky. It **will probably/ definitely rain** later.*

With *be going to* there is often a strong link with the present, and the prediction is often about the near future:

*Look out! You'**re going to spill** the wine!*

4.1C *will/won't be* + verb *-ing*

We use *will/won't be* + verb *-ing* (the future continuous) for a temporary action in progress at a particular point in the future:

*This time next Tuesday afternoon I'**ll be lying** on the beach!*

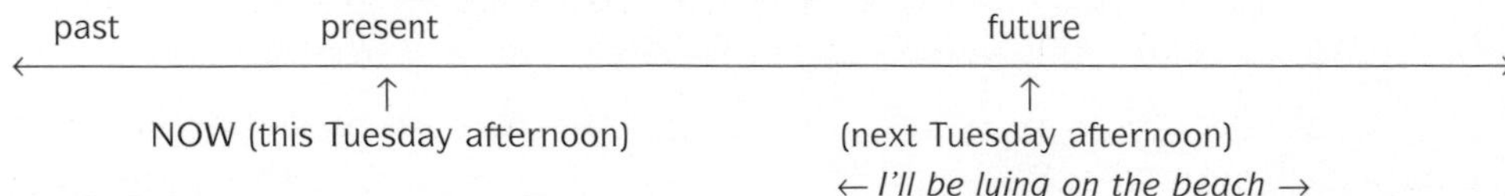

Compare this with the present continuous for a temporary action in the present:

*It's Tuesday afternoon and I'**m lying** on the beach.*

❗ Note that we do not usually use the passive with this form:

✗ ~~*The proposal **will be being presented** at the next meeting.*~~

✓ *The chairman **will be presenting** the proposal at the next meeting.*

❗ We do not use the verb *be* in the continuous:

✗ ~~*Shelley **will be being** in Morocco this time tomorrow.*~~

✓ *Shelley **will be** in Morocco this time tomorrow.*

We can also use *will/won't be* + verb *-ing* (and *will/won't* + infinitive) to make a 'prediction' about something we believe to be the case now (▶ **18.1C**):

*You can't interrupt her now. She'**ll be getting** ready to go on stage, won't she?*

*'What's that noise?' 'It'**ll be** Ron next door. He's learning to play the trumpet.'*

4.1D *will/won't have* + past participle; *will/won't have* + *been* + verb *-ing*

We use *will/won't have* + past participle (the future perfect) to make predictions about actions which we expect to be completed by a particular time in the future:

*He'**ll have had** the operation by May and should be a lot fitter then.*

past	present	future	
←	↑ NOW	↑ *(the operation)*	↑ MAY →

We usually use a time adverb/phrase (such as *soon*, *by then*, *within the next week*) with this kind of prediction. The times can be very close to 'now', e.g.

*You can have my report by the end of the morning. In fact, **I'll have finished** it within the next hour.*

We use *will/won't have* + *been* + verb *-ing* to talk about an action which is still ongoing at a point in the future, to focus on the duration of the action:

*We'**ll have been living** in this house for twenty years in December.*

With verbs such as *live*, *work*, *stay*, which contain the idea of continuity, we can also use *will/won't have* + past participle:

*We'**ll have lived** in this house for twenty years in December.*

❗ We rarely use this form in the passive:

✗ ~~*By July the house will **have been being built** for a year.*~~

✓ *By July they **will have been building** the house for a year.*

4.2 DECISIONS AND INTENTIONS

4.2A *will/won't* + infinitive

We often use *will/won't* + infinitive (the future simple) to talk about a decision made at the time of speaking:

*Oh, our guests are here. **I'll go** and **sort out** some drinks for them.*

*You look tired. **I'll cook** dinner tonight.* (▶ **18.4A**)

In questions asking about decisions, we can use *shall* (with *I* and *we* only):

***Shall I see** you next week, then?*

In speech we stress *will/won't* to indicate determination, especially when the action is decided on or the determination is strengthened at the time of speaking:

*I **<u>will</u> come** with you at the weekend, whatever my parents say!*

*After what has just happened, I **<u>won't</u> believe** a word you say again.*

❗ We do not usually contract *will* to *'ll* with this use, as we usually stress the auxiliary verb, but we can make the contraction when we stress an adverb:

*He'll <u>never</u> **agree** to that!*

4.2B *be going to* + infinitive

We use *be going to* + infinitive for intentions (i.e. for actions that have already been decided on):

*He **is going to study** environmental law next year.*

We can use *be going to* for impersonal intention, e.g. of an authority:

*The Government **is going to** increase VAT in the budget.*

❶ We usually avoid *be going to* with the verbs *go* and *come*:

[*I'm **going to go** home now. **Are** you **going to come**?*]

✔ *I'm **going** home now. **Are** you **coming**?*

We stress *be* or *not* to express determination about something we have already decided on:

*I **am going to** leave. I'm **not going to** stay here forever, so don't try to make me!*

4.3 ARRANGEMENTS

4.3A Present continuous

We use the present continuous (▶ **1.2**) to describe an event in the future which has already been arranged by the time of speaking:

*We're **seeing** a musical at the theatre next week.* (= We've got the tickets.)

Compare this with the use of *be going to*:

*We're **going to see** a musical at the theatre sometime next week.* (not arranged yet; the focus is on our intention)

We usually use the present continuous for future events which involve other people and where we have made some form of commitment, e.g. by buying tickets. However, we can also use this tense for arrangements that don't involve other people. In this case, we see it as an 'arrangement' the speaker makes with him/herself:

*I'm **staying** in tonight. I've got loads of paperwork to do.*

The focus here is on the 'arrangement', i.e. there is no suggestion that the speaker wants to stay in, which is the case when we use *be going to*. Compare:

*I'm **going to stay** in tonight.* (focus on intention)

We also use the present continuous for impersonal plans:

*Computer City has announced that it **is opening** four new shops next month.*

❶ We cannot use this tense with events which are beyond human control, e.g. the weather, because these events are predictions, not intentions or arrangements (▶ **4.1**):

✘ ~~*It's **snowing** tomorrow.*~~

✔ *It's **going to snow** tomorrow./It **will snow** tomorrow.*

4.3B *will/won't be* + verb *-ing*

We can also use *will/won't be* + verb *-ing* (the future continuous) to talk about events that are a result of or part of an arrangement made in the past:

*'How about joining us at the cottage this Sunday?' 'Oh, we can't. We**'ll be coming back** from Edinburgh on Sunday. We're visiting Julianne.'*

*Trains **won't be running** between East Putney and Putney Bridge this weekend due to essential track repairs.*

With this structure the future event is seen as arranged, so we use this as a tactful way of asking about someone's plans or refusing an invitation:

***Will** you **be staying** long?*

*I'm sorry, I can't come to your wedding as **I'll be working** on that day.*

Will you be staying long?

❶ There is, in fact, little difference between this and the use of the present continuous for arrangements. The use of *will/won't be* + verb *-ing* acts to distance the arrangement a little, making it more fixed and less open to change.

4.4 OTHER FUTURE MEANINGS

4.4A Timetables

We can use the present simple to talk about timetabled events:

*The tour **departs** on October 11th for 15 days and costs £495.*

*The car **comes** at eleven to collect the guest speakers and they **arrive** at the hall at eleven thirty.*

4.4B Routine events in the future

We use *will/won't be* + verb *-ing* for future events we see as certain because they are part of a routine, especially when the event continues for a period of time, e.g. a festival, a meeting:

*Winston **will be performing** with his steel band every night of the music festival.*

*We**'ll be having** our weekly meeting tomorrow so I'll present your proposal then.*

The focus in the last example is on the routine nature of the weekly meeting. Compare this with the use of other future forms (all correct English). The present continuous focuses on the arrangement rather than the routine:

*We**'re having** our weekly meeting tomorrow instead of Friday this week.*

The present simple presents the meeting as part of a timetable:

*We **have** our weekly meeting tomorrow so I'll present your proposal then.*

We also often use *will/won't be* + verb *-ing* to say that an event is inevitable:

***I'll be seeing** Mr Kennedy at the court tomorrow – he's always there on Thursdays – so we can discuss your case briefly then.*

We use *will/won't* to express statements of fact about the future:

*Next week **I'll be** 21.*

*The sun **will rise** at 5.30 tomorrow morning.*

4.4C Qualifying future forms

We can make predictions, intentions or decisions stronger or weaker by using certain adverbs, for example *definitely, certainly, probably, possibly* (▶ **24.3C**):

*She'll **definitely** make a fool of herself.*

*The lecture **probably** won't start on time – they rarely do here.*

*I'm **definitely** going to look for another job now!*

*I **certainly** won't give you a lift to the station – it's only down the road!*

We can show our attitude to the future event by using an introductory verb, for example *think, expect, hope, doubt, suppose, promise, guarantee*:

*I **expect** she**'ll call** us from the airport.*

*The Association **guarantees** that 500 tickets **will be** available on the day.*

We usually show negative meaning (e.g. *I won't pass the exam*) at the beginning of the sentence with the introductory verb:

[*I think I **won't pass** the exam.*]

✔ *I **don't think I'll pass** the exam.*

4.4D Time clauses

In time clauses (starting with *when, after, as soon as, once, until*), we do not use *will/won't*, but we use a present form:

✘ ~~***Won't** the park look good once the new trees **will reach** maturity?*~~

✔ ***Won't** the park look good once the new trees **reach/have reached** maturity?*

*Effective penal reform **will not** be achieved until the government **takes** it seriously.*

▶ **Pages 86 and 87 for Round up of future forms**

Practice

The key to these exercises is on page 355.

1 4.1, 4.2

Complete the dialogues according to the cartoons and using the verbs in brackets. Use *will/won't*, *will/won't be* + verb *-ing*, *will/won't have* + past participle or *be going to*.

0 'Can you come to a meeting at three this afternoon?'
'Sorry. I ...*won't have finished*... (finish) all this work by three.'

1 'What can you tell me about my future?
'You .... (meet) a handsome young man!'

2 'What's happening up there?'
'He .... (jump) off the building!'

3 'Is it next week that you're on holiday?'
'Yes. This time next week I .... (sail) on the Mediterranean.'

4 'Is that the phone again?'
'It's all right Mum. I .... (answer) it!'

5 'What is it?'
'He's got a gun. He says he .... (shoot) someone!'

6 'Where's Mum with the shopping? I'm starving!'
'She'll be back by eight. Wait and have dinner with us.'
'Eight! No way! I .... (die) of starvation by then!'

2 4.1, 4.2, 4.3

In each of the sentences below, one or two of the options (A–C) are appropriate. Circle the letter for the option(s) you choose.

1 'Your son has been with his girlfriend for a long time. Any sign of wedding bells?'
'Well, I'm not sure, but I think he ... her to marry him on their holiday next week.'
A asks B will ask C is going to ask

2 'Can I have your report this afternoon?' 'This afternoon? Oh, I don't think I ... by then.'
A 'll have finished B 'm finishing C 'll be finishing

3 Look at the waiter. He's carrying too much. He ... all those plates.
A 's dropping B 's going to drop C 'll be dropping

4 'Do you want to go to the cinema tonight?' 'No, I'm too tired. I ... an early night.'
A 'm having B will have had C 'm going to have

5 Nobody supports my plan to climb Everest. But, believe me, I ... it!
A 'm going to do B will do C 'll have done

6 'I'm really worried about Susan. What do you think has happened?'
'Don't worry. She's probably just caught in traffic. I'm sure she ... here soon.'
A will be B is being C will be being

7 Here's a letter from our holiday representative. They ... a reception in the bar tonight at eight.
A are holding B will have held C are going to hold

8 It ... all day on Sunday, so the party will be in the house, not in the garden.
A will be raining B is going to rain C rains

3 4.1, 4.3, 4.4

For each of the sentences below, write a new sentence as similar as possible in meaning to the original sentence, but using the word given. This word must not be altered in any way. The sentence must include a future form.

0 The manufacturers are certain of a high level of customer satisfaction with this product.
guarantee ...*The manufacturers guarantee that customers will be satisfied with this product*...........

1 Let's stop playing soon – our opponents have so many more points than we do.
going ....

2 Our plane's departure time is at 6.30 in the morning.
leaves ....

3 My great-grandmother celebrates her hundredth birthday next year.
old ....

4 It's unlikely that humans will ever be able to live on the moon.
think ....

5 It's my parents' twenty-fifth wedding anniversary next Saturday.
married ....

6 Come along next Monday afternoon – the band always records on Monday afternoons.
will ....

7 We are one hundred per cent certain of the success of our proposal.
certainly ....

8 The government expects another six thousand people to be in work by the end of the summer.
found ....

9 Do you have any idea of your arrival time on Friday?
arriving ....

10 Our daughter has got a role in the school production of *Miss Saigon* next month.
appearing ....

4 4.2, 4.3, 4.4

Complete the dialogue with verbs from the box. Use suitable forms with future meaning.

arrive	be (x3)	~~come~~	finish (x2)	have	have to	meet (x2)	pick up	work

PAM Can we fix a time for the next meeting? How about the 12th? That's after the sales conference.
ALEX I thought something was happening on that day.
PAM Oh yes, you're right. The people from Head Office (0) ......*are coming*...... .
JOHN What time (1 – *their plane*) .... at the airport? Can we have the meeting in the morning?
PAM No, it's all arranged. I (2) .... them at half past ten, so I (3) .... available at all that day.
ALEX Well, let's have the meeting earlier in June, then. The sales conference (4) .... on the third, doesn't it?
PAM Yes, but we need John's annual figures for the meeting. How are they going, John?
JOHN I'm afraid I haven't started them yet, but I (5) ....on them next week, gathering information.
PAM (6 – *they*) .... ready early in June?
JOHN Well, not really. I (7) .... them by 10 June, but I don't think they (8) .... ready before then.
PAM So, we're looking at the week starting the 17th. How about two o'clock on that day?
ALEX Difficult. I (9) .... lunch with the sales manager of Bowman's. Could we make it three?
PAM John?
JOHN Yes, but I (10) .... the children after school that week, as usual when the nanny's away, so I (11) .... leave here at five thirty. Is that OK?
PAM I think so. Right, so we (12) .... at three o'clock on 17 June, in the boardroom.

5 ALL

Match the sentences (1–9) with the replies (A–J), then complete the replies with the verbs in brackets.

0 There's someone at the door. [D]
1 Mum, I want to get away from John for a while. Can I come and stay with you and Dad? [ ]
2 Anything interesting on the news? [ ]
3 Can I come round and see you this evening? [ ]
4 Have you got any plans for a new TV series? [ ]
5 Is your steak tough again? [ ]
6 Oh no! It's nearly half past and my train's at quarter to! [ ]
7 Have the management made plans to review salaries? [ ]
8 Is the circus timetable sorted out for Saturday? [ ]
9 Have you thought about your day off next week? [ ]

A Yes, they've started the Anglo-Irish tunnel and it .... (be) ready two months early.
B Yes, the clowns .... (start) at eight and then it's the lion tamer at half past.
C It is. This time I .... (complain) to the butcher.
D Don't get up. I ......*'ll answer*...... (answer) it.
E No, sorry. I .... (watch) the football highlights tonight.
F They .... (look at) salaries as usual in the end-of-year review.
G Come on then. I .... (give) you a lift to the station.
H Oh yes, I .... (waterski) next Friday afternoon while you're all working.
I Yes. We .... (film) a new series next year. We've already found the locations and booked the actors.
J Of course, dear. How long do you think you .... (stay)?

6 ALL

Read the article and decide which word or phrase below best fits each space. Circle the letter of the option you choose. The exercise begins with an example (0).

Naturewatch

Mark Rawlings and his team are still in the Andes filming Penny, a puma. They have managed to get quite close to the big cat and gain her trust over the last summer. In this instalment of Mark's video diary, he describes how Penny is currently spending a lot of time with a mate, so Mark and his team are sure that she (0) ... cubs in the spring. If that is the case, they (1) ... much of her over the winter. In fact, they are unlikely to see much of her until the winter (2) ... over anyway, as pumas, like most of the large cats, tend to hide away when the weather is bad. If Penny is pregnant, she (3) ... the cubs by early March and they (4) ... the den about three months later. Although Mark doubts whether she (5) ... out to hunt much in the next few months, he (6) ... until she (7) ... . Once the team (8) ... filming Penny, they (9) ... to North America to track down the grizzly bear, but Mark (10) ... such a pleasant assignment!

	A	B	C
0	A has	(B) is going to have	C will have had
1	A will see	B aren't seeing	C won't see
2	A is	B will be	C is being
3	A is having	B will have had	C will be having
4	A are leaving	B will leave	C leave
5	A will come	B is coming	C will have come
6	A stays	B will have stayed	C is going to stay
7	A reappears	B will reappear	C is going to reappear
8	A will finish	B have finished	C will have finished
9	A are going	B are going to go	C go
10	A thinks it is	B thinks that won't be	C doesn't think that will be

5 The future (2)

We commonly use *will*, *be going to* and present tense forms to talk about the future (▶ **Unit 4**). But we can use a number of other patterns, often with an infinitive, as well as verbs and adjectives that contain future meaning; these are described in this unit, along with ways of talking about the future when seen from a viewpoint in the past.

5.1 EXPRESSIONS WITH FUTURE MEANING

5.1A *be to* + infinitive

We use *be to* in formal English to talk about official arrangements in the future:

*The President **is to hold** an official reception for the visitors.*

This construction is common in writing, especially in news articles:

*Crash investigators **are to release** their findings to the press later today.*

❗ The verb *be* is often omitted in headlines: *President **to hold** official reception.*

We often use *be to* in *if* clauses (▶ **Unit 10**) when we wish to say that the event in the *if* clause is dependent on the event in the main clause happening first:

*If British tennis **is to reach** world standard again, both more money and more commitment will be necessary.* (= More money and commitment must be given first for British tennis to improve.)

We can also use *be (not) to* + infinitive for formal commands and instructions:

*You **are not to disturb** the head teacher while the inspectors are here next week.*

It is quite common to use the passive for instructions with *be to*:

*These pills **are not to be taken** with any other form of medicine.*

5.1B *be due to* + infinitive

We can use *be due to* to talk about an event which forms part of a timetable (▶ **4.4A** present simple). We usually use a time phrase with *be due to*:

*Carriageway repairs on this stretch of the motorway **are due to start** on 26th May.*

When we use *be due to* to talk about a future event, it is possible that the timetable may change, i.e. the event is not totally fixed, as is the case with *be to*:

*New measures to contain asylum seekers **are due to come** into force on 1st August but a case currently before the European court may delay this until the autumn.*

5.1C Expressing the near future

We use *be about to* to talk about an event that we intend or expect to happen in the near future. The event may or may not be planned, but we often use *about to* when evidence in the present indicates that it will happen (*be going to* ▶ **4.1B**):

*Ladies and gentlemen. Please take your seats. The performance **is about to start**.*

*Hurry up, the driver says he can't wait any longer. He**'s about to leave** without us.*

We can stress that the future event is very imminent by adding *just*:

*Come on! The check-in desk **is just about to close**.*

Two other expressions used for talking about the near future are *on the point of* and *on the verge of*. These both mean that something is about to happen. They can be followed by either an *-ing* form or a noun:

*Don't provoke your little brother. You can see he**'s on the point of losing** his temper.*

*Because of the erosion of their habitats, some species **are on the verge of extinction**.*

Some adjectives contain the idea of 'in the near future', e.g. *imminent, forthcoming, impending*. We tend to use these adjectives in more formal English:

*A decision from the judges is **imminent**. We will return to the law court as soon as we have any further news.*

❶ We use *impending* only in attributive position, i.e. before the noun:

✗ ~~*The sensation of doom was **impending**.*~~

✓ *No one could shake off the sensation of **impending** doom.*

❶ We do not usually use time adverbials (e.g. *in an hour*) with the expressions in 5.1C:

✗ ~~*Come in. We're **on the point of** starting dinner **in two minutes**.*~~

5.1D Expressing probability and certainty

We use *be likely to* + infinitive to say that something in the future is probable:

*The payment **is likely to take** ten days. Please contact us if it does not arrive within that time.*

Be unlikely to + infinitive means that it is improbable that something will happen:

*They**'re unlikely to arrive** before six. The traffic is always awful on Fridays.*

We can use *be sure (bound/certain) to* + infinitive to say that something is definitely going to happen:

*The new timetable **is sure to annoy** some of the teachers when they see it.*

*Your application **is bound to fail** if you don't get the divisional director's approval.*

In the negative we put *not* after the adjective:

*Don't worry about Dad – he**'s sure not to find out** about the loan.*

This can sound quite formal, so in casual speech we sometimes rephrase it:

*Don't worry about Dad – **I'm sure he won't find out** about the loan.*

❶ We can use *be sure to* and *be certain to* as imperatives; we don't use *be bound to* in this way:

✗ ~~***Be bound to** give me a call when you arrive at the hotel.*~~

✓ ***Be sure/certain to** give me a call when you arrive at the hotel.*

5.2 VERBS WITH FUTURE MEANING

5.2A Main verbs

Some verbs contain an implied future in their meaning, i.e. we understand that they relate to the future even though we do not use a future form:

verbs	structure	examples
decide, hope, intend, promise, swear	verb + *to* + infinitive	*I **hope to see** everyone at the next Open Day.* *Do you **swear** never **to reveal** any of the secrets of the Magic Circle?*
anticipate, predict, envisage	verb + noun/ *-ing* form	*We **anticipate congestion** on all major routes out of London this weekend.* *Do you **envisage experiencing** any difficulty with this machine?*
arrange, expect, guarantee, plan, undertake	verb + (noun) + *to* + infinitive	*We**'re planning a stay** of only three days.* *We **expect to promote** trainees within two to three years of qualifying.*

5.2B Modal verbs

Many modal verbs can refer to the future, usually expressing a degree of possibility or probability (modal verbs ▶ **Units 16–18**):

*Such financing opportunities **may not be** so readily available in the future.*

*Rankin's latest blockbuster **might win** the Golden Dagger award for crime fiction.*

*Given their expertise and experience, the Swiss team **should triumph** in tomorrow's final.*

5.3 FUTURE IN THE PAST

5.3A *was/were going to* + infinitive

Sometimes we need to describe the future from a viewpoint in the past. We often use *was/were going to* to do this:

*I **was going to get up** early this morning but the alarm didn't go off!*

11.30 p.m. yesterday	6 a.m. today	9 a.m. today
↑ (1)	↑ (2)	↑ (3)

(1) I intend to get up early tomorrow – this is a future plan.
(2) The alarm doesn't go off.
(3) I wake up late. My plan to get up early is now in the past.

When we use *was/were going to* the plan is not usually fulfilled (i.e. it does not happen):

*The fitness club **was going to increase** its annual subscription but so many members protested that it backed down.* (It didn't increase the subscription.)

However, it is possible to describe a past intention that is fulfilled. This is made clear in the context:

*'Thanks for posting my letters.' 'That's OK. **I was going to post** mine anyway.'* (= I did post my letters.)

5.3B Other ways of expressing the future in the past

While *was/were going to* is a very common way of expressing the future in the past, it is possible to transfer any form with future meaning to the past:

present/future form	past form	example
present continuous	past continuous	*We thought they **were arriving** before dinner, but they didn't arrive until midnight.*
will/shall	*would*	*The heating wasn't working and we hoped that the repairman **wouldn't** take long.*
will be + *-ing* form	*would be* + *-ing* form	*Little did we know that we **would** still **be waiting** in three hours' time.*
will have + past participle	*would have* + past participle	*The Cabinet thought the crisis **would have finished** before the election.*
is/are about to/due to	*was/were about to/ due to*	*As he raised his arm she realised that he **was about to strike** her again.*
is/are to	*was/were to*	*We **were to arrive** at the airport at nine, where we **were to have been met** by the tour guide.*

When we transfer present/future forms to the past, they keep the same meaning as they have in the present, that is we use the present continuous to talk about arrangements, so the past continuous also expresses arrangements:

*We **were meeting** them at the concert hall, but we didn't know which entrance they were waiting at.* (unfulfilled arrangement)

❗ With *was/were (due) to* + present infinitive, we don't know if the event happened or not:

*The Professor **was to take up** his chair in October.*

*The exam results **were (due) to arrive** at the school today. We can ring tomorrow to find out whether they have arrived.*

However, *was/were (due) to* + perfect infinitive tells us that the event did not occur:

*The exam results **were (due) to have arrived** at the school today but apparently the exam board has not posted them yet.*

▶ **Pages 86 and 87 for Round up of future forms**

Practice

The key to these exercises is on page 355.

1 5.1

Complete these two short texts using the most appropriate expressions with future meaning.

Here in Augusta the final day of the US Golf Masters (1) .... begin, and we could be (2) .... a historic win. Tiger Woods, who (3) .... start his bid for a place in the history books in forty minutes, could complete the grand slam – winning all four golf masters tournaments in one year. Woods starts today in the lead and he is (4) .... give up that lead easily. This is going to be an exciting day, folks, so be (5) .... book your place in front of the TV and settle down for a thrilling day's viewing!

FILM NEWS

Hollywood's king and queen – Tom Cruise and Julia Roberts – (6) .... star opposite each other in Ridley Scott's new blockbuster.

No interviews or press releases are (7) ...., but rumour has it that the film will be another Roman epic, following hot on the heels of the success of *Gladiator*, Scott's last film. Filming (8) .... start in September, but because of other commitments the two stars are (9) .... join the set until next year. One thing is certain: with that combination of director and stars, the film is (10) .... be a success!

2 5.1, 5.2

Complete this conversation with phrases from the box. Use each phrase only once.

anticipate	are on the point of	expect	guarantee to	hopes to
is about to	is likely to	is sure to	plans to	should

MARY When do Brian's exams start, then?
ANNA Well, he (1) .... start them. The first one is tomorrow in fact.
MARY Do you (2) .... him to do well?
ANNA We think he will. He's taking nine subjects, and he's quite optimistic. He (3) .... pass at least six of them – he's very good at those six subjects. We think that he (4) .... pass two of the others: French and art – he's studied very hard, but he's not naturally gifted in those subjects! We've got no hopes at all for music. He (5) .... fail it. I don't know why the school entered him for it.
MARY What does he want to do next year?
ANNA That depends. If he does well, he (6) .... stay on at school for two years and study sciences.
MARY Can he stay at the same school?
ANNA Well, that's the problem. No, he can't, because his school only takes pupils up to sixteen. But we've just heard that they (7) .... opening the new sixth form college in Fareham. We (8) .... being able to send him there, but we don't know for certain.
MARY And if he doesn't pass enough of the exams?
ANNA Well, he might leave and look for a job. Sandy – you know, my elder sister – says she (9) .... have a vacancy for a trainee in her business, but obviously she can't (10) .... take him. We'll just have to see.

5

3 5.1, 5.2

For each of the sentences below, write a new sentence as similar as possible in meaning to the original sentence, but using the word or phrase given. This word or phrase must not be altered in any way. The exercise begins with an example (0).

0 The result of our appeal against the parking fine should arrive in the post tomorrow.
due ....*The result of our appeal against the parking fine is due tomorrow.*..........

1 Do not disturb the chimpanzees during feeding time.
disturbed ....

2 Turn that music down! It's so loud that it'll definitely wake all the neighbours.
bound ....

3 Scientists in the human genome project feel that they are about to discover the secret of life.
discovering..

4 Will you promise that you won't get drunk again tonight?
not to ....

5 It is probable that the road-sweeping contract will be withdrawn from Dustbugs.
likely to ....

6 Everyone in the village lived in fear of the volcanic eruption, which was imminent.
impending ....

7 The designer believes that he will be able to finish the specifications by tomorrow afternoon.
envisages ....

8 I really don't think that the examiner will accept a handwritten script these days.
unlikely to ....

9 Please make your purchases and proceed to a check-out. The store is going to close in five minutes.
about ....

10 If we want medical research to provide cures for all known diseases, it must be adequately funded.
is ....

4 5.3

Complete the lines of each dialogue, using *was/were going to*, *was/were about to* or *was/were to* and an appropriate ending.

0 'Look, the shoe shop has closed down.'
'Oh, that's a pity. There was a pair of shoes in the window that I liked. I ..*was going to buy them.*..'

1 'Hi, Karen. It's Graham here.'
'Graham, I don't believe it! You must be a mind reader! I was ....'

2 'Where's Dad?'
'He's gone back to work. They had an emergency at the factory.'
'Oh no! I've got some really tough maths homework and he was ....

3 'Ms Sandford. This is the police. We're trying to trace Frank Simmonds. I gather he works for you.'
'Well, today was his first day. He was .... at nine this morning, but he didn't turn up.'

4 'Thanks for coming round. I'm sorry, but there's a spider in my bath.'
'A spider! Is that all? I don't believe it. And I'm starving! When you called we were ....
have dinner.'

5 'Where's Noel? I thought you'd invited him?'
'We did invite him and he was ...., but he has had to work late.'

5 ALL

In this letter some of the lines have a word that must be corrected (example 0), some have a word that must be replaced (example 00), and some are correct (example 000). If a line is correct, put a tick (✓). If a word must be replaced or corrected, underline that word, and write the new, correct word.

Sunnyside Promenade
Barton-on-Sea
Hampshire

Dear Guest

0 The Management of Broadbank Hotel wish to inform you that the hotel is too ....*to*..........
00 close on 5 December this year. It is about to reopen next year as part of the ....*due*..........
000 Value4U chain of hotels. ....✓..........
1 As you know, the Lister family has been involved in Broadbank Hotel for ....
2 over twenty years now and the due closure is a blow to all of us. We realised ....
3 some months ago that we will need to find some kind of financial support for the ....
4 forthcoming season. We started to look at ways of doing this and we were go to ....
5 work with an investment company to upgrade the hotel with the addition of a ....
6 gym, swimming pool and sauna complex. We were on the verge of sign a ....
7 contract, which was to allowed us to retain control of the hotel, but we were ....
8 unable to complete the deal on time. We were likely to send Christmas cards as ....
9 usual to all our regular clients, with information about offers for the spring, but ....
10 of course, that is now not possible. Unfortunately, we are sure to be able to set up ....
11 another hotel in the near future. ....
12 The Value4U chain envisages reopen the hotel by 1 March, and they ....
13 are about to contact you when that happens. It just remains for us to thank you ....
14 for your support in the past, and to wish you every success for the future. We ....
15 hoped to be able to write to you with news of a new venture at some point ....
16 in the not-too-distant future. ....

Round up: Units 4 and 5

The future

use	form	example	►
prediction			
personal	*will/won't*	*He'**ll be** in prison for a long time.*	4.1A
impersonal		*The war **will be** over next month.*	4.1A
prediction with present evidence	*be going to*	*Look at those clouds. It'**s going to snow**.*	4.1B
prediction of an action in progress	*will/won't be* + verb *-ing*	*This time tomorrow we'**ll be sitting** in a Tuscan café.*	4.1C
prediction of an action completed by a point in the future	*will/won't have* + past participle	*I'**ll have finished** this report by 3.30.*	4.1D
prediction of an action still ongoing at a point in the future	*will/won't have* been + verb *-ing*	*She'**ll have been working** there for 25 years next month.*	4.1D
intention			
decision made at the time of speaking	*will/won't*	*I'**ll get** the phone.*	4.2A
intention	*be going to*	*They'**re going to take** voluntary redundancy.*	4.2B
determination	*will/won't*	*I <u>**will**</u> **give up** smoking!*	4.2A
	be going to	*I <u>**am**</u> **going to give up** smoking!*	4.2B
arrangements			
personal	present continuous	*We'**re taking** a month off in the summer.*	4.3A
impersonal		*The bank **is laying off** 200 staff.*	4.3A
arrangement made in the past	*will/won't be* + verb *-ing*	*We'**ll be coming back** from Edinburgh on Sunday.*	4.3B
tactful queries/reason for rejection		***Will** you **be eating** with us?* *I'**ll be rehearsing** tomorrow night.*	4.3B
other future meanings			
'timetable' future	present simple	*The Royal Train **arrives** at 5.45 p.m.*	4.4A
routine events	*will/won't be* + verb *-ing*	*Come for dinner – we'**ll be cooking** for six anyway.*	4.4B
statement of fact	*will/won't*	*He'**ll be** 25 next week.*	4.4B
with adverbs to make stronger, etc.	all forms	*It'**ll probably rain** tomorrow.* *She'**s** definitely **going** to the party.*	4.4C
with verbs of hope, doubt, etc.	all forms	*We **hope** you'**ll be able to come**.* *I **expect** they'**re going to increase** the rate in the budget.*	4.4C
in time clauses	present simple	*He'll stay until you **get** here.* *I'll leave as soon as it **stops** raining.*	4.4D

use	form	example	▶
expressions with future meaning			
official arrangements	*be to*	*They **are to** hold a secret meeting.*	5.1A
timetable	*be due to*	*We**'re due to** collect her at five.*	5.1B
immediate future	*about to*	*The check-in **is about to** close.*	5.1C
	on the point/ verge of	*The building project **is on the point of** completion.*	
	adjectives	*The decision is **imminent**.*	
probability/certainty	*(un)likely to*	*He**'s unlikely to** recognise me.*	5.1D
	bound/sure to	*Your venture **is bound to** fail if you don't prepare fully.*	
verbs with future meaning			
main verbs	*decide, hope, promise, predict,* etc.	*They've **decided** not to buy the house. They're **predicting** snow tomorrow.*	5.2A
modal verb	*may, could,* etc.	*This move **could** lead to war.*	5.2B
future in the past			
	was/were going to	*I **was going to** get up early this morning.*	5.3A
	past continuous	*We thought they **were arriving** before dinner.*	5.3B
	would	*I had hoped you**'d** get here earlier.*	5.3B
	would be + verb *-ing*	*We knew we **would be waiting** for ages.*	5.3B
	would have + past participle	*They thought the crisis **would have finished** before then.*	5.3B
	was/were about to	*I **was about to** tell you when you interrupted …*	5.3B
	was/were to	*We **were to** arrive at nine.*	5.3B
	was/were due to	*The concert **was due to start** at half past seven.*	5.3B
	was/were to have + past participle	*The Queen Mother **was to have accompanied** the others, but she broke her hip the day before.*	5.3B
	was/were due to have + past participle	*I **was due to have started** the treatment yesterday but I couldn't get to the hospital because of the train strike.*	5.3B

6 Negation

There are many different ways of forming negatives in English. Although the most common way is with *not*, we can also use adverbs, quantifiers and prefixes to make the meaning of a sentence or a word negative.

6.1 NEGATIVE STATEMENTS

6.1A Using *not* with verbs

We use *not/n't* with verbs to make the meaning of a sentence negative. We add an auxiliary (*do*, *does*, etc.) in the negative present simple and past simple of all verbs except *be*, and the negative imperative of all verbs:

	affirmative	negative
imperative	*Talk to me!*	***Don't talk** to me!*
be	*He's outside.* *We're waiting for you.*	*He**'s not**/He **isn't** outside.* *We**'re not**/We **aren't** waiting.*
present or past simple	*I like Colombian coffee.* *They finished early.*	*I **don't like** Colombian coffee.* *They **didn't finish** early.*
perfect tenses	*They have arrived.* *They had seen the film.*	*They **haven't arrived**.* *They **hadn't seen** the film.*
modal verbs	*We must leave soon.*	*You **mustn't leave** yet.*
infinitives	*I told you to go.* *To stop now would be silly.*	*I told you **not to go**.* ✗ ~~*I told you don't go.*~~ ***Not to stop** now would be silly.*
participles	*Having seen the film, I understand the hype.*	***Not having seen** the film, I don't understand the hype.*

In short answers with verbs of thinking and believing, e.g. *think*, *hope*, *believe*, *imagine*, we often put *not* after the verb (▶ **35.2D**):

'Has Susannah decided to call her daughter Brittany after all?'
✗ ~~*'I don't hope!'*~~ ✔ *'I hope not!'*

6.1B Using *not* before quantifiers and adjectives

We can use *not* in front of positive quantifiers (e.g. *much*, *many*, *a lot of*) to make the meaning of a clause or phrase negative:

***Not many** people want to be referees – it's a lot of hassle and **not much** money.*

We can use *not* (+ adverb) with adjectives to make the meaning negative:

*Howard found/thought the climb **not (too) difficult** but **not (particularly) easy** either.*

❗ Putting *not* before an adjective weakens the adjective, but it does not give it the same strength as an adjective with the opposite meaning, e.g. *not difficult* does not have exactly the same strength of meaning as *easy*, particularly if we add an adverb after *not* like *too* or *particularly*:

*The maths exam was **easy**.* *The maths exam was **not too difficult**.*
(The speaker is more confident of passing the exam in the first example.)

We can also use *not* before an adjective with a negative prefix (▶ **6.3C**):

*Spanish has a tense system **not dissimilar** to that of English.* (= a bit similar to)
*The tap water here is **not unpleasant** to drink now they've removed the fluoride.* (= not awful, but not nice)

The descriptions above are much less positive than the following:

*Spanish has a tense system **similar** to that of English.*
*The tap water here is **pleasant** to drink now they've removed the fluoride.*

6.1C Uses of *no*

We use *no* to introduce negative replies:

*'Have you been here before?' '**No**, I haven't.'*

We do not combine *no* with a verb to make a negative statement:

✗ ~~*I have **no** been here before.*~~ ✓ *I have **not** been here before.*

We usually use *not* + *any* with a noun to express an absence or lack of something:

*They **won't** get **any** help from Janice.*

However, we can use *no* in front of nouns, instead of *not* ... *any* or *not* ... *a/an*:

*They'll get **no help** from Janice.*

We can often use *no* + noun and *not* ... *a/any* + noun interchangeably, although *no* is usually more emphatic or more emotionally loaded than the neutral *not* ... *a/any*:

*There is**n't any** reason to change policy at this stage.* (neutral statement)

*There's **no** reason to change policy at this stage.* (more emphatic statement)

*She's **not a** dancer.* (statement of fact about her job)

*She's **no** dancer!* (statement of opinion about her ability to dance)

We can use *no* with *different*, *good* and with comparatives:

*Low-impact aerobics is basically **no different from** the normal type, but it's kinder on the legs and feet.* (= very similar to)

*Next-day courier is **no faster than** first-class post.* (= isn't (any) faster than)

*Come on! This café is **no more expensive than** the one down the road. Let's eat!* (= This café charges the same prices as the café down the road.)

6.1D Other *no/not* expressions

There are a number of expressions which we use to give negative meaning to a sentence, e.g. *never*, *neither* ... *nor*, *none*, *not only*, *not* ... *for*, *no sooner* ... *than*:

*The English village is **neither** as pleasant **nor** as unchanging as it is believed to be.*

*The German assault would have lasted longer if it had**n't** been **for** the harsh Russian winter.*

❗ English rarely uses a double negative, i.e. two words with a negative meaning in the same clause, as most people consider this to be incorrect:

✗ ~~*Sorry, but I **don't** know **nothing** about that!*~~

✓ *Sorry, but I **don't** know **anything** about that!* *I know **nothing** about that!*

But double negatives are possible if we intend to make an affirmative:

I don't know <u>nothing</u> about Etruscan history – I know a little about it!

(In spoken English, *nothing* is stressed in this sentence.)

We can put *not only* at the beginning of sentences for emphasis (▶ **34.3B**):

***Not only did they monitor** the landings, they also recorded all their dates and times.*

Note that we use question word order when we use *not only* in this way.

6.1E Negative transfer

When we use verbs like *think*, *suppose* and *believe* to introduce a negative idea, we prefer to make the introductory verb negative, not the verb in the subordinate clause:

[*I think the later train **won't** be cancelled.*]

✓ *I **don't** think the later train will be cancelled.*

If we make the subordinate verb negative rather than the introductory verb, it can express surprise or appear emphatic:

*I **thought** that you **didn't** smoke! When did you start?*

❗ We do not use *hope* in this way:

✗ ~~*We **don't hope** that the reunion will be too painful for you.*~~

✓ *We hope that the reunion **won't be** too painful for you.*

With verbs such as *seem*, *expect*, *appear* + infinitive, we use either of these patterns:

*He **doesn't appear to be** interested.* *He **appears not to be** interested.*

❗ With introductory verbs such as *tell* and *ask* + infinitive, we change the meaning when we make the introductory verb negative:

*The doctor told me **not to** take the pills.* (prohibition)

*The doctor **didn't** tell me to take the pills.* (= The doctor omitted to tell me ...)

6.2 NEGATIVE QUESTIONS

6.2A Form

Negative questions are formed by adding *n't* to a form of *be* or to the auxiliary (▶ **7.1**):

__Haven't__ you seen Harrison Ford's new film yet?
__Isn't__ the mayor opening the new supermarket after all?

To be more formal, we can use *not*. We put this after the subject:

__Is__ the mayor __not__ opening the new supermarket after all?

We can use question words to introduce negative questions:

__Why hasn't__ Stella contacted her solicitor yet?

6.2B Use

We can use negative questions to check or confirm that something is true or has happened, or to ask for agreement. We expect a positive (*yes*) answer:

__Aren't__ you a member of a wildlife organisation? (= I think that you are.)

We also use negative questions to check or confirm that something isn't true, or hasn't happened. We expect a negative (*no*) answer:

You were quick. __Wasn't__ the hairdresser busy? (= I think she wasn't busy.)

Negative questions often express surprise that something isn't true or hasn't happened:

__Haven't__ astronomers __discovered__ a tenth planet? (= I thought that they had.)

We can also use negative questions to express criticism or complaint, often with *why*:

__Didn't__ you __remember__ to post the letter? Honestly, I can't trust you to do anything!
__Why didn't__ you __tell__ me about your new boyfriend?

We can answer negative questions with *yes* or *no*. If a full answer would use an affirmative verb, we use *yes*:

'Hasn't the weather been dreadful recently?' '__Yes__ (it has been dreadful).'

If a full answer would use a negative verb, we use *no*:

'Wasn't the hairdresser busy?' '__No__ (she wasn't busy).'

Both of these examples agree with the speaker. We can also contradict the speaker, but we would then soften the response with an explanation:

'Hasn't the weather been dreadful recently?' 'Well, __no__, I think it's been OK.'
'Wasn't the hairdresser busy?' '__Yes__, she was actually, but she's very fast!'

We can use negative questions to try to persuade someone to do something:

__Won't__ you __come__ with us to the beach tomorrow? It'll be fun.

We also use this form of question to express opinions which expect agreement:

__Don't__ you __think__ that the new shopping centre is really ugly?

6.3 WORDS WHICH CARRY NEGATIVE MEANING

6.3A Restrictive adverbs and quantifiers

Many English words, such as *few*, *little* or *rarely*, have a negative or restrictive meaning (i.e. they reduce the amount, frequency or degree of the word they qualify):

type of word	examples	example sentences
quantifiers	*few, little*	*There are __few__ people who believe you.* *I have __little__ time to watch TV.*
adverbs of frequency	*rarely, seldom, hardly ever*	*The urban fox __seldom__ ventures into gardens during the day.*
adverbs of degree	*hardly, scarcely, barely*	*It is __hardly__ likely that a thug will wait politely for the police!*

The meaning of *few* and *little* is restrictive only without *a/an*. Compare:

Water the fruit frequently as __little__ rain falls at this time of year. (= almost none)
You'd better take an umbrella with you; there's always __a little__ rain at this time of year. (= a small amount)

As these restrictive words are negative in meaning, we use a positive verb with them:

✗ ~~*Many managers **don't hardly** prepare for meetings at all.*~~

✓ *Many managers **hardly prepare** for meetings at all.*

❗ We also use an affirmative question tag with these words (▶ **7.2A**):

*Higher-ranking police officers **rarely** meet the public these days, **do they?***

We can put the adverbs of frequency from the table above before the verb for emphasis (▶ **34.3B**):

***Rarely** did the church bells in our village ring out for something like a wedding.*

6.3B Verbs

Some verbs contain a negative meaning, e.g. *fail, deny, avoid*:

*I **fail** to understand your motivation for doing this.* (= I don't understand)

*Joe **denied** copying the essay from his best friend.* (= said he hadn't copied)

❗ These verbs can be made negative and they can take a negative question tag (▶ **7.2A**):

*The boy **didn't deny** copying the homework.* (= He admitted it.)

*Fran **failed** her driving test again, **didn't she**?*

6.3C Prefixes

We can make verbs, nouns and adjectives negative, with a negative prefix:

***Incomplete** information will delay payment of any benefit due.* (= not complete)

Look at these examples of negative prefixes:

part of speech	prefix	examples
verbs	*dis-*	*dislike, disconnect, disappear, disapprove*
	mis-	*misunderstand, misinform, mislead, misbehave*
	un	*unlock, untie, unpack, uncork, uncover, uncoil*
	de-	*deregulate, defrost, decentralise, dethrone, devalue*
nouns	*anti-*	*anti-freeze, Antichrist, anti-perspirant, anti-climax*
	non-	*nonsense, non-smoker, nonfiction, nonconformist*
	in-	*injustice, inconvenience, inattention, inactivity*
	dis-	*disadvantage, disinformation, dishonesty, disinfectant*
	de-	*decentralisation, deforestation, decriminalisation*
adjectives	*anti-*	*anti-clockwise, anti-smoking, anti-social*
	in- (il-, ir-, im-)	*incomplete, inconvenient, insecure, incredible (illegal, illegible, irrelevant, irregular, impossible)*
	dis-	*dishonest, disobedient, dissimilar, discourteous*
	non-	*non-alcoholic, non-toxic, nonsensical, nonexistent*
	un-	*unfair, uncomfortable, unlikely, unavailable, unusual*

We can use words with a negative prefix in negative clauses:

- Negative verb: *He reached down to the window, but **didn't unlock** it when he heard the cry from outside.* (= didn't open it)
- Negative noun: *It **isn't anti-freeze**, it's anti-perspirant!*
- Negative adjective: *Salaries here are **not unlike** those in the United Kingdom.* (▶ **6.1B**)

He's not disobedient,
just playful.

Practice

The key to these exercises is on page 355.

1 6.1

Rewrite the underlined part of each sentence to make a meaningful negative alternative. There may be more than one way of rewriting some sentences.

0 I'll accept interruptions from you or anyone else while I'm speaking.
........*I'll accept no interruptions*........
Or: ....*I won't accept any interruptions*........

1 We hope that the soldiers experience a lot of resistance when they enter the city.
....

2 After the images of the famine, Geldof urged the nation to turn their TVs off.
....

3 In English, the subjunctive is usually different from the past tense.
....

4 My brother's only just started his electronics degree, so he tried to repair the TV himself when it went wrong last week.
....

5 A great number of songbirds are seen these days, owing to the erosion of their natural habitats.
....

6 In this modern city you get an impression of life in the pre-Capitalist era.
....

7 I was willing to help the children, as they had to take responsibility for the schoolwork they brought home.
....

8 War crimes should be both commonplace and accepted in times of conflict.
....

9 The estimated fee for the project was unreasonable, but I decided to negotiate further.
....

10 I think that our company will be offering aid to the disaster zone this time.
....

11 Sarah has only had a few lessons on the guitar so she's a good guitarist.
....

12 The new twin-turbo engine generates a lot of noise but is especially powerful.
....

2 6.2

Complete the gaps to make negative questions. Use the appropriate form of one of the verbs from the box to form each question. Some of the questions start with *Why* and you may need to add other words.

belong	buy	do	give	~~hear~~	join	take	tell	think

0 'What's Robbie Williams' new single like?'
'........*Haven't you heard it*........ yet? I'm amazed – it's on the radio every five minutes!'

1 'Alice has just applied to join the church choir.'
'.. to it? I thought she joined last year.'

2 'Mr Soames from Brent Trading is coming in on the 6th for a lunchtime meeting.'
'Really? .... your holiday in that week?'
3 'Oh, you're back. I was just about to do the washing-up.'
'.. yet? I've been out for three hours!'
4 'Joe and I are going to the jazz festival on Sunday. .... us?'
'I'm busy on Sunday, I'm afraid, but thanks for asking.'
5 'Sorry, but I can't come to your dinner party tomorrow. I'm double-booked.'
'..? I've already bought all the food!'
6 'We need to get some flowers or something to take with us to the hospital.'
'Oh, ... then? I thought you were going to do that during your lunch break.'
7 '.. those hair extensions look awful on older women?'
'No, actually, I don't. In fact, I'm thinking of having some put in.'
8 'I'm afraid we have some problems with the conference scheduled for Thursday as Harriet Ellis may arrive late.'
'Oh, ... the plenary talk first thing in the morning?'

3 6.3

For each of the sentences below, write a new sentence as similar as possible in meaning to the original sentence, but using the word given. This word must not be altered in any way. The exercise begins with an example (0).

0 Sending someone to prison for defending their own property isn't fair.
injustice ....*Sending someone to prison for defending their own property is an injustice.*........
1 Phil claimed that he had no involvement in the pensions scam.
denied ....
2 If no payment is forthcoming, we will be obliged to remove your connection to the electricity supply.
disconnect ....
3 Hardly anyone from the housing cooperative showed any interest in joining the Neighbourhood Watch scheme.
few ....
4 The fundamental values of the two religions are fairly similar.
dissimilar ....
5 It isn't really possible to capture true colours with this type of video film.
hardly ....
6 It appears that the director deliberately gave the investigators incorrect information.
misinformed..
7 It's best not to talk about topics like politics or religion on a first date.
avoid ....
8 The fact that a great area of trees in the Brazilian rainforests has been cut down has had a devastating effect on the ecosystem.
deforestation..
9 It isn't often that pop stars make it as actors, but Madonna has achieved this.
rarely ....
10 Applications in which we are unable to read the writing will be automatically rejected.
illegible ....

4 6.3

Complete the text using a negative form of the appropriate words from the box.

advantage available convenience courteous cover credible intelligent legal possible usual

This rather (1) .... story from yesterday's news may have escaped your attention.

Customs officials last night (2) .... an attempt at (3) .... entry into Britain by an (4) .... group of immigrants: fleas. The fleas belong to the Cardoso Flea Circus of Australia, who are due to perform this evening at the Edinburgh Festival. The troupe (or the human part of it at least) feels that this is a highly (5) .... way to treat artists. They feel that it is (6) .... for them to cancel the show at this late stage, so despite the (7) .... of having lost their star performers, the show must go on. The flea trainer, Wyman Leung, is currently working with an alternative cast of fleas provided by Cambridge and Bristol Universities, although it is a huge (8) .... to have to work with ordinary cat fleas, rather than the elite strain of crossed cat and kangaroo fleas that were sent back to Australia. The circus didn't even bother trying to train the somewhat (9) .... *pulex irritans* – the human flea.

Home Office spokespeople were all (10) .... for comment.

5 6.1, 6.3

Complete the text below with a word or phrase from the box.

few may not misleading no no intention not for not only not recognising not unlike not wishing noncommittal unwilling

Arts Review

Only a year ago not many people had heard of theatre director Sam Mendes. But since his debut film, *American Beauty*, won five Oscars in March 2000, (1) .... self-respecting cinema-goer would admit to (2) .... the name. (3) .... recent films have received the accolades awarded this film by critics and audiences alike.

(4) .... is Mendes one of the youngest first-time directors of a successful Hollywood film, he is also one of the youngest directors to run his own theatre, the Donmar Warehouse in London's Covent Garden. The small entrance and warehouse-type interior of this theatre is (5) ....: it is (6) .... the Royal Court Theatre of a few years ago, a theatre run by actors for actors and audiences, (7) .... accountants.

Initially, Mendes had (8) .... of going to Hollywood to direct a feature film, but when Steven Spielberg sent him the script of *American Beauty*, he was (9) .... to turn it down. After his Oscar success, the young director was (10) .... about his future. While (11) .... to desert his spiritual home, the Donmar, he (12) .... be able to resist the temptation of another Hollywood film for long.

6 ALL

Find and underline the mistakes in this dialogue. (The first one is given as an example.) Correct the mistakes.

LOUISA Hi, Martin. What's wrong? You look awful.

MARTIN Oh, I've had that horrible flu. It lasted for ages.

LOUISA Didn't you go to the doctor?

MARTIN <u>No, I did</u>. I went last week, but my doctor doesn't know nothing. I asked for that new flu drug – what's it called? ....*Yes, I did.*......

LOUISA Do you mean Relenza?

MARTIN That's it. I asked but he wouldn't give me none.

LOUISA Why?

MARTIN He said that the tests haven't hardly proved that it works. Not for did he refuse to give me Relenza, but he wouldn't give me none other medicine. I think it's because the surgery is over-budget and he doesn't want to spend any more money!

LOUISA If that's the case, it's really unhonest! Have you thought about complaining?

MARTIN No, what's the use? Complaints about doctors rarely have an effect, don't they? Anyway, I suppose there's not much you can do about a virus. He said I should drink plenty of fluids and he didn't tell me to go out until I felt better.

LOUISA How are you feeling now?

MARTIN Not too bad, but I can't taste hardly anything. Well, I think that's an effect of the flu and not a problem with my taste buds!

LOUISA Oh, I don't hope it is! It would be awful not to taste things.

MARTIN I've still got a few chest problems, too. I suppose I should stop smoking.

LOUISA What! Have you stopped smoking through this flu, then? You're crazy, Martin!

MARTIN I know. I guess I'll never be a no-smoker.

LOUISA Perhaps not. Anyway, it lasts a long time, this flu. Not many people don't appreciate that. You think it's gone and you try to get back to normal, then it hits you again.

MARTIN Yes, you're right.

LOUISA Look, I must be going. I don't hope it lasts much longer. 'Bye!

7 Questions

There is a range of issues to take account of in the use of questions in English; these include word order, word choice and intonation. This unit looks at these issues in relation to closed and open questions, tag questions, indirect questions and echo questions. (For negative questions ▶ **6.2**; for indirect questions ▶ **9.3**.)

7.1 CLOSED AND OPEN QUESTIONS

7.1A Form

Questions are either closed or open. Closed questions start with a form of main verb *be*, an auxiliary verb (*be*, *do*, *have*) or a modal auxiliary verb (e.g. *can*, *may*, *will*):

__Is__ your brother staying with his friends in Oxford?
__Will__ you be away for long?
__Should__ your team really have spent £500,000 on one player?

Open questions start with a question word (e.g. *who*, *what*, *where*, *how*):

__What time__ is Alison arriving this evening?

With the simple tenses, *do/does/did* is used as an auxiliary:

__Does__ this box enable me to receive satellite TV as well as digital?
When exactly __did__ the Guggenheim Museum in Bilbao open?

Main verb *be* or an auxiliary verb usually precedes the subject (but ▶ **7.1C**):

__Have you__ registered the birth with the authorities yet?

With more than one auxiliary verb, only the first one precedes the subject:

✗ ~~*How long __had been you__ living there before the war broke out?*~~
✔ *How long __had you been__ living there before the war broke out?*
__Will you have__ finished compiling the figures by the next meeting?

With negative questions, we attach *n't* to the auxiliary verb (▶ **6.2A**):

__Doesn't__ time fly quickly when you're having fun?

7.1B Use

We use closed questions when we want a simple *yes/no* answer:

'Does your sister still live in Canada?' '__Yes__, she does./__No__, not any more.'

We use open questions when we want to find out more information:

'__Why__ did she leave Canada then?' '__She couldn't stand the cold winters.__'

In conversation, we can use statement word order with closed questions, but not with open questions, to check something we think we know or to express surprise. We usually give them a rising intonation:

__You've sent__ the tickets? ↗
__You haven't sent__ the tickets? ↗ *Why not?*
✗ ~~*Why __you haven't__ sent the tickets?*~~
✔ *Why __haven't you__ sent the tickets?*

When we ask questions about opinions and feelings, we often omit *that*:

Do you think (that) the nursery will give me a refund for when Elly was ill?

We usually use the question word *which* when the answer will be one of a limited number of alternatives, usually known to both speaker and listener. We use *what* when there is no limit to the choice:

__Which__ cake do you want to try first? (limited choice of cakes)
__What__ cakes do you like best? (of all cakes; unlimited choice)

When we use a preposition with a question word, we can either put the preposition before the question word (formal use) or at the end of the question (informal use):

__From whom__ did the defendant accept the payment?
__Who__ are you buying the bracelet __for__?

When we precede *who* with a preposition, we change it to *whom*.

7.1C Subject question words

Who, *what* and *which* can be the subject of a verb, as well as the object:

subject ↓ **Who** *invited* object ↓ *Jack? (***Meryl** *did.)* object ↓ **Who** *did* subject ↓ *Meryl invite? (She invited* **Jack**.*)*

If the question word is the subject, the word order is the same as in a statement, i.e. the subject comes before the verb:

Who has been drinking my wine? (*who* = subject)
What happened at the end of the film? (*what* = subject)

We use question word order with a subject question word when we are keen to return to a topic earlier in the conversation and want to get an answer:

*Well, **what** <u>**did**</u> **happen** at the end of the film? You still haven't told me.*

❗ When we use *who*, *what* and *which* as subjects, we use a singular verb, even if they refer to a plural subject:

*'**Who lives** in that amazing chateau?' 'The old **Count and Countess live** there.'*

7.1D Expressing emotion with questions

We can add *-ever* to question words (except *whose*) to add a tone of annoyance or surprise to a question:

***Whatever** have you done to your hair? It looks terrible!*
***However** did they manage to get that ship in the bottle?*

Another, more informal, way of adding surprise or annoyance is with idiomatic phrases such as *on earth*, *the hell*, *in heaven*:

***Why on earth** did John decide to study Chinese?*
***Who the hell** told you that you could take the day off?*

We use *else* with question words when we have some information but would like more.

*'I saw Elena yesterday. She said she'd retired last month.' 'Yes, I'd heard that. **What else** did she say?'*

It is quite common to use a question form when we don't really want an answer. We call this a 'rhetorical question' and we use this kind of question when we want to express amazement or irritation with something:

Have you seen the price of fish at that supermarket? It's outrageous.

We use *What's the point in/use of ... ?* to suggest that a course of action is worthless:

***What's the point in** writing to your MP? It won't make any difference.*
***What's the use of** explaining it all to you if you're not listening?*

7.2 TAG QUESTIONS

7.2A Form (basic patterns)

Tag questions are the short questions which we often attach to the end of a sentence. We form tag questions with *do/does/did* (in simple tenses), or the auxiliary verb. There are three main types of sentence + tag question:

	type	sentence	tag question
mixed tag questions	affirmative + negative tag negative + affirmative tag	*You already **know** Harriet,* *She **hasn't had** the baby yet,*	***don't** you?* ***has** she?*
uniform tag questions	affirmative + affirmative tag	*He **arrived** last night then,*	***did** he?*

If an affirmative sentence contains a negative or 'restrictive' adverb (e.g. *scarcely*, *hardly* ▶ **6.3A**), it takes an affirmative tag:

*There was **hardly** enough food for everyone at the wedding, **was** there?*

Most modal verbs, like auxiliary verbs, are repeated in the tag question:

*Tax returns **can** be submitted on-line now, **can't** they?*
*Parents **shouldn't** expect their children to agree with their opinions, **should** they?*

7.2B Form (exceptions and variations)

There are a number of exceptions and variations in the form of the verb in tag questions:

tag questions after ...	example
I am	*I'm still part of the team,* ***aren't I?***
need (negative)	*He doesn't need to repeat the year,* ***does he?*** (or: *He needn't repeat the year,* ***need he?***)
may/might	*It may/might be fine tomorrow,* ***mightn't it?***
ought to	*We really ought to leave now,* ***oughtn't we?/shouldn't we?***
Let's	*Let's try that new restaurant,* ***shall we?***

Note the following contrasts:

have (British English)	*Oliver has a lot of friends,* ***hasn't he?/doesn't he?***
have (US English)	*Oliver has a lot of friends,* ***doesn't he?***
had (past simple)	*Ali and Stefan had another baby last year,* ***didn't they?***
had (past perfect)	*You had met him before this evening,* ***hadn't you?***

Generally the pronoun in the tag question matches the subject of the sentence:

This *is a good example, isn't* ***it?*** (*This* and *it* are both singular.)
Those *are the flowers for Mum, aren't* ***they?*** (*Those* and *they* are both plural.)
Nothing *ever happens when I'm away, does* ***it?***

But notice these exceptions:

Someone*'s been taking my food again, haven't* ***they?***
Nobody *has phoned, have* ***they****?*

7.2C Use

We use mixed tag questions with a falling intonation, to ask for confirmation:

It's the first of May today, ***isn't it?*** ↘ (The speaker believes that this is true and uses a tag question to check.)

With a rising intonation, mixed tag questions are a genuine request for information:

You haven't talked to Jim yet, ***have you****?* ↗

We use uniform question tags (affirmative sentence + affirmative tag) to respond to something we have heard/seen, as in echo questions (▶ **7.4B**):

'I'm sorry, but I'm going to have to cancel this evening. I'm still at work.'
'Oh, things are still really hectic, ***are they?****'* ↗ (expressing sympathy)

❗ Be careful with this type of tag, as with a rising intonation it can express sarcasm:
'Look. I only paid $120 for this dress – it was so cheap!' 'Oh, $120 is cheap, ***is it****?'*

We answer mixed tag questions in the following way:

- Affirmative tag: *'John isn't experienced enough to do this job, is he?'*
  'No, I don't think he is.' (agreement)/*'Actually, yes, he is.'* (contradiction)
- Negative tag: *'You're staying away for two weeks, aren't you?'*
  'Yes, that's right.' (agreement)/*'No, it's three weeks.'* (contradiction)

7.2D Other functions of tag questions

We can also use tag questions for requests:

You'll bring me back some of those lovely sausages, ***won't you****?*
You couldn't bring me back some of those lovely sausages, ***could you****?*

The choice of tag question after imperatives depends on the function of the sentence:

- Requests: *Pick me up at eight,* ***could you****?*
- Invitations: *Stay another night with us,* ***won't you****?*
- Commands: *Turn the TV off,* ***will you****? Don't annoy Rufus,* ***will you****?*

Don't annoy Rufus, will you?

7.3 INDIRECT QUESTIONS

7.3A Form An indirect question is one question within another question or a statement:

Can you tell me ***how long I'll have to wait to see the doctor****?*

↑ introductory phrase ↑ indirect question

(*How long will I have to wait to see the doctor?*)

Common introductory phrases are *Can/Could you tell me ..., I'd like to know ..., Do you know ...., I wonder*

I'd like to know *if that car is abandoned or not.*

Do you know *which seats give the best leg room on this type of plane?*

❗ In indirect questions we use a statement word order where the subject always precedes the verb or verb phrase:

✗ ~~*Do you know* ***where is the nearest bus stop****?*~~

✓ *Do you know* ***where the nearest bus stop is****?*

✗ ~~*Could you tell me* ***when did he leave****?*~~

✓ *Could you tell me* ***when he left****?*

In indirect questions we can use *whether* instead of *if*. If we use *or not* to imply a choice, we can put it at the end of the clause containing the question, or after *whether* (but not after *if*):

Do you know whether *the date has been confirmed* ***or not****?*

I wonder whether or not *Mum and Dad have got back from the Bahamas yet?*

✗ ~~*Could you let me know* ***if or not*** *the gym is open on Sunday?*~~

✓ *Could you let me know* ***if*** *the gym is open on Sunday* ***or not****?*

We use the same indirect question patterns to report questions (▶ **9.3**):

The police officer ***asked the child whether she could remember her address****.*

7.3B Use We usually use indirect questions to make a question more polite or more tentative:

Do you know where I can find the Impressionist gallery?

This is less abrupt than a direct question:

Where can I find the Impressionist gallery?

7.4 ECHO QUESTIONS

7.4A Form We form echo questions with *be*, the auxiliary verb or a modal verb:

'I'm going to Malaysia on business next week.' ***'Are you (really)?'***

'They didn't give the concert after all last night.' ***'Didn't they?*** *Why not?'*

❗ We don't form echo questions with question words (*what, how, why*, etc.)

It is also possible to form echo questions by repeating the question but replacing part of it with a stressed question word:

'Have you been to the Earth Centre?'

'Have I been to ***what****?'/'Have I been* ***where****?'*

7.4B Use One of the main uses of echo questions is to show interest and to make a conversation 'flow'. We use a rising intonation:

'We went to a really interesting play last night.' ***'Did you?'*** ↗

They can often express surprise, especially with the word *really* or an exclamation:

'We've had wonderful news. Jim's just been promoted.'

'Has he really?'/'Has he? How fantastic!'

We use negative echo questions to show emphatic agreement with the speaker. Here we use a falling intonation:

'That was the best holiday we've ever had!' ***'Yes, wasn't it?'*** ↘

Practice

The key to these exercises is on page 356.

1 7.1

Write each question. Use the prompts in brackets and the replies to help you.

0 (own/white Cadillac/drive/around here) '*Who owns the white Cadillac that drives around here?*'
'Oh, I think the Americans from Harding Road own it.'

1 (applicant/think/be/suitable?) '..'
'Well, I think both applicants are reasonable, but Stephen Wrigley appears the best for this particular post to me.'

2 (give/pigs/that type of feed?) '..'
'We'd only been giving them that particular type of pig feed for about two months.'

3 (tell/you/divorce?) '..'
'I think it was Susan who told me about it, but most people at college seem to know.'

4 (else/do/holiday?) '..'
'We didn't really do much else on the holiday – it was a really small resort.'

5 (persuade/David/stay/team?) '..'
'No, I don't think we could have persuaded him to stay any longer. The counter-offer was far too attractive.'

6 (be/point/complain/faulty goods?) '..'
'There's every point in complaining! How else will shops know that their goods are faulty if people don't complain?'

7 (watch/work/I/be/scuba-diving?) '..'
'Both of the watches are suitable for scuba-diving, but I think you'll find that the Timepiece is more reliable at greater depths.'

8 (accused/steal/getaway car?) '..'
'Your honour, we believe that he stole the getaway car on behalf of the Presley gang, for the robbery of the computer warehouse.'

2 7.2

Complete each question with an appropriate question tag.

1 You'll be able to watch the children for half an hour while I fetch John from work, ...?

2 'I hope you're not doing anything tonight. I've just booked tickets for the circus.' 'Oh, there were tickets left, ...? I thought it would have sold out.'

3 The Consul had been quite cooperative up to this point, ...?

4 We needn't register before the first talk, ...?

5 Be a good girl and pop to the shops for me, ...? We're completely out of cheese.

6 How can you think of marrying her? You've hardly known her five minutes, ...?

7 No one was staffing the west turnstile at the time of the accident, ...?

8 Put some decent trousers on, ...? They won't let you into the restaurant in those old jeans.

9 It seems to me, Minister, that the Government has broken all its pre-election promises regarding the Health Service, ...?

10 'I'll help you with your homework if you want.' 'Oh, you can do calculus, ..., Dad?'

11 Mrs Allison did say that we could take dictionaries into the exam with us, ...?

12 'Ryan didn't go to work yesterday because he was ill.' 'Oh, he was ill, ...? I thought he was watching the football.'

3 7.3

Rewrite each question to make it less direct, but so that it is as similar in meaning as possible to the original question. Begin with the phrases given.

0 Who is responsible for street cleaning in this area?
Could you tell me ......*who is responsible for street cleaning in this area?*......

1 Why did it take you so long to deliver this parcel?
I'd like to know ....

2 Has Harriet finished the minutes of the meeting yet or not?
Can you tell me if ....

3 Why do you keep so many old cars outside your house?
Could I possibly ask you ....

4 When will the new curtains for the hotel suites be ready?
Please let me know ....

5 Will Jonathan be staying for dinner tomorrow evening?
I'd like to know whether ....

6 How often is the bedlinen in the villas changed?
Does the brochure say ....

7 Which metro station should we go to for the Eiffel Tower?
Do you know ....

8 Did Schumacher win yesterday's race or not?
I wonder whether ....

4 7.1, 7.4

Complete B's questions with appropriate verbs and/or question words as necessary. The questions should ask about the underlined parts of A's sentences.

0 A: Come on! I've been waiting out in the cold for ages!
B: Oh, really? ......*How long*...... exactly have you been waiting?

1 A: Someone told me that you've decided to give up the course.
B: Oh, ... that?

2 A: Do you like tabbouleh? I've got some here.
B: Do I ....? I've never even heard of it!

3 A: The new Mayor of London has decided to charge cars to go into the city.
B: ....? Good. I thought he'd never do anything about the congestion.

4 A: I've just been offered two jobs!
B: That's great! .... to take?

5 A: We went to a comedy night at the local pub yesterday, and saw some really good comedians.
B: Oh, ... see?

6 A: It seems that I can't apply for a course at the management college after all.
B: But why ....? I thought anyone could apply, regardless of experience.

7 A: I've just had a letter from Ana.
B: Oh, what does she say?
A: Well, everything's going OK. She's got a job and her mother's recovering well from the operation.
B: That's good. What .... does she say about her family?

8 A: Have you seen my new toy? Look.
B: What .... is it? I've never seen anything like that before!

5 7.2, 7.4

Complete the dialogue with appropriate tag questions or echo questions.

LANDLORD Ms March. Come in. You're the lady who's interested in renting this flat, (1) ....?

MS MARCH That's right.

LANDLORD Well, here it is. This is the living room. It's not looking at its best right now, I'm afraid.

MS MARCH (2) ....? Why not? It looks fine to me.

LANDLORD It's a bit untidy. One of the reasons I'll be pleased to see the back of the current tenants.

MS MARCH On the phone you said that there were two bedrooms, (3) ....?

LANDLORD That's right. Come through. This is the master bedroom.

MS MARCH Mmm, it's nice. But there's no radiator in here, (4) ....?

LANDLORD Er, no, but the electric heater is very efficient.

MS MARCH But expensive? I've heard that electric heaters are very expensive.

LANDLORD (5) ....? I don't think they're that bad. Through here is the second bedroom. It's very large for a second bedroom in a flat of this type.

MS MARCH Yes, (6) ....? It's an excellent size. Oh dear, someone's broken the window in here, (7) ....?

LANDLORD Oh, don't worry about that. I'll get that fixed. This is the bathroom.

MS MARCH Mmm. It's a bit dingy. I don't suppose you could paint it, (8) ....?

LANDLORD Well, we can discuss that later. This is the kitchen. I built it myself.

MS MARCH (9) .... really? It's great!

LANDLORD Yes, though it is in a bit of a mess. Now, let's go back to the living room, (10) ....?

MS MARCH Yes. I think you said the rent was £550 a month, (11) ....?

LANDLORD That's right. Have a look around again by yourself, (12) ...., Ms March? Then we can discuss the details.

MS MARCH OK, I'd like that.

6 7.1, 7.2, 7.3

Read this radio interview and then write the questions the interviewer asks. Use the prompts in the box to help you. Use tags and indirect questions as directed.

- ever/find out/true identity
- how long/exactly/be married
- what/his childhood/be like (indirect)
- ever/find out/who/father was
- it/unusual/famous actors/have lasting marriages (tag)
- younger people/remember him/very different role (tag)
- when/pick up/career again
- what/interrupt/it
- when/start/acting in films (indirect)
- enter/chosen career/quite late (tag)
- which film/consider/best
- Sir Alec/86 (tag)
- win/else
- win/Oscar/for that (tag)

JOHN You'll have heard the news this morning of the death last Sunday of Sir Alec Guinness, one of the greatest British stars of stage and screen. In the studio now is Clare Sands, film critic and biographer of many of the stars.

CLARE Good morning, John.

JOHN Morning, Clare. (1) ....?

CLARE Yes. He was 86 in April, but he had been ill for quite a long time.

JOHN He's survived by a wife and son, I believe. (2) ....?

CLARE It is unusual. Many showbiz marriages are short-lived, but Sir Alec had been married to Merula for a very long time.

JOHN (3) ....?

CLARE For 62 years – quite amazing really.

JOHN It is, isn't it? I understand that Sir Alec came from rather undistinguished roots. (4) ....?

CLARE Well, he was poor, and illegitimate – there's no record of a father on his birth certificate ...

JOHN (5) ....?

CLARE Not really, but when he was fourteen, his mother told him that his real name was Guinness, so he took it.

JOHN But (6) ....?

CLARE No. Of course, the name prompted speculation of links with the Guinness brewing family, but no, he never knew who his father was.

JOHN Mmm. Now, on to his acting. (7) ....?

CLARE Well, he started acting on the stage when he was 20, but his career was interrupted for a few years in 1938.

JOHN (8) ....?

CLARE World War II. He joined the Navy.

JOHN (9) ....? After the war?

CLARE Actually, he appeared in a play in New York before the end of the war.

JOHN We've talked about his stage career. (10) ....?

CLARE Yes. His first film role was in *Great Expectations* in 1946, and he worked a lot in films from then on.

JOHN (11) ...., do you think?

CLARE Oh, I'd say that was *Bridge over the River Kwai*.

JOHN (12) ....?

CLARE Yes, for best actor.

JOHN (13) ....? Any other awards, I mean?

CLARE Well, he was given a special Oscar in 1980, for memorable film performances.

JOHN I'm sure that (14) ....?

CLARE Yes, you mean Obi Wan Kinobi in the original *Star Wars*. He hated the role, but it gave him the money to live well for the rest of his life.

JOHN Thank you, Clare. That's all we've got time for, but thanks for ...

7 ALL

In each space write a suitable word or phrase. There is an example (0) given at the beginning.

0 What's ....*the point*........ in arguing with people who hold very strong opinions?
1 'Did you see Ladysmith Black Mambazo at the charity concert?' 'Did I see .... ? Never heard of them.'
2 Could you tell us .... or not the service has been disrupted?
3 .... did you manage to get home last night? You were so drunk!
4 'Mmm, what .... your pastry so tasty?' 'I use different herbs in it, that's all.'
5 The police .... details of the victim last night, didn't they?
6 I've got a couple of paint samples here. .... colour do you prefer?
7 What's .... of buying all this expensive equipment when you don't know if you'll enjoy the sport?
8 These sitcoms are so formulaic. This one is .... any different from that one we watched yesterday, is it?
9 .... of the available methods did your client pay for her purchases?
10 .... is that, in the corner? She looks as though she's just crawled out from under a bush!

8 Passives, causatives and *get*

We use passive forms for reasons of style and of clarity, as well as of meaning. Mostly the rules of passive formation are straightforward, but it needs to be noted that certain words and structures cannot be used in the passive. Related to the use of forms of *be* in the passive are the causative uses of *have* and *get* and the informal passive use of *get*.

8.1 PASSIVE FORMS

8.1A Basic patterns

The subject of an active verb (e.g. *the judge*) can be the agent of a passive verb. We often don't mention the agent in the passive, but if we do it is introduced with *by*:

The judge ***will read out*** *the names of the winners in alphabetical order.*

The names of the winners ***will be read out*** *in alphabetical order (by the judge).*

Notice that the object of the active verb (e.g. *the names of the winners*) is the subject of the passive verb.

❶ Verbs with no direct object (intransitive verbs) cannot be used in the passive:

✗ ~~*The post* ***has been arrived****.*~~ (passive) ✔ *The post* ***has arrived****.* (active)

Some verbs have two objects, e.g. *The manager offered* ***the customer a refund****.* Either object can be the subject of the passive verb:

The customer *was offered a refund.* or ***A refund*** *was offered to the customer.*

Note that if the object of the passive verb is the indirect object of the active verb (*the customer*) it is usually introduced with a preposition (e.g. ***to*** *the customer*).

8.1B Passive verb forms

We make the passive form of verbs in all tenses by using *be* in the appropriate tense plus the past participle of the main verb:

My bag ***was stolen****.* (= A thief stole my bag.)

The murder ***is being investigated****.* (= The police are investigating the murder.)

Note these comparisons of active and passive forms:

	active	passive
modal verbs: verb + *be* + past participle	*Candidates* ***must answer*** *all the questions.* *They* ***have to take*** *a test.*	*All the questions* ***must be answered****.* *A test* ***has to be taken****.*
modal perfects: verb + *have been* + past participle	*Someone* ***might have stolen*** *it.* *The jury* ***ought to have convicted*** *him.*	*It* ***might have been stolen****.* *He* ***ought to have been convicted****.*
multi-word verbs: We never separate the verb and particle(s) in the passive.	*They* ***took*** *the company* ***over*** *in 2001.*	✗ ~~*The company* ***was taken*** *by them* ***over*** *in 2001.*~~ ✔ *The company* ***was taken over*** *(by them) in 2001.*
make (= force)***/see/hear/ help*** **+ infinitive**: *be* + past participle + *to* + infinitive	*The boss* ***made*** *me* ***work*** *late.* *I* ***saw*** *her* ***take*** *it.*	***I was made to work*** *late.* *She* ***was seen to take*** *it.*
let: *Let* has no passive form so we use a passive form of *allow/permit/give permission*.	*The teacher* ***let*** *us leave early.*	*We* ***were allowed/permitted/ given permission*** *to leave early.*

❶ We avoid using the passive of the perfect continuous tenses. We prefer to use an active form and an impersonal subject, e.g. *they/one* (▶ **27.3**):

✗ ~~*By next month the murder* ***will have been being investigated*** *for over a year.*~~

✔ *By next month* ***they will have been investigating*** *the murder for over a year.*

❗ We usually avoid repeating the same passive auxiliary forms (▶ **19.1A**) in a sentence:

[*The contracts* ***have been signed*** *and* ***have been dated*** *in front of two witnesses.*]

✔ *The contracts* ***have been signed*** *and* ***dated*** *in front of two witnesses.*

8.1C *He/It was said ...*

When we are reporting speech (e.g. *The press said he was innocent*) and we don't want to mention the person whose words are being reported, or we want to describe an impersonal or general feeling, we can use a passive form of the reporting verb. There are two patterns:

- Subject + passive verb + *to* + infinitive:
  He ***was said to be*** *innocent. He* ***was asked to leave.***
- *It* + passive verb + *that* clause:
  It ***was said that*** *he was innocent.*

We use the same pattern with *it* when reporting decisions and general feelings:

It ***was decided/agreed/felt that*** *it would be too costly to take the case to trial.*

We use these passive patterns as an alternative to using an 'empty' subject like *they*:

They said *he was innocent.* (▶ **27.1F**)

(For more information on impersonal *it* ▶ **33.2C**.)

8.1D Verbs not used in the passive

Certain verbs describing states, such as *have* (= own), *be, belong, lack, resemble* and *seem*, cannot be made passive:

✘ ~~*A Ferrari* ***is had*** *by John.*~~ ✔ *John* ***has*** *a Ferrari.* (state)

These verbs cannot be used in the passive even when they describe an action:

✘ ~~*Lunch is being had by John.*~~ ✔ *John's* ***having*** *lunch.*

But the passive can describe a state which is the result of an action. The meaning is similar to an *-ed* participle adjective (▶ **21.2A**):

He went to the payphone to make a call but the phone ***was broken.***

(Somebody had already broken the phone; it was a 'broken' phone.)

Verbs followed by *to* + infinitive usually cannot be made passive:

✘ ~~*Your questions are refused to answer.*~~ ✔ ***I refuse to answer*** *your questions.*

Verbs of wanting and liking, e.g. *want, love, hate* + object + infinitive cannot be made passive:

✘ ~~*He* ***was wanted to leave.***~~ ✔ *She* ***wanted him to leave.***

8.1E Passives with *get*

In informal English, *get* can be used as an alternative to *be* in passive forms which describe actions. We often use *get* to describe an unusual or unexpected action:

'How did he ***get hurt****?'* (= How was he hurt?)

'His hand ***got trapped*** *in the car door.'* (= His hand was trapped ...)

❗ We cannot use *get* to describe states:

✘ ~~*That house* ***gets owned*** *by my uncle.*~~ ✔ *That house* ***is owned*** *by my uncle.* (state)

8.2 PASSIVE *-ING* FORMS AND INFINITIVES

8.2A Passive *-ing* forms

We can use *-ing* forms in the passive, as shown here:

active	passive
-ing **form:**	***being*** **+ past participle:**
I don't like people ***lying*** *to me.* *He enjoys his parents* ***spoiling*** *him.*	*I don't like* ***being lied*** *to.* *He enjoys* ***being spoiled.***
perfect *-ing* form:	***having been*** **+ past participle:**
Having signed *the deal, we went out to celebrate.* ***Not having finalised*** *the quarterly accounts, the auditors were unable to present their report.*	*The deal* ***having been signed****, we went out to celebrate.* *The quarterly accounts* ***not having been finalised****, the auditors were unable to present their report.*

We can use *having been* + past participle and *being* + past participle to refer to the past after certain verbs which are followed by an *-ing* form, e.g. *regret*, *remember*:

We regret ***not having been shown/not being shown*** *the Acropolis.* (= We regret the fact that the tour guide didn't show us the Acropolis.)

I remember ***having been informed/being informed*** *about the assault.* (= I remember that I was informed about the assault.)

8.2B Passive infinitives

Infinitives can be passive (▶ **13.3A**):

to be + past participle:

His dog loves ***to be patted*** *and* ***made*** *a fuss of.*

To be given *the role of Titania was Elizabeth's greatest ambition.*

James was hoping ***to be accepted*** *on the engineering course.*

There is a perfect form:

to have been + past participle:

This ascent is the first ***to have been achieved*** *without the aid of oxygen.*

We use the passive infinitive in reported speech with *ask for* + object (▶ **9.4B**):

Inspector Pascoe ***asked for the prisoners to be held*** *in the cells overnight.*

We can use the passive infinitive (or an active *-ing* form) after *need* (▶ **17.1C**):

That cage really ***needs to be cleaned***. (= *That cage really* ***needs cleaning***.)

8.3 *HAVE/GET* + OBJECT + PAST PARTICIPLE

8.3A Causative use

We use this pattern to describe something which is done for the subject by someone else. We can use it in all tenses. *Get* is usually more informal than *have*:

I ***had the washing machine repaired*** *yesterday.* (= The washing machine was repaired by an engineer.)

Do you ***get your hair done*** *at Ebony's?* (= Is your hair done at Ebony's?)

There is an 'active' version of this pattern with *have* and *get* which means 'cause someone to do something'. The form with *have* is more common in US English:

Have + object + infinitive:

I ***had the mechanic repair*** *my washing machine.*

Get + object + *to* + infinitive:

I will ***get the hairdresser to do*** *my hair this afternoon.*

In British English we can use the *get* + object + *to* + infinitive pattern with a stronger meaning of 'make someone do something':

After numerous letters from our solicitor we finally ***got them to give*** *us a refund.*

8.3B Passive use

We can also use the pattern of *have/get* + object + past participle like a passive to describe something which is done to the subject by someone else, often something unpleasant or unexpected:

Liz ***had her passport stolen***. (= Her passport was stolen.)

John ***got his tyres slashed*** *by some hooligans.*

Out of the blue, Mark ***had his plan approved*** *by the board yesterday.*

8.3C Commands and promises

We can use the causative in imperatives. Here it can be the person spoken to or someone else who will do the action:

Have/Get that mess cleaned up *at once!*

We can use the causative in future statements as commands or promises. Here it can be the subject of the sentence or someone else who will do the action:

Don't worry. ***I'll have the report finished*** *before the board meeting.* (= I will do it or I will get it done.)

8.4 USES OF THE PASSIVE

8.4A Information order

If the subject of a verb is new information, we often make the verb passive so that the new information comes at the end (the information principle ▶ **36.1A**). For example, in the second sentence below, the new information is *Picasso* and *1937*:

[*'Guernica' is a wonderful example of cubist art. In 1937 Picasso painted it.*]

In order to put this new information at the end we make the verb *painted* passive:

'Guernica' is a wonderful example of cubist art. It ***was painted*** *by Picasso in 1937.*

If the subject of a verb is a long phrase or clause, we often make the sentence passive so that the long clause comes at the end:

[*The huge orange sun sinking slowly below the horizon delighted her.*]

She ***was delighted*** *by the huge orange sun sinking slowly below the horizon.*

8.4B The 'unimportant' agent

We often use the passive:

- when the agent (the person or thing which causes an action) is not known:
  She ***was murdered****.* (We don't know who did it.)
- when the agent is obvious from the context or from general knowledge:
  She ***has been sacked****.* (obviously by her employer)
- when the agent is not important or relevant:
  Wars ***have been fought*** *throughout history.* (Who fought them is not important here.)

8.4C Not mentioning the agent

We use the passive when we wish to avoid mentioning the agent (for example, when we don't want to directly blame any specific person, or we want to avoid personal responsibility):

I see the washing-up ***hasn't been done****.*

Oh dear, look, the vase ***has been broken****.*

Don't blame me. Nothing ***can be done*** *about it.*

By omitting the agent we can describe general feelings, opinions or beliefs rather than those of a particular person or group:

São Paulo ***is said to be*** *the fastest-growing city in South America.*

Rio de Janeiro ***has been described*** *as the most beautiful city in the Americas*

8.4D Focusing on issues

The passive is often used in formal English to:

- focus on the issues rather than on the people involved (this is very common in academic and scientific English):
  The research ***was carried out*** *over a period of six months.*
- describe rules and procedures:
  Answers ***must be written*** *in ink.*
  Candidates ***will be interviewed*** *in alphabetical order.*
- describe commercial, industrial and scientific processes:
  Minutes ***are taken*** *and then* ***submitted*** *to the chair for approval.*
  Components ***are*** *electronically* ***tagged*** *and* ***transported*** *to the production line.*
- describe historical, economic and social processes:
  Tribal lands ***were sold*** *over a period of fifty years.*
  The currency ***has been devalued*** *twice since the war.*

Practice

The key to these exercises is on page 357.

1 8.1

Rewrite these sentences using passive forms.

0 Someone might have stolen it. *It might have been stolen.*
1 We will provide refreshments during the interval. ....
2 You should complete the form in black ink. ....
3 We have not tested this product on animals. ....
4 We supply this appliance with a plug. ....
5 Someone has fitted this car with an alarm. ....
6 We arrange our displays in chronological sequence. ....
7 You must wear hard hats while we are carrying out construction work. (two passives) ....
8 We will prosecute all shoplifters. ....
9 Closed circuit cameras are monitoring this area. ....
10 You may find toilet facilities at the rear of block B. ....
11 We will take care of all the formalities. ....
12 The customs officer made me open my suitcases. ....
13 A lot of people say the government is out of touch with public opinion. ....
14 The judge ought to have sent him to prison for life. ....
15 The check-in clerk gave Stephen an upgrade to first class. ....
16 A farmer let us park the caravan in his field overnight. ....
17 They saw him enter the building carrying a shotgun. ....
18 Some people think the proposed legislation is unworkable. ....
19 Someone broke a pane of glass while the boys were playing in the street. ....
20 Their parents have given the twins a puppy for their birthday. ....

2 8.2, 8.3

Choose the word or phrase (A, B, C or D) which best completes each sentence.

0 I don't like .....*A*..... cheated.
A being B to have been C been D get
1 .... been banned from driving, I was unable to rent a car on holiday.
A Getting B Having C Being D To
2 John enjoys being .... around.
A bossing B boss C to boss D bossed
3 They hated not having .... selected for the shortlist.
A been B be C being D get
4 I .... my secretary re-type the memo.
A got B get C had D having
5 She .... her husband to put up some shelves in the kitchen.
A got B had C have D is having
6 They are getting their uncle .... them his cottage in the country.
A lend B lending C to be lending D to lend

7 The minister will have his press officer .... the news tomorrow.
A announce B announced C to announce D being announced

8 Michael deeply regretted not .... selected for the Olympic squad.
A to be B having been C to get D been

9 The Opposition have asked for fuel taxes ....
A be reduced B to get reduced C being reduced D to be reduced

10 We'll .... the builders to move the skip tomorrow morning.
A get B have C be having D getting

11 No problem. I'll .... the figures printed out and on your desk by lunchtime.
A having B be having C have D to get

12 I really didn't expect this project .... completed on schedule.
A having been B to be C being D have

13 The cats love .... cuddled and stroked.
A have B having C to have been D to be

14 Theirs was probably the most glamorous wedding .... featured in the pages of 'Hello' magazine to date.
A getting B to have been C having D have

3 8.3

Choose the most appropriate phrase (A–J) to complete this extract from a guidebook. Five of the phrases will not be needed.

Washington DC Tourist Guide

The White House

The official residence of the President of the United States, (1) .... each year. It is the only residence of a head of state which is open to the public, free of charge, on a regular basis.

The original building dates from 1792 and (2) .... Much of Hoban's original design survives, although the mansion had to be rebuilt after (3) .... in the war of 1814.

The guided tour includes most of the state apartments. (4) .... The private apartments and offices are not open to the public. The tour begins in the East Wing Lobby, an extension to the building which (5) ....

A the British burned the house and many of its valuable contents
B they added in 1942.
C These include the East Room, the Lincoln Bedroom and the State Dining Room.
D the White House, is visited by more than one and a half million tourists
E it and many of its valuable contents were burned by the British
F an Irish-born architect, James Hoban, designed it.
G The East Room, the Lincoln Bedroom and the State Dining Room are included.
H was added in 1942.
I more than one and a half million tourists visit the White House
J was designed by an Irish-born architect, James Hoban.

4 8.3

Match parts 1–3 with A–C in each set.

Set a

1 Have him report to me
2 I had him reported
3 I had him report to me

A because I was his line manager.
B when you see him later.
C to his commanding officer.

Set b

1 We got the computer repaired
2 Get the computer repaired
3 We got the engineer to repair the computer

A or you'll be in trouble.
B after he had fixed the printer.
C because it had broken down.

5 8.1, 8.4

A passive verb form would be more appropriate for ten of the sentences (1–15). Tick (✔) the five sentences which should not be changed. If you think a sentence should be changed, choose the correct reason(s) (A–D) from the list in the box then rewrite the sentence. The first two have been done as examples (0 and 00).

The passive form is more appropriate because:
A the agent is unknown or unimportant
B the agent is obvious from the context or general knowledge
C we are describing rules, processes or procedures
D we prefer to put new information or a long subject clause at the end of a sentence

0 You must dry clean this garment. ......*A/B This garment must be dry cleaned.*....
00 That baby really resembles her mother. ....✔..........
1 The stunning vista of long white beaches backed by verdant hills entranced her.
....
2 Our area sales manager has decided to leave. ....
3 The executioner executed the prisoner at dawn. ....
4 A man who had never known that he had rich relations inherited the estate.
....
5 My parents are staying with us over the weekend. ....
6 The New York flight leaves at six thirty. ....
7 They collect the information from various retail outlets and they enter it onto the database.
....
8 An unknown person has vandalised the lift in our block.
....
9 The ancient Egyptians were superb stonemasons. ....
10 People hardly ever see foxes in daylight. ....
11 People must complete this form in black ink and they must sign it.
....
12 Several members of the international press corps interviewed the terrorists.
....
13 This house used to belong to my aunt. ....
14 The jury convicted the man and the judge sentenced him to fifteen years in jail.
....
15 They heat milk to 110°C and then they rapidly cool it to produce the final pasteurised product.
....

6 8.1, 8.2, 8.3

For each of the sentences below, write a new sentence as similar as possible in meaning to the original sentence, but using the word given. This word must not be altered in any way.

0 The accountants are looking into the matter.
being ....*The matter is being looked into.*........

1 They are delivering Daphne's new car this afternoon.
having ....

2 The athletes will have to pass a series of rigorous drug tests.
be ....

3 The parish council let us use the village hall for our meeting.
allowed ....

4 Having completed the project, we were able to leave early.
been ....

5 We resented the fact that the new manager didn't consult us over the expansion plans.
not having ....

6 I'll instruct the caretaker to open the gates early for you.
have ....

7 They believe the suspect is in hiding somewhere across the border.
believed ....

8 They sacked her for being late so often.
got ....

7 ALL

This text would be improved if at least seven of the verbs were passive. Underline the phrases that should go into the passive and rewrite those sections of the text below.

Solving the Mystery of Hieroglyphics

For almost two thousand years the symbols and inscriptions which people had carved onto the great monuments of ancient Egypt were a complete mystery. They were obviously a kind of writing, but nobody knew what they meant.

Then, in 1799, a French officer discovered a strange stone in the small Egyptian town of Rosetta. It had three types of writing carved into its surface. One of the languages was Greek but the other two were unknown. A year later the British captured the stone and the British moved it to the British Museum in London.

For twenty years the stone lay gathering dust in the museum. Then in 1822 somebody asked a French scientist named Jean François Champollion to look at the stone. He immediately recognised that some of the symbols matched those he had seen on monuments in Egypt. By comparing the Greek words with the Egyptian symbols he was able to work out their meaning. The Egyptian symbols were hieroglyphs, a type of writing in which pictures represent sounds and meanings.

Once somebody had solved the puzzle of their written language it became possible for scholars to decipher the inscriptions on all the great monuments. Thus people finally unlocked the mysteries of Egypt's fabulous history and culture.

Line: ..*1*.. – ....*which had been carved*........
Line: .... – ....
Line: .... – ....
Line: .... – ....
Line: .... – ....
Line: .... – ....
Line: .... – ....

9 Reported speech

When we report what we or other people have said or thought, we can use direct speech (reporting the exact words), but we usually use indirect speech. This unit looks at how we report statements, questions and commands, the variety of reporting verbs and how they are used.

9.1 DIRECT AND INDIRECT SPEECH

9.1A Reporting speech in writing

When reporting speech in literature, authors often use direct speech – the exact words are between inverted commas. We do not use *that* to introduce direct speech:

He leaned towards her and whispered, 'Be sure to lock your door tonight.'

The reporting verb (*said*, *replied*, etc.) can go before the speech in inverted commas, after the speech, or in the middle of it:

***Lovett said**, 'Houston, we have a problem.'*

*'Houston, we have a problem,' **Lovett said**.*

*'Houston,' **said Lovett/Lovett said**, 'we have a problem.'*

When we put the reporting verb after direct speech, it can go before the subject, unless the subject is a pronoun:

✗ ~~*'The operation has been a resounding success,' **said she**.*~~

✔ *'The operation has been a resounding success,' **she said**.*

✔ *'The operation has been a resounding success,' **said the surgeon**.*

In most other forms of writing, such as letters and reports, we prefer indirect speech:

She said the operation had been a resounding success.

9.1B Reporting speech orally

When we are speaking, it is possible, though rare, to quote words directly. We may do this if we want to focus on the exact words spoken: *But did he actually say 'I love you'?* We usually report words using indirect speech in conversations as we do not have punctuation to clearly signal what is the reported speech:

*But did he actually **tell** you **that he loved you**?*

We use indirect speech for statements (▶ 9.2), questions (▶ 9.3) and commands (▶ 9.4).

9.2 INDIRECT STATEMENTS

9.2A Common reporting verbs

There are a number of common introductory verbs used to report statements, which are often followed by *that* (e.g. *say*, *tell*, *add*, *continue*, *answer*, *reply*, *mention*, *remark*):

*For the third time that day, the minister **replied that** it was out of the question.*

We can omit *that* after an introductory verb, and often do in conversation, except after *reply*, *continue*, *answer* and *shout*:

*I **told them** they were barred from the club from now on.*

❗ There are differences in use between *say* and *tell*. We can omit the object or use an indirect object (e.g. *to us*) after *say*, but we use a direct object (e.g. *us*) after *tell*:

✗ ~~*He **said us that** his mobile phone had been out of action all day.*~~

✔ *He **said (to us) that** his mobile phone had been out of action all day.*

✗ ~~*He **told that** his mobile phone had been out of action all day.*~~

✔ *He **told us that** his mobile phone had been out of action all day.*

When we are reporting more than one sentence, it is not necessary to repeat the reporting verb to introduce every new sentence:

*Tom **insisted that** he hadn't been there. He had worked late, and had then gone ...*

We can report our thoughts using reporting verbs such as *think*, *decide* or *imagine*:

*She never **imagined that** it would be so difficult to run for the Senate.*

9.2B Changes of pronoun and adverb

When we report another person's words in indirect speech, we often have to change the pronouns used in the direct speech:

*James added, '**I** really don't understand the problem.'*

*James added that **he** really didn't understand the problem.*

When another person reports James's words, then the pronoun *I* changes to *he*. Similarly, if the place or time of reporting is significantly different from that in the original speech, we often need to make changes to adverbs of place and time (e.g. *now* → ***then**; here* → ***there**; today* → ***that day**; tomorrow* → ***the next day**; yesterday* → ***the day before**; last Monday* → ***the last/previous Monday***):

*Alex said, '**I**'ll meet **you here** again **tomorrow** at 3.30.'*

*Alex said **she** would meet **us there** again **the next day** at 3.30.*

But if the statement is reported on the same day and in the same place, we would say:

*Alex said **she** would meet us **here** again **tomorrow** at 3.30.*

9.2C Changes of tense

When we use indirect speech after a past tense reporting verb (e.g. *said*, *had confirmed*), we usually change the tense in the sentences we are reporting (▶ **9.2D**). We use a tense one step further in the past ('backshift'), so present forms become past forms (e.g. present simple → past simple, present continuous → past continuous):

'I'm leaving in ten minutes.' → *She decided she **was leaving** in ten minutes.*

'We've been living here for years.' → *He revealed they**'d been living** there for years.*

Past forms become past perfect forms (e.g. past simple → past perfect simple):

'It rained really heavily today.' → *Sarah mentioned that it **had rained** really heavily that day.*

❗ The past perfect simple and continuous do not change:

'They'd arrived an hour early.' → *I said they**'d arrived** an hour early.*

9.2D When to change the tense

We do not change the tense of the original words in reported speech when:

- the reporting verb is in a present tense:
  *He says that intelligent life in the universe **does not exist**.*
- the direct speech includes an 'unreal past' (▶ **Unit 11**):
  *'I wish I **were** younger.'* → *Janice said that she wished she **were** younger.*
  ✗ ~~*Janice said that she wished she **had been** younger.*~~

In some cases we can choose to change the tense or not. This often depends on the relationship of the reported event to the time of reporting it. For example, if we report *'I'm going on holiday tomorrow morning'* on the day it is said, we are likely to say:

Susanna said she's going on holiday tomorrow morning.

But reported a few days later, we are more likely to say:

Susanna said she was going on holiday the next morning.

We don't usually change the tense when:

- the action in the indirect speech is still happening or going to happen:
  'I am working on the details of a tentative settlement.' → *The negotiator said **he is working** on the details of a tentative settlement.* (= He is still working on the details.)
- the reported verb expresses a fact or situation that cannot or is unlikely to change:
  *He explained that these animals **roamed** the earth millions of years ago.*
  *He told us that counselling **is not** the answer for everyone.*
- the verb comes after a time conjunction, e.g. *when*, *after*:
  *Martin replied that he had started the job immediately **after** he **left** school.*

Note that in all of these cases, it is also possible to change the tense:

*The negotiator said **he was working** on details of a tentative settlement.*
*He explained that these animals **had roamed** the earth millions of years ago.*
*He told us that counselling **was not** the answer for everyone.*
*Martin replied that he had started the job immediately after he **had left** school.*

❗ We make the tense change if we no longer believe the direct speech statement:

'Where's Tom this evening?'

✗ ~~*'He said he's **going to** join us, but I don't think he will.'*~~

✓ *'He said he **was going to** join us, but I don't think he will.'*

9.2E Modal verbs — We often need to make changes to modal verbs. Where possible, the present form of the modal verb changes to its past form (e.g. *will* → ***would***, *may* → ***might***):

'The new law will be in place soon.' → *She said the new law **would** be in place soon.*

'Publication may be delayed.' → *The editor said that publication **might** be delayed.*

❗ *Shall* becomes *would* when it refers to the future, but *should* when it is a suggestion:

'I shall tell them everything.' → *I decided I **would** tell them everything.*

'Shall we tell the manager?' → *She suggested that they **should** tell the manager.*

We can use both *must* and *had to* in reported speech:

'You must lose twenty kilos!' → *The doctor said that I **must/had to** lose twenty kilos.*

In the negative we can use *mustn't* or *wasn't/weren't to*:

'You mustn't think badly of me.' → *She said we **mustn't/weren't to** think badly of her.*

Ought to, *used to*, *could*, *might*, *would* and *should* do not change when reported.

9.3 INDIRECT (REPORTED) QUESTIONS

9.3A Common reporting verbs — The most common verbs for reporting questions are *ask* and *want to know*:

*The assistant **asked** what type of printer we had, but I don't know.*

*Laura **wanted to know** if anybody had reported the missing person.*

We also use *enquire* for formal questions and *wonder* for 'ask ourselves':

*The reception was boring and Andrzej **wondered** when he could leave.*

9.3B Patterns — We introduce indirect closed questions with *if* or *whether*:

*Lester wondered **if/whether** there was anything better in life.*

We can present alternatives in indirect questions with *whether or not*, but we do not use *if or not*, except by putting *or not* at the end of the question:

✗ ~~*Deborah asked **if or not** there was a lift in the apartment block.*~~

✓ *Deborah asked **whether or not** there was a lift in the apartment block.*

✓ *Deborah asked **whether/if** there was a lift in the apartment block **or not**.*

In indirect open questions we use a question word:

*The nurse asked **when exactly the pain had started**.*

❗ We report negative questions which express surprise or criticism with a 'functional' verb (▶ 9.5A) like *complain*:

'Isn't that stupid?' → ✗ ~~*He **asked if that wasn't stupid**.*~~

→ ✓ *He **complained that it was stupid**.*

9.4 INDIRECT COMMANDS AND REQUESTS

9.4A Common reporting verbs — Verbs used to report commands are *tell*, *order*, *command* and *forbid* (negative):

*When the vet had finished, he **told** them to let the animal sleep.*

*He **forbade** us to pass on any of the information to the authorities.*

We use *ask* for reporting requests, and *beg* or *urge* with urgent requests:

*His secretary **asked** me to come back later.*

9.4B Patterns — In indirect commands we use a reporting verb and *(not) to* + infinitive:

*Several members of the Royal Family **urged** Edward VIII **not to abdicate**.*

We can use *ask for* + passive infinitive if we don't mention the person to whom the command was given:

*The cinema manager **asked for** the culprit **to be brought** to his office.*

9.5 REPORTING VERBS AND THEIR PATTERNS

9.5A Using different reporting verbs

A large number of reporting verbs indicate the function of the original speech, e.g:

'You should stop smoking.' → *He* ***advised*** *her to stop smoking.* (advice)

'If you do that again, I'll call the police.' → *He* ***threatened*** *to call the police.* (warning)

In informal conversation we usually report speech using the introductory verbs *say* and *tell*. In more formal speech and writing, we use a greater variety of introductory verbs:

'I think you should inform the judge.'

Dad ***told*** *me he thought I should inform the judge.*

The lawyer ***advised*** *me to inform the judge.*

9.5B Patterns

There are several different patterns used after reporting verbs:

verb only *'I'm really sorry.'* → *She apologised.*	*agree, apologise, refuse*
verb + (*that*) clause *'I hacked into the company's accounts system.'* → *He admitted* ***(that) he had hacked*** *into the company's accounts system.*	*accept, acknowledge, add, admit, advise, agree, announce, answer*, argue, assert, assume, believe, boast, comment, complain, concede, conclude, confess, continue*, decide, declare, deny, doubt, exclaim, expect, explain, foresee, imagine, imply, insist, know, mention, notice, observe, point out, predict, promise, protest, recommend, remark, repeat, reply*, report, respond, reveal, say, shout*, state, suggest, vow, whisper* (* = *that* is obligatory)
verb + object + *that* clause *'Don't worry. You'll arrive on time.'* → *She reassured me* ***that I would arrive*** *on time.*	*advise, assure, inform, reassure, remind, tell, warn*
verb + *to* infinitive *'We'll pick up the children, if you like.'* → *They* ***offered to pick up*** *the children.*	*agree, demand, guarantee, offer, propose, refuse, swear, threaten, volunteer, vow*
verb (+ optional object) + *to* infinitive *'Please can I use the car?'* → *She* ***asked to use*** *the car.* *'Please let me stay.'* → *She* ***begged us to let*** *her stay.*	*ask (sb), beg (sb), expect (sb), promise (sb)*
verb + object + *to* + infinitive *'You shouldn't say anything.'* → *I* ***advised him not to say*** *anything.*	*advise, allow, challenge, command, compel, encourage, expect, forbid, force, implore, instruct, invite, order, permit, persuade, remind, request, tell, urge, warn*
verb + object + *to* + infinitive + complement *'Muhammad Ali was the greatest boxer ever.'* → *She* ***considers Muhammad Ali to have been*** *the greatest boxer ever.*	*acknowledge, assume, believe, claim, consider, declare, expect, feel, find, presume, suppose, think, understand*
verb + *-ing* form *'I didn't do it.'* → *He* ***denied doing*** *it.*	*admit, apologise for, decide on, deny, mention, recommend, regret, report, suggest*
verb + object + preposition + *-ing* form *'You forged the cheques, didn't you?'* → *They* ***accused me of forging*** *the cheques.*	*accuse sb of, blame sb for, congratulate sb on, thank sb for*

(Note: *sb* = somebody)

Practice

The key to these exercises is on page 357.

1 9.1, 9.2

Four of these six sentences contain mistakes in grammar or punctuation. Tick (✓) the correct sentences, then find and correct the mistakes.

0 'These traffic-calming measures have been put into place for a very good reason,' said he. ....*he said*............
1 The doctor said me that I should really do more exercise. ....
2 Alison decided that she'd have the whole kitchen floor replaced. ....
3 Delia commented that fresh coriander could be found in any good supermarket now. ....
4 The child shouted he wanted to go home to his mother. ....
5 And then the interviewer actually said that's a lie, Minister. ....
6 The new Honda Civic, the salesman added, is one of the most popular small family saloons now. ....

2 9.2

Report these telephone messages. Make sure that you change the tenses, pronouns and adverbs as necessary.

0 'Hi, Mum. It's Lucy here, just phoning to say Happy Birthday. I'm going to be out all afternoon but I'll try you again later.'

Lucy phoned to say ...*Happy Birthday*.... *She said she's going to be out all afternoon but she'll try you again later.*

1 'Elaine, hi. It's Rosemary here. I didn't get to Spanish last night as I'd been out all day and I got home late. I'll ring again to find out what the homework is.'

Rosemary called a couple of days ago. She said ....

2 'Oh, er, hello. This is Christine Reynolds. I'm phoning to find out the results of my blood test. I'm going on holiday tomorrow morning so I'd be grateful if you could ring me back later.'

Doctor, Christine Reynolds left a message earlier today. She said ....

3 'Hello. This is Mr Harrison from Leefield High School. I think we need a chat about some problems your son Joe seems to be having. I'll be at the school until 6.30 if you would like to call me back.'

Mr Harrison from Leefield High phoned earlier. He said ....

4 'Good afternoon. This is Tim at Barrett's Wine Delivery Service. I'm afraid that we can't fulfil your order, as you didn't include credit card details on your order form. We have to have these details, or payment in advance, to fulfil an order. I'll await your instructions.'

Someone called from Barrett's a few days ago. He said ....

3 9.2

Rewrite these sentences in reported speech. Decide whether to change the tenses and adverbs of time and place.

0 'The London Eye is now the most popular tourist destination in London.'
The guidebook states *that the London Eye is now the most popular tourist destination in London.*

1 'I've decided to stay another week as the research is going so well here.'
Professor Jones rang from Vancouver. He said ....

2 'We've got tickets for the opera in New York this weekend.'
Gerry and Louisa told me last week that ....

3 'The smaller islands of the archipelago are mostly uninhabited and very peaceful.'
There are so many people here! But that TV programme a few weeks ago said ....
....

4 'Mum's really ill. I wish we didn't live so far away from her.'
Sharon was really depressed last night. She told me that ....

5 'The house is in a very pleasant cul-de-sac, and there aren't many children or animals there.'
Here's the road. Oh no – it's awful! But the estate agent insisted that ....
....

6 'The accused first met the Wilsons when he decorated their living room.'
In court, the lawyer claimed that ....

7 'Shall we switch to an online banking system for the household accounts?'
My husband suggested that ....

8 'They had been living together secretly for years before they revealed their relationship.'
The newsreader said that the two politicians ....

9 'You mustn't leave your car in these parking bays for more than twenty minutes at a time.'
The traffic warden explained ....

10 'Oh really! There is no such thing as reincarnation!'
The scientist maintained that ....

4 9.3, 9.4

Each of these reported questions and commands contains a mistake. Find the mistakes and correct them.

1 Andy was really excited about the new job and asked if could he start straight away. ....

2 Miriam was running as fast as she was able to, wondering how possibly could she get away from this maniac. ....

3 The Prime Minister asked for the new crime bill to draft as soon as possible. ....

4 The builder told us let the plaster dry completely before we paint it. ....

5 The neighbours asked if or not we had heard anything during the night. ....

6 They informed us where buy the books of tickets for the buses and trains. ....

7 Dad asked me where I'd been all night? ....

8 The salesperson wanted to know what is the problem with the new fax machine. ....

9 Sandra begged to her landlord not to evict her before she had found somewhere else to live. ....

10 Standing in the dank, dark cell, Leyton wondered if he can make contact with the prisoners on either side of him. ....

5 9.2, 9.5

Report each of these statements, using an appropriate verb from the box.

accuse apologise blame consider encourage ~~reassure~~ recommend refuse regret remind suggest warn volunteer

0 My wife: 'Don't worry about the arrangements for the reception. They're all under control.'
My wife reassured me that the arrangements for the reception were all under control.

1 Geraldine: 'I will not take part in the new play.'
....

2 My best friend: 'Don't you ever discuss my problems behind my back again!'
....

3 Pete: 'You should think about going to the new Thai restaurant. It's excellent.'
....

4 The departmental manager: 'It was your fault that we lost the Siemens contract.'
....

5 The disc jockey: 'Oasis were definitely the best band of the nineties.'
....

6 The fan: 'I'm terribly sorry about confusing you with George Michael.'
....

7 The police officer: 'We believe that you have been making obscene phone calls to this office.'
....

8 My friends: 'Come on – you can do the Swimathon with us. You're just as good as we are.'
....

9 Mike's brother: 'I don't mind organising the collection for Mike and Sarah's wedding.'
....

10 The team manager: 'I feel terrible now about contradicting Julie in front of her whole team.'
....

11 The director: 'Let's try this scene a different way, shall we?'
....

12 My mother: 'You had your tonsils taken out when you were about nine, remember?'
....

6 9.1–9.4

Read the article at the top of the next page and then decide which word or phrase below best fits each space. Circle the letter you choose for each option. The exercise begins with an example (0).

	A	B	C
0	A answer	(B) to answer	C that answer
1	A did they spend	B they did spend	C they spent
2	A whether	B what	C if or not
3	A had increased	B was increased	C have increased
4	A they still spending	B 'I still spend ...	C they still spent
5	A changed	B had changed	C has changed
6	A increased	B had increased	C increases
7	A tells	B says us	C tells us
8	A takes	B had taken	C take
9	A or not	B could we get	C we could get
10	A is turning	B was turning	C had turned

Worries about Internet use

A recent survey into Internet use has thrown up some worrying results. The Stanford University survey asked respondents (0) ... a number of questions about their Internet use. It asked how much time (1) ... on the Internet and (2) ... Internet use had affected the amount of time they spent with family and friends. It also enquired whether their Internet use (3) ... the time respondents spent working, either at home or in the office. The answers were interesting, but not unexpected. Two-thirds of the people surveyed responded that (4) ... fewer than five hours a week on the Internet. The survey concludes that the behaviour of these people (5) ... little. However, a quarter of those people who do use the Internet for more than five hours a week claimed that they spend less time with their family and friends. One in four of the total respondents also said that the time they spent working at home (6) ..., benefiting their employers.

Professor of Political Science at Stanford, Norman Nie, (7) ... that we are moving from a world where we know and see neighbours and friends to one where interaction (8) ... place at a distance. He asked rhetorically whether (9) ... a hug or hear a warm voice over the Internet. It seems that the results of the survey prove that the Internet (10) ... people into solitary beings who can't be bothered to call their mother on her birthday.

7 ALL

What did these people say? Rewrite the reported versions of some quotations by famous people in direct speech.

1 Al Capone once complained that he had been accused of every death except the casualty list of the World War.

....

2 President Woodrow Wilson once remarked that he would never read a book if it were possible for him to talk for half an hour with the person who wrote it.

....

3 Pablo Picasso once claimed that age only mattered when one was ageing. He said that as he had arrived at a great age, he might just as well be twenty.

....

4 Jean-Paul Sartre once commented that the world could get along very well without literature and it could get along even better without man.

....

5 A spokesperson from UNESCO stated that since wars had begun in the minds of men, it was in the minds of men that the defence of peace had to be constructed.

....

6 Groucho Marx once asked a club to accept his resignation because he didn't want to belong to any club that would accept him as a member.

....

7 President John F Kennedy once told the American people to ask not what their country could do for them, but to ask what they could do for their country.

....

8 Albert Einstein once said that he knew why there were so many people who loved chopping wood. He explained that in that activity one immediately saw the results.

....

10 Conditionals

Conditional sentences usually consist of two clauses: a conditional clause (or *if* clause) and a main clause (or result clause). The result in the main clause is dependent on the condition in the conditional clause. This unit looks at the basic types of conditional sentence, and some variations on these, and introduces a number of words and phrases used to express conditions.

10.1 GENERAL POINTS ON CONDITIONALS

10.1A Sentence structures

We usually form conditional sentences in one of these basic structures:

if clause → *If I had a car,* main clause → *I would take you.* OR main clause → *I would take you* *if* clause → *if I had a car.*

If we put the *if* clause first, we usually separate the clauses with a comma, especially if one clause is quite long:

If the bill is passed by both parliamentary houses, it becomes law.

We can use *then* in the main clause to emphasise that the result depends on the condition being achieved:

If the bill is passed by both parliamentary houses, ***then*** *it becomes law.*

We can put the *if* clause in the middle of the main clause, but this is rare:

It may be possible, ***if both parties desire it****, to reduce the time scale.*

In conversation we often use only the main clause; the *if* clause is implied:

Actually, it would be pretty difficult. (if we did as you asked)

10.1B Sentence patterns

There are four basic conditional sentence patterns where our choice of tense depends on the time of the condition (past, present or future) and how possible or impossible we think the event is:

zero conditional	Possible at any time, but most commonly in the present: ***If your dog is depressed****, he probably needs more exercise.*
first conditional	Possible in the future: ***If the single flops****, they'll sack their manager.*
second conditional	Impossible in the present/possible (but improbable) in the future: ***If you were a bit nicer****, he wouldn't get so cross.*
third conditional	Impossible in the past: ***If you had answered the door****, she wouldn't have gone away again.*

10.2 ZERO CONDITIONAL

10.2A Patterns

This is also known as the general conditional.

if + present simple — present simple

If *you* ***don't look after*** *tomato plants, they* ***die*** *very quickly.*

We can use other present tenses in both clauses, e.g. present perfect or present continuous:

Prawns ***are*** *very risky to eat if they* ***haven't been kept*** *at the right temperature.*

*If she****'s travelling*** *abroad on business, she always* ***phones*** *me every evening.*

We can use modal verbs in either clause, especially *can* and *may*:

*Prawns **can** be very risky to eat if they haven't been kept at the right temperature.*

*If you **can** read this, you're driving too close to me!*

10.2B Use

We use the zero conditional to talk about events or situations that can occur at any time, and often occur more than once, and their results:

If I eat dairy products, I get red spots on my skin.

If can be replaced by *when* in this type of conditional sentence:

If/When you press this key, the game starts, and when you click here, it stops.

We also use the zero conditional to talk about actions which always have the same result:

If you use a very hot iron on nylon, it melts.

10.2C Related uses

We can use an imperative instead of a present tense in the result clause to give a general instruction:

*If a chip pan sets alight, **throw** a fire blanket, not water, on it.*

10.3 FIRST CONDITIONAL

10.3A Patterns

This is also known as the likely or possible conditional.

if + present simple — *will/won't* + infinitive

*If the museum **charges** for entry, a lot of people **won't be able** to visit it.*

We can use other present tenses in the *if* clause:

*If you**'re coming** on the motorway, you'll need change for the tolls.*

We can also use other future forms in the main clause:

*If the results of the customer survey are favourable, the supermarket **is going to introduce** a new range.*

We can use modal verbs in either clause, especially *can*, *may* and *should*:

*If the regime **can** keep the loyalty of the army, they **may** retain power.*

*If the Spanish team continues to do so well, they **should** win the World Cup.*

It is usually incorrect to use a future form in the *if* clause:

✗ ~~*If the weather will be good tomorrow, we'll have a picnic.*~~

✓ *If the weather **is** good tomorrow, we'll have a picnic.*

However, it is appropriate if *will/won't* refers to willingness or refusal (▶ **18.3A**):

*The company will impose sanctions if the workers **won't abandon** the strike.*

10.3B Use

We use the first conditional to describe possible future events or situations and their results:

If the result of the test is negative, you'll receive notification through the post.

The bank will be starting a recruitment drive if it receives head office approval.

10.3C Related uses

We can use the first conditional to express a variety of functions:

- Commands: *If you get home late, **don't wake** us up!*
  ***Don't forget** to close the windows if you go out, will you?*
- Offers: ***I'll call** the hotel if you **don't have** time.*
- Suggestions: ***Shall** we **go** out tomorrow if the weather**'s** good?*
- Warnings: ***I'll call** the police if you **don't leave** right now!*

Note that we use an imperative in the main clause for commands.

To make this conditional pattern more formal, we can omit *if* and use *should* before the subject:

***Should** you **be** less than delighted with our product, we will refund your money immediately.*

10.4 SECOND CONDITIONAL

10.4A Patterns

This is also known as the unlikely or improbable conditional.

if + past simple — *would/wouldn't* + infinitive

***If** they **wanted** to make an offer, she **would listen** and **think** it **over**.*

We can also use the past continuous or *was going to* in the *if* clause:

*If a celebrity **were staying** in the hotel, security arrangements would be tightened.*

We often use a modal in the main clause, especially *might* or *could*:

*More funding for AIDS research **could** be secured if people were more aware of the dire situation in Africa.*

! With *be* in the *if* clause, we usually use the subjunctive *were* for all persons. You may hear English speakers using *was* as in the first example above. It is becoming accepted today, but you should not use it in formal situations.

[*If the programmer **was** familiar with this language, it would be an easy job.*]

✔ *If the programmer **were** familiar with this language, it would be an easy job.*

! It is possible to use *would* in both clauses in US English but not in British English:

US: *The blockades **wouldn't happen** if the police **would be firmer** with the strikers.*

Br: *The blockades **wouldn't happen** if the police **were firmer** with the strikers.*

10.4B Use

The second conditional has two main meanings.

1 It can describe an improbable future event or situation. The condition is unlikely to be fulfilled because the future event is unlikely to happen:
If the result of the test were positive, we would call you within two days.

2 It can also describe a hypothetical current situation or event, i.e. one which is contrary to known facts. It is therefore impossible to fulfil the condition:
If the police were confident of their case against Sykes, surely they wouldn't hesitate to take him into custody? (= The police aren't confident of their case.)

The choice between the first conditional and Use 1 of the second conditional often depends on how possible the speaker believes an event to be:

*If Mike **rings** the travel agent tomorrow, he might get a cancellation.* (The speaker thinks that it is likely that Mike will ring the travel agent.)

*If Mike **rang** the travel agent tomorrow, he might get a cancellation.* (The speaker thinks it is unlikely that Mike will ring the travel agent.)

10.4C Related uses

We use the second conditional to express a variety of functions:

- Giving advice (with *were*): *If I **were** you, I **would take** her out of that school.*
- Polite requests: *If you **could deal** with this matter, **I'd be** very grateful.*
- Desires/regrets: *If we **didn't have to work** so hard, we **could spend** more time together.*

We can use *should* + infinitive or *were to* + infinitive in the second conditional to emphasise that the condition is unlikely to happen:

*If the printer **should break down** within the first year, we would repair it at our expense.*

*If you **were to listen** more carefully, you might understand a little more.*

We can put *was/were* (*to*) before the subject in order to sound more formal:

***Were** you **to accept** our offer, we could avoid the costs of a court case.*

We do not put *do* or the main verb in front of the subject:

✘ ~~*Did the builders finish the work to schedule, they would receive a bonus.*~~

✔ ***If** the builders **finished** the work to schedule, they would receive a bonus.*

✔ ***Were** the builders **to finish** the work to schedule, they would receive a bonus.*

We can make this condition more formal by placing *should* before the subject (▶ **10.3C**):

***Should** the tickets **fail** to arrive before the departure date, we would arrange to have duplicates waiting at the airport.*

10.5 THIRD CONDITIONAL

10.5A Patterns

This is also known as the past or impossible conditional.

if + past perfect   *would/wouldn't have* + past participle

*If we **had paid** our cleaner more, she **wouldn't have left** us.*

We can use continuous forms in either or both clauses of this conditional:

*If someone **had been teasing** your child so nastily, you would have behaved in the same way.*

We can use a modal in the main clause, usually *might* or *could*:

*It **might have been** easier to break the news if I had known her a bit better.*

*If the spy had intercepted the message, he **could have averted** the crisis.*

❗ In US English, it is possible to use *would have* in the *if* clause. This is becoming more common in British English, although many people consider it incorrect:

US: *If the play **would have finished** on time, we wouldn't have missed the train.*

Br: *If the play **had finished** on time, we wouldn't have missed the train.*

10.5B Use

The third conditional describes a hypothetical situation or event in the past. The past situation or event is contrary to known facts, i.e. it is an unreal or impossible situation:

I would have used your builder if I had managed to contact him. (but I didn't manage to contact him)

10.5C Related uses

We can use the third conditional to express criticism:

*If you**'d been driving** more slowly, you **could have stopped** in time.*

We can put the auxiliary *had* before the subject to create a more literary style:

***Had** the film **been** released in the summer, it would not have been so successful.*

10.6 MIXED CONDITIONALS

Mixed conditionals include the verb forms from two different conditional patterns. These are the two most common mixed patterns.

10.6A Mixed second/third conditional

This conditional describes a hypothetical situation or event in the present, which is contrary to known facts. The result in the main clause refers to the past:

*If the island **were** still a tourist attraction, last week's earthquake **would have caused** far more deaths.* (= The island is no longer a tourist attraction so the earthquake didn't cause a huge number of deaths.)

10.6B Mixed third/second conditional

This conditional describes a hypothetical situation or event in the past, which is contrary to known facts. The result in the main clause refers to the present:

*If Fleming **hadn't discovered** penicillin, there **would be** far more fatalities every year than there actually are.* (= Fleming did discover penicillin so there are fewer fatalities now.)

10.7 ALTERNATIVES TO *IF*

10.7A Negative conditions

We often use *unless* to express a negative condition. It is similar to *if ... not* or *only if*:

***Unless** you've got a doctor's note to say you've passed the medical, they won't allow you to go on the activity holiday.* (= If you don't have a doctor's note ..., they won't allow you ...)

***Unless** they all retreat, the casualty count could be horrendous.* (= The casualty count could be horrendous if they don't all retreat.)

*I wouldn't be willing to help you out again **unless** you paid me.* (= I would help again only if you paid me.)

❶ *Unless* is not always an alternative to *if not*, especially when the negative condition after *if* is contrary to known facts, and in most questions:

✗ ~~*You'd be happier **unless** you had such high expectations.*~~
✓ *You'd be happier **if** you did**n't** have such high expectations.*
✗ ~~*What time shall we leave for the theatre **unless** he turns up?*~~
✓ *What time shall we leave for the theatre **if** he does**n't** turn up?*

We can use *unless* with *not*:

*The college will offer you a place on next year's course, **unless** your school-leaving grade is **not** as predicted.* (= if your school grade is as predicted)
*'Are they going to sell?' '**Not unless** they receive an exceptional offer.'* (= They won't if they don't receive ...)

10.7B Necessary conditions

We use the conjunctions *provided/providing (that)*, *so/as long as* and *on (the) condition (that)* to emphasise that the condition is necessary to the result. They all mean *only if*:

*The system will not have to be drained **provided that** antifreeze has been added.*
*Expenses will be reimbursed **on the condition that** all receipts are submitted.*

❶ We do not use these conjunctions with the third conditional, as they can only refer to present or future conditions:

✗ ~~*We would have had the party there **so long as** they had arranged the catering.*~~
✓ *We'll have the party here, **so long as** you also arrange the catering.*

To express a necessary condition for something to have happened in the past, we use *but for* + noun phrase:

*They would have all perished, **but for** the quick thinking of the driver.* (= ... if it had not been for the quick thinking of the driver)

10.7C Imaginary conditions

We use *Suppose/Supposing (that)* ... and *What if* ... to talk about imaginary conditions.

***Suppose** he asked you to go to the cinema with him, would you go?*

We often omit the result clause with these conjunctions (▶ **11.2D**):

***What if** the money doesn't arrive on time?*

We use *in case* to imagine a future situation. It is not the same as *if*:

*I'll pop round later **in case** you're there.*
(= I don't know if you'll be there.)
*I'll pop round later **if** you're there.*
(= I'll only come if you're there.)

We often use *in case* to imagine a precaution necessary for a situation:

*She gave me the key to get in the house **in case** you were out.*

In case of (+ noun) is more formal, and is often used in instructions:

***In case of** (an) emergency, pull the cord above the bath.*

In case of (an) emergency, pull the cord above the bath.

10.7D Unexpected conditions

We use *even if* to express a condition that is unexpected in the circumstances:

***Even if** they do go down with flu after they've had the vaccination, it's likely to be less serious.*

10.7E Alternative conditions

We use *whether ... or not* to express alternative conditions (for all conditional patterns):

*They'll deliver the furniture **whether** there's someone to receive it **or not**.*

▶ **Pages 138 and 139 for Round up of conditionals, subjunctive and 'unreal' past**

Practice

The key to these exercises is on page 358.

1 10.1–10.4

Write the correct form of the verbs in brackets to complete the conditional sentences in this article. Use modal verbs if you think they are appropriate.

No pain, no gain?

It's January 1st. You're on the bathroom scales, groaning. If you (1) .... (eat) that last piece of Christmas pud, perhaps you wouldn't have put on that extra kilo. Never mind, you can lose it and get fit at the gym!

Or is that the right thing to do? If you're unfit, you (2) .... (stand) a huge chance of injuring yourself in the gym or on the squash court. You must take care before launching yourself into a vigorous exercise routine: if you don't treat your body with respect, it (3) .... (not/function) as you want it to. The knee, in particular, can cause untold problems. We (4) .... (not/have) problems with our knees if we still (5) .... (walk) on all fours, but they're not up to a vertical pounding on the treadmill for an hour a day. All of our joints can cause problems; if you (6) .... (want) to play football safely, make sure you wear the right boots to protect your ankles. Decent coaching (7) .... (be) essential if you're going to take up a racket sport: something as simple as a wrong-size grip can cause tennis elbow.

Many sports injuries are caused by insufficient warm-ups. If everyone spent a few minutes stretching their muscles before exercising, they (8) .... (experience) much less pain during exercise itself. But people can be stubborn about pain when exercising. The phrase 'no pain, no gain' is rubbish. Should you feel pain when you're exercising, you (9) .... (stop) at once!

Sport has so many other hazards, though. Golf, you would think, is relatively harmless. Not so for Anthony Phua, a Malaysian golfer who was killed by getting in the way of his partner's swing. Now, if he hadn't taken up that particular form of exercise in the first place, it (10) .... (happen).

What can you do if you (11) .... (not/want) to risk sport, but you still want to lose weight? Well, it's not all bad news for couch potatoes. If you're happy to lose calories steadily but slowly, just (12) .... (stay) at home: sleeping burns 60 calories an hour, ironing 132 and cooking 190. Just don't eat what you cook!

2 10.3–10.5

Rephrase the information in each paragraph to use a conditional sentence. The first words are given to you in each case, and the first one has been done as an example (0).

South-East Asia faces new smog crisis

0 Forest fires are breaking out all over South-East Asia. Something has to be done to control these fires or the smog crisis of two years ago will be repeated.
There will be a repeat of *the smog crisis of two years ago if nothing is done to control the fires.*

1 The forecast is that the weather will stay dry, but only heavy rain can avert the crisis.
If it doesn't rain, ...
....

2 The government stopped releasing pollution levels in June because it didn't want to frighten off tourists. The tourist industry has not yet suffered.
The tourist industry might..............................
....

3 Government officials are advising people with respiratory problems to wear face masks.
The Government says: 'You should wear ....
....

4 The governments involved didn't take positive action after the 1997 crisis. Environmentalists think this is why the current crisis has happened.
If the governments involved ....
....
....

5 One of the problems is that few of the countries affected have a Ministry of the Environment, so there is no serious environmental protection.
There might be more ....
....
....

3 10.2–10.4

Here are some lines from songs. Each line is a conditional. Match the two halves of the conditional sentence to make the complete line. Be careful – one of the conditionals is incorrect. Can you identify which one?

1 If I could read your mind, love, ...
2 If I had a hammer, ...
3 If I need love, ...
4 If I ruled the world, ...
5 If I were a carpenter, and you were a lady, ...
6 If I were a rich man, ...
7 If looks could kill, ...
8 If you're going to San Francisco, ...
9 If I can't have you, ...
10 If we don't try to save the love we got,

A would you marry me anyway?
B they probably will, in games without frontiers.
C we're gonna lose it.
D be sure to wear some flowers in your hair.
E every day would be the first day of spring.
F what a tale your thoughts would tell.
G I hold out my hand and I touch love.
H I'd hammer out reason.
I I wouldn't have to work hard.
J I don't want nobody, baby.

4 10.4–10.6

Match each *if* clause (1–5) with two possible main clauses (A–L). Then complete the main clauses using the words in brackets. Use modal verbs if appropriate.

0 If Bill Gates hadn't been in the right place at the right time, ...B, E......
1 If athletes today didn't take their training so seriously, ...
2 If John Lennon and Paul McCartney hadn't met, ...
3 If Oppenheimer hadn't discovered how to build an atomic bomb, ...
4 If it weren't possible for scientists to isolate individual genes, ...
5 If the printing press had not been invented, ...

A a cure for cancer .... imminent. **(not/be)**
B he ....wouldn't be.......... the richest man in the world now. **(not/be)**
C Hiroshima and Nagasaki .... **(not/be/destroyed)**
D it .... possible to extend education to most people. **(not/be)**
E Microsoft ..wouldn't have become... a household name. **(not/become)**
F much of our history .... unknown to us. **(be)**
G sport .... so exciting to watch. **(not/be)**
H the Beatles .... **(never/be/formed)**
I the ethical debate around cloning .... an issue. **(not/be)**
J the pop music of today .... very different. **(be)**
K the world .... a more secure and peaceful place. **(be)**
L they .... so many records in recent years. **(not/break)**

5 10.3–10.6

Read each short text and the conditional sentences that follow it. Tick (✔) the correct conditional sentences. (One or two may be correct in each case.) Put a cross (✘) by the incorrect ones. Think about the meaning as well as the grammar.

0 Thanks for looking after the house while I'm away. The only difficulty might be the burglar alarm, which occasionally goes off for no reason. The police always follow up an alarm, but just tell them that it's a bit temperamental.
   A If the alarm goes off, the police will come. ....✔....
   B If the alarm were to go off, the police can come. ....✘....
   C If the alarm should sound, the police will come. ....✔....

1 The crash of the Air France Concorde has now been attributed to a piece of metal on the runway, apparently from a Continental Airlines DC10 which had taken off minutes before. The metal caused one of Concorde's tyres to burst, which in turn ruptured the fuel tank on the left-hand side of the plane.
   A If the runway were swept after each take-off, the disaster might have been averted. ....
   B If the runway had been swept after the DC10 take-off, the disaster could have been averted. ....
   C If the runway hadn't been swept after the DC10 take-off, the disaster might have been averted. ....

2 The government urges that all children and teenagers are vaccinated against meningitis C.
   A If your child had not yet been vaccinated, please make an appointment with the nurse. ....
   B If your child has not yet been vaccinated, please make an appointment with the nurse. ....
   C If your child was not yet vaccinated, please make an appointment with the nurse. ....

3 I haven't seen the result, but Rusedski must have finished his second round match against Pioline by now.
   A If he gets through this one, he'll be delighted. ....
   B If he's got through this one, he'll be delighted. ....
   C If he got through this one, he'd be delighted. ....

4 Try to engage the potential client in conversation as soon as possible, to make it more difficult for him to put the phone down.
  A If the client won't engage, politely thank him for listening and hang up. ....
  B If the client doesn't engage, politely thank him for listening and hang up. ....
  C If the client wouldn't engage, you should thank him for listening and hang up. ....
5 Over ninety-five per cent of people who successfully complete our course find that they recover the course fees within a few months through income from having their work published.
  A Should you not recover the fees within a year of completing the course, we will give you a full refund. ....
  B Did you not recover the fees within a year of completing the course, we would give you a full refund. ....
  C If you hadn't recovered the fees within a year of completing the course, we would give you a full refund. ....
6 In last week's peaceful demonstrations in Burma, one demonstrator was seriously injured when she fell and was trampled by the crowd trying to flee from the water cannons. She is still in hospital in a critical condition.
  A If the demonstrator didn't fall, she might not be in hospital now. ....
  B If the demonstrator hadn't fallen, she might not be in hospital now. ....
  C If the demonstrator hadn't fallen, she might not have been seriously injured. ....

6 10.7

For each of the sentences below, write a new sentence as similar as possible in meaning to the original sentence, but using the words given. These words must not be altered in any way.

0 It would be nice to go to the beach tomorrow.
suppose ....*Suppose we went to the beach tomorrow? That would be nice.*........
1 Perhaps Sophie doesn't like her parents-in-law, but she keeps it to herself.
even if ....
2 After her husband's death, Mrs Jenkins sold the house to her son but insisted that he lived in it himself.
on the condition that ....
3 If you don't request next-day delivery, we will send the goods by normal first-class post.
unless ....
4 Use a power breaker when you mow the lawn as you might cut the electric lead.
in case ....
5 The library computer can tell you about the books you have out on loan, if any.
whether ... or not ....
6 I can't imagine the consequences if the police found out!
what if ....
7 We will only achieve the deadline if you provide all the resources we have requested.
not ... unless ....
8 You will be awarded marks for trying to answer all the questions; not all the answers have to be correct.
whether ... or not ....
9 You're welcome to bring Lucinda, but I don't want her to moan about her work all day.
as long as ....
10 If you hadn't been so stupid in the TV studio, our team would have won the quiz!
but for ....

7 ALL

Read this article and decide which word or words below best fits each space. Circle the letter you choose for each question. The exercise begins with an example (0).

Good news for dog owners!

If you often travel abroad for your holidays, what (0) ... with your beloved pet dog?
Do you put him in a kennel or leave him with friends? One thing is certain, you're extremely unlikely to take him with you, because if you (1) ..., he (2) ... six months in quarantine when you return. A bit of a stiff penalty for two weeks' romping in the Dordogne! But this is set to change soon. From April your dog will be able to travel with you (3) ... he (4) ... a rabies vaccination and is wearing an identification chip. Cara Lewis, spokesperson for the Animal Welfare Society, said, 'This is very good news for all British animal lovers. I know many people who (5) .... take their dogs on holiday with them if only they (6) .... . Indeed, I used to travel to northern France regularly and I (7) ... my dog Wolfie with me every time (8) ... the quarantine regulations.' But Cara also has words of warning: 'Pet owners should remember that there are other considerations when taking animals abroad. (9) ... your animal become disorientated, he (10) ..., so ensure that he is wearing a collar with your holiday address at all times.'

It isn't all good news, however. If you (11) ... to a country outside Western Europe this year, you (12) ... your pet with you – it will be some time before regulations for other destinations are relaxed, if ever.

	A	B	C
0	A will you do	B would you do	Ⓒ do you do
1	A had done	B did	C do
2	A will spend	B has to spend	C would have to spend
3	A providing	B unless	C in case
4	A had	B had had	C has had
5	A could	B will	C would
6	A can	B could	C should be able to
7	A have taken	B will have taken	C would have taken
8	A unless	B but for	C so long as
9	A Should	B Did	C Had
10	A runs away	B should run away	C might run away
11	A will travel	B are travelling	C would travel
12	A don't take	B can't have taken	C won't be able to take

11 The subjunctive and 'unreal' uses of past forms

We use the subjunctive form in certain fixed expressions and after some verbs and adjectives which express the idea of necessity, importance, etc. The subjunctive form can be used to refer to events and situations in the past, present or future. We use it mostly in formal and literary language.

After certain expressions we can also use past tenses to refer to the past, present or future, to describe things which are seen as 'unreal' or unlikely. This is similar to the use of past tenses in conditionals (▶ **Unit 10**). In this unit we look at the way we use past tenses after particular expressions and to express preference and necessity.

11.1 THE SUBJUNCTIVE

11.1A Form and use

The subjunctive form is the same as the infinitive (without *to*). It does not show any marking for tense and can be used to refer to events in the past, present or future. We use it most often in *that* clauses after certain verbs (e.g. *advise*, *ask*, *demand*, *insist*, *propose*, *recommend*, *request*, *suggest*), and after adjectives (e.g. *advisable*, *anxious*, *desirable*, *eager*, *essential*, *important*, *necessary*, *preferable*, *vital*, *willing*), to express the idea that something is necessary or important:

At yesterday's hearing the judge ***insisted*** *(that) Mr Grant* ***give*** *evidence despite his relationship to the accused.*
In future cases it will be ***vital*** *that each party* ***give*** *full disclosure prior to trial.*

We can use passive and negative forms of the subjunctive:

Members of the committee suggested England ***be excluded*** *from future international tournaments.*
Regulations require that officers ***not enter*** *the crime scene without protective clothing.*

The verb *be* has an alternative subjunctive form *were* which is sometimes called the past subjunctive and is used to talk about the imagined present or future (▶ **11.2B**) and in conditionals (▶ **10.4A**).

11.1B Informal alternatives

The subjunctive is used in reported speech, very formal language (e.g. regulations, legal documents) and in poetry:

She insisted that she ***pay*** *her own way.*
We require that all receipts ***be submitted*** *to the committee for approval.*

I know not whether laws ***be*** *right,*
Or whether laws ***be*** *wrong.* (Oscar Wilde)

As the use of the subjunctive is rather formal or literary in British English (it is less formal and more common in US English), British English speakers prefer to use *should* + infinitive or the forms listed below in most situations:

It is vital that every applicant ***complete*** *the form in triplicate.* (subjunctive)
It is vital that every applicant ***should complete*** *the form in triplicate.* (*should* + infinitive)
It is vital that every applicant ***completes*** *the form in triplicate.* (present simple)
It is vital ***for every applicant to complete*** *the form in triplicate.* (*for* + subject + *to* + infinitive)

11.1C Fixed expressions

There are some fixed expressions which use subjunctive forms:

If he doesn't want to see us, then ***so be it****.* (= then let it happen)

Bless *you!*

Long ***live*** *the republic!*

*'There's very little chance of winning this case.' '****Be that as it may****, I'm not going to give up fighting.'* (= Whether that is true or not, I'm not ....)

I'll take it all the way to the Supreme Court ***if need be****.* (= if this is necessary)

11.2 THE 'UNREAL' PAST

11.2A Form and use

After a number of expressions, like *if only*, we use past tenses (active and passive) to describe things in the present, past or future which are imagined or unreal. We sometimes refer to this use of past tenses as the 'unreal' past.

If only I ***was*** *thin.* (= I am not thin but I would like to be thin.)

Other introducing expressions like *if only* are: *It's time ..., What if ..., Suppose/Supposing ..., would rather, would sooner, as if, as though, wish.*

We can use the past simple or the past continuous after these expressions to talk about the imaginary present and future:

- Present: *It's time they* ***were forced*** *to clear up the mess.* (They aren't being forced to clear up at the moment.)
  These kids act as if they ***owned*** *the place.* (They don't own it.)
- Future: *I wish I* ***were coming*** *with you tomorrow.* (I am not coming with you tomorrow.)

We use the past perfect to refer to something unreal in the past:

Suppose the gun ***had been fired*** *at me?* (The gun wasn't fired at me.)

I wish ***I'd never started*** *this course.* (I have started it.)

11.2B *was or were?*

Many speakers prefer to use *were* for all persons when talking about the imagined present or future, especially in more formal situations and in US English. This form is sometimes called the past subjunctive (▶ **11.1A** above) and is also used in second conditional sentences (▶ **10.4**).

Suppose I ***were*** *to announce my candidacy at the next council meeting.*

If only he ***were*** *a little more convincing on the economic issues.*

If I ***were*** *you, I'd think twice before refusing that offer.*

In the above examples we can also use *was* but this is more informal.

11.2C *it's (high/about) time (that)*

We use *it's time* ... to say that something is not happening and it should be:

It's time *we* ***left****.* (= We aren't leaving and we should.)

It's about time *you* ***paid*** *a visit to your grandparents.* (= You should visit them.)

It's high time *that the voice of the people* ***was heard*** *in this House.* (= Their voice isn't being heard and it should be.)

❗ We cannot use a negative after *it's time* ...:

✗ ~~*It's time we* ***didn't*** *stay.*~~

Note that we can also use *it's time to* + infinitive or *it's time for* + object + *to* + infinitive:

I'm afraid ***it's time to put*** *your books away now, children.*

Come on everybody. ***It's time for us to get*** *on the coach.*

11.2D *what if, suppose/ supposing (that)*

We use *what if, suppose/supposing (that)* with the past simple or continuous to ask questions about an imaginary situation in the present or future and its possible consequences. These questions have similar form and meaning to those in second conditional sentences (▶ **10.4, 10.7C**):

__Suppose__ he __asked__ you to marry him, what would you say? (= If he asked you to marry him, what would you say?)

Sentences with these expressions describing an imaginary situation in the past have a similar meaning to third conditional sentences (▶ **10.5**):

__Supposing__ your parents __had refused__, how would you have felt? (= If your parents had refused, how would you have felt?)

And __what if__ he __had been thrown out__ by the landlord? Where would he have gone?

We often use *what if, suppose* and *supposing* to make suggestions:

__Suppose__ you __paid__ the bill for once?

We use a present tense after these expressions to ask about an imaginary situation in the future that we think is likely or probable, or if we want to suggest that it is:

__What if__ the plan __doesn't work__?

__Supposing__ he __gets__ caught at customs? You know how vigilant they can be.

11.2E *would rather/would sooner*

We use *would rather/sooner* with the past simple to describe preferences:

__I'd sooner__ you __gave__ me a cash refund. A credit note's no use to me. (= I would prefer a refund/I wish you would give me a refund.)

They are often used as a polite way to give/refuse permission, or make suggestions:

__I'd rather__ you __didn't smoke__ in here.

I'm not keen on the idea of staying in. __I'd sooner__ we __went out__ clubbing or something.

❗ If the person expressing a preference and the subject of the preference are the same we use an infinitive instead of the past tense. Compare:

__We__'d sooner __you spent__ your bonus on something useful. (past tense: speaker and subject are not the same)

__I__'d rather __spend__ it on something frivolous. (infinitive: speaker and subject are the same)

11.2F *as if/ as though*

We use the past simple after *as if* or *as though* to say that how something appears now does not match with reality:

He talks to the children __as though they were__ imbeciles. (The speaker knows they aren't imbeciles.)

They are acting __as if nothing had happened__. (The speaker knows something has happened.)

But we use a present tense (including the present perfect) after *as if* or *as though* to describe how things seem or appear when there is a possibility that the appearance reflects something real:

He sounds __as if he knows__ what he's talking about. (= Perhaps he does know.)

You look __as though you haven't eaten__ for days. (= You may not have eaten.)

We can use these expressions to be critical, ironic or sarcastic:

It isn't __as if he's__ in any position to pass judgement! (= He probably isn't in a position to do this.)

11.3 *WISH/IF ONLY*

11.3A *wish/if only + past simple*

We use *wish/if only* + past simple to express a desire for something to be different in the present:

__I wish I had__ more free time. (= I don't have much free time, but I would like some.)

The desire can be for something which is actually impossible:

__If only__ I __were__ young again.

11.3B *wish/if only* + past perfect

We use *wish/if only* + past perfect to express a regret about the past, a wish that something different had happened:

*I **wish** that you'**d told** me about this before I booked the tickets.* (= I regret the fact that you didn't tell me about this.)

***If only** he **hadn't been driving** so fast!* (= Unfortunately he was driving very fast.)

11.3C *wish/if only* + *would*

Wish/if only + *would* usually expresses a desire for someone to change their deliberate behaviour in the present or future:

*I **wish** you'**d stop** looking at me like that. It's terribly distracting.* (= You keep looking at me and I want you to stop.)

I wish you'd stop looking at me
like that. It's terribly distracting.
DAD

We often use this form to criticise or complain about something:

*I **wish** you'**d stop** shouting. I'm not deaf you know.*

We can also use the form with inanimate subjects because although we know they have no conscious control over their actions (they are not human), we give them human characteristics for emphatic effect:

***If only** the sun **would come out** so we could get on with the filming.* (= The sun 'refuses' to come out. I want it to come out.)

The change we desire must be possible, even if unlikely. We cannot use *would* for an impossible change, e.g. one which the subject has no control over or a change to the past:

✗ ~~*I **wish** sports cars **wouldn't be** so expensive.*~~ (Cars have no control over their price.)

✓ *I **wish** sports cars **weren't** so expensive.* (+ past simple ▶ **11.3A**)

✗ ~~***If only** nuclear bombs **wouldn't have been invented**.*~~ (a change to the past)

✓ ***If only** nuclear bombs **hadn't been invented**.* (+ past perfect ▶ **11.3B**)

We can't use *would* when the subject of the wish and the subject of the change are the same. Instead we use a past tense, or *could* (▶ **11.3D**):

✗ ~~*I **wish I would be** more energetic.*~~ (Subject of *wish* and *would* are the same.)

✓ ***If only** I **were** more energetic.* ✓ *I **wish** I **could be** more energetic.*

11.3D *wish/if only* + *could (have)*

We use *wish/if only* + *could have* to describe a desire we know is impossible to achieve:

***If only** we **could** see the situation through his eyes.* (We can't.)

We often use the form when we are expressing an impossible desire about ourselves:

*I **wish** I **could** dance but I'm afraid I've got two left feet.*

We can use *could have* (▶ **16.2B**) for a regret about the past. It means 'It would have been nice if ...':

*I **wish** your father **could have been** there to see it all.* (= Unfortunately, he wasn't able to be there.)

11.3E Differences between *wish* and *if only*

If only is often more emphatic than *wish*. Compare these examples:

***If only** we'd seen you coming. We might have braked in time.* (a regret)

*I **wish** we'd seen you coming. We would have put out the red carpet!* (a wish)

For greater emphasis we can put a subject between *if* and *only* in informal English:

***If you only** knew how much trouble you've caused.*

❗ *Wish* can be followed by *that*, but *if only* cannot:

✗ ~~***If only that** you'd told me about it earlier.*~~

✓ *I **wish that** you'd told me about it earlier.*

▶ **Pages 138 and 139 for Round up of conditionals, subjunctive and 'unreal' past**

Practice

The key to these exercises is on page 359.

1 11.1

Study the following extracts. Two of them use appropriate language but four of them use forms which have an incorrect degree of formality. Tick (✔) the two correct extracts and rewrite the remaining four using subjunctives (note you may need to use passive forms).

1 It is vital that claims are submitted to the committee with full supporting documentation.

2 *and then, can you imagine, the boss insisted that I took little James to lunch. I mean, it's not my job to look after the boss's children, is it?*

3 Clause 25.6 of the Treatment of Offenders Act suggests that each offender receives a monthly visit from a probation officer.

4 **May the President have a long life!**

5 **7.30 BBC1**. *Trudy Trouble.* In tonight's hilarious episode Sam suggests that Trudy visits the doctor, with predictably comical results!

6 It is imperative that ear protectors are worn at all times when operating the machine lathes.

2 11.2

Rewrite these sentences using a suitable phrase from the box. Use each phrase only once.

as if she · as though · I'd rather · it's time · it's about time you · suppose I · ~~I'd sooner~~ · they'd rather · what if

0 Taking the later flight would be preferable for me. *I'd sooner take the later flight.*
1 You look awful. Have you been unwell? ....
2 Please don't wipe your feet on the carpets. ....
3 What on earth will happen if they don't accept your explanation? ....
4 We really ought to pay the bill now. ....
5 If I complained to the police, how would they react? ....
6 If they had the choice, I think they'd prefer us to go with them. ....
7 She isn't a member of the club, but she acts like someone who is. ....
8 You should give your parents a call, they must be getting worried by now. ....

3 11.2, 11.3

Read the information in the box then match each statement (1–15) below with one of the speakers Alan (A), Mary (M) or Teresa (T). You can match five statements to each speaker.

A – Alan loves swimming but he doesn't have a pool in his house. M – Mary has a swimming pool in her house. T – Teresa used to own a house with a swimming pool.

1 I wish we had a house with a pool. ....
2 Supposing we got rid of the pool? ....
3 It's high time we changed the water in the pool. ....
4 If only the pool hadn't been so expensive to maintain. ....
5 Suppose we hadn't had a pool for all those years? ....
6 I'd rather we had our own pool. ....
7 People say I sometimes talk as if I had my own swimming pool. ....
8 What if we'd never had a pool? ....
9 If only the children would use our pool more often. ....
10 I wish I could go back to the days when we had our own pool. ....
11 If only we didn't have that great big pool in the back garden. ....
12 I'd sooner we used solar power to heat our pool. ....
13 I wish we could have used our pool more. ....
14 It's about time we built a pool. ....
15 What if we installed a pool in the basement? ....

4 11.2, 11.3

For each of the sentences below, write a new sentence as similar as possible in meaning to the original sentence. Use the words given in bold letters. The words must not be altered in any way. There is an example (0) at the beginning.

0 I regret the fact that we didn't see the band play.
could ....*I wish we could have seen the band play.*........
1 It's a pity that you didn't tell us that you were leaving.
wish ....
2 What would have happened if they hadn't got a receipt?
suppose ....
3 We really should go now.
went ....
4 Unfortunately, I'm not as agile as I used to be.
only ....
5 I'd love to be able to play the piano.
could ....
6 Her constant criticism of me really gets on my nerves.
stop ....
7 Treat my home in the same way that you would treat your own.
though ....
8 I regret not going to university when I was younger.
gone ....
9 She would love to have more friends.
had ....
10 Please don't let the dog sit in the front of the car.
I'd ....

5 11.2, 11.3

Some of these sentences contain mistakes. Tick (✓) the correct sentences; then underline and correct the mistakes.

1 I had rather you didn't take the car; it's just been cleaned. ....
2 It's high time our employer listens to our grievances. ....
3 Supposing I took out my own insurance cover, what did you do about it? ....
4 If we only knew where he was getting the information from. ....
5 I wish I would be a child again. ....
6 He's only a student but sometimes he acts as if he is the teacher. ....
7 I'd sooner die than go out with that creep. ....
8 What if you'll see him at the party? ....
9 It's about time I didn't stay at home; I am twenty-five after all! ....
10 What a mess; you look as though you've been in a fight! ....

6 ALL

Complete the letter with appropriate forms of the words in brackets.

Dear Mrs Grenfell,

I am writing to you in your position as secretary of Cliveden Mansions Residents' Association in connection with the problem of residents leaving bicycles in the common entrance hallway.

My wife and I have yet again been having a lot of trouble with Steve and David Brown, the tenants of flat 16 on the first floor, and we feel it is high time this persistent source of dispute (1) .... (finally/resolve). These tenants own two bicycles which they insist on leaving in the entrance corridor. No doubt you are aware that the leases of all the flats in our building require that the entrance (2) .... (keep clear) of obstruction at all times. The local fire officer has also pointed out to me that under the building regulations the common entrance corridors to flats must be treated as if they (3) .... (be) exits of a public building, and are therefore subject to the same restrictions as those in force in theatres, cinemas, etc. Supposing the corridor (4) .... (block) with bicycles and there was a serious fire? We might all be trapped in our flats.

Apparently last month you told the Browns that they could keep their bicycles there for a temporary period. Well, I certainly wish you (5) .... (not/agree) to that, because they continually use this as an excuse when we ask them to remove the bikes. I have pointed out to them that there is space to store bicycles in the back yard, although I would sooner they (6) .... (keep) the bikes in their own flat as the presence of two mountain bikes might attract thieves. They say that there isn't any space in their flat and I wish I (7) .... (able to) offer them somewhere else. But, as you know, all the space in the bicycle shed is now allocated. Unfortunately they still seem unwilling to move their bikes, and their intransigence is beginning to seem deliberate. It isn't as though we (8) .... (not/tell) them about this on numerous occasions. In fact it has now reached a stage where I feel I must insist that the chairman of the residents' association (9) .... (demand) they remove the bicycles forthwith.

We would rather (10) .... (not/have to/refer) this matter to our solicitors but we feel that if the residents' association is unable to resolve the matter, we will have no alternative.

Yours sincerely,

Howard Blenkinsop

7 ALL

Complete the speech bubbles for the pictures, using the expressions described in this unit.

Round up: Units 10 and 11

Conditionals, subjunctive and 'unreal' past

form	use	example	▶
conditionals			
zero conditional	events that occur at any time or more than once	*If she**'s travelling** abroad on business, she always **phones** me every evening.*	10.2B
	actions that always have the same result	*If you **don't look after** tomato plants, they **die** very quickly.*	10.2B
	general instructions	*If a chip pan **sets** alight, **throw** a fire blanket on it.*	10.2C
first conditional	possible future events or situations and their results	*If the result of the test **is** negative, you**'ll receive** notification through the post.* *The beach party **will go ahead** if the weather **is** fine tomorrow.*	10.3B
	commands, offers, suggestions and warnings	***Shall** we **go** out tomorrow if the weather**'s** good?*	10.3C
second conditional	improbable future events or situations and their results	*If the result of the test **were** positive, we **would call** you within two days.*	10.4B
	hypothetical current situations or events (a condition which is impossible to fulfil)	*If the police **were** confident of their case against Sykes, they **wouldn't hesitate** to take him into custody.*	10.4B
	advice, requests, desires	*If I **were** you, I **would take** her out of that school.*	10.4C
third conditional	hypothetical situations or events in the past (an unreal past situation)	*I **would have used** your builder if I **had managed** to contact him.*	10.5B
	criticism	*If you**'d been driving** more slowly, you **could have stopped** in time.*	10.5C
mixed (second/third) conditional	hypothetical situations or events in the present with a result in the past	*If the island **were** still a tourist attraction, last week's earthquake **would have caused** far more deaths.*	10.6A
mixed (third/second) conditional	hypothetical situations or events in the past with a result in the present	*If Fleming **hadn't discovered** penicillin, there **would be** far more fatalities every year than there actually are.*	10.6B
subjunctive			
the same as the infinitive without *to*	used in formal English to express the idea that something is necessary or important	*At yesterday's hearing the judge insisted Mr Grant **give** evidence despite his relationship to the accused.*	11.1A

form	use	example	▶
'unreal' past			
it's (high/ about) time	to say that something is not happening and it should be	***It's time*** *we left.*	11.2C
what if, suppose/ supposing	to ask questions about an imaginary situation and its possible consequences	***Suppose*** *I asked you to marry me, what would you say?*	11.2D
would rather/ would sooner	to describe preferences (often a polite way to give/ refuse permission, or make suggestions)	***I'd sooner*** *you* ***gave*** *me a refund. A credit note's no use to me.* ***I'd rather*** *you* ***didn't smoke*** *in here.*	11.2E
as if/as though	to say that how something appears does not match with reality (For *as if/as though* with present tenses ▶ 11.2F)	*He talks to the children* ***as though*** *they* ***were*** *imbeciles.* *(He sounds* ***as if*** *he* ***knows*** *what he's talking about.)*	11.2F
wish/if only **+ past simple**	desire for something to be different in the present	*I* ***wish*** *I* ***had*** *more free time.* ***If only*** *I* ***were*** *young again.*	11.3A
wish/if only **+ past perfect**	a regret about the past, a wish that something different had happened	*I* ***wish*** *that you'***d told*** *me about this before I booked the tickets.* ***If only*** *you* ***hadn't been driving*** *so fast!*	11.3B
wish/if only **+ *would***	desire for someone to change their deliberate behaviour in the present and future (often used to criticise or complain)	*I* ***wish*** *you'***d*** *stop looking at me like that. It's terribly distracting.* ***I wish*** *you'***d*** *stop shouting. I'm not deaf you know.*	11.3C
wish/if only **+ *could (have)***	desire which we know is impossible to achieve (including impossible desires about ourselves)	***If only*** *we* ***could*** *see the situation through his eyes.* ***I wish I could*** *dance but I'm afraid I've got two left feet.*	11.3D

12 -*ing* forms and infinitives

The *-ing* and infinitive forms of verbs are very common in English and can act as subjects, objects and complements of verbs. When used like nouns, *-ing* forms are often referred to as 'gerunds'. This unit looks at the use of *-ing* forms and infinitives after certain verbs, determiners, adjectives and nouns, and at the special use of infinitives to describe purpose and result. (For the use of *-ing* and infinitive forms in clauses and phrases and in the passive and perfect forms of participles and infinitives ▶ **Unit 13**).

12.1 -*ING* FORMS

12.1A As subjects and objects

We can use *-ing* forms of verbs in the same way that we use nouns – as the subject, object or complement of a verb. We often refer to *-ing* forms used in this way as gerunds:

__Swimming__ makes you fit.
The whole family has taken up __cycling__.
Her worst habit is __lying__.

Sometimes *-ing* forms can have their own subjects and objects:

I'm looking forward to __my wife returning__. (subject + *-ing* form)
***Meeting new people** is one benefit of **taking evening classes**.* (*-ing* form + object)

We can make a negative with *not* + *-ing*:

***Not getting** a refund on faulty goods is what really annoys me.*

❗ But we use *no* + *-ing* to explain that something is impossible or not allowed:

✗ ~~*There's __not smoking__ in this office/There __isn't smoking__ in this office.*~~
✓ *Could you go outside? There's __no smoking__ in this office.*
There's __no skiing__ here in the summer season. (= Skiing is impossible.)

No Parking (= Parking is not allowed here.)

12.1B -*ing* form patterns

We can use determiners, e.g. *the*, *this*; possessives, e.g. *Peter's*; possessive adjectives, e.g. *his*; or object pronouns, e.g. *him*; before *-ing* forms. Object pronouns are more common in informal English:

***All this complaining** won't get you anywhere, you know.*
***Peter's complaining** didn't do him any good.*
Exorbitant tax rates led to __his leaving__ the country.
Exorbitant tax rates led to __him leaving__ the country. (informal)

We often use an object + *-ing* form after verbs of the senses (▶ **12.3A, 12.3E**):

I __heard Alagna giving__ a marvellous rendition of 'Nessun Dorma'.

❗ We always use the object pronoun after sense verbs:

✗ ~~*Have you __seen our performing__ yet?*~~
✓ *Have you __seen us performing__ yet?*

❗ When we use *the* + *-ing* form and we want to link it with an object, we use *of*:

✗ ~~***The giving presents** is a traditional part of the Christmas festivities.*~~
✓ ***The giving of presents** is a traditional part of the Christmas festivities.*

We also use *-ing* forms as adjectives (▶ **21.2**):

The __remaining__ items will be sold in our January sale.

Many adjectives and nouns are followed by a preposition + *-ing* form (▶ **Unit 15**):

Lara isn't __capable of lying__ and she has no __reason for not telling__ the truth.

12.2 INFINITIVES

12.2A Form

Infinitives with *to* can be the subject, object or complement of a verb:

__To give__ is better than __to receive__. Everyone loves __to win__.

We make a negative with *not* + infinitive:

I tried __not to look__ at the accident.

An infinitive can have its own subject, introduced with *for*:

__For evil to succeed__ it is only necessary for the good to do nothing.

! In informal English we sometimes put an adverb between *to* and the infinitive. This is known as a 'split infinitive' and we usually avoid it in formal English by putting the adverb in another position:

[*The doctor started __to carefully remove__ the bandages.*]

✔ *The doctor started __to remove__ the bandages __carefully.__*

There are also perfect, continuous and passive forms of the infinitive (▶ **13.3A**). If, for example, the person who is doing the action described by the infinitive is not the subject of the sentence, we usually use the passive infinitive:

✘ ~~*The report is __to hand in__ first thing tomorrow morning.*~~

✔ *The report is __to be handed in__ first thing tomorrow morning.*

12.2B Infinitives of purpose and result

We can use an infinitive to describe the purpose or reason for an action:

Cover the turkey in silver foil __to keep__ the meat moist.

__To stop__ the train, pull the lever downwards.

We use *for* before the infinitive when the subject of the infinitive is different from the subject of the sentence:

✘ ~~*She went to WalMart __for to get__ some groceries.*~~

✔ *She went to WalMart __to get__ some groceries.*

✔ *We bought a cage __for John to keep his hamster in__.*

In more formal English we can use *in order* or *so as* + infinitive of purpose:

Interest rates have been raised __in order to reduce__ inflationary pressures.

We have removed the warning signs __so as not to alarm__ members of the public.

The infinitive can also describe a result or something surprising, especially with *only* and verbs such as *find, discover, realise,* etc.:

They queued for hours at the box office __only to discover__ that the show was sold out.

We also use infinitives after *too* and *enough* (▶ **22.2C**) to talk about results:

That blue outfit was __too informal to wear__ to the reception.

There isn't __enough__ (food) __to go__ around, I'm afraid.

12.2C Infinitives after adjectives and nouns

Many adjectives, especially those describing feelings, can be followed by *to* + infinitive (some common examples are in the box below):

We're __thrilled to welcome__ this year's prizewinner onto the podium.

The Bensons are __lucky to be having__ such good weather.

adjective + *to* + infinitive *able/unable, afraid, anxious, ashamed, bound, careful, certain, crazy, curious, due, eager, fit, happy, impossible, likely, lucky, pleased, right, shocked, stupid, sure, surprised, thrilled, welcome, wrong*

Many nouns can be followed by *to* + infinitive (some common examples are in the box below):

She's finally made a __decision to leave__. *Clare would be a __fool to marry__ him.*

noun + *to* + infinitive *attempt, bid, decision, desire, incentive, need, nuisance, opportunity, place, pleasure, reason, time, wish*

! We can use a noun + *to* + infinitive after *there is/are* and *have (got)* to express an obligation:

Don't disturb me, I've got a __report to write__ this evening.

12.3 VERBS FOLLOWED BY *-ING* FORMS AND INFINITIVES

12.3A Verb + *-ing* form

Certain verbs (see box below) can be followed by an *-ing* form, but not by an infinitive:

✗ ~~*I **avoid to travel** in the rush hour whenever possible.*~~

✓ *I **avoid travelling** in the rush hour whenever possible.*

With some of these verbs (marked * in the box below) we can also put an object before the *-ing* form. Compare:

*Can you **imagine wearing** that dress!* (verb + *-ing* form)

*Can you **imagine Jemima wearing** that dress!* (verb + object + *-ing* form)

verb + *-ing* form *admit, appreciate*, avoid*, burst out, can't help*, consider, contemplate, defer, delay, deny, detest*, dislike*, endure*, enjoy*, escape, excuse*, face*, fancy*, feel like, finish, give up, imagine*, involve*, justify*, keep (on), leave off, mention*, mind*, miss*, postpone, practise, prevent*, put off, put sb off, recall*, recommend, resent*, resist*, risk*, save, suggest, tolerate*, understand**

❗ Certain verbs, particularly sense verbs (see box below), are only followed by an *-ing* form when they have an object (▶ **12.1B**):

✗ ~~*In 'Hamlet' the prince **discovers hiding** behind the curtains.*~~

✓ *In 'Hamlet' the prince **discovers Polonius hiding** behind the curtains.*

verb + object + *-ing* form *catch, discover, feel, find, hear, leave, notice, observe, see, spot, watch*

❗ The verbs *advise, allow, forbid* and *permit* are followed by an *-ing* form when they have no object, but an infinitive when they have an object (▶ **12.3B**).

✓ *The doctor **advised taking** a course of antibiotics.*

✗ ~~*The doctor **advised him taking** a course of antibiotics.*~~

✓ *The doctor **advised him to take** a course of antibiotics.*

12.3B Verb + infinitive

Certain verbs can be followed by an infinitive, but not by an *-ing* form (see box below):

✗ ~~*She's **decided applying** for the job.*~~

✓ *She's **decided to apply** for the job.*

Some of these verbs can also have an object before the infinitive (marked * below):

*He doesn't really **expect her to pass** the exam.*

verb + infinitive *afford, agree, aim, appear, arrange[1], ask*, attempt, beg*, campaign[1], care, choose*, consent, dare*, decide, demand, deserve[2], expect*, fail, fight, forget, guarantee, happen, help*, hesitate, hope, intend*, long[1], manage, need*, neglect, offer, pause, plan[1], prepare, pretend, promise, propose, prove, refuse, seem, swear, tend, threaten, trouble*, try, undertake, vow, wait[1], want*, wish*, yearn*

[1] With these verbs we use *for* before the object + infinitive:

✗ ~~*We spent ages **waiting them to arrive**.*~~

✓ *We spent ages **waiting for them to arrive**.*

[2] In British English, we can use *deserve* + *-ing* when it has a passive meaning:

*That naughty child **deserves smacking**.* (= deserves to be smacked)

Some verbs are followed by an infinitive only when they have an object (see box below):

✗ ~~*They **forced to open** our suitcases.*~~ ✓ *They **forced us to open** our suitcases.*

verb + object + *to* + infinitive *advise, allow, cause, command, compel, encourage, forbid, force, get, instruct, invite, leave, oblige, order, permit, persuade, recommend, remind, request, teach, tell, tempt, urge, warn*

Note the special rules about infinitives after *let, make, see, hear, know* and *help* (▶ **8.1B**).

Many of the verbs followed by infinitives are used in reported speech (▶ **Unit 9**).

12.3C Verb + *-ing* form/ infinitive

Some verbs can be followed by an *-ing* form or an infinitive, with no difference in meaning:

*I can't stand **to see/seeing** animals in pain.*

verb + *-ing* form or infinitive *attempt, begin, bother, can't bear, can't stand, cease, continue, deserve, fear, hate, intend, like* (= enjoy), *love, prefer, start*

❶ We usually avoid putting two infinitives or two *-ing* forms together:

[*He wanted **to start to take** lessons.*] ✔ *He wanted **to start taking** lessons.*

We use *to* + infinitive after *would like, would love* and *would hate*:

✘ ~~*When we get there I **would like taking** a nap.*~~

✔ *When we get there I **would like to take** a nap.*

When *like* means 'think something is a good idea', we only use the infinitive. Compare:

*I **like going/to go** to the gym. It's so relaxing.* (= I enjoy visiting it.)

*Because of my weight problem I **like to go** to the gym at least twice a week.* (= I think this is a good idea.)

12.3D Verb + *-ing* form or infinitive

Some verbs can be followed by an *-ing* form or by *to* + infinitive, but there is a difference in meaning:

verb	+ *-ing* form	+ *to* + infinitive
forget/ remember	= forget/remember an earlier action: *Do you **remember going** to school for the first time? I'll never **forget meeting** him.*	= forget/remember to do a future action: *I must **remember to set** my alarm clock tonight. Don't **forget to lock** the back door.*
go on	= continue: *They **went on playing** despite the bad weather.*	= change to another action: *After opening the hospital the Prince **went on to meet** the staff.*
mean	= involves or will result in: *This new job **means living** abroad.*	= intend to do something: *The builders **mean to finish** by Friday.*
regret	= feel sorrow about the past: *I really **regret getting** that tattoo when I was eighteen.*	= announce bad news: *We **regret to inform** you of delays in today's service.*
stop	= finish an action: *They **stopped making** fax machines about ten years ago.*	= finish one action in order to do another one: *We **stopped to get** petrol.*
try	= do something to see what will happen: ***Try using** a screwdriver to get the lid off.*	= make an effort to do something difficult: *We **tried to get** tickets but the show was sold out.*

12.3E Sense verbs

Sense verbs (▶ **1.3C**) can be followed by an object + *-ing* form when we are describing an action in progress or an action that is repeated:

*As I walked past the church I **heard someone playing** Handel's 'Messiah' on the organ.* (The person was in the middle of playing when I walked past.)

*I **saw a young mother slapping** her child.* (She slapped him several times.)

These verbs can be followed by an object + infinitive (without *to*) when we are describing a single action or the action is complete:

*We **saw a young mother slap** her child in the supermarket.* (She slapped once.)

*Last week I **heard them play** the fifth symphony.* (I heard the complete symphony.)

❶ We use *to* + infinitive after a passive sense verb:

*The young mother was **seen to slap** her child.*

12

Practice

The key to these exercises is on page 359.

1 12.1

Underline the mistakes in these sentences and correct them.

0 A great advantage of credit cards is no having to carry cash around all the time. ......*not*..........
1 Have you ever heard my singing *O Sole Mio*? ....
2 We had to come in early for the opening the new extension. ....
3 Constant criticisms led to she resigning from that stressful job. ....
4 You'll have to put that out, sir, this is a not smoking carriage. ....
5 Passengers can find a heated wait room adjacent to platform ten. ....
6 The making a successful soufflé requires expert timing. ....
7 There's not swimming from this beach, the current's too treacherous. ....
8 The argument ended up with we demanding a refund and compensation. ....
9 They stopped to make vinyl records ages ago. ....
10 The crane isn't capable lifting it – it's too heavy. ....

2 12.2

Finish each of the following sentences in such a way that it is as similar as possible in meaning to the sentence before it.

0 I really don't want to see him again.
I have no ....*desire to see him again*..........
1 I want you to hand the report in tomorrow.
The report is ....
2 You can't join the army because you aren't sufficiently fit.
You aren't fit ....
3 He was very worried that he would arrive late.
He was anxious not ....
4 Right now I'm afraid I can't give you an answer.
I am not ....
5 The government closed the borders with the aim of catching the criminals.
In order ....
6 Closing the office was something the manager decided this morning.
The manager made ....
7 I learnt that Amanda was going to marry Ronald, which was surprising.
I was ....
8 They didn't publish the news because they didn't want to frighten the public.
They didn't publish the news so ....
9 Checking the balance on my current account was my main reason for visiting the bank this morning.
I went ....
10 When we got there they had already closed the store for stocktaking!
We got there only ....

3 12.3

Complete the sentences with the correct form of the verbs in brackets.

1 I'm not disappointed, I never really expected .... (pass) the test.
2 Please don't hesitate .... (call) if you have any problems.
3 The doctor recommended .... (avoid) strenuous activity for the first few weeks.
4 The sales team aims .... (exceed) its target by at least five per cent this year.
5 I don't suppose you happened .... (notice) whether there was a cash machine there?
6 How on earth do they justify .... (keep) three dogs in such a small flat?
7 We'd better hurry up; I'd hate .... (arrive) late.
8 Despite all the rejections, Dave's continuing .... (apply) for every vacancy he sees.
9 We discovered an old document .... (lie) under the floorboards.
10 I'll put off .... (call) them until after I've spoken to the personnel officer.
11 You can watch the film if you promise .... (go) to bed straight afterwards.
12 Being a diabetic, I like .... (avoid) anything containing sugar.
13 Thanks very much. Yes, we'd love .... (join) you for dinner on Friday.
14 You really can't help .... (feel) sorry for the poor guy.
15 Passengers are permitted .... (carry) only one piece of hand luggage onto the plane.
16 Jonathan's the one who taught Rachel .... (swim) last summer.
17 Sometimes you have to pretend .... (like) people that you detest.
18 That's strange, I don't recall .... (meet) him at all.
19 The judge will defer .... (pass) sentence until the psychiatric reports have been submitted.
20 Whenever possible, the personnel department likes .... (settle) salary reviews prior to the quarterly board meetings.

4 12.3

Underline the correct form in *italics*.

1 Darling, did you remember *packing/to pack* some spare cassettes for the video camera yesterday?
2 I really regret *leaving/to leave* school so young, it's ruined my career prospects.
3 We tried *pressing/to press* the 'escape' key but the program just wouldn't respond.
4 A suspicious young man was seen *enter/to enter* the building shortly before the incident.
5 As we drove over the river we noticed local women *washing/wash* their clothes in the water.
6 I once heard Karajan *conducting/conduct* the entire Ring cycle – it was wonderful.
7 I stopped *eating/to eat* sugar years ago.
8 Nothing will stop their enquiries, they mean *getting/to get* to the bottom of this strange business.
9 Don't forget *recording/to record* 'EastEnders' tomorrow evening.
10 The woman woke up in the middle of the night, looked out of her window and saw something strange *hovering/hover* over the trees in the park.
11 After a career in the secret service, Ian Fleming went on *achieving/to achieve* fame as an author.
12 Transglobe Airlines regrets *announcing/to announce* the cancellation of today's service to Istanbul due to air traffic restrictions.
13 Do you remember *seeing/to see* that film last summer?
14 If you can't find the information in the manual, try *looking/to look* at our website.
15 We were all exhausted so we stopped *getting/to get* some rest at a motel.

5 12.3

Read the article below and then decide which word or phrase (A–C) best fits each space. The exercise begins with an example (0).

Death in the Air

The death of Emma Christofferson from deep-vein thrombosis allegedly caused by a twenty-hour plane journey has led to calls for an enquiry into so-called 'economy class syndrome'. The cabin crew were shocked (0) .....B..... the previously healthy 28-year-old in a state of collapse at the end of a long-haul flight from Australia to London. A blood clot had spread from her legs to her lungs with fatal results. Experts believe her death is just the latest example of the growing danger posed by (1) ..... for extended periods of time in cramped aircraft seats.

Farol Khan, director of the Aviation Health Institute, (2) ..... to have evidence that more than 6,000 passengers a year die of deep-vein thrombosis (DVT) as a result of long-haul flights. Unfortunately, as symptoms often take some time (3) ....., the link between the condition and flying is not always apparent. But there seems (4) ..... a clear relationship between the occurrence of DVT and the steady reduction in the amount of legroom between seats in economy class cabins. In a bid (5) ..... the number of passengers carried and their consequent profitability, many airlines have squeezed more and more seats into their planes, at the cost of comfort and legroom. And our (6) ..... these uncomfortable conditions is simply based on the fact that we know more seats means lower prices. But with limited opportunities (7) ..... or move around, the blood circulation in passengers' legs (8) ..... to slow down, and blood clots can easily develop. Most at risk are elderly people, sufferers from heart conditions and smokers. But as Emma Christofferson's case shows, even the young and healthy can do little to prevent blood clots (9) ... under these circumstances.

(10) ..... a 'caring, sharing' image is something many airlines are keen on, and some of these have finally (11) ..... to take the problem more seriously by issuing health advice to passengers 'trapped' on their long-haul flights. They usually recommend (12) ..... the legs and feet regularly, and advise (13) ..... walks up and down the aisle at least once an hour. But, as any experienced traveller knows, the aisles on most planes are only just wide enough for the trolleys (14) ..... through. It is often impossible (15) ..... down the aisle (16) ..... to the toilets, let alone (17) ..... exercise.

The truth is that until we are all prepared to (18) ... paying rock-bottom prices for long distance travel, the airlines will have no incentive (19) ..... conditions. And a return to exclusive and expensive air travel is something nobody would (20) ..... advocating.

0 A finding (B) to find C to be found
1 A sitting B to sit C sit
2 A suggests B admits C claims
3 A appearing B to appear C having appeared
4 A being B to be C be
5 A increasing B of increasing C to increase
6 A putting up with B put up with C to put up with
7 A stretching B to stretch C stretch
8 A begins B risks C can't help
9 A occurring B to occur C occur
10 A promoting B to promote C to be promoted
11 A suggested B considered C started
12 A moving B to move C move
13 A taking B to take C take
14 A getting B to get C get
15 A walking B to walk C walk
16 A getting B to get C get
17 A taking B to take C take
18 A give up B fail C refuse
19 A improving B to improve C improve
20 A undertake B choose C contemplate

6 ALL

Complete the letter with suitable forms of words from the box below. The first one has been done as an example (0).

ask	attend	be	bring	buy	cash	cook	fill in	find	join	know
learn	live	~~let~~	make	open	say	see	take	wonder	write	

Dear Mum and Dad,

So my first week at university is over! No lectures this morning so I thought I'd drop you a line (0) ....*to let*...... you know how things are going.

I'm glad (1) .... that everything has worked out fine in the hall of residence. I remembered (2) .... for a room as far away from the lifts as possible (they really are noisy) and they found me a nice comfortable one on the second floor. The room's not very large and I was a bit shocked (3) .... that ten people have to share one bathroom! And it's a good thing you recommended (4) .... my own portable TV set from home as the one in the TV lounge is permanently tuned to the sports channel. There's also a little kitchenette on our corridor, so if I feel like (5) .... something for myself rather than eating in the canteen then that's no problem.

I think (6) .... in a place like this is going to be a lot of fun. There are two other girls from my course here and I plan (7) .... friends with them so that we can help each other with the course work. Everyone else seems very nice.

As Monday was the first day it was devoted to administration, which involved (8) .... lots of forms. I got my student I.D. card and the timetable for this term. I've got a personal tutor and he's arranged (9) .... me next week. The course coordinator persuaded me (10) .... some extra courses which should be interesting. On Tuesday I managed (11) .... a bank account and I deposited my student loan cheque. I tried (12) .... the cheque but the bank said I will have to wait for it to clear. So I'll have to delay (13) .... books and things until next week.

My first few lectures proved (14) .... really fascinating. The lecturers really seem (15) .... what they are talking about. Still, there's a lot of work to do and I can't help (16) .... if I'll be able to keep up with it all, especially with all the distractions here. There are so many clubs and societies, it's incredible. I'm hoping (17) .... the parachuting club, I've always fancied (18) .... how to do that!

Well, I'd better stop now, I'm going (19) .... my first seminar this afternoon, so I've got some preparation to do.

Anyway, I promise (20) .... again soon,

love to everyone, Charlotte

13 Participle and infinitive phrases

Participle phrases (e.g. ***having*** *some time to kill*) can be used in sentences to give extra information or to describe the result, cause or time of the information in the main clause. Extra information phrases are similar to relative clauses (▶ **Unit 31**). Infinitive phrases (e.g. ***to make*** *the best of it*) are used to talk about purpose and, in a similar way to relative clauses, after superlatives and other expressions. (For information on the use of infinitives and *-ing* forms after verbs, nouns, etc. ▶ **Unit 12**.)

13.1 PARTICIPLE PHRASES – FORM AND USE

13.1A Active and passive participles

There are several participle forms which we can use to make phrases:

	active participle	passive participle
simple	X X X X	*(not) repaired*
continuous	*(not) repairing*	*(not) being repaired*
perfect	*(not) having repaired*	*(not) having been repaired*

Participle phrases have active and passive forms but they do not have a tense. Their time reference is usually clear from the verb in the main clause:

Not having a ticket, I won't *be able to go to the concert tomorrow*. (present/future)
Not having a ticket, I wasn't *able to go to the concert yesterday*. (past)

In participle phrases, the active participle (*-ing* form) has an active meaning (see example above) and the passive participle (*-ed* form) has a passive meaning:

They haven't identified the body ***which was found in the Thames***.
They haven't identified the body ***found in the Thames***. (passive participle phrase)

❗ We can't usually use modal verbs in participle phrases:

✗ ~~*The questions* ***must be answered*** *are not easy ones.*~~
✓ *The questions* ***which must be answered*** *are not easy ones*.

Verbs which are not normally used in the continuous, e.g. *be*, *own*, *possess* (▶ **1.3**), can be used in participle phrases:

✗ ~~*Yolanda is rich and* ***is owning*** *six homes.*~~ ✓ *Yolanda is rich,* ***owning*** *six homes.*

13.1B Participle subjects

In many cases, participle phrases do not contain a subject. The subject of the main clause (in **bold** below) usually acts as the subject of the participle phrase:

Moaning with pain, ***the victim*** *was examined by a young doctor.* (= The victim was moaning.)

If the participle phrase follows the object of the main clause then either the object or the subject of the main clause (in **bold** below) can be the subject of the participle phrase, depending on the meaning:

We saw ***her plane*** *coming in to land.* (= The plane was coming in to land.)
The company *has opened a new factory, creating many new jobs.* (= The company has created many new jobs.)

❗ A participle phrase at the beginning of a sentence cannot refer to the object of the main clause:

✗ ~~*Moaning with pain,* ***a young doctor*** *examined the victim.*~~
(= A young doctor was moaning, not the victim.)

13.1C Different subjects

In formal (usually written) English, participle phrases can have a subject which is not the same as the subject of the main clause.

Horns locked, the two stags struggle for mastery.

*I crouched in the alleyway, **my eyes straining** in the darkness.*

13.2 TYPES OF PARTICIPLE PHRASE

13.2A Defining phrases

Participle phrases are an efficient way of giving more information about a noun and can often replace a defining relative clause (▶ **31.1C**). Compare these examples:

*The man is very noisy. **The man lives upstairs.***

→ *The man **who lives upstairs** is very noisy.* (defining relative clause)

→ *The man **living upstairs** is very noisy.* (active participle phrase)

*The portrait was lovely. **The portrait was painted by my brother.***

→ *The portrait **which was painted by my brother** was lovely.* (defining relative clause)

→ *The portrait **painted by my brother** was lovely.* (passive participle phrase)

We can only use a participle phrase to replace a defining relative clause if the subject of the main clause and the relative clause is the same. We cannot use a participle phrase if there is another subject between the relative pronoun and the verb:

✗ *The house **living in** is over a century old.*

✔ *The house **which** we **live in** is over a century old.*

✗ *The man **engaged to** has disappeared.*

✔ *The man **who** Trudy **was engaged** to has disappeared.*

In defining phrases, we only use an active participle phrase (*-ing* form) when we are describing a continuing action or situation. We can't use an *-ing* form for a single completed action:

✗ *The thief **taking her bag** has been arrested.*

✔ *The thief **who took her bag** has been arrested.* (single completed action)

13.2B Phrases of reason, condition and result

Participle phrases can often operate like clauses of reason, condition, result and time:

	full clause	participle phrase
reason	*She will be unable to answer your queries **because she is not qualified.***	***Not being qualified**, she will be unable to answer your queries.*
	***As I hadn't been asked**, I didn't really want to interfere.*	***Not having been asked**, I didn't really want to interfere.*
condition	***If you treat it gently**, the fabric should last for years.*	***Treated gently**, the fabric should last for years.*
result	*The corporation shut down the plant, **with the result that many workers were left unemployed.***	*The corporation shut down the plant, **leaving many workers unemployed.***[1]
time (▶ **13.2C**)	***As we turned the corner** we saw the hospital in front of us.*	***Turning the corner**, we saw the hospital in front of us.*

[1] Note that the result is often not intended:

*I stayed at work rather late, **missing my last train home**.*

13.2C Time phrases

We usually use *-ing* participle phrases when two actions happen at the same time, or one happens immediately after the other. The *-ing* participle usually describes the background or earlier action. This is similar to the use of the continuous aspect for actions in progress (▶ **1.2B**) and background situations (▶ **2.2B**):

***Leaving the motorway**, we noticed an overturned truck on the verge.*

(= As/When we were leaving the motorway, we noticed ...)

***Switching off the lights**, I turned over and buried my head in the pillow.* (= After I switched off the lights, I turned over ...)

In written English an *-ing* participle phrase often describes the setting or background situation:

__Living in Los Angeles__, Brad was one of those ever-optimistic movie wannabes.

❗ When we want to emphasise that one thing happened before another, we can use a perfect participle for the earlier action. The participle phrase can come before or after the main clause:

__Having passed my driving test__, I was able to buy my first car. (= After I had passed my driving test, ...)

I was able to buy my first car, __having passed my driving test__.

The perfect participle can also describe reasons or causes as these usually come before a result (▶ **13.2B** above):

__Having forgotten to take my keys__, I had to borrow a set from my landlord.
(= Because I had forgotten my keys, ...)

13.3 INFINITIVE PHRASES – FORM AND USE

13.3A Active and passive infinitives

We can use the following forms of the verb in infinitive phrases:

	active infinitive	passive infinitive
simple	*(not) to mend*	*(not) to be mended*
continuous	*(not) to be mending*	*(not) to be being mended*
perfect	*(not) to have mended*	*(not) to have been broken*

Infinitive phrases can be active or passive, but they do not show tense. The time reference is shown by the context or by the tense of the verb in the main clause:

The tax bill __will be__ the first item __to be debated__ in the next parliament. (future)

Their proposal __was__ the first one __to be debated__ at yesterday's planning meeting. (past)

But we can use the perfect infinitive for an event that happened before the main clause:

__Not to have acted__ sooner is his greatest regret. (= He regrets he didn't act sooner.)

Her greatest claim to fame is __to have been chosen__ for the last Olympic squad.
(= She is famous now because she was chosen.)

13.3B Subjects and complements

An infinitive phrase can act as the subject or complement of the verb *be*:

__To reach the top__ is their aim.

Their aim is __to reach the top__.

❗ We use *for* with an infinitive phrase if the subject of the infinitive is not the same as the subject of the sentence:

✗ ~~*Their aim is __the team to win__.*~~

✓ *Their aim is __for the team to win__.*

An infinitive phrase can be the subject or complement of a sentence:

__To find her so distressed__ took him by surprise.

They struggled __to keep up their standard of living__.

Sentences with an infinitive phrase as their subject can sound rather formal. We usually prefer impersonal *it* (▶ **33.2**) or an *-ing* form (▶ **12.1**):

__It__ is difficult __to keep up a friendship__.

__Keeping up a friendship__ is difficult.

13.4 TYPES OF INFINITIVE PHRASE

13.4A Defining phrases

We can often replace a relative clause after a superlative, an ordinal number (e.g. *first*), or *one*, *next*, *last* and *only*, with an infinitive phrase:

*The **youngest** person **that entered the programme** was just fourteen.*
→ *The youngest person **to enter the programme** was just fourteen.*
*The window seat is usually the **first** one **which is taken**.*
→ *The window seat is usually the first one **to be taken**.*
*Linda was the **only** one **who stayed for the whole performance**.*
→ *Linda was the only one **to stay for the whole performance**.*

! We usually don't use an infinitive phrase to replace relative clauses containing modal verbs, because the meaning would not be clear:

✗ ~~*He's the only player to save the team from defeat.*~~
✓ *He's the only player **who might save the team from defeat**.*

13.4B Purpose and result phrases

We often use an infinitive phrase to describe a deliberate purpose or aim. This is the infinitive of purpose (▶ **12.2B**):

*Davy took a year out **to see the world and broaden his experience of life**.*

We can use an infinitive phrase to describe discovering something unexpected, especially with *only* (▶ **12.2B**):

*He returned to the field **to find the army in retreat**.*
*Eliza rejoined her friends, only **to discover that Mr Darcy had left**.*

(For infinitives after verbs ▶ **12.3B**, after nouns and adjectives ▶ **12.2C**.)

13.5 USES IN DISCOURSE

13.5A Comment phrases

We sometimes use infinitive and participle phrases to add a comment to something we are saying:

*I'm not very keen on it, **to tell the truth**.*
***Generally speaking**, they're a pretty friendly bunch of people.*
*It wasn't a bad show, **all things considered**.*

We can use an adverb to modify a participle. This describes the particular aspect of something which we are commenting on. The adverb can come before or after the participle:

***Financially speaking**, few of the dot.com companies have a good track record.*
***Compromised artistically**, Picasso felt compelled to leave Paris.*

Note that we can use adverbs in the same way with adjectives (▶ **24.4A**):

*Although **economically successful**, the government is starting to lose popularity.*

13.5B Style

In written English, it is usual to move from the familiar (the current topic) to the new (the information principle ▶ **36.1A**), and to be economical with words and avoid repetition (▶ **35.1A**). Participle and infinitive phrases help us to do these things. Compare these examples:

Steve went home. He noticed a piece of paper which had been left on the doorstep as he walked towards the door.
→ *Steve went home. **Walking towards the door**, he noticed a piece of paper **left** on the doorstep.*
Because Marion didn't have a degree she was the only one who wasn't offered a permanent contract.
→ ***Not having a degree**, Marion was the only one **not to be offered a permanent contract**.*

Practice

The key to these exercises is on page 359.

1 13.1, 13.2

Choose the best participle forms (A–G) to fit into the sentences. One of the forms is not needed.

A giving B not having been given C not giving D having been given
E being given F having given G given

1 The best part ..... to another actor, Josh felt unwilling to continue his involvement in the show.
2 I've always treasured the watch ..... to me on my eighteenth birthday.
3 The police officers stood at either end of the hallway, ... Ray no chance of escape.
4 ..... our tickets to the attendant, we were ushered into the antechamber of the tomb.
5 We are dividing up the grant according to need, the largest amount ..... to the homeless.
6 ..... the mandatory month's notice by the landlord, the tenant was able to stay on in the house.

2 13.1, 13.2

Rewrite the following sentences, replacing the underlined phrase with a suitable participle phrase.

0 As they hadn't been arrested they were able to leave the police station.
Not having been arrested, they were able to leave the police station.
1 She fell asleep while she sat in the armchair.
....
2 Because I can speak Finnish I was able to follow their conversation.
....
3 My brother, who has split up with his wife, wants to move in with me.
....
4 So far nobody has claimed the money we discovered under the floorboards.
....
5 After he had moved out, Danny found it difficult to find a nice place to stay.
....
6 If you leave it for too long, oil paint will form a skin.
....
7 The sea was very rough, which made me feel sick.
....
8 As I am not very good with figures I'll let you do the accounts.
....
9 This is a house which has been built to last forever.
....
10 Provided you wash it at a cool temperature this garment will not shrink.
....
11 People who play loud music late at night can be a real nuisance.
....
12 Because he had been unemployed for so long, Jack despaired of ever finding a job.
....
13 If you give them enough time, the engineers will be able to find the fault.
....
14 The people who lived closest to the river bank were the worst affected.
....
15 Due to the fact that I hadn't registered, I was unable to vote in last week's election.
....

3 13.3, 13.4

Seven of these sentences have mistakes – either an unnecessary extra word or a missing word. Tick [✔] the correct sentences and correct those with mistakes.

1 Study medicine at university you need to pass a biology exam. ....
2 I don't think much of him, be honest with you. ....
3 That was the very first programme to be shown on the new channel. ....
4 We don't want to be the last ones to leave. ....
5 It isn't necessary to be being rich to be happy. ....
6 I was the first one in my family to have been gone to university. ....
7 I'm afraid you aren't the first person to mugged in this neighbourhood. ....
8 She joined the Navy to see the world. ....
9 It's a shame not have seen the fireworks. ....
10 The 'Royale' is the latest fabric to have designed by Silvio Moresco. ....

4 13.3, 13.4

The famous quotations (1–5) are missing infinitive phrases. Match the infinitive forms (A–F) in the box to complete the quotations correctly.

1 'To err is human, ..., divine.' *(Alexander Pope)*
2 'One should eat ....., not live to eat.' *(Molière)*
3 'It is better ..... and lost than never to have loved at all.' *(Samuel Butler)*
4 'To be, or .....: that is the question.' *(William Shakespeare)*
5 'The best thing is ....., but it takes make-up to look natural.' *(Calvin Klein)*

A to have loved
B to look natural
C to live
E to forgive
F not to be

5 13.1–13.4

Use the information in the table to write sentences, inserting an infinitive or a participle phrase. Some sentences can be written in more than one way. The first two have been done as examples.

	action/reason	aim/result/further information
0	The value of the currency fell.	It made foreign holidays more expensive.
	The value of the currency fell, making foreign holidays more expensive.	
00	Hilary got a job in a café.	She was able to make lots of new friends.
	Getting a job in a café, Hilary was able to make lots of new friends.	
1	Carlos joined a dating agency.	He wanted to find a girlfriend.
2	I left my keys at the office.	I couldn't get into my flat last night.
3	Manuela hasn't got a visa.	She can't travel to the USA.
4	My nephew emigrated to Australia.	He wanted to start a new life.
5	A new dam was built across the river.	It flooded thousands of hectares of farmland.
6	The old house had been restored by experts.	It regained its former glory.
7	I wasn't very fit.	I was unable to finish the marathon.
8	Dave and Maria's children had left home.	They felt they should move to a smaller house.
9	They got home early.	They found the place had been burgled.
10	Only one person stayed behind.	It was the caretaker.

6 ALL

Use infinitive and/or participle phrases to rewrite this extract from a TV listings magazine in a more natural way. The parts you need to change are underlined. You may need to change the order of some words. The first phrase has been done for you.

MOVIE OF THE WEEK

The Godfather

<u>It dates from 1971</u> and <u>was directed by Francis Ford Coppola</u>, *The Godfather* won three Oscars. <u>The film lasts almost three hours and is Shakespearean</u> in its scope and ambition. It is the story of a New York mafia family <u>which is headed by Marlon Brando as 'the Godfather'.</u> Although Brando has the title role it is Al Pacino, <u>who plays his troubled son and heir Michael</u>, who steals the show in a masterly performance. <u>As he struggles to reconcile his distaste for crime and brutality with his sense of family honour and duty</u>, Pacino's character embodies the moral dilemma at the heart of the movie. <u>The director intersperses long scenes of family life with shorter sequences of extreme violence in order to achieve his aim of taking the audience on an emotional rollercoaster ride</u>. <u>Because it was shot in explicit detail</u>, this violence may shock some viewers. But anyone <u>who is prepared to put up with this</u> will enjoy a unique dramatic experience. In fact, for many people *The Godfather* is the greatest American film <u>which had been made in the 1970s</u>.

Dating from 1971 ....

....

....

....

....

....

....

....

....

....

....

....

7 ALL

Complete the second sentence so that it has a similar meaning to the first sentence. You must use between three and eight words, including the word given. This word must not be altered in any way. There is an example (0).

0 The first person that arrives in the office in the mornings is usually Gary.
to Gary is usually ......*the first person to arrive*...... in the office in the mornings.

1 Martin is always a great asset at any party because he is so charming.
being .... always a great asset at any party.

2 I took a short computing course following my graduation from college.
having .... a short computing course.

3 Celia's major regret is that she had never made more of her musical abilities.
to .... her musical abilities is Celia's major regret.

4 As she threw open the French windows Mary said 'There's nothing like fresh air!'
throwing 'There's nothing like fresh air!' .... the French windows.

5 The company launched an advertising campaign with the aim of increasing its market share.
to The company .... its market share.

6 Finding the old house in such a derelict state came as a great shock.
find It came as .... in such a derelict state.

7 Frankly, I don't think my clients will ever agree to those prices.
frank I don't think my clients will ever agree ....

8 The shrubs should grow well if you plant them in a sunny spot.
planted .... should grow well.

9 They will probably sell the ground floor flat first.
be They expect the ground floor flat ....

10 My brother is having a lot of trouble finding a decent job as he hasn't had the benefit of a college education.
having .... a college education, my brother is having a lot of trouble finding a job.

11 Sophie was a demanding boss because she was such a perfectionist.
being .... was a demanding boss.

12 The town hall was one of the few buildings that wasn't destroyed in the earthquake.
been The town hall was one of the few .... in the earthquake.

14 Multi-word verbs

A common feature of English is the combination of verbs with prepositions and/or adverbs to create multi-word verbs, e.g. *to put off, to put out, to put up with*. These verbs can be difficult for learners because the meanings often cannot be worked out from the individual words, and there are special rules about the position of objects with these verbs. We sometimes refer to all multi-word verbs as 'phrasal verbs', although there are several different types. (For verbs with dependent prepositions ▶ **Unit 15**.)

14.1 FORM AND USE

14.1A Overview

Multi-word verbs are formed from a verb, e.g. *grow*, plus an adverbial particle, e.g. *away, back, out*, or a prepositional particle, e.g. *on, off, up*. There are four types of multi-word verb and each type has different rules, for example about the use or position of the object:

Type 1 (▶ **14.2A**)	intransitive phrasal verbs, e.g. *take off*: *The plane* ***took off*** *very late.* (There is no object.)
Type 2 (▶ **14.2B**)	transitive phrasal verbs, e.g. *put something off*: *We're* ***putting the party off/putting off the party*** *because of the awful weather.* (The noun object can go before or after the particle.)
Type 3 (▶ **14.3**)	prepositional verbs, e.g. *cope with something*: *How does she* ***cope with all those kids****?* (The object goes after the particle.)
Type 4 (▶ **14.4**)	phrasal–prepositional verbs, e.g. *look forward to something*: *They're* ***looking forward to the holidays***. (The object goes after the particles.)

Learner dictionaries indicate which type a verb is by showing a noun object with the verb:

> **put** sb/sth **off** *phr v* [T] to arrange to do something at a later time or date, especially because there is a problem, difficulty etc: *They've put the meeting off till next week.*

Multi-word verbs form tenses, and are used in questions and negatives and in the passive voice, in the same way as other verbs:

Will *you* ***be putting*** *the party* ***off****?* (future continuous question)

The party ***has been put off*** *until next month.* (present perfect passive)

We never separate the verb and particle in the passive form:

✗ ~~*That story* ***was made*** *by a resentful employee* ***up****.*~~

✓ *That story* ***was made up*** *by a resentful employee.*

We can sometimes form nouns from multi-word verbs. (▶ **25.5A**)

The car ***broke down*** *five kilometres from home.* (multi-word verb)

The ***breakdown*** *happened five kilometres from home.* (noun)

In some cases the order of the verb and particle is reversed in the noun derived from them:

The epidemic first ***broke out*** *in Namibia.* (multi-word verb)

The first ***outbreak*** *of the epidemic was in Zaire.* (noun)

14.1B Formal and informal use

Where a multi-word verb has no exact synonym, e.g. *grow up*, we can use it in formal and informal contexts. However, when there is a single verb with an equivalent meaning, e.g. *think about* (= consider), the multi-word verb tends to be used in informal contexts while the single verb is more formal. Compare these examples:

[*The bank will* ***think about*** *your application in due course.*]
The bank will ***consider*** *your application in due course.* (formal)
[*Honestly, how can you* ***consider*** *money at a time like this!*]
Honestly, how can you ***think about*** *money at a time like this!* (informal)

14.1C Meaning

It is sometimes possible to get an idea of the meaning of a multi-word verb from its particle, because some particles are associated with areas of meaning, for example:

on – starting/continuing/progressing, e.g. *carry on, take on, get on*
out – thoroughness, e.g. *work out, see out, mark out*
up – completion/finality, e.g. *give up, break up, eat up*

❶ However, these areas of meaning can be abstract and may not cover all cases.

14.2 PHRASAL VERBS

14.2A Intransitive verbs

Intransitive phrasal verbs (type 1 ▶ **14.1A**) consist of a verb plus an adverb. Phrasal verbs usually have a meaning which is different from the meaning of the separate parts:

Getting by *on my salary isn't easy!* (= managing)
Rollerblading never really ***caught on*** *in England.* (= became popular)

As intransitive phrasal verbs have no direct object, they cannot be made passive:

✗ ~~*My car* ***broke down*** *the engine.*~~ ✓ *My car* ***broke down****.*

Intransitive phrasal verbs are sometimes used in imperatives:

Watch out*. That floor's not very solid.*
Come on! *I can't wait all day!*

14.2B Transitive verbs

Transitive phrasal verbs (type 2 ▶ **14.1A**) consist of a verb + adverb and have a direct object (either a pronoun or a noun):

It isn't true, I made ***it*** *up. I made up* ***that story****.*

If the object is a noun, it can either be between the verb and particle, or after the particle:

I made ***a story*** *up. I made up* ***a story****.*

If the object is a pronoun, we put it between the verb and particle, but not after the particle:

✗ ~~*I made up* ***it****.*~~ ✓ *I made* ***it*** *up.*

❶ We can't put an adverb between the verb and particle or between the particle and object:

✗ ~~*I paid* ***early*** *back the loan.*~~
✗ ~~*I paid back* ***early*** *the loan.*~~
✓ *I paid the loan back* ***early****.*

❶ We can't put a relative pronoun immediately before or after the particle.

✗ ~~*That's the room* ***which*** *up I did.*~~
✗ ~~*That's the room up* ***which*** *I did.*~~
✓ *That's the room* ***which*** *I did up.*

Some phrasal verbs have a transitive use with one meaning, and an intransitive use with a different meaning. Compare:

The plane ***took off*** *on time.* (*take off*, intransitive = become airborne)
The man ***took off*** *his coat.* (*take something off*, transitive = remove)

14.3 PREPOSITIONAL VERBS

14.3A Form and use

Prepositional verbs (type 3 ▶ **14.1A**) consist of a verb, e.g. *look*, plus a preposition, e.g. *into, at, for*. The combination of the verb and preposition creates a new meaning which can sometimes, but not always, be worked out from the parts:

*She **looked for** her missing passport.* (= searched, tried to find)
*Would you mind **looking into** his complaint?* (= investigating, researching)

These verbs are transitive. We put the noun or pronoun object after the preposition, and not between the verb and preposition (compare with phrasal verbs ▶ **14.2B**):

✗ ~~*We didn't fall **his story** for.*~~ ✗ ~~*We didn't fall **it** for.*~~
✔ *We didn't fall for **it/his story**.*

With prepositional verbs (but not phrasal verbs ▶ **14.2B** above) we can put an adverb between the verb and preposition. But we cannot put an adverb between the preposition and object:

✗ ~~*She parted with **reluctantly** her money.*~~
✔ *She parted **reluctantly** with her money.*

14.3B Special uses

In formal English we sometimes prefer to avoid a preposition at the end of a sentence. With prepositional verbs (but not phrasal verbs ▶ **14.2B** above) we can put the preposition in front of the relative pronouns *whom* or *which*:

*These are the principles (which) our party **stands for**.*
→ *These are the principles **for which** our party **stands**.*
*That's the type of client (whom) I'm **dealing with**.*
→ *That's the type of client **with whom** I'm **dealing**.*

❶ But we cannot put the preposition after *whom* or *which*:

✗ ~~*These are the principles **which for** our party stands.*~~

Some prepositional verbs are mainly used in the passive form (▶ **14.5C**), especially in written English:

*The marketing strategy **is aimed at** a target audience of 18 to 25 year olds.*

14.4 PHRASAL-PREPOSITIONAL VERBS

14.4A Form and use

These verbs (type 4 ▶ **14.1A**) are formed by combining a verb with an adverb and preposition. The combination creates a new meaning which cannot usually be understood from the meanings of the individual parts:

*We **look forward to** hearing from you.* (= anticipate with pleasure)

They are transitive and can be made passive:

*All her employees **looked up to** her.* (active)
*She was **looked up to** by all her employees.* (passive)

We can never use a noun or pronoun object between the particles:

✗ ~~*I can't put up **this treatment/it** with any longer.*~~

We cannot usually put a noun or pronoun object immediately after the verb:

✗ ~~*I can't put **this treatment/it** up with any longer.*~~
✔ *I can't put up with **this treatment/it** any longer.*

The exception is when the verb has two objects, e.g. *let somebody in on something, take somebody up on something*:

*We let **James** in on the plan.* *We took **her** up on her offer.*

❶ We cannot put an adverb before the first particle or after the final particle, but we can use an adverb between the two particles:

✗ ~~*He stands **strongly up for** his principles.*~~ (verb + adverb + particle)
✗ ~~*He stands **up for strongly** his principles.*~~ (particle + particle + adverb)
✔ *He stands **up strongly for** his principles.* (particle + adverb+ particle)

14.5 WORD LIST: COMMON MULTI-WORD VERBS

These tables include all multi-word verbs which occur at least ten times per million words in the Longman Corpus Network. (Below, *sb* = *somebody* and *sth* = *something*.)

14.5A Type 1: intransitive phrasal verbs (▶ 14.2A):

break down (= stop working), *catch on* (= understand/become popular), *come back* (= return), *come in, come on, fall out* (= quarrel), *fall through, fit in, get by* (= manage/cope), *get up, go away, go on* (= continue), *go out, grow up, look out, pass out* (= faint), *shut up, sit down, stand up, stay on* (= remain), *take off, turn up* (= arrive), *wake up, watch out*

14.5B Type 2: transitive phrasal verbs (▶ 14.2B):

act sth out (= perform/demonstrate), *bottle sth up* (= not allow a feeling to show), *bring sth in* (= introduce), *bring sb up* (= rear), *bring sth up* (= mention sth/introduce a topic), *carry sth out* (= perform/undertake), *do sth up* (= restore/redecorate), *fill sth in/out* (= complete in writing), *find sth out* (= discover), *fix sth up* (= arrange), *give sth away* (= reveal), *give sth up* (= stop), *hold sth up* (= delay), *keep sth up* (= maintain), *leave sth/sb out, let sth out* (= release), *look sth up, make sth up* (= invent), *pay sb back, pick sth up* (= collect), *point sth out* (= highlight/explain), *pull sth/sb down* (= demolish, demote), *put sth away, put sth off* (= postpone), *put sth on, put sb up* (= accommodate), *run sb down* (= criticise), *set sth up* (= establish/implement/organise), *take sth over, take sth up, throw sth away, turn sth/sb down* (= refuse), *turn sth/sb out*

14.5C Type 3: prepositional verbs (▶ 14.3A, B):

call for sb, care for sb, come across sth (= encounter), *cope with sth, deal with sth* (= manage, handle), *fall for sth* (= be tricked), *feel like sth, get at sb/sth, get over sth* (= recover from), *get through* (= finish successfully), *go into sth, go with sth* (= match), *lead to sth, look after sb/sth, look at sth* (= observe), *look into sth* (= investigate), *look like sth* (= resemble), *look round sth* (= visit, etc.), *part with sth, pay for sth, rely on sth/sb, run into sb* (= meet by chance), *see to sth* (= organise/manage), *send for sb, stand for sth* (= represent/mean/tolerate), *stick to sth* (= persevere/follow), *take after sb, talk about sth, think about sth* (= consider)

The following prepositional verbs are usually used in the passive:
be aimed at (= intended for), *be applied to, be considered as, be derived from, be known as, be regarded as, be used as, be used in*

14.5D Type 4: phrasal-prepositional verbs (▶ 14.4A):

back out of sth, break in on sth, catch up on sth/sb, catch up with sb, check up on sth/sb, come across as sth (= appear to be), *come down to sth* (= be essentially), *come up with sth* (= invent), *cut down on sth* (= reduce), *do away with sth, drop in on sb, face up to sth* (= confront), *get away with sth, get back to sth* (= return), *get down to sth, get on with sth, get out of sth, give in to sth, go out for sth, go up to sb* (= approach), *keep away from sb/sth* (= avoid), *keep up with sb, look down on sb, look forward to sth* (= anticipate), *look out for sb/sth, look up to sb* (= admire/respect), *make away with sth, move on to sth, put up with sth/sb* (= tolerate), *run away with sb, run off with sth, stand up for sth* (= defend), *turn away from sth, walk out on sth/sb*

The following phrasal-prepositional verbs are usually used in the passive:
be cut off from, be made up of, be set out in

Practice

The key to these exercises is on page 360. All the verbs you need for these exercises can be found in the Word list (▶ 14.5).

1 14.1

Underline the most suitable verb in *italics* in each of these sentences.

1 Don't stop now Liz. *Continue/Go on*, I'm dying to hear the end of the story!
2 In a bid to improve diplomatic relations, the Foreign Office has *arranged/fixed up* a visit by senior embassy staff.
3 The court sentences you to life imprisonment, with the recommendation that you not be *released/let out* for a minimum period of twenty years.
4 Owing to a lack of military support, the United Nations feels unable to *maintain/keep up* its presence in the war-torn province.
5 I don't think your dad trusts me – he's always *observing/looking at* me.
6 You've got to make an effort, darling. You'll never lose weight unless you *reduce/cut down on* the amount of fatty food you eat.
7 The government have announced plans to *abolish/do away with* the disabled person's vehicle allowance in the next budget.
8 My little brother's always getting bullied at school. He just won't *confront/face up to* the other kids.
9 The presidential party will *arrive/turn up* at the palace shortly before luncheon.
10 My best friend always exaggerates – half the things he says are just *invented/made up*!

2 14.2, 14.3

Rewrite these sentences using an appropriate multi-word verb. You must use a pronoun (*it*, *him*, *her*, *them*) to replace the underlined object. In some cases you may have to change the word order. The exercise begins with an example (0).

0 They've postponed the housewarming party until Friday. ...*They've put it off until Friday.*...
1 Would you mind organising the removal yourself? ....
2 I met Steve and Terri quite by chance at the supermarket this morning. ....
3 I've arranged the meeting for ten o'clock tomorrow. ....
4 You're always criticising your colleagues. ....
5 I'm sure the police will investigate the burglary. ....
6 The builders undertook the job very professionally. ....
7 Could you collect the children from school tonight? ....
8 Has Perry recovered from the flu yet? ....
9 She really resembles her parents, doesn't she? ....
10 Would you highlight the advantages for me? ....

3 14.2, 14.3

What are the people saying in the pictures on the next page? Write a short sentence for each situation using multi-word verbs and a suitable pronoun (*it*, *them*, *you*, etc.). All the multi-word verbs you need can be formed from the verbs in brackets and the particles in the box. The first one has been done as an example (0).

PARTICLES: after at down off ~~out~~ up (x2) with

0
NO SMOKING
(put) Please put it out.
4
(go)
1
(take)
5
(pick)
2
Gifts for Special Occasions
(put)
6
MEDICINE
(drink)
3
(take)
7
(look)

4 14.2, 14.3, 14.4

Rewrite the parts of the sentences in brackets with the words in the correct order.

0 Don't (tomorrow/put/until/off/it); do it now. ...*Don't put it off until tomorrow*...
1 Thanks for the invitation; (looking/to/I'm/it/forward). ....
2 The evil witch (frog/prince/the/into/turned/handsome/a). ....
3 I won't have any sugar thank you; (it/I've/up/given). ....
4 There isn't a death penalty any longer; (away/they've/it/done/with). ....
5 He's the footballer (million/a/team/manager/for/the/paid/whom/dollars). ....
6 I have a small trust fund; (by/it/my/was/set/grandfather/up). ....

5 ALL

Read the magazine article below. Then use the information in the text to complete the informal summary on the next page. Use no more than three words for each gap (1–18), including the word in brackets. The words you need are all multi-word verbs and do not occur in the newspaper article. The exercise begins with an example (0).

When anger is healthy

Everyone knows that not allowing oneself to show feelings of anger and resentment can be very unhealthy, leading to stress and long-term feelings of inadequacy and powerlessness. But how do we release our anger without looking foolish or petulant?

The first thing to learn is that expressing your anger and losing your temper are not the same thing at all. One is natural and healthy, the other is destructive and dangerous. We usually admire those who can express their anger calmly, and see them as 'firm but fair' or mature and self-confident. While those who lose their temper appear to be immature, childish, selfish and aggressive.

Mandy Dickson is a psychologist who has established a successful one-day anger workshop that helps ordinary people to learn about and manage their anger. The seminar is not intended for criminals or the mentally ill, but for those ordinary people who feel powerless to control their own tempers.

The first thing Mandy explains is that anger is a natural and normal feeling, and that feeling angry about something is nothing to be ashamed of. But we need to recognise anger when we feel it, and to investigate its true causes. Once we know the real cause of anger we can confront it and begin to do something positive about it. Mandy asks participants to complete a questionnaire about things that make them angry. By comparing these 'triggers' people often discover that the true causes of anger are other feelings, especially fear, disappointment and grief. But because it is not socially acceptable in our culture to openly demonstrate these feelings, we express them as anger. This is particularly true for men who, even in these enlightened times, are expected to hide any feelings of inadequacy or fear and be strong and stoical in all situations.

Having recognised the causes of anger, the first step is to learn how to avoid anger-inducing situations. The next step is to learn how to express one's feelings calmly and firmly. Mandy believes that when we are angry we want other people to understand our anger and sympathise with it. But we often fall into the trap of expressing anger by criticising those around us, when what we really want is their support and empathy. One of the most common causes of anger is when other people fail to behave in a way you expect them to. But as Mandy explains, human beings are not telepathic, they cannot be expected to automatically anticipate other people's desires and wishes. So an essential tool in reducing the occurrence of anger-inducing situations is to always explain exactly what you want and expect from those around you. It is all essentially a question of communication.

We know (0) ......*bottling up*...... (bottle) anger can be unhealthy. But how do we (1) .... (let) our anger without seeming foolish? Expressing anger and losing your temper are different things. One is healthy, the other dangerous. We (2) .... (look) people who express anger calmly, but those who lose their temper (3) .... (come) immature and aggressive.

Mandy Dickson has (4) .... (set) a one-day anger workshop which helps people learn about and (5) .... (deal) their anger. It is (6) .... (aim) ordinary people who don't feel able to control their tempers. She (7) .... (point) that anger is natural and nothing to be ashamed of, but we should recognise it and (8) .... (look) its true causes. Then we can (9) .... (face) it, and begin to do something positive. Participants (10) .... (fill) a questionnaire about things that make them angry. They compare their responses and often (11) .... (find) that the causes are other feelings such as fear or grief. But in our culture it isn't acceptable to (12) .... (act) these feelings in public. Men, in particular, are supposed to (13) .... (cover) these feelings.

Once we know the causes of anger, we must learn how to (14) .... (keep) situations which will induce them. When we are angry we want other people to understand us, but we often make the mistake of (15) .... (run) those around us. Anger is often caused by the feeling that you have been (16) .... (let) by other people. But we can't always expect other people to know our feelings. So the most important way to (17) .... (cut) the number of anger-producing situations is to tell people exactly how we feel. It really all (18) .... (come) communication.

6 ALL

Rewrite John's half of this unnatural telephone conversation in a more natural, informal style. Use the multi-word verbs in the box to replace the underlined verbs and phrases. Replace nouns with pronouns where possible and make any other necessary changes, as in this example:

JOHN (0) I've just <u>demolished</u> the conservatory. ....*I've just pulled it down*....

do sth up · put up with sb · stay up · get on with sb · put sb up · turn sth into sth · look down on sb · put sth up · take sth off · look forward to sth · sit down · take sth up · finish sth off · sort sth out · turn sth down · ~~pull sth down~~

DAVE John, it's Dave. How are things?

JOHN Sorry, I can't hear you. (1) I'll just <u>reduce the volume on</u> the radio. That's better.

DAVE How are things? Still working on the house?

JOHN Yes. (2) We've <u>completed the work on</u> the kitchen and (3) we're <u>renovating</u> the dining room. (4) We're <u>transforming</u> the room into a second bedroom. (5) I've just <u>mounted</u> the wallpaper but I've been having trouble getting it (6) to <u>remain vertically attached</u>.

DAVE I know what you mean. I hate wallpapering.

JOHN (7) And it's all got to be <u>organised and ready</u> by Saturday. Jane's mother is coming and we're (8) <u>providing accommodation for</u> her for a few days.

DAVE I thought you didn't like her.

JOHN (9) We don't <u>interact in a friendly way</u> with each other but (10) I can <u>tolerate</u> her for a few days.

DAVE Why do you dislike her so much?

JOHN (11) I'm sure she <u>regards me as inferior to her</u>. And she's so lazy, I mean she comes in, (12) <u>removes</u> her coat, (13) <u>assumes a seated position</u> and expects us to wait on her hand and foot!

DAVE I see what you mean. Sounds like a nightmare.

JOHN (14) Mm. I think I might <u>commence</u> gardening <u>as a hobby</u> – just to get me out of the house!

DAVE Good idea. Well, I'd better let you get on. And don't forget about our party on Friday.

JOHN (15) Of course not, I'm <u>anticipating the party with pleasure</u>.

15 Dependent prepositions

In English there are many words which are used with particular prepositions. Because the choice of preposition depends on the word and meaning, the prepositions we use are called dependent prepositions. For example, we *accuse someone **of** a crime*, we don't ~~*accuse someone **at** a crime*~~, ~~***by** a crime*~~ or ~~***for** a crime*~~.

There are many verbs which combine with particular prepositions. Some of these are 'prepositional verbs' (e.g. *quarrel **with** someone*) and are explained in detail in Unit 14. Other verbs follow different patterns (e.g. *accuse someone **of** a crime*) which are explained here. There are also many nouns and adjectives which are followed by particular prepositions. (For prepositions and prepositional phrases ▶ **Unit 29**.)

15.1 GENERAL RULES

15.1A Preposition + object

Prepositions after verbs, nouns and adjectives always have an object. The object can be a noun, pronoun or verb.

*I apologised **to my boss/her/the managing director**.*
*I apologised **for arriving** late.*

Note that *to* can be a preposition.

15.1B Preposition + *-ing* form

If the object of a preposition is a verb, it must be an *-ing* form:

✗ ~~*She succeeded **in win** the race.*~~ ✔ *She succeeded **in winning** the race.*

❗ The *-ing* form can have its own subject. This is a noun phrase or an object pronoun:

*I'm looking forward to **my wife returning**.*
*Dad insisted on **us apologising**.*

In formal English we can use possessives rather than nouns or pronouns (▶ **26.1A, 27.1A**):

*The judge granted bail as she felt there was no risk of **the defendant's** absconding.*
*The detective insisted on **our** leaving the crime scene.*

15.1C Preposition or *to* + infinitive

Many adjectives describing feelings and emotions can be followed by a preposition or *to* + infinitive (word list ▶ **15.5D**):

*We were **annoyed at finding** our places taken. He's **keen on learning** archery.*
*We were **annoyed to find** our places taken. He's **keen to learn** archery.*

Some verbs can also be followed by either a preposition or *to* + infinitive, but there may be a change of meaning:

*They don't **agree with** the government's policy.* (= They have a different opinion.)
*I **agreed to help** him fill out the forms.* (= I said that I was willing to ...)

(For verbs + *-ing*/infinitive ▶ **Unit 12**; for participle and infinitive phrases ▶ **Unit 13**.)

15.1D Preposition or *that* clause

Many of the words which describe what we say, think or feel are followed by a preposition + *-ing* form. Some of these words can also be followed by a *that* clause. (For more information on these words ▶ **9.2A, 9.5B**):

*The judge **insisted on** the jury **disregarding** the doctor's testimony.*
*The judge **insisted that** the jury **disregard** the doctor's testimony.*

❗ But prepositions cannot be followed by a *that* clause except with the expression *the fact that*:

✗ ~~*My parents **disapproved of that** my brother left school at sixteen.*~~
✔ *My parents **disapproved of the fact that** my brother left school at sixteen.*

15.1E Preposition + *whether*

We do not use *if* after prepositions, we use *whether*:

✗ ~~*I'm afraid I wasn't aware of **if** she was watching me or not.*~~

✓ *I'm afraid I wasn't aware of **whether** she was watching me or not.*

15.2 VERB + PREPOSITION PATTERNS

15.2A Prepositional verbs

Some verbs combine with a preposition either to create a new meaning or to link a verb with an object. These verbs are called prepositional verbs (▶ **14.3A**).

*They decided to **look into** the problem.* (= to investigate it)

*Tamsin **complained about** the bill.*

*She **apologised for** her outburst.*

Some prepositional verbs also use an extra preposition before an indirect object, e.g. *to the manager* (word list ▶ **15.5A**). Most of these are reporting verbs (▶ **9.5A**):

*Tamsin **complained to** the manager **about** the bill.*

*She **apologised to** the committee **for** her outburst.*

15.2B Verb + object + preposition + *-ing* form

We use object + preposition + *-ing* form after particular verbs to link the verb with the person it affects and the action which is connected to it (word list ▶ **15.5B**):

*The police **accused her of stealing**.*

*His sense of duty **prevented him from leaving**.*

These verbs can be made passive:

*She **was accused of** stealing (by the police).*

*He **was prevented from** leaving (by his sense of duty).*

15.2C Verb + direct object + preposition + indirect object

We can use direct object + preposition + indirect object after particular verbs to link the verb with two objects:

*The tour guide discussed **the day's schedule with us**.*

*Henry explained **it to me** very slowly.*

With some verbs we can change the order of the objects, but in this case different prepositions are used (word list ▶ **15.5B**):

*I **blame** our schools **for** the poor standard of education.* (= blame somebody for something)

*I **blame** the poor standard of education **on** our schools.* (= blame something on somebody)

*The King of Sweden **presented** the physicist **with** the Nobel prize.* (= present somebody with something)

*The King of Sweden **presented** the Nobel prize **to** the physicist.* (= present something to somebody)

❗ These verbs can be made passive. But only the direct object (the one which immediately follows the active verb) can become the subject of the passive verb:

*My teacher explained **it** to **me**.* →

✗ ~~*I was explained it by my teacher.*~~ ✓ ***It** was explained to **me** (by my teacher).*

❗ Unlike some verbs used with two objects (e.g. *give*), with the above verbs we cannot omit the preposition:

He gave it to me. *He gave me it.*

✗ ~~*He explained me it.*~~ ✗ ~~*He explained it me.*~~ ✓ *He **explained** it **to** me.*

✗ ~~*He discussed us it.*~~ ✗ ~~*He discussed it us.*~~ ✓ *He **discussed** it **with** us.*

15.3 NOUN + PREPOSITION

15.3A Noun/verb + preposition

Where a noun is related to a prepositional verb, the noun often takes the same preposition (▶ **15.5C**):

*He **succeeded in** winning the Palme d'Or.* (= to succeed in something)
*We congratulated him on his **success in** winning the Palme d'Or.* (= a success in something)

15.3B Noun only + preposition

But some nouns followed by a preposition are related to verbs which do not take a preposition (▶ **15.5C**):

*The members had a **discussion about** the subscription charges.* (= a discussion about something)
*We **discussed** the subscription charges.* (= to discuss something)
✗ ~~*We discussed about the subscription charges.*~~

Here are examples of other verbs/nouns like this:

*to **demand** something/a **demand for** something*
*to **fear** something/a **fear of** something*

15.3C Noun + preposition + noun

The preposition is usually followed by an *-ing* form or noun. But there are some noun + preposition forms which can only be followed by a noun. (▶ **15.5C**):

✗ ~~*The court issued a **demand for repaying of** the debt.*~~
✔ *The court issued a **demand for repayment of** the debt.*

15.4 ADJECTIVE/PARTICIPLE + PREPOSITION

15.4A Adjective/ noun + preposition

Where an adjective is related to a noun or verb which takes a preposition, the adjective usually takes the same preposition (▶ **15.5D**):

*I expressed my **gratitude for** their assistance. I was **grateful for** their assistance.*
*We **depend on** his generosity. We are **dependent on** his generosity.*

15.4B Adjective + preposition

A lot of adjectives describing feelings and opinions have dependent prepositions:

*My grandfather's very **keen on** trout fishing.*
*Stockbrokers are becoming increasingly **worried about** the news from New York.*

❗ Some of these adjectives are formed from verb participles, e.g. *interested*, *bored*, *scared* (▶ **21.2A**). We use participles + *by* + agent in passive sentences, e.g. *I was really scared by that film* (▶ **8.1A**). Although these adjectives look like participles, they work differently and cannot always be followed with *by*:

✗ ~~*I am **scared by** horror films.*~~ ✔ *I am **scared of** horror films.*
✗ ~~*He is **interested by** philosophy.*~~ ✔ *He is **interested in** philosophy.*

15.4C Preposition choice after participles

In some cases the participle form takes different prepositions depending on the meaning, for example (▶ **29.2D**):

*made **by*** (+ the person/company/process which produced it)
*made **for*** (+ its purpose)
*made **from*** (+ original material which has been transformed)
*made **of*** (+ original material which is still visible)

The wool in Arran jumpers is made by Scottish sheep.

15.5 WORD LIST: DEPENDENT PREPOSITION PATTERNS

(Below, *sb* = *somebody* and *sth* = *something*.)

15.5A Prepositional verb + object + preposition + object (▶ 15.2A)

agree about sth with sb
agree with sb about/over sth
apologise to sb for sth
complain about sth to sb
complain to sb about sth
depend on sb/sth for sth
disagree with sb about/over sth
quarrel with sb about/over sth
rely on sb/sth for sth

15.5B Verb + direct object + preposition + indirect object (▶ 15.2B)

(* These verbs can also follow the pattern: verb + direct object + preposition + *-ing* form.)

*accuse sb of sth**
acquit sb of sth
*advise sb against sth**
advise sb of sth
aim sth at sb
*arrest sb for sth**
*beat sb at sth**
*blame sb for sth**
blame sth on sb
bother sb with sth
*compensate sb for sth**
*congratulate sb for sth** (US English)
*congratulate sb on sth**
*convict sb of sth**
convince sb of sth
criticise sb for sth
cure sb of sth
deprive sb of sth
describe sth to sb
discuss sth with sb
explain sth to sb
help sb with sth
lend sth to sb
make sth for sb
persuade sb of sth
*praise sb for sth**
present sb with sth
present sth to sb
prevent sb from -ing
protect sb from sth
provide sb with sth
provide sth for sb
reassure sb of sth
release sb from sth
rescue sb from sth
rid sb of sth
rob sb of sth
save sb/sth from sth
starve sb of sth
steal sth from sb
stop sb from -ing
strip sb of sth
supply sb with sth
supply sth for/to sb
suspect sb of sth
throw sth at sb (= in order to hit them)
throw sth to sb (= in order for them to catch it)
*warn sb about/against sth**
welcome sb to sth

15.5C Noun + preposition + noun/*-ing* form (▶ 15.3)

(* These nouns can only follow the pattern: noun + preposition + noun.)

advantage of/in
aim of/in
amazement at
anger about/at
annoyance about/at
*answer to**
anxiety about
apology for
attack on
awareness of
belief in
boredom with
craving for
*damage to**
danger of/in
decrease of (+ quantity)
*decrease in**
delay in
delay of (+ duration)
*demand for**
difficulty in
effect of
excitement about/at
expense of
fear of
gratitude for
hope of
idea of
*increase in**
increase of (+ quantity)
insistence on
insurance against
interest in
job of
lack of
matter of
*matter with**
method of
objection to
pleasure of/in
point of/in
possibility of
prelude to
problem of/in
proof of
prospect of/for
purpose of/in
question about/of
reason for
relationship with
satisfaction with
sequel to
*solution to**
success in
surprise at
task of
taste for
thought of
way of
work of
worry about

15.5D Adjective + preposition (▶ 15.4)

(* These adjectives can also be followed by *to* + infinitive.)

absent from
accustomed to
addicted to
afraid of*
amazed at/by
angry, annoyed, furious* at/about* (+ the cause of this feeling)
angry, annoyed, furious with (+ the person who caused this feeling)
anxious about (= feel nervous/worried about sb/sth)
anxious for* (= waiting impatiently for sth)
ashamed of*
astonished at/by
available for (+ purpose)
available to (+ person)
aware of
bad/good at (= ability)
bad/good for (= effect on health)
bad/good to (= behaviour towards/treatment of the object)
based on
bored with
capable of
characteristic of
close to
concerned about (= worried about)
concerned with (= involved in)
conducive to
confident of
content with*
contrary to
convenient for
conversant with
crazy about*
crowded with
curious about*
deficient in
dependent on
devoid of
different to/from
different than (US English)
disgusted with/at
eager for*
engaged in* (= working in/involved in)
engaged to (= promised to marry)
excited about*
faithful to
famous for
fed up with
fond of
fraught with
glad for (= pleased for sb)
glad of (= grateful for sth)
good at/for/to (→ *bad*)
grateful for (+ the cause of this feeling)
grateful to (+ the person who caused this feeling)
guilty of
harmful to
hopeful of
impervious to
impressed with/by
inclined towards
incumbent upon
inherent in
intent on
interested in*
jealous of
keen on*
kind to
lacking in
late for
made by (+ the person/company who produced it)
made for (+ its purpose)
made from (+ original material which has been transformed)
made of (+ original material which is still visible)
nervous of
obedient to
obvious to
opposed to
pleased at/about (+ something general, e.g. your recovery/the inflation figures)
pleased with (+ something personal, e.g. my exam results/my new jacket)
popular with
prone to
proud of*
ready for*
related to
reminiscent of
responsible for
riddled with
scared of
shocked at
short of
similar to
sorry about* (+ the cause of this feeling)
sorry for (+ the person you feel sympathy towards)
subject to
successful in
sufficient for
suitable for
superior to
sure of
terrified of
tired of
typical of
upset about/by/over (+ the cause of this feeling)
upset with (+ the person who caused this feeling)
worried about
worthy of
wrong with

Practice

The key to these exercises is on page 361. You will need to refer to the Word lists (▶ 15.5) to complete these exercises.

1 15.1

Match the sentence beginnings (1–10) with the endings (A–J).

1 Although I had a lot of questions I was afraid ...
2 The passengers' relatives were anxious ...
3 It's not a matter ...
4 We have to face the possibility ...
5 My parents expressed surprise ...
6 We tend to be scared ...
7 As I stepped onto the boat I suddenly felt anxious ...
8 The pupils were scared ...
9 The committee sees no problem ...
10 Ever since that experience at the zoo she's been afraid ...

A ...... of large animals
B ...... at the fact that I'd finally found a job.
C ...... of whether you want to do it or not, it's an order.
D .... that I would make them do the test again.
E ...... to ask them.
F ...... in approving your application for planning permission.
G ...... of things we know little about.
H ...... for news of their loved ones.
I ...... about the lack of life jackets.
J ...... of them not getting here in time.

2 15.2

Complete the sentences with appropriate verbs and prepositions from the boxes. Use each verb only once. Some of the prepositions will be needed more than once. Note that you will need two prepositions in numbers 10–15.

verbs	accuse agree apologise blame convince cure depend disagree explain present prevent quarrel rely stop supply
prepositions	about for from to of on over with

1 Somehow I managed to .... my parents .... my innocence.
2 The subcontractors should be able to .... you .... spare parts.
3 The immigration authorities couldn't .... the refugees .... entering the country.
4 Do you honestly think this faith healer will manage to .... him .... his stutter?
5 The Chief Constable is going to .... Harold .... this year's award for bravery.
6 In my opinion we can .... today's unemployment problem .... the previous government.
7 I'm rather confused; you'd better .... that procedure .... me again.
8 Don't take it out on me; I've never tried to .... you .... doing what you felt was right.
9 I wouldn't dare .... him .... stealing, although I certainly don't trust him.
10 Congress is bound to .... the President .... the increase in federal taxes.
11 I absolutely refuse to .... them .... my comments; they were completely justified.
12 Since the accident he's had to .... his mother .... everything.
13 I'm happy to report that the unions .... us .... the need for wage controls next year.
14 In the event of a power cut you will have to .... the emergency generator .... electricity.
15 Look, just give me the car keys; I don't want to .... you .... this any longer.

3 15.2

Some of these sentences contain grammatical mistakes. Tick (✓) the correct sentences, then find and correct the mistakes.

0 He was accused by fraud of the newspapers.
.... *He was accused of fraud by the newspapers.* ....

1 The firing squad aimed at the condemned man their rifles.
....

2 Our accountant provided us with the end of year accounts.
....

3 The brilliant architect presented us to her imaginative proposals.
....

4 My uncle blames on his hearing problems old age.
....

5 The Prime Minister disagreed with the cabinet over the new welfare scheme.
....

6 Do you agree about her with the corporate sponsorship deal?
....

7 The crippled patient was cured of the doctor's radical new treatment of arthritis.
....

8 Why won't you even discuss her with it?
....

9 The plane was saved from disaster by the quick thinking of the crew members.
....

10 Gerald was accused of the court by lying under oath.
....

4 15.3

Complete the newspaper headlines with appropriate prepositions.

1 SOAP STAR GIVES NO REASON .... DIVORCE

2 Scientists predict success .... battle against cancer

3 Fear .... sunburn keeps children indoors

4 MINISTRY ANNOUNCE SOLUTION .... TRAFFIC JAM NIGHTMARES

5 POSSIBILITY .... MANNED JOURNEY TO SATURN SAY NASA

6 FILM STAR DENIES ATTACK .... PHOTOGRAPHER

7 Renewed prospect .... peace at UN talks

8 PALACE ISSUES APOLOGY .... MISLEADING STATEMENT

9 LITTLE HOPE .... SURVIVORS IN AVALANCHE HORROR

10 Ministers question effect .... violence in Hollywood films

11 SEQUEL .... 'TITANIC' BOMBS AT BOX OFFICE

12 *CONGRESSMAN QUESTIONED OVER RELATIONSHIP .... BIG BUSINESS*

13 PM GIVES JOB .... DRUGS TSAR TO EX POLICE CHIEF

14 NEW WONDER DRUG REDUCES CRAVING .... NICOTINE

15 Travel companies fail to provide insurance .... airport delays

16 *NEW WAY .... FILING TAX RETURNS PROVOKES ANGER IN CITY*

17 WHAT'S THE MATTER .... OUR TEAMS? ASK SOCCER SUPREMOS

18 Government deny belief .... quick fix solutions

19 TASK .... CLEANING UP BEACHES GIVEN TO VOLUNTEERS

20 BANK ANNOUNCES SHOCK INCREASE .... INFLATION FIGURES

5 15.4

For each of the sentences below, write a new sentence as similar as possible in meaning to the original sentence, but using the words given. The words must not be altered in any way.

0 She finds spiders very frightening.
scared ......*She is very scared of spiders.*......

1 Isaac was getting more and more frustrated by his lack of progress.
fed up ....

2 They say the terrorists carried out the atrocities.
responsible ....

3 My students find our film and photography course interesting.
interested ....

4 The public rarely feels sympathy towards politicians caught behaving badly.
sorry ....

5 We found the quality of her singing voice quite astonishing.
astonished ....

6 I don't think he likes spicy food very much.
fond ....

7 Excessive consumption of fried food can have a bad effect on the arteries.
harmful ....

8 I'm afraid I haven't got much change at the moment.
short ....

9 Our neighbour treats her cats remarkably well.
good ....

10 He owes his fame to his performance in *Othello* at the National Theatre.
famous ....

11 I have every confidence in his abilities.
sure ....

12 Thank you for your swift response to my enquiry.
grateful ....

13 My two brothers are not at all like me.
different ....

14 The new legislation covers deregulation of the airline industry.
concerned ....

15 I would love to know how the magician did his tricks.
curious ....

16 My colleague really likes all these new electronic gadgets.
keen ....

17 The daily swim seems to be beneficial to his health.
good ....

18 The research team is working on a brand new project.
engaged ....

19 Unfortunately we don't really expect them to reach the final round.
hopeful ....

20 Inspector Morse believes the blind man committed the murder.
guilty ....

6 ALL

Complete the crossword using the missing words from these sentences.

CLUES ACROSS

1 My client will be able to give .... to your queries at this afternoon's press conference.

3 I was furious .... the teachers for allowing such bullying to carry on unchecked.

4 Since the stroke Lucy has .... on her children for all her basic needs.

11 The class had a stimulating discussion .... the refugee crisis.

12 I feel my main job will be to .... the board of the need for substantial investment.

13 We regret to announce that this evening's flight will be subject to a .... of fifty minutes.

15 The committee .... her for the high standard of her application.

16 We try to .... products for the more discerning customer.

17 Our paper is made .... 100 per cent recycled pulp.

18 We felt that such a rude response was not .... of a person in his privileged position.

CLUES DOWN

2 There will be no problem .... you with all the spare parts you require.

3 I really can't worry about .... he has personal problems or not.

5 The National Health Service seems unable to cope with the increasing .... for high-tech procedures.

6 The manager insisted .... we leave immediately.

7 The trust is going to .... him with a substantial annual income.

8 The beach was .... with happy holidaymakers enjoying the sunshine.

9 I look forward to .... the new sales manager next month.

10 Findler and Outhwaite have agreed .... represent us at the pre-trial hearing.

14 We crowded around the telephone as we were all .... for news of my father's progress.

17 I blame the government .... not recognising the problem soon enough.

16 Modal verbs (1)

can, could, may, might, be able to

Modal verbs can be confusing for learners because individual modal forms can be used to express a number of different meanings. This unit looks at the modals we use to describe ability and possibility, to make deductions, arrangements, suggestions and offers, and to ask for and give permission. (For the use of *can* and *could* with sense verbs ▶ **1.3C**; for the use of modal verbs in conditional sentences ▶ **Unit 10.**)

16.1 ABILITY

16.1A Present and future

We use *can* to describe an ability and *cannot* or *can't* to describe a lack of ability in the present:

*She **can** speak Spanish but she **can't** speak Italian.*

If the present ability is surprising or involves overcoming some difficulty, we can also use *is/are able to*:

*Despite his handicap he **is able to** drive a car.*

❗ We cannot usually use *be able to* with a passive:

✗ ~~*This book **is able to be used** by complete beginners.*~~

✔ *This book **can be used** by complete beginners.*

To emphasise the difficulty or to suggest a great effort (in the present, past or future) we use *manage to*. In more formal English we can also use *succeed in* + *-ing* form:

*Do you think she'**ll manage to** get a visa?*

*The army **succeeded in** defeating their enemy.*

To describe a future ability we use *will be able to*, not *can* (but ▶ **16.3**, **16.4**):

✗ ~~***Can** I speak fluently by the end of the course?*~~

✔ ***Will** I **be able to** speak fluently by the end of the course?*

We also use *be able to* where *can/could* is grammatically impossible, for example:

*I **haven't been able to** drive since I dislocated my wrist.* (with the perfect aspect)

*We love **being able to** talk the local language.* (with *-ing* forms and infinitives)

Another form for *not be able to* is *be unable to*. It is more common in formal English:

*The lawyer **was unable to** persuade the jury of her client's innocence.*

We use *can* (present) and *could* (past) before sense verbs (▶ **1.3C**):

*I think I **can smell** something burning in the kitchen.*

16.1B Past

We use *could* to describe the possession of an ability in the past:

*Mozart **could** play the piano at the age of five.*

❗ To describe the successful use of an ability on a specific occasion we do not use *could*, we use a past tense or *was/were able to*:

✗ ~~*Mike's car broke down but fortunately he **could** repair it.*~~

✔ *Mike's car broke down but fortunately he **was able to** repair it.*

But we can use *could* in questions, and in sentences with limiting adverbs such as *only* or *hardly*:

*'**Could** you fix the computer yourself?' 'No, I **could only** back up the key files.'*

*She was so exhausted she **could hardly** speak.*

We use *couldn't* or *was/were not able to* to describe a lack of ability or success:

*Mozart **couldn't** speak French.*

*Despite being a mechanic, Mike **couldn't** fix his car when it broke down yesterday.*

We use *could/might have* + past participle to describe a past ability which wasn't used or a past opportunity which wasn't taken. The meaning is similar to 'would have been able to' (compare the use of these forms in the third conditional ▶ **10.5**):

*She **could have paid** by credit card but she preferred to use cash.* (= She had the ability to pay by credit card but she didn't use it.)

*I **might have gone** to university after leaving school but I chose to get a job instead.* (= I had the opportunity to go, but I didn't take it.)

We often use these forms to make a criticism:

*You **might/could have told** me about the party!* (= You had the chance to tell me but you didn't.)

We can use *couldn't have* + past participle + comparative adjective when we want to emphasise a past action or feeling:

*They **couldn't have tried harder** to make me feel welcome.* (= They tried very hard.)

*I **couldn't have been more pleased** when I heard about your results – congratulations!* (= I was very pleased.)

16.2 POSSIBILITY, DEDUCTION AND SPECULATION

16.2A Present

We use *can* to describe things which are generally possible (we know they sometimes happen):

*Drinks in restaurants **can** be very expensive.* (= Drinks are sometimes expensive.)

In scientific and academic English we use *may* in the same way:

*Over-prescribing of antibiotics **may** lead to the rapid development of resistant strains.*

To talk about specific possibilities we use *may*, *might* and *could* (but not *can*). The meaning is similar to 'perhaps' or 'maybe':

✗ ~~*There **can** be life on Mars.*~~

✔ *There **may** be life on Mars.* (= Perhaps there is life on Mars.)

*The rash **could** be a symptom of something more serious.* (= Maybe it is a symptom ...)

We use the same forms when we are making a deduction based on evidence or on our experience:

*He always wears smart suits. He **could** be a businessman.*

*'Why isn't she here yet?' 'I don't know. The train **may** be running late.'*

We can use *well* after *may*, *might* and *could* if we think the possibility is quite strong. (If we are very certain of the possibility, we use *must* ▶ **17.5**.)

*Don't worry, the contract **could well** be in the post.* (= It is probably in the post.)

To describe possibilities which depend on certain conditions we use *could* or *might* (▶ **10.4A**):

*She **could** learn much more quickly if she paid attention.* (= She would be able to learn more quickly if she paid attention.)

We use *can* or *could* (but not *may*) to talk about specific possibilities in *wh-* questions or with adverbs such as *only* or *hardly*:

✗ ~~*Who **may** that be at this time of night?*~~

✔ *Who **can/could** that be at this time of night?*

*Where **can/could** that noise be coming from?*

*It **can/could hardly** be the postman, he only comes in the morning.*

*It **can/could only** be Steve. He's the only one with a key.*

We use *might* for a more tentative (less direct) question:

__Might__ the losses be due to currency fluctuations?

We use *can't* or *couldn't* for things which we know are impossible and to make negative deductions:

You __can't__ get blood out of a stone. (I'm sure about this, it's impossible.)

He __couldn't__ be a doctor, he isn't wearing a white coat. (I'm certain he isn't ...)

We also use this form to say that something is impossible because we are unwilling to do it:

I __couldn't__ pick up a spider; they terrify me.

When we think that something is possibly not the case we use *might not* or *may not*:

The shops __may not/might not__ be open today; it's a bank holiday. (Perhaps they are not open.)

❗ In spoken English we often contract *might not* to *mightn't*. We don't usually contract *may not*.

16.2B Past

We use *could* to talk about general possibility in the past (things which sometimes happened):

Teachers __could__ be very strict at my old school. (Sometimes they were strict.)

In scientific and academic English we use *might* in the same way:

Wealthy Victorian families __might__ keep as many as a dozen indoor servants.

We use *could/might have* for a specific past possibility:

She __might have__ done it; she had the opportunity and the motive. (Perhaps she did it ...)

John __could have__ posted the letter. (I'm not sure whether he did or not.)

We also use *might have* for a past opportunity which we know was not taken (► **16.1B**).

I __might have__ gone to drama school, but my parents wouldn't let me. (I had the opportunity but I didn't go.)

We express a negative deduction about the past with *can't have* or *couldn't have* (► **17.5**):

She __can't have__ fixed the computer, it's still not working properly. (I'm sure she didn't fix it.)

When we are less certain we use *may not have* or *might not have*:

We'd better phone them, they __might not have__ heard the news. (Perhaps they haven't heard the news yet.)

We often use *can't have* or *couldn't have* to express surprise or disbelief:

She __couldn't have__ done it; she's such a nice woman.

16.2C Future

If we are certain that something will be possible or impossible in the future we can use *will/won't be able to*:

We'__ll be able to__ travel to the moon, but we __won't be able to__ travel to Mars.

For predictions which are less certain we use *may, might* or *could. Could* usually describes a weaker possibility than *may* or *might*:

The directors __may__ call a stockholders' meeting. (Perhaps they will call a meeting.)

You never know, she __could__ meet someone suitable tomorrow. (It's possible, but unlikely.)

We sometimes use *may/might have* + past participle to talk about a possible completed action by a time in the future (similar to the future perfect ► **4.1D**):

Call me next Tuesday; I __might have finished__ the project by then.

16.3 ARRANGEMENTS, SUGGESTIONS, OFFERS, ETC.

16.3A Arrangements

We use *can*, *could* or *be able to* to describe possible arrangements for a time in the future:

*The doctor **could** see you at six; he **can't** see you before then as he's too busy.*
***I'll be able to** see you after the lesson.*

If the arrangement is uncertain we use *may* or *might*:

*The dentist **might** be free to see you immediately after lunch; I'll have to check the diary.*
*I'm not sure if I'm available; I **may** be working that weekend.*

16.3B Suggestions, offers and requests

The choice of modal verb for suggestions, offers and requests depends on the formality of the situation. *May* and *might* tend to be more formal and tentative than *can* and *could*:

DEGREE OF FORMALITY	offers	requests	suggestions
less formal	***Can** I help you?*	***Can** you close the window?*	*We **can** try that new café.*
	*We **could** do that for you.*	***Could** you pass me the salt?*	*You **could** lose some weight.*
more formal	***May** I help you?* ***Might** I be of some assistance?*	*You **might** get me some milk while you're there.*	*You **might** give John a ring.*

We use *can/could always* for an alternative or more tentative suggestion:

*We **could always** go to the Italian place.*

When we want to make a suggestion with the meaning 'there is no better choice available', we can use the phrase *might as well*:

*Now the children have left we **might as well** sell the house and get something smaller.*

16.4 ASKING FOR AND GIVING/REFUSING PERMISSION

16.4A Present/ future

We use *can/can't* for permission granted or refused by the person being asked and for permission subject to some external authority such as the law:

*'**Can** I use your phone?' 'Yes, of course you **can**./No, I'm afraid you **can't**.'* (I give/refuse permission.)
*You **can't** smoke on the underground.* (The law doesn't allow you to do this.)

In more formal situations we can use *may* and *may not* in the same way:

***May** I interrupt?*
*Candidates **may not** bring calculators into the examination room.*

We use *could* or *might* to ask for permission in a more tentative way (*might* is very formal):

*Excuse me, **could** I leave my coat here?*
***Might** I ask the court for an adjournment at this point?*

16.4B Past

To describe general permission in the past we use *could/couldn't*:

*In the 1950s British children **could** leave school at the age of fourteen.*

But to talk about permission on a specific occasion in the past, we do not use *could*, we use *was/were allowed to*:

✗ ~~*I **could** leave early yesterday.*~~ ✓ *I **was allowed to** leave early yesterday.*

▶ **Pages 198 and 199 for Round up of modal verbs**

Practice

The key to these exercises is on page 361.

1 16.1

Choose a suitable form of *can*, *could*, *be able to*, *manage to* or *succeed in* to complete the sentences below.

1 The manager of the shop was a bit reluctant but in the end I .... get a refund.
2 It was really annoying; I .... get on to any of the websites you recommended.
3 What's her phone number? I .... remember it.
4 Although Stephanie is deaf and mute she .... communicate with the aid of a special computer.
5 They finish the new motorway next month so we .... get to the coast much more quickly.
6 Most of the big hotels were full, but we .... find a room in one of those small guesthouses near the station.
7 Would you speak more slowly? I .... follow what you're saying.
8 I really appreciate .... speak to you so frankly about this.
9 After I move to the country I'm not going to .... visit you so often.
10 Over the last few months the government's fuel tax levy .... generating over a billion pounds in revenue.
11 This new mobile phone is fantastic. It .... be used anywhere in the world.
12 The shopping channel is a real boon for Liz; she adores .... buy clothes at any time of day or night!
13 I .... walk properly since I had that skiing accident.
14 Sadly, many of the indigenous people .... resist the diseases brought by the European settlers.
15 The non-fiction section .... be found on the third floor of the library.

2 16.1, 16.2

Match the situations (A–D) with the sentences (1–4).

A Samantha is going to work at a ticket agency next year.
B Judy went to the theatre yesterday and told the box office clerk that she was a theatre critic.
C Liz went to the theatre yesterday to buy some tickets. They didn't tell her about the special 'free ticket' offer.
D Carol works at a ticket agency.

1 She was able to get free tickets.
2 She can get free tickets.
3 She will be able to get free tickets.
4 She could have got free tickets.

A ☐ B ☐ C ☐ D ☐

3 16.1, 16.2

Match the two parts (1–4 and A–D) to form sentences.

1 He could do it
2 He couldn't do it
3 He might have done it
4 He can't have done it

A – he had plenty of opportunity.
B – he wasn't even in the country.
C – he seems a very capable person.
D – he doesn't look old enough.

4 16.1, 16.2

Finish each of the following sentences in such a way that it is as similar as possible in meaning to the sentence printed before it. You must use a suitable form of *can*, *could*, *may* or *might* in each sentence. The exercise begins with an example (0).

0 I was absolutely thrilled when I heard about your engagement.
I *couldn't have been more thrilled when I heard about your engagement.*

1 I'm very angry with you – you knew I was having problems with the car and you didn't bother to help me!
You ....

2 Twenty years ago my neighbour offered me his apartment for $30,000 but I didn't buy it.
Twenty years ago I ....

3 It would be possible for us to issue the tickets today if you gave us your credit card number.
We ....

4 The service in British restaurants is sometimes quite surly.
The service ....

5 Might the disparity in the figures be due to a computer error?
Is it ....

6 Don't worry, they'll probably be on the next train.
They ....

7 I'm certain he isn't responsible for the error; he looks too experienced.
He ....

8 Perhaps the shuttle bus isn't working at the moment – it is the low season.
The shuttle bus ....

9 It's so annoying. You knew their phone number but you didn't give it to me!
You ....

10 I'm afraid it isn't possible to grow bananas in the British climate.
Unfortunately, you ....

11 Given some luck, our team has a good chance of winning the championship next month.
With any luck ....

12 Perhaps Jim took it; he was in the office all day yesterday.
Jim ....

13 It's possible that the results will have arrived by tomorrow lunchtime.
The results ....

14 Who do you think is making all that noise next door?
Who ....

15 Perhaps there are other intelligent life-forms in the universe.
There ....

16 Thanks to satellite technology, it is now possible to predict hurricanes quite accurately.
We ....

17 The lights are off so maybe he isn't at home.
He ....

18 With a little bit of luck my sister has the potential to be a huge star.
My sister ....

19 They offered Carrie a job in New York, but she didn't want to work there.
Carrie ....

20 I would never be able to live in a house without a garden.
I ....

5 16.1, 16.2

Complete the following article by writing the missing words. Use no more than two words for each space. The exercise begins with an example (0).

The worst experience of my life? I (0) ......*can*...... remember it as if it were yesterday.

I was staying at a beautiful hotel on the coast. My room was on the second floor. It was about two o'clock on my first night when I suddenly woke up. There was a very strong smell of burning but I (1) ..... tell where it was coming from. I jumped out of bed, ran to the door and opened it. I (2) ..... see smoke coming from the staircase. I suppose I (3) ..... tried to run down the stairs, but I knew I wouldn't have made it. It was impossible, the smoke was too dense, I (4) ..... got further than the first landing before choking.

I went back into my room, slammed the door behind me and ran to the window. I had to escape. I (5) ..... jumped out of the window but I felt too scared. It was too high, I needed something to climb down. Suddenly I had a brainwave and ran over to the bed. By tying the bedsheets together I (6) ..... make a kind of ladder. I tied one end of the sheets to the foot of the bed and I threw the other end out of the opened window. Despite my fear of heights I (7) ..... climb out onto the window ledge. A small group of people had gathered on the ground and were shouting encouragement to me.

'Come on,' they said, 'you (8) ..... do it!' I was shaking with fear, but by refusing to look down and concentrating on the rope in my hands I eventually (9) ..... lowering myself from the ledge. Very slowly, putting one hand below the other, I (10) ..... climb down the bedsheet rope to safety.

6 16.3, 16.4

Choose the correct description, A or B.

1 They allowed me to bring my dog.
A They usually allow dogs. B They don't usually allow dogs.

2 The doctor could see you at eleven.
A I'm not sure if she's free at eleven. B I'm suggesting a time for an appointment.

3 Might I borrow your calculator for a moment?
A Talking to your best friend. B Talking to a clerk at the bank.

4 Well, we could always go on the bus.
A I don't really mind how we get there. B I really want to go on the bus.

5 I could wear anything I liked.
A When I worked as a secretary. B On the day I took my secretarial exams.

6 We can have a look at the shops.
A I'm making a suggestion. B I'm describing a future ability.

7 May I interrupt?
A At a formal business meeting. B At a family lunch.

8 You may not bring drinks into the auditorium during the performance.
A It's up to you to decide. B It's forbidden.

9 I might see you after the show.
A I probably will see you. B I'm not sure if I'll see you or not.

10 We might as well go straight home.
A There's nothing better to do. B I really want to go home.

7 ALL

Fill the gaps in the dialogue using a suitable form of *can, could, may, might, be able to, manage to* or *succeed in* and a form of the verb in brackets. The exercise begins with an example (0).

MIKE So how are the wedding arrangements going, Jane?

JANE Not too bad. We're seeing the vicar tomorrow so Harry and I (0) ...*will be able to ask*... (ask) him about hiring the church hall for the reception.

MIKE It would be great if you (1) .... (get) that place, it's an ideal venue.

JANE Yes, I know. Although it (2) .... (be) a bit too small if all our friends turn up!

MIKE It holds about a hundred people, doesn't it?

JANE Well, in fact it (3) .... (accommodate) up to a hundred and twenty-five, apparently. But there are about a hundred and forty on our guest list. It's a bit of a Catch-22 situation because I (4) .... (not/invite) people until the reception is organised, but I (5) .... (not/organise) a venue until I know how many people are coming!

MIKE Some of Harry's cousins live in the States, don't they?

JANE Yes. I'm not sure if they're coming. It's quite an expensive trip so they (6) .... (not/make) it over here. But I'm hoping at least some of them will come.

MIKE They (7) .... (always/get) one of those cheap charter flights. I've seen a lot of them advertised on the Internet recently.

JANE Oh, I think Harry (8) .... (tell) them about that already. He said he'd sent them some Internet links.

MIKE What about catering? Have you made any plans yet?

JANE I've arranged something with *Quality Caterers* in the High Street.

MIKE Oh, I wish I'd known that before! I (9) .... (speak) to Liz Brown for you when I saw her last Tuesday. She's the manager there and she goes to the same tennis club as me. You never know, I (10) .... (even/get) you a discount!

JANE That's a pity. Still, they've given us a pretty good deal. By the way, Mike, there is one favour I wanted to ask you.

MIKE Sure. What is it?

JANE (11) .... (we/borrow) your video camera?

MIKE Of course. You (12) .... (have) the tripod as well, if you like.

JANE Harry dropped his camera when we were in Tenerife. And since we've been back he (13) .... (not/find) anyone around here to fix it.

MIKE What about music at the reception? Are you going to get a band?

JANE No, we (14) .... (not/have) live music at the church hall, it doesn't have a licence. But we (15) .... (have) a disco.

MIKE You (16) .... (always/ask) Jackie Branson, she's got one of those mobile disco things.

JANE I didn't know that! I (17) .... (speak) to her about it yesterday – she was at my aerobics class. I thought she'd given up disc-jockeying ages ago.

MIKE Well, I suppose she (18) .... (give/it/up)when the kids were very young, but I'm pretty sure she's back doing it now.

JANE I expect she'll be at the aerobics class next week; so I (19) .... (ask) her about it then. Oh, that reminds me. Harry wondered why you weren't at football practice on Wednesday.

MIKE It's that awful car of mine – it just wouldn't start on Wednesday. Luckily, Jim down the road (20) .... (fix) it, although it took him two hours!

17 Modal verbs (2)

must, should, ought to, have to, need to

English has a number of different ways of expressing the concepts of obligation and necessity, prohibition, recommendation and logical deduction. This unit looks at the different modal verbs, as well as some common non-modal verbs and phrases, which we use to express these concepts. (For other modal verbs ▶ **Units 16 and 18**).

17.1 OBLIGATION AND NECESSITY

17.1A
Forms

	must	*have (got) to*	*need to*	*should/ought to*
present	*must*	*has/have (got) to*	*need/needs to*	*should/ought to*
past	*had to*	*had (got) to*	*needed to*	*should/ought to have (done)*
future	*must*	*will have to*	*will need to*	*should/ought to*

Must, *should* and *ought to* are modal verbs (unlike *need to* and *have to*). They do not change form in the present tense, nor do they have a past tense or a future form with *will*, nor infinitive or participle forms. As an alternative to *must* or when we can't use *must* (e.g. to refer to the past), we usually use *have to*:

- Past: *The staff and students at the university* ***had to*** *evacuate the campus.*
- Future: *The Council* ***must/will have to*** *find ways of cutting costs next year.*
- Infinitive: *It's difficult* ***to have to*** *stand by and watch your child in pain.*
- Participle: ***Having to*** *listen to hip-hop music all evening is my idea of torture!*

We can express a past meaning of *should* and *ought to* by using a modal perfect:
They really ***should/ought to have consulted*** *their shareholders first.*

Need can be used as a modal verb (without *to*), usually in negatives and questions:
Need *you shout so? I'm right next to you!*
We ***needn't*** *bother making the bed. The maid will do it.*

As an alternative to *need*, we can use *need to* or *have to*:
Do *you* ***need to/have to*** *shout so?*
We ***don't need to/have to*** *bother making the bed.*

We can use *must*, *have to* and *need to* with a passive phrase:
Democracy ***must/has to be seen*** *to work.*
Pulses ***need to be cooked*** *thoroughly to eradicate the toxins in them.*

17.1B
Obligation

We usually express obligation in English with *must* or *have to*:
You ***must*** *arrive in good time for the meeting tomorrow. The MD will be there.*
Everyone ***has to*** *register their name and address in order to be able to vote.*

The difference in meaning between *have to* and *must* can be fine and often depends on whether or not the speaker sees the obligation as one they are imposing. We use *have to* to express an obligation we see as outside our control, e.g. rules imposed by an authority:
Students ***have to*** *wear school uniforms in the sixth form.*

We often use *must* to express an obligation imposed by the speaker:
I ***must*** *get up earlier – I waste so much time in the mornings.*

Must is commonly used for the following situations:

- To give a strong personal opinion: *I believe people* ***must*** *vote at elections.*
- To impose an obligation on oneself: *I really* ***must*** *lose some weight.*
- To give instructions: *The electricity* ***must*** *always* ***be switched off*** *before repairs are attempted.* (In giving instructions, *must* is often used with a passive verb.)

❗ However, *must* expresses a strong obligation and we do not often use it in face to face conversation as it can seem impolite and often inappropriate.

We often use *should* and *ought to* as an alternative to *must* as they express a subjective (often moral) obligation felt by the speaker, but the obligation is weaker than with *must*:

*You **should** treat your neighbours with more respect.*

It is possible to use *need to* to express external obligation, particularly in the future:

*We'**ll need to** get our visas sorted out or we won't be able to stop over in the States.*

We use *have got to* for external obligation like *have to*, but it is more informal than *have to* and more common in speech than in writing (*have got to* is rare in US English):

*What time **have** we **got to** be at the airport tomorrow?*

[*Claim forms **have got to** be date-stamped before payment will be made.*]

✔ *Claim forms **have to** be date-stamped before payment will be made.*

We use *should/ought to* + *have* + past participle for an unfulfilled obligation in the past:

*You really **should have/ought to have registered** before term started.*

*The record was finally released eighteen months later than it **should have been**.*

17.1C Necessity

We can use *need to*, *must* and *have to* to express necessity (i.e. a requirement that results from things other than just commands, rules or laws):

*All living beings **need to/must/have to** take in sustenance in order to live.*

*I really **need to/must/have to** get some more sleep. I'm always exhausted.*

❗ It is possible, though quite rare today, to use *need* without *to* in questions:

***Need** he really play his music so loudly?*

If we want to express a necessity without suggesting who should deal with it, we can use *need* + *-ing* form: *That poor bird – his cage really **needs cleaning**.*

This use has a passive meaning and is similar to the passive infinitive (▶ **8.2B**):

*That poor bird – his cage really **needs to be cleaned**.*

17.1D Other ways of expressing obligation

We can use *be to* for an order from a person in authority (▶ **5.1A**):

*The members of the jury **are to** report to the judge's chambers.*

We use *be obliged to* (US: *obligated to*) or *required to* in formal contexts.

*We're **obliged to** contribute twenty-five per cent of the costs of the repairs.*

*Motorists **are required** by law **to** wear seat belts in the European Union.*

We use *be supposed to* for a lesser obligation and one that is frequently ignored:

*We'**re supposed to** leave our textbooks at school, but we often take them home.*

We use *be liable to* for obligation (often in a legal context):

*Anyone causing damage **will be liable to** pay for all necessary repairs.*

17.2 PROHIBITION AND CRITICISM

17.2A Forms

	must not	***cannot***	**other forms**	***should not/ought not to***
present	*mustn't (have)*	*can't*	*may not* *is/are not allowed to*	*shouldn't* *oughtn't to*
past		*couldn't*	*was/were not allowed to*	*shouldn't have (done)* *oughtn't to have (done)*
future	*mustn't*	*cannot*	*may not* *will not be allowed to*	*shouldn't* *oughtn't to*

17.2B Meaning and use

We use *must not* (usually *mustn't*) to express a prohibition (an obligation not to do something) imposed by the speaker or writer:

*You **mustn't** touch that kettle. It's hot!*

To express a weaker, often moral prohibition, we use *shouldn't* or *oughtn't to*:

*You really **shouldn't/oughtn't to** speak to your mother like that!*

We tend to use *shouldn't* more often than *oughtn't to*.

To express prohibition by an external authority we often use other modal verbs or non-modal expressions. *Mustn't* may appear too strong in these situations:

*Guests **may not** use the pool after 11 p.m.* (formal ▶ **16.4A**)

*Women **can't/aren't allowed to** drive in some Arab countries.* (▶ **16.4A, B**)

❶ It is possible, though not common, to use *must not have* + past participle for a present prohibition which relates to the past:

*Entrants must be aged 16 to 25 and **must not have done** any professional modelling.* (The modelling is in the past, but the prohibition is in the present.)

We use *couldn't* or *wasn't/weren't allowed to* for prohibition in the past:

*We **couldn't** go into the disco because we were too young.*

*Journalists were shown the disused buildings but they **weren't allowed to** enter them.*

We use *shouldn't/ought not to have* + past participle to criticise a past action:

*You **shouldn't have driven** through that red light. You could have caused an accident.*

We usually use *won't be allowed to* or *can't* to express prohibition in the future:

*Let's eat before we go. We **won't be allowed to/can't** take food into the auditorium.*

17.3 ABSENCE OF OBLIGATION OR NECESSITY

17.3A Forms

	not have to	*need not*
present	*do/does not have to*	*need not, do/does not need to*
past	*did not have to*	*did not need to, need not have (done)*
future	*will not have to*	*will not need to, need not*

17.3B Meaning and use

We usually use *don't have to/don't need to* to express a lack of external obligation:

✗ ~~*You mustn't pay to visit most museums in Britain.*~~

✓ *You **don't have/need to** pay to visit most museums in Britain.* (Entrance is free.)

We use *don't need to/needn't* for absence of necessity felt by the speaker. *Needn't* tends to express the speaker's personal opinion more:

*We **needn't/don't need to** put the heating on yet; it's not cold enough.*

We use *didn't have to/didn't need to* for absence of obligation in the past:

*You **didn't have to/didn't need to** finish the washing-up. I could have done it.*

❶ *Need* has two past forms: *didn't need to* and *needn't have done*. We use *didn't need to* when we don't know if the action happened or not:

*We **didn't need to** take warm sweaters, as the weather was so good.* (We don't know if the speaker took warm sweaters or not.)

We use *needn't have* + past participle when the action happened but was unnecessary:

*We **needn't have taken** warm sweaters. We could have used the space in our luggage for more books!* (We know that the speaker took warm sweaters.)

We use *won't have to*, *won't need to* or *needn't* for absence of obligation in the future:

*With one of the new generation of food processors, cooks **won't have to/won't need to/needn't** peel or chop any more.*

17.4 RECOMMENDATION AND ADVICE

17.4A Forms

	must	*should*	*ought to*	*had better*
present	*must (not)*	*should (not)*	*ought (not) to*	*had better (not)*
future	*must (not)*	*should (not)*	*ought (not) to*	*had better (not)*

17.4B Meaning and use

We use *must* for strong recommendations and advice:

*You really **must** read Sebastian Faulks's latest book. It's stunning!*

*You **must** do something about that cough. Please go and see the doctor.*

Note that with this use *must* is usually heavily stressed in speech.

Recommendation or advice with *should* or *ought to* is less emphatic:

Even people as young as twenty-five ***should*** *consider a personal pension.*

Children ***ought not to*** *spend long periods in front of a computer screen.*

We often use *should* and *ought to* with the passive:

The underlying shift in public opinion ***ought not to*** *be exaggerated.*

Had better (not) expresses the best thing to do in a particular situation. It often has a sense of urgency and can be a warning or a threat:

*If the burglars took your keys, you****'d better*** *change the locks in case they come back.*

Your dog ***had better not*** *dig up my rose bush again!*

17.5 LOGICAL DEDUCTION AND PROBABILITY

17.5A Forms

	must	***have (got) to***	***should***
present	*must*	*have (got) to*	*should (not)*
past	*must have* + past participle	*had (got) to*	*should (not) have* + past participle
future	*must*	*have (got) to*	*should (not)*

In this sense, we can also use *must, have to* and *should* with the continuous:

That disco is so loud. You ***must be damaging*** *your ears when you go there.*

You ***have got to be joking****! That was not a foul!*

The accused ***should not have been driving*** *at 80 in a built-up area.*

17.5B Meaning and use

We use *must* for something that we believe to be true because of evidence (i.e. we are making a logical deduction):

This ***must*** *be the place – it's the only restaurant in the street.*

I thought the eclipse was today, but it ***must*** *be happening tomorrow.*

The opposite of *must* in this sense is *can't*, not *mustn't* (▶ **16.2A**):

This ***can't*** *be the place – there's no one inside and there are no lights on.*

It is possible to use *have (got) to* for emphatic logical deduction:

There ***has (got) to*** *be some mistake. I didn't order this furniture.*

We use *must have* + past participle to express a logical deduction about the past:

There was a terrific noise last night. It ***must have been*** *an explosion.*

I couldn't wake you this morning. You ***must have been*** *sleeping really soundly.*

The negative of this is *can't/couldn't have* + past participle (▶ **16.2B**).

Note the difference between the two past forms *must have* + past participle and *had to*:

The Corrs' new single has been played non-stop. You ***must have heard*** *it!* (deduction)

I've always loved The Corrs and when I heard they had a new single out, I ***had to*** *hear it!* (obligation imposed by the speaker)

We use *should/ought to* for probability and *shouldn't/ought not to* for improbability. (For probability with *may* and *might* ▶ **16.2**.) We believe the statement to be true because of our prior knowledge, experience or present evidence:

The plane ***should*** *be landing about now.*

There ***shouldn't*** *be problems with traffic at that time of the evening.*

! We rarely use *should* to 'predict' a negative (unpleasant) situation. Instead we use *will*:

✗ ~~*There* ***should*** *be problems with traffic at that time. The roads* ***should*** *be awful.*~~

✓ *There****'ll*** *be problems with traffic at that time. The roads* ***will*** *be awful.*

We use *should (not)/ought (not) to* + *have* + past participle to talk about the probability of an action in the past:

I don't know where our main speaker can be. He ***should have arrived*** *hours ago.*

▶ **Pages 198 and 199 for Round up of modal verbs**

Practice

The key to these exercises is on page 362.

1 17.1

Complete the dialogue with the best words or phrases from the box. Use each word or phrase once only.

do I have to	had to	has to	have to	having to	must
need to	needs	obliged to	should	supposed to	will have to

BETH Hello. Reception said that you wanted a word with me.

LISA That's right. I'm interested in joining your gym. What (1) .... do?

BETH Take a seat. First, you (2) .... fill in this form. It asks for details about you and your state of health. We want to be sure that you're fit enough to use the gym.

LISA OK ... I have a slight problem with one knee. I twisted it a few weeks ago.

BETH Well, you really (3) .... tell the instructor about that, then he'll make sure that your fitness programme takes account of it.

LISA Fitness programme?

BETH Yes. If you join, you (4) .... have an induction session with one of our fitness instructors. He'll design a programme suited to your level of fitness.

LISA Oh, that's good. Now, it's £30 a month, isn't it?

BETH Well, yes, but that's the special rate if you take out an annual subscription, so you're (5) .... join for the whole year to get that rate. Otherwise it's £40 a month.

LISA I see. Yes, I think I'll join for the year. Is there anything else I should know?

BETH Let's see ... there are some rules, but they're pretty obvious. Of course, everyone (6) .... wear appropriate clothes and footwear. There are lockers outside the gym, so you're not (7) .... take anything in with you, but we don't apply that rule very strictly. You'll probably want to take a towel and a bottle of water in with you anyway: you (8) .... drink plenty of water while you're exercising, to prevent dehydration.

LISA Yes ... are there any restrictions, like (9) .... book time ahead in the evenings?

BETH No. You can use the gym whenever it's open. Obviously, if you think a piece of equipment isn't working properly and (10) .... mending, tell an instructor. Also, for your own good, you (11) .... tell us if you feel unsure about how to use a particular machine.

LISA Of course. Now, the receptionist said I (12) .... provide a photo for the membership card, but I'm afraid I don't have one on me.

BETH That's OK. Bring it next time you come. Until then you can use your receipt as proof of membership.

2 17.1–17.3

Read the letter on the next page and decide which word or phrase below fits each space. In each case, only one answer is possible. Circle the letters you choose. The first one is given as an example (0).

	A	B	C
0	A must not	B cannot	(C) need not
1	A need not have	B must not have	C had to
2	A mustn't have	B shouldn't have	C needn't have
3	A could not	B did not need to	C needed to
4	A are to	B are obliged to	C aren't allowed to
5	A must not	B are liable to	C must
6	A are required to	B do not have to	C need to

	A	B	C
7	A need not	B do not need to	C have to
8	A need to	B do not have to	C must not
9	A are not supposed to	B are not obliged to	C need not
10	A had to	B will have to	C are to
11	A shouldn't be allowed	B oughtn't be allowed	C needn't allowing
12	A need not have been	B must not have been	C did not have to be

Hilverstone Fox Watch

Dear New Member,

Many thanks for your application form for membership of the HFW (Hilverstone Fox Watch). Before I introduce the club to you, I would like to point out that you (0) ... pay your subscription until your membership application has been processed and approved, so those of you who joined at the fete last Saturday (1) ... provided cheques on the spot. Our representative (2) ... accepted your cheques. I am returning them where necessary, with apologies for any inconvenience.

HFW was set up three years ago for two reasons: to lobby for the abolition of fox-hunting – the founder members felt we (3) ... do this as the Hilverstone Hunt is so powerful in this area – but also to provide some protection for the urban foxes here, who (4) ... subsist on household scraps in some cases. Our meetings are fortnightly but please do not feel that you (5) ... attend each one. All our members, however, (6) ... attend six meetings a year and at least two all-night watches. We (7) ... insist upon this to prevent all of the work from falling on the shoulders of a few people.

One or two words of advice: a lot of people interested in foxes attempt to domesticate them by putting food down for them. Please – you (8) ... do this. For one thing, we (9) ... encourage vermin under local by-laws (and foxes are classed as vermin), but also, we (10) ... try to reintroduce these foxes to their natural habitat, as they are not naturally domestic creatures. Please remember also that female foxes with young cubs can be quite aggressive: children in particular (11) ... to go near them at this potentially dangerous time.

Finally, may I remind you that members of HFW (12) ... involved in the Hilverstone Hunt for at least one year prior to joining.

Thank you once again for your interest. I enclose a timetable of our meetings and events for the next three months, and look forward to welcoming you to one of them.

Yours faithfully,
Jonathan Harker

3 17.1–17.4

Complete texts A–C with an appropriate verb or expression. Use the information in the box to help you. The first one is given as an example (0).

REQUIREMENTS OF COURSE			
course	**important**	**advisable**	**unnecessary**
A	keyboarding skills	access to a computer	prior publishing experience
B	previous experience	keyboarding skills	own computer
C	three GCSEs	good level of English	prior publishing experience/computer skills

A DESK-TOP PUBLISHING
Ten-week intensive course for people interested in producing small-scale publications. Applicants for this course (0) ..*must*... have good keyboarding skills but are not (1) .... to have prior publishing experience. If possible, applicants (2) .... have access to a computer and Microsoft Publisher, but there are a limited number of machines available at the college.

B DESK-TOP PUBLISHING
Learn how to self-publish from the professionals! We offer Desk-top Publishing courses to suit all schedules and budgets, from five-week intensive courses to year-long evening courses. You (3) .... have your own computer (on our full-time courses) but you (4) .... have some previous experience in publishing. You (5) .... be able to use a keyboard. Call us on 01202 867349

C DESK-TOP PUBLISHING
One-year course. Applicants (6) .... have previous experience in publishing, as part of the course involves work experience with a local printing company. Equally, you are not (7) .... to have good computer skills as all basic training is provided. A minimum of three GCSEs is (8) .... and applicants (9) .... have a good level of English.

4 17.5

Write four statements making deductions about each picture. Use the words and phrases underneath the pictures. The first one is given as an example (0).

▶

0 (daughter) They must ...*be waiting for their daughter*...
1 (on/train) She can't ....
2 (miss/it) She must ....
3 (child/mother) She must ....
4 (phone/parents) She can't ....

◀

5 (rain) It must ....
6 (slip/banana skin) The man must ....
....
7 (not/wife) She can't ....
8 (ambulance) Someone must ....

5 ALL

For each of the sentences below, write a new sentence as similar in meaning as possible to the original sentence, but using the word(s) given. The word(s) must not be altered in any way.

0 It looks certain that the orchestra's instruments are arriving on a later plane.
must ....*The orchestra's instruments must be arriving on a later plane.*........................

1 I strongly recommend you to try this sundried tomato bread.
must ....

2 There is no obligation to get an international driving licence for this country.
have ....

3 It was stupid of the government to try to break the strike.
should ....

4 I warn you not to chat up my girlfriend again!
had ....

5 We didn't book the table but it didn't matter as there was hardly anyone in the restaurant anyway.
need ....

6 My hair's much too long. I'll have to get it cut soon.
cutting ....

7 It is essential that you disconnect the gas supply before removing the boiler.
be disconnected ....

8 The management will not permit latecomers to enter the theatre until there is a suitable break.
allowed ....

9 Why do we have to state ethnic origin on official forms these days?
required ....

10 There can be no doubt that the solicitor has received the information by now.
must ....

11 It probably won't be difficult to get tickets for the first night.
should ....

12 It is essential that patients have not eaten or drunk anything for three hours before the operation.
must ....

6 ALL

Underline six more mistakes to do with modal verbs or expressions from this unit, then correct them.

Minutes of Holmefield NeighbourCare meeting

Sergeant Dibden reminded us that we don't have to tackle a burglar if one enters our home as this can be very dangerous. He also reminded us that we are supposed by law to inform the police and our insurance companies of all keyholders after a break-in. ....*mustn't*.......

Mrs Sanders from Twyfield Close reported that she had been burgled two afternoons before. The burglar should have got in through an open downstairs window, although at that time of day there must be plenty of people around who witnessed the break-in. You'd better report it to the police if you saw anything as it's our civic duty.

Mr Harrison from Dukes Avenue was concerned that he hadn't taken up an invitation from a security company to assess his house for security risks, but he was relieved to discover from Sergeant Dibden that he needn't have invited them anyway, as the police can do security checks.

Finally, remember, if you need speak to a police officer, you can call Sergeant Dibden at Holmefield police station at any time.

18 Modal verbs (3)

will, would, shall

Learners of English often think of *will* as a way of expressing the future (▶ **Unit 4**) and of *would* as a word which is used mainly in conditional sentences (▶ **Unit 10**), but we use both of these modal verbs to express a number of other meanings. This unit also looks at *shall* which, although it is the least-used modal in English, we can use to express a variety of meanings.

18.1 PREDICTION AND CERTAINTY

18.1A Predictions about the future

We use *will/won't* to make predictions about the future (▶ **4.1A**):

*He's been found guilty of murder. He'**ll** be in prison for a long time.*
*You must work hard for this exam. It **won't** be easy.*

18.1B Past predictions about the future

Sometimes we wish to express a prediction about the future that someone made in the past. For this we often use *would/wouldn't* (*would* is the past form of *will*):

*We had to hurry to get him to the hospital. We knew it **would** be too late otherwise.*

This use of *would* is related to the use of *would* in reported speech (▶ **9.2E**):

*I'm sure the Lions **will** win the rugby series this year.* → *She was sure the Lions **would** win the rugby series.*

18.1C Certainty about the present

We make confident 'predictions' about the present based on our knowledge or previous experience (or on current expectations) with *will/won't*:

*'Rachel's in Turkey at the moment.' 'I hope she's taken some winter clothes because it **won't** be warm at this time of year.'*

Compare this use of *will* and the present simple. We use the present simple to state a fact without expressing an opinion as to the certainty or otherwise of the event:

*Janet isn't here at the moment. She'**s** in France.* (Fact – the speaker knows it's true.)

To say that we believe something is certain, we use *will/won't*:

*It's five o'clock. Janet'**ll** be in Paris now.* (Certainty – the speaker believes it's true.)

To express a certainty about something ongoing (i.e. where we would use the present continuous for a fact), we use *will/won't + be + -ing* form:

*Jason is sympathetic because he knows his successor **will be having** a hard time at the moment.*

18.1D Certainty about the past

To refer to something which we feel certain has happened (but do not actually know), we use *will have* + past participle:

*We sent the invitations on Monday, so they **will have received** them by now. Why hasn't anyone replied?*

This is similar to *must have* + past participle (▶ **17.5B**):

*We sent the invitations on Monday, so they **must have received** them by now.*

We use *won't have* + past participle to refer to something which we feel certain has not happened:

*We sent the invitations by second-class post. They **won't have received** them yet.*

❗ We do not use *mustn't have* + past participle in this way (▶ **17.5B**, ▶ **16.2B**), but we can use *can't have*:

✘ ~~*We sent the invitations by second-class post. They **mustn't have received** them yet.*~~
✔ *We sent the invitations by second-class post. They **can't have received** them yet.*

18.2 CHARACTERISTICS, HABITS AND ROUTINES

18.2A Present

We often use *will/won't* to talk about actions that have become so routine that they are predictable:

*Every lesson is the same: he'**ll** sit down, get his books out and then he'**ll** start giving us instructions. He **won't** greet us or show any interest in us.*

We can extend this use of *will* to talk about habits and characteristics:

*The public **will** always side with the nurses in any dispute.*

*The dominant male of the group **will not** tolerate the presence of other males.*

We can also use the present simple to describe characteristics and habits:

*The public always **sides with** the nurses in any dispute.*

*The dominant male of the group **does not tolerate** the presence of other males.*

We often use *will* when talking about the characteristics of capacity or ability:

*The Olympic stadium in Sydney **will** hold 110,000 people.*

*This model **will** do 0 to 100 kilometres per hour in eight seconds.*

It is also possible to use *can* and the present simple for these last two uses with no change in meaning:

*The Olympic stadium in Sydney **can hold/holds** 110,000 people.*

*This model **can do/does** 0 to 100 kilometres per hour in eight seconds.*

We use *will* (not the present simple) to describe an annoying habit or to make a criticism:

*We enjoy going out with Frank and Carol, but they **will argue** in public!*

❶ We do not contract *will* when we use it to describe an annoying habit – we stress it:

✗ ~~*Geoff'**ll** leave the lights on when he's last out of the office.*~~

✓ *Geoff **will** leave the lights on when he's last out of the office!*

We often use *will/won't* to criticise inanimate objects in this way:

*Whatever I do, my car **won't** start first time on cold mornings.*

To state a simple fact with no (or little) annoyance, we use the present simple:

*My car **doesn't start/never starts** first time on cold mornings.*

My car won't start first time on cold mornings.

18.2B Past

We use *would/wouldn't* to talk about habits in the past (▶ **2.5B**):

*Every lesson was the same: he'**d** sit down and get his books out, then he'**d** start giving us instructions. He **wouldn't** greet us or show any interest in us.*

We can use *would/wouldn't* to criticise or talk about annoying habits in the past:

*I miss Dad, even though he **would** always tell me how to run my life!*

❶ We do not usually contract *would* to *'d* when we use it in this way; we stress it:

*When Alan was a toddler he **would** cling on to me whenever a stranger came in.*

However, we do not always stress *would* when it is followed by an adverb:

*My boss was awful: he'**d invariably** find something for me to do at five o'clock.*

We can use *would/wouldn't* to talk about inanimate objects (▶ **18.2A**):

*The car **would** never start on winter mornings when we were in Sweden.*

18.3 WILLINGNESS AND REFUSAL

18.3A Present/future willingness and refusal

We use *will* to express willingness to do something:

*The doctor **will** act as a witness to your signature. She doesn't mind doing that sort of thing.*

We can use it to express *be willing to*. In this sense, we can use *will/won't* in the *if* clause of a first conditional (▶ **10.3A**):

*If you'**ll** take a seat for a moment, Mr Franks will be with you soon.* (If you are willing to take a seat for a moment, ...)

We use *won't/shan't* to express unwillingness or refusal to do something:

*The PA **won't** book my flights. She says it isn't in her job description.*
*'Go and buy some milk, will you, love?' 'No, I **shan't**. I'm busy.'*

18.3B Past willingness and refusal

We use *would/wouldn't* to show willingness or refusal in the past. We use *would* in the affirmative only to refer to general willingness (i.e. a habit):

*Dad **would** always help us with our maths homework.*

❗ We do not use *would* in the affirmative to express willingness to do something on a single occasion in the past:

✗ ~~*The tour guide was very helpful. She **would contact** the Consulate for me when I lost my passport.*~~

✔ *The tour guide was very helpful. She **contacted/offered to contact** the Consulate for me when I lost my passport.*

We can use *would not* for refusal on a single occasion in the past:

*The shop assistant **wouldn't** change this jumper for me, even though I hadn't worn it.*

18.4 OTHER USES OF *WILL/SHALL/WOULD*

18.4A Offers and promises

We can use both *will* and *shall* to make offers. We use *will* in the affirmative, both to make offers to do something ourselves and on behalf of other people:

*Sit down. I'**ll** wash up this evening.*
*Your car sounds a bit rough. Harry **will** take a quick look at it, if you like.*

We use *shall* in questions to make more tentative offers than with *will* in the affirmative:

***Shall** I wash up this evening?*

We use *will* to make promises:

*My government **will** turn round the economy and reduce unemployment.*

We can use *would*, *will* or *won't* when we offer something to another person:

***Would** you have/like some more of the pie?* (neutral)
***Will** you have some more of the pie?* (neutral)
***Won't** you have some more of the pie?* (more encouraging)

18.4B Suggestions

We use *shall* in questions with *we* to make suggestions:

***Shall we** go out for a curry tonight?* (= Why don't we ...?/How about ...?)

To ask for suggestions or advice, we can use *shall* with a question word:

***What shall we** do about Tom if he doesn't get into a university?*

US English uses *should* in preference to *shall* for suggestions:

*Let's decide what to do this evening. **Should we** go bowling?*

❗ We use *shall* in question tags after *let's* (▶ **7.2B**):

***Let's** forget about it now and talk about something else, **shall we**?*

❗ We use *would* in suggestions or responding to invitations if we want to be more tentative or distant:

*It **would** be a good idea to get together one evening.*
*'Come to dinner on Sunday.' 'That **would** be nice. I'll let you know.'*

18.4C Requests

We often make requests with *will*. These requests are informal and we usually use them only with people we know quite well (*can* ▶ **16.3B**):

__Will__ you give me a call when you get to the hotel?

We use *would* to make requests more tentative or polite, or to request things of people we do not know so well:

__Would__ you lend me the car tomorrow night, Dad?

__Would__ you fill in this form, please, sir? (*could* ▶ **16.3B**)

We can make a request more insistent by using *will you* as a question tag:

Come and look at this, __will you?__

If we make a request in this way, we do not expect the answer to be 'no':

Pick up my suit from the cleaner's when you're out, __will you?__

18.4D Orders and instructions

We use *will* and *shall* for orders and formal instructions. We use *shall* for more formal instructions, especially in official documents:

You __will/shall__ all stay behind for thirty minutes and clean this room.

The secretary __shall__ minute the proceedings of each meeting.

We also use *shall/will* for rules, for example of examinations and competitions:

The judge's decision __shall__ be final.

18.4E Disagreeing

We can use *would/wouldn't* to show disagreement in a polite way:

I __wouldn't__ say that.

I __wouldn't__ go that far.

18.4F Expressing desires and preferences

We often use *would* with verbs of liking and preference (*like*, *love*, *prefer*, etc.) to express desires and preferences which we think we can realise:

We__'d love__ to come to your wedding on 6th September. Thank you for the invitation.

I__'d prefer__ to lose weight by a tried and tested method than by a new trendy diet.

We can use *would* with *rather* to express a preference (▶ **11.2E**):

Our delegates __would rather not__ stay at the conference centre.

❗ Note that we can use an object with these forms:

I __would like you__ to listen to me when I'm talking!

18.5 HYPOTHETICAL *WOULD*

18.5A Hypothetical desires about the present/future

We use *would* with *be* or verbs of liking and wishing to express a desire for the present or future. Fulfilment of the desire is impossible or improbable:

It __would be__ so nice to live by the sea. (The speaker doesn't live by the sea.)

I __would prefer__ to be a man. (The speaker is a woman.)

To state a simple fact, we use the present simple:

It __is__ nice to live by the sea.

We can use the present simple (*like*) to talk about something we currently like and do, but we use *would like* to talk about an unfulfilled desire:

I __like__ to stay in five-star hotels. (I do stay in five-star hotels and enjoy it.)

I __would like__ to stay in five-star hotels. (I don't stay in them, but it's my desire.)

Wish + *would* expresses a desire for another person (not) to do something:

I __wish you wouldn't__ talk with your mouth full! (▶ **11.3C**)

18.5B Hypothetical desires about the past

If we want to comment on a hypothetical situation in the past, we use *would/wouldn't* + *have* + past participle:

It __would have been__ a good idea to notify us in advance of your intentions.

(= The person did not notify anyone in advance.)

❗ British English often uses the perfect infinitive here (▶ **13.3A**):

[*It would have been a good idea __to have notified__ us in advance ...*]

▶ **Pages 198 and 199 for Round up of modal verbs**

Practice

The key to these exercises is on page 362.

1 18.1, 18.2

Complete these dialogues with *will*, *won't*, *would*, *wouldn't*, + *have* if necessary, and a form of the verbs in the box. The first one is given as an example (0).

argue	~~be~~	come	have	hold	prepare	say	start	stop	watch	work

0 'Sue says she's enjoying the job but she's putting on weight.'
'Yes, that ....*will be*.... because of all those long business lunches.'

1 'Are you having problems with your new camera?'
'Yes, the flash .... in semi-darkness, only when it's fully dark.'

2 'Shop assistants used to be more polite, didn't they?'
'Yes, a few years ago they .... always .... "please" and "thank you" and smile.'

3 'Surely there are too many people here to get on one plane?'
'No, a jumbo jet .... easily .... over 300 people.'

4 'I hope Josh is OK at that summer camp. He might be homesick.'
'Don't worry about him. He .... a great time!'

5 'Do you think that the jury will acquit Nick?'
'I hope so. I'm sure that his lawyer .... a solid defence.'

6 'I don't think this new secretary is as good as Janice was.'
'I don't know. Janice .... always .... whenever you pointed out errors in her typing.'

7 'The new horse at the riding stables seems to be working out very well.'
'Quite well, but he .... and eat whenever he gets the opportunity!'

8 'Oh no, I've just noticed a mistake in the headline for the front page article!'
'Phone the printers. They .... printing it yet – they don't print until early morning.'

9 'What happened after the car broke down?'
'Well, we knew that traffic .... along that road so late, so we slept in the car.'

10 'Why are you and Jack arguing so much these days?'
'He takes me for granted. He .... TV every evening and ignore me completely.'

2 18.2, 18.3

Rewrite the underlined parts of this phone conversation, using *will*, *won't*, *would* and *wouldn't*.

JAKE 020 7543 9216.

ALICE Hi, Jake. It's Alice here.

JAKE Alice, how nice to hear from you!

ALICE Actually, Jake, I'm phoning to ask you for some advice.

JAKE (0) <u>I'm willing to help you</u> if I can, of course. ....*I'll help you*..........

ALICE Your mother receives help from the Council, doesn't she? Can you tell me what (1) <u>they agree to do</u> and what (2) <u>they don't agree to do</u> for older people?
(1) ....
(2) ....

JAKE Yes, of course. Mum has a home help. She comes three times a week. (3) <u>She's perfectly happy to do light cleaning</u> and (4) <u>she's willing to get the shopping</u>, but (5) <u>she refuses to do anything heavy</u>.
(3) ....
(4) ....
(5) ....

ALICE That's fair enough. What about cooking?

JAKE Well, when she first started (6) <u>she was happy to prepare supper</u> when she came, but she stopped that after a few weeks. ....

ALICE Why was that?

JAKE You know my mum. (7) <u>She insists on saying exactly what she thinks</u>. Apparently the home help used to make Italian food and Mum didn't like it. (8) <u>She refused to eat it</u>. Why are you asking, anyway? ....

ALICE It's Dad. He can't move around very easily now. The neighbours are great, they (9) <u>make a habit of popping in</u> now and again but (10) <u>he's unwilling to ask them for help</u> if he's in trouble. ....

JAKE Mmm. You can understand that.

ALICE Oh, but he's so impatient. I take him to the shops once a week, but yesterday (11) <u>the car refused to start</u> and I was about half an hour late. (12) <u>Was he willing to wait for me?</u> No, (13) <u>he insists on trying to cope by himself</u>! He went to the shops and collapsed on the way there. ....

JAKE Oh, dear. It's a worry, isn't it? Look, (14) <u>if you don't mind waiting for a few minutes</u>, I'll look out the phone number for the right person at social services. ....

3 18.4

Complete the dialogues below the pictures. Use *will*, *shall* or *would*.

0

STUDENT 1: *Will you pass me the dictionary, please?*
STUDENT 2: Yes, here you are.

1

WOMAN: ....
FRIEND: I won't, thanks. I'm trying to lose weight.

2

TEACHER: ....
....
STUDENTS: Oh, Miss, not another essay for homework! We've already written two this week.

3

MAN: ....
WOMAN: Oh, yes, please! We always need someone to take the minutes.

4

POLICE OFFICER: ....
THIEF: Come with you? No, why should I?

5

MAN: I don't understand what you want from me!
WOMAN: ....
MAN: But I <u>do</u> respect you!

4 18.1, 18.4, 18.5

Read the article and then decide which word or phrase A, B or C below best fills each space. Circle the letter you choose for each question. The exercise begins with an example (0).

Words, words, words

The words that caught the mood of the decade are all there in a book published yesterday – *clone, concentration camp, gene, depression* – except that the decade was not the 1990s; these words (0) ... current in the 1900s.

The *Guinness Book of the Twentieth Century* cites lists of buzzwords for each decade of the last century. At the outset of the 20th century, few people would have guessed that it (1) ... more language change than ever before. Of course, before the days of the communications revolution language evolved much more slowly. Many people today (2) ... language not to change at all, but that is an unrealistic dream in the age of the global village.

Words you (3) ... every day, such as *chatline* and *trainers*, (4) ... only thirty years ago. And a word as universal as *teenager* gained common currency only in the 1940s. Words change in meaning too: a scientist in the 1960s (5) ... *clone* to refer only to plants. And anyone who asked '(6) ... we watch the soap tonight?' would have encountered total incomprehension before the Second World War. (*Soap* was what you washed with.)

There is a more worrying side to this, if you consider that new coinage reflects the society it comes from. Only twenty years ago few people (7) ... *stalking, ethnic cleansing* or *road rage* – concepts that the world (8) ... perhaps be better without. It (9) ... nice to think that the 21st century (10) ... us happier words, but don't hold your breath!

0	(A)	would have been	B	would be	C	will have been
1	A	will bring	B	brought	C	would bring
2	A	would rather	B	would prefer	C	will prefer
3	A	will hear	B	will be hearing	C	will have heard
4	A	would not have been recognised	B	would not be recognised	C	will not recognise
5	A	wouldn't understand	B	will be understanding	C	would have understood
6	A	Won't	B	Would	C	Shall
7	A	shall have understood	B	would have understood	C	will have understood
8	A	would	B	will	C	shall
9	A	will be	B	would be	C	would have been
10	A	would bring	B	would have brought	C	will bring

5 18.4, 18.5

Read the statements from people who have or have had a disadvantaged life. Complete the sentences, expressing the people's desires and regrets about the past. Use the word in brackets.

0 We don't have running water in our homes. We have to collect water from the stream or from a pipe in the village. **(like)**
Aisha ....*would like to have running water in her home.*....

1 We live in a wooden shack outside the city. It's very small but eight of us live in it. It's my dream to live in a real house. **(prefer)**
Pedro ....

2 In my country we have to pay for medicine and a lot of people can't afford it. The government should provide free medicine. **(like)**
Esther ....

3 Every day I go into the town and I beg in the streets for money. Obviously I don't like going begging, but we need the money. **(rather)**
Sun-Li ....

4 I wear the same clothes every day. I look at models in magazines and I'm very envious of their beautiful clothes. **(be nice)**
Hana thinks it ....

5 I live in a village just outside a big city. The village is OK, but rich people from the city come and dump their rubbish in our village. It's dreadful! **(wishes)**
Sunil ....

6 I didn't go to school. My family couldn't afford to send me. So now I can only get a badly-paid job. It's such a pity, because I enjoy learning new things. **(been good)**
Maria thinks it ....

6 ALL

There are nine more mistakes in this text connected with the language in this unit. Underline the mistakes and correct them.

I'll never forget the day my life changed. It was a normal day – in those days I shall (*would*) do my homework straight after school so that I could go and listen to pop music at Janice's after dinner. So I was sitting in front of the fire, trying to keep warm. Mum was ironing. I looked at the clock.

'Dad's late,' I remarked to Mum.

'It's Thursday. He'd be visiting Granny.'

My grandmother lived in a cold, draughty cottage on the moors. Mum and Dad wanted her to move in with us, but our house was very small, and she won't. They knew that the cold winter months would have hastened her death – she already suffered from chronic bronchitis – but she was a stubborn old woman who will insist on her independence.

'Won't it be nice if we had some money? We could buy a big house and Granny could have a flat of her own in it. I hate being poor.'

'Oh, pet, I shan't say we're poor. We're not as well off as some, but we've got a roof over our heads and food in our bellies.' Mum would always see the best in every situation. It really annoyed me! 'Will I make a nice cup of tea? Your Dad would be frozen when he gets in. He'll want to save the bus fare so I'm sure he's walked all the way from your grandmother's.'

At that moment, the door opened and Dad walked in, waving a slip of paper.

'Forget the tea, Mary. We're going out tonight. First prize in the lottery. We're rich!'

Round up: Units 16–18

Modal verbs

function	time	form	example	▶
ability	present	*can*	*She **can** speak Spanish but she **can't** speak Italian.*	**16.1A**
		is/are able to	*Despite his handicap he **is able to** drive a car.*	
	past	*could*	*Mozart **could** play the piano at the age of five.*	**16.1B**
		was/were able to	*Mike's car broke down but he **was able to** repair it.*	
possibility	present	*may, might, could*	*There **may** be life on Mars.* *The rash **could** be a symptom of something more serious.*	**16.2A**
	past	*could have, might have*	*She **might have done** it; she had the opportunity and the motive.*	**16.2B**
	future	*will be able to*	*We**'ll be able to** travel to the moon but we **won't be able to** travel to Mars.*	**16.2C**
arrangements	future	*can, could, be able to*	*The doctor **could** see you at six; he **can't** see you before then as he's too busy.*	**16.3A**
permission	present/ future	*can, can't*	***'Can** I use your phone?' 'No, I'm afraid you **can't**.'*	**16.4A**
	past	*allowed to*	*I **was allowed to** leave early yesterday.*	**16.4B**
obligation	present	*have (got) to*	*Students **have (got) to** wear school uniform here.*	**17.1B**
		must	*I **must** get up earlier.*	**17.1B**
		need (to)	*Do we **need to** get a visa for the USA?*	**17.1B**
		should	*You **should** respect your neighbours.*	**17.1B**
	past	*had to*	*We **had to** report to reception by four.*	**17.1B**
	future	*will have to, will, need to*	*We**'ll have to/'ll need to** get our visas sorted out.*	**17.1B**
necessity	present	*must, have to, need to*	*All human beings **must/have to/need to** have enough sleep.*	**17.1C**
	past	*had to, needed to*	*Cave dwellers **had to/needed to** hunt in order to survive.*	**17.1C**
	future	*will have to, will need to*	*You**'ll have to/'ll need to** work harder than that.*	**17.1C**
prohibition	present/ future	*must not*	*You **mustn't** touch that kettle!*	**17.2B**
		cannot, may not	*Guests **can't/may not** use the pool after 11 p.m.*	**17.2B**
		should not	*You **shouldn't** speak to me like that!*	**17.2B**
	past	*could not*	*We **couldn't** go because we were too young.*	**17.2B**
past criticism		*should (not) have*	*You **shouldn't have driven** through that red light.*	**17.2B**

function	time	form	example	►
absence of obligation or necessity	present	*do not have to, do not need to*	*You **don't have to/don't need to** pay to visit most museums in Britain.*	17.3B
	past	*did not have to, did not need to, need not have*	*You **didn't have to/didn't need to** finish the job. We **needn't have taken** sweaters as it was so warm there.*	17.3B
	future	*will not have to, will not need to*	*You **won't have to/won't need to** ask the doctor to sign this form.*	17.3B
advice/ recommendation	present/ future	*must*	*You really **must** read 'Birdsong'!*	17.4B
		should	*You **should** consider a private pension.*	17.4B
		had better	*You'**d better** change the locks straight away.*	17.4B
logical deduction	present/ future	*must, have to*	*This **must/has to** be the place.*	17.5B
		cannot	*This amount **can't** be correct.*	17.5B
	past	*must have*	*That noise **must have been** an explosion.*	17.5B
		cannot have	*She **can't have done** it – she wasn't even here.*	17.5B
probability	present/ future	*should*	*The plane **should** be landing now.*	17.5B
	past	*should have*	*What's happened to the boys? They **should have arrived** hours ago.*	17.5B
certainty	present	*will*	*It **won't** be warm at this time of year.*	18.1C
	past	*will have*	*They'**ll have received** the invitations by now.*	18.1D
routines	present	*will*	*He'**ll** come in and he'**ll** start giving instructions.*	18.2A
	past	*would*	*He'**d** come in and he'**d** start giving instructions.*	18.2B
habits	present	*will*	*The public **will** always side with the nurses.*	18.2A
	past	*would*	*Dad **would** always tell me how to run my life.*	18.2B
characteristics	present	*will*	*The stadium **will** hold about 110,000 people.*	18.2A
	past	*would*	*The car **wouldn't** start on cold mornings.*	18.2B
willingness/ refusal	present	*will, won't*	*The doctor **will** act as a witness.*	18.3A
	past	*would, wouldn't*	*The shop **wouldn't** change this jumper.*	18.3B
other functions	present/ future	*will, shall*	*I'**ll** wash up this evening. **Shall** I wash up this evening?*	18.4A
		shall	***Shall** we go out for a curry?*	18.4B
		will	***Will** you give me a call?*	18.4C
		would	***Would** you fill in this form, please?*	18.4C
		will, shall	*You **will/shall** all stay after school tonight.*	18.4D
hypothetical desires	present/ future	*would*	*It **would** be nice to live by the sea.*	18.5A
	past	*would have*	*It **would have been** a good idea to notify us in advance.*	18.5B

19 Auxiliaries, *have (got)*, *do*

Be, *have* and *do* can be used as main verbs (*I **have** a new car*) or as auxiliary verbs (*I **have** sold my old car*). We use forms of *have* as auxiliary verbs in perfect tenses, forms of *be* in continuous tenses and passives, and forms of *do* in questions and negatives. In this unit we look at these auxiliary functions, at the use of *have* and *do* as main verbs, the use of *do* for emphasis, and at *have* and *have got*.

19.1 AUXILIARY VERBS

19.1A Uses

There are three auxiliary verbs in English: *have*, *be* and *do*. We use *have* and *be* to make perfect, continuous and passive forms of tenses:

*I **haven't** seen her for ages.*
*John **is** working very hard these days.*
*The flat **is** watched by the surveillance team twenty-four hours a day.*

We use forms of *do* to form questions, negatives and negative questions in the present and past simple:

***Do** you enjoy going to the theatre?*
***Did** they like the new place?*
*The thermostat **doesn't** work any more.*
*We **didn't** go to Corfu after all.*
***Doesn't** the thermostat control the heating?*
***Didn't** you go to Ibiza?*

❗ We don't use auxiliary verbs with modal verbs, e.g. *must*, *can*, *should*:

✗ ~~***Do** we must pay excess baggage on this?*~~
✔ *Must we pay excess baggage on this?*
✗ ~~*We **didn't** could wear high heels at my old school.*~~
✔ *We couldn't wear high heels at my old school.*

❗ We don't usually repeat the same subject and auxiliary verb in a sentence:

[***We were** watching television and **we were** laughing at Mr Bean's antics.*]
✔ ***We were** watching television and laughing at Mr Bean's antics.*

We sometimes omit auxiliary verbs in newspaper headlines:

Terrorist arrested in dawn raid. (= A terrorist was arrested ...)

We often omit subjects and auxiliary verbs when we are writing notes or postcards:

Enjoying my holiday. Flying back next week. (= I am enjoying ... I am flying ...)

But we don't omit auxiliaries if doing so would make the meaning unclear:

[*Dave going to come to party but tied up.*] (= Dave is coming.)
✔ *Dave **was** going to come to the party but **he's** tied up.* (= Dave isn't coming.)

We also use *be*, *have* and *do* as substitute words in text (▶ **35.2B, 35.3B**) and in inversion (▶ **34.3B**).

19.1B Contracted forms

We often contract *not* and the auxiliaries *have* and *be*. In writing we use an apostrophe (') to represent the missing letter(s):

full form	*is*	*are*	*has*	*have*	*had*	*not*
contracted form	*'s*	*'re*	*'s*	*'ve*	*'d*	*n't*

We don't combine contracted auxiliaries with a contracted form of *not*:

*I **have not** seen it.*
✗ ~~*I'**ven't** seen it.*~~ ✔ *I **haven't** seen it* or, ***I've** not seen it.*

But in spoken English and when we represent speech in writing we can combine contracted auxiliaries, e.g. *'ve*, and contracted *not* with modal verbs:

*He **shouldn't've** done it.* (= He should not have done it.)

❶ You may hear *ain't* instead of *am/is/are not* used in conversation and in popular songs. This form is considered incorrect by most English speakers:

[*I **ain't** going to the party.*] (= I am not going to the party.)

❶ We don't contract *was*:

✘ ~~*He's watching television when she arrived.*~~

✔ *He **was** watching television when she arrived.*

In formal English we don't use contractions when there is more than one subject:

✘ ~~*The Army and the Navy've launched a recruitment drive.*~~

✔ *The Army and the Navy **have** launched a recruitment drive.*

❶ The contraction for *has* and *is* is the same: *'s*. Similarly, the contraction for *had* and *would* is the same: *'d*. The context tells us which auxiliary is being used:

*He**'s** taken a long lease.* (= has taken) *He**'s** taking a holiday.* (= is taking)

*He**'d** known her for ages.* (= had known) *He**'d** know what to do.* (= would know)

❶ We usually avoid using contractions in very formal English:

[*Clauses 10–15 **don't** apply in the case of valuables stolen from vehicles.*]

✔ *Clauses 10–15 **do not** apply in the case of valuables stolen from vehicles.*

19.2 EMPHASIS

19.2A Stressing the auxiliary

To make a sentence, which includes an auxiliary, more emphatic in speech we stress the auxiliary verb (underlined in the examples).

*Fancy seeing you again. It **has** been a long time!*

*Don't beat around the bush. **Did** you or **didn't** you take it?*

*That holiday's done wonders; you **are** looking well!*

But if the auxiliary is preceded by a modal verb then we stress the modal:

*That's absolutely ridiculous; you **must** have seen something!*

19.2B Inserting *do*

Present simple and past simple phrases, which do not contain an auxiliary, can be made more emphatic by adding a form of *do*:

*I'm very sorry sir. We **do** try our best to comply with most passenger requests.*

*The witness is hazy on the details, but she **did** notice a scar on his forearm.*

We can also emphasise imperatives with *do*:

***Do** shut up.*

We often use this pattern to make polite suggestions or offers:

***Do** sit down and make yourself comfortable.*

***Do** let me help you with that heavy case.*

19.3 *HAVE* AND *DO*

19.3A *have* and *do* as main verbs

Have and *do* can be used in the same way as other main verbs:

*He **didn't have** any brothers or sisters. When **do** you **do** the washing?*

In British English we can use *have* without auxiliary *do* in questions and negatives:

***Has** the government any real intention of addressing the crime problem head on?*

*I **haven't** a clue what they're talking about.*

❶ We don't usually use the passive of main verb *have*. When we do, it has the meaning 'be tricked or cheated':

*You paid $100 for a T shirt! You**'ve been had**!* (= You've been cheated.)

Have and *do* can combine with particles to make multi-word verbs (▶ Unit **14**):

*You're **having** me **on**! I don't believe he's going to **do** the house **up** by himself.*

(For *have/get something done* and *have somebody do something* ▶ **8.3A**.)

19.3B Meanings of *have*

We use *have* to describe many different states, e.g. possession, inclusion, relationship:

*The chairman of the board **has** a Gulfstream executive jet.* (possession)

*Our latest computer **will have** a number of upgradeable components.* (inclusion)

*I **have** two older brothers.* (relationship)

(We do not use *have* in continuous or passive forms with these meanings ▶ **19.4A**.)

We can use *have* + noun to talk about experiences and actions:

*He **has a headache** every time he eats blue cheese.* (= He suffers from a headache ...)

*We're **having chicken** with cashew nuts.* (= We're eating chicken ...)

We can use *have* + noun when we want to give extra information by using adjectives:

They raced up the hill. The race was exhausting.

*They **had an exhausting race** up the hill.*

I'm going to swim in the sea tomorrow. It will last a long time and be invigorating.

*I'm going to **have a long, invigorating swim** in the sea tomorrow.*

Sometimes we use *have* + noun when there is no single verb in English for the action or experience we want to describe. (For more about *have* and *take* + noun ▶ **20.1C**):

*You **have an appointment** with the accountants at four.*

*I **had a brainwave** on the bus coming here.*

*The children often **have nightmares** after thunderstorms.*

❗ *Won't have* and *wouldn't have* can be used to mean 'not tolerate':

*I **won't have** anyone smoking in my house.*

19.3C Meanings of *do*

Do can have several meanings. We often use *do* to talk about actions in general:

*What did you **do** this morning?*

We can use *do* meaning 'carry out/complete a task':

*Sarah's **doing** something for her boss.* (= is carrying out a task)

*Right. That's **done** at last.* (= A task has been completed.)

There are many fixed expressions with *do*:

*What **does he do**?* (= What's his job?)

*That child **could do with** a good telling off.* (= deserves/needs)

*Five minutes **will do** if you're rushed for time.* (= be sufficient)

(For different expressions with *make* and *do* ▶ **20.1B**.)

19.4 *HAVE GOT*

19.4A *have got* = *have*

We use *have got* as an alternative to *have* to express possession and similar states in the present (▶ **19.3B**). *Have got* is more common than *have* in informal British English:

[*He has a car but he hasn't a garage to keep it in.*]

✔ *He**'s got** a car but he **hasn't got** a garage to keep it in.*

In formal written English we can use *have got*, but *have* is more usual:

[*Applicants have got three months in which to complete and return the forms.*]

✔ *Applicants **have** three months in which to complete and return the forms.*

❗ We usually use a form of *have*, not *have got*, to talk about past or future possession:

[*I had got a pet labrador when I was a child.*]

✔ *I **had** a pet labrador when I was a child.* (= possessed)

[*I'm going to have got a nice cottage by the seaside when I retire.*]

✔ *I'm **going to have** a nice cottage by the seaside when I retire.* (= going to possess)

❗ *Have got* and *have* do not have continuous or passive forms when they mean 'possess':

✘ ~~*He is having (got) a car.*~~ ✘ ~~*A car has been got by him.*~~ ✔ *He **has got** a car.*

In US English *have got* is used mainly in speech, and the negative and question forms are not common.

(For *have (got) to* to express obligation, etc. ▶ **17.1B**)

19.4B *have got ≠ have*

Have got is also the present perfect form of the verb *get*. It can mean *has become*, *has obtained*, *has received*, etc. Compare:

*She's **got/has** a degree in chemistry and works at the lab.* (= possesses)

*She's just **got** a degree and hopes to get a job in a lab.* (= has just obtained)

We can use *have got* as an infinitive with these present perfect meanings but not with the meaning of 'possess':

perfect infinitive	✔ *I hope **to have got** the results by March.* (= to have obtained) ✘ ~~*She has always wanted **to have got** a car.*~~ (= to possess)
modal/auxiliary verb + perfect infinitive	✔ *She **must have got** a terrible shock.* (= must have received) ✘ ~~*Members **can have got** two cards each.*~~ (= possess) ✔ *She **will have got** the keys by next week.* (= will have obtained) ✘ ~~*While she is working for Blake's, Cassandra **will have got** a company car.*~~ (= possess)

We can use *had got* with the meaning 'had obtained/received', etc:

*He'**d got** a certificate from the doctor so he could claim sick pay.* (= had obtained)

In US English the past participle form of *get* when it means 'has become/obtained/received', etc. is *gotten*:

*Hollywood movies **have gotten** more and more violent in recent years.*

We don't use *have got* in these ways:

to describe actions	✘ ~~*Can you answer the phone? I've got a shower.*~~ ✔ *Can you answer the phone? I'**m having** a shower.*
in short answers (ellipsis ▶ 35.3)	*'Do you have/Have you got anything vegetarian?'* ✘ ~~*'Yes, we have got.'*~~ ✔ *'Yes, we **do/have**.'*
in tag questions (▶ 7.2)	✘ ~~*You've got two brothers, haven't you got?*~~ ✔ *You've got two brothers, **haven't you**?*
with *used to*	✘ ~~*We used to have got a place in the country.*~~ ✔ *We **used to have** a place in the country.*

I've got a shower.
I'm having a shower.

Practice

The key to these exercises is on page 362.

1 19.1

There is one auxiliary verb missing from each of these sentences. Rewrite the sentences using a suitable auxiliary verb. Whenever appropriate, use contracted forms. If two contracted forms are possible, in conversational speech for instance, write both.

0 He could not seen them do it.
He couldn't have seen them do it. *He couldn't've seen them do it.*

1 I been waiting here for hours.

2 They trying to find a nice hotel for two hours last night.

3 She will not returned by the time the show starts.

4 Protection under this policy not include items of an aggregate value exceeding $500.

5 He might not known that it was you at the door.

6 their boss not realise that they are under a lot of pressure?

7 James got better despite the fact that he not been taking his medication for weeks.

8 she not appreciate how upset he was?

9 We regret to inform you that the bank unwilling to extend credit facilities in this case.

10 Hilary not expecting you until this evening.

11 They really should told you about their decision.

12 The documents requested from your solicitor have not received and we are therefore obliged to cancel your contract forthwith.

2 19.2

The words in these sentences have been jumbled up. Write the sentences correctly then match them to the descriptions in the box.

A Emphatic sentences	**B** Imperatives	**C** Suggestions/offers

0 seat/do/a/take
Do take a seat. *C*

1 to/drink/do/yourself/help/a

2 himself/to/behave/did/promise/he/in/future

3 attention/do/young/pay/man

4 good/run/enjoy/the/park/the/dog/a/does/around

....

5 off/do/your/take/feet/table/the

....

6 quiet/keep/do

....

7 us/come/join/do/and

....

8 do/at/yourself/home/make

....

9 a/lot/manage/Jane/did/to/lose/of/weight/quite

....

10 Disney/the/the/do/children/love/really/channel

....

3 19.3

For each of the sentences below, write a new sentence as similar as possible in meaning to the original sentence, but using the word given in bold. The word must not be altered in any way.

0 He's going to restore the house himself.
up *He's going to do the house up himself.*

1 I don't know what the answer is.
clue ....

2 Don't forget you are due to see the sales manager at ten o'clock.
appointment ....

3 Does Your Honour have any further instructions on this matter?
has ....

4 How does Clare earn a living?
do ....

5 She won't allow anybody to use bad language at the dinner table.
have ....

6 He's been deceiving you.
on ....

7 Will this piece of fabric be suitable for the new curtains?
do ....

8 This floor needs a good wash.
with ....

9 You've been tricked!
had ....

10 It isn't quite finished yet.
done ....

11 What was on the menu for your staff lunch last week?
did ....

12 I think he's in the middle of an asthma attack.
having ....

4 19.4

The following dialogue and the hotel brochure below each contain at least six phrases which can be replaced by forms of *have* or *have got*. Find the phrases and rewrite them. Use contractions whenever appropriate, and only use *have* if *have got* is either not appropriate or not grammatically correct.

SARA New hairstyle, Liz?

LIZ Yes. <u>I use this marvellous new hairdresser.</u>

SARA Really?

LIZ Mm. Jane Lindsay, she owns a place in the high street.

SARA But I thought you went to that place next to the post office.

LIZ No, I used to, but the woman who did my hair emigrated to Australia last month.

SARA Oh? Well, your new woman's certainly very original! Your hair contains extensions, doesn't it?

LIZ Yes, they're great, aren't they?

SARA Very distinctive. I've always wanted to possess extensions but I've never had the nerve to ask for them. Was it expensive?

LIZ Not really. She's doing a special offer. You can receive three hairstyling sessions for the price of two – if you bring a friend along.

SARA Bring a friend?

LIZ Yes. There is an appointment for you there at two o'clock tomorrow afternoon. My treat!

Glenforth Hotel

Situated in the heart of the beautiful Scottish Highlands, the Glenforth Hotel offers the discerning guest the ultimate in luxury and gracious living.

Dining We possess a Michelin-starred restaurant offering the best in cordon bleu cuisine featuring a variety of locally-sourced organic ingredients.

Leisure facilities Would you enjoy indulging in a relaxing swim or sauna? Our guests can obtain free membership of the adjacent Glenforth Health Centre which includes a fully-equipped gymnasium, heated indoor pool and sauna/steam rooms.

Babysitting service If your family contains small children you will be able to take advantage of our unique babysitting service. We employ several fully-qualified local nannies who are able to take care of your children for an evening.

Sports For those of our guests that enjoy fishing, the hotel has acquired the fishing rights on a three-mile stretch of the river Glenswift, which is teeming with a large number of salmon, trout and bream.

(Note: in formal written texts like the one above it would be considered inelegant style to use the same words, e.g. *have* and *have got*, too often.)

Line 2 I've got this marvellous new hairdresser.

5 ALL

Choose the most appropriate form (A or B) to complete each sentence.

1 .... just closing the doors as she rushed into the bank.
A They were B They're

2 The committee is of the opinion that such a case .... provided for under Article 7 of the treaty.
A is not B isn't

3 You're quite wrong. I know it was dark, but he really .... the outline of the burglar's face – I'm sure of it!
A saw B did see

4 'Listen, Burt. He .... done it. He's been with me at the betting shop all day.'
A couldn't've B could not have

5 Mandy's marrying old Benson? You're .... me on!
A having B doing

6 Clients wishing to take up this offer must .... an address within the European Union.
A have B have got

7 You ought to visit Emily; .... a wonderful flat overlooking the river.
A she got B she's got

8 OK then. The rear stalls .... if you haven't got any seats in the front circle.
A will do B do

9 He's got one of those new WAP mobile phones, ...
A hasn't he got? B hasn't he?

10 Today's headlines. British and French authorities .... a joint anti-smuggling initiative.
A 've announced B have announced

11 He told you he was a millionaire and you believed him! You've ....!
A been done B been had

12 The great thing about Laura is that she's always been able .... a laugh at her own expense.
A to have B to have got

13 I look a mess; I could really .... a new haircut.
A do B do with

14 Once the computer centre is built the college is hoping to .... a steady stream of applicants eager to improve their computing skills.
A have got B have

15 I couldn't tell you what Bill looks like now, we .... seen him for ages.
A 'ven't B haven't

20 Confusing verbs

Some pairs of verbs in English are subtly different from each other and so can be a source of confusion for learners. This is because the pairs, e.g. *make* and *do*, *lay* and *lie*, have similar meanings but are used to describe different kinds of actions or situations. These are 'false synonyms'. In other cases there are verb pairs which cause problems because we use them to describe similar situations even though they have opposite meanings, e.g. *borrow* and *lend*. These are 'opposite pairs'. In this unit we look at the verb pairs which are most often confused. (For *say* and *tell* ▶ **Unit 9**.)

20.1 FALSE SYNONYMS

Several verbs appear to have similar meanings but are used differently.

20.1A *make* and *do*

Make often means 'create' or 'produce':

Aunt Alice is going to ***make*** *the bridesmaids' dresses.*
Gouda cheese ***is made*** *in Holland.*

Make often expresses the idea of building and constructing:

The multinationals ***are making*** *a lot of products in the developing world these days.*

We also use *make* to describe a process of change. The meaning is similar to 'become' or 'cause to be':

The spare bedroom ***has made*** *a wonderful office for Deirdre.* (= has become)
Those new drugs seem to ***make*** *him very lethargic.* (= cause him to be)

Make + object + infinitive (without *to*) means 'force' or 'command':

The police officer ***made me empty*** *my pockets.*

Make has a number of idiomatic meanings such as 'earn' and 'keep an appointment':

He ***makes*** *$1000 a week on the oil rigs.*
I can't ***make*** *it on Friday; I'm in a meeting all day.*

We often use *do* to describe an activity or to mean 'carry out/complete a task':

What are we going to ***do*** *for your birthday?* (= take part in an activity)
You can go out after you've ***done*** *your homework.* (= you've completed)

(For more information about the uses of *do* ▶ **Unit 19**.)

We can use *do* + determiner + *-ing* form to describe regular tasks at home or at work:

There isn't much in the fridge as I haven't ***done the shopping*** *yet.*
We ***do the stocktaking*** *every Wednesday morning.*

20.1B Expressions with *make* and *do*

There are several multi-word verbs with *make* or *do* (▶ **Unit 14**):

Don't believe a word he said, he ***made*** *it all* ***up***. (= invented)
The government ***did away with*** *the death penalty in the sixties.* (= abolished)

❗ There are a number of fixed expressions with either *make* or *do*:

✗ ~~*It's time to* ***do a decision***.~~
✓ *It's time to* ***make a decision***.
✗ ~~*Who* ***made your hair***?~~
✓ *Who* ***did your hair***?

Here are some of the most common expressions with *make* and *do*. (Note that in the table below, *sb* = somebody and *sth* = something.)

make		
an attempt	*an exception*	*a noise*
an appearance	*an excuse*	*an offer*
an appointment (= arrange)	*a fire*	*a plan*
arrangements	*a fortune*	*a point*
a bed	*friends (with sb)*	*a profit*
a (phone) call	*a fuss*	*progress*
a charge (for sth)	*a gesture*	*a promise*
a choice	*a good/bad job of sth*	*a remark*
a comment	*a habit of sth*	*a sound*
a contribution	*a journey*	*a speech*
a decision	*a list*	*a start (on sth)*
a difference	*a living*	*a suggestion*
a discovery	*love*	*time (for sth/sb)*
an effort	*a mess*	*trouble*
an enemy of sb	*a mistake*	*war*
an enquiry	*money*	*a will*

do		
your best (= try hard)	*an experiment*	*the laundry*
business (with sb)	*sb a favour*	*military service*
the cleaning/cooking/ironing/washing (up)	*good* (= help other people)	*research*
a course	*sb some good* (= make sb better/healthier)	*the shopping*
some damage	*your hair/face/nails*	*sport*
the dishes	*harm*	*your teeth* (= brush/clean)
your duty	*the homework/housework*	*well/badly* (= be successful/unsuccessful)
an exam/a test	*yourself an injury*	
an/some exercise	*a job*	

20.1C *have/take* + noun

We can describe some actions with either *have* or *take*; in other cases we only use one of these verbs:

have		***take***		***have*** **or** ***take***
an appointment (= an existing arrangement)	*lunch/dinner/a meal*	*account of*	*part (in)*	*a bath/shower*
an argument	*a quarrel*	*action*	*a photo(graph)*	*a break*
a baby	*a race*	*advantage (of)*	*place*	*an exam/test*
a care	*a row*	*a breath*	*power*	*a guess*
a chance (to do sth)	*a/the right (to)*	*care (of)*	*precedence (over)*	*a holiday/a vacation*
a chat	*a say*	*a chance*	*responsibility (for)*	*a look*
a dance	*something to eat*	*a decision*	*a risk*	*a nap*
a drink	*a talk*	*a dislike to sth/sb*	*root*	*a rest*
an effect (on sth)	*a think*	*effect*	*sides (with sb)*	*a seat*
a fall	*(no/the) time*	*exception (to)*	*a step/steps*	*a sip*
a fit	*a wash*	*the form of medicine/drugs*	*the trouble (to)*	*a stroll*
a go	*a word (with)*	*a message*	*years/months/weeks/days/hours, etc.*	*a swim*
an/no/any idea		*offence (at sth)*		

20.1D *been/gone*

The two past participle forms, *gone* and *been*, are used with similar but slightly different meanings. In British English we use *been*, not *gone*, when we express the idea of visiting or going somewhere and then leaving or returning:

Jane's just got back. ✘ ~~*She's **gone** to the doctor's.*~~

✔ *She's **been** to the doctor's.* (= She went and then came back.)

We use *gone*, not *been*, when someone has gone somewhere but not yet come back:

Jane isn't here right now. ✘ ~~*She's **been** to the doctor's.*~~

✔ *She's **gone** to the doctor's.* (= She went there and hasn't returned.)

For both of these situations, *gone* is commonly used in US English.

20.1E *lay/lie*

To lay expresses an action; it means to put something or someone down in a flat position. *To lie* describes a state of being in a horizontal position. Compare:

*You will find the process easier if you **lay** all the parts on a worksurface.* (action)
*I think I'll just **lie** on the sofa until my headache goes.* (state/position)

There is also the verb *lie* meaning 'to say something that isn't true':

*That child **lies** all the time.* (= says things which are not true)

Notice that these three verbs have different forms:

infinitive	past tense	past participle	present participle
lay (= action)	*laid*	*laid*	*laying*
lie (= state)	*lay*	*lain*	*lying*
lie (= tell lies)	*lied*	*lied*	*lying*

*They've **laid** new carpet throughout the house.*
*We've been **laying** artificial grass on the new football pitch.*
*We found the old photographs **lying** in a drawer.*
*Yesterday I was so tired that I **lay** on the bed all morning.* (past simple of *lie*)

20.1F *speak/talk*

Speak and *talk* have very similar meanings and are often equally appropriate:

*I'm going to **talk/speak** to my teacher about it after the lesson.*

We usually use *speak*, not *talk*, for formal speeches when a person in authority is addressing an audience:

✘ ~~*The Prime Minister **talked** to Parliament this morning.*~~

✔ *Before the election the President **spoke** to the nation on television.*

We use *speak*, not *talk*, to refer to languages:

✘ ~~*Anatoly **talks English** with an accent.*~~ ✔ *Anatoly **speaks English** with an accent.*

We use *talk* for long conversations:

✘ ~~*We were up half the night **speaking**!*~~ ✔ *We were up half the night **talking**!*

There are a number of expressions with *speak* or *talk*:

*Could you **speak up**. I can't hear you.* (= talk louder)
*I'd like to **talk about** our new sales strategy.* (= explain/discuss)
*You're **talking nonsense**.* (I strongly disagree with what you are saying.)

20.1G *raise/rise/arise*

Raise refers to the action of someone or something lifting, increasing or moving something else in an upward direction. *To rise* only refers to the movement itself:

*The government has been urged **to raise** corporation tax rates to match those in other European Union states. Rates are predicted **to rise** by ten per cent.*

❗ Because *raise* refers to an action done to something or someone else it always has a direct object:

✘ ~~*Fares will **raise** next year.*~~ ✔ *They will **raise the fares** next year.*

Rise cannot have an object:

✘ ~~*They will **rise the fares** next year.*~~ ✔ *Fares will **rise** next year.*

In formal English we sometimes use *arise* to refer to problems or difficulties occurring:

*Tissue rejection is a problem which can **arise** in this procedure.*

❶ *Arise* does not have an object:

✗ ~~*Let's hope nobody **arises that issue**.*~~ ✔ *Let's hope that issue doesn't **arise**.*

Note that these verbs have different forms:

infinitive	past tense	past participle	present participle
raise	*raised*	*raised*	*raising*
rise	*rose*	*risen*	*rising*
arise	*arose*	*arisen*	*arising*

20.1H *rob/steal*

We use *rob* to refer to the person or place that suffered the robbery; we use *steal* to refer to what was taken:

✗ ~~*Thieves **stole** my uncle.*~~ ✔ *Thieves **robbed** my uncle.*

✗ ~~*A gang **stole** the head office.*~~ ✔ *A gang **robbed** the head office.*

✗ ~~*They **robbed** his gold watch.*~~ ✔ *They **stole** his gold watch.*

We can use the preposition *from* to link *steal* to a person or place:

*Colonel Blood **stole** the crown jewels **from** the Tower of London in 1665.*

We can use the preposition *of* to link *rob* with the thing which was taken:

*No man has the right to **rob** another **of** his freedom.*

20.2 OPPOSITE PAIRS

Some verbs act as 'mirror images' of each other. They describe the same event from different sides.

20.2A *borrow/lend*

If you want to use something that belongs to someone else you can *borrow* it *from* them. The owner of something can *lend* it *to* you for a certain period:

*'Dad, could we **borrow** your electric drill?' 'Sorry. I've already **lent** it **to** Michael.'*

20.2B *bring/take* (and *fetch*)

Bring means to take someone or something with you to the place you are now, to your home, or to the place/event you have been talking about:

*I've **brought** the pliers you said you needed.*

*When are you going to **bring** your new boyfriend to meet us?* (to our house)

*Jane and I got lost on the top of the mountain and we had to stay there till morning. Fortunately Jane had **brought** some food and water.*

Take means to move someone or something away from the place you are now, away from your home or away from the place/event you have been talking about:

*I can't find the cheque book – Dennis must have **taken** it when he left this morning.*

*When are you **taking** me to meet your parents*? (away from here to their home)

❶ The choice of verb depends on the situation of the speaker:

*Are you **bringing** your scuba gear?* (on our holiday)

*Are you **taking** your scuba gear?* (on your holiday)

*I **brought** the car to work today.* (I am at work now.)

*I **took** the car to work today.* (I am not at work now.)

Fetch means to collect someone or something from another place and bring it to the place you are now, to your home or to the place you are talking about. We don't use *bring* with this meaning of 'collecting':

✗ ~~*Could you **bring** the children from school on Monday?*~~

✔ *Could you **fetch** the children from school on Monday?* (= go to the school and bring them home)

20 Practice

The key to these exercises is on page 363.

1 20.1

Rewrite the sentences using suitable forms of *make* or *do*.

0 What activities are you planning for next week? *What are you doing next week?*
1 Heavy rains have led to parts of the road becoming impassable. ....
2 We're going to have the roof repaired next spring. ....
3 It's all part of the research I'm carrying out for my dissertation. ....
4 I'm rather busy this evening so I won't be able to meet you at the cinema. ....
5 The old pond has become a wonderful paddling pool for the kids. ....
6 How can you talk to me like that after all I've achieved for you! ....
7 Are you going to take any more aerobics classes? ....
8 In many countries women still earn less money than men for the same work. ....
9 They forced the hostages to walk for three days without food or water. ....
10 They've been producing Rolls Royce cars in the same factory for forty years. ....

2 20.1

Complete the sentences with a suitable form of *have* or *take*.

1 You sometimes have to wait a year or two for the plants to really .... root in the soil.
2 Unless a cheque is received by return of post we will have no option but .... steps to recover the disputed sums through the courts.
3 I can't help you with that, I'm afraid; I .... absolutely no idea when it comes to electrics.
4 You want to become a doctor at your age? It .... years to get through a medical degree.
5 Do you mind if I .... a quick wash before we sit down to eat?
6 She's very worried about the takeover. Perhaps you should .... a chat with her about it.
7 And what makes you think you .... the right to lecture me on morality?
8 I'm not feeling too good today; I .... the most almighty row with my girlfriend last night.
9 In the latest developments in the civil war it appears that the rebel army .... power in the southern provinces.
10 I can't think why you're so reluctant to go. Come on, ... a risk for once!
11 We regret to announce that Alvin Claymore is unable .... part in tonight's performance owing to ill health.
12 The residents insist on .... their say; they're going to demand a public meeting with the housing committee.
13 With any luck the new policing initiative .... a positive effect on the appalling crime rate around here.
14 I know I'm old-fashioned but I do .... exception to all the bad language on TV these days.
15 You really can't put this off any longer; you must .... a decision on the Knowlson case today.

3 20.1

Replace each of the underlined phrases in the text with an expression containing a suitable form of *make* or *do* plus a word or phrase from the box. Add any necessary words. The first one is given as an example (0).

bad job	charge	decision	fuss	journey	mistake	promise	start
~~best~~	good	laundry	research	shopping	trouble	up	

HIGHLAND HELL

This month Jeremy Vegal's 'Hotel Road Test' is the Trent Castle Hotel in Scotland.

In the bad old days, Scottish country hotels had a reputation of being cold, draughty and dour places which tried hard to make their guests feel as unwelcome as possible. 0 *did their best* Well, the tourist industry has moved on and we at *TravelDetective* felt it was time to see if the winds of change blowing through the British hotel world had yet reached our northern extremities. From the catalogues and brochures, it seems that every castle in Scotland has turned itself into a hotel, and it was difficult to reach a conclusion about which one to try. In the end we settled for a little-known but promising place deep in the Highlands. 1 ……………

So, full of optimism, I travelled north on the overnight sleeper, jumped into a cab and headed east to the Trent Castle Hotel. 2 …………… I had investigated and I knew that the place had been converted from a sixteenth-century fortress about five years ago. 3 …………… From the outside it certainly looked the part with tall granite walls and looming turrets overlooking the dark waters of Lochtrent. But the owners had clearly committed an error with their work on the interior. 4 …………… Rather than warm and welcoming, it was just as grim and forbidding as the outside.

I got to my room and, always eager to test a hotel's efficiency, I began by calling 5 …………… room service and asking for my clothes to be washed. 6 …………… It took forty-five minutes for the chambermaid to arrive, and when she did, she happily informed me that the hotel would impose a fee approximately equivalent to the gross national 7 …………… product of the average third-world nation for each item of clothing I wished to have cleaned. Never one to complain, I politely declined the offer of instant 8 …………… bankruptcy and decided to ask the woman about the possibility of an extra blanket or ten, as the temperature in my room was hovering around zero and it was only the middle of the afternoon. She guaranteed to bring one straight away, 9 …………… and that was the last I was to see of her for my entire visit.

Anxious to find some warmth, I decided to try out the hotel sauna, sure that some dry heat would be healthy for me. 10 …………… But when I asked the receptionist about the location of this heavily advertised facility, she looked at me as though I had invented it. 11 …………… 'Been closed for months,' she announced. 'If you want something to do you could always go out and buy some things, 12 …………… there's a lovely souvenir shop six miles down the road.' The prospect was deeply unexciting.

'Look,' I said, 'I don't want to cause difficulties, 13 …………… but the sauna *is* advertised in your brochure.'

'Oh, that thing's full of mistakes,' she replied, 'The printers really messed it up.' 14 …………… Rather like the owners, I thought to myself ...

4 20.1

In the following texts some lines (1–17) have a mistake with the verb and some lines are correct. Find and underline any incorrect verbs and write the correct verb form, then tick (✔) the correct lines. The exercise begins with two examples (0) and (00).

US RATE RISE

0 The Chancellor returned from this month's meeting of the 'Group ......✔......
00 of Six' with news that interest rates are to be <u>rised</u> by an average of ......*raised*......
1 half a percentage point in the United States. While the Chancellor ....
2 has gone in Dallas city markets have been feverish with rumours of ....
3 even higher increases. The US dollar has been laying at an all-time ....
4 low for several weeks and the American trade deficit has been rising ....
5 steadily. The Chairman of the Federal Reserve has been to Tokyo to ....
6 discuss the problems which have arose from pressure in Congress to ....
7 tackle the deficit. He will be in Japan until next Tuesday. ....

PRICELESS TREASURE DISAPPEARS

8 The Benton Horde, a priceless collection of ancient Roman silver, has ....
9 disappeared from its display cabinet in the British Museum. At today's ....
10 emergency press conference, Museum director Alan Woods talked of ....
11 his theory that the treasures had probably been robbed by a professional ....
12 gang on behalf of a specific collector as the silver is too well-known to ....
13 be sold on the open market. Ten museums have been stolen in the last ....
14 six months and the number has been raising steadily over the last few ....
15 years. The Benton Horde is one of Britain's most important collections ....
16 of Roman silver. It was found in 1926, having laid undiscovered for ....
17 almost sixteen centuries beneath a Sussex field. ....

5 20.2

Choose the best word in *italics* for each sentence.

1 We'd better order a taxi to *bring/take* us to the airport next week.
2 My uncle *borrowed/lent* me the money to buy my first car.
3 Shall I *bring/take* my holiday photos when I come over on Saturday?
4 Is there any chance of you *bringing/fetching* the kids from their swimming lesson tonight?
5 The car isn't here, I'm *borrowing/lending* it to my sister for the week.
6 My boyfriend went to Japan on a business trip and *brought/took* me a fantastic MP3 player.
7 Can I *borrow/lend* your dictionary? I left mine at home.
8 When my girlfriend left me she *brought/took* my entire CD collection.
9 Would you like me to *fetch/bring* your car from the garage this afternoon?
10 Is there any chance I could *borrow/lend* your calculator over the weekend?

6 ALL

Choose the correct label, A or B, for each picture.

1

A 'Of course I love you darling, but when are you taking me to meet your parents?'
B 'Of course I love you darling, but when are you bringing me to meet your parents?'

2

A Poor Jenny, she always ends up doing the dishes.
B Poor Jenny, she always ends up making the dishes.

3

A They've robbed the cash machine, officer.
B They've stolen the cash machine, officer.

4

A I'm afraid Steve's just been to Texas.
B I'm afraid Steve's just gone to Texas.

5

A They're exhausted, they've been laying all morning.
B They're exhausted, they've been lying all morning.

6

A He's always borrowing her clothes.
B He's always lending her clothes.

21 Adjectives

Adjectives in English seem straightforward as they do not change their form except when they are comparatives or superlatives (▶ **Unit 22**). But the different positions of adjectives, e.g. *concerned residents* or *residents concerned*, and the sequence of groups of adjectives can cause difficulty. This unit looks at these areas and at the use of participle and compound adjectives. (For modification of adjectives ▶ **Unit 23**.)

21.1 ADJECTIVE PATTERNS

21.1A Form and use

Adjectives are words which give extra information about nouns. They do not change their form to show number or gender:

*The hero was played by a **young boy**. Several **young girls** took the secondary roles.*

Many adjectives are formed from other words; notice the spelling changes:

+ ic	***+ (i)al***	***+ able***	***+ ful***	***+ ent***	***+ ive***
history → historic	politics → political	fashion → fashionable	beauty → beautiful	depend → dependent	effect → effective

+ ous	***+ less***	**participles** (▶ 21.2A)	**compounds** (▶ 21.2C)
danger → dangerous	hope → hopeless	interesting interested	home-made red-hot

Adjectives can sometimes act as nouns when they describe a particular group or characteristic (▶ **28.1B**). We usually use the definite article and a plural verb:

***Old** people are becoming more numerous. = **The old are** becoming more numerous.*

❗ We cannot use the possessive *'s* with adjectives used as nouns or make them plural:

✗ ~~*The government is looking at **the disabled's** problems.*~~

✔ *The government is looking at the problems of **the disabled**.*

✗ ~~*The **Japaneses** enjoy a high standard of living.*~~

✔ ***The Japanese** (or **Japanese** people) enjoy a high standard of living.*

❗ When we make a brief comment in conversation we often use *what* + adjective + noun or *how* + adjective:

*What an **amazing** story*! ✗ ~~*What amazing!*~~ ✔ ***How amazing**!*

21.1B Attributive position

Most adjectives can be used in front of a noun (attributive position), or after a linking verb, e.g. *be* (predicative position):

- Attributive: *We've just seen an **exciting film**.*
- Predicative: *That film **was exciting**.*

❗ But there are some adjectives which we usually only use in one position. Some classifying adjectives (which describe what type of thing something is) and emphasising adjectives are mainly used before a noun (see the table below):

✗ ~~*The plant they are building outside the town is **chemical**.*~~

✔ *They're building a **chemical** plant outside the town.*

Adjectives usually used in attributive position:	
classifying adjectives	*chemical, chief, criminal, elder, entire, eventual, former, industrial, local, lone, main, maximum, medical, national, nuclear, only, outdoor/indoor, principal, social, sole, underlying, whole*
emphasising adjectives	*mere, sheer, utter*

21.1C Predicative position

Adjectives in predicative position are usually the complement of a linking verb (e.g. *be, become, feel, seem* ▶ **30.2B**):

When she heard the noise Mary ***became*** *very* ***uneasy****.*

However, after certain verbs of thinking and feeling (i.e. *consider, find, think*) we can omit the linking verb:

I ***consider/find*** *him (to be) very* ***reliable****.*

Many adjectives beginning with the letter *a* and adjectives describing health and feelings are not usually used before nouns; we use them in predicative position:

✗ ~~*Try not to disturb the* ***asleep*** *children.*~~

✓ *Try not to disturb the children; they are* ***asleep****.*

Adjectives usually used in predicative position:	
beginning with *a*	*ablaze, afloat, afraid, alight, alike, alive, alone, aloof, ashamed, askew, asleep, awake, aware*
health and feelings	*content, fine, glad, ill, pleased, poorly, ready, sorry, sure, upset, (un)well*

❗ There are some fixed phrases/idioms in which we use normally predicative adjectives before a noun with a special meaning, e.g. *glad tidings, an ill wind, a ready wit, a sorry state, an upset stomach.*

Some predicative adjectives have equivalent words which can be used before a noun:

They are doing experiments on ***live*** *animals/animals which are* ***alive****.*

predicative	*alive*	*afraid*	*alike*	*asleep*	*ill*
attributive	*live/living*	*frightened*	*similar*	*sleeping*	*sick*

21.1D Adjectives after nouns, pronouns, etc.

We use adjectives after indefinite words like *something, anyone, no one, nothing, somewhere*, etc.:

✗ ~~*I'm looking for* ***cheap something****.*~~

✓ *I'm looking for* ***something cheap****.*

Some adjectives, including some ending in *-able* and *-ible*, can follow a noun if the noun follows a superlative adjective or *the first/last/next/only*:

They say she's ***the oldest woman alive****.*

I'm afraid that's ***the last ticket available****.*

Adjectives that are followed by a prepositional phrase, e.g. *interested* ***in something****, suitable* ***for somebody*** (▶ **15.5D**), go after, not before, a noun:

✗ ~~*The project will appeal to* ***interested in ecology students****.*~~

✓ *The project will appeal to* ***students interested in ecology****.*

This is similar to a reduced relative clause (▶ **31.1G**). We can also use a full relative clause with the adjective in predicative position (▶ **21.1C**):

The project will appeal to ***students*** *who are* ***interested in ecology****.*

❗ Some adjectives have a different meaning when used before or after a noun:

The meeting was full of ***concerned*** *residents.* (= worried)

The students ***concerned*** *were a small minority.* (= who took part/were involved)

I'm afraid we have ***opposite*** *points of view.* (= contrasting)

We used to live in the house ***opposite****.* (= physically facing/across from us)

The ***present*** *chairman is getting on a bit.* (= current/existing now)

We took a vote of all members ***present****.* (= physically there)

Responsible *parents have been outraged by this show.* (= caring/conscientious)

The person ***responsible*** *will be caught and punished.* (= who did the action)

He gave us a ridiculously ***involved*** *excuse.* (= complicated)

The president gave medals to all those ***involved****.* (= who took part)

21.2 PARTICIPLE (*-ING* OR *-ED*) ADJECTIVES

21.2A Position

We often use *-ing* and *-ed* participles as adjectives. We usually use them in the same positions as other adjectives (▶ **21.1B**):

A win, even by only one goal, would be a ***satisfying*** *result.*
I never find fast food very ***satisfying****.*
Recommendations from ***satisfied*** *customers got our business off the ground.*
We follow up every complaint from customers ***dissatisfied*** *with our service.*

Some participle adjectives (see the table below) can be used on their own before or after a noun:

The ***chosen*** *song features innovative use of digital sampling.*
The song ***chosen*** *may be a disappointment to lovers of traditional ballads.*

❗ But some participle adjectives (see the table below) can only be used after a noun:

✘ ~~*Please dispose of your cigarettes in the* ***provided*** *ashtrays.*~~
✔ *Please dispose of your cigarettes in the ashtrays* ***provided****.*

before or after a noun	*affected, chosen, identified, infected, remaining, selected, stolen*
only after a noun	*applying, caused, discussed, found, provided, questioned, taken*

21.2B Use

When we use participles as adjectives, *-ing* participles have an active meaning and *-ed* participles have a passive meaning:

I always seem to play for the ***losing*** *team.* (= the team which is losing)
She found the ***lost*** *ring under the sofa.* (= the ring which had been lost)

We often use participles as adjectives to describe feelings or opinions. We use *-ing* participles to describe a feeling that something causes:

It was a ***frightening*** *film.* (= it frightened us/it made us feel afraid)

We use *-ed* participles to describe a feeling that someone experiences:

I felt ***frightened*** *when I watched that film.* (= I was frightened/I experienced fear)

❗ Inanimate objects cannot have feelings so we don't usually use *-ed* adjectives about feelings to describe them:

✘ ~~*The report into the Paddington rail crash was rather* ***worried****.*~~
✔ *The report was rather* ***worrying****.* (= The report made readers feel anxious.)

We can use *that/those* with all participle adjectives with a meaning like 'the one/the ones that ...' (▶ **28.2A, B**). In this pattern we use *that* to refer to a thing and *those* to refer to things or people:

The easiest route is ***that taken*** *by Amundsen.* (= the one which was taken by)
Those living *in temporary accommodation will be rehoused within three months.* (= those people who are living in)
I feel sorry for ***those left*** *behind.* (= Those people that are left behind.)

(For more information on participles in phrases ▶ **Unit 13**.)

21.2C Compounds

We sometimes combine participles with other words to make compound adjectives. The participle usually comes last. Notice the use of hyphens when the compound adjective is used before a noun:

This Japanese maple is a particularly ***slow-growing*** *variety.*
Handel's 'Xerxes' was a ***rarely-performed*** *opera until relatively recently.*
Interest in Latino music is no longer confined to a ***Spanish-speaking*** *audience.*
The marines made a ***death-defying*** *leap over the cliff edge.*

21.3 GROUPS OF ADJECTIVES

21.3A Adjective order

We often use more than one adjective to describe a noun. The order of adjectives generally follows this sequence of categories:

*The 747's refurbished interior features **fantastic soft grey leather** seats.*

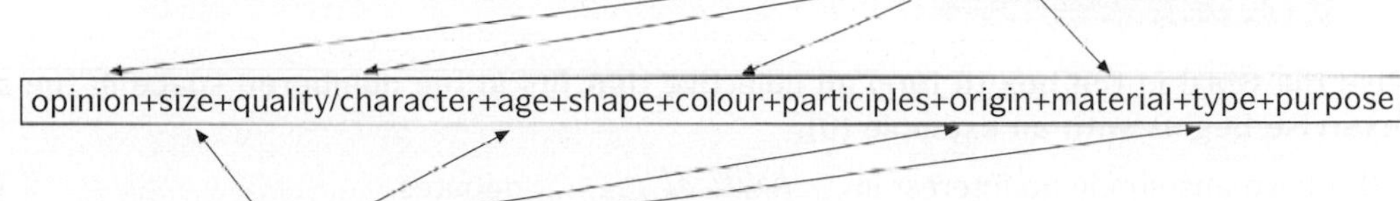

*For sale: **small, old, French carriage** clock.*

We always put the category which is most permanent or important (usually 'type' or 'purpose') next to the noun:

✗ ~~*The builders took out the gas **heating** antiquated system.*~~
✔ *The builders took out the antiquated gas **heating** system.*

And we put opinion adjectives before all others:

✗ ~~*I've just bought this new mobile **fantastic** phone.*~~
✔ *I've just bought this **fantastic** new mobile phone.*

❗ We don't usually use more than three or four adjectives before a noun. If we want to give more information we can use additional clauses:

[*It's a **charming small nineteenth-century French brass carriage** clock.*]
✔ *It's a **charming small French carriage** clock, made of brass and dating from the nineteenth century.*

21.3B Paired adjectives

If two adjectives describe different parts of the same thing we put *and* between them.

✗ ~~*The **chrome steel** facade glinted in the sunlight.*~~
✔ *The **chrome and steel** facade glinted in the sunlight.* (= Some parts were chrome, some parts were steel.)

We always use *and* between two colours:

✗ ~~*The players will be wearing **blue red** shirts for this match.*~~
✔ *The players will be wearing **blue and red** shirts for this match.*

We can use *and* between two adjectives which describe similar aspects of something:

*She's looking for a **stable and long-lasting** relationship.*

When two adjectives describe contrasting aspects of the same thing we put *but*, *yet* or *though* between them:

*The flat was located in a **rundown but central** part of town.*
*Group therapy can be a **simple yet effective** solution to this sort of problem.*

21.3C Using commas and *and*

When there are several adjectives in predicative position we usually put *and* before the last one:

*I'm afraid the hotel was **ancient**, **dirty** and **overpriced**.*

With longer lists of adjectives of the same category before a noun we can use commas and put *and* before the last adjective, or we can simply list the adjectives:

*I found him a **friendly, knowledgeable and dedicated** guide.*
*I found him a **friendly knowledgeable dedicated** guide.*

We don't use *and* before the last adjective when the adjectives are of different categories:

✗ ~~*We enjoyed sitting in the **fantastic soft grey and leather** seats.*~~
✔ *We enjoyed sitting in the **fantastic soft grey leather** seats.*

Practice

The key to these exercises is on page 363.

1 21.1

Use the word in the box to form an adjective that fits in the numbered space in the sentence. The exercise begins with an example (0).

0 I have absolutely no interest in ....*political*........... debates.
1 Entry to the single currency zone is .... on meeting several financial criteria.
2 Most public car parks now have special parking bays for the ....
3 John F Kennedy enjoyed a .... rise to fame in the 1960s.
4 Our lives are ruled by .... bureaucrats who seem to be answerable to no one.
5 It was more than funny, it was absolutely .... !
6 People claim the rise of popular culture has had a .... effect on national identity.
7 There are few things more .... than people who shout at waiters.
8 They say the .... love their pets more than their children.
9 I've made my mind up and any attempt to change it is ....
10 The soil in this valley is particularly ....
11 As a teenager I went through a very .... phase.
12 Unfortunately, a sense of moral duty seems to be becoming increasingly .... these days.
13 Orange and lemon trees are .... in this part of Spain.
14 Two weeks in the Bahamas for less than a hundred dollars? That's .... !
15 There's no point carrying on, the situation is ....
16 The compass will only work when laid on a .... surface.
17 That documentary on drug smuggling was a fine example of .... journalism.
18 Dry cleaning is often the only .... way to deal with stubborn stains.
19 Some of his pathetic excuses were downright ....
20 According to recent statistics the .... have Europe's highest per capita income.

0 politics
1 depend
2 able
3 meteor
4 face
5 hysteria
6 destroy
7 disagree
8 Britain
9 point
10 fertility
11 argue
12 fashion
13 plenty
14 believe
15 hope
16 horizon
17 investigation
18 effect
19 laugh
20 Holland

2 21.1

Look at these pairs of sentences. Tick (✓) those which are grammatically correct and cross (✗) those which are incorrect. In some cases both sentences are correct.

	A		B	
1	Cost is the chief factor.	☐	The cost factor is chief.	☐
2	This is the principal argument.	☐	This argument is principal.	☐
3	He had an ashamed feeling.	☐	He felt ashamed.	☐
4	That's a ridiculous idea.	☐	That idea is ridiculous.	☐
5	The village has a local post office.	☐	The village post office is local.	☐
6	It was sheer madness.	☐	The madness was sheer.	☐
7	You have a ready dinner.	☐	Your dinner is ready.	☐
8	He had an alone sensation.	☐	He sensed he was alone.	☐
9	We're building an indoor pool.	☐	The pool we are building is indoor.	☐
10	You have very alike children.	☐	Your children are very alike.	☐
11	That was a silly comment.	☐	That comment was silly.	☐
12	She's a mere beginner.	☐	That beginner is mere.	☐
13	They are afraid people.	☐	Those people are afraid.	☐
14	We have maximum security here.	☐	Here the security is maximum.	☐
15	He's my ill brother.	☐	My brother is ill.	☐

3 21.1

Indicate the correct position for the adjective or phrase in brackets, as in the example. The word the adjective/phrase describes is underlined.

0	There was <u>nothing</u>/in the book.	(original)
1	Many of the <u>portraits</u> are in the Prado Museum.	(painted by El Greco)
2	There was <u>something</u> about her behaviour.	(inexplicable)
3	They gave an <u>explanation</u> which simply served to confuse the jury.	(involved)
4	I'm afraid six o'clock is the only <u>appointment</u>.	(available)
5	The <u>state of affairs</u> is unlikely to continue for much longer.	(present)
6	I'm afraid the <u>person</u> is on holiday at the moment.	(responsible for recruitment)
7	They've started having late night parties in the <u>apartment</u>.	(opposite)
8	<u>Anyone</u> would be deeply offended by that harrowing documentary.	(sensitive)
9	Don't worry about getting receipts, the <u>amounts</u> are very small.	(concerned)
10	<u>Flower buds</u> often turn black and rot away.	(damaged by frost)

4 21.2

Study the numbered options in *italics* in this text. Underline the correct options. Note that in some cases both options are correct.

Airport hell

Results of a recent survey of international air travellers have revealed (1) *alarmed/alarming* discrepancies in the levels of (2) *comfort and service provided/provided comfort and service* at many leading airports around the world. A (3) *staggered/staggering* 75 per cent of (4) *interviewed those/those interviewed* felt that airports were failing to provide a (5) *relaxed/relaxing* and efficient environment.

Airports in Britain and the United States came in for particular criticism. Fewer than one in ten people were fully (6) *satisfied/satisfying* with the (7) *provided service/service provided* at leading airports in these countries. Researchers point to the enormous growth in

passenger numbers in the last twenty years, a (8) *continued/continuing* trend which has not been reflected in a corresponding growth in airport facilities.

By contrast, airports in the growing economies of south-east Asia and the Pacific have received far higher satisfaction ratings. Many (9) *questioned passengers/passengers questioned* felt that these airports, which are generally more modern than their equivalents in the West, usually offered (10) *enhanced/enhancing* check-in facilities and a more pleasant environment when compared to their competitors.

A (11) *discussed key factor/key factor discussed* in the report is the way in which airports deal with flight delays. The better airports have found ways to cope with (12) *bored/boring* passengers, ranging from television lounges to children's activity areas. (13) *Delayed/Delaying* passengers seem to appreciate small details such as comfortable seating and the availability of a wide range of refreshments. (14) *Affected passengers/Passengers affected* were less likely to complain if their children were (15) *amused/amusing* and they were able to find inexpensive cafés and bars.

5 21.2

Improve these sentences by rewriting them using compound participle adjectives to replace the underlined phrases. Use suitable forms of one word from each box to form the compound adjectives and make any changes necessary to grammar and word order.

brilliant car digital home film fast rare ~~rapid~~ slow technology well

colour drive know manufacture visit enhance ~~expand~~ go grow make move

0 São Paulo is a city which is getting bigger very quickly.
São Paulo is a rapidly-expanding city.

1 Northumberland is a part of England which people don't go to very often.

2 They were soon engulfed by the water which was flowing very quickly.

3 In recent times changes which are caused by technical developments have had a profound impact on working practices.

4 The oak is a tree which doesn't get bigger very quickly.

5 Australian parrots have plumage which is a mixture of bright red, yellow and green.

6 The Midlands is Britain's main region that produces automobiles.

7 The Hubble space telescope has produced pictures which are improved by electronic means that have amazed the public.

8 There is a segment of the public that visits cinemas that will always want to see corny adventure movies.

9 The new wing will be opened by a TV personality whom many people have heard of.

10 The desserts which are produced by ourselves are the main feature of our restaurant.

6 21.3

Rewrite these jumbled sentences with the words in the correct order. As a clue the first word of the sentence has a capital letter.

0 terraced/in/Victorian/They/a/live/house/wonderful
They live in a wonderful Victorian terraced house.

1 wine/It's/ancient/jar/a/Greek/priceless/ceramic

2 new/a/centre/Our/has/fantastic/school/state-of-the-art/computer

3 superb/textured/the/She/ten/sales/found/metres/dark/blue/of/velvet/in

4 Italian/It/upholstery/luxurious/features/leather

5 orange/for/study/We've/a/lovely/chosen/inexpensive/and/wallpaper/green/the

7 ALL

All these sentences contain mistakes. Find the mistakes and rewrite the sentences correctly. In some cases you may need to add, remove or change words; in others, you may need to change the word order.

0 The house was draughty, and damp cold.
The house was draughty, damp and cold.

1 Sylvia had a warm, gentle but friendly personality.

2 They've just bought a little Persian beautiful cat.

3 That documentary about racism was truly horrified.

4 This was the taken route by the original explorers.

5 The wealthies seem to have all the power in our capitalist societies.

6 The book is bound to appeal to fascinated by crime readers.

7 We comforted the afraid children after their terrifying ordeal.

8 On many questions my father and I have opinions opposite.

9 They've chosen a blue yellow colour scheme for their kitchen.

10 The injured bird appeared to have a breaking wing.

11 The boat has an aluminium and glass-fibre unique hull.

12 I'm afraid the city was noisy though overcrowded.

13 A new form of licensing is the proposed by parliament solution.

14 No punishment is severe enough for the responsible person for these crimes.

15 We are an action group acting on behalf of parents who are lone.

16 It was difficult because we had to choose between two alike alternatives.

17 Tall anyone will find these seats cripplingly uncomfortable.

18 Living in Scotland viewers may experience poor reception due to weather conditions.

19 Karen found her new job to be well paid and challenged.

20 The movie is a moving fast account of events during the Gulf War.

22 Comparison

Gradable adjectives (▶ **23.1**) can be used to make comparisons. The rules for the production of comparative and superlative forms of adjectives are generally straightforward but there can be difficulties with spelling, exceptions in use, and the different phrases which accompany them. This unit also describes ways of making comparisons without using comparative and superlative forms, e.g. with *like* and *as*.

22.1 COMPARATIVE AND SUPERLATIVE ADJECTIVES

22.1A Form and use

Hot Dog €1.50 Hamburger €2.75

Fishburger €2.75 Cheeseburger €3.95

We use comparative adjectives to compare two (or more) things or people, and superlative adjectives to distinguish one thing or person from a number of others. This table shows the forms of comparative and superlative adjectives and the basic patterns they are used in:

	comparative adjectives	**superlative adjectives**
adjectives with one syllable: *cheap*	adjective + *-er* (+ *than*): *The hamburger is **cheaper** (**than** the cheeseburger).*	*the* + adjective + *-est*: *The hot dog is **the cheapest**.*
ending in silent *-e*: *safe*	omit final *-e*: *saf**er***	omit final *-e*: *the saf**est***
ending in a consonant + *y*: *dry*	change *y* to *i*: *dr**ier***	change *y* to *i*: *the dr**iest***
ending in a single vowel + a single consonant: *big*	double the final consonant: *bi**gg**er*	double the final consonant: *the bi**gg**est*
adjectives with two or more syllables: *expensive*	*more* + adjective: *The hamburger is **more expensive** (than the hot dog).*	*the most* + adjective: *The cheeseburger is **the most expensive**.*
irregular adjectives *good/bad* *far* *old*	 *better/worse* *further/farther* *older/elder*	 *the best/worst* *furthest/farthest* *oldest/eldest*

We can use *than* to introduce a clause after a comparative adjective:

*Los Angeles is **bigger than I expected it to be**.*

We can use other phrases between a comparative adjective and a *than* clause:

*Burgers were **more expensive in this restaurant** than in the others we visited.*

❶ If the object of the comparison is a pronoun without a verb we usually use an object pronoun (▶ **27.1D**). If there is a verb we use a subject pronoun:

[*I'm taller than he.*] ✔ *I'm taller than* ***him***. ✔ *I'm taller than* ***he is***.

❶ When we have two or more adjectives with *more* in a list, we usually only use *more* once:

[*Lester and Graves were* ***more hardworking and more determined*** *than the others.*]

✔ *Lester and Graves were* ***more hardworking and determined*** *than the others.*

When we refer to a place or group we use *in* not *of* after superlatives.

✘ ~~*New York is one of the largest cities* ***of*** *the world.*~~ ✔ *...* ***in*** *the world.*

✘ ~~*He's by far the cleverest student* ***of*** *his class.*~~ ✔ *...* ***in*** *his class.*

But in formal English we can put an *of* phrase at the beginning of the sentence, before the superlative.

Of *the students in his class, he is the cleverest.*

22.1B Exceptions

There are some exceptions to the rules of form and the patterns of use listed above. One-syllable adjectives ending in *-ed* and the adjectives *real*, *right* and *wrong* form the comparative and superlative with *more* and *most* (they do not take *-er* and *-est*):

✘ ~~*I was* ***boreder*** *than I was on the flight to Sydney.*~~

✔ *I was* ***more bored than*** *I was on the flight to Sydney.*

Many two-syllable adjectives ending in *-ly*, *-y*, *-ow*, *-r* and *-l*, and the adjectives *common*, *handsome*, *mature*, *pleasant*, *polite*, *simple* and *stupid* can have either *more* and *most* or *-er* and *-est*:

The photographer wanted something ***more lively*** (or ***livelier***).

Your son needs to develop a ***maturer*** (or ***more mature***) *attitude to his work.*

When we add a negative prefix to two-syllable adjectives ending in *-y* (e.g. *happy* – *unhappy*) they can still take *-er* and *-est*:

He's ***the unhappiest*** *man in the world.*

❶ In informal spoken English we sometimes use a superlative adjective when we are only comparing two things, especially if the two things make a set:

I've got two cars but the Mercedes is ***the best***.

22.1C Irregular adjectives

We can use *elder* and *eldest* (instead of *older* and *oldest*) to talk about people's ages, especially people in the same family, but we can't use *elder* immediately after a verb:

Their ***eldest/oldest*** *son went to Harvard. Mary is* ***the eldest/the oldest***.

✘ ~~*My sister is* ***elder*** *(than me).*~~ ✔ *My sister is* ***older*** *(****than*** *me).*

Note that we don't use *elder* and *eldest* to talk about the age of things:

✘ ~~*This is the* ***eldest***~~ *house in the street.* ✔ *This is* ***the oldest*** *house in the street.*

We use *further* or *farther* to talk about a 'greater distance':

John's house is the ***farther*** *one.*

I've moved ***further away*** *from my parents.* (= a greater distance away)

❶ We use *further* (not *farther*) with the meaning of 'extra' or 'more':

Let me know if you have any ***further*** *questions.* (= extra/more)

22.1D Emphasis and strength

Most one-syllable adjectives can also form the comparative and superlative with *more* or *most* instead of *-er* or *-est*. We usually use this form for emphasis in spoken English:

You should be ***more proud*** *of the things you've already achieved.* (= prouder)

I think this is the one she is ***the most proud*** *of.* (= proudest)

Comparatives can be made stronger or weaker by inserting a word or phrase in front of them:

- Stronger: *even*, *(very) much*, *far*, *a lot*, *lots* (informal), *considerably*, *a great deal* (formal) + comparative:
  The cheeseburger's ***even more expensive than*** *the fishburger.*
- Weaker: *a little*, *slightly*, *a bit* (informal), *somewhat* (formal) + comparative:
  The hot dog's ***a bit cheaper than*** *the hamburger.*

We can make a superlative weaker or stronger in the same way.

- Stronger: *by far*, *easily* (informal) + superlative:
  *He's **by far the cleverest** student in his class.* (= He is much cleverer than the others.)
  *She's **easily the best** programmer in the company.* (informal) (= She is much better than the others.)
- Weaker: *one of*, *some of* + superlative:
  *New York is **one of the largest** cities in the world.* (= There may be some larger.)

22.1E Equality

To say that two things are equal we can use patterns like *is* + *no* + comparative or *is not* + *any* + comparative:

*The fishburger is **no more expensive than** the hamburger.* (= They are the same price.)
*The fishburger **isn't any cheaper than** the hamburger.* (= They are the same price.)

22.1F *less* and *least*

We use *less* and *least* as the opposite of *more* and *most*. We use these words with all adjectives including one-syllable adjectives:

*I prefer the paisley pattern; it's **less bold than** the others.*
*The hot dog is **the least expensive**.*

❗ But in informal English we usually prefer to make negative comparisons of this kind with *not as ... as* (▶ **22.2B**):

*I prefer the paisley pattern; it is**n't as bold as** the others.*

(For the use of *more/most/less/least/* with nouns ▶ **25.4A**, **B**.)

22.2 ADJECTIVES WITH *AS*, *SO*, *TOO*, *ENOUGH* AND *SUCH*

22.2A *as ... as*

We can say that two things are equal by using *as* + adjective + *as*. (Also ▶ **22.3D**):

*The hamburger is **as expensive as** the fishburger.*

We make this comparison more emphatic with *just*:

*We really shouldn't have gone; it's **just as bad as** I predicted it would be!*

To say that things are almost equal we use *just about*, *about*, *almost* or *nearly*:

*I've had **just about as much as** I can take.*
*She's **nearly as old as** I was when I got married.*

22.2B *not as ... as*

We make a negative comparison with *not as/so* + adjective + *as*:

*The hot dog is**n't as expensive as** the hamburger.* (= The hot dog is cheaper.)

We can modify this comparison with *nearly* or *quite*:

*The hot dog is**n't nearly so expensive as** the cheeseburger.* (= It is much cheaper.)
*The hot dog is**n't quite as expensive as** the hamburger.* (= It is slightly cheaper.)

In informal spoken English we can use *not anything like*, *nothing like* or *nowhere near* + *as* + adjective:

*The fishburger is**n't anything like as expensive as** the cheeseburger.*
*The fishburger's **nothing like** (or **nowhere near**) **as expensive as** the cheeseburger.*

22.2C *so*, *too* and *enough*

We use another type of 'comparison' when we describe the result of a particular quality or characteristic. We can use several structures:

- *so* + adjective + (*that*) clause:
  *I'm afraid I can't identify her. It was **so dark (that)** I couldn't see her face.* (= It was very dark. The result was that I couldn't see her face.)
- *too* + adjective (+ *for/to* phrase):
  *It was **too dark** (for me) (to see her face).*
- (*not*) adjective + *enough* (+ *for/to* phrase):
  *It wasn't **light enough** (for me) (to see her face).*

A more formal alternative to these forms is *so* + adjective + *as to* phrase:

*It was **so dark as to** make it impossible to see her face.*

22.2D *as* and *such*

We can use *as* and *such* to introduce a comparison. There are two patterns:

- *as* + adjective + *a* + noun + *as*:
  It wasn't ***as bad a result as*** *I'd expected.* (= It was a better result than I'd expected.)
- *such a* + adjective + noun + *as* (or *that* clause):
  It wasn't ***such a bad result as*** *I had expected.*
  It was ***such a dark night that*** *I couldn't really see her face.*

22.3 OTHER TYPES OF COMPARISON

22.3A Progressive comparison

We can describe how something increases or decreases by repeating the same comparative two or sometimes three times, putting *and* between the forms:

Her visits to the country to see her son became ***rarer and rarer***. (= increasingly rare)
As the illness progressed the patients grew ***more and more*** *detached from reality.*
Marching into the sunset, the figures became ***smaller and smaller and smaller***.

22.3B Combined comparison

To describe how a change in one thing causes a change in another, we can use two comparative forms with *the*. Note the use of the comma after the first clause:

The longer *you leave it,* ***the worse*** *it'll get.*

We sometimes omit the verb *be* in the clauses:

The more sophisticated *the product,* ***the more substantial*** *the potential profit.*

22.3C Contrastive comparison

When we contrast two related qualities, we always use *more* (not *-er*):

✗ ~~*I'm sadder than disappointed.*~~ ✓ *I'm* ***more sad than*** *disappointed.*
Her eyes are ***more green*** *than grey.*

We can also use *not so much … as* or *rather than*:

I'm ***not so much*** *disappointed* ***as*** *sad.*
Her eyes are green ***rather than*** *grey.*

22.3D *like* and *as*

We often describe something by comparing it to something else which has similar qualities. These comparisons are known as 'similes'. There are two forms:

- *as* + adjective + *as*:
  Listening to her was about ***as interesting as*** *watching paint dry.*
  (In informal English we sometimes omit the first *as*: *She looks* ***white as*** *a sheet.*)
- *like* + noun or verb phrase:
  The cruise ship was ***like a skyscraper lying on its side***.

There are many idioms in which we use these two patterns:

You're ***as white as a sheet****; I think you'd better see a doctor.*
I feel full of energy today – I ***slept like a log*** *last night.*

❗ We use *like* (not *as*) before a noun when we are making a comparison between two things which seem similar:

✗ ~~*You look* ***as a man*** *who's seen a ghost!*~~ ✓ *You look* ***like a man*** *who's seen a ghost!*
When Mike puts on his dark suit he looks ***like a waiter***. (= He resembles a waiter.)

❗ We use *as* (not *like*) before a noun when we are describing someone's job, role or identity, or something's function:

✗ ~~*Simon's working* ***like a waiter*** *during the summer vacation.*~~
✓ *Simon's working* ***as a waiter*** *during the summer vacation.* (This is his job.)
Use your payroll number ***as a password*** *for the computer.* (This is its function.)

❗ We can also describe something by comparing it with something similar without using *like* or *as*; this is known as a 'metaphor':

We hope the new treaty will form ***a bridge*** *between our two nations.* (*a bridge* = metaphor for *a link*)

Metaphors are common in poetry and literary English:

Sometimes too hot the ***eye of heaven*** *shines.* (*eye of heaven* = metaphor for *the sun*)

22 Practice

The key to these exercises is on page 364.

1 22.1

Fill the gaps with appropriate comparative and superlative forms of the adjectives in the box. Add *than* and *the* if necessary.

dry	keen	fat	bored	good	loose	real	~~safe~~	tidy
	bad	big	pretty	wet	scared	wrong	far	

0 I'm rather worried about the side effects of aspirin. Can you recommend a ......*safer*..... alternative?
1 And now we come to the award for .... actor in a leading role.
2 It's been raining non-stop. I wouldn't be surprised if this turns out to be .... July on record!
3 The authenticity of dialogue and setting often makes low-budget films seem .... the somewhat artificial version of reality in Hollywood movies.
4 In medieval times people rarely travelled long distances. For most peasants .... they would ever travel would be to the local market town.
5 In our study children on a diet high in dairy products tended to be considerably .... average.
6 Now that I'm employing a cleaner the house has become a lot .... it ever used to be!
7 This skirt's much too tight on the hips. I need something with a .... fit.
8 DiCaprio was awful! I think that's .... performance I've ever seen him give.
9 I don't mind the Mediterranean summer because it's a .... heat than you find in the tropics.
10 They say the great pyramid at Giza is .... structure to survive from the ancient world.
11 I like all Mozart's operas but I think *Don Giovanni* is the one I am .... on.
12 We inherited two paintings from my grandmother. Of the two, I'd say the landscape is ....
13 I know all murder is wrong, but don't you agree that it's .... to murder a child than to murder an adult?
14 .... I've ever felt was when Joe and I were flying over the Himalayas and we hit a storm; it was absolutely petrifying.
15 That play was so tedious. I was .... watching that than I was when I spent three hours trapped in that lift last year!

2 22.1, 22.2

Match each sentence (1–7) with a sentence with the same meaning from A–G.

1 It's slightly cheaper.
2 It's much cheaper.
3 It isn't anything like as cheap.
4 It's just as cheap.
5 It's by far the cheapest.
6 It isn't quite as cheap.
7 It isn't as cheap.

A It's considerably more expensive.
B It's the least expensive.
C It's more expensive.
D It's somewhat less expensive.
E It's no more expensive.
F It's slightly more expensive.
G It's nothing like as expensive.

3 22.1, 22.2

Tick (✔) the best explanation, A or B.

1 The prices on the menu aren't nearly as expensive as I expected.
A Prices are a little cheaper than I expected. ☐
B Prices are much cheaper than I expected. ☐

2 It looks as if your new car isn't any more reliable than the old one!
A Both cars are equally unreliable. ☐
B The new car is slightly less reliable than the old one. ☐

3 Of all the teams in the league, theirs is the least successful.
A Their team is the most unsuccessful. ☐
B Their team is less successful than some of the others. ☐

4 They said it was one of the most powerful earthquakes ever.
A No other earthquake was as powerful. ☐
B There may have been more powerful earthquakes. ☐

5 The new tax regulations are somewhat more rigorous than last year's.
A The new regulations are much more rigorous than last year's. ☐
B Last year's regulations were slightly less rigorous. ☐

6 I have to say that the hotel wasn't quite as luxurious as the brochure claimed.
A The hotel was much less luxurious than the brochure claimed. ☐
B The hotel was slightly less luxurious than the brochure claimed. ☐

7 This is by far the best seat in the plane. There's loads of legroom.
A No seat in the plane is better. ☐
B Other seats may be equally good. ☐

8 She isn't anything like as snobbish as you said.
A She is less snobbish than you said. ☐
B She isn't snobbish. ☐

9 I'm afraid your figures are no more accurate than the ones Rachel gave me.
A Your figures are less accurate than Rachel's. ☐
B Your figures and Rachel's figures are equally inaccurate. ☐

10 As far as Daniel's job is concerned, things are about as bad as they can be.
A Daniel's job could get worse. ☐
B Daniel's job couldn't be any worse than it is. ☐

4 22.2, 22.3

Complete each sentence so that it means the same as preceding one(s). Use the words in brackets but do not change the words given in any way.

0 As students get closer to their exams they become more nervous. (**the ... more**)
The closer students ....*get to their exams, the more nervous they become.*..........................

1 The lecture was very boring. As a result I fell asleep. (**so ... that**)
The lecture ....

2 The tickets sold out within days because the concert was so well publicised. (**such ... that**)
It was ....

3 The wording of the document is very complicated. It's incomprehensible. (**so ... as to**)
The wording of the document ....

4 I couldn't find my contact lens because it was very dark. (**too**)
It was ....

5 My friends claimed that the exhibition was interesting but I found it pretty dull. (**exhibition**)
It wasn't as ....

6 She's slightly angry but she's very disappointed. **(than)**
She's ....

7 Approaching the church, we noticed the sound of the bells becoming increasingly loud. **(and ... and)**
Approaching the church, we noticed the sound of the bells ....

8 As dogs get older they become less aggressive. **(the less)**
The older dogs ....

9 My son can't get a place at kindergarten because he's too young. **(enough)**
My son isn't ....

10 Their remarks were only slightly insulting, but they were extremely inaccurate. **(not so much)**
Their remarks ....

5 22.3

Match the situations (1–15) with the similes (A–P). Then use the similes to rewrite the sentences. You may need to use a good dictionary for this exercise.

A	like a cat on a hot tin roof	I	like hot cakes
B	like a trooper	J	as a fiddle
C	like a lamb to the slaughter	K	as a feather
D	like a bull in a china shop	L	as ice
E	like a bear with a sore head	M	as the grave
F	like a log	N	as a sheet
G	like a chimney	O	as a mule
H	like a rocket	P	~~as the hills~~

0 Stonehenge is incredibly ancient, more than 4,000 years old. *(P) Stonehenge is as old as the hills.*
1 She's a heavy smoker. ....
2 He's incredibly clumsy and often breaks things. ....
3 I slept really soundly last night. ....
4 It's absolutely freezing in here! ....
5 She so naive, she doesn't realise what a dangerous situation she's going into.
....
6 My grandmother may be 85 but she's incredibly fit and healthy.
....
7 Do you feel all right? You're very pale. ....
8 He's terribly nervous, he can't keep still for a moment. ....
9 She's in a foul mood this morning, shouting at and arguing with everyone.
....
10 Our new car goes really fast. ....
11 My new flatmate never stops swearing. ....
12 Once the lights were out the dormitory became eerily quiet. ....
13 She doesn't need to diet, she weighs hardly anything! ....
14 Once the old man has made his mind up he never changes it, whatever you say.
....
15 These new mobile phones are selling amazingly well. ....

6 ALL

Complete the following article. Use only one word for each space (1–20). Read through the whole text before you begin writing. The exercise begins with an example (0).

CONSUMER REPORT

HAIR CONDITIONERS

For this week's consumer test we've been looking at the (0) .....*most*..... popular choices of competing hair conditioner. We chose the three (1) ....-selling brands: Supremesoft, Vitabalm and ActiveShine, and gave them to our panel of ordinary consumers to try for a month.

Supremesoft ★★

At $2.99 for 250ml Supremesoft is the (2) .... expensive of the three brands. But, surprisingly, price is no guide to quality as this brand was (3) .... more effective (4) .... the cheaper brands. On the other hand, the panel felt the packaging was (5) .... upscale than the competitors, and the conditioner itself had an attractive colour and scent. But these advantages weren't significant (6) .... to compensate for the extra cost.

Vitabalm ★

Vitabalm is the (7) .... of the tested brands ($1.99 for 250ml). Our consumers thought the packaging wasn't (8) .... attractive (9) .... the others and the conditioner had what one tester described as 'a rather chemical smell'. It was (10) .... as effective as the others in dealing with tangled hair, but testers with dry hair found that it wasn't rich enough (11) .... give their hair any extra body. And everyone agreed that it was (12) .... harsh to be useable on a daily basis.

ActiveShine ★★★

This brand emerged as the (13) .... all-round value for money. It had a strong smell, rather (14) .... an antiseptic cream, but the smell was not (15) .... strong as to be off-putting. Testers found that it was just as effective with greasy hair as with dry hair and it was (16) .... far the most successful with flyaway hair. ActiveShine doesn't have (17) .... a rich composition as Supremesoft, but our testers found that (18) .... more they used it, the (19) .... noticeable the effect on their hair, so it was considered to be just as effective (20) .... the others in the long term.

So, at around $2.50 for 250ml ActiveShine receives this month's three-star rating.

23 Gradable and ungradable adjectives

Adjectives are 'describing' words. Most adjectives have a meaning which can be made stronger or weaker; these are called 'gradable adjectives'. Other adjectives have a meaning which is extreme or absolute and cannot easily be made stronger or weaker. These are called 'ungradable adjectives'. The differences in the way we use these two kinds of adjectives can cause problems even for advanced students. This unit looks at these different types of adjective and the ways in which we can modify their meaning. (For adjective use in general ▶ **Unit 21**; for adjectives used in comparisons ▶ **Unit 22**.)

23.1 MODIFYING GRADABLE ADJECTIVES

23.1A Gradable and ungradable adjectives

Gradable adjectives represent a point on a scale. For example, *cheap* and *expensive* are adjectives on the scale of 'how much something costs'. Ungradable adjectives represent the limits of a scale (▶ **23.2A** below).

ungradable adjectives (limit of the scale)	*free*	*freezing*	*vast/enormous*
↑ **gradable adjectives** ↓	*(very cheap)* *cheap* *(not very cheap)* *(a bit expensive)* *expensive* *(very expensive)*	*cold* *hot*	*large* *small*
ungradable adjectives (limit of the scale)	*priceless*	*boiling*	*minute/tiny*

We can make comparative and superlative forms from all gradable adjectives:

23.1B Strengthening the adjective

We can make gradable adjectives stronger with *very*, but not with the adverb *absolutely*:

✗ ~~*That new jacket looks **absolutely expensive**.*~~
✓ *That new jacket looks **very expensive**.*

There are several other modifiers which we use to strengthen the meaning of these adjectives: *so*, *rather*, *really*, *extremely*, *terribly*, *most* (formal), *pretty* (informal):

Last night's match was ***terribly exciting****.*
I felt ***pretty upset*** *after the accident.* (informal)
The chapter on the early sonnets was ***most instructive****.* (formal)

We often use less common adverbs to modify certain gradable adjectives. Although *very* is commonly used to strengthen any adjective, your English will sound more fluent and natural if you learn to use other combinations of adverb and adjective:

I was ***bitterly disappointed*** *at my exam results.*
My brother is ***painfully shy****.*
The students in this school are ***highly intelligent****.*

Note that we can often only use certain adverbs with certain adjectives (for commonly used combinations ▶ **23.4**).

23.1C Weakening the adjective

Gradable adjectives can usually be made weaker by the words *fairly*, *slightly*, *a (little) bit* (informal) and *somewhat* (formal):

I've been feeling ***slightly dizzy*** *all morning.*
My friend was ***a bit drunk****.* (informal)
The police reported that the man was ***somewhat inebriated****.* (formal)

In conversation, *a bit* is a useful way to make a critical remark more polite:

You're ***a bit overdressed****, aren't you?*

We can use *not very* and *not at all* to weaken gradable adjectives after the verb *be*:

The end of term test ***wasn't very long*** *and it* ***wasn't at all difficult****.*

23.1D *quite*

With gradable adjectives *quite* usually means 'fairly' but can have other meanings. The different meanings are only apparent in spoken English as they are dependent on stress and intonation:

The lecture was ***quite interesting****.* (unmarked = fairly interesting)
quite ***interesting*** (stress on adjective = more interesting than the speaker expected)
quite *interesting* (stress on adverb = less interesting than the speaker expected)

(For *quite* with ungradable adjectives ▶ **23.2B**.)

23.2 MODIFYING UNGRADABLE ADJECTIVES

23.2A Ungradable adjectives

Ungradable adjectives (e.g. *enormous*, *vast*, *tiny*, *priceless*, *free*) have a meaning which represents the limit of a scale. For example the limits of the scale of 'how much something costs' (▶ table in **23.1A**) are *free* (= it costs nothing) and *priceless* (= its cost is too great to be counted). Ungradable adjectives are not usually used in comparatives and superlatives (but ▶ **23.2D**), and we do not use *very* to make them stronger:

✗ ~~*The Ming vases are* ***more priceless*** *than the Egyptian mummies.*~~
✔ *The Ming vases are* ***more valuable*** *than the Egyptian mummies.*
✗ ~~*Entrance to the museum is* ***very free****.*~~
✔ *Entrance to the museum is* ***absolutely free****.*

23.2B Intensifying the adjective

A common way to intensify the meaning of ungradable adjectives is with the adverb *absolutely*. We use this device to add emphasis in spoken and informal English; it is not common in writing:

I couldn't swim in the sea; the water was ***absolutely freezing****.*
The show was ***absolutely fabulous****.*

When we use *quite* with ungradable adjectives, it has a similar meaning to 'completely', emphasising the strength of the adjective:

The tenor's performance was ***quite amazing****.*
You're ***quite correct****.*

Although we use *absolutely* with many ungradable adjectives, there are some adjectives which are never intensified with *absolutely* and some where we prefer to use other intensifying adverbs such as *completely*, *totally* and *utterly*. There are no grammar rules which explain these combinations so it is best to learn them as vocabulary items (► 23.4).

*I'm afraid your answer is **completely wrong**.*
*Since the accident Henry has been **totally deaf** in one ear.*
*Susan was **utterly appalled** by her husband's dishonesty.*

We can also use *a most* before ungradable adjectives used before a noun:

*Hilary has **a most amazing** hairstyle.*

23.2C *almost, nearly*, etc.

We do not usually make ungradable adjectives weaker by using the modifiers *fairly*, *slightly*, *a (little) bit*, *somewhat* or *not very*:

✗ ~~*Their favourite possession is a **slightly priceless** Satsuma vase.*~~
✗ ~~*I wouldn't recommend the show; it's **not very fabulous**.*~~

But we do use *almost*, *nearly*, *practically* or *virtually* to indicate a point close to the absolute meaning of ungradable adjectives:

*He never turns the heating on – it's **practically freezing** in there.*
*The battery in my calculator is **almost dead**.*
*After six months with the disease he was **nearly deaf** and **virtually blind**.*

23.2D Comparatives and superlatives

Because ungradable adjectives represent the limit of a scale, they are not usually used in comparatives and superlatives. However, in spoken English many 'ungradable' adjectives can be used gradably when we are comparing similar things at one end of a scale and can then be used in comparisons:

*I've never been **more exhausted** than I was after the New York marathon.*
*That was **the most delicious** meal you've ever cooked!*

With comparatives of this type we often use *still more* or *even more*:

*Their house is **even more enormous** than Richard's!*

23.3 MODIFYING ADJECTIVES IN INFORMAL ENGLISH

23.3A *really, real*, etc.

There are several modifiers which we use with both gradable and ungradable adjectives to make their meaning stronger. The most common in informal English is *really*:

*That film was **really exciting**. It's **really freezing** in here!*

In informal US English *real* can be used instead of *really*:

*That watch looks **real expensive**.*

Expressions such as *nice and* and *good and* can be used to intensify many adjectives:

*The hotel was **nice and clean**. I'll come when I'm **good and ready**.*

In very informal English, *dead* and a number of slang words (e.g. *bleeding*) can be used as intensifiers:

*The rollercoaster ride was **dead scary**.*

! We usually do not use these colloquial modifiers in formal English:

[*Her Majesty was **dead interested** in the traditional Maori dancing*.]
[*The bank is **really sorry** about having to refuse your application for a loan*.]

23.3B Gradable and ungradable

Some adjectives can have both gradable and ungradable meanings, depending on whether the speaker feels the adjective describes an absolute quality or one which is relative to something else:

*I'm afraid there are no rooms – the hotel is **full**.* (ungradable = completely full)
*The hotel's **very full** but I think I can get you a single room for tonight.* (gradable = has many guests but there is still some space)

Other adjectives like this are: *empty, beautiful, black, delicious, new, possible*.

23.4 COMMON ADVERB + ADJECTIVE COLLOCATIONS

These collocations are taken from the British National Corpus. (Below, 'sb' = *somebody* and 'sth' = *something*.)

adverb +	adjective
bitterly	*cold, disappointed, divided, hostile, humiliated, hurt, opposed, resented, resentful, upset*
completely	*acclimatised, alone, different, drained, empty/full, extinguished, immune (from/to sth), incapable (of sth), incomprehensible, lost, negative, new, open (with sb)* (= honest), *overlooked, revised, right/wrong, untenable*
deeply	*ashamed, attached (to sb/sth)* (= strong feeling for), *conscious, conservative, depressed, disappointed, disturbed, divided, embedded, embittered, hurt, indebted (to sb), ingrained, in love with, involved, involved (in sth), lamented, meaningful, moving, religious, rutted*
entirely	*absent, beneficial, clear, different, false, fitting, free, global, impersonal, loyal, new, obvious, serious, unconvincing, unexpected*
heavily	*armed, booked, built, censored, criticised, embroiled (with sb/sth), flavoured, guarded, involved (in sth), muscled, polluted, populated, protected, publicised, regulated, represented, scented, soiled, taxed*
hideously	*bad, burnt, deformed, disfigured, disfiguring, effective, embarrassing, expensive, injured, lurid, mangled, scarred, swollen, ugly, unhygienic*
highly	*commended, contagious, controversial, critical, dependent, developed, educated, enjoyable, flexible, intelligent, mobile, paid, personal, polished, political, popular, publicised, qualified, recommended, regarded, relevant, resistant, respected, significant, skilled, specialised, technical, toxic, trained, unlikely, valued, volatile*
painfully	*acute, aware, evocative, learned, loud, obvious, self-conscious, sensitive, shy, slow, small, sparse, thin*
perfectly	*arranged, balanced, capable, fitting* (= appropriate), *formed, genuine, good, healthy, normal, placed, proper, rational, reasonable, (all) right, safe, still, straightforward, understandable, valid*
seriously	*damaged, exposed, hit* (= damaged), *ill, impaired, rich, threatened, undermined, wealthy*
totally	*abandoned, abused, alien, anaemic, decent, destroyed, different, embarrassed, harmless, homogeneous, honest, impervious (to sth), inadequate, incompetent, integrated, irresistible, logical, new, normal, overpowering, stiff, surprising, unacceptable, unbelievable, undefined, unjustified, wasted*
utterly	*abandoned, alone, appalled, careless, dejected, destroyed, devoted (to sb), different, disastrous, fearless, futile, impossible, irresistible, lacking, ruthless, tragic, unacceptable, unattainable, unquestioning, useless, wrecked*

Practice

The key to these exercises is on page 364.

1 23.1, 23.2

Put each adjective into the correct box below. Each box will contain ten adjectives.

amazing attractive cold correct dead enormous exciting expensive extinct fascinating freezing good interesting huge large minute paralysed shy sick ugly

ungradable adjectives	gradable adjectives

2 23.1, 23.2

Use the words in the box below to rewrite each sentence, making it either stronger or weaker according to the instructions. Use each word once only. The exercise begins with an example (0).

virtually very somewhat a bit highly absolutely ~~slightly~~ fabulously fairly

Make these sentences weaker:

0 The dress I bought yesterday is damaged. *The dress I bought yesterday is slightly damaged.*
1 These days mobile phones are inexpensive. ....
2 Be careful changing gear; the gearstick's stiff. ....
3 The inscription on the tomb was indecipherable. ....
4 Many of the Inca religious ceremonies were bloodthirsty. ....

Make these sentences stronger:

5 Jane's flat was freezing last night. ....
6 This new computer game sounds interesting. ....
7 Hilary's new boyfriend is rich. ....
8 Victory in our next game seems unlikely. ....

3 23.1–23.3

Match the labels (A–D) with the sentences (1–6). Some labels may be used more than once.

A US English **B** formal **C** informal **D** very informal

1 We were wearing the same outfit! It was dead embarrassing. ....
2 The cave paintings were real impressive. ....
3 I thought Dave's behaviour was a bit bizarre last night. ....
4 The professor's lecture was most illuminating. ....
5 Francis Bacon's later works were somewhat disturbing. ....
6 These new engines are pretty reliable. ....

4 23.1, 23.2, 23.4

Read the article below and decide which word (A–C) best fits each space (1–10). The exercise begins with an example (0).

Fakes found in major museums

Oscar White Muscarella, a (0) ... respected archeologist at New York's Metropolitan Museum, claims that more than 1,250 forgeries are on display in the world's leading museums and art galleries. In his latest book Muscarella specifically names 37 forgeries in the Louvre, 16 in the British Museum and 45 in his own museum in New York. Muscarella's earlier claims have been heavily (1) ... by some museum officials who are (2) ... opposed to his arguments. But Muscarella has (3) ... good scientific evidence for his claims, showing that over 40 per cent of the objects examined by the Oxford Thermo-luminescence laboratory are fakes. The reason for the quantity of forgeries is (4) ... simple. Because many of the objects in our museums were found by amateurs and illegally exported from their countries of origin they have no official provenance or documented history. Museums are painfully (5) ... of this embarrassing problem and as a result they have been known to overlook the lack of written records before accepting or buying antiquities. This makes it (6) ... impossible to detect forgeries, especially if they are accurate copies. But in fact many forgeries are (7) ... obvious as they are often copied from a photograph which only shows the front of an object. When examining the back of the forgery they can look (8) ... different from the original. But museum officials tend to be (9) ... conservative and hate to question objects which have been sitting in their collections for many years.

Muscarella specialises in the ancient Middle East, and this is the area of archaeology in which he has found so many forgeries. But his research has had the effect of undermining the reputation of some of our most (10) ... regarded institutions, and this should be of concern to anyone who values our cultural heritage.

0 A absolutely (B) highly C very
1 A discussed B rejected C criticised
2 A bitterly B highly C rather
3 A perfectly B absolutely C somewhat
4 A virtually B quite C really
5 A conscious B understanding C aware
6 A very B virtually C pretty
7 A a bit B entirely C deeply
8 A completely B absolutely C almost
9 A heavily B dead C deeply
10 A very B highly C absolutely

5 23.3, 23.4

Six of these sentences contain mistakes. Tick (✔) the correct sentences, then find the mistakes and correct them.

1 We thought the state rooms in the White House were real impressive! ....

2 I'm afraid there's nothing to eat; the fridge is very empty. ....

3 The tour bus is completely full so I've only got six seats left to offer you. ....

4 I love these 'awayday' tickets; they're nice and cheap. ....

5 We chose the hotel because it was very recommended by our neighbours. ....

6 If you were really serious about your studies, you would have given up that evening job. ....

7 Everyone in our class loves Jackie – she's dead friendly. ....

8 Jack was a very built man with massive shoulders and a menacing stare. ....

9 I found the funeral ceremony absolutely moving. ....

10 The Ambassador would be really delighted to accept this honour on behalf of the President. ....

6 ALL

This box contains eight groups of gradable and ungradable adjectives with similar meanings. There are four adjectives for each group in the box below. Complete the gaps in the table. The example for *nice* is provided.

annoyed boring ~~brilliant~~ delighted diminutive diverting ecstatic engaging exhilarated ~~fabulous~~ famished ~~fantastic~~ fascinating furious happy hungry interesting irate irritated little ~~lovely~~ minute ravenous scarce starving stultifying tedious tiny uncommon uninteresting unique unusual

	gradable adjectives			ungradable adjectives		
1 dull	....	....	....	....		
2 small	....	....	....	....		
3 amusing	....	....	....	....		
4 rare	....	....	....	....		
5 angry	....	....	....	....		
6 nice	*lovely*	xxx	xxx	*fabulous*	*fantastic*	*brilliant*
7 pleased	....	xxx	xxx	....	....	....
8 peckish	....	xxx	xxx	....	....	....

7 ALL

The writer of this letter has made mistakes with some of the adjectives she has used. Find the mistakes and substitute suitable alternative adjectives from the table in exercise 6. You can only change the adjectives, everything else must remain the same. There are 14 unsuitable adjectives in the letter, including the example.

HOTEL PALMERA
BARCELONA

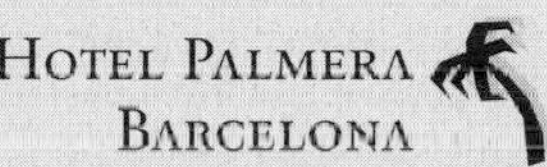

Dear Susanna,

Having an absolutely ~~nice~~ time here in Barcelona. The weather has been wonderfully hot and sunny with hardly a cloud in the sky. Our hotel is in the Gothic quarter – it's very minute but quite comfortable. The staff are all very friendly and helpful – we got back from a club at 3 a.m. a couple of days ago – all of us were absolutely hungry of course – and the doorman kindly offered to make us all sandwiches! Steve wasn't impressed (as usual!), he was actually fairly furious because they didn't have granary bread!

We've seen most of the sights in the city. Karen was absolutely pleased when we went to the 'Sagrada Familia' – she loves Gaudi's work. It's certainly a totally rare building. And Steve was very ecstatic about going to the Maritime Museum – he seems to find anything to do with boats utterly interesting. I can't understand it myself. I was absolutely annoyed when he suggested we stay there over lunch time – especially as I was a bit famished at the time (not surprising after two very tedious hours of looking at dusty old ships! It was even more stultifying than that afternoon we spent with the VAT inspectors – if you can imagine such a thing!)

The street life here is very fascinating. We've spent a lot of time wandering around and staring at the street performers. Luckily there are lots of pavement cafés and it's very fabulous to simply while away the time watching the world go by.

Anyway, I hope things are going well at the office, although I can't say I'm very exhilarated at the thought of getting back there next week!

Lots of love

Jackie

Line 2 ~~nice~~ fabulous

24 Adverbs

Adverbs are words which modify or give extra information about verbs, adjectives, other words or whole clauses. This unit examines the form and use of adverbs, including adverb pairs with very similar forms, as well as adverbs and adjectives with the same form. This unit also looks at the position of adverbs which modify verbs and at those adverbs which convey a viewpoint or attitude, or modify a whole sentence.

24.1 FORM

24.1A Forms of adverbs

Some adverbs are not derived from other words, while others are formed by adding suffixes (e.g. *-ly*) to other words, or are formed from groups of words. These are some common examples of adverbs (note spelling):

not formed from other words	*just, well, soon, too, quite, still*
fixed phrases	*kind of, of course, at last*

formed from other words	
adjective + *-ly*	*tragic* → ***tragically***, *excitable* → ***excitably***, *easy* → ***easily***, *real* → ***really***
noun/preposition + *-ward(s)/-wise*	*home* → ***homeward***, *after* → ***afterwards***, *price* → ***pricewise***, *health* → ***healthwise***
compounds	*some* + *times* → ***sometimes***

24.1B Confusing forms

In some cases adverbs have the same forms as adjectives; in other cases two different adverbs are derived from the same adjective:

Adverbs which have the same form as adjectives:
close, dead, fast, fine, long, low, pretty, short, straight, wide, wrong

Common adverbs from the same base, with different meanings:	
direct (= without stopping) *We flew* ***direct*** *from La Guardia to Houston.*	*directly* (= immediately/very soon) *Don't go. I'll be with you* ***directly***.
late (= not on time/not early) *The plane arrived* ***late*** *due to bad weather.*	*lately* (= recently) *She's been rather ill* ***lately***.
high (= to a great height) *He lifted it* ***high*** *over his head.*	*highly* (= extremely) *Arsenic is* ***highly*** *toxic.*
hard (= with a lot of effort/severely) *He braked* ***hard*** *when he saw the cat.*	*hardly* (= scarcely, almost not) *We* ***hardly*** *know our neighbours.*
right (= direction/correctly) *Turn* ***right*** *at the crossroads.* *Try to do it* ***right*** *this time!*	*rightly* (= correctly in my opinion) *The tribunal* ***rightly*** *condemned the war criminals.*
free (= without paying) *We got into the concert* ***free***!	*freely* (= without limitation or control) *Sheep roam* ***freely*** *over the hills.*
deep (= to a great depth/distance) *We explored* ***deep*** *into the jungle.*	*deeply* (= thoroughly) *I'm* ***deeply*** *ashamed of my behaviour.*

❗ There are a few adjectives which look like adverbs, e.g. *friendly*, *lonely*, *cowardly* (▶ **Unit 21**). We cannot make these adjectives into adverbs in the usual way. We use alternative words or phrases, or the adjective with *manner* or *way*:

✗ ~~*He left **cowardlyly**, sneaking out the back door.*~~

✓ *He left **like a coward** ...* ✓ *He left **in a cowardly way** ...*

We use some common adjectives as adverbs in informal conversational English, although some speakers consider this incorrect:

[*They sell things very **cheap** in that market.*]

In informal US English *real* and *good* can be used instead of *really* and *well*:

*She's a **real** nice girl. The team's running **good** this season.*

24.2 USE

24.2A Modifying, and adding information

The most common use of adverbs is to modify adjectives; the adverb usually comes before the adjective:

*I thought his answers were **pretty good** on the whole.*

Some adverbs, e.g. *really*, *almost*, *quite*, *pretty*, can modify another adverb:

*The French team did **really well** in the first round.*

Certain adverbs, e.g. *quite*, *roughly*, *about*, *approximately*, can also modify following noun phrases, prepositional phrases and numbers:

*Her news came as **quite a shock**.*

*In our school **roughly fifty** students have mobile phones.*

A key use of adverbs is to add information about the time, manner or place of an action or state described in a sentence (▶ **24.3**):

*He hit the ball **hard** and **this time** it flew **into the back of the net**.*

Note that we can use noun phrases (*this time*) and prepositional phrases (*into the back of the net*) as adverbs.

We can use adverbs with *as*, *so*, *too*, *enough*, etc.:

*She performed **so enthusiastically that** the judges overlooked her inexperience.*

*We missed the bargains because we didn't get there **soon enough**.*

Some adverbs are used in conversation to show the speaker's attitude (▶ **24.4B**).

24.2B Using adverbs in comparisons

We can use adverbs in comparatives and superlatives, usually with *more* and *most*:

*In the lottery draw red balls seem to come up **more frequently** than yellow ones.*

*Of all the relatives at Gran's funeral I think Uncle Ralph felt her loss **most deeply**.*

Adverbs which do not end in *-ly* take the same comparative and superlative forms as adjectives (▶ **22.1A**):

*If you tuned the engine **more often** the car would go **faster**.*

Note that the comparative and superlative forms of the adverb *well* are *better* and *best*.

24.3 POSITION OF ADVERBS IN SENTENCES

24.3A The three positions

The position of an adverb depends on its meaning and the word or phrase it is modifying. Adverbs which modify adjectives, other adverbs and noun phrases have fixed positions (▶ **24.2A** above), but adverbs which modify a verb or add information about how, when or where something happens can take several positions in a sentence. We call these 'front position' (before the subject), 'mid position' (next to the verb ▶ **24.3C** below) and 'final position' (after the object or complement):

front ↓ mid ↓ final ↓

***These days** I **probably** take my health **much more seriously**.*

❶ If the object or complement of a verb is very long we can put a final position adverb before it:

*These days I take **much more seriously** all those things I used to take for granted.*

24.3B Front position

We can use many adverbs in this position. We often use adverbs which link or contrast with information in the previous sentence:

*I've been incredibly busy this week. **Yesterday** I worked more than twelve hours.*

After negative adverbs (e.g. *never*), or after adverbs of time and place followed by a verb of movement or position, we put the verb before the subject (inversion ▶ **34.3**):

***Never** have I seen such a disturbing sight.*

***Here** lies the body of our late lamented sovereign.*

❶ We do not use adverbs of definite frequency, e.g. *daily*, *weekly*, in front position:

✘ ~~*Monthly I get paid.*~~ ✔ *I get paid **monthly**.*

24.3C Mid position

This is the usual position for adverbs of indefinite frequency, adverbs of degree, adverbs of certainty, one-word adverbs of time, *even* and *only*:

adverbs of indefinite frequency	*always, frequently, generally, hardly ever, never, normally, occasionally, often, rarely, seldom, sometimes, usually*
adverbs of degree	*absolutely, almost, completely, entirely, just, hardly, partly, quite, rather, really, slightly, totally*
adverbs of certainty	*certainly, definitely, probably*
one-word adverbs of time	*already, finally, immediately, just, now, no longer, soon, still, then*

With a simple verb we put the adverb between the subject and the verb, but with simple forms of *be* the adverb goes after the verb:

✘ ~~*She **arrives always** by taxi and she **always is** on time.*~~

✔ *She **always arrives** by taxi and she **is always** on time.*

If there is a modal or auxiliary verb we put the adverb after the (first) auxiliary verb:

*We'**ve never** been to the Greek islands. You **can just** see the coast.*

*Sea eagles **have occasionally** been seen around Loch Lomond.*

These adverbs go after *do* or *not*:

*They **don't really** understand my point of view.*

❶ But we put *sometimes*, *still*, *certainly*, *definitely* and *probably* before a negative auxiliary:

✘ ~~*I **don't sometimes** understand his arguments. He **hasn't still** convinced me.*~~

✔ *I **sometimes don't** understand his arguments. He **still hasn't** convinced me.*

In spoken British English, if we want to emphasise an auxiliary verb or a simple form of *be*, we can put a mid-position adverb before it. The auxiliary/verb (underlined) is usually stressed:

*You **really** <u>don't</u> understand me at all!* *But she **never** <u>is</u> on time!*

Compare:

*I don't **really** like him.* (unmarked position = I slightly dislike him.)

*I **really** <u>don't</u> like him.* (emphatic position = I hate him.)

We can do this in US English even when we are not emphasising the verb:

*Madonna **never** has been shy of image changes.*

❶ We do not use other time adverbs (definite time or frequency) in mid position:

✘ ~~*We **every day** buy our lunch at that sandwich bar on the corner.*~~

But we can do this in news reports:

*The Federal Reserve **today** announced an immediate rise in interest rates.*

24.3D Final position

The most frequent position for adverbs in English is the end of the sentence. It is the usual position for *yet*, *a lot*, *any more*, *any longer*, *too*, *as well*:

✗ ~~*They aren't **any more** selling it.*~~ ✔ *They aren't selling it **any more**.*

We usually put adverbs of manner (which describe *how* something is done) and adverbs of definite frequency (▶ **24.3B**) in this position:

✗ ~~*He **well** plays the guitar.*~~ ✔ *He plays the guitar **well**.*

Adverbs of manner which end in *-ly* (except *badly*) can go in final or mid position:

*Harry **painstakingly** counted out the coins and arranged them **neatly** into piles.*

❗ We don't use *hardly ever* or *never* in final position:

✗ ~~*They watch television **hardly ever**.*~~ ✔ *They **hardly ever** watch television.*

❗ If we put *often*, *rarely* and *seldom* in final position, we must use *very* or *quite*:

✗ ~~*These days I eat desserts **rarely**.*~~ ✔ *These days I eat desserts **very rarely**.*

If there are several adverbs in final position, we usually follow a sequence of adverbs of manner, then place, and finally time:

*The statue was lifted **(carefully)(onto the plinth)(before the ceremony)**.*

24.4 SENTENCE ADVERBS

24.4A Viewpoint adverbs

Adverbs can describe the particular aspect of something we are commenting on:

***Economically**, the current government has been a resounding success.* (= The government has successfully managed the economy.)

*Although **economically successful**, the government is starting to lose popularity.*

24.4B Attitude/ sentence adverbs

Adverbs such as *clearly*, *honestly*, *obviously*, *surprisingly*, *understandably* can express our attitude towards an action:

*You've **obviously** been eating too many sweets, young man!* (This is a logical deduction which is clear to anybody.)

We can also use these adverbs in conversation to introduce, extend, or make a comment on a topic or opinion. We usually put these 'sentence adverbs' at the front or end of the sentence, separated by a comma:

***Incidentally**, I noticed they were looking for new players down at the Red Lion.*

*I don't think he knows what he's talking about, **frankly**.*

❗ There are a number of these adverbs where the meaning is not always obvious:

adverb	meaning
admittedly	This probably qualifies or contradicts what I have just said/heard.
apparently	This is something I believe to be true or have heard, although I'm not certain it is correct.
fortunately	This is something positive which contrasts with something else I have said/heard. I am pleased about this.
frankly	This is my true opinion, although it may be shocking.
incidentally/ by the way	I am changing the subject – this is some information which is not directly connected with the previous information.
understandably	One can sympathise with this.

❗ Some adverbs, e.g. *naturally* and *clearly*, can be used as sentence adverbs and also as adverbs of manner. Note the different meanings:

*Despite being in a zoo, the animals behaved quite **naturally**.* (= in a natural way)

***Naturally**, wild animals behave quite differently in captivity.* (= what is expected)

*The teacher answered the question **clearly** and precisely.* (= in a clear way)

***Clearly**, the teacher didn't answer the question.* (This is obvious.)

Practice

The key to these exercises is on page 365.

1 24.1

Underline the correct option in *italics*.

1 He slapped him *friendly/in a friendly way* on the back.
2 Does that flight go *direct/directly* or is there a stopover?
3 Many of the senior staff are *right/rightly* concerned about their pensions.
4 There's been a lot of talk about European integration *late/lately*.
5 Our new cellphone fits *easy/easily* into the average-sized pocket.
6 The path leads *straight/straightly* to the front door.
7 *Healthy/Healthwise*, stress is probably the most serious problem facing people today.
8 Animals are now able to wander *free/freely* throughout the game reserve.
9 In late spring the gulls nest *high/highly* on the cliff face.
10 The remains of the Spanish galleon lie *deep/deeply* under the ocean.
11 The minister will begin by giving a statement. *After/Afterwards,* you will be able to put your questions to him directly.
12 Jackson came pretty *close/closely* to winning that last race.
13 You'll never get better if you don't eat – you've *hard/hardly* touched your dinner!
14 In the Denver play-offs the Miami team did *real/good* well.
15 Some of these kids drive their cars far too *fast/fastly*.

2 24.2

Complete the second sentence so that it has a similar meaning to the first sentence. You must use between three and six words, including the word given in bold. This word must not be altered in any way. The exercise begins with an example (0).

0 Karen did really well in the test.
highly Karen ......*was highly successful*...... in the test.
1 The car started to accelerate as we turned the corner.
go As we turned the corner the car ....
2 She really didn't expect to win so much money.
quite Winning so much money came .... surprise.
3 Evolution is slower during periods of climatic stability.
happens Evolution .... during periods of climatic stability.
4 We didn't get there in time to hear the overture.
soon We wanted to hear the overture but we didn't get ....
5 More or less three-quarters of our students are fee-paying these days.
roughly These days .... our students pay fees.
6 In the USA only a few people have heard of our products.
entirely Our products are .... in the USA.
7 She gave such a moving performance that we were virtually in tears.
so She performed .... we were virtually in tears.
8 Mr Skidmore had a deeper involvement than any of the other directors.
most Of all the directors, Mr Skidmore was ....
9 In terms of politics, I felt most of the participants were biased.
politically In my opinion most of the participants ....
10 I couldn't have made my answers to the questionnaire any more honest than I did.
as I answered the questionnaire .... I could.

3 24.3

Tick (✓) all those adverbs which can complete the sentences and cross (✗) those that cannot. In one case none of the adverbs will fit.

1 Clarice .... opened the door to the secret compartment.
A slowly B last week C probably
2 We don't .... know the identity of the masked stranger.
A still B really C certainly
3 You can .... see the coast from this point.
A definitely B just C as well
4 Our next door neighbours go there ....
A as well B hardly ever C a lot
5 .... the boss gives me a hard time.
A Every day B Daily C Sometimes
6 I get the feeling you haven't .... understood my point.
A entirely B really C probably
7 The public don't .... respond in the ways advertisers expect them to.
A sometimes B any longer C always
8 I haven't been to the cinema ....
A yet B often C very often
9 Alarming signs of radiation leakage have been .... reported around the power station.
A often B this week C always
10 .... have I been subjected to such outrageous demands.
A Never B Rarely C Frequently
11 I'm afraid the bank does not .... permit such large overdrafts.
A generally B any longer C any more
12 The patient .... reacts to any kind of bright light.
A badly B immediately C usually
13 He plays the saxophone ....
A too B quite rarely C never
14 The data from those sensors isn't .... reliable.
A absolutely B sometimes C always
15 She treats her children ....
A carefully B well C badly

4 24.3

Rewrite these sentences putting the words and phrases in brackets in the best order. Note that none of these sentences are emphatic. The exercise begins with an example (0).

0 My parents (allowed/hardly ever) us to (late/on weekdays/stay up).
My parents hardly ever allowed us to stay up late on weekdays.
1 Taking advantage of a gap between the players, Owen kicked the ball (into the net/just before half time/skilfully). ....
2 Foxes (often/be seen/can) scavenging (on the streets of London/at night).
....
3 David (well/behaves/quite) when he is at home but he (at school/causes trouble/often).
....
4 The post (arrive/sometimes/on time/doesn't) in this part of the city.
....
5 Jennifer (immediately/didn't/recognise) the man waving (at the end of the show/frantically/from the balcony). ....

6 We (unable/are/usually) to offer refunds on the spot, but we will examine (thoroughly/before the end of the week/your claim). ....

7 These children (never/have/given/been/probably) the opportunities we all take for granted.
....

8 Access to the Internet (no longer/is) available (on weekday mornings/free of charge/at our libraries).
....

9 Such losses (have/would/normally/avoided/been) by the use of back-up devices.
....

10 Many of the old masters had assistants who would prepare the oil pigments (each morning/by hand/in their studios). ....

5 24.3

Make the answers in these mini-dialogues more emphatic by rewriting them with the adverb in brackets in a suitable position. Make any other changes that are necessary. The exercise begins with an example (0).

0 'Lucy hasn't turned up yet again.'
'I know. She is unreliable, isn't she?' (**really**) *'I know. She really is unreliable, isn't she?'*

1 'Admit it. You took that money out of the till.'
'I'm sorry. I don't know what you are talking about!' (**really**) ....

2 'How ridiculous! They can't fit us in on Saturday because they're full.'
'But that place is full on Saturday evenings!' (**always**) ....

3 'Isn't it strange that he never mentions his wife. Don't you wonder why?'
'Yes, I have wondered about that.' (**often**) ....

4 'Laurence won't even let us discuss your proposal.'
'I'm not surprised. He doesn't listen to my ideas.' (**never**) ....

5 'How bizarre. The customs officer really went through my luggage with a fine-tooth comb!'
'That's not unusual; the customs officers are quite thorough.' (**usually**) ....

6 'You must have some idea of his whereabouts.'
'I'm sorry but we don't know where he is.' (**honestly**) ....

7 'I think you should swallow your pride and apologise to them.'
'Come off it. You can't expect me to just cave in like that.' (**really**) ....

8 'Take a break? Give yourself space? What are you on about?'
'You don't have a clue what I'm talking about, do you?' (**absolutely**) ....

9 'Downloading that software seems to be taking an awfully long time.'
'I'm afraid these programs do take a long time to download.' (**sometimes**) ....

10 'Look. It's midday and Tabitha still isn't here.'
'Well, she is in the office before noon these days.' (**rarely**) ....

6 24.1, 24.4

Make this dialogue more natural by using suitable adverbs from the box to replace each of the expressions in *italics* (each adverb can only be used once and not all the adverbs will be needed).

admittedly	apparently	by the way	clearly	exactly	fortunately	frankly	ideally
naturally	obviously	reasonably	really	still	seriously	understandably	

STEVE Not a bad party last night. Lots of old faces from college were there.

CLARE (1) *That sounds interesting; can you tell me more?* ....

STEVE Yeah. Lizzie was there with her new husband. (2) *This is something I've heard although it may not be true*, ... he's something very high up and important in the civil service.

CLARE Yes, I've heard that too. (3) *This is my true opinion, although it may be shocking* ...., I never really expected her to marry anyone successful. She was always so scruffy and laid back. She was never into social status or anything like that.

STEVE (4) *It is a logical deduction* .... she's changed her outlook on life. I mean, she was very smartly dressed and she kept telling me all about how much money their new house had cost.

CLARE (5) *Do you expect me to believe that?* ....

STEVE Yes, she was really bragging about it.

CLARE Well she never used to be interested in money at all. (6) *This probably contradicts what I've just said* .... she did like eating out and travelling.

STEVE (7) *What I'm about to say isn't really related to what we've been discussing* .... your old flame Simon was at the party.

CLARE Was he? I haven't seen him for ages.

STEVE (8) *As one would expect* ...., he couldn't stop asking me questions about you.

CLARE I think he still hopes that we might get back together one day.

STEVE (9) *That is completely accurate* ....

CLARE Well, not much chance of that! Oh, was that obnoxious old creep Douglas Jarrold there?

STEVE I'm afraid so. (10) *I'm pleased about this* ...., he was right over the other side of the room so I didn't have to talk to him. He was trying to chat up Mary Bracknell. I can't think why.

CLARE (11) *This is obvious* ...., he still fancies her.

STEVE Maybe. She certainly wasn't very interested in him, (12) *which one can sympathise with* ....

CLARE Strange how some people never change, isn't it?

7 ALL

Rewrite these sentences using all the adverbial expressions in brackets.

0 The press office advised us not to discuss the matter. (before the conference/last week/publicly)
Last week the press office advised us not to discuss the matter publicly before the conference.

1 Ruined, the owner of the business agreed to sell the premises. (reluctantly/within the month/financially/rather) ....

2 There is nothing better than collapsing. (onto a sofa/probably/at the end of the day/lazily)
....

3 Controlled, this effective new drug can reduce blood pressure. (amazingly/within hours/carefully/dramatically) ....

4 We regret having to announce the suspension of all staff working in our subsidiary. (currently/under the circumstances/in San Diego/deeply) ....

5 We seem to get the chance to talk. (about these things/seriously/these days/rarely)
....

6 Many of my colleagues disapprove of my scheme to update the accounting procedures (thoroughly/over the next quarter/unfortunately/in the sales department)
....

25 Nouns and noun phrases

English nouns generally present few problems for the advanced learner but some aspects of countability and noun–verb agreement can be problematic. This unit looks at these aspects, as well as at plural nouns and at the nominalisation of verbs into nouns. (For compound nouns ▶ **Unit 26**; for nominalisation of adjectives ▶ **21.1A**.)

25.1 BASIC POINTS

25.1A Form and meaning

English nouns only change their form when they are plural (▶ **25.2A**, **B**) and to show possession (▶ **26.1**).
Nouns can be countable or uncountable (▶ **25.3A**), and concrete (*table*, *child*, *station*, *food*, *storm*) or abstract (*hope*, *responsibility*, *anger*, *efficiency*, *consternation*).

25.1B Gender

Nouns do not have grammatical gender in English. Some have a 'natural' gender, e.g. *woman* = female, *father* = male. Most nouns for jobs do not imply a gender. To specify gender, we have to say, e.g. *a woman doctor*. However, some nouns for jobs and roles do refer to males or females, often by their suffix, e.g. *business**man*** (male), *manager**ess*** (female). It used to be common to use the *-man* suffix to refer to people of both sexes:

*That's the view of Sheila Davison, **chairman** of the Institute of Public Relations.*

A lot of people avoid this now, especially if referring to a woman, and prefer a form with no implicit gender, e.g. *chair*, or to match the suffix to the person, e.g. *chairwoman*:

*That's the view of Sheila Davison, **chair(woman)** of the Institute of Public Relations.*

25.2 SINGULAR AND PLURAL NOUNS

25.2A Regular plurals

In writing, most English nouns form the plural with *-s*. This is true of nouns which end in most consonants (e.g. *road* → *road**s***, *bag* → *bag**s***, *town* → *town**s***) and the vowels *a* and *e* (e.g. *area* → *area**s***, *rope* → *rope**s***). But note these variations:

noun	plural form	examples
ending in consonant + *y*: BUT vowel + y:	+ *ies* + *s*	*family* → *famil**ies***, *party* → *part**ies*** *tray* → *tray**s***, *monkey* → *monkey**s***
ending in *-ch*,[1] *-s*, *-sh*, *-x*, *-z*:	+ *es*	*watch* → *watch**es***, *boss* → *boss**es***, *fox* → *fox**es***, *waltz* → *waltz**es***[2]
ending in consonant + *o*: BUT vowel + *o*:	+ *es* + *s*	*potato* → *potato**es***, *hero* → *hero**es***[3] *radio* → *radio**s***, *video* → *video**s***

[1] If the pronunciation of *ch* is /k/, add *-s* only: *patriarch* → *patriarch**s***.
[2] Note these exceptions of vowel + *z*: *quiz* → *quiz**zes***, *fez* → *fez**zes***.
[3] Some words ending in *-o*, especially words from other languages, take *-s* only: *piano* → *piano**s***, *photo* → *photo**s***, *kilo* → *kilo**s***, *adagio* → *adagio**s***.

25.2B Irregular plurals

English does not have very many irregular plurals. Here are some examples:

noun	plural	examples
ending in *-f* or *-fe*	usually + *ves*[1]	*leaf* → *lea**ves***, *loaf* → *loa**ves***
foreign nouns	varies according to origin of word:	Latin origin: *terminus* → *termin**i***, *datum* → *dat**a***, *vertebra* → *vertebr**ae*** Greek origin: *crisis* → *cris**es***, *phenomenon* → *phenomen**a***

noun	plural	examples
other irregulars	+ *(r)en*: change of vowel: no change in plural:	*child* → ***children***, *ox* → ***oxen*** *woman* → ***women***, *foot* → ***feet*** *sheep* → ***sheep***, *craft* → ***craft*** (e.g. boat)

[1] Several words ending in *-f* and all those ending *-ff* just take *-s*: *chief* → ***chiefs***, *belief* → ***beliefs***, *cliff* → ***cliffs***. Some words ending in *-f* take either plural ending: *scarf* → ***scarfs/scarves***. You can check irregular plurals in a dictionary.
You may sometimes see plurals formed with an apostrophe, especially with dates and abbreviations: *1960's, some GP's*. This is quite common and may be considered correct in informal writing, but it is considered incorrect in formal written English.

25.2C Nouns with no singular form

Some English nouns are more common in the plural form. These occur in a number of categories (▶ **25.4** for agreement with verbs):

- Clothing: *clothes, jeans, trousers, pyjamas, trunks, dungarees*
- Tools/equipment: *scissors, glasses* (= spectacles), *scales, handcuffs, pliers*
- Games: *dominoes, darts, cards, bowls*
- Subjects/activities: *physics, maths, politics, economics, aerobics, athletics*
- Other: *goods, whereabouts, remains, thanks, news, stairs, proceeds*

These nouns may have a singular form with a different meaning or as part of a compound noun (▶ **26.3C**): *a glass* (e.g. wine glass), *a pyjama party, a dartboard*

25.3 COUNTABLE AND UNCOUNTABLE NOUNS

25.3A Use

Countable nouns are usually concrete nouns and they can be 'counted': *a computer, three computers*. Uncountable nouns cannot be 'counted': *oil, beauty, fruit*. We do not use *a/an* with uncountable nouns, and we do not make them plural:

✗ ~~*The Asthma Helpline will be able to give you **an advice/some advices**.*~~
✓ *The Asthma Helpline will be able to give you **(some) advice**.*

❗ There are some differences between British English and US English: *accommodation* (uncountable in British English)/*accommodation**s*** (countable in US English).
Some determiners change according to whether the noun is countable or not (▶ **28.3**):

*For good health we should eat **a few vegetables** every day, as well as **a little fruit**.*
*It is also advisable to drink **less alcohol** and eat **fewer sweet things**.*

❗ In informal English it is possible to use *less* rather than *fewer* with countable nouns, although many people consider this to be incorrect:

[*You should eat **less sweet things**.*] [*There are **less people** here than yesterday.*]

Less is always correct if it refers to a 'whole', e.g. a period of time (▶ **25.4C**):

*The flight takes **less than three hours**.* (three hours = a period of time)

25.3B Countable and uncountable meanings

Some nouns can be countable or uncountable, but have different meanings:

noun	countable meaning	uncountable meaning
coffee[1]	*I'd love **a coffee**, please.* (= a cup of coffee)	Do you drink **coffee**? (= the liquid)
chicken[2]	*I'll buy **a chicken** for dinner tonight.* (= the whole bird)	*Would you like **some chicken** for dinner?* (= a part/the dish)
drawing[2]	*This is **an amazing drawing** by Leonardo.* (= a picture)	*My son is very good at **drawing**.* (= the activity)
stone[2]	*Someone threw **a stone** at our window.* (= one item)	*In this flat landscape of scrub and **stone** …* (= the material)

[1] This applies to all drinks: *tea/a tea, beer/a beer, lemonade/a lemonade*
[2] There are other examples of the same type as these, but not all nouns of the type can

be both countable and uncountable: *a duck/duck*, *a fish/fish*, but not ~~*a beef*~~, ~~*a pork*~~; *a painting/painting*, *a sculpture/sculpture*, but not ~~*an art*~~, ~~*a poetry*~~; *a paper/paper*, *a rock/rock*, but not ~~*a wool*~~, ~~*a cotton*~~

25.3C Quantifying uncountable nouns

We can refer to a specific example of an uncountable noun with determiner + countable noun + *of* + uncountable noun. Common countable nouns in this pattern are *piece* and *bit*:

*The Council will remove **two pieces of unwanted furniture** if desired.*
*Did you hear **that** interesting **bit of gossip** about Susan?*

Other common nouns used in this way are: *a slice of bread/meat/cheese/cake*; *an item of news/furniture/clothing*; *a lump of sugar/coal*; *a cup of coffee/tea*.
We can sometimes make an uncountable noun countable when we want to express 'different types' of the noun:

***The wines of Australia** are now of similar quality to many from France.*

We can make some uncountable abstract nouns countable if we refer to a specific type of the noun, for example, *distrust* → *a deep distrust*, *a distrust of accountants*. This is common with nouns connected with emotions. We do not make these nouns plural:

***Jealousy** is an enormously destructive emotion.*
*She felt **an incomprehensible jealousy** when she saw him with her daughter.*

25.4 AGREEMENT

25.4A Subject + verb + object/complement

In English the verb usually agrees with the subject even if the verb is separated from its subject by prepositional phrases, relative clauses, brackets or commas:

***The petrol station** across the road from the new shops **has** just cut its prices.*

However, if the verb is a long way from the subject but is closer to a complement (▶ **30.2B**), it is possible to agree the verb with the complement. Compare:

***The most exciting event was** the rowing finals.*
***The most exciting event** in the Sydney Olympics for most British viewers **was/were** the rowing finals.*

The same can apply after *what* used to introduce a relative:

***What** the Board needs to address now **is/are** the terms of the redundancies.*

25.4B Two subjects/plural subject + verb

We usually use a plural verb with two subjects linked by *and* or *both ... and*:

***Mum and Dad were** hoping that you'd join them this evening.*
***Both the doctor and the surgeon have** advised me to have my gall bladder out.*

❗ However, we use a singular verb if we consider the two items as one concept:

✗ ~~***Fish and chips are** one of the most common English dishes.*~~
✓ ***Fish and chips is** one of the most common English dishes.*

Titles of books, films, etc. take a singular verb, even if they are plural nouns:

***Hitchcock's film 'The Birds' is** based on a story by Daphne du Maurier.*

When we link two items by *or*, the verb usually agrees with the second of the items:

*Either **my brother or my parents are** going to bring the sleeping bags.*

25.4C Noun ending in *-s* + verb

Some uncountable nouns end in *-s* but take a singular verb. These often concern illness (*measles*, *mumps*), sport (*aerobics*, *gymnastics*) or study (*mathematics*, *politics*):

***German measles is** a particularly dangerous illness for pregnant women.*
***Politics is** a topic best avoided with people you don't know well.*

Some nouns refer to one object divided into two parts and take a plural verb, e.g. *scissors*, *trousers*, *scales* (▶ **25.2C**):

***Scissors are** used to cut the jeans.*

❗ A plural subject describing a single entity, e.g. measurement, can take a singular verb:

✗ ~~***Two metres aren't** particularly tall these days.*~~
✓ ***Two metres isn't** particularly tall these days.*
***Twenty-four hours is** a long time in politics.*

25.4D Collective noun + verb

We can use either a singular or a plural verb with most collective nouns, i.e. nouns referring to a group of people, animals or things, e.g. *family, government, group, staff, team, band, class, jury*. A singular verb presents the collective noun as a 'whole' entity:

The family has agreed that the funeral should be held in Ireland.

A plural verb presents the noun as a group of individuals, e.g. family members:

The family are all gathering here for Christmas.

A large number of proper nouns fall into this category, e.g. *the United Nations*:

The United Nations has agreed to deploy a peacekeeping force.

The United Nations are in disagreement on this issue.

! Unlike British English, US English prefers a singular verb in these cases.

In English we prefer to use a singular verb after a collective noun if we use *a/an* rather than *the*:

A team of inspectors is visiting the prison tomorrow afternoon.

A few collective nouns always take a plural verb, e.g. *cattle, police, people*:

The police are investigating his accusation of fraud.

An adjective used as a collective noun always takes a plural verb (▶ **21.1A**):

The middle-aged have a lot to offer employers, if only they would see it.

It is common to use a plural verb after nouns such as *the majority, a number, a couple*, when these are followed by *of* + a plural noun:

The majority of the people were pleased to see the government fall.

25.5 NOMINALISATION

25.5A Verb → noun

It is possible to make verbs into nouns in English by adding a suffix, e.g. *-ion, -ment, -er*: *educate → education, establish → establishment, teach → teacher*.

It is also possible to use many verbs as nouns, especially in informal English:

*Can't you open that? Shall I give it **a try**?*

*I'll take you to the station if you give me **a shout** when you're ready.*

! This does not apply to every verb. It is best to check in a good dictionary.

It is also possible to make nouns from multi-word verbs. The particle often (but not always) precedes the verb in the noun form:

*The epidemic first **broke out** in Zaire. → The first **outbreak** of the epidemic ...*

*The plane **took off** very smoothly. → The **takeoff** was smooth.*

*The car **broke down** five kilometres from home. → The **breakdown** happened ...*

25.5B Verb phrase → noun phrase

It is sometimes more concise and elegant, especially in written English, to use noun phrases rather than verb phrases to express an idea:

- Verb phrase: ***The committee decided** to open the playground to all children. This was welcomed by the local schools.*
- Noun phrase: ***The committee's decision/The decision of the committee** to open the playground to all children was welcomed by the local schools.*

The noun phrase is often made up of two nouns linked by a preposition:

verb phrase	noun phrase
They released the video in 1998.	*The release **of** the video in 1998 ...*
The law was amended last week.	*The amendment **to** the law last week ...*
The war drained the country's resources.	*The war was a drain **on** the country's resources.*

An adverb in a verb phrase changes to an adjective if the verb is nominalised:

*The girl shouted **loudly** and attracted the attention she wanted.*

*The girl's **loud** shouts attracted the attention she wanted.*

Practice

The key to these exercises is on page 366.

1 25.1, 25.2

Complete the crossword from the clues below.

CLUES ACROSS

1 plural of *quay*
5 neutral form of *chairman*
6 singular of *media*
7 singular of *wharves*
10 plural of *formula*
12 singular of *heroes*
15 plural of *monarch*
16 plural of *mosquito*

CLUES DOWN

2 plural of *sheriff*
3 neutral form of *manageress*
4 plural of *quiz*
8 plural of *address*
9 plural of *flamingo*
11 plural of *goose*
13 plural of *crisis*
14 singular of *oases*

2 25.2, 25.3

Underline the correct words or phrases in *italics* to complete this article.

Cookery Corner

In today's Cookery Corner I'd like to address a request from Mrs Parkinson of Suffolk for (1) *an information/information* about which type of (2) *chocolate/chocolates* to use in cooking. Well, Mrs P, my (3) *advice is/advices are* always to use the best possible chocolate you can find. It's the same principle as with (4) *wines/wine*: in cooking always use (5) *an equivalent quality/equivalent quality* to what you eat or drink. With chocolate, the reason for this is that higher quality chocolate will always give your cakes and sweets (6) *better/a better* taste. To judge the quality of chocolate, look at the amount of cocoa in the chocolate. Good quality chocolate has more cocoa solids and (7) *less sugar/fewer sugars*. For the best taste choose chocolate with a high cocoa (8) *contents/content* – never (9) *fewer than/less than* 70 per cent cocoa solids and as much as 80 per cent if possible. It goes without saying that you should also use other (10) *ingredient/ingredients* of the highest quality, too. If, for example, you're using coffee in your chocolate recipe, always use (11) *a strong, fresh coffee/strong, fresh coffee*. If you're making (12) *a cake/cake*, use the right kind of (13) *flours/flour*, and always weigh the ingredients on your kitchen (14) *scale/scales*. Believe me, if you follow these simple rules, the next time you bake a chocolate cake, there won't be (15) *a lump/a slice* left over!

3 25.5

Read this draft of a newspaper article, then complete the rewritten sections of the article below with a noun or noun phrase. The first one is given as an example (0).

St Andrew's Hospital Trust has recently confirmed that a fresh wave of food poisoning has broken out in the Scottish resort, and this has alarmed everyone who lives in the town. A spokesperson stated that the illness was not serious and could be easily treated. This appeased community leaders but they requested further reassurances that the authorities were doing everything within their control to contain the spread. The hospital authority has announced that it will investigate fully the causes of this epidemic. As a recent investigation into a similar outbreak concluded that the cause was poor meat hygiene in a local butcher's shop, local shopkeepers are concerned about what will come out of the pending investigation. The leader of the Shopkeepers' Association, Len Murphy, suggested that the source of the epidemic might be hospital kitchens, which has angered hospital staff. The kitchen staff at the hospital have now called for a strike of hospital auxiliaries across the region, which is likely to have severe financial consequences for the health authority.

(0) ....*The recent confirmation*.. by St Andrew's Hospital Trust of (1) .... of food poisoning in the Scottish resort has alarmed (2) ....
A (3) .... that the illness was not serious and could be easily treated appeased community leaders, but they requested further reassurances that the authorities were doing everything within their control to contain the spread. The hospital authority has announced (4) .... into the causes of this epidemic. As (5) .... of a recent investigation into a similar outbreak cited poor meat hygiene in a local butcher's shop as the cause, local shopkeepers are concerned about (6) .... of the pending inquiry. (7) .... by the leader of the Shopkeepers' Association, Len Murphy, that the source of the epidemic might be hospital kitchens has angered hospital staff. (8) .... by kitchen staff at the hospital for a strike of hospital auxiliaries across the region is likely to have severe financial consequences for the health authority.

4 25.1–25.4

Find fifteen more mistakes, or places where the style could be improved, in this text. Underline the mistakes and correct them. The exercise begins with two examples.

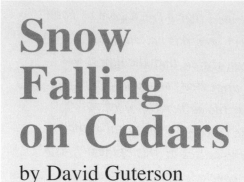

Snow Falling on Cedars

by David Guterson

Snow Falling on Cedars open in the courthouse of San Piedro, a small sleepy island off the Pacific coast of the north-west United States. Underneath the courtroom windows, four tall narrow archs of a leaded glass, a drama which will divide the island's communitys are unfolding. The defendant stands erect in the dock; the local press and the jurors – farmers, grocers, builders, fisher wifes – await the start of this trial. Kabuo Miyamoto is accused of the murder of Carl Heine, a young fisherman. The alleged crime by a young man of Japanese descent stirs up the emotions of the islanders and questions their believes and their politic. It takes place in the 1950's, and not many years has passed since the Japanese bombing of Pearl Harbour and the horrors of World War II. Although the Japanese on San Piedro was eager to defend their adopted country against the country of their ancestors, some people in the community were unable to forgive Japan its role in the War, and the trial causes their deeply-held prejudicies to surface.

Snow Falling on Cedars is not only one of the best mysterys of recent years, but it raises issues which affects us all. However, it ends with a great optimism. David Guterson has succeeded in combining the best from both classic and populist American literatures into a spellbinding art. Buy and read this beautiful novel.

opens

arches

5 25.3, 25.4

Fill the gaps in these sentences with *a*, *an*, nothing (–) or the correct form of a suitable verb. If there are two possible answers, put both possibilities.

1 Have you put .... pepper in this dish? I like plenty of seasoning.
2 What he'd really like us to buy him for his birthday .... some new Nike trainers.
3 Rickets .... a disease caused by a deficiency of vitamin D.
4 I first felt the desire to visit Venice when looking at .... painting by Canaletto.
5 You can't hold a classical concert in the village hall; the acoustics .... terrible!
6 A large number of police officers .... present at the demonstration last week in case of trouble.
7 At present 10,000 kilometres .... the longest walking competition held in the Olympics.

8 'What have we got for supper?' 'Salmon. I got .... huge fish at the fishmonger's for only five pounds.'
9 Either the twins or John, the eldest brother, ... going to make a speech at the Golden Wedding party.
10 My brother thinks that economics .... really interesting. I disagree.
11 Saudi Arabia, along with most of the oil-producing nations, ... voted to raise the price of crude oil again.
12 That band .... always had a reputation for performing better in the studio than live.
13 Both my brother and sister .... lived in this town all their lives.
14 We developed .... passion for Baroque music at university.
15 Roast beef and Yorkshire pudding .... definitely still the favourite of many British people!

6 ALL

Finish each of the following sentences in such a way that it is as similar as possible in meaning to the sentence printed before it. The exercise begins with an example (0).

0 The drama school is always looking out for new talent.
The drama school is always on ....*the lookout for new talent.*..

1 I heard some fascinating news on the radio this morning.
I heard a fascinating ....

2 The police used handcuffs to restrain the aggressive young man.
Handcuffs ....

3 A few roads in the Brighton area have been affected by the recent floods.
A small number ....

4 OK. I'll call the bank tomorrow and check our balance.
OK. I'll give ....

5 The medical profession considers that children eat too many sweet and fatty things today.
The medical profession considers that children should ....

6 It didn't take us ten minutes to get here from the station.
It took us ....

7 A lot of people have taken up our new offer, which has delighted us.
We have been delighted by the ....

8 We've got quite a lot of unwanted furniture since we moved to the smaller house.
We've got several ....

9 The management expects all staff to attend the meeting tomorrow afternoon.
All staff ....

10 They should now address the questions of VAT and fuel tax.
What ....

11 A lot of the older men sit in cafés and play dominoes.
Dominoes ....

12 We launched the new women's magazine in April and it was a great success.
The ....

13 In a democracy the government is elected by the people.
In a democracy the people ....

14 The teachers were boosted by the fact that the parents agreed to help fund the new playground.
The teachers were boosted by the parents' ....

26 Possessives and compound nouns

We can show the relationship between two nouns by using possessive forms or compound nouns. There are two basic possessive forms: the genitive (*'s* – e.g. *the **company's** shareholders*) and the *of* structure (e.g. *the shareholders **of the company***). This unit describes the forms and uses of the genitive and explains how we choose between this and *of* phrases. It also contrasts the use of possessives and compound nouns.

26.1 FORM AND MEANING

26.1A Possessive forms

We can indicate the possessive form of a noun by adding *'s* (the genitive form ▶ **26.1B**) or we can use the *of* structure (noun + *of* + noun):

*There was a scratch on my car**'s** paintwork.*
*There was a scratch on the paintwork **of** my car.*

❗ We usually use the definite article before an *of* structure (except with the 'double possessive' ▶ **26.1D**):

✗ ~~*… on a paintwork of my car.*~~ ✗ ~~*… on paintwork of my car.*~~
✔ *… on the paintwork of my car.*

There are possessive forms of pronouns and also possessive adjectives (▶ **27.1A**):

*You can't use that card, it's **mine**.*
*Oh sorry. I didn't realise it was **your** personal photocopy card.*

26.1B *'s* – basic rules

These are the key rules about which form of the genitive (*'s/s'/'*) to use:

singular noun: add *'s*	*house → house's bus → bus's*
singular proper noun ending in *-s*: add *'s* or an apostrophe (') only	*Mr James → Mr James's house/Mr James' house*
regular plural noun: add an apostrophe only	*boys → boys' buses → buses'*
irregular plural noun (not ending in *-s*): add *'s*	*men → men's children → children's*
one, somebody, everyone, each other, etc.: add *'s*	*one's house somebody's house nobody's house everyone's rights each other's houses*

26.1C *'s* – special rules

We can have two genitives together:

*We were beginning to get fed up with our neighbour**'s** tenant**'s** loud music.*

If the meaning is clear from the context, we can use the genitive without a following noun:

*That isn't my handwriting. It's Selina**'s**.* (= Selina's handwriting)

If the possessive form consists of a compound noun (▶ **26.3C**) or two or more nouns which form a single team or group we put the *'s* on the last noun only:

*Are you coming to my **brother-in-law's** party?* (compound noun)
*I'm a great fan of **Lerner and Lowe's** musicals.* (They wrote as a single team.)

❶ When the nouns do not form a single group we must use *'s* with both nouns:

Schrodinger's and Heisenberg's versions of quantum mechanics had seemed different. (two versions of the theory)

If the possessive noun is part of a short phrase (without a verb in it), we usually put the *'s* at the end of the phrase:

✗ ~~*The **man's in the corner** dog began to bark.*~~

✓ *The **man in the corner's** dog began to bark.* (= The dog belonging to the man in the corner ...)

26.1D
The double possessive (*of* structure + genitive)

We can use the genitive form and the *of* structure in the same phrase (the double possessive) when we want to make the first noun specific, but at the same time show that it is one of several. We usually use the indefinite article with this pattern:

*I heard the story from **a friend of my brother's**.* (= from one of my brother's friends)

We do not always include the genitive *'s* on the second noun:

*They got a tip off from **a friend of the owner**.*

❶ The double possessive is common with pronouns. We always use the possessive pronoun:

✗ ~~*She's a friend of us.*~~ ✗ ~~*She's a friend of our.*~~

✓ *She's **a friend of ours**.* (= We have several friends. She is one of them.)

26.2 THE GENITIVE (*'S*) OR *OF* STRUCTURE

26.2A
The genitive

We usually use the genitive *'s* (and not the *of* structure) to express the following ideas:

use	example
referring to general ownership, or possession of somebody's home	*Have you seen Sheila**'s** new car?* *We'll be at Mum**'s** soon.* (= Mum's house)
referring to people and animals (especially with proper nouns ▶ **28.1E**), and to personal/professional relationships and human qualities	*Sheila is Harold**'s** youngest daughter.* *Do you like Snap**'s** new collar?* *Have you met the boss**'s** new secretary?* *John**'s** intransigence is a pain.*
referring to location in time (but not with dates)	*Have you seen the poem in today**'s** 'Observer'?* ✗ ~~*It was in 19th December's paper.*~~
referring to the origin of something, for example where it comes from or who made it	*Oil is Saudi Arabia**'s** biggest export.* *The 'St Matthew Passion' is Bach**'s** most profound work.*
referring to a quantity or measure, for example of duration, distance or value (We can also use compound nouns ▶ **26.3C**.)	*There will be an hour**'s** delay.* *The hotel was ten minutes**'** drive from the beach.*
in expressions for value/quantity with *worth*	*Could you give me a pound**'s** worth of chips?*
with the names of shops, companies and people/places that provide a service	*I'm getting the Thanksgiving shopping at Macy**'s**.* (= Macy's department store) *Was there anything nice at the butcher**'s** this morning?* (= the butcher's shop)
in certain fixed expressions	*She was at death**'s** door. For God**'s** sake!* *For pity**'s** sake! For heaven**'s** sake!*

26.2B The *of* structure (noun + *of* + noun)

We usually use the *of* structure (and not the genitive *'s*) in the following situations:

use	example
with abstract nouns (e.g. *science*) and when we are referring to inanimate things	*I've been studying **the** philosophy **of** science.* *We set up our base camp at **the** bottom **of** the mountain.*
when the noun is followed by a verb phrase or clause which defines it	*The players ignored **the** jeers **of** the women standing in the front row.*
when we refer to a specific date	*It was destroyed in **the** fire **of** 1666.*
with long or complex phrases, even when we are referring to people	*A man was sentenced to death for **the** murder **of** an English tourist, Monica Cantwell.*
certain fixed expressions and titles	*He's **the** President **of** the United States.* ***The** Prince **of** Wales is to visit Iceland.*

26.2C Either pattern

We can usually use the genitive *'s* or the *of* structure to express the following ideas:

use	example
referring to a quality that something possesses or displays (but we prefer to use the genitive with human qualities)	*We were amazed by the ship**'s** sheer size.* *We were amazed by **the** sheer size **of** the ship.*
referring to the subject of something, its topic or theme (▶ **26.2D**)	*The Queen**'s** portrait has caused dismay.* ***The** portrait **of** the Queen has caused dismay.*
with human creations such as countries, organisations, cities, institutions, machines, vehicles, buildings, etc. (The genitive is more common.)	*Radio City Music Hall is one of New York**'s** most famous theatres.* *Plane trees are a common sight on **the** streets **of** London.*
expressing a reason or purpose with *sake* (but note exceptions ▶ **26.2A** above)	*We agreed to make a go of it for **the** sake **of** the children/for the children's sake.*

26.2D Genitive + *of* structure

The genitive and the *of* structure can describe different types of relationship such as ownership, origin and subject. To avoid confusion when we are describing more than one relationship between nouns in a phrase, we prefer to use the *'s* genitive for the origin, owner or creator, and the *of* structure for the subject or topic:

✗ ~~*I wasn't convinced by **the quarrel's description of the witness**.*~~

✔ *I wasn't convinced by **the witness's description of the quarrel**.*

(*the witness* = the person who made the description; *the quarrel* = the topic of the description)

*One of our most popular exhibits is **Van Dyck's portrait of King Charles**.*

(*Van Dyck* = the creator of the portrait; *King Charles* = the subject of the portrait)

We can also combine possessive forms with prepositions (▶ **Unit 28**) to describe a number of different relationships:

*Have you seen **the National Gallery's** portrait **of King Charles** by Van Dyck?*

↑ ownership (*'s*) — ↑ subject (*of* structure) — ↑ creator (preposition)

26.2E New information with the *of* structure

We can use the *of* structure to put new information at the end of a sentence (for more on the information principle ▶ **36.1A**). Compare:

American presidential candidate Robert Kennedy was assassinated in 1968.

✗ ~~*He was former president John F Kennedy**'s** younger brother.*~~

✔ *He was **the** younger brother **of** former president John F Kennedy.* (The new information is the reference to John F Kennedy.)

26.3 SPECIFYING OR CLASSIFYING POSSESSIVES AND COMPOUND NOUNS

26.3A Specifying or classifying possessives

Possessive forms of nouns can describe two types of relationship. In most cases we use possessive nouns as 'specifying' words, showing a relationship with something specific, such as a person or place (underlining = stressed word):

Marion washed the ***children's clothes*** *every Thursday.* (= the clothes belonging to Marion's children)

In other cases, possessive nouns can describe a 'classifying' relationship, describing the type of thing something is (underlining = stressed word):

Janice decided to open a shop specialising in ***children's clothes***. (= clothes designed for any children to wear)

We use adjectives in a different way depending on which type of relationship the possessive form is describing. With specifying possessives the adjective only describes the noun following it:

She was suspicious of her ***wealthy brother's girlfriend***. (= Her brother is wealthy.)

She didn't like her ***brother's wealthy girlfriend***. (= His girlfriend is wealthy.)

But when we use adjectives in front of a possessive noun with a 'classifying' meaning, the adjective describes the whole phrase, not just the possessive noun which follows it:

Janice's shop had a large selection of ***hand-made children's clothes***. (= The children's clothes are hand-made, not the children.)

26.3B Other classifying relationships

We use *of* and other prepositions to describe classifying relationships such as type of content, subject, source and purpose.

I've got a marvellous book ***of short stories*** *by Somerset Maugham.* (content)

The kids have been watching a film ***about rollerblading***. (subject)

I'm hoping to buy a sofa ***from that Swedish store***. (source)

Our uncle's company manufactures lubricants ***for ball-bearings***. (use/purpose)

! We do not use a possessive if there is a compound noun with the same meaning:

✗ ~~*I bought a new racquet at the* ***sport's shop***~~.

✓ *I bought a new racquet at the* ***sports shop***. (*sports shop* is a compound noun)

26.3C Compound nouns

Compound nouns are words which have been created by combining two nouns which are related to each other. They are similar to classifying possessives because the first noun 'classifies' the second noun, it describes it or tells us its purpose:

dressmaker (= maker of dresses) *fashion magazine* (= magazine about fashion)

Compound nouns can be written as a single word (*dressmaker*), two separate words (*fashion magazine*) or two words joined by a hyphen (*waste-bin*). There are no rules for this and it is best to check in an up-to-date dictionary.

Compound nouns can also be formed by combining nouns with verbs or adjectives:

- noun + verb: *windsurfing* *fire-eater* *Thanksgiving* *screwdriver*
- verb + noun: *cookbook* *rocking chair* *filing cabinet* *swimsuit*
- adjective + noun: *highway* *blackbird* *real estate* *easy chair*

! Some compound nouns are formed from multi-word verbs (▶ **Unit 14**). They usually follow the same order as the verb, but there are a few exceptions:

turn out → turnout *spill over → overspill* *turn down → downturn*

We can also make compound nouns from time expressions (▶ **26.2A**):

a three-week holiday *a four-hour delay* *a ten-minute drive*

! Be careful with compound nouns describing containers. The compound form only describes the container itself, not its contents. Compare these examples:

- In a shop: *I'd like a dozen Royal Doulton* ***tea cups***. (compound noun – cups designed to hold tea)
- In a café: ✗ ~~*I'd like a* ***tea cup*** *and a Mars bar, please.*~~
  ✓ *I'd like a* ***cup of tea*** *and a Mars bar, please.* (= tea in a cup)

Practice

The key to these exercises is on page 366.

1 26.1

Rewrite the sentences using genitive forms. The exercise begins with an example (0).

0 The stories Steve told and the stories Jane told were completely different.
Steve's and Jane's stories were completely different.
1 I'm sure this bag belongs to somebody. ....
2 Let's go to the shop the girls own. ....
3 That is the hotel belonging to Mr Hollis. ....
4 I love the operettas of Gilbert and Sullivan. ....
5 It's the fault of nobody. ....
6 They had respect for the opinions of each other. ....
7 The dog belonging to my next-door neighbour never stops barking.
....
8 I'm fed up with the hopeless inefficiency of the secretary of my boss.
....
9 The personality of my mother and the personality of my father are very alike.
....
10 These aren't my keys, they are the keys belonging to my flatmate.
....
11 The new Act of Parliament will protect the right of everyone to privacy.
....
12 The toilet for men is over there on the right. ....
13 I've just inherited the house belonging to the brother of my grandmother.
....
14 The opinions of residents of sink estates are rarely taken into consideration.
....
15 The dance routines of Fred Astaire and Ginger Rogers are legendary.
....

2 26.1

Eight of these sentences contain mistakes. Tick (✔) the correct sentences, then find and correct the mistakes.

1 Elizabeth is a good friend of him. ....
2 I'm really fed up with my landlord's wive's endless complaints about noise. ....
3 As the English say, ones' home is ones' castle. ....
4 You should pay attention to what he says; he's a close associate of the managing director. ....
5 Don't blame him; it was mine own fault. ....
6 She's been put in charge of childrens' activities at the summer camp in Maine. ....
7 Since they got married they've only been interested in each other. ....
8 My brother's-in-law's parents have decided to emigrate. ....
9 We don't know him very well; he's just an acquaintance of us from our university days. ....
10 There's something wrong with that buses' brake lights. ....

3 26.2

Choose the correct alternative, A or B. In some cases both options are correct.

1 What did you do ...
A at the course's end?
B at the end of the course?

2 Have you met ...
A Sam's new girlfriend?
B the new girlfriend of Sam?

3 ... is a constant source of inspiration.
A Barcelona's architecture
B The architecture of Barcelona

4 I need to visit ...
A the doctor's surgery.
B the surgery of the doctor.

5 Some debris got caught under ...
A the conveyor belt's wheels.
B the wheels of the conveyor belt.

6 Our organisation strives towards ...
A poverty's elimination.
B the elimination of poverty.

7 The Ninth Symphony is arguably ...
A Beethoven's greatest work.
B the greatest work of Beethoven.

8 ... is the search for personal fulfilment in a hostile world.
A The novel's theme
B The theme of the novel

9 He's taking ... from his job at the university.
A a year's sabbatical
B a sabbatical of a year

10 ... sometimes drives me up the wall.
A My husband's impatience
B The impatience of my husband

11 Throughout the flight we had to put up with ...
A the children sitting in the back row's antics.
B the antics of the children sitting in the back row.

12 The most senior clergyman in the Church of England is ...
A Canterbury's Archbishop.
B the Archbishop of Canterbury.

13 We're going to hold the party at ...
A Michael's place.
B the place of Michael.

14 ... was an important turning point in French history.
A 1789's revolution
B The revolution of 1789

15 Researchers have been amazed by the ... to mutate when attacked.
A virus's ability
B ability of the virus

16 The vet wasn't very pleased with ...
A Fido's progress.
B the progress of Fido.

17 Her doctoral thesis investigates ... in medieval China.
A Confucianism's spread
B the spread of Confucianism

18 The blessing will take place at ...
A the Twelve Apostle's church.
B the church of the Twelve Apostles.

19 Why can't you just hand in your notice, ...
A for heaven's sake!
B for the sake of heaven!

20 ... are generating a lot of excitement at the Paris fashion shows.
A Galliano's latest designs
B The latest designs of Galliano

4 26.3

Use the words (1–15) in the box to form compound nouns that fit in the same numbered gaps in the text. You will need to add the second part of the compound yourself. The exercise begins with two examples (0) and (00).

Today's consumer guide looks at (0) ....*laptop*.... computers. The range of these portable computers on the market can be daunting, but a good place to start is computer magazines. These often contain useful (00) ......*buyer's guides*.... and reviews of models currently on the market. Suppliers of the leading (1) ..... often sell their products at cut prices through these magazines. If you decide to buy by (2) ..... you will find the advertisements a good source of bargains. And if you pay by (3) ..... you will automatically be insured. But if you need help in choosing a model, it might be better to shop in the (4) ....., where you can ask a (5) ..... for impartial guidance and advice.
You should make a (6) ..... of the features and facilities you require, and these will depend to a large extent on the way you plan to use your machine. If you use a lot of graphics (7) ..... you'll need a fast processor, a large (8) ..... and a high-definition screen. If you are only going to be using the machine for (9) ....., processor speed will not be so important, but you will want a comfortable and sturdy (10) ..... .
Almost everyone these days needs to access the Internet in order to use e-mail and cruise the (11) ....., so look for a high-speed modem. Be aware of the input and (12) ..... devices you want; CD and floppy disk drives usually come as standard, but you may want a DVD drive or a PC-card slot.
Once you have checked all these features you can compile a (13) ..... of models you are interested in. Check that your chosen models include comprehensive (14) ..... and ask your supplier about warranties and (15) ..... service.

0 lap
00 buyer's
1 brand
2 mail
3 credit
4 high
5 shop
6 check
7 soft
8 hard
9 word
10 key
11 world
12 out
13 short
14 instruction
15 after

5 26.3

Which explanation is correct, A or B?

1 Stephanie loved her beautiful daughter's sports car.
   A Stephanie's daughter was beautiful.
   B The car belonging to Stephanie's daughter was beautiful.
2 There's a new doctor's surgery on the corner of Greenford Street.
   A The doctor has recently qualified.
   B The surgery has recently opened.
3 She inherited a wonderful wooden doll's house.
   A The doll is made of wood.
   B The house is made of wood.
4 The company manufactures low-cost nurses' uniforms.
   A The nurses earn low wages.
   B The uniforms aren't expensive.
5 Gary didn't think much of his new boss's management techniques.
   A Gary has a new boss.
   B Gary's boss has some new management techniques.

6 Bill and Suzy found hiring a well-educated children's nanny was worth every penny.
  A Their nanny was well-educated.
  B Their children were well-educated.
7 I managed to find a place in the 24-hour supermarket's parking lot.
  A The supermarket is open 24 hours.
  B The parking lot is open 24 hours.
8 Dave was often embarrassed by his aggressive flatmate's comments.
  A Dave's flatmate was aggressive.
  B His flatmate's comments were aggressive.
9 My uncle is restoring a redundant tax inspector's office in Newcastle.
  A Some tax inspectors have been made redundant in Newcastle.
  B The office in Newcastle is no longer required by the tax inspectors.
10 Who's going to look after our sick neighbour's puppy?
  A Our neighbour is sick.
  B Our neighbour's puppy is sick.

6 ALL

Use compound nouns to complete the sentences. The compound nouns you need can be formed by combining words from each of the boxes below. Then rewrite these sentences using appropriate possessive forms to replace the phrases in brackets. In two sentences the phrase in brackets does not need to be changed.

land down horse news bank traffic data out rail ~~filing~~ wind five-minute walking

jam fit ~~cabinet~~ robber stick turn agent surfer racing walk lord ways bases

0 The only thing missing from (the office belonging to my boss) is a ....
  The only thing missing from my boss's office is a filing cabinet.
1 Could you pop down to the .... and pick up (the evening paper that Charles orders).
  ....
2 That silver-topped .... belongs to (one of the friends that I have).
  ....
3 The (private beach of the hotel) is only a .... from here.
  ....
4 The (privatisation organised by the government) of the .... is going ahead next year.
  ....
5 The .... wouldn't allow (the girlfriend of his tenant) to move in.
  ....
6 (The pension fund of my father) has been badly affected by the .... in the value of blue-chip stocks ....
7 Clare bought a beautiful new .... for (the wedding of the sister of her brother-in-law).
  ....
8 The .... managed to ignore (the screams of the crowd) lining the beach.
  ....
9 Whenever we are over at (the house belonging to Dad) we seem to spend the entire time watching .... on the television. ....
10 The .... refused to accept (the jurisdiction of the legal system) over him.
  ....
11 (The firm my wife works for) specialises in setting up .... for insurance companies.
  ....
12 The .... was caused by the volume of cars setting out for the south coast at (the start of the bank holiday). ....

27 Pronouns

Pronouns are words which we substitute for nouns in order to avoid repetition. This unit explains how English uses subject and object pronouns, reflexive and reciprocal pronouns, and indefinite pronouns. (For determiners used as pronouns ▶ **28.2**, **28.3**; for relative pronouns ▶ **31.2A**; for more on pronouns as substitutes for nouns ▶ **35.2**.)

27.1 PERSONAL PRONOUNS

27.1A Form

We use personal pronouns to refer to both people and objects. (This unit also looks at possessive adjectives.)

subject pronouns	object pronouns	(possessive adjectives)	possessive pronouns	reflexive pronouns (▶ 27.2)
I	*me*	*my*	*mine*	*myself*
you	*you*	*your*	*yours*	*yourself/yourselves*
he	*him*	*his*	*his*	*himself*
she	*her*	*her*	*hers*	*herself*
it	*it*	*its*	(no pronoun)	*itself*
we	*us*	*our*	*ours*	*ourselves*
they	*them*	*their*	*theirs*	*themselves*

27.1B Use

After we mention a person or an object once, or if the context makes it clear who or what we are referring to, we usually use pronouns to refer to them.
We use subject pronouns instead of a noun as the subject of a verb:

*Paul Allen plans to set up a rock music museum. **He** was a founder of Microsoft.*

We use object pronouns instead of a noun as a direct or indirect object:

- Direct object: *I met Julian yesterday. I like **him**, don't you?*
- Indirect object: *Those books belong to Julian. Can you give them to **him**, please?*

We use possessive adjectives before a noun to express 'belonging':

- Adjective: *Did the neighbours leave that here? It looks like **their** deckchair.*

We use possessive pronouns instead of a possessive adjective + noun:

- Pronoun: *No, it's not their deckchair. It's **ours**! Don't you recognise it?*

27.1C Omission/inclusion of pronouns

English does not usually omit pronouns, especially subject pronouns:

*We can expect carol singers; **they** often come at this time of year.*

But it is incorrect to use a noun + pronoun together as the subject of a verb:

✗ ~~*E-mails **they** have become a real nuisance.*~~ ✔ *E-mails have become a real nuisance.*

We do not use object pronouns in infinitive phrases or relative clauses if the object has already appeared in the same sentence:

✗ ~~*Those plastic cakes look good enough to eat **them**.*~~
✔ *Those plastic cakes look good enough to eat.*
✗ ~~*That's the play I told you about **it**.*~~ ✔ *That's the play I told you about.*

27.1D Subject and object pronouns

There are some cases where we can use either an object pronoun or a subject pronoun. After *as* and *than* in comparative patterns, we use the subject pronoun only in very formal English; the object pronoun is more common:

- Formal: [*The ski instructor didn't ski any better **than I**.*]
- Informal: *The instructor didn't actually ski any better **than me**.*

After *as* and *than*, we can use a subject pronoun with an auxiliary or modal verb (▶ **22.1A**):

The ski instructor didn't ski as well ***as I do/did/can****.*

We usually use the object pronoun in short responses: *'Who's there?' 'It's* ***us****.'*

After *It is* we use the subject pronoun in formal language, the object in informal:

- Formal: ***It is they*** *who asked for the music to be turned down.*
- Informal: ***It's them*** *who asked for the music to be turned down.*

When we have a noun and pronoun, or two pronouns together, we tend to put the speaker last (possibly out of politeness):

You and I *are both invited to the pro-celebrity golf match, if you fancy it.*

However, if we have a noun and pronoun where the pronoun does not refer to the speaker, we usually put the pronoun first:

Don't you think we should let ***him and his wife*** *decide when to come?*

❶ We should use object pronouns after a preposition, although in informal English you may hear the subject pronoun:

✗ ~~*They're sending the new consignment over for* ***Tom and I*** *to check.*~~

✔ *They're sending the new consignment over for* ***Tom and me*** *to check.*

27.1E Modifying pronouns

In some exclamations we modify object pronouns, usually with an adjective:

Look what I've done! ***Silly me!*** ***Lucky old him/her****.*

We can use a noun after a pronoun to clarify who or what we are referring to:

I want ***you boys*** *to report to the Head after this class!*

Then ***she, Mrs Vincent****, got up and asked everyone to leave at once.*

27.1F Uses of *he*, *she* and *it*

We use *it* to refer to animals, things, ideas, or actions, and not usually to people unless to refer to an unborn or young baby (if the sex is unknown):

Mary brought her new baby into the shop yesterday – ***it****'s very cute.*

We use *it* as an 'empty' subject (▶ **33.2**):

*'Who can that be at the door?' '****It****'s my neighbour. He often calls this late.'*

It *has been several years since sultry singer Sade was last in the spotlight.*

We use *he* and *she* to refer to people and also to animals, especially domestic pets:

We had to take our dog, Damon, to the vet yesterday. ***He****'s got ear mites.*

The fact that English distinguishes gender with *he, him, his* and *she, her, hers* can cause difficulty in deciding which form to use after a subject or object not clearly of either gender. *He, him* or *his* used to be most common, but many people now object to this. Ways to avoid using *he, him* and *his* include the use of *he/she* (*him/her, his/her*) in writing, or *they* (*them, their*) or plurals in speech or writing:

A doctor always makes decisions according to the best of ***his/her/their*** *knowledge.*

Doctors *always make decisions according to the best of* ***their*** *knowledge.*

We often use *they* (*them, their*) after indefinite pronouns:

'Someone called you from Grant's Garage.' 'Oh, did ***they*** *leave* ***their*** *name?'*

27.1G *one*

We use *one* or *ones* to avoid repeating countable nouns:

Do you prefer the dark chocolates or the light ***ones****?*

We do not use *one* to replace uncountable nouns:

✗ ~~*Do you prefer white rice or brown* ***one****?*~~ ✔ *Do you prefer white rice or brown?*

We can use *one/ones* after *the* and adjectives, but not immediately after *a/an*:

✗ ~~*I'd like a loaf of bread. Can you pass me* ***a one*** *from the top shelf?*~~

✔ *I'd like a loaf of bread. Can you pass me* ***one*** *from the top shelf?*

These are interesting fossil specimens. This is an ***amazing one****.*

We do not use *one/ones* when we refer to an item that has previously been defined. Compare:

I need a drink, a large ***one****.* (= any drink)

Where's my drink? Oh, there ***it*** *is.* (= my drink – a defined drink)

27.2 REFLEXIVE AND RECIPROCAL PRONOUNS

27.2A Reflexive pronouns

Reflexive pronouns are formed with *self/selves* (▶ **27.1A**). We usually use reflexive pronouns when the subject and object are the same person or thing:

✗ *~~Quick! The baby's burnt her.~~* ✔ *Quick! The baby's burnt **herself**!*

Compare:

*Ben treated **him** to an ice cream.* (*him* = someone else, not Ben)
*Ben treated **himself** to an ice cream.* (*himself* = Ben)

After prepositions we use an object pronoun to refer to the subject when it is clear who or what it refers to; otherwise we use a reflexive pronoun. Compare:

*Jim emerged from the underground station and looked **around him**.* (*him* = Jim)
*Jane was upset. Alexa was really annoyed **with her**.* (her = Jane)
*Jane was upset. Alexa was really annoyed **with herself**.* (herself = Alexa)

We use reflexive pronouns to refer to the subject after verbs with dependent prepositions (▶ **15.2**):

*Politicians have to **believe in themselves** if they expect the people to believe in them.* (We use *them* here as the subject of *to believe in them* is *the people* and not *politicians*.)

We can use either the object pronoun or the reflexive to refer to the subject after *as (for)*, *like*, *but (for)* and *except (for)*:

*Howard made sure that everyone except **him/himself** had a drink, as he was driving.*

27.2B Idiomatic use of reflexive pronouns

Some verbs take the reflexive in English where it may not seem logical, and where similar verbs in other languages may not take the reflexive, e.g. *enjoy yourself*, *help yourself*, *acquaint yourself (with)*, *behave yourself*:

*Did the children **behave themselves** while we were out?* (= behave well)
***Help yourself** to the food, won't you?* (= take as much food as you want)

The phrase *by yourself/himself*, etc. means 'alone' or 'without help':

*We've decided to go on holiday **by ourselves** next year.*

❗ There are many verbs which take a reflexive in other languages but do not usually do so in English, e.g. *wash*, *dress*, *feel*, *remember*, *hurry*:

✗ *~~I don't feel myself very well today.~~* ✔ *I don't feel very well today.*

27.2C Emphatic use of reflexive pronouns

We can use reflexive pronouns to emphasise the subject or object of a sentence. The pronoun can come after the subject, after the auxiliary (if there is one) or verb, after the object or at the end of the sentence:

I have used this technique on a number of occasions.
↑ ↑ ↑ ↑
myself

We can use the reflexive pronoun either at the beginning or the end of a sentence and separated by a comma to mean 'as far as I'm concerned':

***Myself**, I don't like the new fashion for flared trousers.*
*I don't like the new fashion for flared trousers, **myself**.*

We use *(all) (by) myself/yourself*, etc. to emphasise 'without any help' or 'completely alone':

*The garden looks amazing. Did you do it **(all) (by) yourself**?*

27.2D Reciprocal pronouns

Compare the use of reciprocal pronouns (*each other/one another*) and reflexive pronouns:

*Steve and Elaine blamed only **themselves** for the break-up of their marriage.* (They both blamed the two of them and nobody else.)
*Steve and Elaine blamed **each other** for the break-up of their marriage.* (Steve blamed Elaine and Elaine blamed Steve.)

Each other usually refers to two subjects, *one another* to more than two, though we tend to use the two forms interchangeably in informal English:

*He spoke fast and his words tumbled out, tripping over **each other/one another**.*

❗ Don't use a reflexive or an object pronoun where a reciprocal pronoun is needed:

✗ ~~*So, we'll see ourselves/us at the fountain at half past one tomorrow.*~~

✓ *So, we'll see* ***each other*** *at the fountain at half past one tomorrow.*

27.3 'IMPERSONAL' PRONOUNS

27.3A *you, we, they*

When we wish to express general feelings and opinions (i.e. not necessarily those of the speaker), we can use *you, we* or *they*:

You *can wear whatever* ***you*** *like to go to the theatre these days.*

If we wish to include ourselves, it is better to use *we*:

We *can wear whatever* ***we*** *like to go to the theatre these days.*

If we wish to exclude ourselves, it is better to use *they*:

They *behave really badly at football matches nowadays.*

We also use *they* to refer to people in authority:

Did you know ***they****'ve put the parking charges up again?*

27.3B *one*

We use *one* in formal language to mean people generally including ourselves:

One *can sympathise with the sentiments behind the actions of the strikers.*

We can use *one* as a subject or object pronoun, and as a reflexive pronoun:

One tends to learn to fend for ***oneself*** *if one lives alone.*

❗ The use of *one* to mean 'I' is considered unnecessarily formal:

[***One*** *would like to attend the ceremony, but* ***one*** *is too busy.*]

❗ US English rarely uses *one*, but prefers *you* (▶ **27.3A**).

27.4 INDEFINITE PRONOUNS AND ADVERBS

27.4A Form and use

person	object	place	manner
someone/body[1]	*something*	*somewhere*	*somehow*
anyone/body	*anything*	*anywhere*	*anyhow*[2]
everyone/body	*everything*	*everywhere*	
no one/body[3]	*nothing*	*nowhere*	

Any, *some*, *every* and *no* combine with nouns or adverbs to form pronouns (or adverbs):

[1] We use *-one* and *-body* interchangeably.

[2] *anyhow* is informal and is similar to *anyway*: ***Anyhow****, as I was saying ...*

[3] We usually write *no one* as two words, we write *nobody* as one word.

These pronouns and adverbs do not refer to a specific person, place, etc.:

They were miles from ***anywhere – no one*** *would hear her scream.*

We use *some* compounds when we are thinking of a particular unspecified person, place or thing, but we use *any* compounds when we are thinking of people, places or things in general:

'What would you like for your birthday?'

'Oh, ***anything****.'* (= no particular present)

'Well, there's ***something*** *I would like ...'* (= a particular present)

❗ *Any + one/thing/where* is not negative:

Anyone *would hear her scream.* (= any people in the area)

We use *any + one/thing/where* with the meaning 'it doesn't matter who/what/where':

'Where shall I sign the card?' 'Oh, ***anywhere*** *you like.'*

If we use these pronouns and adverbs as subjects, they take a singular verb:

Everything *is going smoothly and NASA expects to launch the shuttle as scheduled.*

We can use these pronouns with modifiers, e.g. adjectives or *else*:

Tony decided to do ***something active*** *about his problems.*

Something else *you become aware of all over the Basque country is the bracken.*

Practice

The key to these exercises is on page 367.

1 27.1

Read the article below and replace the underlined words with a suitable pronoun or possessive adjective. The first one is given as an example (0).

Bernard Warner is a fishmonger. Mr Warner sells fish – lots of (0) ~~fish~~ ......*it*...... – and (1) Mr Warner .... sometimes sells lobsters. When the lobster arrived in his shop, (2) the lobster .... didn't strike (3) Mr Warner .... as being particularly odd. (4) The lobster .... was a little paler than most others of (5) the lobster's .... species, but perhaps it was just a bit old. Mr Warner left his shop to go on holiday as planned. (6) Mr Warner's shop .... was a family shop and he knew (7) the shop .... was in good hands.

En route to Majorca, Mr Warner picked up the in-flight magazine. (8) The magazine .... fell open at an article about albino lobsters. These very rare lobsters are just paler versions of a normal lobster. (9) Albino lobsters .... are also very valuable: (10) an albino lobster .... caught off the American coast was sold for £15,000; another, bigger (11) albino lobster .... was insured for £20,000.

As soon as he reached his destination, Mr Warner raced to a phone. 'Don't sell that lobster!' he told his family firm. But it was too late. (12) The lobster .... had already been sold. Mr Warner couldn't believe his bad luck. A diner somewhere had eaten the prize catch and (13) the diner .... had had no idea at all of (14) the animal's .... value. After 40 years as a fishmonger (15) Mr Warner .... had thought that no one knew the business better than (16) Mr Warner ...., but he had never come across (17) an example .... of those lobsters before! Mr Warner said that he now knows what it's like when a person wins the lottery only to realise that (18) that person .... have thrown away the ticket!

2 27.1, 27.3

Rewrite all of the underlined phrases in this dialogue to correct the mistakes with the pronouns. Some of the underlined pronouns are grammatically incorrect; others may be considered too formal or old-fashioned. In some cases you will just need to change the order of the pronouns. The first one is given as an example (0).

MILES 352 87641. Hello.

PHOEBE Hi, Miles. (0) It is I, Phoebe. ....*It's me*..........

MILES Hi, Phoebe, how are things?

PHOEBE Not too bad. (1) Me and Justin have had colds, but we've still been going in, (2) a teacher can't desert his class! ....

MILES You should take time off, you know. (3) One can't carry on working if one isn't feeling well. ....

PHOEBE I know what you mean, but (4) it's we teachers who always get the blame if the kids don't learn enough and fail their exams, so (5) one can't take too much time off. Talking of colds, have you had (6) a one this year yet? ....

MILES No, I think (7) I and Jenny have been really lucky so far. ....

PHOEBE Yes, you have. Listen, Miles, I'm actually phoning to find out if (8) Jenny and you would be interested in joining the amateur operatic society in the village (9) with Justin and I. ....

MILES You're joking, aren't you? You know that you and Justin sing much (10) better than we, and anyway, Jenny thinks the society is really snobbish, so she won't be interested. ....

PHOEBE Perhaps (11) one does get a lot of middle-class people there, but they're always friendly. (12) If anyone new comes in, he's always made welcome. ....

MILES I don't know ... when is it, anyway?

PHOEBE The season starts on Thursday evening.

MILES Oh, we can't come then. Our dog Samson is having a minor operation that day and (13) we want to be with it in the evening in case the anaesthetic hasn't worn off properly. ....

PHOEBE Oh, (14) poor old he! I hope it goes OK, and I quite understand. (15) One can't be too careful with animals. OK, let's get together another time then. I'll give you a buzz soon. ....

3 27.2, 27.3

In each pair of sentences below, one or both sentences are correct. Tick (✓) the correct sentences and cross (✗) the incorrect ones. Where both sentences are correct, choose an explanation from the box for the difference between them. You can use the explanations more than once.

A The pronouns refer to different people.
B There is no difference in meaning at all.
C The difference is one of emphasis.
D One sentence is more formal or more dated than the other.

0 a You can get tickets for the whole of the city transport network here. ...✓...
  b One can get tickets for the whole of the city transport network here. ...✓... [D]
1 a Alicia and Charles blamed themselves for the break-up of their marriage. ....
  b Alicia and Charles blamed each other for the break-up of their marriage. .... ☐
2 a Ewan is thinking of bringing some work with him. ....
  b Ewan is thinking of bringing some work with himself. .... ☐
3 a We all give each other small presents at the Christmas party. ....
  b We all give one another small presents at the Christmas party. .... ☐
4 a Ouch! That radiator is really hot. I've burnt myself! ....
  b Ouch! That radiator is really hot. I've burnt me! .... ☐
5 a We're going to miss the bus. Quick, let's hurry ourselves! ....
  b We're going to miss the bus. Quick, let's hurry! .... ☐
6 a The paint effect you've used on the wall is great. Did you do it yourselves? ....
  b The paint effect you've used on the wall is great. Did you do it by yourselves? .... ☐
7 a Will we be able to find each other amongst all the people at the concert hall? ....
  b Will we be able to find ourselves amongst all the people at the concert hall? .... ☐
8 a The girl's coach rebuked herself for missing some very easy shots. ....
  b The girl's coach rebuked her for missing some very easy shots. .... ☐
9 a I thought the Government supported GM food. Didn't the PM say that? ....
  b I thought the Government supported GM food. Didn't the PM say that himself? .... ☐
10 a Most people find this style of art depressing. As for me, I think it's stimulating! ....
  b Most people find this style of art depressing. As for myself, I think it's stimulating! .... ☐

4 27.4

Underline the correct alternative in *italics* in these sentences. In two sentences both alternatives are acceptable; in these sentences, underline both of them.

1 You can't have lost the tickets. They've got to be *anywhere/somewhere*!
2 I haven't got a clue where I am! Isn't there *anyone/no one* here who could direct me to the Stakis Hotel?
3 *Is/Are* everyone here now? We'll start the tour straight away then.
4 There is hardly *anybody/nobody* to be seen on the streets of the centre after dusk.
5 Peter decided that he needed to do *constructive something/something constructive* with his life.
6 The kidnap victims were blindfolded, driven into the country and thrown from the car miles from *somewhere/anywhere*.
7 It is essential that we locate *someone/somebody* who can repair this machine within the next 48 hours.
8 The mayor is caught in the city traffic. We've *somehow/anyhow* got to find a way to get her here fast.
9 'What would you like to drink?' 'Oh, *something/anything*. Whatever you're having will be fine.'
10 That new chess champion from the Ukraine is amazing. *Anyone/No one* can beat him!
11 *Anyhow/Anyway*, I must be going now. I've got lots to do this morning.
12 The ball can bounce *anywhere/somewhere* between the inner tramlines, but if it bounces outside them, you lose the point.

5 ALL

Read this extract from a book and complete it with a suitable pronoun or possessive adjective which best fits each space. In the book the author, an American, describes his first visit to England.

It must be said that Dover was not vastly improved by daylight, but I liked (1) .... I liked (2) .... small scale and cosy air, and the way everyone said 'Good morning', and 'Hello', and 'Dreadful weather – but it must brighten up', to (3) ...., and the sense that this was just (4) .... more in a very long series of fundamentally cheerful, well-ordered, pleasantly uneventful days. (5)........ in the whole of Dover would have any particular reasons to remember 21 March 1973, except for (6)........ and a handful of children born that day.

I didn't know how early (7) .... could decently begin asking for a room in England, so I thought (8) .... would leave (9) .... till mid-morning. With time on (10) .... hands, I made a thorough search for a guesthouse that looked attractive and quiet, but friendly and not too expensive, and at the stroke of ten o'clock presented (11) .... on the doorstep of the (12) .... I had carefully selected, taking care not to discompose the milk bottles. (13) .... was a small hotel that was really a guesthouse, indeed, was really a boarding-house.

I don't remember (14) .... name, but I well recall the proprietress, who showed (15) .... to a room, then gave (16) .... a tour of the facilities and outlined the many complicated rules for residing there. This was all bewilderingly new to me. Where I came from, (17) .... got a room in a motel, spent ten hours making a lavish and possibly irredeemable mess of (18) ...., and left early the next morning. This was like joining the army.

6 ALL

Read the article below. Some of the lines are correct (examples 0 and 000), some have a wrong word that must be replaced (example 00) and some have an unnecessary word (example 0000). If a line is correct, tick (✓) it. If a word must be replaced or omitted, underline it and write its replacement if necessary at the end of the line. There are four examples at the beginning (0, 00, 000 and 0000).

0	In Manchester, UK, twelve-year-old Andrew and his friends kick a ball to	✓
00	themselves after school every day. It is Andrew's ambition to play football	*each other*
000	for Manchester United. In Pakistan, Asma, also twelve, stitches the balls that	✓
0000	Andrew and his friends play with them. It is Asma's ambition to become a	–
1	teacher. That ambition is as unattainable for her as is Andrew's for them.	....
2	In recent years the use of child labour in producing footballs has become	....
3	an issue which it fuels public indignation. About 80 per cent of match-grade	....
4	footballs are produced in Pakistan, many of their by children. But is this	....
5	necessarily a bad thing? Work can be a way for children to gain skills and	....
6	increase them choices. Many families in Pakistan are extremely poor; they	....
7	need to find money everyhow and many children have to work. Stitching	....
8	footballs is safe, easy work, which it can be done at home, fitted around the	....
9	child's schooling. Anyone wants the children in Pakistan to go to school	....
10	more than them do. But, as one child says, 'If we are to go to school instead	....
11	of work, one must give us money'.	....
12	At a conference organised to address the problem of children having to	....
13	work, children theirselves were asked to give opinions. A girl from Peru	....
14	commented, 'Anybody must get together to fight the real problem – poverty	....
15	– not working children.' Children at the conference felt that they herself	....
16	should be consulted, as adult decisions are often wrong for them. For	....
17	example, many Bangladeshi children they suffered in the mid-1990s when a	....
18	US Bill threatened to ban imports made by it: clothing manufacturers in	....
19	Bangladesh sacked all children under fourteen, and many of themselves were	....
20	forced to take less well-paid, more harmful work, including prostitution.	....

28 Determiners

Determiners are words that precede nouns, e.g. articles, demonstratives, quantifiers and possessive adjectives. Articles can be a problem area in English for students even at advanced level, especially for those whose own language has a very different article system. This unit covers articles, demonstratives and quantifiers.

28.1 ARTICLES

28.1A Basic rules

Articles (*a/an*, *the*) precede nouns and some other words in a noun phrase, e.g. *few*, *little*, adjectives. The article is usually the first word in a noun phrase, but note:

- *all/both/half + the*: ***all the*** *information*, ***both the*** *twins*
- *quite/rather/such/what/half + a/an*: ***quite a*** *difficult problem*

We use the indefinite article (*a/an*) with singular countable nouns: ***a*** *garage*, ***an*** *opinion*. We use the definite article (*the*) with singular countable nouns (***the*** *garage*), with plural nouns (***the*** *latest computers*) and uncountable nouns (***the*** *purest water*). We can omit *the* with uncountable and plural nouns (▶ **28.1D**).

28.1B Naming, describing and classifying

We use *a/an* when we name or describe something:

*That's **a** scarab beetle. 'What's that?' 'It's **an** enormous anthill.'*

We use *a/an* when we refer to one example of a class or a species:

An *African elephant has larger ears than **an** Indian elephant.*

We use *the* to refer to the whole class or species:

The *African elephant has larger ears than **the** Indian elephant.*

However, it is more common to refer to the whole class with the plural:

African elephants have larger ears than Indian elephants.

❗ We do not use *a/an* to refer to a whole class rather than individual examples:

✗ ~~*Ruthless poachers hunt **an elephant** for the valuable ivory of its tusks.*~~

✔ *Ruthless poachers hunt **the elephant** for the valuable ivory of its tusks.*

✔ *Ruthless poachers hunt **elephants** for the valuable ivory of their tusks.*

We can also use *the* with an adjective to refer to a class of people (▶ **21.1A**):

The homeless *will be removed from the streets and placed in hostels.*

28.1C Known or unknown topics

We use *a/an* when the topic (noun) is not known to our listener/reader; we use *the* when it is known. Therefore, we usually use *a/an* for the first reference to a topic in a text, but then use *the* for subsequent references:

A *new travel guide has advised would-be tourists to Morecambe that it is a place to avoid. ... **The** guide paints a bleak – if not third-world – picture.*

We do not always have to mention something for it to be known to the listener. We consider that it is known in the following situations:

situation	example
something is unique	*We are in danger of permanently damaging **the** Earth.*
superlatives	*Muhammad Ali is **the** greatest heavyweight boxer ever.*
the context makes it 'known'	*'Has Edward arrived yet?' 'Yes, he's in **the** dining-room.'* (= the dining-room of the house we are in)
a defining phrase makes it 'known'	*Oasis is **the** Manchester band **that shot to fame in the early 1990s**.*
a prepositional phrase makes it 'known'	*Meet me in **the** café **next to the underground station near my house**.*

28.1D General and specific

With plural nouns we use either *the* or no article. We don't use an article when we want to refer to a group or class in general (▶ **28.1B**). Compare:

__Tourists__ are often blamed for changing the character of a place. (= all tourists)
Did you notice what __the tourists__ in the cathedral were doing? (= specific tourists)
It is commonly accepted today that brown __bread__ is good for you.
Did you remember to get __the bread__ out of the freezer?

We only use an article before an abstract noun if we wish to make an abstract noun more specific, e.g. to talk about a particular type of *hope*:

✘ ~~*It is impossible to live in a world without __the hope__.*~~
✔ *It is impossible to live in a world without __hope__.* (hope in general)
__The hope of finding a cure for cancer__ drives a lot of medical research.

Nouns such as *church*, *hospital*, *school* do not take an article if we think of their purpose, i.e. *church* as a place of worship, or *school* as a place of learning:

Fewer people attend __church__ regularly now than twenty years ago.
Can children leave __school__ at fourteen in your country?

If we think of the physical place or building, we use an article:

The collection for restoring __the church__ has almost reached its target.
Is there __a school__ in the village or do the children have to go to the town?

28.1E Other common uses of articles

a/an	jobs, nationalities and beliefs: *I'm __a__ structural engineer. Helmut's __an__ Austrian. Cat Stevens became __a__ Muslim.*[1]
	numbers: ***a*** *hundred thousand*
	prices, speeds, etc: *two dollars __a__ kilo, 20km __an__ hour*

[1] We can use these without an article if we put the noun before the person's name:
__Irishman__ Eddie Jordan has put together a team of great quality and spirit.

the	some geographical names: plurals (***the*** *United States*, ***the*** *US*), areas (***the*** *West*), mountain ranges (***the*** *Pyrenees*), oceans or seas (***the*** *Pacific Ocean*, ***the*** *Black Sea*), rivers (***the*** *Rhone*)
	musical instruments: *She plays __the__ violin.*
	the media: *All our family work in __the__ theatre.*[2]
	in some comparative phrases: ***the*** *more* ***the*** *merrier, all* ***the*** *better*
	in front of superlatives and *first, last, next, only, same, right, wrong*: ***the*** *most dangerous profession,* ***the*** *last time,* ***the*** *only one*
	in measurements: *You can buy saffron by __the__ gram.*
	physical environments: *I prefer __the__ town to __the__ country.*
	newspapers: ***the*** *Times,* ***the*** *Herald Tribune,* ***the*** *Daily Mirror*
	dates when spoken: ***the*** *tenth of May*

[2] We often use *television*, *cinema*, etc. without an article to refer to the art or entertainment form: *She works in television. I'm studying film in my final year.*
If we refer to a specific item we use the article:
Don't put flowers on __the__ television. Have you seen __the__ new film by Ridley Scott?

no article	proper names: *James, Chris Graham, Mr Jones*[3]
	names of most countries, mountains, lakes: *Japan, Mount Everest, Lake Victoria*
	substances, liquids and gases: *Cooking oil is simply liquid fat.*
	materials: *This blouse is made of silk.*
	political or business roles: *Lagos became President of Chile in 2000.*
	transport: *We're going by rail to London, then by plane.*
	times and seasons: *at night, in summer, at dusk*[4]

no article	meal(time)s: *Have you had breakfast? See you at lunch.* sports: *She plays both tennis and squash very well.* illnesses: *He's got lung cancer. She's had German measles.*

[3] We use *a/an* if we want to make a name less specific:
*A **Mr Jones** came to see you this afternoon.* (I don't know which Mr Jones.)
We can make a name more specific by using *the*:
***The Mr Jones** with the stutter came to see you.* (The stutter identifies this Mr Jones.)
[4] Although we don't usually use an article with seasons, it is possible to use *the*: *in **the** spring/**the** summer*, and note that we use *the* with parts of the day: *in **the** afternoon*.
❗ We usually use a possessive adjective (not *the*) to refer to parts of the body:
*Put **your** hand up if you know the answer.*

28.2 DEMONSTRATIVES

28.2A Used as adjectives

We can use demonstratives, *this/that* (singular) and *these/those* (plural), as adjectives before nouns to refer to someone or something known to both speaker and listener:
*'I'm not sure which shoes to buy.' 'Well, I think **these** shoes are lovely.'*

	close	distant
space	*Do you recognise **this** man?* ***These** parrots can live to over 70.*	*I've seen **that** man before.* *Can you see **those** birds in the tree?*
time	*What are you doing **this** weekend?* *There's so much crime **these** days.*	*Do you remember **that** weekend?* *There were no drugs in **those** days.*

We use them to distinguish between close and distant things (in both space and time):
In very informal speech we can use *this* or *these* instead of *a/an* or *some*, often to introduce a topic or start telling a story:
***This** woman came up to me in the bank and asked if she could borrow …*

28.2B Used as pronouns or intensifiers

We can use demonstratives as pronouns to refer to a noun, a thing or idea (▶ **35.2A**):
***This** is a really wonderful cup of tea. What kind is it?*
*Alan says he's giving up his job to travel the world. I think **that**'s stupid.*
We can use *this* to talk about a situation that we are experiencing:
***This** is the worst recession we have seen for more than ten years.*
We can use demonstratives as a more formal alternative to *the one(s)*:
*Hundreds of Brixton residents turned out to welcome Tyson to their borough. **Those** who had bothered were rewarded by a 40-minute walkabout.*
In certain expressions, we can use *this* or *that* instead of *so* to intensify an adjective:
*I've never known a winter **this** cold before. So you think you're **that** clever, do you?*

28.3 QUANTIFIERS

28.3A Common quantifiers and their use

Quantifiers are determiners which describe the quantity of something. Notice the use of *of* or *of the* shown in the table:

quantifier	+ singular noun	+ plural noun	+ uncountable noun
no		*I've got **no** coins.*	*I've got **no** money.*
none of the		***none of the** details*	***none of the** information*
neither	***neither** cat*	***neither** of the cats*	
either	***either** twin*	***either** of the twins*	
any	***any** document*	***any** (of the) documents*	***any** (of the) information*[1]
both		***both** (of the) awards*[2]	

quantifier	+ singular noun	+ plural noun	+ uncountable noun
few/little		*(a)* ***few*** *(of the) sweets*[3]	*(a)* ***little*** *(of the) water*[3]
half	***half*** *(of) the task*	***half*** *(of) the tasks*	***half*** *(of) the work*
some		***some*** *(of the) jewels*	***some*** *(of the) jewellery*
several		***several*** *(of the) episodes*	
a lot of	***a lot of the*** *conference*	***a lot of*** *(the) ideas*	***a lot of*** *(the) time*
many/much		***many*** *(of the) chairs*	***much*** *(of the) furniture*
most	***most*** *of the holiday*	***most*** *(of the) apples*	***most*** *(of the) fruit*
each	***each*** *applicant*	***each*** *of the applicants*	
every (one of)	***every*** *page*[4]	***every one of*** *the pages*	
all	***all*** *(of) the problem*	***all*** *(of) the problems*	***all*** *(of) the trouble*

[1] We often use quantifiers (except *none* and *a lot*) directly before a noun:
It is impossible to nominate ***both candidates*** *for the Vice-presidency.*

With most quantifiers, using *of the* before a plural or uncountable noun changes the meaning of the noun from general to specific:
I'd like ***some*** *jewellery.* (general, we don't know which jewellery)
I'd like ***some of the*** *jewellery.* (specific, a particular set of jewellery)

[2] With *both* we can omit *of* before *the*: ***Both*** *(of) the candidates believed they had won.*

[3] For the difference between *little/few* and *a little/a few* (▶ **6.3A**).

[4] Note the difference between *each* and *every*. Both quantifiers describe 'more than one'; we can use *each* to refer to two things, but not *every*:
✗ ~~*She was wearing a fine gold chain on* ***every*** *ankle.*~~
✓ *She was wearing a fine gold chain on* ***each*** *ankle.*
But: *She was wearing a ring on* ***every*** *finger.*

We usually use *some* in positive sentences, *any* in questions and negatives:
You've got ***some*** *interesting ideas, but have you got* ***any*** *money to back them?*

We can use *any* in positive sentences with the meaning 'it doesn't matter which':
You won't catch any fish here. ***Any*** *fisherman will tell you that.*

! It is possible to use *some* in questions where we have some expectation that the answer will be positive:
Is ***some*** *of the information useful?* (I expect that a part of it is.)
Is ***any*** *of the information useful?* (I have no idea if it is useful or not.)

28.3B Quantifiers as subjects

We can use quantifiers (except *no* and *every*) without a noun as subject of the clause:
The vote was split: ***half*** *were in favour of the motion,* ***half*** *were against it.*

When used as subjects some quantifiers take a singular verb, and some take a plural verb. Others are used with a singular or plural verb, depending on the noun they substitute or modify. Look at the table:

always singular[1]	*each, either, much* ***Much of the research has*** *already been completed.*
always plural	*both, several, a few, many* *Some visitors to the new gallery are enthusiastic but* ***many have*** *expressed their disappointment*
singular or plural	*any, half, some, a lot, all* ***Some of the information is*** *considered top secret.* ***Some of us are*** *hiring a minibus to go to the match.* *'We can't get many books to the schools in the outback.' 'Don't worry.* ***Any (books)*** *are better than none.'*

[1] The quantifiers *neither* and *none* take a singular verb with plural nouns, though a plural verb is now accepted in speech and informal writing:
None of the students is/are *willing to accept the increase in coursework.*

Practice

The key to these exercises is on page 367.

1 28.1

Read this story and fill in the gaps with the correct article: *a/an*, *the* or – (no article). For one gap you will need a possessive adjective.

I first experienced terror when I was seven. My mother lived in London, but after a brief liaison with (1) .... soldier from the United States she became pregnant and fled to (2) .... country. (At that time, fifty years ago, it was considered shameful to be a single parent.) A great aunt of hers lived in (3) .... cottage in (4) .... North Wales, and there she was able to bring me up in (5) .... peace, pretending that she was a widow. (6) .... locals were all very friendly to us and accepted us without question, and I had (7) .... blissful childhood.

One day I arrived home from (8) .... school to find my mother clutching (9) .... telegram, in floods of tears. (10) .... telegram informed her that her father – my grandfather – had died. His funeral would be in three days and we had to go to London. I had never been outside (11) .... village and I was really excited at the thought of going to (12) .... capital city. So, two days later, we boarded a train to London. It was (13) .... first time I had been on a train and I could barely contain (14) .... excitement of such an adventure. Several hours later we arrived. I clutched my mother's hand as we stepped down from the train. (15) .... station was full of people rushing home from (16) .... work and it was quite dark. Now (17) .... fear was starting to creep into my mind. Then, suddenly, we were in (18) .... street outside the station. I had never seen so many people, buses and cars, nor heard so much noise. I was terrified. I opened (19) .... mouth and the wail that I let escape was one of (20) .... sheer terror.

2 28.1

Complete these short sentences with an appropriate article: *a/an*, *the* or – (no article).

1 He's got .... asthma.
2 The ring is just a band of .... gold.
3 It prints seven pages .... minute.
4 Let's have a weekend in .... mountains.
5 She's at .... work.
6 It's in .... Tasman Sea.
7 Sorry – it's .... wrong answer.
8 It appeared in .... *New York Times*.
9 She's always been .... Catholic.
10 What's for .... dinner?
11 We're going on a day trip by .... coach.
12 They're flying to .... Seychelles.
13 It's .... best solution.
14 Can you ski on .... Mont Blanc?
15 It's quite warm there in .... winter.
16 We all need .... oxygen.
17 We've had over .... dozen applicants.
18 She works in .... television.
19 It's all .... better if you can come early.
20 He was crowned .... king.

3 28.2

Complete the dialogue with a demonstrative adjective or pronoun from the box.

this (x3)	that (x4)	these (x1)	those (x2)

ROB What's on TV tonight, do you know?
JENNY No. Why don't you look in the paper you're reading?
ROB (1) .... paper doesn't have TV listings.
JENNY Oh, right. Well try (2) .... one on the shelf, over there.
ROB OK ... yes, let's see. There's nothing much on (3) .... days at all, is there? It's all soaps and detective series.

JENNY Mmm. I thought there was always a serious documentary on Tuesday evenings. (4) .... one last week on homelessness was really interesting.

ROB Yes, you're right. There's one on travellers. Listen. (5) .... is awful. 'Although landowners may lose income while travellers are on their land, there is no fast route to evicting them. (6) .... who go through the courts often have to take out more than one injunction before the matter is settled.'

JENNY Well, what do you expect? The travellers need somewhere to live, like the rest of us. The government should give them land.

ROB (7) ....'s no solution, is it? They want to travel, not to settle.

JENNY How do you know? There was (8) .... story in my magazine about travellers from years ago and the encampments they made – they were allowed to settle down then.

ROB Yes, but in (9) .... days there was more free land. Land is (10) .... valuable today, people use every bit of it and don't want travellers on their land.

JENNY Mmm, well why don't we turn the TV on and find out what the documentary says?

4 28.1, 28.2

Match one of the sentences or beginnings of sentences in each pair (1–8) with a continuation of the sentence or conversation from the list below (A–I).

A I don't know him. Do you?
B Could I have a closer look at it, please?
C It's a basic human right.
D You just have to shop around.
E It's the tallest type of tree in the world.
F She took journalism and media studies.
G ~~You know, the one where Chris works.~~
H You know, the one that we couldn't get last week.
I I've never come across one so talkative before!

0 a Let's meet in a wine bar.
b Let's meet in the wine bar. ....b.... + ...G....
1 a My sister went to university.
b My sister went to the university ... . + ...
2 a The cat communicates a lot of desires and emotions.
b This cat communicates a lot of desires and emotions. .... + ...
3 a Dr Richards called to speak to you.
b A Dr Richards called to speak to you. .... + ...
4 a People shouldn't be denied freedom.
b People shouldn't be denied the freedom ... . + ...
5 a A giant redwood once grew to over 70 metres.
b The giant redwood can grow to more than 70 metres. .... + ...
6 a Let's get a video out this evening.
b Let's get that video out this evening. .... + ...
7 a You can pay a lot less for a car these days.
b You could pay a lot less for a car in those days. .... + ...
8 a This is an interesting specimen.
b That's an interesting specimen. .... + ...

5 28.3

For each of these questions, either one or two alternatives (A–C) are correct. Circle the letters of all the correct alternatives.

1 I haven't seen .... of those films, so I don't mind which one we go to.
A any B no C either
2 You shouldn't slouch like that. It puts .... of pressure on one hip and leg.
A much B a lot C all
3 At this stage, ... information would have been a step in the right direction.
A little B some C any
4 The Fitness Room would like to invite .... of its patrons to enter the annual fitness challenge.
A all B every C some
5 .... witnesses responded to the police appeal after the accident.
A No B None C Any
6 .... of the women who attended the demonstration was willing to give us an interview.
A No B None C Many
7 We would like to add that .... medallion is inscribed with the name of its lucky owner.
A each B every C either
8 Only .... of the news today has been about the election.
A half B a little C a few
9 We guarantee that .... item of the dinner service will be replaceable for a period of ten years.
A each B every C all
10 We are delighted to be able to welcome .... the competition winners to the gala evening.
A both B either C all

6 ALL

Complete the article with the words from above each paragraph. (– = no article)

a all the the the The this your – –

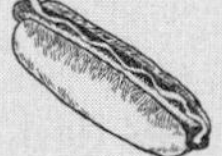

FOOD FRIGHTS

Planning a big day out this summer? It's not just the rides that could turn your stomach!

The risk of food poisoning should be the last thing on (1) .... mind when you're enjoying a quiet day out (2) .... summer. But, in (3) .... UK, there were around 95,000 reported cases of (4) .... food poisoning in (5).......... last year alone – a four-fold increase on the number of reported cases just ten years ago.

We checked food safety at 13 of our top tourist attractions. We tested the food on offer and inspected hygiene standards at restaurants, cafés and kiosks on site. Standards were generally poor. About (6) .... third of the 65 food samples we bought failed to meet satisfactory microbiological guidelines. Sandwiches came out worst – in five of (7) .... 25 samples we bought we found food-poisoning bacteria. But, to judge from our inspections, the results are not that surprising. Only one in seven food outlets passed (8) .... of our inspection criteria. (9) .... majority of problems we came across were staff-related, and showed a lack of training in (10) .... food safety.

each half most the the these these This – –

What we found

At (11) .... tourist attraction we bought a selection of sandwiches and other food products. Our tests revealed specific food-poisoning bacteria in five of (12) .... sandwiches. High levels of other general bacteria were also found in more than (13) .... of the sandwiches – while (14) .... bacteria don't make you ill, they do point to (15) .... poor hygiene practices.

Five sandwiches contained food-poisoning bacteria at levels that are not satisfactory according to guidelines. (16) .... could cause food-poisoning – (17) .... children, elderly people and pregnant women are particularly vulnerable. We've informed (18) .... food outlets and tourist attractions concerned; (19) .... (but not all) have taken positive action as a result of (20).......... disturbing findings.

7 ALL

Read the following text. In most lines there is an unnecessary word, a word missing or an incorrect word. For each numbered line (1–23), identify the mistake and write the correct word in the space on the right. Some lines are correct. Indicate these with a tick (✔). The exercise begins with three examples.

Magnum past and present

0 Magnum is a co-operative of nearly sixty photographers with offices in New ....✔........
00 York, London, Paris and Tokyo. A co-operative was founded in 1947 by ......A → The......
000 photographers the Robert Capa, Henri Cartier-Bresson, George Rodger and ......~~the~~......
1 David Seymour. All them had been involved in the Second World War. ....
2 Rodger had walked hundreds of miles through forest to escape Japanese ....
3 in the Burma. And Seymour received a medal for his work in American ....
4 intelligence. ....
5 However, all of founders of Magnum had been photographers for ....
6 some time. Photographic work they were famous for dated back further. ....
7 Capa's photos of the Spanish Civil war were called 'finest pictures of ....
8 front-line action ever taken.' ....
9 They all appreciated an importance of showing the world what really ....
10 happens during this major conflicts and world crises, so they decided to ....
11 produce the best documentary photography at this time. Cartier-Bresson ....
12 once commented 'Some photographers tell the news step by the step as ....
13 if making an accountant's statement.' He and Magnum, on the other hand, ...
14 felt that the news had to be shown in that way that would engage most ....
15 the people who are unable to experience world-changing events at first-hand. ....
16 Tragically, within a decade of the start of Magnum, the half of its original ....
17 founders died while covering other wars. However, agency had started to ....
18 employ other top-class photographers and its work was sure to continue. ....
19 Today, Magnum is some goal for many young photographers. It still ....
20 produces the finest documentary photographs of world events. Recent ....
21 coverage has included the events in Balkans and the tribal wars in East ....
22 Africa, and while Magnum photographers cover these events, we will all be ....
23 able to appreciate both best and worst of humanity. ....

29 Prepositions

Prepositions are a common cause of confusion for learners, often because each preposition has a number of different uses. This unit looks at the uses of a range of prepositions, and the difficulties they can present. (For prepositional and phrasal verbs ▶ **Unit 14**; for prepositions dependent on nouns, verbs and adjectives ▶ **Unit 15**.)

29.1 INTRODUCTION

29.1A Basic information

A preposition describes the relationship between two or more things. It can link nouns, verbs or adjectives before the preposition with a noun or pronoun after it:

Now, let's move on to [*item six*] ***on*** [*the agenda*].

Be careful. The hem of your dress is [*dragging*] ***along*** [*the floor*].

John's got an appraisal tomorrow. He's really [*anxious*] ***about*** [*it*].

Prepositions can be one word only, e.g. *of*, *throughout*, or more words, e.g. *because of*:

We got fewer dollars this week ***because of*** *the drop in the exchange rate.*

29.1B Prepositions and adverbs

There is no difference in form between prepositions and many adverbs, but there is a difference in use: a preposition has an object but an adverb does not. Compare:

Did you ever travel ***before the war****, Dad?* (preposition)

I have a strange feeling that I've been here ***before****.* (adverb)

We can modify prepositions with adverbs (the adverbs in the example are in bold):

The pub is ***almost*** *at the end of the street,* ***just*** *before the traffic lights.*

29.2 MEANING AND USE

29.2A Position

vertical relationships ↑↓	*above, after, below, beneath, down, on, on top of, over, under, underneath, up*

Above and *over* have similar meanings, as do *below* and *under*. We usually use *above* or *below*:

The refuge is in the hills ***above*** *the town.*

The temperature was ***below*** *freezing last night.*

But we use *over* or *under* in the following cases:

- When one thing covers another:
  The clouds hung low ***over*** *the hills. He disappeared* ***under*** *the water.*
- When horizontal movement is suggested:
  Are we going to fly ***over*** *the Alps?*
- With prices, ages, speeds, distances and quantities, where we mean *more than* or *fewer/less than*:
  ✗ ~~*The conference was very badly attended:* ***below*** *two hundred people came.*~~
  ✔ *The conference was very badly attended:* ***under*** *two hundred people came.*

We use *above* or *below* to talk about 'level' or 'rank':

Is the position of Managing Editor ***above*** *or* ***below*** *that of Editorial Director?*

It is also possible to use *after* in this sense:

His opinion is second only ***after*** *the Managing Director's.*

Note the use of *up* and *down*:

John lives a few houses further ***up/down*** *the hill from us.*

We generally use *beneath* in idiomatic phrases:

Your behaviour towards my new husband was really ***beneath contempt****!*

horizontal relationships ←→	*against, along, alongside, around, at, beside, between, by, in, near, next to, on, on the left/right of*

We use *at* with a point in space, e.g. ***at*** *the bus stop*, ***at*** *8 Baker Street*; we use *on* with a surface or a line, e.g. ***on*** *the table*, ***on*** *the river*, ***on*** *Oxford Street*; and we use *in* with something that surrounds, e.g. ***in*** *the wood*. We use different prepositions depending on how we see a place. Compare:

The group will meet at 7.30 ***at*** *the sports centre.* (= either inside or outside)

The group will meet at 7.30 ***in*** *the sports centre.* (= inside)

❶ Also: ***at*** *the corner of the street* (= a point) but ***in*** *the corner of the room* (= inside).

We usually use *in* with countries, cities or towns. We use *on* with streets, roads, avenues, etc., and we use *at* with the names of squares if we think of the 'address', and *in* if we think of the square as 'surrounding' us:

✘ ~~*The film premiere this year will take place* ***on*** *Leicester Square* ***at*** *London.*~~

✔ *The film premiere this year will take place* ***at*** *Leicester Square* ***in*** *London.*

The trees ***in*** *Leicester Square don't look very healthy.*

We use *at* when we refer to gatherings of people: ***at*** *a party*, ***at*** *a conference*.

We use *beside* and *alongside* to express proximity along a line:

Warehouses were built ***beside/alongside*** *the motorway.*

'facing' relationships ▸◂	*across, after, before, behind, facing, in front of, opposite, over*

We use *in front of* or *behind* to describe the spatial relationship of two things, one after the other on a line and facing the same way:

front
A ↑
back
front
B ↑
back

A is ***in front of*** *B. B is* ***behind*** *A.*

In front of and *behind* can also be used for metaphorical, not literal, position:

Christopher is really ***behind*** *his brother in terms of academic development.*

Before and *after* can refer to position in some contexts:

Karen's nephew appears ***before/in front of*** *the magistrates this afternoon.*

You'll be called first as my name is ***after*** *yours on the list.*

Opposite, *facing*, *across* and *over* have the meaning of 'on the other side of' but with *across* and *over* we have to state on the other side of what, e.g. a road, a river:

I'll meet you in the café ***opposite/facing*** *the theatre.* (= on the other side of the road)

I'll meet you in the café ***across/over*** *the road from the theatre.*

❶ The difference between *opposite/facing* and *in front of* is that the items on the 'line' are not facing in the same direction, as in the diagram above, but are facing each other:

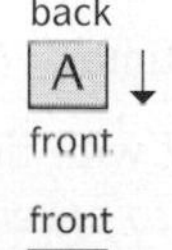

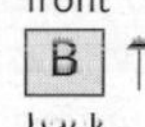

A is ***facing/opposite*** *B. A and B are* ***facing/opposite*** *each other.*

29.2B Movement and direction

vertical movement *down (to), off, on, onto, over, up (to)*

We use these prepositions for movement up or down:

Keep to the right as you go ***down*** *the stairs.*

Look at Johnny's knee – he's just fallen ***off*** *his bike.*

We *get on* or *off* a bus, plane, train, boat and bike but *into* and *out of* a car.

We can use *over* for a movement up and then down an obstacle:

The burglar leapt ***over*** *the garden fence as he ran away from us.*

passing movement *across, along, down, over, past, through, up*

We use *along* for movement in a line, e.g. *along a river/road*:

You can spend a pleasant afternoon strolling ***along*** *the canals in Amsterdam.*

We also often use *up* and *down* with roads and rivers (meaning 'along'):

Go ***up*** *the road to the corner, and the cinema is on the left.*

We use *across* for movement from one side to the other of something on a 'surface', e.g. *across the river/road/field*. We use *through* for movement inside something, e.g. *through a room/tunnel*:

You walk ***across*** *the playing field to the wood then you go* ***through*** *the wood …*

Over is similar to *across* (one side to the other) but it incorporates the idea of *above*:

Are we going to fly ***over*** *the Alps on the way to Italy?*

We use *past* for a movement from one side to the other of something, next to it:

I was startled by a huge bird that flew ***past*** *my window this afternoon.*

movement in one direction *around, at, away from, down, down to, from, into, onto, out of, to, towards, up, up to*

We can use both *to* and *at* after certain verbs, e.g. *throw, shout*. *To* suggests that the recipient of the action is willing but *at* that he/she is not willing:

Can you throw that book ***to me****, please?* (I am willing.)

Don't throw stones ***at the cat****!* (The cat is unwilling.)

We can use *up to* or *towards* when we approach someone or something, but we use only *up to* if we actually reach the person/thing:

✗ ~~*Do you think I can go* ***towards*** *him and ask for his autograph?*~~

✓ *Do you think I can go* ***up to*** *him and ask for his autograph?*

✓ *The scientist moved quietly* ***towards*** *the group of grazing animals.*

We can use *up (to)* and *down (to)* for movement north or south within a country:

We've just come ***down to*** *Canberra from Darwin.*

We can express a circular movement with *(a)round*:

We drove ***(a)round*** *the roundabout three times before we took the correct exit.*

We can also use the prepositions of movement in a less literal way:

A system of charges has been introduced ***into*** *the Health Service.*

29.2C Time

point in time *at, in, on*

We use *at* with times, special periods (e.g. celebrations) and in some phrases:

at *five to seven*, ***at*** *Christmas*, ***at*** *night*, ***at*** *the weekend* (US English ***on*** *the weekend*)

We use *in* with parts of the day, months, seasons, years, centuries, etc.:

in *the evening*, ***in*** *December*, ***in*** *1999*, ***in*** *the winter*, ***in*** *the twentieth century*

We use *on* with days and dates, including special days:

on *Thursday*, ***on*** *(the morning of) the 31st of October*, ***on*** *Christmas Day*

We sometimes omit the preposition if we use *about* or *around*, to be less specific:

Let's meet at the station (at) ***about*** *six; there's a train at ten past.*

We can supply the materials (on) ***around*** *Thursday next week.*

In US English and informal British English, we can also omit *on* before days:

Great news! The travel agent can get us on a flight that leaves ***Wednesday****.*

We do not use the prepositions *at*, *on* or *in* immediately before adverbs or adverbial phrases such as *today*, *tomorrow*, *last/this/next week*:

✗ ~~*The new soap opera on BBC2 is starting* ***on*** *tomorrow.*~~

✓ *The new soap opera on BBC2 is starting tomorrow.*

before or after *after, before, by, past*

We can use *after* or *past* to mean 'later than':

There's no point in going to the party now; it's ***after/past*** *eleven o'clock.*

We use *before* to mean 'before a time', and we use *by* to mean 'before or at a time':

Applications must be submitted ***before*** *30th November.* (= on the 29th or earlier)

Applications must be submitted ***by*** *30th November.* (= on the 30th or earlier)

❗ The adverbial phrases *in time* (with time to spare) and *on time* (at the right time, often fixed) have different meanings:

The wedding car arrived ***in time*** *but the bride wasn't ready.* (= time to spare)

I want to arrive right ***on time*** *at the church. It's not done for the bride to arrive before the groom.* (= not early or late)

duration *as from/of, between, during, for, from ... till/until/up to, in, inside, since, through(out), until/till, up to, within*

We can use a number of different prepositions to talk about duration:

As of *next Monday, we will have to suspend flexible working arrangements* ***until*** *further notice.*

The long flowing style – of hair and clothes – was fashionable ***during/through(out)*** *much of the seventies.*

This volcano hasn't erupted ***since*** *1935.*

The motorway widening was successfully completed ***within/in/inside*** *four months.*

British English uses *from ... to* to express the start and end points of a period of time, but US English uses *through*:

I'll be staying at the Hilton ***from*** *Friday* ***to*** *Monday.*

I'll be staying at the Hilton Friday ***through*** *Monday.*

29.2D Other meanings

reason *because of, due to, for, from, out of, owing to, through*

The 10.00 service to Bath has been cancelled ***due to/owing to*** *staff shortage.*

Huge numbers of people in the Third World die ***from*** *starvation every day.*

Many parents sacrifice their own material wealth ***out of*** *the desire to give their children everything.*

The fire started ***through*** *careless disposal of a cigarette end.*

means *by, by means of, in, via, with*

We use *by* or *with* to introduce an instrument:

Negotiations were held ***by*** *phone between the client and his solicitor.*

The victim was killed ***by*** *a bullet to the head/****with*** *a sawn-off shotgun.*

We also use *by* for the agent (or originator) of something:

It's a painting ***by*** *Van Gogh. He completed it during his stay in Arles.*

Note the difference between *by* and *of* here:

It's a painting ***of*** *Van Gogh. It's actually not a very good likeness of him.*

We use *in* when we refer to the means we use to achieve something:

Complete the form ***in*** *pencil. He prefers to paint* ***in*** *watercolour.*

purpose *for, towards*

I want an opener that can be used ***for*** *opening bottles of beer as well as wine.*
We're saving all of this extra income ***towards*** *a round-the-world trip next year.*

comparison *against, as, beside, between, contrary to, than, (un)like*

We use *against, beside* and *contrary to* to make a contrast:
Look at this year's sales figures ***against*** *last year's; they're so much better.*
Beside *her sister, Laura was positively plain.*
The Davis Cup final was won by the French team, ***contrary to*** *expectations.*
We use *between* to differentiate (usually *the difference between*):
You won't be able to tell the difference ***between*** *butter and this spread.*
We can use *like* to make a comparison, but we use *as* to express a role:
She behaves ***like*** *a director, but she's really only a secretary.*
Speaking ***as*** *a director of the company, I believe we should sell the shares.*

inclusion and exclusion *among, as well as, besides, between, beyond, inside, instead of, out of, outside, under, within, without*

We usually use *between* with only two objects and *among* with more than two:
For women, the distinction ***between*** *work and leisure is less clear-cut.*
The terminals are ***among*** *the biggest single development sites in Europe.*
Note the uses of the following prepositions which have the meaning of exclusion:
Are there any issues remaining ***besides*** *that of the roof repairs?*
I'm afraid that changes to the curriculum are ***beyond/outside/out of*** *our control.*

exception *apart from, barring, but for, except (for), save*

Everyone is invited to the conference dinner, ***except (for)/apart from/save*** *those who have bought 'day' tickets only.*
Except and *except for* can both be used after phrases containing determiners such as *all, every, no*:
Julian did very well in all his exams ***except (for)*** *geography.*
Except for *one question on calculus, Julian got all the maths questions right.*
However, when the prepositional phrase contradicts the main idea of the sentence, we use *except for* :
Trulli emerged from the wreckage of the car uninjured ***except for*** *a broken thumb.*
We use *but for* to mean 'if not for':
The house would have been destroyed ***but for*** *the quick thinking of the firefighters.*

contrast ▶ 32.2 *despite, for all, in spite of*

Despite/In spite of/For all *his grand ways, he was really no better off than the rest of us.*

material *from, of, out of, with*

We use different prepositions when we describe the material from which something is made (*made* ***(out) of****, made* ***from****, made* ***with*** ▶ **15.4C**).
We use *of* when the original material is still visible:
a dress made ***of*** *silk*   *a jacket made* ***of*** *leather*   *a table* ***of*** *the finest mahogany*
We use *from* when the original material has been transformed:
ice cream made ***from*** *strawberries*   *toilet rolls made* ***from*** *recycled paper*

We use *with* when we refer to a filling or an ingredient:

*vine leaves stuffed **with** rice* *rice pudding made **with** cream*

We use *of* in metaphorical phrases:

*a man **of** iron* *a heart **of** gold*

benefit	*for, for the sake of, on behalf of*

***On behalf of** our shareholders, I'd like to thank all of you who voted in favour of the merger.*

*I think we should move to the country **for the sake of** the children.*

reporting	*according to*

We do not use *according to* to report our own feelings or opinions:

✗ ~~*Holograms aren't a real art form, **according to** me.*~~

✓ ***According to** many art critics, holograms aren't a real art form.*

✓ *Holograms aren't a real art form, in my opinion.*

29.3 PREPOSITIONAL PHRASES

29.3A Form

A prepositional phrase consists of a preposition and the word(s) that follow it. The most common words that follow prepositions are nouns and pronouns:

*sleep **on** [the floor]* *comparisons **between** [Clinton and Kennedy]* *it's **for** [you]*

We can also use *-ing* forms, adverbs or *wh-* clauses after prepositions:

***As well as** [helping] us to move into the house, John bought us a great present.*

*Please don't interfere in any way **with** [what I have written in the introduction].*

A prepositional phrase can include a determiner before the noun or *-ing* form:

*The head teacher doesn't approve **of** [his arrangements] with a local band.*

We can't use a *that* clause after a preposition:

✗ ~~*The government managed to pass the bill through Parliament, **despite that** it had a low majority.*~~

✓ *The government managed to pass the bill through Parliament, **despite** its low majority/**despite** having a low majority/**despite the fact that** it had a low majority.*

Nor can we use an infinitive phrase, except with the prepositions *except*, *but* and *save*:

*Please come straight home – don't stop **except to** phone us.*

29.3B Stranded prepositions

A 'stranded preposition' is a preposition on its own at the end of a clause or sentence. English commonly uses stranded prepositions in:

- Questions: ***Who** are you coming to the party **with**?*
- Relative clauses: *I've been offered the job in London **that** I applied **for**!*
- The passive: *What **is** your coat **made from**?*
- Infinitive clauses: *That man is impossible **to work with**!*

We sometimes keep the preposition and object together in formal language:

*We have been unable to offer you the position **for which** you applied.*

❗ We do not precede the relative pronoun *that* with a preposition:

✗ ~~*We have been unable to offer you the position **for that** you applied*~~

Practice

The key to these exercises is on page 367.

1 29.1

Rewrite the sentences. Put the words in brackets in the correct order.

1 The people in the earthquake zone were encouraged to [area/away/from/get/the] while there was still time. ....
2 Water will be made available [and/crisis/for/hospitals/schools/the/throughout]. ....
3 The acting and the costumes were excellent, [as/but/for/plot/the], it was ridiculous! ....
4 It must have been raining really hard. All [are/through/passers-by/soaked/the]. ....
5 This year's award for excellence in the industry will be collected [behalf/of/on/winner/the] by the chairman of the Design Foundation. ....
6 The rescuers pulled the dog [a/by/from/means/of/rope/the/well]. ....
7 Can you pass me the pasta pan? It's [cupboard/of/on/right/the/top]. ....
8 The journey time has been reduced [hours/just/three/to/under]. ....
9 'You're late. You weren't on the train that was derailed, were you?' 'No, [one/after/the/mine/just/was]. ....
10 Didn't you recognise her? She was sitting [almost/beard/man/opposite/the/the/with]. ....

2 29.2

Underline the best alternative in *italics*.

1 Our son, James Christopher, was born *in/on* the morning of 2nd March.
2 Don't forget that your final assignment must be handed to your tutor *– /on* next Monday.
3 The soldiers didn't arrive at the village *on/in* time – the rebels had already burned the remaining houses.
4 Don't be late for the Philharmonia concert – you know they always start dead *on/in* time.
5 There has been no sign of the birds *until/since* nightfall.
6 David Mamet's latest play will be showing on Broadway October *up to/through* December.
7 Payment of your electricity bill is now four weeks overdue. If we do not receive payment *on/by* 31st July, we shall refer the matter to the court.
8 As he opened the shop at 7.30 in the morning, Mr Charles was attacked *by/with* a baseball bat.
9 The definitive photograph *of/by* Marilyn Monroe is the one where she is standing over an air vent.
10 Alexander Graham Bell worked *as/like* a teacher for much of his life.
11 It was impossible to find anything of importance *between/among* the dead man's papers.
12 It is the duty of governments today to take seriously the threat of global warming, *in spite of/for the sake of* future generations.
13 *Except/Apart* for a few less experienced individuals, all of the recent applicants were taken on.
14 This publication is made *of/from* paper from sustainable forests.
15 Letters of application for this post should be completed *in/with* handwriting.

Complete the following article with the most appropriate prepositions. The preposition may consist of more than one word. The exercise begins with an example (0).

End of the road

It was late afternoon when we drove (0) .*into*. the little town. We had driven (1) .... 400 kilometres in the morning and most of it had been (2) .... thick fog. We were tired and decided to find a hotel – we didn't know how far it might be to the next town. We parked, got (3) .... the car and stretched – a walk would be very welcome. We left our luggage (4) .... the car boot and walked (5) .... the already empty car park to a narrow but fast-flowing stream. A five-minute stroll (6) .... a tree-lined avenue (7) .... the stream took us (8) .... the town square. It was a beautiful old square with a fountain (9) .... the middle and arcades (10) .... three sides. We looked up at terraces of interesting-looking restaurants (11) .... the arcades and then back down at entrances to fascinating little shops (12) .... them.

We had no idea where to look for a hotel or a pension in this sleepy town, so we walked (13) .... an old man sitting (14) .... a bench by the fountain. He pointed us in the direction of a narrow alleyway and told us we'd find the best hotel (15) .... the little road. It seemed unlikely, but we followed his advice and sure enough, (16) .... the other end of the alleyway, (17) .... two picturesque old houses, was a sign saying 'hotel'. Just (18) .... the hotel, (19) .... the other side of the street, was a house covered in the most colourful flowers, and I immediately hoped that we might be able to see the house from our bedroom window. (20) .... the hotel reception, a cool, dark room with a bar (21) .... one corner, we asked about a room. Our satisfaction was complete when we realised that even the best room in the hotel was (22) .... $50.

We looked at the room, decided to take it and went down to the lounge, where we stopped for a delicious cappuccino. Soon dusk was falling, so we handed the room key (23) .... the receptionist and told him we'd be back with our luggage in ten minutes. As we walked (24) .... the narrow streets, we discussed what we would do the next day and how long we'd stay in the little town. Imagine our horror when we arrived (25) .... the car park to find it completely empty – our car and all of our luggage had been stolen!

4 29.3

In most of the lines of the following text, there is one word or phrase missing. For each line 1–14, indicate where the word should be (use ⁄\) and write the missing word in the spaces on the right. Some lines are correct. Indicate these lines with a tick (✓). The exercise begins with two examples (0 and 00).

0 One of the changes in entertainment in recent years has been the arrival of ....✓..........
00 alternative comedy. In this type of comedy, performers work with ⁄\ is considered ....*what*.......
1 to be taboo or controversial. It's a very strong kind of humour, the main aim ....
2 which is the desire to shock people out their comfortable complacent lives and ....
3 make them think about is important in life today. Some of the most common ....
4 subject areas that alternative comedians work are politics, sex and religion. ....
5 Alternative comedy takes place mainly in adult clubs and comedy venues; ....
6 because of the that it questions and threatens the establishment, public TV ....
7 channels have been reluctant to give it much air time, except try to boost ratings ....
8 occasionally among certain audience sectors. In fact, whenever alternative ....
9 comedy has appeared on prime time TV, viewers with children have complained ....
10 about being somehow corrupted by the nature of the humour. Of course, this ....
11 kind of comedy is not intended for children at all, nor is it really the older, ...
12 established families with children that it is aimed. Fortunately for alternative ....
13 comedians, the section of society it *is* intended – younger people who themselves ....
14 question the values and priorities of society – continue to support it. ....

5 ALL

Underline the correct word or phrase in *italics*. In some cases, both may be correct.

No, you're not looking at a scene (1) *from/out of* a James Bond movie! The futuristic buildings in this photo really exist. They are part of the Eden Project – one of the most spectacular (2) *in/of* the Millennium projects.

The Eden Project is located (3) *at/in* Cornwall, England, in a former clay pit (4) *above/over* 50 metres deep. It consists of two enormous domes, a large open area and a visitor centre. The Eden Project functions (5) *as/like* a 'storeroom' for a huge number of plants from (6) *across/all over* the world. The two collections of domes house plants and trees (7) *from/for* the tropical and temperate regions (8) *of/in* the world, while the open area accommodates more local species.

The Eden Project is much more (9) *as/than* a storeroom, however. It is a centre (10) *for/on* education, art and science, showing us ways in (11) *which/that* plants are vital to the world's existence, and promoting understanding of the delicate balance (12) *between/among* using and conserving plant life. As well as (13) *offer/offering* a visitor attraction (14) *to/for* people of all ages, the Eden Project provides a focus both for scientific research and for education, (15) *including/inside* exciting experiences for children, such as walking (16) *through/in* a rainforest (17) *outside/without* leaving England.

In the year 2000, the Eden Project was in the final stages (18) *at/of* construction. (19) *Contrary to/Unlike* most projects of this scale, the Eden Project opened its doors to visitors (20) *for/during* that building stage. (21) *For/Since* several months visitors were able to experience the challenges that lie (22) *under/behind* the building of such a project and get a taste of (23) *what/which* was to come. (24) *From/In* spring 2001 this living theatre opened fully to the public and for (25) *under/below* £10, everyone can now experience the diversity of the world's plants.

Prepositions are missing from the following three stories. Use the prepositions in the box above each story to fill the gaps.

according to	across	between	by	from	in	on	to

A BAD EXPLORER

A man (1) .... Kentucky, USA, had a dream that would take him away from the rolling hills of his home state. The dream: to row (2) .... the icy Bering Strait (3) .... Alaska and Russia, (4) .... a bathtub! Unfortunately, the dream was not completely fulfilled. (5) .... the explorer, 'I took four gallons of peanut butter along, but (6) .... the morning of the fourth day, it had gone solid. (7) .... late afternoon, although the sun was still high, the sea went rather thick. Next morning I was frozen in.' No problem. He abandoned the bathtub and walked (8) .... land.

at	behind	in	instead of	into	like	under	with

Some stupid thieves

(9) .... the town of Vang, Norway, a group of professional thieves were carrying out a carefully planned robbery. Everything was going (10) .... clockwork. They broke into a company (11) .... night, located the safe and set up some explosives that would blow the door of the safe off, allowing them to get to the money inside. After setting the fuse, they ran (12) .... the next room, crouched (13) .... the wall and waited for the explosion. It came a few seconds later. The safe door was blown off. So was the roof. In fact, the entire building collapsed, trapping the robbers, still crouching in the next office, (14) .... the rubble of the destroyed building. There had been just one problem they had not foreseen: (15) .... money, the safe had been filled (16) .... dynamite.

about against along at between during in in into
of off on on on on with

Self-help crime prevention

A Western businessman living (17) .... Japan had been warned (18) .... pickpockets in the Tokyo subways. These notorious thieves operated (19) .... the crowded rush hour. They had a habit (20) .... grabbing wallets just as the subway doors were closing, leaving the victim helpless (21) .... the train while they disappeared with the loot.

One morning the businessman was (22) .... his usual subway stop when the train pulled in. He got on, and sure enough, just as the train doors were about to close, he felt a man rub (23) .... him. In a panic, the businessman reached for his wallet. It was gone! He looked up as the doors began to close and saw that a man had just got (24) .... the train. The man was looking at him triumphantly.

Thinking fast, the businessman pushed his hands (25) .... the closing doors and grabbed the thief's jacket. The doors closed, with the thief still (26) .... the platform but (27) .... the lapels of his jacket trapped (28) .... the tight grip of the businessman. As the train began to pull away, the expression (29) .... the thief's face changed. He began screaming as he ran (30) .... the platform with the train. Finally, he held onto a post and his lapels tore away from his jacket. As the train moved (31) .... the tunnel, the businessman was satisfied that at least he had frightened the thief.

When he reached his office, he called his wife to get his credit card numbers so he could cancel them. 'But honey,' she said, 'I've been waiting to call you. You left your wallet (32) .... the dressing table when you went to work today.'

30 Word order and verb patterns

Word order in English is very important in signalling the relationships between the different elements within a sentence. Although the subject usually precedes the verb in English, there are many different ways of ordering the other elements in the sentence. This unit examines word order in sentences, as well as the most common verb patterns in English and the way we link clauses to make complex sentences.

30.1 WORD ORDER IN ENGLISH

30.1A Sentence word order

Word order shows us which element of the sentence is the subject and which is the object. In affirmative sentences, the subject is usually first, followed by the verb:

Sarah really enjoys [*a hot dog*] *(for tea occasionally).*

↑ subject ↑ verb ↑ object

❗ This is not the same as:

A hot dog really enjoys Sarah (for tea occasionally).

The main part of the example above (i.e. outside the brackets) shows subject–verb–object word order (SVO). There are, however, occasions when we change this word order. In questions, we usually place a verb (main or auxiliary) before the subject (▶ **Unit 7**):

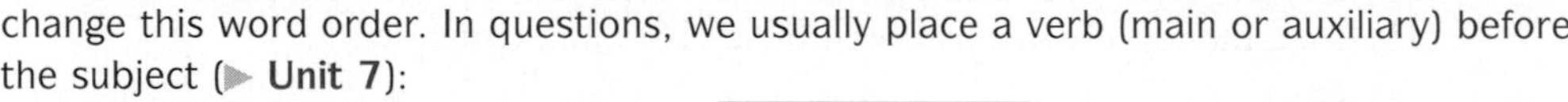

*Is **the Prime Minister** discussing* [*the issue of debt*] *with the Cabinet?*

↑ auxiliary verb ↑ subject ↑ main verb ↑ object

We also change the order when we place adverbs such as *never, seldom, rarely* (▶ **34.3B**) at the beginning of the sentence for stylistic reasons:

*'**Never** in the field of human conflict was so much owed by so many to so few.'*

(For more on word order with adverbs ▶ **Unit 24**.)

30.1B Variations

Apart from the variations mentioned (▶ **30.1A**), a number of patterns can follow verbs in English. Note that even verbs with similar meanings can take different patterns:

I said that you could go. (verb + clause)

I told you that you could go. (verb + indirect object + clause)

She told me a lie. (verb + indirect object + direct object)

❗ The indirect object is often a person who receives something (*a lie*, in the example above) and it is often introduced by a preposition (▶ **30.2C**).

30.2 VERB PATTERNS

30.2A Verb only (intransitive verbs)

Some verbs do not have an object. These are intransitive verbs:

They've arrived! *The cup shattered.*

We can use adverbs or prepositional phrases with these verbs:

*They've arrived **there**! The cup shattered **into hundreds of tiny shards of glass**.*

*After admitting the charge, the politician apologised **to all his constituents**.*

Some common intransitive verbs are: *come, fall, go, happen, lie, sleep, swim, wait*.

Some verbs can be intransitive or transitive (used with an object ▶ **30.2C** below):

The door ***opened****.* (intransitive) *He* ***opened the door****.* (transitive)

The meat ***burnt****.* (intransitive) *The cook* ***burnt the meat****.* (transitive)

Some common verbs that can be transitive or intransitive are: *begin, break, change, close, continue, dry, finish, hang, hurt, move, separate, stand, start, stop, tear, turn*.

❗ Sometimes the two uses of a verb can have very different meanings:

He ***ran*** *to catch the bus.* (intransitive = moved quickly)

He ***ran the new software*** *to show us how it worked.* (transitive = operated)

In modern usage, some transitive verbs are used as intransitive verbs:

I don't know why you're bothering with those boots – they won't ***sell****.*

And some intransitive verbs are used as transitive verbs:

In order to survive we need to ***grow the business*** *by 100 per cent within two years.*

30.2B Verb + complement

Some verbs are followed by complements (not objects). A complement is usually a noun phrase or an adjective that identifies, describes or gives information about the subject:

George Carey has become [***the new Archbishop of Canterbury***].

My grandmother has become [***very forgetful recently***].

↑ subject ↑ verb ↑ complement

Some common verbs which introduce complements are *be, become, appear, keep* (+ adjective), *remain, taste, make*:

You don't want to ***remain a shop assistant*** *all your life, do you?*

A quiet afternoon at home would ***make a nice change****.*

Chris was very good – he ***kept quiet*** *all through the boring sermon.*

After *seem, appear, look, feel* and *sound* we can use an adjective to describe the subject:

The whole group ***seemed very keen****. Marie's new outfit* ***looked fantastic****!*

We can also use a noun phrase to describe the subject after these verbs:

That ***sounds a wonderful idea****! Your suggestion* ***seems the best solution****.*

❗ However, when we use a noun phrase after *seem* or *appear* to identify (rather than describe) the subject, we have to use *to be* to introduce the noun phrase:

✗ ~~*Surprisingly, the young fresh-faced boy seemed the boss.*~~

✔ *Surprisingly, the young fresh-faced boy* ***seemed to be the boss****.*

A complement can also describe the object of a verb. In this case, the object comes before the complement:

The committee named [*Frances*] [***President***].

The journey made [*the children*] [***fractious***].

↑ subject ↑ verb ↑ object ↑ complement

We often use verbs of naming, e.g. *name, call, elect*, with this pattern:

The President finally decided to call [*his new dog*] [***Buddy***].

We can use a noun or an adjective as the complement after verbs such as *think, keep, consider, prove, call, find*:

Although he was twenty, Katherine still ***considered*** [*him*] [***a child/childish***].

Many critics ***call*** [*Kevin Costner's 'The Postman'*] [***his worst movie yet***].

We can use an adjective as a complement in the same pattern in a number of idiomatic phrases after verbs such as *drive, send* and *turn*:

The noise of the planes flying over us at night ***drives*** [*me*] [***crazy***]!

The new aftershave from Givenchy is guaranteed to ***send*** [*women*] [***wild***].

Did you see his expression? It could ***turn*** [*milk*] [***sour***]!

30.2C Verb + object(s)

Transitive verbs have a direct object, which can be a noun or a pronoun:

We discussed [*the problem/it*] *at great length.*

subject verb object

The object can also be an *-ing* form (with or without a prepositional phrase):

The instructor suggested ***practising*** *(****on the nursery slopes first****).*

We can omit the object after some transitive verbs where the context is clear:

Geoff was mortified to find that he ***had failed*** *(the test) again.*

Some common transitive verbs which can omit the object are *answer*, *ask*, *drink*, *eat*, *enter*, *fail*, *leave*, *pass*, *play*, *practise*, *sing*, *study*, *wash*, *win*, *write*.

In English a number of verbs can take two objects, e.g. *give*, *bring*, *buy*, *show*. These verbs take a direct object and an indirect object and there are two possible patterns:

The judges gave [*the enormous marrow/it*] [*first prize*].

subject verb indirect object direct object

The judges gave [*first prize*] [*to the enormous marrow*].

subject verb direct object indirect object

✗ ~~*The judges gave to the enormous marrow first prize.*~~

❗ If we put the direct object first, we introduce the indirect object with a preposition (either *to* or *for*). We do not vary from this.

If the indirect object is a pronoun, we prefer to put it before the direct object:

[*The Shakespearean actor brought a certain amount of class to us.*]

✔ *The Shakespearean actor brought us a certain amount of class.*

Which pattern we use often depends on what information in the sentence is new. We prefer to put new information at the end of the sentence (▶ **36.1A**).

30.2D Verb + prepositional phrase

We can use a prepositional phrase after intransitive verbs (▶ **30.2A**):

The train departed [***from platform 9***] *– but we were waiting* [***on platform 5***]*!*

subject verb prepositional phrase

We can also use prepositional phrases after transitive verbs:

He carefully removed [*the egg*] [***from the nest***].

subject verb object prepositional phrase

We do not usually change the order of object + prepositional phrase in this pattern, unless the object is very long (▶ **36.1B**):

✗ ~~*He carefully removed from the nest the egg.*~~

✔ *He carefully removed from the nest* ***the three fragile blue-speckled eggs and the one chick that had already hatched****.*

30.2E Verb + verb

Many verbs can be followed by another verb (▶ **12.2A**):

The consultant refused to take responsibility for the decision.

subject verb verb

We can use a direct object between the verbs:

We require [*all students*] *to attend the pre-sessional English course.*

subject verb direct object verb

With some verbs we do not need *to*, for example, modal verbs, auxiliary verbs, semi-modals (*need* and *dare*), and *make* and *let*:

He ***daren't leave*** *early without my permission.*

Let *the dish* ***stand*** *for at least a minute after removing it from the microwave.*

We can use the verb *help* with or without *to*:

*The volunteers **helped (to) provide** support and comfort to the refugees.*

30.2F Verb + clause — Verbs can be followed by *that* clauses or *wh-* clauses (those which start with a question word). We often use *that* clauses after verbs of speaking and thinking:

The staff agreed [*that redundancies were the only course of action*].

(*The staff* = subject; *agreed* = verb; *that redundancies were the only course of action* = clause)

❗ We can omit *that* after the verbs mentioned above:

The warden told the visitors (that) the prisoner did not want to see them.

Examples of *wh-* clauses are indirect questions (▶ **7.3**):

I couldn't meet you. You didn't tell [*me*] [*when you were arriving*].

(*You* = subject; *didn't tell* = verb; *me* = object; *when you were arriving* = clause)

❗ *Wh-* words can be followed by *to* + infinitive after verbs such as *show, explain, teach*:

*Is it common for people to teach their children **how to** drive here?*

30.3 LINKING CLAUSES

30.3A Coordination — We can link clauses of equal value (i.e. both can stand on their own) with *and*, *but* or *or*. With these conjunctions we can often put either of the clauses first:

*We can pay in one lump sum **or** we can pay in instalments.*
*We can pay in instalments **or** we can pay in one lump sum.*

If the subject is the same in both clauses, we can omit it in the second clause (▶ **35.3A**):

He rang the doorbell and knocked on the door.

We can also use the 'two-part' conjunctions *both ... and, either ... or, neither ... nor* and *not only ... but (also)*:

*At the French Open Hewitt **both** proved his return to form **and** won the only Grand Slam title to have evaded him.*

30.3B Subordination — When we link a main clause with a subordinate clause (i.e. dependent on the main clause), we use conjunctions (*when, if, although*). With subordinate clauses we cannot usually change the order of the events in the clauses without changing the meaning:

1 *The flowers were delivered* [*just **after** she left*]. (she left = first event)

(*The flowers were delivered* = main clause; *just after she left* = subordinate clause)

2 *She left* [*just **after** the flowers were delivered*]. (flower delivery = first event)

(*She left* = main clause; *just after the flowers were delivered* = subordinate clause)

It is, however, usually possible to change the order of the clauses themselves:

*Just **after** she left the flowers were delivered.* (= same as 1 above)
*Just **after** the flowers were delivered, she left.* (= same as 2 above)

Common types of subordination are:

- *that* or *wh-* clauses: *Didn't the notice say **when the water was going to be cut off**?*
- Adverbial clauses, e.g. of condition (▶ **Unit 10**) or contrast (▶ **Unit 32**):
  *There may well be more accidents in future **if air traffic continues to grow**.*
  ***Although the Aztecs were rich and powerful**, the Spanish conquistadors overpowered them.*
- Relative clauses, introduced by pronouns, e.g. *who, which, that* (▶ **Unit 31**):
  *It was surprisingly not their latest CD **that went platinum**, but the one before.*
- Comparative clauses (▶ **Unit 22**): *With the strength of the pound at present we paid less for our holiday this year **than we did last year**.*

30 Practice

The key to these exercises is on page 368.

1 30.1

Choose the correct sentence, A or B, for each cartoon. In some cases both sentences are correct.

1 A The dog chased the cat down the garden.
  B The cat chased the dog down the garden.

2 A John thought Harriet was wonderful.
  B Harriet thought John was wonderful.

4 A Our priceless Ming vase broke the picture of Uncle Albert when it fell on it.
  B The picture of Uncle Albert broke our priceless Ming vase when it fell on it.

3 A Mary said Kevin was an idiot.
  B 'Kevin,' said Mary, 'was an idiot.'

5 A Jerry has become a real little devil.
  B A real little devil has become Jerry.

2 30.1, 30.2

Each sentence below contains one mistake with word order. Rewrite the sentence correctly.

0 The military regime denied to the world's press access.
  ......*The military regime denied access to the world's press.*......

1 When he made out his will, Mr Smithson refused to leave anything his estranged son.
  ....

2 Geoff originally believed Susan when he told her he was having long business meetings after work.
  ....

3 Please leave by the door your shoes before entering the temple.
  ....

4 The Management recommends that you keep safe your valuables by handing them in at Reception.
  ....

5 The invitation doesn't tell what we should wear at the reception us.

....

6 The new President of the United States has been elected George W Bush.

....

7 It is said that our thinking power really improves studying philosophy.

....

8 She carefully placed the 24-carat gold, diamond-encrusted engagement ring that her fiancé had just bought her onto her finger. ....

9 The course director insists on attending at least 80 per cent of classes the first-year students.

....

10 Prizes can be claimed by sending the form and proof of purchase us, at the address below.

....

3 30.2

Read the newspaper article and then choose the best phrase (A–P) to complete each space. Write the letter of the chosen phrase in the space. Some of the answers do not fit at all. The exercise begins with an example (0).

Children at risk from mental illness

A recent study has shown that levels of mental illness (0) ..G.. The study claims that mental problems such as depression and anxiety (1) ... . One of the reasons given for this is the current obsessive preoccupation of parents with their children's safety. Parents today consider the streets (2) ... , so children are taken from home to school and back, and their parents rarely let them (3) ... . This preoccupation has two causes: fear of traffic accidents and anxiety about child molesters and murderers on the streets. Parents' fears make (4) ... about the outside world and children in turn miss the normal adventures of everyday life. In addition, they don't learn (5) ... with other children. Over-anxious children often become (6) ... and their fears are therefore realised and even increased. It is a vicious circle. It is a fact, however, that children could be experiencing (7) ... . While parents may think a child molester lurks (8) ... , this is not supported by statistics: very few children are attacked by people they don't know. The fear of traffic accidents is certainly more real but is something that needs to be addressed by society in general. Some cities in The Netherlands, for example, have created (9) ... and pedestrian-friendly zones, where cars, if allowed at all, must give priority to people and bicycles. Children can therefore play (10) ... .

There are, however, critics of this study. Many child psychologists believe that (11) ... enough to cause mental problems. They consider the problems more likely (12) ... family breakdown in modern society.

A their children anxious
B are affecting one in five youngsters
C this lack of independence not to be
D traffic-free zones
E how to form relationships
F this lack of independence is not
G ~~in children are rising~~
H these fears unnecessarily
I to be a result of
J more safely in these areas
K go out on their own
L their children to be anxious
M too dangerous for their children
N victims of bullies
O round every corner
P being too dangerous for children

4 30.2

Rewrite the jumbled phrases to make sentences with the correct word order.

1 named/Samantha/their first daughter/the couple

....

2 to stand/when he arrives/visitors/expects/His Excellency

....

3 to stay/a legal assistant/I wouldn't like/for long

....

4 brought/to the team/Amanda/all her expertise

....

5 brought/the team/Amanda/all her expertise

....

6 has become/a very inexperienced salesman/the Sales Manager

....

7 into the box/sparkling, diamond encrusted/he placed/18-carat gold ring/carefully wrapped/the

....

8 provided/all rubbish/please/in the bins/put

....

9 let/to/your parents/all-night parties/do/go/you/?

....

10 the grenade/removed/the paratrooper/the pin/from/carefully

....

11 so her daughter/the bracelet/bought/for her/Susan liked/it

....

12 all day long/their resistance/stand/the prisoners/they/to/made/reduce

....

13 of destruction/all sick/the scenes/us/made/in the film

....

14 an easy programme/trying/first/recommended/the trainer

....

5 30.3

Match the clauses in A and B to make sentences, using a linking word from the box to join them. Decide if each sentence contains co-ordinated clauses or a subordinate clause, and write C or S.

after   and   even though   if   or   so   than   that   ~~when~~

A

0 Did the doctor say exactly
1 It was the finest portrait
2 Some of the passengers were causing trouble
3 The holiday will be automatically cancelled
4 The policeman was rushed to hospital
5 We can either go camping
6 Maurice Greene won the gold medal
7 Our car broke down last week
8 The whole class would rather go to the cinema

B

a the pilot diverted the plane to the nearest airport. ....
b stay in a cheap hotel. ....
c we only bought it two months ago. ....
d he smashed the World and Olympic Records. ....
e he had been stabbed in the park. ....
f the artist had ever painted. ....
g see a play at the theatre. ....
h you'll be able to go back to work? ...*+ when (S)*..
i we don't receive the balance on the due date. ....

6 ALL

Nine of these sentences contain mistakes. Tick (✓) the correct sentences and correct the mistakes.

1 The wind knocked the vase off the table and it broke thousands of pieces. ☐

....

2 The attitude of some shopkeepers today makes me absolutely furious! ☐

....

3 The children seemed content to remain to be tenants in their parents' house. ☐

....

4 I can't understand what's happened. There appears some mistake. ☐

....

5 The whole teaching staff found the new head teacher very inefficient and positively offensive. ☐

....

6 No wonder you can't get a table for tonight – we recommended book the restaurant at least a week in advance. ☐

....

7 The winning team proudly showed to their gathered fans their trophy. ☐

....

8 The voice over the loudspeaker explained us the problem. ☐

....

9 I don't know the way to the library. Can you tell me to go? ☐

....

10 The young boy looked around and gingerly placed back in its correct position the gold watch. He wouldn't steal it after all. ☐

....

11 The neighbours very kindly helped move us our furniture into the new house. ☐

....

12 The smell of fish cooking drives absolutely wild my cats! ☐

....

7 ALL

Fill each gap in this text with no more than three words.

Few things are more detested by drivers than the 'Denver Boot' – the wheel clamp. Motorists in many countries consider (1) .... one of the most odious inventions ever. Everyone dreads the consequences of finding one of these on their car – phoning the clamping company, waiting (2) .... to arrive, paying the fine for removing the clamp, and then, on top of that, paying the original parking fine!

One inventive motorist recently found an ingenious way of releasing his car, however, (3) .... cause any damage at all to the clamp or his car. A local shopkeeper takes up the tale: 'This motorist came back to his car and found a clamp on the wheel. He seemed (4) .... a mild-mannered man, but this had obviously made him really (5) ...., as he started muttering and swearing under his breath. Then he calmed down. He took out a mobile and phoned the clamping company and they told him (6) .... would be there in 45 minutes, which obviously didn't please him. Then he had an idea. He took a match and started fiddling with the car tyre. I realised that he was (7) .... the air escape from the tyre. Then he got the jack out of the car boot and jacked up the car – the clamp then slid off the wheel with no problems! (8) .... he had carefully placed (9) .... on the pavement, he pumped his tyre back up, smiled at me, got in the car and drove off. Five minutes later the clampers arrived to find no car and an undamaged clamp. I explained to them (10) .... he had done it and they were absolutely furious! It was hilarious!'

31 Relative clauses

Relative clauses are subordinate clauses (▶ **30.3B**) which refer to the noun of the main clause, identifying it or adding extra information. There are two types of relative clause: defining clauses (identifying the noun or classifying it as part of a group) and non-defining clauses (adding information about the noun). This unit examines both types of relative clause and the pronouns and adverbs used to introduce relative clauses.

31.1 RELATIVE CLAUSES

31.1A Form and use

Relative clauses are subordinate clauses introduced by relative pronouns, such as *that*, *which* or *who* (▶ **31.2**). These clauses give information about someone or something in the main clause. Compare these examples:

*I used to live in one of **those houses**. They have now been demolished.*

*I used to live in one of **those houses** that have now been demolished*.

main clause — relative clause

The relative pronoun is the subject or object of the relative clause (▶ **31.1B**). It is therefore unnecessary to repeat the noun from the main clause or introduce a personal pronoun to replace it:

✗ ~~*I used to live in one of those houses that **they** have now been demolished.*~~

We usually put the relative clause as close as possible to the noun it refers to, otherwise the meaning may not be clear:

✗ ~~*Jack has prepared his favourite dish from Jamie Smith's recipe book, **which he is about to eat**.*~~

✔ *Jack has prepared his favourite dish, **which he is about to eat**, from Jamie Smith's recipe book.*

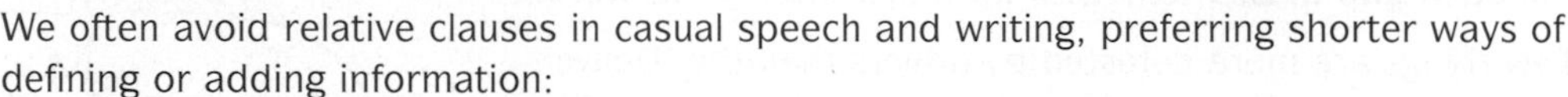

We often avoid relative clauses in casual speech and writing, preferring shorter ways of defining or adding information:

*People **who come from Wales** are often quite musical.* (relative clause)
***Welsh** people are often quite musical.* (adjective)
*People **from Wales** are often quite musical.* (prepositional phrase)

31.1B Subjects and objects

A relative pronoun can be the subject of a relative clause:

*Last week I saw that film **which** won all the Oscars.*

subject relative pronoun

Here, the pronoun is the subject of the relative clause (***the film** won the Oscars*), even though it is the object of the main clause (*I saw **the film***).

A relative pronoun can also be the object of a relative clause:

*Last week I saw the film **which** you made at college.*

object relative pronoun

Here, the pronoun is the object of the subordinate clause (*you made **the film***).

In defining relative clauses (▶ **31.1C**) we can omit the relative pronoun when it is the object of the relative clause, but not when it is the subject:

✗ ~~*Last week I saw the film won all the Oscars.*~~

✔ *Last week I saw the film you made at college.*

31.1C Defining relative clauses

A defining relative clause identifies or classifies a noun or pronoun in the main clause:

- Identifying relative clause: *Is this the book* ***that you were looking for****?*
- Classifying relative clause: *Would all those* ***who have booked dinner*** *please go to the restaurant now?*

(In the second example, the relative clause classifies the members of a group.)

In defining relatives, the relative clause gives information which is necessary for the sense of the sentence. In the first example above, if we say just *Is this the book?*, this does not convey the key meaning of the whole sentence, i.e. the book that you were looking for.

We often use defining relative clauses to describe an important quality of someone or something:

Van Gogh was an artist ***who used a lot of bold, vibrant colours****.*

We often use a relative clause with the same pattern for emphasis, with introductory *it* (▶ **34.1B**):

It *is always violent crime* ***that*** *provokes the most extreme reaction from the public.*

31.1D Non-defining relative clauses

We usually use non-defining relative clauses to add extra information about the subject of a main clause:

ITV's News at Ten, ***which occupied the mid-evening slot for many years****, was a very popular programme.*

(main clause = *ITV's News at Ten was a very popular programme.*)

We can also use non-defining relative clauses to show consecutive actions:

Heskey passed the ball to Owen, ***who scored a magnificent goal****.*

We use non-defining relative clauses mainly in writing and formal speech.

31.1E Punctuation and pausing

We usually use commas to separate the relative clause from the main clause in non-defining relatives, but we do not use them in defining relatives:

The tribespeople, ***who traded with the settlers,*** *retained their land.* (All of the tribespeople retained their land, and, incidentally, they traded with the settlers.)

The tribespeople ***who traded with the settlers*** *retained their land.* (Only some of the tribespeople retained their land – this defines a group.)

The use of commas reflects the way we say the two types of relative clause. In defining relative clauses, there is no pause between the main clause and the relative clause:

We asked for the double room ***which had a sea view****.*

In non-defining relatives, there is a short pause after the main clause or between the two parts of the main clause:

We were given a lovely double room ( ), ***which had a sea view****.*

I first met Harry Gardiner ( ), ***who eventually became my father-in-law*** *( ), at a Law Society meeting.*

31.1F Prepositions with relative clauses

We can use prepositions with relative pronouns. Where we put the preposition depends on formality (▶ **29.3B**):

- Informal: *Have you seen the little case* ***that/which*** *I keep my contact lenses* ***in****?*
- Formal: *This system provides a case* ***in which*** *the contact lenses can be kept.*

❗ We do not put a preposition before the relative pronoun *that*:

✗ ~~*This system provides a case in that the contact lenses can be kept.*~~

❗ If we put a preposition before *who*, the pronoun always becomes *whom*. Compare:

The people ***who*** *this report is addressed* ***to*** *will have to consider carefully the consequences of the proposed cuts.*

The people ***to whom*** *this report is addressed will have to consider carefully the consequences of the proposed cuts.*

We can often use *where* (for places) or *when* (for times) instead of *which* + preposition (▶ **31.2A**):

This is the house ***where*** *I grew up/****which*** *I grew up in/****in which*** *I grew up.*

31.1G Reduced relative clauses

We often 'reduce' a relative clause, i.e. we shorten it by omitting the pronoun and verb. We can do this with a participle phrase (▶ **13.1, 13.2**):

Marilyn was the woman ***living in the flat underneath us at the time****.* (= … who lived/was living in …)

The clauses ***struck out of the agreement*** *were all unimportant.* (= … which were struck out/which we struck out …)

Another possibility is to use an infinitive phrase (▶ **13.3, 13.4**):

Newton was the first person ***to really understand*** *the laws of gravity.* (= … who really understood …)

31.2 RELATIVE PRONOUNS AND ADVERBS

31.2A General use

This table lists relative pronouns and adverbs and how they can be used:

	used for	used as			
pronouns		subject	object	defining	non-defining
[1] *who*	people, animals	✔	✔	✔	✔
whom	people	✘	✔	✔	✔
[2] *which* *which*	objects, animals ideas	✔ ✔	✔ ✔	✔ ✘	✔ ✔
[3] *that*	people, objects, animals	✔	✔	✔	✘
[4] *whose*	relationships, possessions	✔	✔	✔	✔
[5] no pronoun	people, things, animals	✘	✔	✔	✘
adverbs					
[6] *where*	places	✔	✔	✔	✔
[7] *when*	times	✔	✔	✔	✔
[8] *why*	reasons	✔	✔	✔	✔
nominal pronoun					
[9] *what*	objects, ideas (means the thing that)	✔	✔	✔	✘

Notes on the table:

1 We sometimes use *who* to refer to animals, particularly domestic pets:

Is Sheba the dog ***who*** *was run over and nearly killed last year?*

Whom is formal and we rarely use it in speech. We now mainly use it after prepositions (▶ **31.1F**):

I am referring to the person with ***whom*** *you were seen on that evening.*

2 Note that we always use *which* (not *who*) to refer to inanimate objects. We can also use *which* to refer to the 'idea' of a whole clause:

When he came home, he was unusually attentive, ***which*** *made her very suspicious.*

Here, *which* refers to the fact that 'he was unusually attentive'.

3 We can use *that* to refer to people or objects, but we usually prefer to use *who* for a person when the pronoun is the subject of the relative clause:

Ms Harrison is the lawyer ***who/that*** *has been chosen to represent you.*

❗ We do not use *that* in non-defining relative clauses:

✘ ~~*This offer,* ***that will not be repeated,*** *must end next week.*~~

❗ In US English *that* is more common than *which* or *who* in defining relative clauses.

4 It is possible, though not very common, to use *whose* to refer to objects.
It would only be possible to colonise planets ***whose*** *atmosphere contained enough oxygen to sustain human life.* (= the atmosphere of which)

5 We often omit a relative pronoun when it refers to the object of a defining relative clause (▶ **31.1B**):
The girl ***(who)*** *I met in the florist's was at the party.* (= I met the girl.)
We cannot omit the pronoun if it is the subject of the clause:
✘ ~~*The girl works for the florist in the High Street was at the party.*~~
✔ *The girl* ***who*** *works for the florist in the High Street was at the party.*
! We cannot omit an object relative pronoun in non-defining relative clauses:
✘ ~~*Last year's winner presented the cup, each holder keeps for the year.*~~
✔ *Last year's winner presented the cup,* ***which*** *each holder keeps for the year.*

6 We can use *which* or *that* + a preposition instead of *where* (▶ **31.1F**):
Mozart's birthplace and the house ***where*** *he composed 'The Magic Flute' are both now museums.*
Mozart's birthplace and the house ***that*** *he composed 'The Magic Flute'* ***in*** *are both now museums.*

7 We can use *that* as an alternative to *when* in defining relative clauses:
I remember – it was the day ***when/that*** *the heatwave started.*
We can use *which* or *that* + a preposition instead of *when* (▶ **31.1F**):
The attacks continued up to the day ***on which*** *the agreement was signed.*

8 The only noun which takes *why* as a relative pronoun is *reason*:
Sometimes he thought her clear morality was the reason ***why/that*** *he loved her.*
We can use *which* + *for* instead of *why*:
High taxation is often the main reason ***for which*** *governments fall.*
! It is possible to use relative adverbs without the noun to which they refer:
It's (the place) ***where*** *that rock festival is held every year.*

9 We use *what* to mean 'the thing that/which'. The clause containing *what* is a nominal clause, i.e. the whole clause acts as a noun, either a subject or an object. While *what* isn't used in the same way as *that* or *which* it can fulfil the same functions as the other relative pronouns:
Why don't you tell the police ***what*** *you told me yesterday?*
In this example *what you told me yesterday* is the object of the verb *tell*. It means the same as:
Why don't you tell the police the story (that) you told me yesterday.
We cannot use *what* to replace *who*, *which* or *that*:
✘ ~~*It was the money what I wanted, not the fame.*~~
✔ *It was the money (that) I wanted, not the fame.*
This could be expressed as:
The money was ***what*** *I wanted, not the fame.* (= the thing that I wanted)

31.2B Modifying a relative pronoun/ adverb

We often use modifiers, such as *all of* and *many of* before *which* or *whom* in a non-defining relative clause to refer to the subject or object of the clause:
The supermarket removed from the shelves all of its jars of tomato puree, ***several of which*** *were found to contain fragments of glass.*
The college entered over a hundred students for the exam, ***all of whom*** *passed.*
We interviewed fourteen applicants for the post, ***none of whom*** *we thought suitable.*

31.2C *Whichever, whenever,* etc.

In defining relative clauses we can modify the pronoun or adverb with *-ever* to give the meaning of *anything*, *anyone*, *anywhere*, etc.:
Use ***whichever*** *phone you want – they all have outside lines.*
I'd like to meet ***whoever*** *did that to the garden hedge!*
You can put the photo ***wherever*** *you think it looks best. I don't mind.*

Practice

The key to these exercises is on page 368.

1 31.1

Match each headline (1–10) with a sentence (A–J). Then write one sentence containing a relative clause (defining or non-defining) to combine each headline and sentence that accompanies it. Use the present perfect tense in the main clause.

0 SCIENTISTS DISCOVER NEW WONDER-CURE FOR CANCER
1 BODY OF MAN FOUND IN RIVER SEVERN
2 FASHION ICON QUANT LEAVES BUSINESS
3 GLOBAL WARMING CONFERENCE ENDS WITHOUT AGREEMENT
4 IRVINE NARROWLY MISSES FORMULA 1 WORLD CHAMPION TITLE
5 HAND COUNT OF VOTES CONTINUES
6 LONDON ZOO REMAINS OPEN
7 POLITICIAN HANDS IN RESIGNATION
8 SIZE 16 MODEL WINS NEW ESTÉE LAUDER CONTRACT
9 MADONNA'S UK HOME BURGLED

A He was disgraced in a financial scandal.
B They were spoiled in the recent US presidential election.
C His contract with Ferrari finishes at the end of the season.
D It was held in The Hague.
E She shares the house with her British husband, Guy Ritchie.
F It was in danger of closing through lack of funds.
G She refused to diet to a size 12.
H The man jumped off the Severn Bridge.
I ~~They have been studying cancer genes for years.~~
J She is famous for inventing the mini-skirt.

0 Scientists *(I) who have been studying cancer genes for years have just discovered a new wonder-cure for cancer.*

1 The body of a man ....

2 The fashion icon Mary Quant ....

3 The global warming conference ....

4 Formula 1 driver Eddie Irvine ....

5 The hand count of votes ....

6 London Zoo ....

7 The politician ....

8 The size 16 model ....

9 Madonna's house in the UK ....

2 31.1

Choose the best sentence to describe each cartoon.

1 A The burglar, who fell off the ladder, was arrested by the police.
B The burglar who fell off the ladder was arrested by the police.

3 A I decided to buy the microwave oven which had a grill inside.
B I decided to buy the microwave oven, which had a grill inside.

2 A The customers who arrived after nine o'clock weren't allowed into the sale.
B The customers, who arrived after nine o'clock, weren't allowed into the sale.

4 A We stopped at the only pub in the village which had a front garden.
B We stopped at the only pub in the village, which had a front garden.

3 31.2

Complete the following article by writing each missing relative pronoun or adverb in the space provided. Use only one word for each space.

TV Choice

Jack of Hearts

Jack of Hearts is a new six-part drama series (0) *which/that* comes to our screens this week. It has been given the prime Wednesday evening 9.30 slot, (1) .... shows that the network has faith in its latest creation. The first episode opens to a scene (2) .... a young man is being chased. He stops at a phone box and makes a desperate call. This calls wakes up a man (3) .... most viewers will recognise as Keith Allen – the slightly sleazy unshaven Cockney (4) .... characters are usually less than wholesome. This time, however, he is on the right side of the law, playing a probation officer with a complicated professional and personal life, both of (5) .... form the main themes of the series. The writers have managed to find a different angle on his personal problems. At the centre of these problems is his stepdaughter, for (6) .... he attempts to keep the household together. His relationship with the girl's mother, (7) .... seems to be a bad-tempered, grumpy woman, is further compromised later in the series (8) .... she joins the staff of a college at (9) .... she meets a former lover. Thus the ground is prepared in this first episode for a series (10) .... may help to lift British summertime TV out of its regular slump.

4 31.1

This article has too many relative clauses in it. Change the underlined parts so that you don't use a relative clause. The first one has been done for you.

Controversial school to close

Brockenhurst School, which opened as an educational experiment in 1974, is to close this summer. All the teachers (0) who are currently employed by the school will be relocated to other schools in the area (1) which have staff vacancies. Brockenhurst was founded by (2) Sir Patrick McDonald, who comes from Inverness, at a time when new educational theories were welcomed by the establishment and experiments in education were supported. However, in recent years, such initiatives have been frowned upon as successive governments have urged a 'back-to-basics' approach.

The school currently employs 28 teachers, (3) all of whom come from the holistic school of education. Most of the teachers have been at the school for at least 15 years. There are approximately 780 students (4) who are of different ages at the school, and they will all transfer to schools in the region. Staff (5) who are currently living at the school will be found alternative housing by the local council.

Sir Patrick was the first person (6) who was informed of the government's decision and he passed the bad news on to staff and students at a meeting (7) which was held last week. Sir Patrick, who is 62, has decided to take early retirement. Although Sir Patrick himself was unavailable for comment, a spokesperson for the school told us, 'We are all very sorry about the closure. For over 25 years we have run an establishment (8) which has been dedicated to making learning a rich and enjoyable experience. All the staff and students (9) who have been participating over the years will agree that this is a sad day not only for the local community but for education in this country as a whole.'

(0) *currently employed by the school*
(1) ....
(2) ....
(3) ....
(4) ....
(5) ....
(6) ....
(7) ....
(8) ....
(9) ....

5 ALL

Complete the article at the top of the page opposite with an appropriate relative pronoun or adverb (if necessary) and a phrase from the box. Use each phrase once only. Write the letter of each phrase (A–I) in the spaces (1–8).

pronouns	phrases
who	A raise huge amounts of money
whose	B only the privileged can take part
whom	C ~~most of us can only dream about~~
where	D activities are as diverse as
which	E she was able to raise so much
why	F women hire private jets to go shopping
that	G has given nearly $200 million
	H you often can't find a cab
	I they wear only once

Women who rule New York

There is another world in New York beyond the tourist attractions and the high-rise blocks (0) ....*which C*........ . It's a world (1) .... and pay several thousand dollars for a dress (2) .... These are women for whom one of the modern-day necessities is having a personal car and driver in New York, (3) .... These women, however, are not only interested in designer clothes and facelifts, but they are also serious philanthropists, many of (4) .... for charity. Brooke Astor, for example, is a 97-year-old socialite (5) .... to charitable causes in the last 40 years. This 'Queen of New York Society', (6) .... visiting elementary schools and attending charity dinners, has raised $4 million in one evening alone. In an explanation of (7) ...., she admits that she tries to stimulate competition amongst her wealthy and famous guests. This is a rarified life in (8) ...., but which does a lot of good for the less fortunate.

6 ALL

Read the following text. In most lines, there is an unnecessary word, a word missing or a punctuation error. For each numbered line 1–22, identify the mistake and write the correct version in the space on the right. Some lines are correct. Indicate these lines with a tick (✓). The first two lines are examples (0 and 00).

0 Tourism today is an industry has grown so much in recent years that in many ....*which*........
00 countries it provides the greatest single contribution to the country's revenue. ....✓........
1 But is it always a good thing? Mass tourism which is a relatively recent ....
2 phenomenon, brings with it a whole raft of problems. First, it means that a ....
3 country's economy may rely on an industry which it is wholly seasonal, with ....
4 the consequence that the huge numbers of people work in tourism during the ....
5 season have no income during the rest of the year. Some find wherever work ....
6 they can, but others may turn to a government is already receiving lower ....
7 revenues for support. ....
8 Second, it is true that in many countries tourists are destroying the very ....
9 sights they flock to see them. They take home pieces of an ancient monument ....
10 or of a coral reef which will gradually result in erosion of the attractions and ....
11 therefore of the industry. While this kind of destruction may be wholly ....
12 unintentional, a certain type of tourist what wants only a 'good time' can be ....
13 very destructive in a different way: they drink too much, pick fights and ....
14 destroy the clubs and bars where they are drinking in. Obviously, it is then ....
15 this behaviour by that the local community judges all members of that ....
16 nationality group, creating enmity between races rather than fostering ....
17 empathy, what should be one of the main advantages of tourism. ....
18 Finally, there are many places tourism is threatening a well established ....
19 way of life: people that whose livelihoods traditionally come from older ....
20 industries, such as agriculture or fishing, are finding new jobs and wealth in ....
21 the over-developed tourist regions, but at what cost? It is sometimes difficult ....
22 to understand exactly which a country gains from tourism. ....

32 Contrast

English can express contrasts: with conjunctions, adverbs and prepositions. Knowing exactly how to use each type of contrast is one of the more advanced points of English. This unit looks at the most common ways of contrasting information.

32.1 CONJUNCTIONS OF CONTRAST

32.1A Expressing difference

A contrast between two clauses can be one simply of difference between the ideas expressed in them. The most common way of expressing a simple difference in English is with *but*:

Life expectancy in Japan is now over 80 ***but*** *it is several years lower in the UK.*

Other conjunctions which express simple differences are *while*, *whereas* and *whilst*. *While* is more informal than *whereas*; *whilst* is very formal:

Reds and yellows are warm colours, ***whereas*** *blues and greens are cool.*

While *only 84 people died on the railways last year, more than 5,000 died on the roads.*

We can put a clause starting with *while*, *whilst* or *whereas* either before or after the main clause, but a clause starting with *but* has to come second:

I've got two sisters, ***while*** *my best friend has got two brothers.*

While *I've got two sisters, my best friend has got two brothers.*

✗ ~~***But*** *I've got two sisters, my best friend has got two brothers.*~~

✔ *My best friend has got two brothers* ***but*** *I've got two sisters.*

The clause introduced by the conjunction is usually the one which carries more emphasis or introduces something new to the discourse (▶ **36.1**).

❶ We always separate clauses with *while*, *whereas* and *whilst* with a comma. This is not usually necessary when we use *but*.

32.1B Expressing opposition or surprise

There is another type of contrast in English, where the idea of one clause is in some way opposing the idea of the other, and which often expresses an element of surprise. For example, we may feel that it is surprising to pay a lot of money for a meal in a restaurant and to find that the food is awful, or to fail an exam after studying hard:

Although *we paid an enormous amount of money for the meal, the food was terribly disappointing.*

Derek failed the exam ***but*** *he had studied really hard for it.*

Derek failed the exam, ***although*** *he had studied really hard for it.*

We use the conjunctions *but*, *(al)though* and *even though* to introduce the fact or idea in opposition to information in the main clause.

Note that the subordinate clause can precede the main clause:

Although *he had studied really hard for the exam, Derek failed it.*

❶ Remember that *but* does not introduce a subordinate clause and that a clause starting with *but* cannot precede the other clause in the sentence (▶ **32.1A**):

✗ ~~***But*** *he had studied really hard for the exam, Derek failed it.*~~

It is often possible to start either clause in a sentence with a conjunction, depending on which clause has the information we consider 'surprising' and which we want to focus on. Compare these examples:

Little is known about the artist's early life ***although a lot has been found out about his later life****.*

A lot has been found out about the artist's later life, ***although little is known about his early life****.*

In the first example, the writer probably feels that it is surprising that a lot is known about the artist's later life when little is known about his early life, but in the second, it is the lack of knowledge about the artist's early life which is surprising.

Though is a more informal alternative to *although*:

*I enjoyed the exhibition, **though** I thought it was rather badly organised.*

Even though adds emphasis to the subordinate clause:

*Psychosis is also part of this debate, **even though** problems arising from it affect a relatively small number of people.*

❗ Do not use *even although* or *even* by itself:

✗ ~~*She loves him, **even although** he is violent.*~~

✗ ~~*She loves him, **even** he is violent.*~~

✓ *She loves him, **even though** he is violent.*

❗ Do not confuse *even though* and *even if* (▶ **10.7D**):

*I'm going to apply for the job, **even though** it pays very little.* (fact)

*I'm going to apply for the job, **even if** it pays very little.* (I don't know what it pays.)

A more formal conjunction of contrast is *yet*:

*These exclusive villas are only a five-minute walk from the busy centre of the resort, **yet** they are a haven of peace and tranquillity.*

32.1C Other patterns with *although, even though* and *though*

We can use these conjunctions with an adjective instead of a clause:

*The necklace, **even though** (it was) staggeringly expensive, would match the dress perfectly.*

***Though** exhausted after the drive home, Shelley cooked a meal for them all.*

*Her face, **although** deathly pale, was as stern as ever.*

We can use *though* after an adjective, with verbs such as *be, look, seem*:

*Beautiful **though** she is, you must be sure that you love her for herself.*

Compare this with the use of *although* as a conjunction:

***Although** she is beautiful, you must be sure that you love her for herself.*

We can use *though* at the end of a sentence to make a contrast with the sentence that precedes it (▶ **32.3B**).

32.2 PREPOSITIONS OF CONTRAST

We can use the prepositions *despite* and *in spite of* to express contrast. They are more formal than *(al)though*:

***Despite** the depressed gold price, mine production rose in most areas last year.*

As these are prepositions, they do not introduce clauses:

✗ ~~***In spite of she saw me** in the car, she didn't wave or say hello.*~~

✓ ***Although** she saw me in the car, she didn't wave or say hello.*

✗ ~~***Despite** the plane left an hour late, we arrived at our destination on time.*~~

✓ ***Though** the plane left an hour late, we arrived at our destination on time.*

These prepositions can be followed by a noun or an *-ing* form:

***Despite** often **offering** poor conditions and basic salaries, charities rarely have problems in recruiting staff.*

To introduce a clause with *despite* or *in spite of*, we have to add *the fact that*:

***In spite of the fact that** the final rehearsal had gone so badly, the first night was a great success.*

32.3 ADVERBS OF CONTRAST

32.3A Formality We can use sentence adverbials, e.g. *however, nevertheless, still, on the other hand, on the contrary*, to make a contrast between sentences, but mainly in more formal speech and writing:

*A dog may be a good companion for the elderly. **However**, the need to take it for walks may be a disadvantage.*

Nevertheless/nonetheless is more formal than *however*:

*The new version of Windows is not problem-free. **Nevertheless**, it is still an improvement on the previous one.*

We use commas to separate these adverbials from the sentence.

We use *even so* in the same way, often to express a particularly surprising contrast:

*The last attempt to swim the Channel ended in disaster. **Even so**, more swimmers than ever are training to achieve this difficult feat.*

More informal adverbs of concession are *still, all the same* and *mind you*:

*Our latest designs are not really as innovative as the competition. **Still**, they will certainly be popular, as they are realistically priced.*

*I know it's not late. I have to go, **all the same**.*

*The new programme about dinosaurs is a bit far-fetched. **Mind you**, it's a lot more interesting than most of the other programmes on TV right now.*

32.3B Position All of the adverbs of contrast can be placed at the beginning of the contrasting sentence:

*One way of selecting candidates is a written editorial test. **On the other hand**, an informal interview can often be more informative.*

We can also put them after the subject or verb of the contrasting sentence:

*Little is known about Shakespeare's early life in Stratford. His years in London, **however**, are well documented./... are, **however**, well documented.*

The adverb *though* can be put at the end of the contrasting sentence:

*We haven't had a lot of success with the garden this year. The weather was much hotter than usual, **though**.*

Nevertheless and *nonetheless* are not commonly used at the end of a sentence; we tend to use them at the beginning of the sentence. But we often use *even so* at the end of a sentence. Look at these examples:

Last year the government turned away more asylum seekers than ever before.

- ***Nonetheless**, the public considers that too many are allowed to stay.*
- *The public, **however**, considers that too many are allowed to stay.*
- *The public considers that too many are allowed to stay, **even so**.*

The informal adverb *still* can appear at the beginning of the sentence, but not the end, and *all the same* and *mind you* are common at both the beginning and the end:

I know it's far too expensive for someone on my income.

- ***Still**, it's worth it!*
- ***All the same**, it's worth it!*
- *It's worth it, **all the same**!*
- ***Mind you**, it's worth it!*
- *It's worth it, **mind you**!*

Practice

The key to these exercises is on page 369.

1 32.1

Combine each sentence in A with a suitable contrasting sentence from B, using the conjunction given in brackets.

A

0 Cliff Richard's Christmas single went straight to the top of the charts. ...*c*...
1 Many people believe that capital punishment is a deterrent to serious crime. ....
2 We usually consider it healthy to eat lots of fruit. ....
3 I enjoy having people to stay. ....
4 The main medium of communication on the Internet is English. ....
5 Iain Banks's early novels were considered quite strange. ....
6 I tend to drink more white wine. ....
7 Global warming is often considered the main factor in current climate fluctuations. ....

B

a Many web sites now operate in other languages. (although)
b Too much can produce an excess of acid in the stomach. (but)
c ~~He is reviled by much of the pop music establishment. (even though)~~
d Climate change has long been a feature of the Earth's development. (yet)
e It actually makes little difference to the crime rate. (on the contrary)
f My husband prefers red. (whereas)
g I always appreciate the peace when they have gone. (though)
h His later books are more mainstream and accessible. (while)

0 ...*Cliff Richard's Christmas single went straight to the top of the charts, even though he is reviled by much of the pop music establishment.*...

2 32.1, 32.2

For each of the sentences below, write a new sentence as similar as possible in meaning to the original sentence, but using the word given.

0 Malcolm's teeth were bothering him again, even though he had recently visited the dentist.
despite ...*Malcolm's teeth were bothering him again, despite the fact that he had recently visited the dentist.*...

1 Very little of the remaining stock sold, despite the low prices in the sale.
even though ....

2 The ailing magazine tried introducing several new features. Nevertheless, circulation continued to drop.
although ....

3 Although this may seem difficult now, you'll soon wonder why it caused so many problems.
though ....

4 In spite of her insistence that all was well, I knew that something was wrong.
fact ....

5 The Scots won the battle, even though they had a far smaller force.
despite ....

6 Despite the fact that the critics hated it, Archer's latest book was well received by the public.
being ....

3 32.3

Six of these sentences contain a mistake in word order or formality. Tick (✓) the two correct sentences and correct the mistakes in the others.

1 I think that I did quite well in the computing exam. It was more difficult than though I expected.
2 We were expecting a basic but pleasant apartment. On the contrary, what we got was little more than a hovel.
3 Strictly no pets are allowed in the hotel rooms. Guide dogs for the blind may be permitted with prior permission from the management, mind you.
4 Julian's just had a shocking cold. It didn't last long, still.
5 Office supplies may be ordered as necessary. However, all orders must be copied to the Accounts Department.
6 I know you'd like us to be godparents to little Emily. We'd rather all the same not.
7 That new kid at the nursery is a right little pain. He really gets on your nerves. Nevertheless, we've got to do our best by him.
8 Writing more than the required number of words will not attract a higher mark. You may be penalised for failing to follow on the other hand the rules.

4 ALL

Which of the sentences in these pairs are alternative ways of saying the same thing? Which pairs have different meanings? Put a tick (✓) in the correct box. The exercise begins with an example (0).

0 A In spite of the fact that this computer costs less, it's as good as the other one.
B Despite its lower price, this computer is as good as the other one.
same ☑ different ☐

1 A Despite the awful weather, the parade was a success.
B Although the weather was awful, the parade was a success.
same ☐ different ☐

2 A Brilliant as he is, he can't find a suitable job.
B Though he is brilliant, he can't find a suitable job.
same ☐ different ☐

3 A Even though I went to the party, I didn't see her.
B Even if I went to the party, I wouldn't see her.
same ☐ different ☐

4 A The new museum is extremely popular. It hasn't made any money yet.
B The new museum is extremely popular, yet it hasn't made any money.
same ☐ different ☐

5 A This ice cream is very sweet and rich, though it's not very fattening.
B This ice cream is very sweet and rich. It's not very fattening, though.
same ☐ different ☐

6 A The waiters in this restaurant are notoriously rude. However, customers keep coming back.
B The waiters in this restaurant are notoriously rude. Even so, customers keep coming back.
same ☐ different ☐

7 A Even as we complained, the noise continued.
B Even though we complained, the noise continued.
same ☐ different ☐

8 A We were at the Norfolk Hotel, while the rest of the group was at the Grange.
B While we were staying at the Norfolk Hotel the rest of the group moved to the Grange.
same ☐ different ☐

9 A Though delighted at her sister's success, Vicky couldn't help feeling somewhat envious.
B Despite her delight at her sister's success, Vicky couldn't help feeling somewhat envious.
same ☐ different ☐

10 A Men usually have good spatial awareness, whereas women's linguistic skills are often better.
B Whereas men usually have good spatial awareness, women's linguistic skills are often better.
same ☐ different ☐

11 A 'Mary threatened to leave last night. She's still here now.'
B 'Mary threatened to leave last night. Still, she's here now.'
same ☐ different ☐

12 A Chicken pox is much milder in children than in adults. It's still not pleasant, mind you.
B Chicken pox is much milder in children than in adults. All the same, it's still not pleasant.
same ☐ different ☐

5 ALL

Complete each gap in the text with a conjunction or preposition from the box.

~~Although~~	but	despite	Despite	even though	however	However	Nevertheless
On the contrary	though	whereas	While	Yet			

The Elgin Marbles

The Elgin Marbles are statues which date back to the 5th century BC. (0) ...*Although*... they were created in Greece and were located there until the late 18th century, they are now exhibited in the British Museum, London.

The statues used to be in Athens (1) .... they were bought in 1799 by the Englishman Lord Elgin, who wanted to bring them back to Britain as part of his personal art collection. (2) ...., on the sea voyage back to England, the ship carrying them was sunk and the 'Marbles' were temporarily lost. It would be an incredibly expensive operation to recover them. (3) ...., Elgin did so, and (4) .... he was a very rich man, he placed himself in enormous debt. (5) .... his own desires, he had to sell the Marbles to the British Government to recover his losses and they were housed in the British Museum, where they have remained ever since.

In recent times, (6) ...., the statues have become the subject of debate between Britain and Greece and, indeed, among British historians and archaeologists. (7) .... the Greek authorities have requested the return of the Marbles on many occasions, the request has always been refused. There are arguments on both sides. Some people believe that it would be foolish to return them, valid (8) .... the Greek request may be, because of the pollution that is affecting the Parthenon and the possibility of earthquakes in Greece. Restored to the Parthenon, the Marbles could be exposed to damage, (9) .... they are safe in the British Museum.

Of course, there are equally compelling arguments for their return, especially on the moral level. It cannot be denied, (10) .... the material safety the statues enjoy in Britain, that they are part of the Greek heritage. Many people also refute the argument that Athens would not be a safe place for them. (11) ...., they claim that if the statues were returned to Greece, a new state-of-the-art building would be constructed to house them, where they would be both safe and in their rightful environment. Furthermore, the British authorities have long used the argument that works of art should not be subject to 'ownership', but should be kept where they are accessible to most people. (12) .... in the past they have returned a number of cultural artefacts from other civilisations to their origins.

The argument continues, and is likely to do so for some time in the future.

33 Introductory *there* and *it*

In this unit we look at the use of *it* and *there* as 'empty' subjects to introduce new information or the main content of a sentence. We can also use them to manipulate the position of subjects, objects and clauses in sentences. This allows us to describe or report things in an indirect way and to create a more impersonal style often found in formal English. (For information on the pronoun *it* ▶ **27.1F**; for the use of *it* to introduce cleft sentences ▶ **34.1B**)

33.1 INTRODUCTORY *THERE*

33.1A Use

We use *there* as an 'empty' subject + *is/are* to introduce new information and/or to say that something exists or happens:

If you're looking for a café; ***there's*** *one opposite the station.* (new information)
[*Fifty-one states exist in the USA.*] ***There are*** *fifty-one states in the USA.*
[*Three murders happen in the film.*] ***There are*** *three murders in the film.*
[*Is a bank situated near here?*] ***Is there*** *a bank near here?*

We often use *there is/are* to introduce or describe a character or place, or to 'set the scene' when telling a story or joke:

At the top of the hill ***there's*** *a small café with wonderful views over the bay.*
There's *an Englishman, an Irishman and a Scotsman who go into a bar ...*

❗ *There is/are* is usually followed by an indefinite noun phrase, not a definite noun phrase (▶ **28.1A**):

✗ ~~*In the hotel lobby* ***there is the cash machine****.*~~ (definite noun phrase)
✓ *In the hotel lobby* ***there is a cash machine****.* (indefinite noun phrase)

But we can use *there is/are* with definite noun phrases when we are reminding someone of something we/they already know, or pointing something out:

✓ *Don't forget* ***there's a/the cash machine*** *in the lobby if you run out of money.* (reminding somebody of something you/they know)
✓ *Look,* ***there's a/the cash machine****, next to the porter's desk.* (pointing something out)

33.1B Form

We can use all forms of *be* after *there,* including modal forms:

Once upon a time ***there were*** *three little bears.*
There will be *an interval of twenty minutes during the performance.*
There must have been *a thousand applicants for the post.*

The form of *be* agrees with the complement:

There ***is*** *only* ***one answer*** *to this question.*

There ***were*** ***two ways*** *out of the building.*

❗ But in conversational English, we sometimes use *there is* with a plural complement:
There's *two ways we can do this.*

33.1C Special patterns

There + *be* can be followed by a noun + participle phrase (▶ **13.1, 13.2**):

__There's__ a strange old man __sitting in the corner__.

__There are__ two scales of temperature __used in science__.

❗ When we are describing a single action we use a full relative clause:

✗ ~~*In 1755 __there was__ an earthquake __destroyed much of Lisbon__.*~~

✓ *In 1755 __there was__ an earthquake __which destroyed much of Lisbon__.*

In formal English, verbs with future meaning, e.g. *anticipate, expect, envisage, intend* (▶ **5.2A**), can be followed by *there* + *to be/being*:

The organisers didn't expect (__there to be__) quite such an overwhelming response.

We don't anticipate (__there being__) any resistance from the anti-hunting lobby.

33.1D Words and expressions after *there* (+ *be*)

We commonly use *there* (+ *be*) with the following words and expressions:

there + *be* + quantifiers (*any, some, much, many, several*, etc. ▶ **28.3A**)	***Are there any more** issues outstanding?* ***There are several** ways we can tackle this.*
there + *be* + indefinite pronouns (*somebody, nothing*, etc. ▶ **27.4A**)	*I've had a good look and **there's nothing** to report.* ***Isn't there somebody** here who can help us?*
there + *be* + *bound/certain/expected/ likely/sure/supposed* + *to be*	*If the government goes ahead **there's sure to be** an outcry from the miners.* *Hang on, **there was supposed to be** a television in the room.*
there + *be* + *problem/difficulty/ trouble* + *-ing* form	✗ ~~***There won't be** any trouble **to get back**.~~ ✓ ***There won't be** any trouble **getting** back.*
there + *appear/happen/seem(s)/tend/ used* + *to be*	***There used to be** a house at the end of the common.* *Researchers noticed that **there tends to be** a higher number of influenza cases in warm winters.*
there + a passive reporting verb (e.g. *is said to be, is thought to be*) + an indefinite noun phrase (This is used to describe a general feeling or belief.) (compare *it* ▶ **33.2C**)	***There are thought to be** several other senior officers implicated in the cover-up.* *In Zaire alone, **there are believed to be** more than a million sufferers of the disease.*
In formal written English we can use *there* + *arise/arrive/come/emerge/ enter/exist/follow/live/occur/remain/ result/sit/stand/take place*	*Deep inside her **there arose** a desperate hope.* *At the crime scene **there remained** little in the way of physical evidence.* ***There follows** a full list of our current terms and conditions of trading.*

33.2 INTRODUCTORY/IMPERSONAL *IT*

33.2A Use

We can use *it* as an 'empty' subject. This is a grammatical device to introduce or identify something later in the phrase. It is followed by a definite noun phrase (▶ **28.1**):

'Who's that?' '__It's__ Alan.'

Hello, __it's__ Steve here. Could I speak to Jane?

'What's worrying you?' '__It's__ the children.'

It can refer to one or many things, but grammatically it is always singular:

✗ ~~*It are Alan and Margaret at the door.*~~

✓ ***It's** Alan and Margaret at the door.*

We use *it* + *be* to introduce information about the following topics:

weather/environment	***It'll be*** *cold in Edinburgh at this time of year.* ***It was*** *damp and foggy in London that autumn.*
time/dates	***It is*** *eight o'clock in the morning.* *Thank goodness* ***it's*** *Friday today.*
conditions/situations	***It's*** *so quiet and peaceful here.* ***It was*** *becoming increasingly dangerous.*
distance	***It's*** *quite a long way to the nearest town.*

33.2B Common expressions with *it*

We use *it* before *seems as if/though* and *looks as if/though* to describe impressions and probability:

It seems as if *we've known each other for years.* (This is my impression.)
It looks as though *I'm going to fail the test.* (I think it's probable.)

We can also use *it* as an 'empty' object after certain verbs to introduce a following clause:

like/hate/love + it + when/that clause (This is used to describe likes and dislikes.)	***I hate it when*** *people stare at me.* *We* ***love it when*** *the grandchildren come over.*
would appreciate it + if clause (This is used to make a polite request.)	*I* ***would appreciate it if*** *you could fax your response as a matter of urgency.*
owe/leave it to somebody + infinitive clause	*We* ***owe it to him to try*** *and find a resolution.* *We* ***leave it to you to suggest*** *a suitable date.*
think/find/consider + it + adjective/noun/preposition phrase + *that* clause	*I* ***find it intolerable that*** *we have no recourse in law.* *He* ***thought it a pity that*** *they hadn't contributed to the fund.* *I* ***consider it in your own best interests that*** *you leave immediately.*

33.2C Impersonal *it*

We sometimes want to describe our attitudes, feelings and opinions without mentioning ourselves directly. We can use *it* + *be* as an impersonal way to introduce these phrases. This is less direct than sentences beginning with *I think/feel/believe* and allows us to present opinions as though they were impersonal general feelings or even objective facts. We also use this device in academic writing where there is a convention that ideas should be presented in an impersonal way.
There are several patterns that we use:

it + *be* + adjective + *-ing* form (We use this in informal English.)	***It was lovely meeting*** *you at last.*
it + *be* + adjective + *that* clause	***It isn't surprising that*** *she left you.* ***It is remarkable that*** *so few of the patients suffered side effects.*
it + *be* + adjective + infinitive clause	***It's wonderful to sit*** *out here under the stars.* ***It was possible to recognise*** *regularities in the patterns of soil distribution.*
it + verb or modal verb phrase (usually passive) + *that* clause (We use this in formal written English.)	***It has been shown that*** *most of the patients improved noticeably.* ***It should be noted that*** *the majority of the responses were positive.*

It + a passive reporting verb describes impersonal or general feelings. It also allows us to report someone's words without mentioning the speaker/s. We use a verb clause after the verb, not a noun phrase (compare ▶ **33.1D**):

It was said *(that) he was innocent.*
It is believed *(that) the rebels are about to attack the capital.*

33.2D Uses of *it* in discourse

If the subject of a sentence is a long clause we can use *it* as an 'empty' subject so that we can put the long subject at the end:

It *was hard to believe* ***that he had behaved so appallingly.*** (= That he had behaved so appallingly was hard to believe.)

This device also helps us put new information in the end focus position (▶ **36.1A, B**):

It *really hurts me* ***to be going away***. (= To be going away really hurts me.)

It can also be an 'empty' object (▶ **33.2A**), anticipating a later clause. This allows us to combine several pieces of information into one sentence, again putting new information at the end:

We leave ***it*** *to the reader* ***to appreciate what this will mean***. (= The reader can appreciate what this will mean. We leave it to the reader to do this.)
She thought ***it*** *a pity/sad* ***that he hadn't joined in the festivities***. (= He hadn't joined in the festivities. She thought that was a pity.)

❗ We don't usually use *it* as an 'empty' object when the main verb is not followed by an adjective or by a noun or preposition phrase:

✗ ~~*She thought **it** that he hadn't joined in the festivities.*~~
✓ *She thought that he hadn't joined in the festivities.*

We also use *it* to introduce cleft sentences (▶ **34.1B**):

It *isn't just his outlandish sense of humour that I'm complaining about.*

Practice

The key to these exercises is on page 370.

1 33.1

Rewrite the following sentences using *there*.

0 Such a strong reaction was not anticipated by the protestors.
The protestors did not expect there to be such a strong reaction.

00 Getting a visa won't be difficult.
There won't be any difficulty getting a visa.

1 More than a million species of insects exist in the world.

2 A grandfather clock was ticking in the background.

3 At Hiroshima in 1945 an event happened which shook the whole world.

4 Two further suspects are thought to be under arrest.

5 They are bound to react badly to the news.

6 A statement by the Prime Minister now follows.

7 Present in the compound were two forms of amino acid.

8 Does Osaka have an underground railway?

9 A massive sell-off of high-tech shares is likely in the next few days.

10 From the middle of the forest emerged a strange hooded figure.

11 In this case, securing a conviction should be no trouble.

12 Is nobody here able to help us?

13 Illustrated in our brochure are ten new holiday destinations.

14 Do you have a buffet car on the train?

15 In this bad weather a poor turnout for the election is certain.

16 Hanging over the bed was a beautiful antique tapestry.

17 People think at least two leading politicians are involved in the scandal.

18 We don't envisage any adverse reaction from viewers.

2 33.2

This text can be improved by rewriting one sentence from each paragraph with impersonal/introductory *it*. Underline the sentences that can be improved and rewrite them. The first one has been done as an example.

The Beach

by Alex Garland

Now a movie starring Leonardo DiCaprio.

People say that somewhere in the tropical waters of Asia there is a perfect beach on an uninhabited island. Rich in animal and plant life, surrounded by virgin jungle and watered by sweet underground springs, the beach could be the setting for an idyllic and easy life.

The Beach is the story of a young man who yearns for, seeks out and eventually finds just such a place. But to discover that far from being the source of contentment and inner fulfilment that he expects, the beach turns out to be a place of savage violence, terror and death, comes as a shock.

Alex Garland takes the reader on an exotic journey from the steaming tourist-packed dives of the Khao San Road in Bangkok to the drug-infested islands of the remote seas around Thailand. Not to be impressed by the author's skill in describing the unfamiliar oriental locations and his ability to empathise with the obsessions of today's young backpacking 'new-age' travellers is difficult.

Taking in illegal drug plantations, memories of the Vietnam war, sexual jealousy, shark-infested waters, the psychological dynamics of communal living and the clash of cultures, Garland spins a tale which both seduces and shocks the reader. What gives the novel its haunting sense of unease and horror is the author's unique blend of these disparate elements.

It is a thriller with all the traditional ingredients, an exotic location, a central mystery, good versus evil, and dangers around every corner. There is a strong sense of good and evil in the book, but to decide who is right and who is wrong Garland leaves to the reader. There are few moral certainties in this exotic corner of the world.

Events unfold at great speed, and be warned, to put this book down once you have started it is impossible. With an international cast of well-observed characters Garland creates a nail-biting narrative that keeps the reader hooked until the final bloody climax.

It is said that somewhere in the tropical waters of Asia there is a perfect beach on an uninhabited island.

....

....

....

....

....

....

3 ALL

For each of the sentences below, write a new sentence as similar as possible in meaning to the original sentence, but using a form of *it* or *there* and the word given. This word must not be altered in any way. The exercise begins with an example (0).

0 I think Steve might win the race.
though *It looks as though Steve might win the race.*

1 Such an overwhelming demand for tickets wasn't anticipated by the organisers.
being ……………………………………

2 She may well marry him.
seems ……………………………………

3 People think many other politicians are involved in the scandal.
thought ……………………………………

4 I would like you to send me your up-to-date retail price list.
appreciate ……………………………………

5 Fifty students applied for the scholarship.
applicants ……………………………………

6 They say he hates publicity.
said ……………………………………

7 We're not surprised that their children are so badly behaved.
surprising ……………………………………

8 In this paper we will demonstrate that DNA strands can be replicated.
demonstrated ……………………………………

9 We are selling twelve detached houses with double garages on this estate.
sale ……………………………………

10 To be nominated for this award makes me feel greatly honoured.
honour ……………………………………

4 ALL

Eight of these short extracts from conversations at a museum would be improved with the use of *it* or *there*. Two of the extracts do not need to be changed. Tick (✓) these two extracts, then rewrite the others.

1 DAVE How far's the café from here?
GUIDE The distance isn't far; you'll find it at the other end of the Egyptian Gallery.

2 GUIDE Ladies and gentlemen, this is the Gutenburg Bible. People believe this is the first book to be printed in Europe.

3 JACK Isn't this the head of Queen Nefertiti?
MARY Yes. She was the aunt of Tutankhamun.

4 KARL Do you have many Impressionist paintings here?
GUIDE Yes, more than thirty examples hang in the East wing.

5 JACK What an amazing statue.
MARY That Rodin produced such a superb piece of work all by himself is hard to believe.

6 DAVE This fifteenth-century portrait looks brand new!
SUE Yes, the impression is that the painting has been rather over-enthusiastically restored.

7 GUIDE On your left you will see a fine example of late Renaissance sculpture.

8 JACK You know Van Gogh never sold a single painting.
MARY I'm really surprised that people didn't appreciate his genius during his lifetime.

9 DAVE We've been here two hours and we're not even halfway round the museum.
SUE I know; but to see everything in one trip is impossible.

10 KARL Which one's the Titian, Jane?
JANE The Titian is in that place, next to the sculpture.

5 ALL

The words *it* or *there* are missing from eleven of these sentences. Tick (✓) the sentences which are correct and rewrite the others with *it* or *there* in the correct place.

1 She found strange that he'd never heard of such a famous historical character.
.....

2 Was really such a long wait between trains?
.....

3 We always have lots of visitors but tend to be more in the summer months.
.....

4 Rarely were such extreme methods required.
.....

5 The director leaves to the viewer to decide who is guilty and who is innocent.
.....

6 They assured us that would be no trouble getting a refund if the goods were faulty.
.....

7 It wasn't their behaviour that annoyed me, but their attitude.
.....

8 You know really gets on my nerves when she talks like that.
.....

9 Commonly believed myths are not necessarily true.
.....

10 What's incredible is that might have been so many more fatalities.
.....

11 I find impossible to conceive that someone with his track record would be so careless.
.....

12 In 1666 was a fire which destroyed a large part of London.
.....

13 We would appreciate if you submitted your estimate to our head office.
.....

14 Getting to the airport on time is the least of our worries.
.....

15 Grandpa loves when the children ask for his advice.
.....

34 Emphatic structures and inversion

We often emphasise a particular part of a sentence, perhaps to contradict what someone else has said or for dramatic effect. In speech we can do this with stress and intonation alone, but we can also do this by changing the position of elements in a sentence in speech and in writing. In this unit we look at the ways we can manipulate grammar to emphasise something, by splitting one sentence into two parts (cleft sentences) or by bringing the element we want to emphasise to the beginning (fronting).

34.1 CLEFT SENTENCES

34.1A Form and use

'Cleft' means divided. In a cleft sentence, information which could be given in one clause is divided into two parts, each with its own verb:

Vanessa has made the greatest impact. (normal sentence: single clause, one verb)

[*It is Vanessa*] [*who has made the greatest impact*]. (cleft sentence: two clauses, two verbs)

This gives extra emphasis to part of the sentence. We often use this pattern to emphasise some piece of new information, to give explanations or to make a contrast with a previous statement (the emphasised information is in **bold**):

All of the Redgrave family are gifted actors. But it is ***Vanessa*** *who made the greatest impact in the world of feature films.*

'I remember your uncle taking us to the fair.' 'No, it was ***my father*** *that took us there.'*

34.1B *it* cleft sentences

It cleft sentences have this structure:

it + a form of *be* (+ *not* and/or adverb) + **emphasised word/phrase** + *that/which/who* clause

It [isn't just] **his outlandish sense of humour** [that I'm complaining about].

We can use this pattern to emphasise the subject or the object of a simple sentence, or an adverbial phrase, or a prepositional phrase:

sentence	*Mike took Sally to the party on Saturday.*
emphasising the subject	*It was* ***Mike*** *who took Sally to the party on Saturday.*
emphasising the object	*It was* ***Sally*** *(that) Mike took to the party on Saturday.*
emphasising the adverbial	*It was* ***on Saturday*** *(that) Mike took Sally to the party.*
emphasising the prepositional phrase	*It was* ***to the party*** *(that) Mike took Sally on Saturday.*

In informal English we can use *when* and *where* clauses, but we do not use *how* or *why*:

It was ***in January*** *when I got the test results.*

It's ***in Green Street market*** *where we'll find the best bargains.*

✘ ~~*It was greed why he did it.*~~ ✔ *It was because of greed that he did it.*

✘ ~~*It is using a calculator how he does it.*~~ ✔ *It is by using a calculator that he does it.*

❶ We cannot use *it* clefts to highlight the action or a verb complement in a sentence. We use *wh-* clefts (▶ **34.1C**) to do this:

✘ ~~*It was taking Sally to the party that Mike did.*~~ ✔ *What Mike did was take Sally ...*

✘ ~~*It is totally unscrupulous that they are.*~~ ✔ *What they are is unscrupulous.*

34.1C *wh-* cleft sentences

We can use this pattern to highlight the action in a sentence. For example, if we want to highlight Mike's action of taking Sally to the party:

wh- clause + a form of *be* + **emphasised word or phrase**

What Mike did was ***take Sally to the party***.

In these sentences *what* means *the thing(s) that*. The *wh-* clause must contain a verb. To highlight the action we use a form of *do* in the *wh-* clause. The highlighted phrase usually contains a bare infinitive (example above) or *to* + infinitive:

What Mike did was ***to take Sally to the party***.

If the highlighted verb is in the continuous or perfect, the form of *do* matches it:

The boys aren't leaving Sandy at home. They are taking him to the match.

→ *What the boys are doing is* ***taking Sandy to the match***.

Old members are absent but the new members have taken their seats in the assembly.

→ *What the new members have done is* ***taken their seats in the assembly***.

We can also use *wh-* clefts to highlight a verb complement. For example, if we want to highlight the complement *stingy* in the sentence *Jean and Bob are stingy*, we can say:

*wh-*clause + *is* + **emphasised complement**

What Jean and Bob are is ***stingy****!*

We use this pattern most often when we want to express our opinion of something or somebody using an adjective:

'Do you think Jean and Bob are a bit cautious with their money?'

'Cautious? What they are is downright ***stingy****!'*

34.1D Other types of cleft sentence

We can use *wh-* clauses with *when*, *where*, *why* and *who* to highlight a person, a place, a time and a reason, but we usually use an introductory noun phrase (underlined below). The *wh-* clause acts like an ordinary relative clause:

✗ ~~*Who we forgot to invite was Ian.*~~ ✓ *The one (who) we forgot to invite was* ***Ian***.

person	*The guy who told me about the new club was Zack.*
place	*The house where I used to live is near here.*
time	*The day (when) we left was the saddest day of my life.*
reason	*The reason (why) they never told me is they don't trust me.*

We can emphasise an item (described by a noun phrase or a verb phrase) with *the (only/last) thing* or *all*:

The thing I most disliked about the movie was ***the scene in the graveyard***.

The only thing we want is ***a chance to air our grievances***.

The last thing we did was ***pack the kettle***.

All we're asking for is ***to be given a chance***.

We can also use *the (only) thing* with a negative verb:

The thing we ***won't do*** *is* ***repair goods bought in other shops***.

The only thing we ***didn't find*** *was* ***the key to the cellar***.

34.1E Reversed cleft sentences

We can reverse the order of the parts in *wh-* cleft sentences and put the emphasised part at the beginning:

Taking Sandy to the match *is what the boys are doing.*

Zack *was the guy who told me about the new club.*

There is a form in spoken English similar to a reversed cleft using *this* and *that*:

We have to get off ***here***. → ***This*** *is where we have to get off.*

They told me ***the same thing***. → ***That****'s what they told me.*

❗ We only use reversed *it* clefts in a formal literary style. We put the emphasised part before *it*:

And thus ***Cezanne*** *it was that took the first steps on the road to Impressionism.*

34.2 FRONTING

34.2A Fronting objects and complements

In spoken English we sometimes want to make a strong contrast with something in a previous statement. We can do this with objects and complements by 'fronting' them (moving them to the front of the clause), which makes them more emphatic:

'She's such a lovely person; so friendly and reliable.'
['She may be friendly but she isn't reliable.'] → *'**Friendly** she may be, but **reliable** she isn't!'*

We can also front demonstrative pronouns for emphasis:

*I disagree with **that.*** → ***That** I disagree with.*

We can use fronting to help the flow of spoken or written information by putting the known information at the beginning of the sentence (the information principle ▶ **Unit 36**):

*The house was large and sprawling, with two wings and a dark attic. Hilary spent most of her time in the drawing room or the garden. **The attic** she rarely visited.*

34.2B Fronting adjective phrases; *also* and *such*

When we want to start a sentence with known information or we want to make an emphatic comparison with information in a previous sentence, we can use a comparative or superlative phrase at the beginning. We use a form of the verb *be* followed by the subject (inversion ▶ **34.3A**):

*The first band was dire. **Much more exciting** was Red Heat, the second group to play.*
*Many of the monuments are truly awesome. **Best of all** is the Colosseum.*
*The actors were a mixed bunch. **Least inspiring** of the lot was Pacino.*

We can use a similar pattern with *also* and *such*:

*Members of the royal family attended the funeral. **Also** at the service were several ambassadors.*
*They led a life of abject poverty. **Such** is the fate of most illegitimate children in this province.*

We can emphasise an adjective by using *so* + adjective + a form of *be* + subject + a *that* clause:

***So intense** was the heat (that) the firefighters were unable to enter the building for two hours.*

34.2C Fronting adverbials and infinitives; *as* and *though*

We can put known information at the beginning of a sentence by putting adverbial phrases describing position or place (e.g. *At the back of the house*), verbs of position and movement (e.g. *stand, attach, lie*) and *to* + infinitive forms in the front position, with inversion of the subject and verb *be* (▶ **34.3A**):

***At the back of the house** was an untidy garden, much of which was taken up by a large and unkempt lawn. **Standing in the corner of the garden** was a massively overgrown silver birch tree which towered over the roof of the garage. **Attached to the roof** was an unsightly FM aerial.*
*For years I have been writing to the President in the White House. **To meet him** is my most fervent wish.*

We can also front an infinitive form when it 'echoes' an earlier verb:

He said he would arrive on time.
And he did (arrive on time).
→ *And **arrive** on time he did.*

We can front verbs and adjectives using *as* and *though*:

***Battered though** he was, he never lost his will to succeed.*
***Try as** she might, she simply couldn't open the jam jar.*

Try as she might, she simply couldn't open the jam jar.

34.3 INVERSION

34.3A Subject–verb inversion

We sometimes put a verb or verb phrase in front of the subject after adverbs of place (e.g. *on, in, here, there, outside, opposite*) and adverbs of time (e.g. *next, then, first, now, finally*). We can use a form of *be* or verbs of place and movement (e.g. *stand, sit, lie, come, go, climb, run, sail, fly*) before the subject. We often use this pattern to form a link with the information in the previous sentence, and it is common in formal English:

place adverbs + *be* or verbs of place/movement	***Here lies*** *the body of our late lamented sovereign.* *On one wall there was a beautiful rambling rose.* ***Opposite stood*** *an ancient oak tree over a charming wishing well.*
time adverbs + *be* or verbs of place/movement	*For the first hour the teams seemed evenly matched.* ***Then came*** *the turning point in the game as Ed scored.* *That was the final instalment.* ***Next is*** *the news.*

❶ We don't use inversion if the subject of the clause is a pronoun:

Here comes the bus. ✗ ~~*Here comes it.*~~ ✓ *Here* ***it*** *comes.*

We can also use inversion in *as* and *than* clauses in formal English:

Mr Slater is expecting a pay rise, ***as are*** *several other salesmen in the team.*

I'm afraid her proposals are no more feasible ***than are*** *those James presented.*

We also use inversion in certain fixed expressions, often with subjunctives (▶ **11.1C**):

So be *it.* ***Long live*** *the king!*

34.3B Subject–auxiliary inversion

We sometimes put an auxiliary (*do, have, should, can*, etc.) before the subject in statements; the rest of the verb phrase follows the subject. We use this pattern of inversion for emphasis in the following cases:

after adverbs with 'restrictive'/ negative meaning (e.g. *hardly, scarcely, rarely, little, never*)	***Little*** *did we realise the true extent of his involvement.* ***Never*** *have I seen such a disturbing sight.* ***Hardly*** *had I arrived when Suzy collared me.*
only + time expression or prepositional phrase	***Only later*** *did he manage to get permission.* ***Only with a great deal of effort*** *was he able to escape.*
(in) no way, at no time, under no circumstances, on no account	***No way*** *am I going to wear that!* (informal) ***Under no circumstances*** *can refunds be given.*
not + *only*/time expression/ person or thing	***Not only*** *is he late, he hasn't even brought a present.* ***Not since the sixties*** *has a pop group won such acclaim.* ***Not a single stone*** *was left unturned in the search.*
no sooner … than	***No sooner*** *had we set out* ***than*** *the skies opened.*
clauses beginning with *neither* or *nor*	*They have no intention of paying and* ***neither*** *have we.* *We couldn't face the customers and* ***nor*** *could the boss.*
clauses beginning with *may* which describe a strong wish	***May*** *he live to regret this decision!*
after fronted comparisons, *also, such* and *so* (▶ **34.2B**)	*The captain is refusing to play under these conditions and* ***so*** *is the rest of the team.*

❶ Expressions with *no, not*, etc. not listed above (e.g. *no doubt*) cannot be inverted:

✗ ~~***No doubt*** *will he give us a key.*~~ ✓ ***No doubt*** *he will give us a key.*

❶ We do not invert the subject and auxiliary after *only* if there is no time expression or prepositional phrase immediately after it:

✗ ~~***Only*** *can members park there.*~~ ✓ ***Only*** *members can park there.*

✓ ***Only on Sundays*** *can members park there.*

Note there are other uses of inversion: Negation ▶ **Unit 6**; Questions ▶ **Unit 7**; Reported speech ▶ **Unit 9**; Conditionals ▶ **Unit 10**.

Practice

The key to these exercises is on page 371.

1 34.1

Read the information in the box then complete the replies. Each reply must contain a cleft sentence. The exercise begins with an example (0).

> Nick turned up late for work on Monday because he got stuck in a traffic jam on the ring road. Luckily Nick has a mobile phone so he was able to phone his boss and warn her that he would be late. She was furious but managed to reschedule an important meeting for the afternoon.

0 'Didn't the boss turn up late on Monday?'
'No, it ......*was Nick who turned up*........ late on Monday.'

1 'Nick was late because he overslept, wasn't he?'
'No, it .... that he was late.'

2 'How on earth did Nick let the boss know he'd be late?'
'Well, what .... call her from his mobile phone.'

3 'Wasn't Nick late on Wednesday?'
'No, ... that he was late.'

4 'Nick's boss had to start the meeting without him, didn't she?'
'No, what she .... the afternoon.'

5 'Didn't Nick get stuck in a traffic jam in the town centre?'
'No, not the town centre; it .... got stuck.'

6 'Didn't the boss have to reschedule that meeting because the client didn't turn up?'
'No, it .... had to reschedule the meeting.'

7 'Nick rang the boss to give her the sales figures, didn't he?'
'No, it .... that he rang her.'

8 I heard the boss was a little annoyed with Nick for being late.
'No, she wasn't "a little annoyed". What ....!'

2 34.1

For each of the sentences below, write a new sentence as similar as possible in meaning to the original sentence, but using the words given in bold.

0 Sebastian left the job because of the long working hours.
why *The reason why Sebastian left the job was the long working hours.*

1 We have to wait here.
this ....

2 We just need five minutes to fix it.
all ....

3 Jennifer started the strike.
person ....

4 I'm not questioning his dedication.
isn't ....

5 These men are totally ruthless.
what ....

6 I used to live around the corner.
the place ....

7 It was your next door neighbour who complained.
the one ....

8 We inherited everything except the house.
only thing ....

9 You know the sales assistant told me exactly the same thing.
that's ....

10 I want you to copy this down in your notebooks.
to do ....

11 First of all we checked the insurance details.
first thing ....

12 The climbers reached the peak at six o'clock.
was ....

13 We're taking the au-pair with us.
doing ....

14 Before leaving we switched off the power supply.
last thing ....

15 They moved to Andalucia because of the climate.
reason ....

16 The company has imposed a ban on private e-mails.
has done ....

17 The only thing we want is our money back.
all ....

18 Our boss told us the news.
it ....

19 I want you to appreciate that it's not my fault.
what ....

20 The introduction of stamp duties led to the loss of the American colonies.
that ....

3 34.2

Make these sentences more emphatic by 'fronting' part of them. Do not use any additional words.

0 I can't stand hypocrisy. ..... *Hypocrisy I can't stand!* .....
1 Though he was exhausted, he managed to reach the finishing line. ....
2 My life's ambition is to make the pilgrimage to Mecca. ....
3 The ninth symphony is his most sublime work. ....
4 I really can't accept that proposal. ....
5 An enormous gold Buddha was placed on the altar. ....
6 The Cresta Run is much more challenging for the dedicated skier. ....
7 Several sharp criticisms of ministerial conduct were also included in the report. ....
8 An old man was lying in the shop doorway. ....
9 It proved impossible to get to the bottom of the mystery. ....
10 The pilot couldn't regain control because the damage was so severe. ....

4 34.3

In twelve of the following sentences there are mistakes with word order and missing auxiliaries. Tick (✓) the correct sentences and then find the mistakes and correct them.

1 They're going to complain about this and so are we. ☐
2 Little we knew the full extent of his involvement in the fraud. ☐
3 The sales director is resigning and so most of the marketing team are. ☐
4 I tried to get there by nine, only was there a traffic jam on the motorway. ☐
5 Over there stood the three-metre tall statue of Lenin. ☐
6 The embassy refuses to intervene. Well, so it be. ☐
7 Tomorrow the first day is of the rest of your life. ☐
8 Long live the glorious republic! ☐
9 No way is the boss treating me like that and getting away with it! ☐
10 Under no circumstances latecomers will be admitted to the auditorium. ☐
11 Armando and Josepha are quite destitute and such the condition is of many of the refugees. ☐
12 Now the time is for wise investors to think seriously about buying Treasury Bonds. ☐
13 Rarely had we encountered such friendly and positive attitudes. ☐
14 Oh look – here comes the procession at last. ☐
15 Not since Kubrick's *2001* a director has made such an intellectually challenging sci-fi movie. ☐
16 The government's proposals are unrealistic, as those are of the opposition. ☐
17 Opposite this house ran the old city walls. ☐
18 Only with the greatest of luck he managed to escape from the rising flood waters. ☐
19 May John and Carol have a long and happy life together. ☐
20 No doubt didn't he realise the consequences of his actions. ☐

5 ALL

Rewrite the replies in these mini-dialogues to make them more emphatic by using suitable structures (cleft sentences, fronting or inversion) to emphasise the underlined items. The exercise begins with two examples (0) and (00).

0 'That dress looks expensive.'
'No, the shoes were expensive, not the dress.' ...*'No, it's the shoes that were expensive, not the dress.'*...

00 'Did Darren help you with the decorating?'
'No, he did the wallpapering, nothing else.' ...*'No, the only thing he did was the wallpapering.'*...

1 'Jerry says Liz is going to quit her job at the bank.'
'I find that really hard to believe.' ....

2 'You look as though you're destroying that rose bush.'
'No, I'm just cutting off the dead flower heads.' ....

3 'Are you sure you brought everything with you?'
'We left the personal stereo behind, that's all.' ....

4 'Didn't you own a Volkswagen Golf once?'
'No, my brother owned one.' ....

5 'He said the speech would shake them up a bit.'
'And it certainly did shake them up.' ....

6 'I thought the car chase and the scene in the airport were brilliant.'
'But the explosion on the jumbo jet was best of all.' ....

7 'I think we should try to give them first aid.'
'No, we should wait for the ambulance to arrive.' ....

8 'So what was so awful about the view from your hotel room?'
'Well, a huge electricity pylon was standing right outside the bedroom window.' ....

9 'You've always wanted to buy a cottage in the country, haven't you?'
'Yes, my greatest ambition has always been <u>to own a cottage</u>.' ....

10 'You're all leaving on Saturday, aren't you?'
'No, we're going <u>on Friday</u>.' ....

6 ALL

In the following magazine article ten emphatic sentences have been changed and underlined. Rewrite the sentences in their original emphatic form using the clues in brackets. The first one has been done as an example (0).

RAP JUMPING? NO WAY, JOSÉ!

I'm quite sporty and I love a new challenge, especially if it's a little bit risky. I often try out new things with my friends Tony and Bruce. (0) <u>In fact Bruce told me about his new hobby</u> – rap jumping. (1) <u>I've done bungee jumping before</u> – that's the sport where you jump off a crane or bridge with your feet attached to a long length of elastic – so I had some idea what he was talking about. Bruce promised me that (2) <u>rap jumping was more exciting and a lot more dangerous than bungee jumping</u>, and (3) <u>he didn't tell me too much about it to keep me in suspense</u>. So of course I was dying it give it a go.

(4) <u>But Tony actually took me for my first rap jump</u>. (5) <u>He's the real daredevil</u>. We went to the top of this tall building which had a sort of gantry overhanging the edge. (6) <u>I could see a rope and a harness hanging from the gantry</u>.

'Oh, I understand,' I said to Tony, 'I get into the harness and then lean back over the edge and lower myself down – it's like abseiling.'

'No, no,' said Tony, '(7) <u>You lean forward and walk down</u>.'

I began to feel a little sick. I don't normally suffer from a fear of heights because I avoid it by looking up or sideways. (8) <u>I can't cope with seeing the ground</u>. The idea of going over the edge facing downwards was just too much for me. '(9) <u>I'm not doing that</u>,' I announced.

Well, would you have done it?

0 (*it*) ......*In fact it was Bruce who told me about his new hobby*......
1 (fronting) ....
2 (*not only*) ....
3 (fronting) ....
4 (*it*) ....
5 (*the one*) ....
6 (*all*) ....
7 (*What*) ....
8 (*It's*) ....
9 (*No way*) ....

35 Aspects of cohesion

Both spoken and written English use certain devices to keep the meaning clear and to express it more economically. These devices include ways of avoiding repetition, either by choosing alternative (and usually shorter) words and phrases or by missing out words, phrases or clauses. This unit looks at what can be omitted and which words and phrases can be used to substitute for others. In the examples in this unit, **bold** shows substitute words, and shading indicates words which have been replaced by substitution. We use < > to show omitted words.

35.1 TYPES OF TEXT REFERENCE

35.1A Substitution and ellipsis

Substitution and ellipsis are both devices for avoiding the unnecessary repetition of words or phrases in speech or writing. Substitution consists of replacing one word or phrase with another. This is a sentence without substitution:

Labour voted for the proposals and the Liberals voted for the proposals too.

Here is the same sentence with substitution:

Labour voted for the proposals and the Liberals ***did*** *too.*

In ellipsis, we leave out words or phrases altogether:

Mike left at about the same time as Jane <left>.

We can leave out or replace nouns, verbs and entire clauses. The following example uses a pronoun to substitute for *resorts*, and leaves out the verb phrase *it is found*:

[*The best skiing is found not at big resorts but it is found at small resorts.*]

The best skiing is found not at big resorts but at small ***ones****.*

Verbs and verb phrases are often replaced by a form of the auxiliary *do*:

'Hadn't we better look into the interest rates first?' 'It's OK. I've already ***done*** *it.'*

35.1B Using substitution and ellipsis

We usually replace or omit words or phrases which have previously been mentioned:

The managers in our company have often adopted production processes which give rise to unsatisfying jobs because it is cheaper for ***them*** *to* ***do so****.*

It is clear that *them* refers to *the managers* and *do so* refers to the phrase *have often adopted production processes which give rise to unsatisfying jobs*. Referring back in a text to a previously mentioned item is known as 'anaphoric reference':

The Museum's lifelike new dinosaur will surely enhance ***its*** *status amongst children.*

We can use substitution to refer to items mentioned further back than in the same sentence, as long as there is no ambiguity:

She had a vast collection of antique clocks, which she kept in a small room devoted to her hobby. While most of ***them*** *dated from the Victorian era, she had a few smaller* ***ones*** *which dated back to the early 19th century.*

It is clear that *them* and *ones* relate to *clocks*, as there is no other plural noun in the context to which they could refer. We avoid substitution and ellipsis if there is a possible ambiguity, as below, where there are two plural nouns in the first sentence:

She had a vast collection of antique clocks and an equally large collection of Victorian dolls. [*She had quite* ***a few*** *from the Victorian era but also some smaller* ***ones*** *from the early 19th century.*]

Here, we don't know whether *a few* and *ones* refer to *clocks* or *dolls* or to both.

It is also possible to use a substitute word to refer to something later in the sentence. This has the effect of creating an atmosphere of suspense and is often used in dramatic or literary language. This is known as 'cataphoric reference':

Its *eyes glinting like steel and* ***its*** *mouth salivating, the predator prepared to strike.*

35.2 SUBSTITUTION

35.2A Substitution of a noun or noun phrase

The most common substitutes for nouns or noun phrases are pronouns (▶ **Unit 27**), such as personal pronouns (subject, object, possessive or reflexive ▶ **27.1A**):

*John came into the room. **He** was wearing a light blue silk suit.*
*Ben and Alice were refreshingly independent of each other. While Ben's politics were far to the left, Alice made it known that **hers** were centre right.*

We can use the pronouns *one/ones* (to refer to singular/plural countable nouns) after adjectives or demonstratives (▶ **27.1G**):

*I'd like a sweet sherry please and John would like a **dry one**.*
*Davis appeared in numerous major films but practically no **great ones**.*
*Which colour would you prefer for the bathroom suite, **this one** or **that one**?*

We don't use *one* for uncountable nouns; instead, we omit the noun:

✗ ~~*I really like sweet sherry but my husband prefers dry **one**.*~~
✔ *I really like sweet sherry but my husband prefers dry <sherry>.*

We can also use the demonstrative pronouns (▶ **28.2B**) without *one/ones*:

*Which colour would you prefer for the bathroom suite, **this one** or **that**?*
*It is possible to respect both your own opinions and **those** of other people.*

It is also possible to replace a noun or noun phrase with a quantifier, e.g. *some, all, each, none, either, neither, both, other, a few, enough* (▶ **28.3B**):

*The boys went out night after night and **some** did not return.*
*The doctor suggested I should try aspirin or ibuprofen, but **neither** worked.*

35.2B Substitution of a verb or verb phrase with *do*

We can use a form of *do* to avoid repeating a present or past simple verb:

*At the time, they lived very near to where I **did**.*

Using a form of *do* is particularly common in comparison clauses:

*She doesn't know any more than I **do**.*
*He doesn't help as much as she **does**.*

We also use *do* to avoid repeating the main verb in coordinate clauses:

*Mary sent him a text message and I **did** too.*
*Dad never learnt a foreign language and Mum **didn't** either.*

With coordinate clauses where the action is the same in both, as above, we can also use the inverted pattern *so/neither* + *do/does/did* + subject (▶ **34.3B**):

*She really enjoyed the thrill of the open road, and **so did** her husband.*
*Dad never learnt to speak any other languages, and **neither did** Mum.*

We use the same pattern with *so, not either* and *neither/nor* to agree with the speaker in short answers:

*'I **saw Jane** yesterday.' 'Oh, yes, **so did** I.'*
*'I didn't have enough money'. '**Neither/Nor did** I.'/'I **didn't either**.'*

We can omit *do* and use the object pronoun, usually with *too, neither, nor*, in informal speech:

*'I **saw Jane** yesterday.' '**Me, too!**'*
*'Julian was at the meeting about the new road scheme yesterday.' '**Him too**?'*
*'I didn't want to go.' '**Me neither**.'/'**Nor me**.'*

35.2C Substitution of a verb or verb phrase with *do so/it/that*

We can often use *do so/it/that* to replace a verb phrase which describes a single, specific action. In this use, *do so* tends to be more formal than *do it/that*:

*Margaret had been trying to pluck up the courage to confront her son about the money, and she was just about to **do so/it** when the doorbell rang.*

We usually use *do it/that* (and not *do so*) when the subject of the verb changes:

I was unable to contact the barrister about the court appearance.
[Can the clerk do so tomorrow?] ✔ *Can the clerk **do it/that** tomorrow?*

❗ We use *that* (and not *it*) to emphasise an action. In this use, we stress *that*:

*'Why don't you just lie to him?' 'Oh, I couldn't do **that**!'*

We prefer to use *do so* (and not *do it/that*) when we are referring to an activity rather than a single, specific action:

Anyone wishing to interrupt with questions should feel free to ***do so****.*
When you want to get fit, you should only ***do so*** *within a planned exercise programme.*

We do not usually use *do so/it/that* to replace verbs which refer to events outside our control, e.g. *believe, lose, forget*. We use *do* only:

Michael still believes fiercely that no one is evil – just as he ***did*** *when he was younger.*
I always said you'd lose that mobile phone and now you ***have done****!*
She told me not to forget the cake in the oven, but I ***did****.*

35.2D Substitution of a clause

We use verbs like *expect/think/imagine/believe* with *so* to express an opinion, belief or intention, without repeating the preceding statement or question. We usually try to avoid using the same verb in the answer:

'Do you ***think*** *WAP phones will ever catch on?' ['I think* ***so****.'] 'I* ***expect so****.'*
'I wonder if privatising the post office will make the postal service more efficient.'
'I ***hope so****!'/'I* ***don't believe so****, myself.'*

❗ We do not use a *that* clause after *so*:

'Do you know if John is coming this evening?'
✗ ~~*'I think* ***so (that) he is****.'*~~ ✔ *'I think* ***so****.'/'I think (****that) he is****.'*

To express a negative response, we tend to make the verb negative and use *so*:

'Are you coming to the party tomorrow?' ✗ ~~*'I think not.'*~~ ✔ *'I* ***don't think so****.'*

It is possible, though archaic, to use these verbs with *not* to respond in the negative. It is still sometimes used in a formal context:

'Was the document countersigned by two witnesses?' 'I ***believe not****.'*

An exception to this is *hope*. We do not use the *not ... so* pattern but use *hope not*:

'It's going to rain!' ✗ ~~*'Oh, I don't hope so!'*~~ ✔ *'I* ***hope not****.'*

❗ We do not use *so* or *not* after expressions of certainty or doubt. We prefer to use *it*:

'Do you think it'll rain?' ✗ ~~*'I'm certain of so.'*~~ ✔ *'I'm* ***certain of it****.'*
'Do you think interest rates will go down this month?' ✗ ~~*'I doubt so.'*~~ ✔ *'I* ***doubt it****.'*

We use the pronouns *it, this* or *that* to refer back to a previous clause:

I forgot his birthday again and he was really upset about ***it****.* (= forgetting his birthday)
Many of the latest models have been recalled because of a fault in the steering. ***This*** *has caused embarrassment to the manufacturers.*
'He really doesn't know what he's talking about!' 'Oh, why do you say ***that****?'*

We substitute *if* and *whether* clauses with *if so* (affirmative) and *if not* (negative):

Can you check whether that contract has arrived and, ***if so****, send it out to Mr Andrews?*
He asked the guests if they wanted an evening meal, and ***if not****, whether he could bring them sandwiches in their rooms.*

We can use *so* at the beginning of a short answer when we agree to a statement with a certain amount of surprise:

*'They've put a new statue in front of the palace.' '****So*** *they have!'*

❗ Be careful not to confuse this use with *So did I* or *I did so* (▶ **35.2B, C**).

35.3 ELLIPSIS

35.3A Omitting a noun/pronoun

We often omit nouns or pronouns in the second of two coordinate clauses (▶ **30.3A**):

Lucy went up to the bar and <she> asked for a coffee.
We were totally exhausted but <we> felt satisfied with our day's work.

In casual spoken English we can also omit *and* when the subject is the same:

Sandy was feeling really bored, <and he> didn't know what to do with all the extra time he'd now got.

❗ We do not leave out pronouns in subordinate clauses (▶ **30.3B**):

At night she was so tired that she fell asleep as soon as she got into bed.

We can omit subject pronouns at the beginning of short sentences in casual English:

<I> Must go now. It's getting late.

'Is your brother coming with us?' '<I> Hope not!'

35.3B Omitting a verb

We can often omit a verb to avoid repeating it:

She attracts the attention of the local yobbos and he <attracts> the suspicions of the villagers.

Generally we do not omit the auxiliary or modal. Look at this table:

form	change	example
present/past simple verb	omit main verb in *and* clauses	*I like John and he <likes> me.*
auxiliary + main verb	omit main verb	*He was looking for a job, or at least, he said he **was** <looking for one>.* *'Have you seen my glasses?' 'Yes, I **have** <seen them>. They're here.'*
modal + main verb	omit main verb	*I can speak Spanish and Mary **can** <speak Spanish> too.*
compound verb forms	omit second/third auxiliary or only the main verb	'Couldn't anybody have been warned about the problem?' 'Yes, the captain **could** <have been warned>/**could have** <been warned>/**could have been** <warned>.'

In coordinate clauses where the second clause is very similar in pattern to the first, we leave out the auxiliary as well:

Since the divorce I've lived in London and my husband <has lived> in Cambridge.

❗ We can introduce a new modal in order to add interpretation (in this case deduction) but still not repeat the main verb:

*'Has Mary arrived yet?' 'She **must have** <arrived>. There's her coat.'*

We also omit verbs in comparison clauses as in the table above, but it is possible in comparison clauses to omit auxiliary and modal verbs as well in the subordinate clause:

You look older than my mother <does>.

*House prices have dropped much less than share prices <have done>/**have** <done>.*

*Most European teams can now play more interesting football than the British teams <can play>/**can** <play>.*

*I've been working here longer than you <have been doing>/**have** <been doing>/**have been** <doing>.*

❗ If the comparison clause begins with a pronoun and we omit the verb phrase completely, we use an object pronoun rather than a subject pronoun (▶ **27.1D**):

You look older than she does. → *You look older than **her**.*

35.3C Omitting infinitives or *wh-* clauses

We can omit an infinitive phrase when the meaning is clear:

Geri had intended to complete the degree after the birth of her child, but she soon realised she wouldn't be able to <complete it>.

He didn't win the competition even though he had expected to <win it>.

After most verbs which are followed by *to* + infinitive, such as *ask, forget, promise* and *want* and *would like* in *if* or *wh-* clauses, we can omit *to*:

'You don't have to take the children to the cinema, you know.' 'But I promised <to>.'

'Shall we go to the cinema tonight?' 'Yes, if you want <to>.'

In questions and embedded questions, we often use the question word only and omit the clause:

'Dr Angelo said he was going on a call this afternoon.'

*'Did he say **where** <he was going>?' 'No, he didn't say where.'*

35

Practice

The key to these exercises is on page 372.

1 35.1, 35.2

There are several substitute words in this text, in *italics*. Find the word or phrase that each one refers to and write it below. The exercise begins with an example (0).

The clock on the platform was showing midnight as the train drew in. Miriam checked (0) *her* ticket against the sign on the window, opened the door to Coach H, climbed in and shut (1) *it* gently behind her.

The train was already reaching (2) *its* highest speed, thundering across country towards Warsaw, when Miriam dropped (3) *her* bags in the correct compartment. She thought briefly of the few kilometres already behind her and (4) *the many* ahead, then she bent to her bags. She lifted the two small (5) *ones* onto the overhead rack, but the large one was a different matter, so she pulled (6) *it* close to her seat and sat down.

Alone in the carriage, she contemplated her future. She hadn't expected (7) *this* so soon, but the job opportunity in Warsaw had come up unexpectedly. She'd always wanted to return to the city of her birth and (8) *that* of her parents, but hadn't thought she would (9) *do it* within two weeks of leaving college. At first she had discounted the job, so far away from home, and her parents had (10) *done so* too, but they had all spoken to her prospective employers at length on the phone, after (11) *which* all (12) *their* concerns were laid to rest. Miriam closed her eyes and allowed the rhythm of the speeding train to lull her to sleep.

0 her = ...*Miriam*.....
1 it = ...
2 its = ...
3 her = ...
4 the many = ...
5 ones = ...
6 it = ...
7 this = ...
8 that = ...
9 do it = ...
10 done so = ...
11 which = ...
12 their = ...

2 35.2

Complete this dialogue with the correct substitute words. (There may be more than one possibility.)

JENNA Have you seen the new clothes shop in the High Street?
SOPHIE The (1) .... opposite the station, you mean?
JENNA Yes, that's right. I went in (2) .... yesterday. It's fantastic! It's full of designer seconds and (3) .... of them are from really famous fashion designers.
SOPHIE Which (4) ....?
JENNA Oh, people like Nicole Farhi.
SOPHIE Wow! I love (5) ....! But you said seconds. Is there anything wrong with the clothes?
JENNA I couldn't find anything wrong with them. I don't know why these clothes are called seconds sometimes.
SOPHIE No, (6) .... Did you buy anything?
JENNA No, not yesterday. I tried on a really nice dress but it was a bit tight, so I'm going to lose a bit of weight first.
SOPHIE You're always saying (7) ....!
JENNA I know, but this time I'm really going to (8) .... Anyway, I said I'd give up smoking last year and I (9) .... Oh, I nearly forgot. Are you going to the conference next week?
SOPHIE I expect (10) .... I don't think I can get out of it.
JENNA Didn't you say you wanted to get a new suit before the next conference?

SOPHIE Oh, (11) .... I did! Perhaps I'll pop in to the shop at the weekend and see what they've got.

JENNA Well, if you (12) ...., give me a ring first. I've got some discount vouchers for ten per cent off and I can let you have (13) ....

SOPHIE (14) ....'s really nice of you. OK, I'll call you Saturday morning if I decide to go there and, if (15) .... I'll see you at the conference.

3 35.3

Cross out the words in these sentences that can be omitted. Cross out as many words as you can.

1 I told the students they could either take the exam in June or they could take it in December.
2 We can go to the theatre tonight if you want to go to the theatre.
3 The children were delighted with the Christmas lights and they wanted to see them turned on again.
4 Even though it is possible to go skiing in Scotland, the British have always been worse skiers than most Europeans have been.
5 'Why hasn't the new shopping centre been opened yet?' 'But it has been opened.'
6 'Will Julie be going to the club's New Year's party this year?' 'I think she gets back from holiday on 30th December, so she could be going.'
7 'Is the new restaurant in the High Street open on Sunday evenings?' 'I don't know. It might be open on Sunday evenings. The old one was open on Sunday evenings.'
8 We haven't earned any money this summer. I really expected us to earn some.
9 The young woman plays the violin and her brother plays the cello.
10 He told me that he was going to leave his wife and I asked him why he was going to leave her.
11 Baxter's sick tonight, which is unfortunate as he can play better than all the others can.
12 We thought that the old woman had been looking after the house, but she can't have been looking after it as she was in hospital at the time.

4 35.2, 35.3

Read the following text about the Inuit system of adoption, then complete these two tasks:

A Mark three more omissions with ⋏ and write the omitted words. The first omission is given as an example (0).

B Underline eleven more substitute words, then write the words they replace. The first substitution is given as an example (00).

0 The Inuit system of child adoption, although ⋏ archaic, appears much more humane ....*it is*....
00 than our <u>own</u> in the so-called civilised world, where childless couples must apply ....*system*....
1 through faceless agencies for the opportunity to adopt. They must undergo a series of ....
2 intrusive interviews and examinations and, if successful, will then be put on a waiting ....
3 list for an unspecified period of time. An Inuit couple wanting to adopt simply makes ....
4 it known and soon enough they will receive a call from a woman who is prepared to ....
5 give up her child. This may be because she already has too many children and does ....
6 not want another one, or the call may come from a relative or friend who wishes to ....
7 help someone less fortunate than themselves. Traditionally, the couple would be ....
8 asked if they would like the child and, if so, a simple handover would take place. ....
9 Today, however, this has been replaced by bureaucracy in the form of civil ....
10 registration, although the tradition itself has not. It survives even at the end of the ....
11 twentieth century. ....

5 ALL

In each of these pairs or groups of sentences, at least one of the choices is correct, and two or three may be. Tick the correct ones.

1 A He just came in and he sat down without even saying hello. ☐
B He just came in and sat down without even saying hello. ☐

2 How about packing up now and hitting the beach for an hour?
A Uh no, I don't really want. ☐
B Uh no, don't really want to. ☐
C Uh no, I don't really want to. ☐

3 Did you know that your son hasn't been to school for over a week, Mr Greene?
A But that's impossible! He must! ☐
B But that's impossible! He must have! ☐
C But that's impossible! He must have been! ☐

4 A You play the piano much better than the usual pianist. ☐
B You play the piano much better than the usual pianist plays. ☐
C You play the piano much better than the usual pianist does. ☐

5 I've decided to resign from the drama group.
A Why? ☐
B Why have you decided? ☐
C Why have you decided to do that? ☐

6 Barbara takes in stray dogs and cats, but she's much fonder of cats.
A She considers them far too obsequious. ☐
B She considers dogs far too obsequious. ☐

7 We love going to the Greek islands but we try to avoid ...
A the ones that attract the jet set. ☐
B the that attract the jet set. ☐
C those that attract the jet set. ☐

8 Adults often like hot, spicy food, whereas ...
A children usually prefer mild food. ☐
B children usually prefer mild. ☐
C children usually prefer mild one. ☐

9 All my American friends expected their team to win most of the track medals ...
A and we did too. ☐
B and we did it too. ☐
C and we did so too. ☐

10 Look! Jason can walk on his own!
A Oh, so he can! ☐
B Oh, so can he! ☐

6 ALL

Read the text below and think of the word which best fits each space (1–18). Use only one word in each space. In some cases you do not need to add a word at all (write '–' in these spaces). There are two examples at the beginning (0) and (00).

Have you ever sent an e-mail to a friend from work? Or have you sent a joke one (0) ...–... to a colleague on the office computer? Well, think again. (00) ...this... is exactly what Rupert Beverly and David Pennington (1) ...., and now they wish they hadn't (2) ....! They were sacked from an engineering company in the north of England for doing just (3) ....

Hang on – you may think – this is one small company in the UK. But (4) .... happens not only in less-regulated small companies but in large multinational (5) .... too. Eight sales staff at Cable and Wireless have recently lost (6) .... jobs after a complaint about an e-mail. Management claimed that it could have been construed as offensive, and while the sacked workers agreed that perhaps it could (7) ...., they insist that (8) .... wasn't pornography, as they knew it was a sackable offence to download this.

Regulations governing this area vary from country to country: at present the law in the USA allows companies to monitor staff e-mails and while (9) .... in the UK is currently not so strict, it looks as though it will follow the US model. In Germany, however, the law does not allow 'spying' on employees' personal e-mail, but at least one multinational (10) .... based there is taking advantage of the UK regulations by sending all e-mails to the UK to be monitored.

Civil rights organisations are concerned that monitoring e-mails infringes personal liberty and that it also undermines trust in the working environment. (11) .... want management to intercept and monitor e-mails only when (12) .... necessary, and to be able to prove that (13) .... was indeed necessary to do (14) ....

And what of Rupert and David? Well, (15) .... claim for unfair dismissal was rejected: the tribunal found that the company was within (16) .... rights to sack employees for sending joke e-mails, and also, more worryingly, (17) .... for the time wasted in (18) .... it. Watch out, Big Brother really is watching you now!

7 ALL

Read this text which has repetition. Correct to improve the style, using substitution and ellipsis.

Most people enjoy listening to music but few people realise the important ~~effects~~ and largely positive effects listening to music can have on us. We know that certain types of music are used to influence our emotions and influence our behaviour. For example, airlines use soothing music before a flight to relax passengers, especially passengers who may feel nervous about flying. You may have noticed how shops often play fast, rousing music (if you haven't noticed, you probably shop at the more old-fashioned type of store) – playing fast and rousing music tends to make us feel happier and more likely to spend money!

Music is also being used now as a psychiatric therapy. It seems to be particularly useful for eating disorders and addictions, but it is also useful for sufferers of post-traumatic stress syndrome. People attending group therapy sessions are invited to bring along their favourite tracks. Not everyone does, but the people who bring them along play them for the group. Playing them for the group creates a sense of belonging, as well as creating a more relaxed atmosphere for the therapy session.

36 Features of discourse

There are several principles and conventions which we follow in discourse (texts or conversations). This unit looks at how we organise information when we speak or write and the implications of this for word order, grammar and vocabulary. The unit goes on to describe other discourse features such as the use of linking words between sentences, stylistic devices and the choice of words appropriate to their context of use.

36.1 ORDERING INFORMATION

36.1A The information principle

When speaking in English we usually sequence words so that we move from something known (already mentioned or obvious from the context) at the beginning of the sentence to something new at the end:
(in these examples, known information is underlined, new information is in **bold**)

information obvious from the context → *you*; new information → ***John***

*'Do you know where **John** is?'*

*'He's in **the garden**.'*

information already mentioned → *He*; new information → ***the garden***

Notice how the pronoun *He* refers back to *John*; this kind of economic use of language is called 'cohesion' (▶ **Unit 35**).
When writing in English we usually organise the information in the same way that we do in speaking. Starting sentences with information which relates back to something already mentioned helps the text to 'flow' more smoothly and makes it easier for the reader to understand it:

*Another striking feature of the capital's squares and parks are **the plane trees**. The plane tree can reach **35 metres in height** and has **leaves similar to those of the maple**. It has a **vigorous and robust habit** and is **highly resistant to cold and air pollution**. These features make it **an ideal choice for city parks in northern Europe**.*

We do not usually put new information at the beginning (but ▶ **36.1C, D** below).

36.1B The end-weight principle

In English we prefer to put long and complex phrases at the end of a sentence. English prefers sentences to be 'light' at the beginning (before the main verb) and 'heavy' at the end. Long complex clauses also often contain new information, so this principle and the information principle reinforce each other:

*A striking feature of the central areas of the capital are **the elegant classical squares which were originally laid out by aristocratic developers in the eighteenth century**.*

Sentences with a heavy clause at the beginning can seem clumsy and be difficult to understand:

[***The elegant classical squares which were originally laid out by aristocratic developers in the eighteenth century*** *are a striking feature of the central areas of the capital.*]

❗ But the information principle is more important in text than the end-weight principle, so we can put a heavy clause at the beginning of a sentence if it contains familiar information linking it to the preceding text:

London has many public parks and squares which date from previous centuries. ***The elegant classical squares which were originally laid out by aristocratic developers in the eighteenth century*** *are a striking feature of the central areas of the capital.*

36.1C Focus

In English we can show which part of a sentence or clause contains the most important point or 'focus' by moving the important point to the beginning or end of the sentence – these are the two positions which appear most important to a reader or listener.

In this example *Jim* and *nightclub* are the focus – they seem the most important issues:

Jim *invited Lucy to the* ***nightclub****.*

If we want to put the focus on an item that doesn't naturally come at the beginning or end of the sentence (e.g. *Lucy*) we have to manipulate the grammar to bring the item to the front focus position. We call this 'fronting' (▶ **34.2**). For example, we can use cleft sentences (▶ **34.1**):

It was Lucy *that Jim invited to the nightclub.*

Lucy *was the girl that Jim invited to the nightclub.*

Similarly, we can give focus to something by moving it into the end focus position:

The girl that Jim invited to the nightclub was ***Lucy****.*

36.1D Contrast and emphasis

We sometimes need to break the principles of word order to create effects of emphasis and contrast. Because word order in English is usually fixed, we can emphasise something by moving it to an unfamiliar position. We often do this with adverbial expressions (▶ **34.2C**), objects and complements (▶ **34.2A**), and *that* and *to* infinitive phrases (▶ **34.1E**, **13.3**, **13.4**, **13.5**):

The facade of the house was blank and austere. [*But it was ornate and luxurious* ***inside****.*] → ***But inside*** *it was ornate and luxurious.*

[*I may be* ***old***], *but I'm not stupid.* → ***Old*** *I may be, but I'm not stupid.*

Priscilla invariably rejected impoverished suitors. [*Her only ambition was* ***to marry for money****.*] → ***To marry for money*** *was her only ambition.*

(For more information on word order with verbs ▶ **Unit 30**; with adverbs ▶ **Unit 24**.)

36.1E Manipulating grammar and vocabulary

In order to follow the ordering principles (▶ **36.1A, B** above) when we are writing we have to choose suitable vocabulary and grammar. As the subject usually comes at the beginning of a sentence in English the simplest way to organise a sentence is to choose a subject which links with the previous information:

Whenever possible, we pack all our furniture in ***flat packages****.* [***Transport*** *becomes cheaper because less space is taken up by* ***a flat pack*** *than a bulky one.*] → ***A flat pack*** *takes up less space than a bulky one, which means that transport becomes cheaper.*

We sometimes use a noun which summarises the previous information (for more information on 'nominalisation' ▶ **25.5B**):

The rioters threw petrol bombs at the embassy. ***<u>The situation</u>*** *was getting out of hand.*

We can choose alternative verbs or use the passive (▶ **8.4A**) so that the appropriate subject comes at the beginning:

Our neighbours got a good price for their ***car****.* [*The local garage bought it from them.*] → *They sold* ***it*** *to a local garage./****It*** *was bought by a local garage.*

'Guernica' *is a wonderful example of cubist art.* [*In 1937 Picasso painted* ***it****.*] → ***It*** *was painted by Picasso in 1937.*

We can also use introductory *it* (▶ **Unit 33**) and participle and infinitive phrases (▶ **Unit 13**) to put the familiar information at the beginning and new information at the end:

Fleming's behaviour was inexplicable. ***It was hard to believe*** *that he had become this savage with a bare knife.*

Steve went home. ***Walking towards his door****, he noticed a piece of paper left on the doorstep.*

36.2 DISCOURSE DEVICES

36.2A Linking expressions

We use various words and phrases at the beginning of a sentence to express a relationship between what we are about to say and what we have just said. (We also use words to link clauses within a sentence; for more information about these ▶ **30.3A, B**). The table below contains some common examples of sentence linkers:

types	examples	discourse examples
additive linkers (giving extra information)	*Furthermore,*[1] *Similarly,*[1] (= in the same way), *In addition, On top of this, What's more,*	*You can save yourself a full five per cent of interest with our new credit plan.* ***Furthermore****, we are offering no repayments for a year to customers who sign up before the end of the month.*
adversative linkers (introducing information which contrasts with what has been mentioned previously) [2]	*However,*[1] *Nevertheless,*[1] (= despite this) *On the other hand,*	*Your counsel has made a convincing case in mitigation, Mr Belgrave.* ***Nevertheless****, we feel that in a case of this gravity the only appropriate option is a custodial sentence.*
causal linkers (introducing the result of previous information)	*Consequently,*[1] *It follows from this,*[1] *For this reason, As a result, So,*	*Your repayments are now three months in arrears.* ***Consequently****, we have no option but to withdraw credit facilities immediately.*
temporal linkers (expressing a relationship of time or sequence with the previous information)	*Then, After that, An hour later, Finally, At last*	*The troops trudged for weeks through the snowy wastes.* ***Finally****, as they were nearing the point of exhaustion, they saw the faint lights of the city on the horizon.*

[1] We usually use these linkers in more formal English.

[2] These are often adverbs of contrast. (▶ **32.3B**)

36.2B Reference

A key feature of continuous text and of conversation is the use of reference words (▶ **Unit 35**) which tie different sentences together by making cross references backwards and forwards in the text. We generally do not repeat the same words:

Professor John Doherty gave the lecture this morning. [***Professor John Doherty's*** *theme was endorphin production in mammals.*]

We tend to avoid doing this because repetition is boring for the reader or listener and it is not considered stylish. A better alternative is partial repetition:

✔ *... Doherty's theme was endorphin production in mammals.*

We can often use a pronoun or replacement word which refers back to the earlier item:

*... His/****The lecturer****'s theme was endorphin production in mammals.*

We can also use pronouns or other substitute words (▶ **35.2**) and in some cases we can omit the repeated information (▶ **35.3**).

36.2C Parallelism

Although we try to avoid repeating words when we are writing a text (▶ **36.2B** above), a useful way of making a text cohesive is to use similar grammar in different sentences, for example the same tense or aspect, similar word order or repeating a particular grammatical form:

She is probably going to *fail the exam. And* ***she is probably going to*** *blame her teacher.*

Your world. ***To live*** *and sleep in.* ***To cook*** *and eat in.* ***To take*** *a shower, watch TV or maybe do some work in.*

❶ We avoid sudden changes in grammar as this often looks clumsy and it can make a written text difficult to understand:

[*I can't wait to lie on the sand. Swimming in the sea is great. To sunbathe is something I would love to do as well.*]

✔ *I can't wait to be lying on the sand, sunbathing and swimming in the sea.*

If we want to create a dramatic effect or make a strong contrast, we can repeat an unusual grammatical pattern. But we usually only use this device in narrative and fiction because in less literary contexts it can seem inappropriate:

Rarely had I *seen such a ramshackle boat. And* ***never had I*** *actually been expected to get on board one.*

36.2D Appropriate language

A key feature of the use of language which is appropriate to its context is the choice of vocabulary. Most English words are 'neutral' and we can use them in any situation. But some words are only appropriate, for example, in a formal situation and others only in an informal context. Compare these examples which say the same thing in different registers:

The ***show starts*** *at nine o'clock.* (neutral)
The ***performance commences*** *at nine o'clock.* (formal)
The ***show kicks off*** *at nine.* (informal)

Certain forms and grammatical patterns are more suitable for formal situations, e.g. passives (▶ **8.4D**), subjunctives (▶ **11.1B**), infinitive phrase subjects (▶ **13.3B**) and non-defining relative clauses (▶ **31.1D**). There are other patterns which we usually use for more informal situations, e.g. passives with *get* (▶ **8.1E**), sentences ending with prepositions (▶ **14.3B**), using verbs as nouns (▶ **25.5A**) and *it* cleft sentences with *when* and *where* (▶ **34.1B**).

Here is another set of examples which differ not only in choice of vocabulary but also in the choice of grammatical patterns:

I'm afraid I can't come because I'm busy tonight. (neutral)
I regret that I am unable to attend due to a prior engagement. (formal)
Sorry I can't make it but I'm a bit tied up tonight. (informal)

❶ In written English we usually do not mix formal and informal language in the same text unless we want to create a comic or ironic effect:

[*The Minister was unable to attend the reception* ***because he was a bit tied up****.*]

✔ *The Minister was unable to attend the reception* ***due to a prior engagement****.*

Practice

The key to these exercises is on page 372.

1 36.1

In the following passages the underlined phrases or sentences (0–7) do not conform with text writing principles. The main problem is the order of information. Rewrite these sentences appropriately, changing the grammar as necessary. The exercise begins with an example (0).

The Hubble Space Telescope

The Hubble Space Telescope was put into orbit by the American space shuttle *Discovery* in April 1990. (0) The earth is orbited by it at an altitude of 610 kilometres. (1) The light from space is not affected by interference from the earth's atmosphere at this height. As a result the Hubble telescope is at least ten times more accurate than telescopes on the ground and has a much greater range. (2) In our search for distant stars and planets this makes it the most useful tool.

The telescope is named after the most influential astronomer of the twentieth century, Edwin Hubble. Working at the Mount Wilson Observatory in Pasadena, (3) his close observation of the Andromeda Galaxy was used by the American astronomer to develop the theory that the universe is expanding. (4) Directly based on his ideas is the Big Bang theory, now accepted as the most likely explanation of the creation of the universe.

The Hubble Space Telescope has not had a smooth history. (5) Scientists at NASA discovered that the main mirror had become distorted and could not be used with any accuracy only two months after it went into orbit. Rather than abandon the project, NASA decided to find a way to resolve this problem. (6) COSTAR (corrective optics space telescope axial replacement) was the name of the solution. This was a device which contained ten smaller mirrors designed to compensate for the distortion in the telescope's main mirror. It cost $360 million to develop the technology and more than 30 hours of spacewalks by astronauts to fix the device. (7) The Hubble Space Telescope is now working correctly and sending its astonishing data back to earth, the repairs were completed in January 1994.

0 *It orbits the earth at an altitude of 610 kilometres.*
1 ....
2 ....
3 ....
4 ....
5 ....
6 ....
7 ....

2 36.1

Choose the best alternative, A or B, according to text ordering principles.

1 The witness gave the police details of her assailant's appearance. ... circulated throughout the metropolitan district.
   A The description was
   B The details of her assailant's appearance were

2 Della Jones, one of our best-loved singers, is well known for her opera repertoire. ...
   A Her greatest operatic roles have included Rosina in *Il Barbiere di Siviglia* and the title role in *La Cenerentola*.
   B Rosina in *Il Barbiere di Siviglia* and the title role in *La Cenerentola* are included among her greatest operatic roles.

3 One of the great comic stars of the 1960s was Walter Matthau. ...
   A Particularly noteworthy was Jack Lemmon's film work with him.
   B His film work with Jack Lemmon being particularly noteworthy.

4 If you're looking for a quiet holiday, forget about Ibiza. ...
   A It may be sun-drenched and beautiful but it isn't peaceful!
   B Sun-drenched and beautiful it may be, peaceful it isn't!

5 Elizabeth inherited a kingdom torn by religious strife. ...
   A Her first action was to try and pacify the rival fanatics.
   B Pacifying the rival fanatics was her first action.

6 Potential residents will find everything they need in the Dinglewood rest home in Harwich. ...
   A Among its features are twenty-four hour nursing care and luxurious private rooms.
   B Luxurious private rooms and twenty-four hour nursing care are among its features.

7 But I had nothing to do with it, Your Honour. ...
   A My twin brother was the one the police saw outside the warehouse.
   B The police saw my twin brother outside the warehouse.

8 Built in 1078 by Bishop Gundulf for William the Conqueror, the Tower of London is one of the oldest landmarks in the city. ...
   A Today its main claim to fame is the recently built Jewel House containing the fabulous crown jewels of Great Britain.
   B The recently built Jewel House containing the fabulous crown jewels of Great Britain is its main claim to fame today.

9 Birch trees can reach 30 metres in height and have a very vigorous growth pattern. ...
   A Damage can be caused to drains and house walls if they are too close to the particularly fast-growing roots.
   B The roots are particularly fast-growing and can cause damage if they are close to drains and house walls.

10 My rather unconventional sister turned up in the middle of the night without any warning. ... soon sent our peaceful little household into total turmoil.
   A My sister arriving unexpectedly in the night
   B Her sudden arrival

3 36.2

There is one mistake in each extract, 1–10. Some mistakes are incorrect linking words, some are incorrect use of vocabulary or grammar, and some are due to unnecessary repetition. Find each mistake and correct it.

1 *Dave – I'm off to Mum's for the weekend. Don't forget to activate the burglar alarm if you go out! See you Monday. Love Jane*

....

2 London is a vast sprawling metropolis containing millions of people over an area of several thousand square kilometres, much of which consists of endlessly monotonous suburbs. Consequently, many of the individual districts seem to have retained their own distinct and almost village-like identities.

....

3

Swimming in the morning and skiing in the afternoon. Dining on seafood in the evening and to fall asleep to the sound of lapping waves at night. There's nowhere like Andalucia. Call now for our brochure.

....

4

Ralph felt the icy wind on his back and wrapped his scarf more tightly around his neck. It was surprising how chilly the icy wind could be once one got a few miles out to sea.

....

5

Local residents are ready to take the matter to the police and the authorities. Nevertheless, they are going to write to their member of parliament to insist on a public inquiry into the affair.

....

6

To make a recording first insert a blank tape into the machine. Then select the channel you wish to record and set the counter to zero. You ought to press the red 'record' button and at the same time press the 'play' button.

....

7

8.00 Tonight's episode of *Changing Rooms* features a brave married couple from Darlington. The brave married couple allow their rather ham-fisted neighbours to redecorate their recently rebuilt conservatory in what the programme makers describe as 'tropical' style!

....

8

Policyholders wishing to make a claim under Section 3 should be prepared to provide receipts of purchase for all items. Items for which receipts cannot be provided will not be eligible for reinstatement except in really special circumstances and at the absolute discretion of the insurers.

....

9

To have made one great album is easy. To have made two is not so hard. But having made three is a rare feat indeed in today's easy-come, easy-go music business. Yes, Radiohead have pulled off the hat trick!

....

10

We moved into the new house today. Everything went pretty smoothly. The furniture van arrived bang on the dot of 10 and we spent an exhausting three hours unloading. At first, at one o'clock we were able to sit down on our own sofa in our own new living room!

....

4 ALL

Read the text about Paul Robeson and match the underlined phrases and sentences (1–8) with the features (A–H). (Note that underlined items 1–4 match text features A–D, and underlined items 5–8 match features E–H.) Write the numbers in the boxes.

Features

A Putting familiar information at the beginning by using a noun. ☐
B Giving extra focus to information by putting it at the front of the sentence. ☐
C Repeating a grammatical structure to give extra emphasis (parallelism). ☐
D Using a linking word to make a contrast with information in the previous sentence. ☐
E Familiar information at the beginning, new information at the end (the information principle). ☐
F Using a substitute word to avoid repetition. ☐
G Putting familiar information at the beginning by using the passive. ☐
H Long and complex phrases at the end (the end-weight principle). ☐

Paul Robeson was the first African American to gain international success in the 'white' world of Hollywood movies. He was born in 1898, the son of a Methodist minister and a runaway slave. (1) Highly intelligent, he won a scholarship to Columbia University where he qualified as a lawyer. (2) But there were few opportunities for black lawyers in the New York of the nineteen twenties and Robeson decided to pursue a career on the stage. He soon became one of the biggest stars on Broadway, taking the leading role in Eugene O'Neill's play *The Emperor Jones* in 1924. (3) Applauded for his acting ability and acclaimed for his remarkable physical presence on stage, Robeson went on to show the world his greatest talent, his superb deep bass singing voice, by taking the role of Joe in Jerome Kern's hit musical *Show Boat* in 1927. After a successful run in this musical he changed direction again by tackling Shakespeare, achieving rave reviews for his portrayal of Othello.

(4) Success on Broadway inevitably led to Hollywood and Robeson made his screen debut in the film version of *The Emperor Jones* in 1933. Word of his abilities soon spread outside the United States and (5) in 1935 the actor moved to England, where he starred in *Sanders of the River* and *King Solomon's Mines*.

Back in America Robeson starred in *Show Boat*, singing his famous song *Ol' Man River*. (6) A recording and singing career followed with Robeson popularising traditional negro spirituals, a form of religious folk song developed by black slaves in the American South. Robeson became increasingly involved in politics and in the nineteen fifties made a visit to the Soviet Union. It was an era of strong anti-communist feelings in America and when Robeson returned home his passport was cancelled and he was forced to stay in the United States for the next six years. (7) He was blacklisted by Hollywood and was unable to find work. (8) Robeson left the States in 1958 and began a new career as a concert performer in Europe. But he became seriously ill in the sixties and returned to New York. He died in Harlem in 1976.

5 ALL

Use the following notes to prepare a short article for a reference book about the samurai. Write one sentence only for each numbered set of notes, using connecting words and phrases as appropriate. You may add words and change the form of the words given in the notes but do not add any extra information. The first point has been expanded for you as an example (0).

The samurai – Warriors of Japan

0 s. = warrior class – founded by first 'shogun' (military ruler) Yoritomo – 1180
1 worked for shogun (wartime) ; employed by large landowners, ('daimyo') in peace
2 many rights & privileges: right to carry swords/ride horses etc.
3 exchange for rights: owed absolute loyalty > their daimyo (even extent expected – commit suicide when d. died)
4 this tradition – part of 'bushido' (= 'The Way of the Warrior'): strict code of honour – stressed importance: self-discipline & bravery
5 bushido based on peaceful beliefs of Zen Buddhism; despite this – helped s. become most ruthless, feared & brutal warriors in Asia
6 s. reached peak importance & influence – civil wars (16th century) – fought for rival warlords
7 peaceful years (after 1603) s. gradually lost military importance & many became administrators (not soldiers)
8 1867 last shogun (Tokugawa Keiki) resigned; Japan began modernise military forces; conscription & western army structure (introduced 1872)
9 s. no longer needed/wanted = result; remaining s. in Satsuma decide mount rebellion against government
10 Satsuma rebellion = disaster for s. – finally defeated by Imperial Army 1877

0 *The samurai were a warrior class founded by the first 'shogun' or military ruler, Yoritomo, in 1180.*

Key to diagnostic tests

Check your answers to the exercises in the diagnostic tests. Circle the reference numbers at the end of the line (e.g. ▶ **5.1C**) for any mistakes you made. Then turn to the relevant unit and study the sections where you made the mistakes.

TEST 1

1 enjoys, watches ▶ **1.1A, B, C**
2 doesn't use ▶ **1.1A, B**
3 Does, usually change ▶ **1.1A, C**
4 smokes ▶ **1.1C, 1.2C**
5 is staying ▶ **1.1C, 1.2B**
6 take ▶ **1.1C**
7 am feeding ▶ **1.1C, 1.2C**
8 does not usually send ▶ **1.1C**
9 mix, put ▶ **1.1D**
10 are turning ▶ **1.2D**
11 get, says ▶ **1.1E**
12 isn't playing ▶ **1.2B**
13 comes ▶ **1.2B**
14 are always losing ▶ **1.2C**
15 consists of ▶ **1.3A**
16 Do you think ▶ **1.3B**
17 are you thinking ▶ **1.3B**
18 is being ▶ **1.3B**
19 are tasting ▶ **1.3C**
20 guarantee ▶ **1.3D**
▶ **Unit 1, pages 46 to 53**

TEST 2

1 swim ▶ **2.1A**
2 stopped ▶ **2.1A**
3 jumped ▶ **2.1B**
4 ruled ▶ **2.1B**
5 were growing, was ▶ **2.2B**
6 were experiencing ▶ **2.2B**
7 was leaving ▶ **2.2D**
8 were working ▶ **2.2C**
9 had been running ▶ **2.2C**
10 was taking ▶ **2.2D**
11 had taken ▶ **2.3B**
12 had been ▶ **2.3B**
13 had already started ▶ **2.3C**
14 climbed ▶ **2.3C**
15 had expected ▶ **2.3D**
16 had been declining ▶ **2.4B**
17 had only used ▶ **2.4C**
18 use to have ▶ **2.5A**
19 used ▶ **2.5B**
20 used to be ▶ **2.5C**
▶ **Unit 2, pages 54 to 61**

TEST 3

1 has stood ▶ **3.1B, 3.2A**
2 wrote ▶ **3.1B, 3.2B**
3 didn't see ▶ **3.1D, 3.2B**
4 has increased ▶ **3.1D**
5 has spent ▶ **3.1D, 3.2D**
6 has surrounded ▶ **3.1E**
7 thought ▶ **3.2E**
8 have been eating ▶ **3.3B**
9 has welcomed ▶ **3.3B, 3.4A**
10 has risen ▶ **3.4C**
11 ~~have been waited~~ → have waited/have been waiting ▶ **3.1A, 3.3A**
12 ~~since two years~~ → for two years ▶ **3.1B**
13 ~~were~~ → have been ▶ **3.1B, 3.2B**
14 ~~already announced~~ → has already announced ▶ **3.1C**
15 ~~has imposed~~ → imposed ▶ **3.1D, 3.2D**
16 ~~have been~~ → were ▶ **3.1D, 3.2A**
17 ~~is growing~~ → has been growing/has grown ▶ **3.3B, 3.1B**
18 ~~has been playing~~ → has played ▶ **3.3B, 3.4B**
19 ~~I've travelled~~ → I've been travelling ▶ **3.3C, 3.4C**
20 ~~has been recording~~ → has recorded ▶ **3.3C, 3.4D**
▶ **Unit 3, pages 62 to 69**

TEST 4

1 will find ▶ **4.1A**
2 'll probably sell ▶ **4.1A, 4.4C**
3 are going to win ▶ **4.1B**
4 's going to rain ▶ **4.1B**
5 'll be skiing ▶ **4.1C**
6 'll have been married ▶ **4.1D**
7 'll have been living/'ll have lived ▶ **4.1D**
8 'll just finish/'m just going to finish ▶ **4.2A, B**
9 shall we have ▶ **4.2A**
10 will come/am going to come ▶ **4.2A, B**
11 'm going to spend ▶ **4.2B**
12 're going to build ▶ **4.2B**
13 is coming ▶ **4.3A**
14 'm staying ▶ **4.3A**
15 'll be making/'re going to make ▶ **4.3B, 4.2B**
16 will you be staying/are you going to stay ▶ **4.3B, 4.2B**
17 takes off ▶ **4.4A**
18 will be/is ▶ **4.4B, A**
19 will be playing ▶ **4.4B**
20 pay ▶ **4.4D**
▶ **Unit 4, pages 72 to 79**

TEST 5

1 b ▶ **5.1A**

2 a ▶ **5.1A**

3 a ▶ **5.1B**

4 c ▶ **5.1C**

5 b ▶ **5.1C**

6 a ▶ **5.1D**

7 b ▶ **5.2A**

8 a ▶ **5.3A**

9 c ▶ **5.3B**

10 b ▶ **5.3A**

11 b, c ▶ **5.1A, B**

12 a, b ▶ **5.1A, D**

13 b, c ▶ **5.1C**

14 a, c ▶ **5.1C**

15 a, b ▶ **5.1C**

16 a, b ▶ **5.1D**

17 b, c ▶ **5.2A**

18 a, b ▶ **5.2A, B**

19 a, b ▶ **5.3A, B**

20 a, c ▶ **5.3A, B**

▶ **Unit 5, pages 80 to 85**

TEST 6

1 a, b ▶ **6.1A, C**

2 b, c ▶ **6.1A, E**

3 a, c ▶ **6.1B, 6.3C**

4 a, c ▶ **6.1C**

5 b, c ▶ **6.1C, 6.3A**

6 a, b ▶ **6.1D**

7 a, c ▶ **6.1E**

8 a, b ▶ **6.1E**

9 a, c ▶ **6.2B**

10 b, c ▶ **6.2B**

11 b, c ▶ **6.3A**

12 a, c ▶ **6.3A**

13 not to leave ▶ **6.1A**

14 Not having seen ▶ **6.1A**

15 Not many/Few ▶ **6.1B**

16 neither to go on a cruise nor to visit the Pyramids. ▶ **6.1D**

17 don't believe that there is/believe that there isn't ▶ **6.1E**

18 Haven't you seen ▶ **6.2A**

19 didn't deny/admitted ▶ **6.3B**

20 dishonest ▶ **6.3C**

▶ **Unit 6, pages 88 to 95**

TEST 7

1 ~~What means 'heliotrope'?~~ → What does 'heliotrope' mean? ▶ **7.1A**

2 ~~you had been~~ → had you been ▶ **7.1A**

3 ✔ ▶ **7.1B**

4 ~~What did happen?~~ → What happened? ▶ **7.1C**

5 ✔ ▶ **7.1C**

6 ✔ ▶ **7.1D**

7 ~~Yes,~~ → No, ▶ **7.2A**

8 ~~don't we?~~ → shall we? ▶ **7.2B**

9 ✔ ▶ **7.2C**

10 ~~what time does the train from Croydon arrive?~~ → what time the train from Croydon arrives? ▶ **7.3A**

11 ~~if or not the tree roots will affect~~ → if the tree roots will affect the foundations (or not)/whether or not the tree roots will affect ▶ **7.3A**

12 ✔ ▶ **7.3A**

13 ~~Could you tell me where~~ (*too formal/tentative for situation*) → Where did ▶ **7.3B**

14 ~~Did they?~~ → Didn't they? ▶ **7.4A**

15 ✔ ▶ **7.4B**

16 won't they? ▶ **7.2A**

17 oughtn't we?/shouldn't we? ▶ **7.2B**

18 need she?/does she? ▶ **7.2B**

19 is he? ▶ **7.2C**

20 will you? ▶ **7.2D**

▶ **Unit 7, pages 96 to 103**

TEST 8

1 A pay rise has been offered to the workers. ▶ **8.1A**

2 The entire fleet is being overhauled. ▶ **8.1B**

3 The contestants were made to dress in ridiculous outfits. ▶ **8.1B**

4 We should have been warned in advance. ▶ **8.1B**

5 Advice having been taken, it was decided not to proceed. ▶ **8.2A**

6 To be buried at sea was my father's final wish. ▶ **8.2B**

7 We regret not having been/being informed of the landlord's decision. ▶ **8.2A**

8 I have/get my car serviced every six months./I have the garage service my car every six months. ▶ **8.3A**

9 We will have the carriers return the goods to your clients by Friday./We will have the goods returned to your clients by the carriers by Friday. ▶ **8.3A**

10 Susy's getting her car repaired free of charge! ▶ **8.3B**

11 Get that computer repaired as soon as you possibly can. ▶ **8.3C**

12 The bathroom hasn't been cleaned for weeks! ▶ **8.4C**

13 a ▶ **8.1E**

14 b ▶ **8.1C, 8.4C, D**

15 b ▶ **8.1D**

16 a ▶ **8.1D**

17 a ▶ **8.4A**

18 b ▶ **8.4B, D**

19 a ▶ **8.1A**

20 a ▶ **8.4B**

▶ **Unit 8, pages 104 to 111**

TEST 9

1 ~~said she.~~ → she said. ▶ **9.1A**

2 ~~He told that~~ → He said that/He told us/me that ▶ **9.2A**

3 ~~I felt I~~ → she felt she ▶ **9.2B**

4 ~~tomorrow morning~~ → the next/following morning ▶ **9.2B**

5 ✔ ▶ **9.2C** (*also possible:* when he gets home ▶ **9.2D**)

6 ~~she had still been young.~~ → she was/were still young. ▶ **9.2D**

7 ✔ ▶ **9.2D**

8 ~~said if~~ → asked if/wanted to know if ... ▶ **9.3A**

9 ~~had started the pain.~~ → the pain had started. ▶ **9.3B**

10 ~~if or not there was a swimming pool at the villa.~~ → whether or not there was a swimming pool at the villa/if there was a swimming pool at the villa or not. ▶ **9.3B**

11 ~~don't abdicate.~~ → not to abdicate. ▶ **9.4B**

12 ~~to have taken part~~ → taking part/having taken part ▶ **9.5B**

13 (that) he would remember 1st March 2000 as a great day for the nation. ▶ **9.2B, C**

14 (that) publication might be delayed by one week. ▶ **9.2E** (*also possible:* may be delayed ▶ **9.2D**)

15 (that) I must/had to lose at least 20 kilos./to lose at least 20 kilos. ▶ **9.2E**

16 (that) intelligent life does not exist in our universe. ▶ **9.2D**

17 (that) the Ming Dynasty lasted/had lasted for almost 300 years. ▶ **9.2D**

18 when she/we wanted the sofa to be delivered. ▶ **9.3B**

19 that it was stupid behaviour for a cyclist. ▶ **9.3B**

20 to do at least four hours' training a day. ▶ **9.4B, 9.5B**

▶ **Unit 9, pages 112 to 119**

TEST 10

1 ✔ ▶ **10.1A**

2 If the bill is passed by both parliamentary houses, then it becomes law. (*insert comma*) ▶ **10.1A**

3 ~~had~~ → have ▶ **10.1B, 10.3, 10.4**

4 ✔ ▶ **10.2A**

5 ✔ ▶ **10.2B**

6 ~~will charge~~ → charges ▶ **10.3A**

7 ~~Are you unhappy~~ → If you are unhappy/Should you be unhappy ▶ **10.3C, 10.4C**

8 ✔ ▶ **10.3A**

9 ✔ ▶ **10.3A** (*or:* the transfer takes ▶ **10.2A**)

10 ~~are~~ → were ▶ **10.4A** (*or:* ~~would~~ → will ▶ **10.3A, B**)

11 ✔ ▶ **10.4A, C**

12 ~~was~~ (*often considered incorrect*) → were ▶ **10.4A**

13 ~~would have waited~~ → had waited ▶ **10.5A, B** (*but* ✔ *in US English*)

14 ~~hadn't been~~ → had been ▶ **10.5B**

15 ~~wouldn't renew~~ → wouldn't have renewed ▶ **10.6A**

16 ✔ ▶ **10.6B**

17 ~~unless you made~~ → if you didn't make ▶ **10.7A**

18 ✔ ▶ **10.7C**

19 ~~Even they~~ → Even if they ▶ **10.7D**

20 ~~whether we take remedial steps now.~~ → whether or not we take remedial steps now./whether we take remedial steps now or not. ▶ **10.7E**

▶ **Unit 10, pages 120 to 129**

TEST 11

1 ✔ (*or:* ~~were~~ → was) ▶ **11.2B, C**

2 ~~would have~~ → had ▶ **11.3C**

3 ✔ ▶ **11.1A,B**

4 ✔ ▶ **11.3E**

5 ~~didn't act~~ → stopped acting ▶ **11.2C**

6 ~~would have been~~ → had been/could have been ▶ **11.3C**

7 ~~lives~~ → live ▶ **11.1C**

8 If only I had known. (omit *that*) ▶ **11.3E**

9 b ▶ **11.2A, 11.3B**

10 a ▶ **11.2C**

11 a ▶ **11.2D**

12 b ▶ **11.2F**

13 b ▶ **11.3A**

14 a ▶ **11.3D**

15 started doing/did your homework. ▶ **11.2C**

16 had been invited, would you have gone? ▶ **11.2D**

17 didn't bring that smelly dog into this house. ▶ **11.2E**

18 wear natural fabrics. ▶ **11.2E**

19 he knows what he is talking about. ▶ **11.2F**

20 would stop talking with your mouth full. ▶ **11.3C**

▶ **Unit 11, pages 130 to 137**

TEST 12

1 no parking ▶ **12.1A**

2 to succeed ▶ **12.2A**

3 to make ▶ **12.2B**

4 helping ▶ **12.1A**

5 his leaving (him leaving *is acceptable in informal English*) ▶ **12.1B**

6 to boost ▶ **12.2B**

7 to find ▶ **12.2B**

8 to help ▶ **12.2C**

9 meeting ▶ **12.3A**

10 the children seeing ▶ **12.3A**

11 to write ▶ **12.2C**
12 seeing/to see ▶ **12.3C**
13 to set ▶ **12.3D**
14 to hurt ▶ **12.3D**
15 making ▶ **12.3D**
16 dancing ▶ **12.3D**
17 to announce ▶ **12.3D**
18 building ▶ **12.3E**
19 ~~The dispensing medical~~ → The dispensing of medical ▶ **12.1B**
20 ✔ ▶ **12.1B**
21 ~~is sure to looking~~ → is sure to look/be looking ▶ **12.2C**
22 ~~found making~~ → found him making ▶ **12.3A**
23 ~~taking~~ → to take ▶ **12.3A**
24 ~~the judge ordered to pay~~ → the judge ordered us/you/him/her/them to pay ▶ **12.3B**
25 ✔ ▶ **12.3C**

▶ **Unit 12, pages 140 to 147**

TEST 13

1 Not owning ▶ **13.1A, 13.2B**
2 author ▶ **13.1B**
3 bought ▶ **13.2A**
4 to walk ▶ **13.2A, 13.4A**
5 opening ▶ **13.2C**
6 for the company ▶ **13.3B**
7 to find ▶ **13.4B**
8 speaking ▶ **13.5A**
9 having been refused ▶ **13.1A, C, 13.2B**
10 Not being ▶ **13.1A, 13.2B**
11 Serviced ▶ **13.1A, 13.2B**
12 completed ▶ **13.1C**
13 left ▶ **13.2A**
14 Not having kept ▶ **13.2B, C**
15 Living ▶ **13.2C**
16 Having passed ▶ **13.2C**
17 not to have applied ▶ **13.3A, 13.4A**
18 to sell ▶ **13.4A**
19 to access ▶ **13.4B**
20 to be ▶ **13.5A**

▶ **Unit 13, pages 148 to 155**

TEST 14

1 was made up by him. ▶ **14.1A**
2 Keep it up. ▶ **14.2B**
3 stick strictly to ▶ **14.3A, 14.5C**
4 go with it. ▶ **14.3A, 14.5C**
5 ran into him ▶ **14.3A, 14.5C**
6 which our movement stands for./for which our movement stands. ▶ **14.3B**
7 put up with it. ▶ **14.4A**
8 let her in on it. ▶ **14.4A**
9 ~~by head office over~~ → over by head office ▶ **14.1A**
10 ~~breakout~~ → outbreak ▶ **14.1A**
11 ~~left by his ex-girlfriend out~~ → left out by his ex-girlfriend ▶ **14.1A**
12 ~~not give away~~ → not reveal (give away *is an inappropriate verb in a formal context*) ▶ **14.1B**
13 ~~activate~~ → turn on/switch on (activate *is an inappropriate verb in an informal context*) ▶ **14.1B**
14 ~~down the floor and~~ → down (on the floor) and ▶ **14.2A**
15 ✔ ▶ **14.2A**
16 ~~took off the ground at incredible speed.~~ → took off (from the ground) at incredible speed. ▶ **14.2A, B, 14.5A**
17 ~~brought recently in~~ → recently brought in ▶ **14.2B, 14.5B**
18 ✔ ▶ **14.3B, 14.5C**
19 ✔ ▶ **14.4A**
20 ✔ ▶ **14.4A, 14.5D**

▶ **Unit 14, pages 156 to 163**

TEST 15

1 ~~apologise to~~ → apologise to her/him ▶ **15.1A**
2 ~~sit~~ → sitting ▶ **15.1B**
3 ✔ ▶ **15.1B, 15.5D**
4 ~~to~~ → with ▶ **15.1C**
5 ~~astonished at that her boyfriend had behaved~~ → astonished that her boyfriend had behaved/astonished at her boyfriend having behaved ▶ **15.1D**
6 ~~if~~ → whether ▶ **15.1E**
7 ~~quarrelled his wife~~ → quarrelled with his wife ▶ **15.2A**
8 ~~on you their party costumes.~~ → on you for their party costumes. ▶ **15.2A, 15.5A**
9 ✔ ▶ **15.2B**
10 ✔ ▶ **15.2C**
11 ~~provide Sam for a room~~ → provide Sam with a room/provide a room for Sam ▶ **15.2C, 15.5B**
12 ~~me all the details.~~ → all the details to me. ▶ **15.2C**
13 ✔ ▶ **15.3A**
14 ~~demanded for~~ → demanded ▶ **15.3B**
15 ~~growing.~~ → growth. ▶ **15.3C, 15.5C**
16 ✔ ▶ **15.4A, 15.5D**
17 ~~furious by~~ → furious at/about ▶ **15.4B, 15.5D**
18 ~~scared by~~ → scared of ▶ **15.4B**
19 ✔ ▶ **15.4B**
20 ✔ ▶ **15.4B, 15.5D**

▶ **Unit 15, pages 164 to 173**

TEST 16

1 ~~can~~ → will be able to ▶ **16.1A**
2 ~~can't have been able~~ → haven't been able ▶ **16.1A**
3 ~~is able to be~~ → can be ▶ **16.1A**
4 ✔ ▶ **16.1B**
5 ~~could~~ → was able to ▶ **16.1B**
6 ~~could warn~~ → could have warned ▶ **16.1B**
7 ✔ ▶ **16.1B**
8 ~~can't~~ → couldn't ▶ **16.1B**
9 ~~can~~ → may/might/could ▶ **16.2A**
10 ~~could be~~ → could have been ▶ **16.2B**
11 ✔ ▶ **16.2A**
12 ~~can~~ → could/may/might ▶ **16.2A**
13 ✔ ▶ **16.2A**
14 ~~May you get~~ → Could/Might you get/Is it possible you will get ▶ **16.2A**
15 ✔ ▶ **16.2A**
16 ✔ ▶ **16.2C**
17 ~~couldn't steal~~ → couldn't have stolen ▶ **16.2B**
18 ~~can~~ → could/might ▶ **16.2A**
19 ✔ ▶ **16.3A**
20 ✔ ▶ **16.3A**
21 ~~Am I able to use~~ → Can/Could/May/Might I use ▶ **16.3B, 16.4A**
22 ✔ ▶ **16.3B**
23 ~~could~~ → was able to ▶ **16.4B**
24 ✔ ▶ **16.3B**
25 ~~might not~~ → may not/can't ▶ **16.4A**

▶ **Unit 16, pages 174 to 181**

TEST 17

1 Having to ▶ **17.1A**
2 ought to ▶ **17.1A, B**
3 have to ▶ **17.1B**
4 have to ▶ **17.1B**
5 shouldn't have ▶ **17.1B**
6 need ▶ **17.1C**
7 are supposed to ▶ **17.1D**
8 couldn't go ▶ **17.2A, B**
9 are not allowed to ▶ **17.2B**
10 must not have ▶ **17.2B**
11 needn't ▶ **17.3A**
12 don't have to ▶ **17.3B**
13 didn't need to show ▶ **17.3B**
14 better ▶ **17.4A**
15 should ▶ **17.4B**
16 had better not ▶ **17.4B**
17 be raining ▶ **17.5A**
18 shouldn't ▶ **17.5B**
19 must have ▶ **17.5B**
20 had to have ▶ **17.5B**

▶ **Unit 17, pages 182 to 189**

TEST 18

1 would be ▶ **18.1B**
2 'll be driving ▶ **18.1C**
3 won't have started ▶ **18.1D**
4 will eat/eat ▶ **18.2A**
5 will act ▶ **18.3A**
6 won't book ▶ **18.3A**
7 would always help ▶ **18.3B, 18.2B**
8 would not reveal ▶ **18.3B**
9 Shall I make ▶ **18.4A**
10 shall we do ▶ **18.4B**
11 Would you be ▶ **18.4C**
12 would like ▶ **18.5A**
13 b ▶ **18.1A**
14 a ▶ **18.1C**
15 a ▶ **18.2A**
16 b ▶ **18.2B**
17 b ▶ **18.4D**
18 b ▶ **18.4E**
19 a ▶ **18.5A**
20 b ▶ **18.5B**

▶ **Unit 18, pages 190 to 197**

TEST 19

1 ~~were painting the staircase and were tiling the bathroom.~~ → painting the staircase and tiling the bathroom. ▶ **19.1A**
2 ~~its~~ → it's ▶ **19.1B**
3 ✔ ▶ **19.2B**
4 ~~to have got~~ → to have ▶ **19.4B**
5 ✔ ▶ **19.3B**
6 ~~He's watching~~ → He was watching. ▶ **19.1B**
7 ✔ ▶ **19.1B**
8 ~~have got~~ → have/get ▶ **19.4B**
9 ~~really do some~~ → really do with some ▶ **19.3C**
10 ✔ ▶ **19.2B**
11 ~~A shower was had by John~~ → John had a shower ▶ **19.3B**
12 ✔ ▶ **19.3A**
13 ~~can have got~~ → can have ▶ **19.4B**
14 ~~gotten~~ → got (*in British English*) ✔ (*in US English*) ▶ **19.4B**
15 ~~have got~~ → have ▶ **19.4B**

▶ **Unit 19, pages 200 to 207**

TEST 20

1 makes ▶ **20.1A**
2 has made/makes ▶ **20.1A**
3 have done ▶ **20.1A**
4 had made ▶ **20.1A**
5 do ▶ **20.1A**
6 doing ▶ **20.1B**
7 do ▶ **20.1B**
8 make ▶ **20.1B**
9 taken ▶ **20.1C**
10 took ▶ **20.1C**
11 been ▶ **20.1D**
12 lie ▶ **20.1E**
13 laid ▶ **20.1E**
14 lay ▶ **20.1E**
15 speaks ▶ **20.1F**

16 spoke ▶ **20.1F**
17 talking ▶ **20.1F**
18 raise ▶ **20.1G**
19 arisen ▶ **20.1G**
20 rising ▶ **20.1G**
21 stole ▶ **20.1H**
22 lend ▶ **20.2A**
23 bringing ▶ **20.2B**
24 took ▶ **20.2B**
25 fetching ▶ **20.2B**

▶ **Unit 20, pages 208 to 215**

TEST 21

1 ~~historics~~ → historic ▶ **21.1A**
2 ~~young's~~ → young ▶ **21.1A**
3 ✔ → **21.1A**
4 ~~What amazing!~~ → How amazing!/What amazing news! ▶ **21.1A**
5 ~~A plant being built outside the town is chemical.~~ → A chemical plant is being built outside the town./The plant being built outside the town is a chemical one. ▶ **21.1B**
6 ~~the asleep children~~ → the sleeping children/the children who are asleep ▶ **21.1C**
7 ~~alive animals~~ → live/living animals/animals who/which/that are alive ▶ **21.1C**
8 ~~negative anything~~ → anything negative ▶ **21.1D**
9 ✔ ▶ **21.1D**
10 ✔ ▶ **21.1D**
11 ~~involved people~~ → people involved ▶ **21.1D**
12 ✔ ▶ **21.2A**
13 ~~provided security boxes~~ → security boxes provided ▶ **21.2A**
14 ~~worried~~ → worrying ▶ **21.2B**
15 ~~lost~~ → losing ▶ **21.2B**
16 ~~speaking Spanish~~ → Spanish-speaking ▶ **21.2C**
17 ~~dining mahogany table~~ → mahogany dining table ▶ **21.3A**
18 ~~Victorian wonderful~~ → wonderful Victorian ▶ **21.3A**
19 ✔ ▶ **21.3B**
20 ~~well-informed and honest, capable.~~ → well-informed, honest and capable ▶ **21.3C**

▶ **Unit 21, pages 216 to 223**

TEST 22

1 ~~slimer~~ → slimmer ▶ **22.1A**
2 ~~than I~~ → than me/than I am ▶ **22.1A**
3 ✔ (*but also* ~~much more lively~~ → much livelier) ▶ **22.1B**
4 ~~realer~~ → more real ▶ **22.1B**
5 ✔ ▶ **22.1B**
6 ~~most proudest~~ → proudest/the most proud ▶ **22.1B, D**
7 ✔ (*but also* ~~the most unhappy~~ → the unhappiest) ▶ **22.1B**
8 ✔ ▶ **22.1F**
9 ~~eldest~~ → oldest ▶ **22.1C**
10 ✔ ▶ **22.1C**
11 ~~lots~~ → a lot/considerably/much/a great deal/even/far more ▶ **22.1D**
12 ~~of~~ → in ▶ **22.1A**
13 ~~worse~~ → bad ▶ **22.2A**
14 ✔ ▶ **22.3A**
15 ~~angrier~~ → more angry ▶ **22.3C**
16 Of all the modems (in our catalogue), the *Hyperlink* is by far the fastest/the fastest by far. ▶ **22.1D**
17 Jan is no better/Jan is no worse than Lucy at tennis. ▶ **22.1E**
18 Getting a made-to-measure suit was not nearly as expensive as I expected. ▶ **22.2B**
19 It was so cold that I couldn't open the lock. ▶ **22.2C**
20 The more frustrated he becomes, the angrier he gets. ▶ **22.3B**

▶ **Unit 22, pages 224 to 231**

TEST 23

1 ✔ ▶ **23.1A**
2 very enormous ▶ **23.2A**
3 ✔ ▶ **23.1B**
4 more boiling ▶ **23.2A**
5 slightly huge ▶ **23.2C**
6 ✔ ▶ **23.2D**
7 ✔ ▶ **23.2C**
8 ✔ ▶ **23.3A**
9 ✔ ▶ **23.3A**
10 absolutely ugly ▶ **23.1B**
11 ✔ ▶ **23.3B**
12 slightly free ▶ **23.2C**
13 c ▶ **23.1B**
14 c ▶ **23.1B**
15 a ▶ **23.1B**
16 b ▶ **23.1C**
17 a ▶ **23.2B**
18 a ▶ **23.2B**
19 b ▶ **23.2C**
20 c ▶ **23.1D**

▶ **Unit 23, pages 232 to 239**

TEST 24

1 highly ▶ **24.1A, B**
2 deep ▶ **24.1B**
3 roughly fifty ▶ **24.2A**
4 faster ▶ **24.2B**
5 Yesterday I only slept ▶ **24.3A, B**
6 I get paid weekly, ▶ **24.3B**
7 Here lies the tomb ▶ **24.3B**
8 usually arrives ▶ **24.3C**
9 is often ▶ **24.3C**
10 still don't ▶ **24.3C**
11 trading any longer ▶ **24.3D**
12 hardly ever go out. ▶ **24.3D**
13 behaved badly ▶ **24.3D**
14 I thought his performance was pretty good. ▶ **24.2A**
15 The patient's body is now almost entirely free of symptoms. ▶ **24.2A**

16 These days I probably take my health more seriously. ▶ **24.3A**

17 She's my worst enemy and I really don't like her./She's really my worst enemy and I don't like her. ▶ **24.3C**

18 Emotionally rejected, Harriet turned to food for comfort./ Rejected emotionally, Harriet turned to food for comfort. ▶ **24.4A**

19 Incidentally, I bumped into your brother at the supermarket. ▶ **24.4B**

20 I understood everything because the teacher answered the question clearly. ▶ **24.4B**

▶ **Unit 24, pages 240 to 247**

TEST 25

1 ✔ ▶ **25.1B**

2 pianos ▶ **25.2A**

3 phenomena ▶ **25.2B**

4 MPs ▶ **25.2B**

5 kitchen scales ▶ **25.2C**

6 advice ▶ **25.3A**

7 fewer (less *is possible only in informal English*) ▶ **25.3A**

8 a stone ▶ **25.3B**

9 ✔ ▶ **25.3C**

10 ✔ ▶ **25.4A**

11 has ▶ **25.4A**

12 is ▶ **25.4B**

13 was ▶ **25.4B**

14 it's ▶ **25.4C**

15 is ▶ **25.4C**

16 ✔ ▶ **25.4D**

17 ✔ ▶ **25.4D**

18 a shout ▶ **25.5A**

19 The attack on the Minister was ▶ **25.5B**

20 outbreak ▶ **25.5A**

▶ **Unit 25, pages 248 to 255**

TEST 26

1 ~~on a side~~ → on the side ▶ **26.1A**

2 ✔ ▶ **26.1B**

3 ~~their's~~ → their ▶ **26.1A**

4 ✔ ▶ **26.1C**

5 ✔ ▶ **26.1C**

6 ~~sister's in law's~~ → sister-in-law's ▶ **26.1C**

7 ~~Lennon's and~~ → Lennon and ▶ **26.1C**

8 ✔ (*but also* of Professor Grigson's) ▶ **26.1D**

9 ~~a friend of me~~ → a friend of mine ▶ **26.1D**

10 ~~the new car of Hilary~~ → Hilary's new car ▶ **26.2A**

11 ~~the youngest daughter of Mr Granger~~ → Mr Granger's youngest daughter ▶ **26.2A**

12 ~~the local paper of today~~ → today's local paper ▶ **26.2A**

13 ✔ ▶ **26.2A**

14 ✔ ▶ **26.2A**

15 ✔ ▶ **26.2A**

16 ~~the house of my brother~~ → my brother's (house) ▶ **26.2A**

17 ✔ ▶ **26.2A**

18 ~~for the sake of heaven~~ → for heaven's sake ▶ **26.2A**

19 ~~anthropology's history~~ → the history of anthropology ▶ **26.2B**

20 ~~crowd's cheers~~ → cheers of the crowd ▶ **26.2B**

21 ~~April the thirteenth's morning~~ → the morning of April the thirteenth ▶ **26.2B**

22 ~~the famous serial killer's arrest~~ → the arrest of the famous serial killer ▶ **26.2B**

23 ✔ ▶ **26.2C**

24 ✔ ▶ **26.2C**

25 ~~the short stories' collection of Graham Greene~~ → the/a collection of short stories by Graham Greene/Graham Greene's collection of short stories ▶ **26.2D**

26 ~~my expensive wife's car~~ → my wife's expensive car ▶ **26.3A**

27 ✔ ▶ **26.3A**

28 ~~estate's agent's~~ → estate agent's ▶ **26.3B**

29 ~~maker of dresses~~ → dressmaker ▶ **26.3C**

30 ✔ (*but also* one year's sabbatical) ▶ **26.3C**

▶ **Unit 26, pages 256 to 263**

TEST 27

1 ~~its~~ → the dog's (dishes) ▶ **27.1A**

2 ~~our!~~ → ours! ▶ **27.1A, B**

3 ~~E-mails they have become~~ → E-mails have become ▶ **27.1C**

4 ~~to eat them~~ → to eat ▶ **27.1C**

5 ✔ ▶ **27.1D**

6 ~~you and I~~ → you and me ▶ **27.1D**

7 ✔ ▶ **27.1E**

8 ~~a one~~ → one ▶ **27.1G**

9 ~~I've enjoyed very much~~ → I've enjoyed it/myself very much. ▶ **27.2A**

10 ~~in remembering themselves what~~ → in remembering what ▶ **27.2B**

11 ✔ ▶ **27.2C**

12 ~~themselves~~ → each other ▶ **27.2D**

13 ✔ ▶ **27.3A**

14 ~~seem~~ → seems ▶ **27.4A**

15 a ✔ b ✘ c ✔ ▶ **27.1C**

16 a ✔ b ✘ (*too formal*) c ✔ (*but only if the household is mainly female*) ▶ **27.1F**

17 a ✔ (*but unlikely if the speaker is the pet owner*) b ✔ c ✘ ▶ **27.1F**

18 a ✔ b ✘ c ✔ ▶ **27.2A**

19 a ✔ b ✔ c ✘ ▶ 27.2D
20 a ✔ b ✔ c ✔ ▶ 27.3A
▶ **Unit 27, pages 264 to 271**

TEST 28

1 the ▶ **28.1B**
2 The ▶ **28.1C**
3 the ▶ **28.1C**
4 the ▶ **28.1C**
5 – ▶ **28.1D**
6 the ▶ **28.1D**
7 – ▶ **28.1D**
8 a ▶ **28.1E**
9 the ▶ **28.1E**
10 – ▶ **28.1E**
11 an ▶ **28.1A**
12 a ▶ **28.1C**
13 A/– ▶ **28.1E**
14 those ▶ **28.2A**
15 This/A ▶ **28.2A (28.1C)**
16 this ▶ **28.2B**
17 any/some ▶ **28.3A**
18 All ▶ **28.3A**
19 both/both of ▶ **28.3A**
20 Much/A lot ▶ **28.3B**
▶ **Unit 28, pages 272 to 279**

TEST 29

1 b ▶ **29.2A**
2 c ▶ **29.2A**
3 b ▶ **29.2A**
4 b ▶ **29.2A**
5 b ▶ **29.2B**
6 c ▶ **29.2C**
7 b ▶ **29.2C**
8 a ▶ **29.2C**
9 c ▶ **29.2D**
10 a ▶ **29.2D**
11 c ▶ **29.2D**
12 c ▶ **29.3A**
13 ✔ ▶ **29.1A, 29.2B**
14 by means of ▶ **29.2D**
15 just behind ▶ **29.1B**
16 up to ▶ **29.2B**
17 because of the solicitors' involvement/because (of the fact that) solicitors became involved ▶ **29.3A**
18 ✔ ▶ **29.3A**
19 Apart from dismantling the lighting, ▶ **29.3A**
20 that I applied for/for which I applied ▶ **29.3B**
▶ **Unit 29, pages 280 to 289**

TEST 30

1 a ✔ c ✔ ▶ **30.1B, 30.2C, F**
2 a ✔ b ✔ ▶ **30.2A**
3 b ✔ c ✔ ▶ **30.2B**
4 a ✔ c ✔ ▶ **30.2B, D**
5 b ✔ c ✔ ▶ **30.2B**
6 a ✔ b ✔ ▶ **30.2C**
7 a ✔ c ✔ ▶ **30.2E, B**
8 b ✔ c ✔ ▶ **30.2E**
9 the Duke really loves the Princess ▶ **30.1A, 30.2C**
10 Could you provide a formal quote? ▶ **30.1B, 30.2C**
11 Katharine kept her marriage to Duncan a secret ▶ **30.2B**
12 John named the yacht Bettina ▶ **30.2B**
13 brought the company a certain amount of class ▶ **30.2C**
14 Will you show them the way to the motorway? ▶ **30.2C**
15 the magician pulled a rabbit from his hat ▶ **30.2D**
16 the visitors that the prisoner didn't want to see them ▶ **30.2F**
17 Can you show me how to use this machine? ▶ **30.2F**
18 she was well-qualified and had enough experience/she had enough experience and was well-qualified ▶ **30.3A**
19 is much brighter than the previous one ▶ **30.3B**
20 We left as soon as the first act was over. ▶ **30.3B**
▶ **Unit 30, pages 290 to 297**

TEST 31

1 that ▶ **31.1C, 31.2A**
2 which ▶ **31.1D, 31.2A**
3 which ▶ **31.1F**
4 which ▶ **31.2A**
5 whom ▶ **31.2A**
6 which ▶ **31.1D**
7 whose ▶ **31.2A**
8 what ▶ **31.2A**
9 when ▶ **31.2A**
10 wherever ▶ **31.2C**
11 ~~which this shop makes them~~ → which this shop makes ▶ **31.1A**
12 ~~Jack has prepared his favourite dish from Delia Smith's recipe book, which he is about to eat.~~ → Jack has prepared his favourite dish, which he is about to eat, from Delia Smith's recipe book ▶ **31.1A**
13 ~~bars have got toffee in the middle?~~ → bars which/that have got toffee in the middle?/ bars with toffee in the middle? ▶ **31.1A, B, 31.2A**
14 ~~St Andrew's Hospice which opened last year.~~ → St Andrew's Hospice, which opened last year. ▶ **31.1D, E**
15 ~~the city where I grew up in.~~ → the city where I grew up./the city which/that I grew up in. ▶ **31.1F**
16 ~~the residents who living here~~ → the residents who are living here/the residents living here ▶ **31.1G**
17 ~~a genuine Ming vase, that was worth~~ → a genuine Ming vase, which was worth ▶ **31.2A**
18 ~~The bank robbery what I told you about~~ → The bank robbery that/which I told you about ▶ **31.2A, 31.1B**

19 ~~the main reason which governments fall.~~ → the main reason why governments fall. ▶ 31.2A

20 ~~most of them proved~~ → most of which proved ▶ 31.2B

▶ **Unit 31, pages 298 to 305**

TEST 32

1 ~~even though~~ → but ▶ 32.1A

2 ✔ ▶ 32.1A

3 ~~But they'd travelled round the world, they had~~ → They'd travelled round the world but they had/Although they'd travelled around the world, they had ▶ 32.1B

4 ✔ ▶ 32.1B

5 ~~she had served although~~ → although she had served ▶ 32.1B

6 ~~Even although~~ → Even though ▶ 32.1B

7 ~~even they have had~~ → even though they have had ▶ 32.1B

8 ~~They are a haven of peace and tranquillity yet.~~ → Yet, they are a haven of peace and tranquillity. ▶ 32.1B

9 ✔ ▶ 32.1C

10 ~~Ideal the house may appear~~ → Ideal though the house may appear ▶ 32.1C

11 ~~In spite of he had~~ → In spite of the fact that he had/In spite of having/Although he had ▶ 32.2

12 ~~Despite she was a woman~~ → Despite the fact that she was a woman/Despite being a woman/Although she was a woman ▶ 32.2

13 ✔ ▶ 32.2

14 ~~Although the fact that the machine~~ → Although the machine/Despite/In spite of the fact that the machine ▶ 32.2

15 ~~Nonetheless~~ → Mind you/Still/All the same ▶ 32.3A

16 ~~However a dog may be a good companion for the elderly, the need to take it for walks~~ → A dog may be a good companion for the elderly. However, the need to take it for walks ▶ 32.3B

17 ~~Australian, by contrast, champagne~~ → Australian champagne, by contrast/By contrast, Australian champagne ▶ 32.3B

18 ✔ ▶ 32.3B

19 ~~They will certainly be popular as they are realistically priced, still.~~ → Still, they will certainly be popular as they are realistically priced. ▶ 32.3B

20 ✔ ▶ 32.3B

▶ **Unit 32, pages 306 to 311**

TEST 33

1 there was ▶ 33.1B, 33.1A

2 there will be ▶ 33.1B

3 there was ▶ 33.1D

4 It's ▶ 33.2A

5 It's ▶ 33.2A

6 There ▶ 33.1D

7 it's ▶ 33.2A

8 There's ▶ 33.1D

9 there being ▶ 33.1C

10 It ▶ 33.2B

11 There are ▶ 33.1D

12 it is ▶ 33.2C

13 there ▶ 33.1D

14 there is ▶ 33.1D

15 it ▶ 33.2D

16 it is ▶ 33.2C

17 it ▶ 33.2B

18 there's ▶ 33.1D

19 it's ▶ 33.2A

20 there to be ▶ 33.1C

▶ **Unit 33, pages 312 to 319**

TEST 34

1 It was the shellfish that made Jasmine sick. ▶ 34.1B

2 It was the office keys (that) Greg lost./It was Greg that lost the office keys. ▶ 34.1B

3 What he's doing is approaching the problem from an entirely new angle. ▶ 34.1C

4 What they've done is unforgivable! ▶ 34.1C

5 The reason (why) I came by bus is (that) my car has broken down. ▶ 34.1D

6 All I want is a second chance. ▶ 34.1D

7 Zack was the guy who told me about the new club. ▶ 34.1E

8 This is where we have to leave our bags and coats. ▶ 34.1E

9 That's what they told me. ▶ 34.1E

10 Lucky in love he isn't! ▶ 34.2A

11 Much more interesting were the interactive displays. ▶ 34.2B

12 Also at the ceremony was the Lord Chancellor. ▶ 34.2B

13 So intense was the heat (that) the firefighters were unable to enter the building. ▶ 34.2B

14 Stuck to my windscreen was a parking ticket. ▶ 34.2C

15 Defeated though they were, they managed to keep smiling. ▶ 34.2C

16 Beside the river bank stands a gnarled old oak tree. ▶ 34.3A

17 Next is/it's the midnight movie. ▶ 34.3A

18 Seldom has the government suffered such an overwhelming defeat. ▶ 34.3B

19 No sooner had we arrived than they announced that the show was cancelled. ▶ 34.3B

20 Under no circumstances can refunds be given. ▶ **34.3B**

▶ **Unit 34, pages 320 to 327**

TEST 35

1 She ▶ **35.1A, 35.2A**

2 those/the ones ▶ **35.2A**

3 ones ▶ **35.2A**

4 They/All of them/They were all ▶ **35.2A**

5 did ▶ **35.2B**

6 neither do I/nor do I/I don't either/me neither ▶ **35.2B**

7 do so/do it/do that ▶ **35.2C**

8 it/that ▶ **35.2C, D**

9 not ▶ **35.2D**

10 if not/if they're not ▶ **35.2D**

11 ~~but they are to be found in small, backstreet restaurants~~ → but in small, backstreet ones ▶ **35.1A**

12 ~~They were~~ → The girls were ▶ **35.1B**

13 ~~I prefer red one.~~ → I prefer red. ▶ **35.2A**

14 ~~so we did~~ → so did we ▶ **35.2B**

15 ~~'So did I.'~~ → 'So I did.' ▶ **35.2C**

16 ✔ ▶ **35.3A**

17 ~~because tore a muscle~~ → because he tore a muscle ▶ **35.3A**

18 ~~Well, they must~~ → Well, they must be ▶ **35.3B**

19 ✔ ▶ **35.3B**

20 ~~that he had wanted to put through~~ → that he had wanted to ▶ **35.3C**

▶ **Unit 35, pages 328 to 335**

TEST 36

1 b ▶ **36.1A**

2 a ▶ **36.1B**

3 a ▶ **36.1D**

4 b ▶ **36.1B**

5 b ▶ **36.1E**

6 a ▶ **36.1C**

7 b ▶ **36.1E**

8 b ▶ **36.2A**

9 c ▶ **36.2A**

10 f ▶ **36.2A**

11 e ▶ **36.2A**

12 g ▶ **36.2B**

13 j ▶ **36.2C**

14 k ▶ **36.2C**

15 n ▶ **36.2D**

▶ **Unit 36, pages 336 to 343**

Key to practice exercises

1

1 1 am standing 2 are dying 3 believe 4 aren't doing 5 are clearing 6 do 7 aren't planting 8 understand 9 say 10 are always using/always use 11 don't have 12 aren't asking

2 1 houses 2 are trying out 3 don't eat 4 display 5 are currently showing 6 come 7 brings 8 come, don't take 9 are always complaining (always complain *is possible, but less likely because of the suggestion of annoyance*) 10 Is the orchestra playing 11 provides 12 do you consider

3 1 Judge blocks ban on tobacco adverts/blocks tobacco adverts ban 2 Police chief admits errors during President's visit 3 Radio 1 outshines rivals 4 Fox-hunting bill does not achieve support needed/ necessary support 5 India snubs Pope on eve of visit 6 DiCaprio film-makers face protest over beach

4 1 is minding 2 is knocked down 3 survives 4 becomes 5 buys 6 hides 7 intends 8 is recovering 9 is suffering from 10 puts 11 demands 12 do not know

5 1 A 2 A 3 B 4 B 5 A 6 B 7 A 8 A 9 A 10 B

6 1 ✔ 2 ~~Appeals the idea~~ → Does the idea appeal 3 ✔ 4 ✔ 5 ~~are hearing~~ → hear/can hear 6 ✔ 7 ~~there is lying~~ → there lies 8 ~~We're inviting~~ → We invite 9 ✔ 10 ~~currently develop~~ → are currently developing 11 ✔ 12 ✔ 13 ✔ 14 ~~are rising~~ → rise 15 ~~shelter~~ → shelters 16 ✔ 17 ~~build~~ → are building 18 ✔ 19 ~~now show~~ → are now showing 20 ✔ 21 ✔ 22 ✔

2

1 1 D 2 E 3 C 4 B 5 A 6 E 7 C 8 A 9 D 10 B

2 1 was standing, saw 2 was blowing, set off 3 felt/was feeling, collapsed, pressed, settled down 4 spent, were cooking 5 were living, hit 6 soared, announced 7 was getting up, decided 8 left, was having/had 9 took, managed 10 ran into, mentioned

3 1 A 2 B 3 A 4 A 5 B 6 B 7 B 8 A

4 1 turned 2 had just left 3 had taken 4 had expelled 5 had eaten 6 had been practising 7 had already booked 8 had been working 9 had hoped 10 had been suffering

5 1 ✔ 2 ~~did hear~~ → heard 3 ✔ 4 ~~build~~ → built 5 ✔ 6 ~~use to~~ → used to 7 ~~would have~~ → had 8 ✔ 9 ~~was telling~~ → told 10 ✔ 11 ~~were becoming~~ → became 12 ~~had helped~~ → helped 13 ~~watched~~ → watching 14 ✔ 15 ~~were sending~~ → sent 16 ✔ 17 ✔ 18 ~~had published~~ → published

6 1 was 2 used to think/ thought 3 was 4 had lived/ lived/had been living 5 were/was 6 had met 7 would get up/used to get up 8 had been enjoying/had enjoyed 9 became/was becoming 10 got out 11 had been painting 12 returned 13 had drawn 14 had recently been asked 15 began 16 was beating down/beat down 17 sat down 18 had been publishing/had published 19 had been amputated 20 had always wanted

3

1 1 B 2 B (A *is acceptable in US English*) 3 A 4 B 5 A 6 A 7 B 8 A 9 A 10 B

2 1 Most of the workers have been/worked here since 1996/since the factory opened. 2 The guest performers have all arrived. 3 We have visited the new theme park three times (so far). 4 Everyone in my family has learnt the basics of First Aid. 5 The latest novel by the young Indian writer Arundhati Roy is the best she has ever written. 6 The panel has not yet decided about the technical irregularities.

3 1 1A, 2B 2 1B, 2A 3 1A, 2B 4 1A, 2B 5 1B, 2A

4 1 have unearthed 2 have been digging 3 found 4 contained 5 has been trying 6 perished 7 existed 8 walked 9 have been found 10 has discovered 11 has been 12 were discovered 13 has produced 14 has allowed

5 1 has been 2 has become 3 has now started 4 was born 5 moved 6 completed 7 began 8 appeared 9 got 10 has since made 11 went on 12 moved 13 has made 14 have been 15 has never been 16 marked 17 has been directing 18 has directed 19 has lived/has been living 20 married

6 *Suggested answers* 1 He has become one of the most highly paid Hollywood actors, and he has written filmscripts. 2 Willis was born in Germany in 1955, to a father who was in the US army and a German mother. 3 The family moved back to the United States, to New Jersey, in 1957. 4 He

went to Montclair State College in New Jersey, where he got a role in a play called *Heaven and Earth*, then he left school and started acting. 5 His first main role was David Addison in the hit TV show *Moonlighting*, for which he won Emmys and Golden Globe awards. 6 His first hit film was *Die Hard*, which was made in 1988, and he has made two sequels since then. 7 Willis has been starring/has starred mainly in violent action films since *Die Hard,* although he has also made different types of film, such as *Twelve Monkeys* in 1995 and *The Sixth Sense* in 1999. 8 He has made more than forty films, many of which have been commercial successes. 9 He has had a severe stutter since childhood, but acting has helped him to overcome it as it is not a problem in front of an audience. 10 He was married to Demi Moore for ten years, until their separation in 1998, and they had three children together.

4

1 1 will meet/are going to meet 2 's going to jump 3 'll be sailing 4 'll answer 5 's going to shoot 6 'll have died/'ll be dying

2 1 B, C 2 A 3 B 4 A, C 5 A, B 6 A 7 A, C 8 A, B

3 1 ... our opponents are going to win! 2 Our plane leaves at 6.30 in the morning. 3 My great-grandmother will be one/a hundred years old next year. 4 I don't think that humans will ever be able to live on the moon. 5 My parents will have been married for twenty-five years next Saturday. 6 ... the band will be recording (then). 7 Our proposal will certainly be/is certainly going to be (one hundred per cent) successful. 8 (The government expects that) another six thousand will have found work by the end of the summer. 9 When/What time will you be arriving/are you arriving on Friday? 10 Our daughter is appearing in the school production of *Miss Saigon* next month.

4 1 does their plane arrive 2 'm meeting 3 won't be/'m not going to be 4 finishes 5 'll be working/'m going to work 6 Will they be 7 'll have finished 8 'll be 9 'm having/'ll be having 10 'm picking up/'ll be picking up 11 'll have to 12 're meeting/'ll meet

5 1 J 'll be staying 2 A is going to be 3 E 'll be watching/'m going to watch/'m watching 4 I 're filming/'ll be filming 5 C 'm going to complain/'ll complain 6 G 'll give 7 F 'll be looking at 8 B start 9 H 'll be waterskiing

6 1 C 2 A 3 B 4 B 5 A 6 C 7 A 8 B 9 A (B *is possible*) 10 C (B *is possible*)

5

1 1 is about to 2 on the verge/point of 3 is due to 4 unlikely to 5 sure to/certain to 6 are to 7 imminent 8 is due to 9 unlikely to 10 bound to/certain to

2 1 is about to 2 expect 3 hopes to 4 should 5 is sure to 6 plans to 7 are on the point of 8 anticipate 9 is likely to 10 guarantee to

3 1 The chimpanzees are not to be/should not be disturbed during feeding time. 2 It's bound to wake all the neighbours. 3 ... they are on the point/verge of discovering the secret of life. 4 Will you promise not to get drunk again tonight? 5 The road-sweeping contract is likely to be withdrawn from Dustbugs. 6 Everyone in the village lived in fear of the impending volcanic eruption. 7 The designer envisages finishing/being able to finish the specifications by tomorrow afternoon. 8 (I really think) the examiner is unlikely to accept a handwritten script these days. 9 The store is about to close. 10 If medical research is to provide cures for all known diseases, it must be adequately funded.

4 1 ... (just) about to/going to call you. 2 ... going to help me. 3 ... to start/to have started 4 ... (just) about to/going to 5 ... going to come/coming

5 1 ✔ 2 ~~due~~ → imminent/forthcoming/impending 3 ~~will~~ → would 4 ~~go~~ → going 5 ✔ 6 ~~sign~~ → signing 7 ~~allowed~~ → allow/have allowed 8 ~~likely~~ → going/due 9 ✔ 10 ~~sure~~ → unlikely 11 ✔ 12 ~~reopen~~ → reopening 13 ~~about~~ → sure/bound/certain 14 ✔ 15 ~~hoped~~ → hope 16 ✔

6

1 1 We hope that the soldiers don't experience 2 not to turn their TVs off 3 the subjunctive is usually no different/not usually different 4 didn't try to repair the TV himself 5 Not a great number of/Not many songbirds 6 you get no/don't get any impression of life 7 I was not willing/unwilling to help the children 8 neither commonplace nor accepted 9 The estimated fee for the project was not unreasonable 10 I don't think that our company will be offering aid 11 she's not a good guitarist 12 is not especially powerful

2 1 Doesn't she (already) belong to it? 2 Aren't you taking your holiday in that week? 3 Haven't you done it yet? 4 Why don't you join us?/Won't you join us? 5 Why didn't you tell me? 6 Oh, didn't you buy any, then? 7 Don't you think those hair extensions look awful on older women? 8 Isn't she/Is she not giving ...

3 1 Phil denied that he had any involvement ... 2 ... we will be obliged to disconnect your/the electricity supply. 3 Few (people) from the housing ... 4 ... are not dissimilar. 5 It is hardly possible to capture ... 6 ... deliberately misinformed the investigators. 7 It's best to avoid (talking about) topics ... 8 The deforestation of the Brazilian rainforests has had ... 9 Pop stars rarely/Rarely do pop stars make it as actors, but ... 10 Illegible applications will be automatically rejected.

4 1 incredible 2 uncovered 3 illegal 4 unusual 5 discourteous 6 impossible 7 inconvenience/disadvantage 8 disadvantage/inconvenience 9 unintelligent 10 unavailable

5 1 no 2 not recognising 3 Few 4 Not only 5 misleading 6 not unlike 7 not for 8 no intention 9 unwilling 10 noncommittal 11 not wishing 12 may not

6 Line 5 ~~nothing~~ → anything Line 7 ~~none~~ → any Line 9 ~~haven't~~ → have Line 10 ~~Not for~~ → Not only Line 10/11 ~~he wouldn't give me none other~~ → he wouldn't give me any other/he would give me no other Line 13 ~~unhonest~~ → dishonest Line 16 ~~don't~~ → do Line 17 ~~didn't tell me~~ → told me not Line 20 ~~can't~~ → can Line 22 ~~don't hope it is~~ → hope not Line 25 ~~Have~~ → Haven't Line 27 ~~no-smoker~~ → non-smoker Line 29 ~~don't appreciate~~ → appreciate Line 32 ~~don't hope it lasts~~ → hope it doesn't last

7

1 1 Which applicant/Which of the applicants do you think is (most) suitable? 2 How long had you been giving the pigs that (type of) feed for? 3 Who told you about my/our divorce? 4 What else did you do on the/your holiday? 5 Could/Couldn't you have persuaded David to stay in the team (any longer)? 6 What's the point in/Is there any point in complaining about faulty goods? 7 Which watch will work (better) while I'm scuba-diving?/Will both watches work while ... 8 For whom did the accused steal the getaway car?/Why did the accused steal the getaway car?/Who did the accused steal the getaway car for?

2 1 won't you? 2 were there? 3 hadn't he/she? 4 need we? 5 will you?/could you?/would you? 6 have you? 7 were they? 8 will you?/can't you? 9 hasn't it? 10 can you? 11 didn't she? 12 was he?

3 1 I'd like to know why it took you so long to deliver this parcel. 2 Can you tell me if Harriet has finished the minutes of the meeting yet or not? 3 Could I possibly ask you why you keep so many old cars outside your house? 4 Please let me know when the new curtains for the hotel suites will be ready. 5 I'd like to know whether Jonathan will be staying for dinner tomorrow evening. 6 Does the brochure say how often the bedlinen in the villas is changed?/how often the bedlinen is changed in the villas? 7 Do you know which metro station we should go to for the Eiffel Tower? 8 I wonder whether or not Schumacher won yesterday's race./whether Schumacher won yesterday's race or not.

4 1 Oh, who told you that? 2 Do I like what? 3 Has he (really)? 4 Which one are you going to take? 5 Oh, who did you see? 6 But why can't you?/But why not? 7 What else ... 8 What on earth/the hell/in heaven

5 1 aren't you? 2 Isn't it? 3 didn't you? 4 is there? 5 Have you?/Are they? 6 isn't it? 7 haven't they? 8 could you? 9 Did you really? 10 shall we? 11 didn't you? 12 won't you/will you

6 1 Sir Alec was 86 years old, wasn't he? 2 It's unusual for famous actors to have lasting marriages, isn't it? 3 How long exactly had they been married? 4 Can you tell us what his childhood was like? 5 Did he ever find out his true identity? 6 did he ever find out who his father was? 7 He entered his chosen career quite late, didn't he? 8 What interrupted it? 9 When did he pick up his career again? 10 Do you know when he started acting in films? 11 Which film is considered (his) best, do you think? 12 He won an Oscar for that, didn't he? 13 Did he win anything else? 14 I'm sure that younger people remember him in a very different role, don't they?/will remember him in a very different role, won't they?

7 1 who/what 2 whether 3 However/How/How on earth/the hell/in heaven 4 makes 5 released/published 6 Which 7 the use 8 hardly/scarcely 9 By which 10 Who on earth/in heaven/the hell/Who/Whoever

8

1 1 Refreshments will be provided during the interval. 2 The form should be completed in black ink. 3 This product has not been tested on animals. 4 This appliance is supplied with a plug. 5 This car has been fitted with an alarm. 6 Our displays are arranged in chronological sequence. 7 Hard hats must be worn while construction work is being carried out. 8 All shoplifters will be prosecuted. 9 This area is being monitored by closed circuit cameras. 10 Toilet facilities may be found at the rear of block B. 11 All the formalities will be taken care of. 12 I was made to open my suitcases. 13 The government is said to be out of touch with public opinion./It is said the government is out of touch with public opinion. 14 He ought to have been sent to prison for life. 15 Stephen was given an upgrade to first class./An upgrade to first class was given to Stephen. 16 We were allowed/permitted/given permission to park the caravan in a farmer's field overnight. 17 He was seen to enter/entering the building carrying a shotgun. 18 The proposed legislation is thought to be unworkable./It is thought that the proposed legislation is unworkable. 19 A pane of glass was/got broken while the boys were playing in the street. 20 The twins have been given a puppy for their birthday./A puppy has been given to the twins for their birthday.

2 1 B 2 D 3 A 4 C 5 A 6 D 7 A 8 B 9 D 10 A 11 C 12 B 13 D 14 B

3 1 D 2 J 3 A 4 C 5 H

4 Set a: 1 B 2 C 3 A
Set b: 1 C 2 A 3 B

5 1 D She was entranced by the stunning vista of long white beaches backed by verdant hills. 2 ✔ 3 B The prisoner was executed at dawn. 4 D The estate was inherited by a man who had never known that he had rich relations. 5 ✔ 6 ✔ 7 C Information is collected from ... and entered into the database. 8 A The lift in our block has been vandalised. 9 ✔ 10 A/B Foxes are hardly ever seen in daylight. 11 C This form must be completed in black ink and signed. 12 D The terrorists were interviewed by several members of the international press corps. 13 ✔ 14 B The man was convicted and sentenced to fifteen years in jail. 15 C Milk is heated to 110°C and then rapidly cooled to produce the final pasteurised product.

6 1 Daphne is/will be having her new car delivered this afternoon. 2 A series of rigorous drug tests will have to be passed. 3 We were allowed to use the village hall ... 4 The project having been completed, we were able to leave early. 5 We resented not having been consulted over the expansion plans. 6 I'll have the caretaker open the gates early for you. 7 The suspect is believed to be in hiding ... 8 She got sacked/got the sack for being late so often.

7 *Any seven of the following*
Line 4 a strange stone was discovered Line 6 the stone was captured Line 7 and moved to the British Museum Line 9 was asked to look Lines 12/13 hieroglyphs, in which sounds and meanings are represented by a type of writing. Line 14 the puzzle of their written language had been solved Lines 14/15 possible for the inscriptions on all the great monuments to be deciphered. Lines 15/16 thus the mysteries of Egypt's fabulous history and culture were finally unlocked.

9

1 1 ~~said me~~ → said to me 2 ✔ 3 ✔ 4 ~~shouted he wanted~~ → shouted that he wanted 5 ~~said that's a lie, Minister~~ → said, 'That's a lie, Minister.' 6 'The new Honda Civic,' the salesman added, 'is one of the most popular small family saloons now.'

2 *Most likely answers*
1 that she hadn't got to Spanish the night before because she had been out all day and had got home late. She said she'd ring again to find out what the homework was. 2 that she was phoning to find out the results of her blood test. She said that she's /she was going on holiday in the morning, so she'd be grateful if you could ring her back later. 3 he thinks/thought we need/needed a chat about some problems Joe seems/seemed to be having. He said he'll/he'd be at the school until 6.30 if we'd like to call him back. 4 (that) they couldn't fulfil your/our order, as you/we hadn't included/didn't include credit card details on your/our order form. He said they have/had to have these details or payment in advance to fulfil an order. He said he'd await your/our instructions.

3 *Most likely answers*
1 he's decided to stay another week as the research is going so well there. 2 they had got tickets for the opera in New York at the weekend. 3 the smaller islands of the archipelago were mostly

uninhabited and very peaceful. 4 her mum was/is really ill. She said that she wishes they didn't live so far away from her. 5 the house was in a very pleasant cul-de-sac, and there weren't many children or animals here. 6 the accused had first met the Wilsons when he decorated/had decorated their living room. 7 we should switch to an online banking system for the household accounts. 8 had been living together secretly for years before they revealed their relationship. 9 that we mustn't/weren't to leave our car in those parking bays for more than twenty minutes at a time. 10 there is no such thing as reincarnation.

4 1 ~~could he~~ → he could 2 ~~possibly could she~~ → she could possibly 3 ~~to draft~~ → to be drafted 4 ~~told us let~~ → told us to let 5 ~~if or not~~ → if 6 ~~where buy~~ → where to buy 7 ~~all night?~~ → all night. 8 ~~is the problem~~ → the problem was 9 ~~begged to her landlord~~ → begged her landlord 10 ~~can~~ → could

5 1 Geraldine refused to take part in the new play. 2 My best friend warned me never to discuss her problems behind her back again. 3 Pete recommended (going to) the new Thai restaurant. 4 The departmental manager blamed me for losing the Siemens contract. 5 The disc jockey considers Oasis to have been the best band of the nineties. 6 The fan apologised for confusing him with George Michael. 7 The police officer accused him of making obscene phone calls to the office. 8 My friends encouraged me to do the Swimathon with them. 9 Mike's brother volunteered to organise the collection for Mike and Sarah's wedding. 10 The team manager regrets contradicting Julie in front of her whole team. 11 The director suggested trying the scene a different way. 12 My mother reminded me that I had had my tonsils taken out when I was about nine.

6 1 C 2 A 3 A 4 C 5 C 6 B 7 C 8 A 9 C 10 A

7 *Possible answers (and actual quotations)* 1 Al Capone: 'I've been accused of every death except the casualty list of the World War.' 2 President Woodrow Wilson: 'I would never read a book if it were possible for me to talk half an hour with the person who wrote it.' 3 Pablo Picasso: 'Age only matters when one is ageing. Now that I have arrived at a great age, I might just as well be twenty.' 4 Jean-Paul Sartre: 'The world could get along very well without literature; it could get along even better without man.' 5 A spokesperson from UNESCO: 'Since wars began in the minds of men, it is in the minds of men that the defence of peace must be constructed.' 6 Groucho Marx: 'Please accept my resignation. I don't want to belong to any club that will accept me as a member.' 7 President John F Kennedy: 'Ask not what your country can do for you; ask what you can do for your country.' 8 Albert Einstein: 'I know why there are so many people who love chopping wood. In this activity one immediately sees the results.'

10

1 1 hadn't eaten 2 stand 3 won't function/might not function/may not function 4 wouldn't have 5 walked 6 want 7 is 8 would/might experience 9 must stop 10 wouldn't/couldn't have happened 11 don't want 12 stay

2 1 If it doesn't rain, the crisis will not be averted/we will not be able to avert the crisis. 2 The tourist industry might have suffered if the government had not stopped releasing pollution levels in June/had continued to release pollution levels. 3 'You should wear a face mask if you have/suffer from respiratory problems.' 4 If the governments involved had taken positive action after the 1997 crisis, the current crisis might/would not have happened. 5 There might be more serious environmental protection if more of the countries affected had a Ministry of the Environment.

3 1 F 2 H 3 G 4 E 5 A 6 I 7 B 8 D 9 J 10 C

4 1 G wouldn't be/might not be, L wouldn't have broken/might not have broken 2 H would/might never have been formed, J would/might be 3 C would not have been destroyed, K would/might be 4 A might/would not be, I would not be 5 D would not have been, F would be

5 1 A ✔ B ✔ C ✘ 2 A ✘ B ✔ C ✘ 3 A ✘ B ✔ C ✘ 4 A ✔ B ✔ C ✘ 5 A ✔ B ✘ C ✔ 6 A ✘ B ✔ C ✔

6 1 Even if Sophie doesn't like her parents-in-law, she keeps it to herself. 2 After her husband's death, Mrs Jenkins sold the house to her son on the condition that he lived in it himself. 3 Unless you request next-day delivery, we will send the goods by normal first-class post. 4 Use a power breaker when you mow the lawn in case you cut the electric lead. 5 The library computer can tell you whether you have any books out on loan or not/

whether or not you have any books out on loan. 6 What if the police found out? 7 We will not achieve the deadline unless you provide all the resources we have requested. 8 You will be awarded marks for trying to answer all the questions, whether the answers are correct or not. 9 You're welcome to bring Lucinda as long as she doesn't moan about her work all day. 10 But for your stupidity in the TV studio, our team would have won the quiz!

7 1 B 2 C 3 A 4 C 5 C 6 B 7 C 8 B 9 A 10 C 11 B 12 C

11

1 1 ~~are submitted~~ → be submitted 2 ✔ 3 ~~receives~~ → receive 4 ~~May the President have a long life!~~ → Long live the President! 5 ✔ 6 ~~are worn~~ → be worn

2 1 You look as though you've been unwell. 2 I'd rather you didn't wipe your feet on the carpets. 3 What if they don't accept your explanation? 4 It's time we paid the bill. 5 Suppose I complained to the police? 6 They'd rather we went with them. 7 She acts as if she was/were a member of the club. 8 It's about time you called your parents.

3 1 A 2 M 3 M 4 T 5 T 6 A 7 A 8 T 9 M 10 T 11 M 12 M 13 T 14 A 15 A

4 1 I wish you'd told us that you were leaving. 2 Suppose they hadn't got a receipt? 3 It's (about) time we went. 4 If only I was/were as agile as I used to be. 5 I wish/If only I could play the piano 6 I wish she would stop criticising me. 7 Treat my home as though it was/were your own. 8 If only/I wish I had gone to university. 9 She wishes she had more friends. 10 I'd rather/sooner you didn't let the dog sit in the front of the car.

5 1 ~~had~~ → would 2 ~~listens~~ → listened 3 ~~did~~ → would 4 ✔ 5 ~~would be~~ → could be/were 6 ~~he is~~ → he was/he were 7 ✔ 8 ~~you'll see~~ → you see/you saw 9 ~~I didn't stay at home~~ → I left home 10 ✔

6 1 was finally resolved 2 be kept clear 3 were 4 was/were blocked 5 hadn't agreed 6 kept 7 was/were able to 8 haven't told 9 demand 10 not have to refer/we didn't have to refer

7 A I'd rather/sooner do something slightly less dangerous! B Long live freedom! C It's (high) time you changed your phone! D I wish/If only you would tidy up this room! E I wish/If only I was/were taller! F He treats that dog as if/as though it was human!

12

1 1 ~~my~~ → me 2 ~~opening the~~ → opening of the 3 ~~she~~ → her 4 ~~not~~ → no 5 ~~wait~~ → waiting 6 ~~making a~~ → making of a 7 ~~not~~ → no 8 ~~we~~ → us/our 9 ~~to make~~ → making 10 ~~capable lifting~~ → capable of lifting

2 1 to be handed in tomorrow. 2 enough to join the army. 3 to arrive late. 4 able to/allowed to/permitted to/free to give you an answer right now. 5 to catch the criminals the government closed the borders. 6 a decision to close the office this morning. 7 surprised to learn that Amanda was going to marry Ronald. 8 as not to frighten the public. 9 to the bank this morning to check the balance on my current account. 10 to find/discover they had already closed the store for stocktaking!

3 1 to pass 2 to call 3 avoiding 4 to exceed 5 to notice 6 keeping 7 to arrive 8 to apply 9 lying 10 calling 11 to go 12 to avoid 13 to join 14 feeling 15 to carry 16 to swim 17 to like 18 meeting 19 passing 20 to settle

4 1 to pack 2 leaving 3 pressing 4 to enter 5 washing 6 conduct 7 eating 8 to get 9 to record 10 hovering 11 to achieve 12 to announce 13 seeing 14 looking 15 to get

5 1 A 2 C 3 B 4 B 5 C 6 A 7 B 8 A 9 A 10 A 11 C 12 A 13 A 14 B 15 B 16 B 17 B 18 A 19 B 20 C

6 1 to say 2 to ask 3 to find 4 bringing 5 cooking 6 living 7 to make 8 filling in 9 to see 10 to take 11 to open 12 to cash 13 buying 14 to be 15 to know 16 wondering 17 to join 18 learning 19 to attend 20 to write

13

1 1 D 2 G 3 A 4 F 5 E 6 B (*Extra unnecessary phrase is C.*)

2 1 sitting in the armchair 2 Being able to speak Finnish 3 having split up with his wife 4 discovered under the floorboards 5 Having moved out 6 Left for too long 7 making me feel sick 8 Not being very good with figures 9 built to last forever 10 Washed at a cool temperature 11 People playing loud music late at night 12 Having been unemployed for so long 13 Given enough

time 14 The people living closest to the river bank 15 Not having registered

3 1 ~~Study~~ → To study 2 ~~be honest~~ → to be honest 3 ✔ 4 ✔ 5 ~~to be being rich~~ → to be rich 6 ~~to have been gone~~ → to have gone 7 ~~to mugged~~ → to be mugged 8 ✔ 9 ~~not have seen~~ → not to have seen 10 ~~to have designed~~ → to have been designed

4 1 E 2 C 3 A 4 F 5 B

5 1 Carlos joined a dating agency to find a girlfriend. 2 Having left my keys at the office, I couldn't get into my flat last night. 3 Not having a visa, Manuela can't travel to the USA. 4 My nephew emigrated to Australia to start a new life. 5 A new dam was built across the river, flooding thousands of hectares of farmland./A new dam having been built across the river, thousands of hectares of farmland were flooded. 6 Having been restored by experts, the old house regained its former glory./The old house had been restored by experts, regaining its former glory. 7 Not being very fit, I was unable to finish the marathon. 8 Their children having left home, Dave and Maria felt they should move to a smaller house. 9 They got home early to find the place had been burgled. 10 The only person to stay behind was the caretaker.

6 (*Participle and infinitive clauses underlined*)
Dating from 1971 and directed by Francis Ford Coppola, *The Godfather* won three Oscars. Lasting almost three hours, the film is Shakespearean in its scope and ambition. It is the story of a New York mafia family headed by Marlon Brando as 'the Godfather'. Although Brando has the title role it is Al Pacino, playing his troubled son and heir Michael, who steals the show in a masterly performance. Struggling to reconcile his distaste for crime and brutality with his sense of family honour and duty, Pacino's character embodies the moral dilemma at the heart of the movie. To achieve his aim of taking the audience on an emotional rollercoaster ride the director intersperses long scenes of family life with shorter sequences of extreme violence. (or: The director intersperses long scenes of family life with shorter sequences of extreme violence to achieve his aim of taking the audience on an emotional rollercoaster ride.) Shot in explicit detail, this violence may shock some viewers. But anyone prepared to put up with this will enjoy a unique dramatic experience. In fact, for many people *The Godfather* is the greatest American film (to have been) made in the 1970s.

7 1 Being so charming, Martin is 2 Having graduated (from college) I took 3 Not to have made more of 4 said Mary, throwing open 5 launched an advertising campaign to increase 6 a great shock to find the old house 7 to those prices, to be frank. 8 Planted in a sunny spot, the shrubs 9 to be the first (flat) to be sold/to be sold first. 10 Not having had the benefit of 11 Being such a perfectionist, Sophie 12 buildings not to have been destroyed/buildings that had not been destroyed

14

1 1 Go on 2 arranged 3 released 4 maintain 5 looking at 6 cut down on 7 abolish 8 face up to 9 arrive 10 made up

2 1 Would you mind seeing to it/sorting it out yourself? 2 I ran into them at the supermarket this morning. 3 I've fixed it up for ten o'clock tomorrow. 4 You're always running them down. 5 I'm sure the police will look into it. 6 The builders carried it out very professionally. 7 Could you pick them up from school tonight? 8 Has Perry got over it yet? 9 She really looks like them/takes after them, doesn't she? 10 Would you point them out for me?

3 (*Suggested answers*) 1 He takes after you. 2 Put it down! 3 Please take it off. 4 It doesn't go with it. 5 Pick it up! 6 Drink it up. 7 Look at them!

4 1 I'm looking forward to it 2 turned the handsome prince into a frog/turned the frog into a handsome prince 3 I've given it up 4 they've done away with it 5 for whom the team manager paid a million dollars 6 it was set up by my grandfather

5 1 let out 2 look up to 3 come across as 4 set up 5 deal with 6 aimed at 7 points out 8 look into 9 face up to 10 fill in/fill out 11 find out 12 act out 13 cover up 14 keep away from 15 running down 16 let down 17 cut down 18 comes down to

6 1 I'll just turn the radio down 2 We've finished off the kitchen 3 we're doing up the dining room 4 We're turning it into a second bedroom 5 I've just put the wallpaper up 6 stay up 7 sorted out 8 putting her up 9 get on with each other 10 put up with her 11 looks down on me 12 takes her coat off 13 sits down 14 I think I might take up gardening 15 looking forward to it

15

1 1 E 2 H 3 C 4 J 5 B 6 G 7 I 8 D 9 F 10 A

2 1 convince, of 2 supply, with 3 prevent/stop, from 4 cure, of 5 present, with 6 blame, on 7 explain, to 8 stop/prevent, from 9 accuse, of 10 disagree/agree with, over/about 11 apologise to, for 12 depend/rely on, for 13 agree with, about/over 14 rely/depend on, for 15 quarrel with, about/over

3 1 The firing squad aimed their rifles at the condemned man. 2 ✔ 3 The brilliant architect presented her imaginative proposals to us/presented us with her imaginative proposals. 4 My uncle blames his hearing problems on old age. 5 ✔ 6 Do you agree with her about the corporate sponsorship deal? 7 The crippled patient was cured of arthritis by the doctor's radical new treatment. 8 Why won't you even discuss it with her? 9 ✔ 10 Gerald was accused by the court of lying under oath/of lying under oath by the court.

4 1 for 2 in 3 of 4 to 5 of 6 on 7 of 8 for 9 of 10 of 11 to 12 with 13 of 14 for 15 against 16 of 17 with 18 in 19 of 20 in

5 1 Isaac was getting more and more fed up with his lack of progress. 2 They say the terrorists are responsible for the atrocities. 3 My students are interested in our film and photography course. 4 The public rarely feels sorry for politicians caught behaving badly. 5 We were was astonished at/by the quality of her singing voice. 6 I don't think he's (very) fond of spicy food. 7 Excessive consumption of fried food can be harmful to the arteries. 8 I'm afraid I'm short of change at the moment. 9 Our neighbour's remarkably good to her cats. 10 He is famous for his performance in *Othello* at the National Theatre. 11 I'm (completely/very) sure of his abilities. 12 I am grateful for your swift response to my enquiry. 13 My two brothers are (very) different from me. (US: *different than*) 14 The new legislation is concerned with deregulation of the airline industry. 15 I'm curious about/to know how the magician did his tricks. 16 My colleague is keen on all these new electronic gadgets. 17 The daily swim seems to be good for him/his health. 18 The research team is engaged in a brand new project. 19 We aren't hopeful of them/their reaching the final round. 20 Inspector Morse believes the blind man is guilty of the murder.

6 **Across**: 1 answers 3 with 4 depended 11 about 12 convince 13 delay 15 praised 16 make 17 from 18 worthy
Down: 2 supplying 3 whether 5 demand 6 that 7 provide 8 crowded 9 meeting 10 to 14 eager 17 for

16

1 1 managed to 2 couldn't/wasn't able to 3 can't 4 is able to/can 5 will be able to 6 were able to/managed to 7 can't 8 being able to 9 be able to 10 has succeeded in 11 can 12 being able to 13 haven't been able to 14 were unable to/weren't able to/didn't manage to 15 can

2 A 3 B 1 C 4 D 2

3 1 C 2 D 3 A 4 B

4 1 You could/might have helped me (with the car)! 2 Twenty years ago I could/might have bought that apartment for $30,000. 3 We could issue the tickets today if you gave us your credit card number. 4 The service in British restaurants can be quite surly. 5 Is it possible that the disparity in the figures is due to a computer error? 6 They could/might/may (well) be on the next train. 7 He can't/couldn't be responsible for the error; he looks too experienced. 8 The shuttle bus might/may not be working at the moment ... 9 You could/might have given me their phone number! 10 Unfortunately, you can't grow bananas in the British climate. 11 With any luck our team could/might win the championship next year. 12 Jim might/could have taken it ... 13 The results may/might have arrived by tomorrow lunchtime. 14 Who can/could be making all that noise next door? 15 There may/could/might be other intelligent life-forms in the universe. 16 We can now/are now able to predict hurricanes quite accurately thanks to satellite technology. 17 He may/might not be at home; the lights are off. 18 My sister could/might be a huge star with a little bit of luck. 19 Carrie could/might have worked in New York ... 20 I couldn't/could never live in a house without a garden.

5 1 couldn't 2 could 3 could have/might have 4 couldn't have/wouldn't have 5 could have/might have/may have 6 was able to/managed to 7 was able to/managed to 8 can 9 succeeded in 10 managed to/was able to

6 1 B 2 B 3 B 4 A 5 A 6 A 7 A 8 B 9 B 10 A

7 1 could get/were able to get/managed to get 2 might be/may be/could be 3 can accommodate 4 can't invite 5 can't organise 6 might/may not make 7 could always get 8 might/may have told 9 could have spoken 10 might even have got 11 Could/Can we borrow 12 can/could have 13 hasn't been able to find 14 can't have 15 can have 16 could always ask 17 could have spoken 18 might/could have given it up 19 will be able to ask/can ask/could ask 20 was able to fix/managed to fix

17

1 1 do I have to 2 have to 3 must 4 will have to 5 obliged to 6 has to 7 supposed to 8 should 9 having to 10 needs 11 need to 12 had to

2 1 A 2 B 3 C 4 B 5 C 6 A 7 C 8 C 9 A 10 B 11 A 12 B

3 1 required 2 should 3 need not/do not have to 4 must 5 should 6 need not/do not have to 7 required/obliged 8 required/necessary 9 should

4 1 She can't have been on the train. 2 She must have missed it. 3 She must be the child's mother. 4 She can't have phoned her parents. 5 It must have been raining. 6 The man must have slipped on the banana skin. 7 She can't be his wife. 8 Someone must have phoned for an ambulance.

5 1 You must try this sundried tomato bread. 2 You don't have to get an ... 3 The government should not have tried to ... 4 You had better not chat up ... 5 We didn't need to book the table as ... 6 My hair's much too long. It needs cutting soon. 7 The gas supply must be disconnected before you remove the boiler/before the boiler is removed. 8 Latecomers will not be allowed to enter the theatre ... 9 Why are we required to state ... 10 The solicitor must have received ... 11 It should not be difficult ... 12 Patients must not have eaten or drunk anything ...

6 Line 3 ~~supposed~~ → obliged/required Line 6 ~~should have got in~~ → must have got in Line 7 ~~there must be~~ → there must have been Line 8 ~~You'd better report it~~ → You should/ought to report it Line 12 ~~needn't have invited~~ → didn't need to invite Line 14 ~~need~~ → need to

18

1 1 won't work 2 would always say 3 will easily hold 4 will be having 5 will have prepared 6 would always argue 7 will stop 8 won't have started 9 wouldn't come 10 will watch

2 1 they will do 2 they won't do 3 She'll do light cleaning 4 she'll get the shopping 5 she won't do anything heavy 6 she would prepare supper 7 She will say (exactly) what she thinks. 8 She wouldn't eat it. 9 will pop in 10 he won't ask them for help 11 the car wouldn't start 12 Would he wait for me? 13 he will try to cope by himself 14 if you'll wait for a few minutes

3 *Suggested answers:* 1 Will you/Won't you have another piece/some more cake? 2 You will all write the/this essay for homework. 3 Shall I take the minutes? 4 Will/Would you come with us, please (Sir)? 5 I would like you to respect me.

4 1 C 2 B 3 A 4 A 5 C 6 C 7 B 8 A 9 B 10 C

5 1 Pedro would prefer to live in a real house. 2 Esther would like the government to provide free medicine. 3 Sun-Li would rather not go begging in the streets. 4 Hana thinks it would be nice to have some beautiful clothes. 5 Sunil wishes that rich people from the city wouldn't dump their rubbish in the village. 6 Maria thinks it would have been good to go to school.

6 Line 6 ~~He'd be visiting~~ → He'll be visiting Line 8 ~~she won't~~ → she wouldn't Line 9 ~~would have hastened~~ → would hasten Line 11 ~~will insist~~ → would insist Line 12 ~~Won't it be~~ → Wouldn't it be Line 14 ~~I shan't say~~ → I wouldn't say Line 16 ~~Will I make~~ → Shall I make Line 17 ~~would be frozen~~ → will be frozen Line 18 ~~he's walked~~ → he'll have walked

19

1 1 I've been waiting 2 They were trying 3 She won't have/won't've returned 4 this policy does not include (*no contraction – formal English*) 5 He mightn't have known/He mightn't've known (*in spoken English*) 6 Doesn't their boss realise 7 he hadn't been taking 8 Didn't/Doesn't she appreciate 9 the bank is unwilling (*no contraction – formal English*) 10 Hilary's not expecting/Hilary isn't expecting/Hilary wasn't expecting 11 They really should've told 12 have not been received (*no contraction – formal English*)

2 1 Do help yourself to a drink. C 2 He did promise to behave himself in future. A 3 Do pay attention, young man. B 4 The dog does enjoy a good run around the park. A 5 Do take your feet off the table. B 6 Do keep quiet. B 7 Do come and join us. C 8 Do make yourself at home. C 9 Jane did manage to lose quite a lot of weight. A 10 The children really do love the Disney channel. A

3 1 I haven't (got) a clue what the answer is./I don't have a clue ... 2 Don't forget (that) you have (got) an appointment with the sales manager at ten o'clock. 3 Has Your Honour any further instructions on this matter? 4 What does Clare do (for a living)? 5 She won't have (anybody using) bad language at the dinner table. 6 He's been having you on. 7 Will this piece of fabric do for the new curtains? 8 This floor could do with a good wash. 9 You've been had! 10 It hasn't been/Isn't quite done yet. 11 What did you have for your staff lunch last week? 12 I think he's having an asthma attack.

4 Line 4 ~~she owns~~ → she's got Line 11 ~~Your hair contains extensions, doesn't it?~~ → You've got extensions, haven't you? Line 13 ~~to possess~~ → to have Line 16 ~~can receive~~ → can have Line 19 ~~There is an appointment for you~~ → You've got an appointment Line 22 ~~possess~~ → have Line 24 ~~indulging in~~ → having Line 25 ~~can obtain~~ → can have Line 26 includes → has Line 27 ~~your family contains~~ → If you have/you've got Line 28 ~~employ~~ → have Line 30 ~~has acquired~~ → has/has got Line 31 ~~is teeming with~~ → has

5 1 A 2 A 3 B 4 A 5 A 6 A 7 B 8 A 9 B 10 B 11 B 12 A 13 B 14 B 15 B

20

1 1 Heavy rains have made parts of the road impassable. 2 We're going to have the roof done next spring. 3 It's all part of the research I'm doing for my dissertation. 4 I'm rather busy/I'm doing something this evening so I won't be able to make the cinema/make it. 5 The old pond has made a wonderful paddling pool for the kids. 6 How can you talk to me like that after all I've done for you! 7 Are you going to do any more aerobics classes? 8 In many countries women still make less (money) than men for the same work. 9 They made the hostages walk for three days without food or water. 10 They've been making Rolls Royce cars in the same factory for forty years.

2 1 take 2 to take 3 have 4 takes/will take 5 have 6 have 7 have 8 had 9 has taken 10 take 11 to take 12 having 13 will have 14 take 15 take

3 1 make a decision 2 made a journey 3 done (some) research 4 made a mistake 5 made a start 6 laundry to be done 7 make a charge 8 make a fuss 9 made a promise 10 do me good 11 made it up 12 do some shopping 13 make trouble 14 made a bad job

4 1 ✔ 2 ~~gone~~ → been 3 ~~laying~~ → lying 4 ✔ 5 ~~been~~ → gone 6 ~~arose~~ → arisen 7 ✔ 8 ✔ 9 ✔ 10 ~~talked~~ → spoke 11 ~~robbed~~ → stolen 12 ✔ 13 ~~stolen~~ → robbed 14 ~~raising~~ → rising 15 ✔ 16 ~~laid~~ → lain 17 ✔

5 1 take 2 lent 3 bring 4 fetching 5 lending 6 brought 7 borrow 8 took 9 fetch 10 borrow

6 1 A 2 B 3 B 4 A 5 A 6 B

21

1 1 dependent 2 disabled 3 meteoric 4 faceless 5 hysterical 6 destructive 7 disagreeable 8 British 9 pointless 10 fertile 11 argumentative 12 unfashionable 13 plentiful 14 unbelievable 15 hopeless 16 horizontal 17 investigative 18 effective 19 laughable 20 Dutch

2 1 A ✔ B ✘ 2 A ✔ B ✘ 3 A ✘ B ✔ 4 A ✔ B ✔ 5 A ✔ B ✘ 6 A ✔ B ✘ 7 A ✘ B ✔ 8 A ✘ B ✔ 9 A ✔ B ✘ 10 A ✘ B ✔ 11 A ✔ B ✔ 12 A ✔ B ✘ 13 A ✘ B ✔ 14 A ✔ B ✘ 15 A ✘ B ✔

3 1 Many of the portraits painted by El Greco are 2 There was something inexplicable 3 They gave an involved explanation 4 the only appointment available./the only available appointment. 5 The present state of affairs 6 the person responsible for recruitment is on holiday 7 in the apartment opposite. 8 Anyone sensitive would be 9 the amounts concerned are very small. 10 Flower buds damaged by frost often

4 1 alarming 2 comfort and service provided 3 staggering 4 those interviewed 5 relaxed/relaxing 6 satisfied 7 service provided 8 continuing 9 passengers questioned 10 enhanced 11 key factor discussed 12 bored 13 Delayed 14 Affected passengers/Passengers affected 15 amused

5 1 Northumberland is a rarely-visited part of England. 2 They were soon engulfed by the fast-moving water. 3 In recent times technology-driven changes have had a profound impact on working practices. 4 The oak is a slow-growing tree. 5 Australian parrots have brilliantly-coloured plumage. 6 The Midlands is Britain's main car-manufacturing region. 7 The Hubble space telescope has produced digitally-enhanced pictures that have amazed the public. 8 There is a segment of the film-going public that will always want to see corny adventure movies. 9 The new wing will be opened by a well-known TV personality. 10 The home-made desserts are the main feature of our restaurant.

6 1 It's a priceless ancient Greek ceramic wine jar. 2 Our school has a fantastic new state-of-the-art computer centre. 3 She found ten metres of superb dark blue textured velvet in the sales. 4 It features luxurious Italian leather upholstery. 5 We've chosen a lovely inexpensive orange and green/green and orange wallpaper for the study.

7 1 ~~but~~ → and 2 ~~a little Persian beautiful cat~~ → a beautiful little Persian cat 3 ~~horrified~~ → horrifying/horrific 4 ~~the taken route~~ → the route taken 5 ~~wealthies~~ → wealthy 6 ~~to fascinated by crime readers~~ → to readers fascinated by crime 7 ~~afraid~~ → frightened 8 ~~opinions opposite~~ → opposite opinions 9 ~~blue yellow~~ → blue and yellow 10 ~~breaking~~ → broken 11 ~~aluminium and glass-fibre unique hull~~ → unique aluminium and glass-fibre hull 12 ~~though~~ → and 13 ~~the proposed by parliament solution~~ → the solution proposed by parliament 14 ~~responsible person~~ → person responsible 15 ~~parents who are lone~~ → lone parents 16 ~~two alike alternatives~~ → two similar alternatives/two alternatives which were alike 17 ~~Tall anyone~~ → Anyone tall 18 ~~Living in Scotland viewers~~ → Viewers living in Scotland 19 ~~challenged~~ → challenging 20 ~~moving fast~~ → fast-moving

22

1 1 the best 2 the wettest 3 more real than 4 the furthest/farthest 5 fatter/bigger than 6 tidier than 7 looser 8 the worst 9 drier 10 the biggest 11 (the) most keen/keenest 12 the prettier/prettiest 13 more wrong 14 The most scared 15 more bored

2 1 D 2 G 3 A 4 E 5 B 6 F 7 C

3 1 B 2 A 3 A 4 B 5 B 6 B 7 A 8 A 9 B 10 B

4 1 The lecture was so boring that I fell asleep. 2 It was such a well-publicised concert that the tickets sold out within days. 3 The wording of the document is so complicated as to be incomprehensible. 4 It was too dark to find my contact lens. 5 It wasn't as interesting an exhibition as my friends had claimed. 6 She's more disappointed than angry. 7 Approaching the church, we noticed the sound of the bells becoming louder and louder and louder. 8 The older dogs get, the less aggressive they become. 9 My son isn't old enough to get a place at kindergarten. 10 Their remarks were not so much insulting as inaccurate.

5 1 G She smokes like a chimney. 2 D He's like a bull in a china shop. 3 F I slept like a log last night. 4 L It's as cold as ice in here. 5 C She's like a lamb to the slaughter. 6 J She's as fit as a fiddle. 7 N You're as white as a sheet. 8 A He's like a cat on a hot tin roof. 9 E She's like a bear with a sore head this morning. 10 H Our car goes like a rocket. 11 B My new flatmate swears like a trooper. 12 M Once the lights went out it was as quiet as the grave. 13 K She doesn't need to diet, she's as light as a feather. 14 O The old man is as stubborn as a mule. 15 I These new mobile phones are selling like hot cakes.

6 1 best/top 2 most 3 no 4 than 5 more 6 enough 7 cheapest 8 as 9 as 10 just/almost/about 11 to 12 too 13 best 14 like 15 so 16 by 17 such 18 the 19 more 20 as

23

1 **Ungradable**: amazing correct dead enormous extinct fascinating freezing huge minute paralysed
Gradable: attractive cold exciting expensive good interesting large shy sick ugly

2 1 fairly inexpensive 2 a bit stiff 3 virtually indecipherable 4 somewhat bloodthirsty 5 absolutely freezing 6 very interesting 7 fabulously rich 8 highly unlikely

3 1 D 2 A, C 3 C 4 B 5 B 6 C

4 1 C 2 A 3 A 4 B 5 C 6 B 7 B 8 A 9 C 10 B

5 1 ✔ 2 ~~very empty~~ → completely empty 3 ~~completely full~~ → very full 4 ✔ 5 ~~very recommended~~ → highly recommended 6 ✔ 7 ✔ 8 ~~very built~~ → heavily built 9 ~~absolutely moving~~ → deeply moving 10 ~~really delighted~~ → highly delighted

6 1 **gradable**: boring, tedious, uninteresting **ungradable**: stultifying 2 **gradable**: diminutive, little, tiny **ungradable**: minute 3 **gradable**: diverting, engaging, interesting **ungradable**: fascinating 4 **gradable**: scarce, uncommon, unusual **ungradable**: unique 5 **gradable**: annoyed, irate, irritated **ungradable**: furious 7 **gradable**: happy **ungradable**: delighted, ecstatic, exhilarated 8 **gradable**: hungry **ungradable**: famished, ravenous, starving

7 Line 4 ~~very minute~~ → very small/tiny Line 6 ~~absolutely hungry~~ → absolutely famished/starving Lines 7/8 ~~fairly furious~~ → fairly annoyed/angry Line 9 ~~absolutely pleased~~ → absolutely delighted Lines 10/11 ~~totally rare~~ → totally unique Line 11 ~~very ecstatic~~ → very pleased/happy Line 12 ~~utterly interesting~~ → utterly fascinating Line 13 ~~absolutely annoyed~~ → absolutely furious Line 14 ~~a bit famished~~ → a bit hungry Line 16 ~~stultifying~~ → boring/uninteresting/tedious Line 18 ~~very fascinating~~ → very amusing/diverting Line 20 ~~very fabulous~~ → very nice/lovely Lines 22/23 ~~very exhilarated~~ → very happy/pleased

24

1 1 in a friendly way 2 direct 3 rightly 4 lately 5 easily 6 straight 7 Healthwise 8 freely 9 high 10 deep 11 Afterwards 12 close 13 hardly 14 real 15 fast

2 1 started to go faster (and faster) 2 as quite a 3 happens more slowly 4 there soon enough 5 roughly three-quarters of 6 almost entirely unheard of/unknown 7 so movingly that 8 (the) most deeply involved 9 were politically biased 10 as honestly as

3 1 A ✔ B ✘ C ✔ 2 A ✘ B ✔ C ✘ 3 A ✔ B ✔ C ✘ 4 A ✔ B ✘ C ✔ 5 A ✔ B ✘ C ✔ 6 A ✔ B ✔ C ✘ 7 A ✘ B ✘ C ✔ 8 A ✔ B ✘ C ✔ 9 A ✘ B ✘ C ✘ 10 A ✔ B ✔ C ✘ 11 A ✔ B ✘ C ✘ 12 A ✘ B ✔ C ✔ 13 A ✔ B ✔ C ✘ 14 A ✔ B ✘ C ✔ 15 A ✔ B ✔ C ✔

4 (*Note: These answers follow the guidelines for sequence in the Reference section*)
1 Taking advantage of a gap between the players, Owen kicked the ball skilfully into the net just before half time.
2 Foxes can often be seen scavenging on the streets of London at night. 3 David behaves quite well when he is at home but he often causes trouble at school. 4 The post sometimes doesn't arrive on time in this part of the city.
5 Jennifer didn't immediately recognise the man waving frantically from the balcony at the end of the show. 6 We are usually unable to offer refunds on the spot, but we will examine your claim thoroughly before the end of the week. 7 These children have probably never been given the opportunities we all take for granted. 8 Access to the Internet is no longer available free of charge at our libraries on weekday mornings.
9 Such losses would normally have been avoided by the use of back-up devices. 10 Many of the old masters had assistants who would prepare the oil pigments by hand in their studios each morning.

5 1 'I'm sorry. I really don't know what you are talking about!' 2 'But that place always is full on Saturday evenings!' 3 'Yes, I often have wondered about that.' 4 'I'm not surprised. He never does listen to my ideas.' 5 'That's not unusual, the customs officers usually are quite thorough.' 6 'I'm sorry but we honestly don't know where he is.' 7 'Come off it. You really can't expect me to just cave in like that.' 8 'You absolutely don't have a clue what I'm talking about, do you?' 9 'I'm afraid these programs sometimes do take a long time to download.'
10 'Well, she rarely is in the office before noon these days.'

6 1 Really? 2 Apparently 3 Frankly 4 Obviously 5 Seriously? 6 Admittedly 7 By the way 8 Naturally 9 Exactly 10 Fortunately 11 Clearly 12 understandably

7 1 Financially ruined, the owner of the business rather reluctantly agreed to sell the premises within the month.
2 There is probably nothing better than collapsing lazily onto a sofa at the end of the day/At the end of the day there is ... 3 Carefully controlled, this amazingly effective new drug can dramatically reduce blood pressure within hours/can reduce blood pressure dramatically within hours/this dramatically effective new drug can amazingly reduce 4 Under the circumstances we deeply regret having to announce the suspension of all staff currently working in our subsidiary in San Diego. 5 We rarely seem to get the chance to talk seriously about these things these days.
6 Unfortunately, many of my colleagues thoroughly disapprove of my scheme to update the accounting

procedures in the sales department over the next quarter.

25

1 **Across**: 1 quays 5 chair 6 medium 7 wharf 10 formulae 12 hero 15 monarchs 16 mosquitoes
Down: 2 sheriffs 3 manager 4 quizzes 8 addresses 9 flamingos 11 geese 13 crises 14 oasis

2 1 information 2 chocolate 3 advice is 4 wine 5 an equivalent quality 6 a better 7 less sugar 8 content 9 less than 10 ingredients 11 strong, fresh coffee 12 a cake 13 flour 14 scales 15 a slice

3 1 an outbreak 2 the town's population/the townspeople/ the town's residents 3 A spokesperson's statement 4 a full investigation 5 the conclusion 6 the outcome 7 The suggestion/A suggestion 8 The call

4 Line 3 ~~a leaded glass~~ → leaded glass Line 4 ~~communitys~~ → communities Line 4 ~~are unfolding~~ → is unfolding Line 5 ~~fisher wifes~~ → fisher wives Line 8 ~~believes~~ → beliefs Line 9 ~~politic~~ → politics Line 9 ~~1950's~~ → 1950s Line 9 ~~has passed~~ → have passed Line 11 ~~was eager~~ → were eager Line 13 ~~prejudicies~~ → prejudices Line 15 ~~mysterys~~ → mysteries Line 16 ~~which affects~~ → which affect Line 16 ~~a great optimism~~ → great optimism Line 18 ~~literatures~~ → literature Line 18 ~~a spellbinding art~~ → a spellbinding work of art

5 1 – 2 are/is 3 is/was 4 a 5 are 6 were 7 is 8 a 9 is 10 is 11 has 12 has/have 13 have 14 a 15 is

6 1 item/piece of news on the radio this morning. 2 were used to restrain the aggressive young man. 3 of roads in the Brighton area were affected by the recent floods. 4 the bank a call tomorrow and check our balance. 5 eat fewer sweet and fatty things. 6 less than ten minutes to get here from the station. 7 uptake of our new offer. 8 items/pieces of unwanted furniture since we moved to the smaller house. 9 are expected to attend the meeting tomorrow afternoon. 10 they should now address are/is the questions of VAT and fuel tax. 11 is played by a lot of the older men in cafés. 12 launch of the new women's magazine in April was a great success. 13 elect the government. 14 agreement to help fund the new playground.

26

1 1 I'm sure this is somebody's bag. 2 Let's go to the girls' shop. 3 That is Mr Hollis's/ Mr Hollis' hotel. 4 I love Gilbert and Sullivan's operettas. 5 It's nobody's fault. 6 They had respect for each other's opinions. 7 My next-door neighbour's dog never stops barking. 8 I'm fed up with the hopeless inefficiency of my boss's secretary/my boss's secretary's hopeless inefficiency. 9 My mother's and (my) father's personalities are very alike. 10 These aren't my keys, they are my flatmate's (keys). 11 The new Act of Parliament will protect everyone's right to privacy. 12 The men's toilet is over there on the right. 13 I've just inherited my grandmother's brother's house/the house belonging to my grandmother's brother. 14 Residents of sink estates' opinions/Sink estates' residents' opinions are rarely taken into consideration. 15 Fred Astaire and Ginger Rogers' dance routines are legendary.

2 1 ~~him~~ → his 2 ~~wive's~~ → wife's 3 ~~ones' home is ones' castle~~ → one's home is one's castle 4 ✔/managing director's 5 ~~mine~~ → my 6 ~~childrens'~~ → children's 7 ✔ 8 ~~brother's in-law's~~ → brother-in-law's 9 ~~us~~ → ours 10 ~~buses'~~ → bus's

3 1 B 2 A 3 A, B 4 A 5 A, B 6 B 7 A 8 A, B 9 A 10 A 11 B 12 B 13 A 14 B 15 A, B 16 A 17 B 18 B 19 A 20 A

4 1 brand names 2 mail-order 3 credit card 4 high street 5 shop assistant 6 checklist 7 software 8 hard disk 9 word processing 10 keyboard 11 world-wide web 12 output 13 shortlist 14 instruction manuals 15 after-sales

5 1 A 2 B 3 B 4 B 5 A 6 A 7 A 8 A 9 B 10 A

6 1 Could you pop down to the newsagent and pick up Charles'/Charles's evening paper. 2 That silver-topped walking stick belongs to a friend of mine. 3 The hotel's private beach is only a five-minute walk from here. 4 The government's privatisation of the railways is going ahead next year. 5 The landlord wouldn't allow his tenant's girlfriend to move in. 6 My father's pension fund has been badly affected by the downturn in the value of blue-chip stocks. 7 Clare bought a beautiful new outfit for her brother-in-law's sister's wedding/the wedding of her brother-in-law's sister. 8 The windsurfer managed to ignore the screams of the crowd lining the beach. 9 Whenever we

are over at Dad's (house) we seem to spend the entire time watching horse racing on the television. 10 The bank robber refused to accept the legal system's jurisdiction/the jurisdiction of the legal system over him. 11 My wife's firm specialises in setting up databases for insurance companies. 12 The traffic jam was caused by the volume of cars setting out for the south coast at the start of the bank holiday.

27

1 1 he 2 it 3 him 4 It 5 its 6 It/His 7 it 8 It 9 They 10 one 11 one 12 It 13 he/they 14 its 15 he 16 him/he/he did 17 one 18 they/he

2 1 Justin and I 2 teachers can't desert their class/a teacher can't desert their class 3 You can't carry on working if you aren't feeling well 4 it's us teachers 5 we/you can't take too much time off 6 one 7 Jenny and I 8 you and Jenny 9 with Justin and me 10 better than us/we do 11 we/you do get 12 If anyone new comes in they're always made welcome 13 we want to be with him in the evening 14 poor old him 15 You can't be too careful with animals

3 1 a ✔ b ✔ A 2 a ✔ b ✘ 3 a ✔ b ✔ B 4 a ✔ b ✘ 5 a ✘ b ✔ 6 a ✔ b ✔ B 7 a ✔ b ✘ 8 a ✔ b ✔ A 9 a ✔ b ✔ C 10 a ✔ b ✔ B

4 1 somewhere 2 anyone 3 Is 4 anybody 5 something constructive 6 anywhere 7 someone/somebody 8 somehow 9 anything 10 No one 11 Anyhow/Anyway 12 anywhere

5 1 it 2 its 3 each other/one another/everyone/body else 4 one 5 No one/Nobody 6 me/myself 7 one/you 8 I 9 it 10 my 11 myself 12 one 13 It 14 its 15 me 16 me 17 you/one 18 it

6 1 ~~them~~ → him 2 ✔ 3 ~~which it fuels~~ → which fuels 4 ~~their~~ → them 5 ✔ 6 ~~them~~ → their 7 ~~everyhow~~ → somehow 8 ~~which it can~~ → which can 9 ~~Anyone~~ → No one 10 ~~them~~ → they 11 ~~one~~ → someone/they 12 ✔ 13 ~~theirselves~~ → themselves 14 ~~Anybody~~ → Everybody 15 ~~herself~~ → themselves 16 ✔ 17 ~~children they suffered~~ → children suffered 18 ~~it~~ → them 19 ~~themselves~~ → them 20 ✔

28

1 1 a 2 the 3 a 4 – 5 – 6 The 7 a 8 – 9 a 10 The 11 the 12 the 13 the 14 the 15 The 16 – 17 – 18 the/a 19 my 20 –

2 1 – 2 – 3 a 4 the 5 – 6 the 7 the 8 the 9 a 10 – 11 – 12 the 13 the 14 – 15 –/the 16 – 17 a 18 – 19 the 20 –

3 1 This 2 that 3 these 4 That 5 This 6 Those 7 That 8 this 9 those 10 that

4 1 a+F 2 b+I 3 b+A 4 a+C 5 b+E 6 b+H 7 a+D 8 b+B

5 1 A, C 2 B 3 B, C 4 A, C 5 A 6 B 7 A, B 8 A, B 9 A, B 10 A, C

6 1 your 2 this 3 the 4 – 5 the 6 a 7 the 8 all 9 The 10 – 11 each 12 the 13 half 14 these 15 – 16 This 17 – 18 the 19 most 20 these

7 1 All them → All of them 2 ~~Japanese~~ → the Japanese 3 ~~the Burma~~ → Burma 4 ✔ 5 ~~of founders~~ → of the founders 6 ~~Photographic work~~ → The photographic work 7 ~~finest pictures~~ → the finest pictures 8 ✔ 9 ~~an~~ → the 10 ~~this~~ → these 11 ~~this~~ → that 12 ~~step by the step~~ → step by step 13 ✔ 14 ~~that way~~ → a way 15 ~~most the people~~ → most of the people 16 ~~the half~~ → half 17 agency → the agency 18 ✔ 19 some goal → the goal 20 ✔ 21 ~~in Balkans~~ → in the Balkans 22 ✔ 23 best → the best

29

1 1 get away from the area 2 for schools and hospitals/hospitals and schools throughout the crisis 3 but as for the plot 4 the passers-by are soaked through 5 on behalf of the winner 6 from the well by means of a rope 7 right on top of the cupboard 8 to just under three hours 9 mine was the one just after 10 almost opposite the man with the beard

2 1 on 2 – 3 in 4 on 5 since 6 through 7 by 8 with 9 of 10 as 11 among 12 for the sake of 13 Except 14 from 15 in

3 1 over 2 through/in 3 out of 4 in 5 across 6 along 7 by/next to 8 into/to 9 in 10 on/around 11 on top of/above 12 under(neath)/beneath/below 13 up to 14 on 15 up/down/in 16 at 17 between/opposite 18 opposite 19 on 20 In/At 21 in 22 under 23 to 24 through/along 25 at

4 1 ~~main aim which~~ → main aim of which 2 ~~people out their~~ → people out of their 3 ~~about is~~ → about what is 4 ~~comedians work are~~ → comedians work with/on are 5 ✔ 6 ~~the that~~ → the fact that 7 ~~except try~~ → except to try 8 ✔ 9 ✔ 10 ~~about being~~ → about them being 11 ✔ 12 ~~it is aimed~~ → it is aimed at 13 ~~it is~~

~~intended~~ → it is intended for 14 ✔

5 1 from/out of 2 of 3 in 4 over 5 as 6 across/all over 7 from 8 of/in 9 than 10 for 11 which 12 between 13 offering 14 to/for 15 including 16 through/in 17 without 18 of 19 Unlike 20 for/during 21 For 22 behind 23 what 24 From/In 25 under

6 1 from 2 across 3 between 4 in 5 According to 6 on 7 By 8 to 9 In 10 like 11 at 12 into 13 behind 14 under 15 instead of 16 with 17 in 18 about 19 during 20 of 21 on 22 at 23 against 24 off 25 between 26 on 27 with 28 in 29 on 30 along 31 into 32 on

30

1 1 B 2 A, B 3 A, B 4 B 5 A

2 1 refused to leave his estranged son anything. 2 Susan originally believed Geoff 3 Please leave your shoes by the door 4 that you keep your valuables safe 5 doesn't tell us what we should wear at the reception. 6 George W Bush has been elected the new President 7 that studying philosophy really improves our thinking power. 8 She carefully placed onto her finger the 24-carat gold, diamond-encrusted engagement ring that her fiancé had just bought her. 9 The course director insists on first-year students attending at least 80 per cent 10 by sending us the form and proof of purchase

3 1 B 2 M 3 K 4 A 5 E 6 N 7 H 8 O 9 D 10 J 11 F 12 I

4 1 The couple named their first daughter Samantha. 2 His Excellency expects visitors to stand when he arrives. 3 I wouldn't like to stay a legal assistant for long. 4 Amanda brought all her expertise to the team. 5 Amanda brought the team all her expertise. 6 A very inexperienced salesman has become the Sales Manager. 7 He placed into the box the carefully wrapped, sparkling, diamond encrusted 18-carat gold ring. 8 Please put all rubbish in the bins provided. 9 Do your parents let you go to all-night parties? 10 The paratrooper carefully removed the pin from the grenade./removed the pin from the grenade carefully. 11 Susan liked the bracelet so her daughter bought it for her. 12 They made the prisoners stand all day long to reduce their resistance. 13 The scenes of destruction in the film made us all sick. 14 The trainer recommended trying an easy programme first./recommended first trying an easy programme.

5 1 – that – f (S) 2 – so – a (S) 3 – if – i (S) 4 – after – e (S) 5 – or – b (C) 6 – and – d (C) 7 – even though – c (S) 8 – than – g (S)

6 1 ~~broke thousands~~ → broke into thousands 2 ✔ 3 ~~remain to be tenants~~ → remain tenants 4 ~~appears some mistake~~ → appears to be some mistake 5 ✔ 6 ~~recommended book~~ → recommended booking/ recommended that you book 7 ~~showed to their gathered fans their trophy~~ → showed their trophy to their gathered fans 8 ~~explained us the problem~~ → explained the problem to us 9 ~~tell me to go?~~ → tell me where to go? 10 ~~placed back in its correct position the gold watch~~ → placed the gold watch back in its correct position 11 ✔ 12 ~~drives absolutely wild my cats!~~ → drives my cats absolutely wild!

7 1 it (to be) 2 for them/for someone 3 which didn't 4 to be 5 angry/annoyed/ furious 6 (that) they 7 letting 8 After/When 9 it/the clamp 10 how

31

1 1 H The body of a man who jumped off the Severn Bridge has been found in the River Severn. 2 J The fashion icon Mary Quant, who is famous for inventing the mini-skirt, has left her business. 3 D The global warming conference, which was held in The Hague, has ended without agreement. 4 C Formula 1 driver Eddie Irvine, whose contract with Ferrari finishes at the end of the season, has narrowly missed gaining the Formula 1 World Champion title (today). 5 B The hand count of votes which/that were spoiled in the recent US presidential election has continued. 6 F London Zoo, which was in danger of closing through lack of funds, has remained open. 7 A The politician who was disgraced in a financial scandal has handed in his resignation. 8 G The size 16 model who refused to diet to a size 12 has won the new Estée Lauder contract. 9 E Madonna's house in the UK, which she shares with her British partner, Guy Ritchie, has been burgled.

2 1 B 2 A 3 B 4 A

3 1 which 2 where 3 who/ whom/that 4 whose 5 which 6 whom 7 who 8 when 9 which 10 which/that

4 1 with staff vacancies 2 Sir Patrick McDonald, from Inverness 3 all from the holistic school of education.

4 of different ages 5 currently living 6 to be informed of the government's decision
7 (held) last week
8 dedicated to 9 participating over the years

5 1 where F 2 (that/which) I
3 where H 4 whom A
5 who G 6 whose D
7 why F 8 which B

6 1 ~~tourism which~~ → tourism, which 2 ✔ 3 ~~which it is~~ → which is wholly seasonal
4 ~~people work~~ → people who work 5 ~~wherever work~~ → work wherever 6 ~~government is already receiving~~ → government which/that is already receiving/government already receiving 7 ✔ 8 ✔
9 ~~to see them.~~ → to see.
10 ~~reef which~~ → reef, which
11 ✔ 12 ~~tourist what wants~~ → tourist who/that wants
13 ✔ 14 ~~where they are drinking in.~~ → where they are drinking./that/which they are drinking in. 15 ~~that~~ → which
16 ✔ 17 ~~what~~ → which
18 ~~places tourism~~ → places where/in which tourism
19 ~~that whose~~ → whose
20 ✔ 21 ✔ 22 ~~which~~ → what

32

1 1 e Many people believe that capital punishment is a deterrent to serious crime. On the contrary, it actually makes little difference to the crime rate. 2 b We usually consider it healthy to eat lots of fruit but too much can produce an excess of acid in the stomach.
3 g I enjoy having people to stay, though I always appreciate the peace when they have gone./I always appreciate the peace when they have gone, though.
4 a The main medium of communication on the Internet is English, although many web sites now operate in other languages. 5 h Iain Banks's early novels were considered quite strange, while his later books are more mainstream and accessible. 6 f I tend to drink more white wine, whereas my husband prefers red. 7 d Global warming is often considered the main factor in current climate fluctuations. Yet climate change has long been a feature of the Earth's development.

2 1 Very little of the remaining stock sold, even though the prices in the sale were very low. 2 Although the ailing magazine tried introducing several new features, circulation continued to drop.
3 Difficult though this may seem now, you'll soon wonder why it caused so many problems. 4 In spite of the fact that she insisted (that) all was well, I knew that something was wrong. 5 The Scots won the battle, despite their smaller force./despite having a far smaller force.
6 Despite being hated by the critics, Archer's latest book was well received by the public.

3 1 ~~than though I expected~~ → than I expected, though 2 ✔
3 ~~mind you~~ → however/on the other hand 4 ~~It didn't last long, still.~~ → Still, it didn't last long. 5 ✔ 6 ~~We'd rather all the same not.~~ → We'd rather not, all the same./All the same, we'd rather not.
7 ~~Nevertheless~~ → Still/All the same/Mind you 8 ~~You may be penalised for failing to follow on the other hand the rules.~~ → On the other hand, you may .../You may, on the other hand .../... be penalised, on the other hand, for .../... for failing to follow the rules, on the other hand.

4 1 same 2 same 3 different
4 different 5 same 6 same
7 different 8 different
9 same 10 same
11 different 12 same

5 1 but 2 However
3 Nevertheless 4 even though
5 Despite 6 however
7 While 8 though 9 whereas
10 despite 11 On the contrary 12 Yet

33

1 1 There are more than a million species of insect in the world. 2 There was a grandfather clock ticking in the background. 3 At Hiroshima in 1945 there was an event which shook the whole world.
4 There are thought to be two further suspects under arrest.
5 There is bound to be a bad reaction to the news (from them). 6 There now follows/There will now be a statement by the Prime Minister. 7 There were two forms of amino acid present in the compound./Present in the compound there were two forms of amino acid. 8 Is there an underground railway in Osaka? 9 There is likely to be a massive sell off of high-tech shares in the next few days. 10 From the middle of the forest there emerged a strange hooded figure./There emerged a strange hooded figure from the middle of the forest. 11 In this case, there should be no trouble securing a conviction. 12 Is there nobody here able to help us?/Is there nobody here who can help us? 13 There are ten new holiday destinations illustrated in our brochure.
14 Is there a buffet car on the train? 15 In this bad weather there is certain to be a poor turnout for the election./There is certain to be a poor turnout for the election in this bad

weather. 16 There was a beautiful antique tapestry hanging over the bed.
17 There are thought to be at least two leading politicians involved in the scandal.
18 We don't envisage there being any adverse reaction from viewers.

2 (*Suggested rewriting in italics*) *The Beach* is the story of a young man who yearns for, seeks out and eventually finds just such a place. *But it comes as a shock to discover that, far from being the source of contentment and inner fulfilment that he expects, the beach turns out to be a place of savage violence, terror and death.*

Alex Garland takes the reader on an exotic journey from the steaming tourist-packed dives of the Khao San Road in Bangkok to the drug-infested islands of the remote seas around Thailand. *It is difficult not to be impressed by the author's skill in describing the unfamiliar oriental locations and his ability to empathise with the obsessions of today's young backpacking 'new-age' travellers.*

Taking in illegal drug plantations, memories of the Vietnam war, sexual jealousy, shark-infested waters, the psychological dynamics of communal living and the clash of cultures, Garland spins a tale which both seduces and shocks the reader. *It is the author's unique blend of these disparate elements which gives the novel its haunting sense of unease and horror.*

It is a thriller with all the traditional ingredients, an exotic location, a central mystery, good versus evil, and dangers around every corner. *There is a strong sense of good and evil in the book, but Garland leaves it to the reader/ but it is left to the reader to decide who is right and who is wrong.* There are few moral certainties in this exotic corner of the world.

Events unfold at great speed, and be warned, it is impossible to put this book down once you have started it. With an international cast of well-observed characters Garland creates a nail-biting narrative that keeps the reader hooked until the final bloody climax.

3 1 The organisers didn't anticipate there being such an overwhelming demand for tickets. 2 It seems (as if/as though) she's going to marry him./It seems she may marry him. 3 There are thought to be many other politicians involved in the scandal./It is thought that there are many other politicians involved in the scandal. 4 I would appreciate it if you would/could send me/if you sent me your up-to-date retail price list. 5 There were fifty applicants for the scholarship. 6 It is said he hates publicity. 7 It isn't surprising that their children are so badly behaved. 8 In this paper it will be demonstrated that DNA strands can be replicated.
9 There are twelve detached houses with double garages for sale on this estate. 10 It is a great honour to be nominated for this award.

4 1 ~~The distance isn't far~~ → It isn't far 2 ~~People believe this is~~ → It is believed to be 3 ✔
4 ~~more than thirty examples hang~~ → there are more than thirty examples 5 ~~That Rodin produced such a superb piece of work all by himself is hard to believe~~ → It is hard to believe that Rodin produced such a superb piece of work all by himself. 6 ~~the impression is that the painting~~ → it looks/ seems as if/as though the painting 7 ✔ 8 ~~I'm really surprised~~ → It's (really) surprising 9 ~~to see everything in one trip is impossible.~~ → it's impossible to see everything in one trip. 10 ~~in that place~~ → there

5 1 She found it strange that he'd never heard of such a famous historical character.
2 Was there really such a long wait between trains? 3 We always have lots of visitors but there tend to be more in the summer months. 4 ✔ 5 The director leaves it to the viewer to decide who is guilty and who is innocent. 6 They assured us that there would be no trouble getting a refund if the goods were faulty. 7 ✔
8 You know it really gets on my nerves when she talks like that. 9 ✔ 10 What's incredible is that there might have been so many more fatalities. 11 I find it impossible to conceive that someone with his track record would be so careless. 12 In 1666 there was a fire which destroyed a large part of London. 13 We would appreciate it if you submitted your estimate to our head office. 14 ✔ 15 Grandpa loves it when the children ask for his advice.

34

1 1 No, it was because of the traffic jam that he was late.
2 Well, what he did was (to) call her from his mobile phone.
3 No, it was on Monday that he was late. 4 No, what she did was (to) reschedule the meeting for the afternoon.
5 No, not the town centre; it was on the ring road that Nick got stuck. 6 No, it was

because Nick was late that she had to reschedule the meeting. 7 No, it was to warn her that he would be late that he rang her. 8 What she was was furious!

2 1 This is where we have to wait. 2 All we need is five minutes (to fix it). 3 The person who started the strike was Jennifer./Jennifer was the person who started the strike. 4 It isn't his dedication (that) I'm questioning. 5 What these men are is totally ruthless. 6 The place where I used to live is around the corner. 7 The one who complained was your next door neighbour./Your next door neighbour was the one who complained. 8 The only thing we didn't inherit was the house./The house was the only thing we didn't inherit. 9 That's exactly what the sales assistant told me. 10 What I want you to do is (to) copy this down in your notebooks. 11 The first thing we did was (to) check the insurance details. 12 It was at six o'clock (that) the climbers reached the peak./It was six o'clock when ... 13 What we're doing is taking the au-pair with us. 14 The last thing we did (before leaving) was (to) switch off the power supply. 15 The reason (why) they moved to Andalucia was the climate./The climate was the reason (why) they moved to Andalucia. 16 What the company has done is imposed a ban on private e-mails. 17 All we want is our money back. 18 It was our boss who told us the news. 19 What I want you to appreciate is that it's not my fault. 20 It was the introduction of stamp duties that led to the loss of the American colonies.

3 1 Exhausted though he was, he managed to reach the finishing line. 2 To make the pilgrimage to Mecca is my life's ambition. 3 His most sublime work is the ninth symphony. 4 That proposal I really can't accept. 5 Placed on the altar was an enormous gold Buddha. 6 Much more challenging for the dedicated skier is the Cresta Run. 7 Also included in the report were several sharp criticisms of ministerial conduct. 8 Lying in the shop doorway was an old man. 9 To get to the bottom of the mystery proved impossible. 10 So severe was the damage that the pilot couldn't regain control.

4 1 ✔ 2 ~~we knew~~ → did we know 3 ~~and so most of the marketing team are~~ → so are most of the marketing team 4 ~~was there~~ → there was 5 ✔ 6 ~~so it be~~ → so be it 7 ~~Tomorrow the first day is~~ → Tomorrow is the first day 8 ✔ 9 ✔ 10 ~~latecomers will~~ → will latecomers 11 ~~such the condition is~~ → such is the condition 12 ~~the time is~~ → is the time 13 ✔ 14 ✔ 15 ~~a director has made~~ → has a director made 16 ~~as those are~~ → as are those 17 ✔ 18 ~~he managed to escape~~ → did he manage to escape 19 ✔ 20 ~~didn't he~~ → he didn't

5 1 That I find really hard to believe. 2 No, what I'm doing is cutting off the dead flower heads. 3 All we left behind was the personal stereo./The only thing ... 4 No, it was my brother (who owned one). 5 And shake them up it certainly did. 6 (But) best of all was the explosion on the jumbo jet. 7 No, what we should do is wait for the ambulance to arrive. 8 Well, (standing) right outside the bedroom window was a huge electricity pylon. 9 Yes, to own a cottage has always been my greatest ambition. 10 No, it's (on) Friday that we're going.

6 1 Bungee jumping I've done before. 2 not only was rap jumping more exciting than bungee jumping, it was also a lot more dangerous./ rap jumping was not only more exciting but also a lot more dangerous than bungee jumping. 3 to keep me in suspense he didn't tell me too much about it 4 But it was Tony who actually took me for my first rap jump. 5 He's the one who's the real daredevil. 6 All I could see was a rope and a harness hanging from the gantry. 7 What you do is lean forward and walk down. 8 It's seeing the ground that I can't cope with. 9 No way am I doing that!

35

1 1 it = the train door 2 its = the train's 3 her = Miriam's 4 the many = kilometres 5 ones = bags 6 it = the large bag 7 this = the job opportunity/her move to Warsaw 8 that = birth 9 do it = return to Warsaw 10 done so = discounted 11 which = speaking to her prospective employers 12 their = Miriam's and her parents'

2 1 one 2 it/there 3 some/all/most/many 4 ones 5 her 6 neither/nor do I 7 that 8 do it 9 did 10 so 11 so 12 do 13 one/some/them 14 That 15 not/I don't

3 1 I told the students they could either take the exam in June or ~~they could~~ take it in December. 2 We can go to the theatre tonight if you want ~~to go to the theatre~~. 3 The children were delighted with the Christmas lights and ~~they~~ wanted to see them turned on again. 4 Even though it is possible to go skiing in Scotland, the British have always been worse skiers than most Europeans ~~have been~~. 5 'Why hasn't the new shopping centre been opened yet?' 'But it has ~~been opened.~~' 6 'Will Julie be going to the club's New Year's party this year?' 'I think she gets back from holiday on 30th December, so she could be ~~going~~.' 7 'Is the new restaurant in the High Street open on Sunday evenings?' 'I don't know. It might be ~~open on Sunday evenings~~. The old one was ~~open on Sunday evenings~~.' 8 We haven't earned any money this summer. I really expected us to ~~earn some~~. 9 The young woman plays the violin and her brother ~~plays~~ the cello. 10 He told me that he was going to leave his wife and I asked him why ~~he was going to leave her~~. 11 Baxter's sick tonight, which is unfortunate as he can play better than all the others ~~can~~. 12 We thought that the old woman had been looking after the house, but she can't have ~~been looking after it~~ as she was in hospital at the time.

4 **A**
line 4 – if *they are* successful; *they* will then ... line 7 – *she* does not ... line 12 – has not *been replaced*
B
line 1 – They = childless couples line 4 – it = that they want a child line 4 – they = the couple line 5 – her = the woman's; This = that she is prepared to give up her child line 5 – she = the woman line 6 – one = child line 7 – themselves = the person/people willing to give up a child line 8 – they = the couple line 8 – if so = if they would like the child line 9 – this = a simple handover line 10 – It = the tradition

5 1 A ✔ B ✔ 2 A ✘ B ✔ C ✔ 3 A ✘ B ✔ C ✔ 4 A ✔ B ✘ C ✔ 5 A ✔ B ✘ C ✔ 6 A ✘ B ✔ 7 A ✔ B ✘ C ✔ 8 A ✔ B ✔ C ✘ 9 A ✔ B ✘ C ✘ 10 A ✔ B ✘

6 1 did 2 – 3 that 4 this 5 ones 6 their 7 – 8 it 9 that 10 – 11 They 12 – 13 it 14 so/it 15 their 16 its 17 – 18 doing

7 *Sample answer*
Most people enjoy listening to music but few realise the important and largely positive effects it can have on us. We know that certain types of music are used to influence our emotions and behaviour. For example, airlines use soothing music before a flight to relax passengers, especially those who may feel nervous about flying. You may have noticed how shops often play fast, rousing music (if you haven't, you probably shop at the more old-fashioned type of store) – this tends to make us feel happier and more likely to spend money!

Music is also being used now as a psychiatric therapy. It seems to be particularly useful for eating disorders and addictions, but also for sufferers of post-traumatic stress syndrome. People attending group therapy sessions are invited to bring along their favourite tracks. Not everyone does, but those who do (so) play them for the group. This/Doing so creates a sense of belonging, as well as a more relaxed atmosphere for the therapy session.

36

1 1 At this height, the light from space is not affected by interference from the earth's atmosphere. 2 This makes it the most useful tool in our search for distant stars and planets. 3 the American astronomer used his close observation of the Andromeda Galaxy to develop the theory that the universe is expanding. 4 The Big Bang theory, now accepted as the most likely explanation of the creation of the universe, is directly based on his ideas. 5 Only two months after it went into orbit scientists at NASA discovered that the main mirror had become distorted and could not be used with any accuracy. 6 The solution was named COSTAR (corrective optics space telescope axial replacement). 7 The repairs were completed in January 1994 and the Hubble Space Telescope is now working correctly and sending its astonishing data back to earth.

2 1 A 2 A 3 B 4 B 5 A 6 A 7 A 8 A 9 B 10 B

3 1 ~~activate~~ → turn on 2 ~~Consequently~~ → Nevertheless/However/ Nonetheless, etc. 3 ~~to fall asleep~~ → falling asleep 4 ~~the icy wind~~ → the wind/it 5 ~~Nevertheless~~ → Furthermore/ In addition, etc. 6 ~~You ought to press~~ → Press 7 ~~The brave married couple~~ → The couple/They 8 ~~really special~~ → exceptional 9 ~~having made three~~ → to have made three 10 ~~At first~~ → Finally/At last, etc.

4 A 4 B 1 C 3 D 2 E 8 F 5 G 7 H 6

5 1 Although they worked for the shogun in wartime, they were employed by the large landowners, the daimyo, in times of peace. 2 They had many rights and privileges including the right to carry swords and ride horses. 3 In exchange for these rights they owed absolute loyalty to their daimyo, even to the extent that they were expected to commit suicide when their daimyo died. 4 This tradition was part of 'bushido' or 'The Way of the Warrior': a strict code of honour which stressed the importance of self-discipline and bravery. 5 Despite the fact that bushido was based on the peaceful beliefs of Zen Buddhism, it helped the samurai to become the most ruthless, feared and brutal warriors in Asia. 6 The samurai reached their peak of importance and influence in the civil wars of the sixteenth century, when they fought for rival warlords. 7 In the peaceful years after 1603, the samurai gradually lost their military importance, and many became administrators rather than soldiers. 8 In 1867, the last shogun Tokugawa Keiki resigned and Japan began to modernise its military forces with the introducton of conscription and a western army structure in 1872. 9 As a result the samurai were no longer needed or wanted and the remaining samurai in Satsuma decided to mount a rebellion against the government. 10 The Satsuma rebellion was a disaster for the samurai, who were finally defeated by the Imperial Army in 1877.

Index

The Index references below refer to section and sub-section headings in the explanation sections. For example 16.1A is unit 16 explanation, sub-section 1A.